SELF-ABANDONMENT TO DIVINE PROVIDENCE

and

LETTERS OF FATHER DE CAUSSADE ON THE PRACTICE OF SELF-ABANDONMENT

SELF-ABANDONMENT TO DIVINE PROVIDENCE

Also known as
ABANDONMENT TO DIVINE PROVIDENCE

by

Father J. P. de Caussade, S.J.

and

LETTERS OF FATHER DE CAUSSADE ON THE PRACTICE OF SELF-ABANDONMENT

*Translated from the standard French edition of
Father P. H. Ramiere, S.J. by*
Algar Thorold

Newly edited by
Father John Joyce, S.J.

With an Introduction by
Dom David Knowles
Regius Professor of Modern History at the
University of Cambridge

TAN BOOKS AND PUBLISHERS, INC.
Rockford, Illinois 61105

Nihil Obstat: Adrianus van Vliet, S.T.D.
                  Censor Deputatus

Imprimatur: ✠ E. Morrogh Bernard
                  Vicar General
                  Westminster
                  February 14, 1959

Apart from the "Spiritual Counsels" (Part II, Book VIII), newly translated by Father John Joyce, S.J., the writings of Father de Caussade here collected in one volume have previously been published separately: Part I under the title *Self-abandonment to Divine Providence* (1933); Part II, Books I-III, under *The Spiritual Letters of Father J. P. de Caussade, S.J.* (1934); Part II, Books IV-V, under *Ordeals of Souls* (1936); Part II, Books VI-VII under *Comfort in Ordeals* (1937). The Introduction by Dom David Knowles originally appeared in the first of these four volumes.

ISBN: 0-89555-312-0

Library of Congress Catalog Card No.: 86-51602

Printed and bound in the United States of America.

TAN BOOKS AND PUBLISHERS, INC.
P.O. Box 424
Rockford, Illinois 61105

1987

INTRODUCTION
By Dom David Knowles

THE treatise on Self-abandonment is a spiritual classic of the
first order. It was a mannerism of Lord Macaulay to erect in
every department of history and letters a hierarchy of excellence
—the half-dozen greatest Athenians, the five greatest epic
poems, and so forth—a poor substitute, so his detractors say, for
true criticism. We all do the like at times, I imagine, and if we
set ourselves to choose the ten greatest spiritual guides since St
Bernard—a magnificent list, indeed, including St Teresa, St
John of the Cross and St Francis de Sales—it would without a
doubt be necessary to find a place for Père de Caussade. Certainly few apart from the saints have received such unstinted
praise from all parts of the Church of today. In France two of
the judges best qualified to speak, Père Garrigou-Lagrange and
M. Henri Bremond, have repeatedly spoken of him in terms of
reverent admiration. A still greater testimony, as well to the
depth and sureness of his teaching as to his value as a living,
helping force, is experience itself. How many souls, both in
France and (though in smaller numbers) in this country, have
found in Caussade their greatest stay—perhaps their only resource—at a particular period of their spiritual life. How many
others have found, not this, but—sure token of a classic—a
steady friendship to which they can return again and again, not
at a period of crisis but during the ordinary flow of life. *L'Abandon*
then is a book for all those who, in St Benedict's words, truly seek
God. It has been translated and printed not to be explained or
to be criticized, but to be read, and for the majority of readers of
the kind Caussade would have desired, no introduction is necessary.

Yet since he is still an unknown figure to many Englishmen;
since to some who read widely he is bound to challenge comparison with others; since, in fine, despite his discursive exterior
he has a clearly defined doctrine for us to learn, there seems room
for a word of introduction which endeavours to give, in his own

words, the main lines of his teaching, and to indicate what masters he himself appears to have been willing to follow.

I. Very little is known of the life of Caussade, and since Abbot Chapman has set out this little in an article in the *Dublin Review* in January 1931 (which also appeared as an introduction to Caussade's *Dialogues on Prayer*),[1] we may pass at once to consider his spiritual teaching. It has come down to us in three books: *L'Abandon*; the above-mentioned treatise in the form of dialogues on prayer; and a considerable number of letters to a small group of correspondents, almost all religious of the Visitation. The treatise and the letters, although they throw very valuable light on Caussade's mind, do not add in any essentials to the teaching of *L'Abandon*, which, as in form it is undoubtedly his masterpiece, so in matter is the very kernel of his doctrine.

Père de Caussade's spiritual teaching was derived from two extremely pure sources, St Francis de Sales and St John of the Cross. That he should be beholden to St Francis was only to have been expected. Bremond has shown us how deep was St Francis's influence on French religious thought in the century that followed his death, and Caussade received this influence from at least two different directions. We know from his own words how great was the influence of Bossuet upon him. Bossuet, though by no means wholly Salesian, knew St Francis well and took from him a number of leading ideas. Several of these, and above all abandonment to divine Providence and confidence in God, are precisely those which most attract Caussade. But another source of influence was probably still more potent. Caussade, like all directors, must have learnt much from his penitents, and these were, for the most part, nuns of the Visitation. He would naturally wish to express himself in an idiom with which they were familiar and steep himself in the writings of their lawgiver, and we are not surprised to find many traces of resemblance, both doctrinal and verbal, between him and St Francis.[2]

[1] See also Biographical Note, p. xix below.

[2] Cf. *The Love of God*, viii, 3–7, 14; ix, 1–6, 15; *Conferences*, ii, xv. I owe these references to Père Garrigou-Lagrange, O.P., *La Providence* (Desclée, 1932), p. 231. See also Bousset, *Etats d'oraison*, viii, 9.

Indeed, the two phrases which recur most frequently in his treatises and letters—abandonment to divine Providence and the value of the present moment—are peculiarly Salesian, and it is noteworthy that whereas the Carmelite school, following St Teresa and St John, when speaking of the death to self use by choice the evangelical words "poverty", "renunciation" and "death", Caussade instinctively turns to "abandonment", "trust" and "acquiescence". Yet in speaking of Salesian influence we must make a distinction. The mode of expression, as is well known, if not the whole method, of St Francis underwent a remarkable development as the result of his experience with the Visitation at Annecy, and in particular with the way of helplessness and desolation by which St Jane Frances was led. The deepest and most intimate chapters of the *Love of God* are of an entirely different colour—one had almost said, of an entirely different culture—from the *Introduction*, the early letters and even some of the *Conferences*. It is to this later period, the Visitandine, Chantal period, that Caussade is related, and the tone of *L'Abandon* is in many places almost precisely that of the deepest chapters of the *Love of God*.

The second great source of Caussade's doctrine is the school of Carmel, and especially St John of the Cross. During his maturity the long-dormant interest of the Church as a whole had been reawakened by St John's canonization in 1726. In Spain a serious attempt was made to print a critical edition of his works, and in any case his doctrine was now placed beyond the breath of calumny. There are specific references to him in the dialogues on prayer, but one does not get the impression that Caussade used him as a guiding textbook, and I am not aware that Caussade was thrown often into direct contact with Carmelites. Nevertheless, his mystical theology, as we shall see, squares exactly with the scheme set out in the *Ascent* and the *Dark Night* and treated as classic by the Carmelite theologians. This agreement is all the more remarkable because it is implicit rather than explicit. Caussade does not, of preference, throw the same aspects or moments of the spiritual life into high light; his compositions are not in the same key as St John's; he has not that peculiar Carmelite family likeness which Anne of Jesus, let us

say, shares both with St John and with St Teresa of Lisieux. Yet
I think there can be no doubt that his doctrine, as formulated in
L'Abandon, can be equated with St John's far more fully than can
St Francis's or Père Grou's. Perhaps equation is not the best term,
Caussade's achievement is rather one of synthesis. He, and he
alone of the great French spiritual writers, superimposes on the
Salesian teaching of self-abandonment and simplicity the typi-
cally Carmelite emphasis on grace as a dynamic force, enlight-
ening and cleansing the soul.

We look, and, so far as I am aware, we look in vain, for another source of influence on Caussade. Within his own Society,
and in France, there had been a succession of eminent directors
who drew their inspiration from the great Lallemant. Caussade
cannot, one would think, have been unaware of this tradition
or unsympathetic to it. His outlook is, in fact, very close to that
of the Lallemant school, and not at all close to that of Rodriguez and Bourdaloue. Yet so far as I have noticed he makes no
direct reference to Lallemant; certainly there is in *L'Abandon* no
trace of emphasis on the points so dear to Lallemant himself—
the sharp opposition of active and contemplative, the exposition
of the gifts of the Holy Ghost, the insistence on the need for a
"second conversion".

We may now look a little more closely at the leading ideas of
Caussade's teaching, and the whole system into which they fit.
Chief amongst them is, of course, the one which gives its title to
the present treatise—the word Caussade has made peculiarly
his own—*L'Abandon*.[1] The translator has decided to render this
by the compound English word "self-abandonment". This is
probably as near as our language can get to the French word,
but his readers must ultimately learn from Caussade's whole
body of teaching the full meaning of the term. For the moment,
it is important to remember that "self-abandonment" does not
for him directly signify the active, ascetic renunciation of self,
self-love and self-will. This process, rightly emphasized by all
ascetical writers and occupying a very large place in Carmelite

---

[1] In Littré's *Dictionnaire* the first quotation of *abandon* is from Bossuet, and
he gives as the meaning; *remise entre les mains de*. His résumé of the growth of
the word's usage is as follows: *remettre, céder, confier, laisser aller, délaisser*.

spirituality, occupies a relatively minor place in Caussade's thought, not because he neglects, but because he assumes it. His "self-abandonment" is, in its primary sense, an acceptance of the will of God, a submission to it. On the second page of the book our Lady's *Fiat mihi* is given us as our exemplar. But the meaning of the word, as his doctrine develops, deepens still further. Two common uses of the word in English may help us to an appreciation. We speak of a swimmer abandoning himself to the waves or to the current. He may or may not wish to swim against, across or with them; in any case he finds that his independent efforts are useless or needless, and he abandons himself to the waters. We speak of one abandoning himself to grief. From this motive or that, by distraction or compulsion, with hope of success or without it, he has kept grief from mastering him. He now opens his heart to it and becomes all grief. It masters him and yet it is what his heart desires. If we substitute the divine action for the waters of the sea or of sorrow in these two phrases, we shall have a faint, inaccurate conception of the deepest meaning of Caussade's "self-abandonment"—inaccurate because in the case of co-operation with grace the human liberty and, at least normally, the human effort is still, and must be, present.

But let us return to the root meaning of "self-abandonment". Acceptance of the will of God, whether signified to us by command, counsel and inspiration, or manifested by the ordinances of divine Providence, is the duty of every Christian. It is a virtue; it may be taught and practised by repeated acts. But "self-abandonment" in Caussade's vocabulary means something more. It means the real, effective gift to God of all the powers of the soul. It means the attitude, the outlook of a soul so given. It means the state of a soul caught up, so to say, in God's machinery, for whom the supernatural life is more real than the natural. *Vivo ego, jam non ego.* Caussade's first editor, the saintly Père Ramière, S.J., tells us that the treatise, as he printed it, is a mixture of letters and conferences taken down by one of the audience. The order and divisions which we now have are Ramière's, not Caussade's. His aim was to divide matter which would be useful to all souls from that which would primarily be of use only to advanced souls. In the first division he tried to collect instructions for acquiring the virtue of abandonment; in the second, advice for those who were in the state of abandonment. This division serves its purpose to some extent, but it does not really correspond to any development in Caussade's thought. In his *Letters*, indeed, we see how he speaks to beginners and those not in religion, but *L'Abandon* is addressed in its entirety to souls of whom he is certain—chosen souls, contemplatives.

II. We have, then, to find in Caussade the outlines of a theory of mystical theology. Let us first hear his aim:

I wish to show all that they may lay claim, not to the same distinct favours, but to the same love, the same self-abandonment, the same God . . . and to eminent sanctity.

Let us not distress or refuse anyone, or drive any away from eminent perfection. Jesus calls all to perfection. . . . If we knew how to leave God's divine hand free to act, we should attain the most eminent perfection. All would attain it, for it is offered to all.

The last sentences show clearly enough that by perfection and sanctity Caussade means the complete perfection of a fully purified soul. Its origin is in sanctifying grace:

The presence of God which sanctifies our souls is that indwelling of the Holy Trinity which is established in the depths of our hearts when they submit to the divine will.

And its end is:

To form Jesus Christ in the depth of our hearts.

We for our part have to do no more than give our whole heart really to God:

The free gift which he asks from our hearts consists of abnegation, obedience and love ; the rest is God's affair.

In other words there

is but one thing to do : to purify our hearts, to detach ourselves from creatures, and abandon ourselves entirely to God,

because

The divine action . . . can only take possession of a soul in so far as it is empty of all confidence in its own action.

That is the pure doctrine of St John, as is also this:

> *To do all this in a holy manner, you have but to change your heart.*
> *What is meant by the heart is the will.*

In this process of detachment, the purely natural activities of the reason must give way to supernatural faith:

> *Our understanding wishes to take the first place among the divine*
> *methods; it must be reduced to the last.*

Likewise the life of the senses must go:

> *We must kill our senses and be stripped of them; their destruction*
> *means the reign of faith,*

and faith must take their place:

> *Faith is what I preach, self-abandonment, confidence and faith;*
> *willingly to be the subject and instrument of divine action. . . . Faith*
> *gives the aspect of heaven to the whole earth, it is by faith that the heart*
> *is ravished, transplanted . . . faith only reaches the truth without seeing*
> *it; it touches what it does not perceive.*

And so:

> *The life of faith is nothing but the continual pursuit of God through*
> *everything that disguises, disfigures, destroys and, so to say, annihilates*
> *him.*

When we have given ourselves to God, he begins to work upon us, not by developing our natural gifts and instincts:

> *This work* (of the Holy Spirit) *is not accomplished by way of our*
> *own cleverness or intelligence, or subtlety of mind, but by way of our*
> *passive self-abandonment to its reception. . . .*

We remember St John's axiom: "Contemplation is to receive."[1] Caussade continues:

> *All we have to do is to receive what we are given and allow ourselves*
> *to be acted upon . . .*

for

> *God teaches the heart not by ideas, but by pains and contradictions.*

[1] *The Living Flame* (Baker, 1912), p. 82.

xi

And therefore:

> *In order to reach the highest stage of perfection, the crosses sent by Providence, which are provided by their state at every moment, open to them a surer and far quicker road than extraordinary states and works.*

But this self-abandonment, we must remember, is itself the work of God:

> *While he strips of everything the souls who give themselves absolutely to him, God gives them something which takes the place of all; of light, wisdom, life and force: this gift is his love,*

and love leads to a greater self-abandonment:

> (The soul) *abandoned by creatures knows only how to abandon itself and place itself in the hands of God by a love which is most real, most genuine and most active although it has been silently infused into the soul.*

The theological justification of this self-abandonment, its method and its excellence, takes up a series of pages at the beginning of the treatise which both for pure beauty of style and sustained eloquence of pleading is a masterpiece of literature.

So far, in these passages which have been taken from the early pages of the book, Caussade has been insisting that abandonment of self-will and the throwing of the soul open to divine action are all in all, and that the divine action is present—and should be perceptible to the eye of faith—in every event of life, and that no single external circumstance is more than a temporary instrument of God's action which shows us God's will here and now. In what follows he proceeds to look a little more carefully at God's more intimate action. If our first task is to realize that God is in everything, the next is to realize that he is more particularly in everything that crosses the natural self:

> *The doctrine of pure love can only be learned through the action of God, and not as the result of our own activity of mind. God instructs the heart by sufferings and contradictions, not by ideas. . . .*

(We are approaching the traditional doctrine of passive purification.)

To possess this science, it is necessary to be disengaged from all particular goods; and, to arrive at this detachment, it is necessary to be really deprived of these goods. Thus, it is only by mortifications of all sorts, by trials and deprivations of all kinds, that we can be established in pure love. We must reach the point at which the whole of creation is nothing to us and God everything.

The soul which began by seeing and using creatures by a purely natural light, must end by seeing and using them by a purely supernatural light, and before this can happen they must become nothing to it. Hence all created things must be reduced:

First to nothing and then to the point they have to occupy in God's Order.

This is, almost verbally, the doctrine of St Francis:

It is love which, entering into a soul to make it happily die to itself and live to God, bereaves it of all human desires. . . . Theotimus, he who has forsaken all for God ought to resume nothing but according to God's good pleasure. . . . God commanded the prophet Isaias to strip himself naked; and he did so . . . and then, the time prefixed by God having expired, he resumed his clothes. Even so are we to . . . die with our Saviour naked upon the cross, and rise again with him in newness of life.[1]

This applies to all the soul's sight of itself, and of its way, aims and progress:

(God) desires an entire handing over the soul to him. If one has the conviction that his guidance is good, one has no longer faith nor self-abandonment.

The waters are indeed deepening; we are in the Night of the Spirit, the night of faith and hope:

Previously, the soul saw by its own ideas and lights how the plan of its perfection was working out; this is no longer the case when it is in this condition. . . . God now communicates himself to it as Life, but is no longer before its eyes as the Way and the Truth. The Bride seeks the Bridegroom in the night: he is behind her and holds her in his hands.

[1] *The Love of God*, ix, 16.

xiii

Introduction

We are also in the night of love:

> *A far more grievous trial for a soul who desires nothing but to love its God, is the impossibility in which it finds itself of assuring itself that it loves him. . . .*

and again:

> *To steal God from a heart which desires but God, what a secret of love! It is indeed a great secret of love, for by that means (and only by that means is it possible) pure faith and pure hope are established in a soul,*

and he gives the reason in words which St John could not better:

> *The more one appears to lose with God, the more one gains; the more he deprives us of the natural, the more he gives us of the super-natural. We loved him a little for his gifts; when these are no longer perceptible, we arrive at loving him for himself alone.*

This summary of Caussade's teaching will have shown how traditional is his outlook and how closely he is in agreement with the great mystical theologians of the Dominican and Carmelite schools. Especially is this the case in his assumption throughout that for the growth of a soul to perfection the passive purifica-tions are absolutely necessary, whether they take the form of ordinary or extraordinary sufferings, or whether they are part of the direct action of God on the soul, infusing purifying light. Caussade, in *L'Abandon*, is scarcely occupied at all with "states" of prayer or a defence of contemplation. He was in fact speaking to contemplatives and therefore had no need to be. But it is pos-sible to extract from his *obiter dicta* a perfectly consistent theory. We have seen that he equates perfection with self-abandonment and proclaims that both may be aimed at by all:

> *Let us teach all simple and God-fearing hearts self-abandonment to the divine action . . . let us not distress or drive away anyone from the path of eminent perfection. Jesus calls all to it.*

And this perfection is the full, supernatural flower of the Chris-tian life, disclosed in St Paul's epistles. It is the life of the saints; there is not another "mystical" perfection beyond; this *is* mysti-cal perfection:

> *All souls would arrive at supernatural, sublime, wonderful, inconceivable states of prayer. . . . Yes, if one could only leave the hand of God to do its work, one would reach the most eminent perfection. All souls would reach it, for it is offered to all.*

And while he insists that for this perfection there is no need of states, works or favours which are theologically speaking "abnormal" or "extraordinary", since:

> *In order to reach the highest stage of perfection, the crosses sent them by Providence, with which their state of life supplies them at every moment, open to them a far surer and swifter path than extraordinary states and works,*

yet he is equally insistent that the way and grace to which he invites are *de facto* uncommon and eminent:

> *I wish to make all see that they can aim . . . at eminent sanctity. What are called extraordinary and privileged graces are so called solely because few souls are faithful enough to make themselves worthy of them.*

The careful reader of the two last extracts in their context will surely feel that the distinction between what is strictly extraordinary (the *gratiae gratis datae*, visions, the gift of prophecy and the like) and what is *de facto* extraordinary because eminent and therefore uncommon (sanctity and contemplation) has rarely been grasped more clearly or expressed more lucidly.

Indeed, the perfect agreement here as elsewhere—it is more than agreement, it is a real and pervading similarity of soul—between Caussade and St Teresa of the Infant Jesus[1] is most striking and consoling. It is well known that St Teresa took for her master St John of the Cross and was a living exemplar of his doctrine. But in the manner of her presentation of the message—in her "secret", in her "little way"—she reminds us far more of Caussade, whom, so far as I am aware, she had not read. No one at all familiar with the *Histoire d'une Ame* can fail to note the general resemblance; it will be enough here to underline some of the distinctively personal features of the saint which are anticipated in *L'Abandon*. Her very definition of the "little way" is in words that might be his:

[1] St Thérèse of Lisieux, *The Little Flower.*

> *The little way is one of spiritual childhood, of confidence and complete self-abandonment.*

Her devotion to the Infancy and Passion of our Lord, it will be remembered, did not spring, as it does with the majority of Christians, from the natural love and sympathy that childhood and suffering evoke, but from the peculiarly pure faith in the supernatural, challenged and called out, so to say, by the divinity veiled in Nazareth and still more impenetrably veiled— annihilated, in Caussade's word—in the Passion. We find the same devotion in *L'Abandon*:

> *Ask Mary, Joseph, the wise men, the shepherds: they will tell you that they find in this extreme poverty a something which renders God greater and more lovable. The deficit of the senses increases and enriches faith : the less there is for the eyes, the more for the soul. . . . The life of faith is nothing but a perpetual pursuit of God through everything that disguises, disfigures, destroys him and, if we may use the word, annihilates him.*

We think at once of the most characteristic traits of St Teresa's autobiography—of her ever-growing capacity to see, in the light of faith, the supernatural significance of apparently ordinary incidents in her own life and the lives of those dear to her. How gladly would she have made her own these lines of Caussade:

> *The history of that divine drama which consists in the life led by Jesus in holy souls . . . can only be guessed at by our faith. . . . The holy souls are the paper, their sufferings and actions are the ink. The Holy Spirit, with the pen of his activity, writes in them a living gospel.*

And the following paragraphs—among Caussade's finest— might well be taken as a complete summary of her life:

> *Their life, though extraordinary in its perfection, shows nothing on the outside but what is common and very ordinary : they fulfil the duties of religion and of their state ; others, as far as appearances go, do the same as they. Examine the rest of their lives : you will find nothing striking or special ; they are made up of the ordinary course of events. What distinguishes them—the dependence in which they live on*

the will of God which arranges everything for them—does not fall under observation. . . . When God gives himself to the soul in this way, the ordinary sequence of life becomes extraordinary. This is why nothing extraordinary appears outwardly; because it is extraordinary in itself and consequently does not need the ornament of marvels which have nothing to do with it.

A final point may be noted. It has often been remarked that the great contemplatives, whatever theological formation they may have received, all use the same language when speaking of the action of grace on the soul. Caussade is no exception, and though he never develops a theory, his scheme of thought is consistent. I will give some of the most typical passages without comment, to direct the attention of those who may be interested in the subject. His leading thesis is as follows:

God and the soul perform together a work the success of which depends entirely on the divine Workman, and can be compromised only by the soul's infidelity.

He explains this at greater length elsewhere:

The soul (of the contemplative), *like a musical instrument, receives nothing and produces nothing except in so far as the intimate operation of God occupies it in a state of passivity or applies it to some external action. Such external application is accompanied by a co-operation which from the soul's side is free and active but from God's side is infused and mystical.*

And so, as the soul grows in grace and self-abandonment,

It forms insensibly a habit of acting always by the instinct (so to speak) of God,

and thus:

The unique and infallible movement of the divine action always applies the soul in its simplicity exactly, and it corresponds always very perfectly to this intimate direction. . . . Sometimes it does this with advertence and sometimes without, being moved by obscure instincts to speak, act and abstain without other reasons,

and so:

We must learn to let ourselves go passively under the divine action,

> *allowing the Holy Spirit to act in our interior, without knowing what he is doing, and even being content not to know.*

It need scarcely be repeated that Caussade is speaking here the wisdom of God among the perfect; by them he will be understood; the rest of us may reverence his words even where we do not fully appreciate their meaning.

And so, I think, we may approach Père de Caussade—"the incomparable Caussade", as Bremond calls him—looking back to St John of the Cross and St Francis de Sales and forward to St Teresa of the Infant Jesus. If I have, in these pages of introduction, extracted and emphasized almost solely those sentences in which he outlines his theories, it is because a teacher must ultimately be judged by the great principles of his doctrine. But it is not the least merit of Caussade that he may be read by those to whom theory means little, and who ask of a book nothing but that it may lead them to God.

1933

A BIOGRAPHICAL NOTE

JEAN PIERRE DE CAUSSADE was born in 1675 and entered the Jesuit novitiate in Toulouse at the age of eighteen. After spending a year or so in the novitiate he was sent to teach classics in the Jesuit college in Aurillac. In 1702 he began his theological studies, was ordained priest in 1705, completed his theological studies the following year and took his final vows in 1708. From 1708 to 1714 he taught grammar, physics and logic in the Jesuit college in Toulouse, and then ceased teaching in order to devote himself to the itinerant career of a missioner and preacher.

Between the years 1715 and 1729 he was stationed successively in the residences of Rodez, Montauban, Auch, Clermont, Annecy, Puy and Beauvais. For the next two years he was in Lorraine, and it was during this period that he made his first contact with the nuns of the Order of the Visitation in Nancy, to whom we are indebted for having preserved his letters and the notes of his conferences. In 1731 he was sent as spiritual director to the seminary in Albi, but two years later was back in Nancy in charge of the Jesuit Retreat house there. During his seven years in this office he gave frequent conferences to the Visitation nuns and undertook the personal direction of several of them. The Superior of the convent at this time was Mother de Rosen to whom many of his letters were written. She was a woman of great intelligence and culture, and of high mystical attainments, like her trusted junior, Sister de Vioménil.

In 1740 Fr de Caussade was back in Toulouse. Then from 1741 to 1743 he was Rector of the Jesuit college in Perpignan, and for the following three years he occupied a similar post in the college in Albi. His letters during these years show him struggling with wry humour to resign himself to the office of superior which he seems to have heartily disliked. In 1746 he returned to the House of Professed in Toulouse and acted as spiritual director in the seminary there. His blindness, which appears to have been threatening him for some years, grew worse, but he bore it with courageous fortitude and in the spirit of his own great principle of self-abandonment to the will of God. He died in 1751 at the age of seventy-six.

Apart from his letters and conference notes which were preserved by the nuns of the Visitation, Caussade's contemporaries appear to have left no note of him beyond the bare statement of his whereabouts as given above. His career seems to have been typical of most other men of his Order, and again typically his name occurs once only in the Jesuit menology in a passing allusion in a biographical account of his better-known colleague, P. Antoine. Yet in spite of this lack of contemporary evidence we can gain a good impression of the man from his works.

The only book he published in his own lifetime was the "Spiritual Instructions on the various states of prayer according to the teaching of Bossuet" (published in English under the title of *On Prayer* by Burns Oates and Washbourne). This book appeared anonymously in 1741 at Perpignan and was for a time attributed to his popular contemporary, P. Antoine, S.J. The style is dry and in the form of a catechism, but it betrays profound spiritual discernment and his own abiding preoccupation with the deeper problems of the spiritual life. Possibly also it was written to combat any suspicion of his being a Quietist, for the spiritual world of France was still shaking from the great controversy between the two Archbishops, Bossuet and Fénelon, in which the latter had been overwhelmed, and had later been condemned by Rome for Semi-Quietism.

But Caussade reveals himself more clearly in the Treatise on Self-abandonment and in his Letters. The history of these works is somewhat peculiar. They were not published by Caussade himself or even during his lifetime. The Treatise was put together from notes of his conferences which the nuns of the Visitation convent in Nancy took down and circulated among their other convents. After some years these notes were published in various mutilated forms until Fr Ramière, S.J., took the work in hand, putting them into logical order and publishing them together with the Letters in 1861. Since that time they have gone through no less than twenty-five editions, with slight emendations and additions.

In the Treatise we get a good picture of Caussade. His clarity, fluency and ease of style show us a man who is master of his subject. He is also passionately in earnest about it and passionately eager to communicate it to others. There is nothing cold or formal about him; indeed at moments his burning zeal and conviction lift his style to a moving and urgent eloquence.

In his Letters he shows himself to be not only a teacher but also a man who fervently practises the art of prayer for himself, and has suffered and passed through the tremendous experiences of the spiritual life in his own soul. His direction of souls in these lofty and difficult ways is authoritative and firm with the authority that comes from profound study and intimate personal experience. But beneath his intensity and his almost relentless drive there is always the calm serenity and poise of a well-balanced character, and the human kindliness of a sensitive director of souls.

The style is the man, and from the style of the Letters we get a picture of a man of delightful spontaneity, of verve and vigour, but tender, sympathetic and humorous. He is subtle but logical, humble but sure, straight, forceful and firm yet gently persuasive and always encouraging and patient. Obviously Caussade was a man of fine natural character and charm, and of high spiritual attainments and mystical gifts. No wonder his Treatise and Letters have become one of the favourites among spiritual classics.

Perhaps a warning should be given to readers of the Letters. We must remember that these were written for the most part to nuns who were already far advanced in the spiritual life, and so they take for granted the essential but elementary fundamentals of religious life. These of course are of first importance and must not be neglected or underestimated by even the most advanced, and much less so by beginners like ourselves. But, read with this caution in mind, the Letters can be enjoyed and used by everyone.

JOHN JOYCE, S.J.

CONTENTS

Introduction, *by Dom David Knowles*   v

A Biographical Note, *by John Joyce, S.J.*   xix

PART ONE

SELF-ABANDONMENT TO DIVINE PROVIDENCE

Book I

THE VIRTUE OF SELF-ABANDONMENT

Chap.

  1. Sanctity consists in fidelity to the order established by God and in self-abandonment to his action   3

  2. The divine action works unceasingly at the sanctification of souls   18

Book II

THE STATE OF SELF-ABANDONMENT

  1. The nature and excellence of the state of self-abandonment   42

  2. The duties of souls whom God calls to the state of self-abandonment   55

  3. Trials accompanying the state of self-abandonment   71

  4. Of the paternal assistance with which God surrounds the souls who abandon themselves to him   84

PART TWO

LETTERS ON THE PRACTICE OF SELF-ABANDONMENT

Book I

THE ESTEEM AND LOVE OF SELF-ABANDONMENT

Letter

1. The happiness and unalterable peace of the soul that abandons itself to God 109
2. Self-abandonment is the quickest way to reach pure love and perfection 110
3. Application of this to the writer. The profound peace which he enjoys through self-abandonment in the midst of business worries 112
4. The same subject 114
5. The same subject 115
6. Self-abandonment softens the hardship of loneliness 116
7. The happiness gained from self-abandonment by a community of Poor Clares 117
8. Motives for our self-abandonment on God's side— The divine grandeur and goodness 118
9. A further motive for self-abandonment to God: his paternal Providence 121
10. The same subject 123
11. The mutual good wishes of souls who seek nothing but God 125

Book II

THE PRACTICE OF THE VIRTUE OF SELF-ABANDONMENT

1. Principles and practices of self-abandonment 127
2. A general plan of the spiritual combat 131
3. The first work of God in the soul 132

Letter

4. The practice of self-abandonment in general   133
5. On the means of acquiring self-abandonment   134
6. General directions   136
7. The same subject   139
8. The prayer of souls called to a life of self-abandonment—Some wise advice on prayer   140
9. The same subject: The danger of illusion in the prayer of recollection   142
10. The same subject   144
11. The practice of self-abandonment in different states of the soul   146
12. The Practice of self-abandonment through peace of soul   150
13. The same subject   152
14. The practice of self-abandonment in time of consolation   156
15. The same subject   160
16. The same subject   162
17. Docility to interior inspirations of the Holy Spirit: Peaceful waiting   166
18. How we should moderate our desires and fears   168
19. How to tend towards simplicity   169
20. The same subject   170
21. Diverse attractions of grace   172
22. Self-abandonment in the trials to which a vocation is subjected   174
23. The same subject   175
24. The same subject   177
25. The same subject   179
26. Self-abandonment in regard to one's occupations and undertakings   180
27. Self-abandonment in the acceptance of offices   181
28. The same subject   182
29. The same subject applied to the writer himself   183
30. Self-abandonment in illness   184
31. The same subject   186
32. Bearing with one's neighbour and oneself   187

Contents

Letter

  33. Bearing with oneself   188
  34. Preparation for the sacraments, prayers, reading;
        instruction on behaviour   189
  35. Programme for a time of rest in the country   190
  36. Life and death—Consolations and ordeals   192
  37. The same subject   194

Book III

OBSTACLES TO SELF-ABANDONMENT

  1. Feelings of vanity—Recurring infidelities   196
  2. The failings of beginners   201
  3. Interior troubles voluntarily entertained; weakness   202
  4. The same subject   206
  5. Love of relations   213
  6. Too friendly attachments   215
  7. The same subject   216
  8. Active natures   217
  9. Excessive eagerness of good desires   219
  10. Haste in pious reading   220
  11. Indiscreet and undisciplined zeal   221
  12. Dislike of accepting privileges ordered by superiors   223
  13. The same subject; attachment to one's own opinions   224
  14. Dislike of self-revelation   226
  15. Discouragement   227
  16. Fear of failure and of making oneself conspicuous   228

Book IV

FIRST ORDEAL OF SOULS CALLED
TO THE STATE OF SELF-ABANDONMENT—
ARIDITY, HELPLESSNESS, AVERSION

  1. Ordeals as a whole—General instruction   233
  2. Interior vicissitudes   240

Letter

3. The same subject—Self-abandonment 241
4. Darkness—Helplessness 243
5. Helplessness—Distractions 246
6. The same subject—Interior rebelliousness—
   Spiritual poverty 250
7. Darkness—Insensibility 253
8. Dryness—Distractions during prayer 257
9. Distractions—Weariness—Outbursts of feeling 260
10. Aversion—Idleness 263
11. Powerlessness—Remembrance of former faults—
    Weariness—Fears 264
12. The uses of ordeals—Behaviour to be followed 268
13. The same subject 272
14. The same subject 275
15. The same subject 278
16. The same subject 282
17. The same subject 285
18. The same subject 288
19. Usefulness of ordeals, even when they are punish-
    ments 290
20. Deep peace as the result of these ordeals 292
21. The same subject 294

Book V

NEW ORDEALS—
SUFFERINGS, AFFLICTIONS, PRIVATIONS

1. Sickness and its usefulness—Rules to be followed 298
2. Suffering of various kinds 299
3. Public calamities and disasters 301
4. Antagonistic dispositions and characters 302
5. The same subject 304
6. Vexations of various kinds 305
7. The same subject—Rules to be followed 307
8. Vexations caused by good people 308
9. The same subject 309

Contents

Letter

10. Seeing God in our trials   310
11. Loss of human support   311
12. A director's departure   312
13. The same subject   313
14. Self-abandonment in ordeals of this kind   315
15. Usefulness of these afflictions   317
16. The same subject   320
17. Behaviour to be shown in these ordeals   322
18. The same subject   324
19. Happiness of souls abandoning themselves to God in their afflictions   326

Book VI

CONSEQUENCES OF ORDEALS—FEAR OF GOD'S DISFAVOUR

1. Temptations, fears of yielding to them   328
2. Fear of temptations themselves   329
3. Description of the state of a tempted soul, and of God's plans for it   330
4. Sundry temptations   334
5. Fear of lacking submission to God   335
6. Fear of displeasing God can sometimes be the result of self-love   340
7. Fear of lacking goodwill   343
8. Fear of loving creatures more than God   347
9. Fear of displeasing God and misleading his creatures   348
10. Fear of not making progress and of not doing enough penance   350
11. Fears concerning confessions   352
12. The same subject   353
13. Fear about contrition   354
14. General confession   355
15. The same subject—Various fears   356
16. The same subject—Various fears   357
17. Pangs of Conscience—Rebelliousness of the passions   360

Letter
18. The same subject   363
19. The same subject—Relapses   364
20. Despondency in ordeals—Distractions—Resentment   365
21. The same subject   367
22. Realization of our wretchedness—Exterior vexations   369
23. Past faults   371
24. Lamentable results of our imprudence   375
25. Rules to be followed in spiritual ordeals   377
26. The same subject   379

Book VII

ULTIMATE ORDEALS—AGONY AND
MYSTICAL DEATH—THEIR FRUITS

1. Spiritual nakedness—Self-obliteration. The temptation to despair   384
2. The same subject   389
3. Interior prostration   393
4. The same subject   394
5. Emptiness of heart   395
6. The same subject—Grief redoubled   396
7. The same subject   398
8. Violent temptations   401
9. Annihilation and spiritual agony   404
10. Mystical death; its usefulness   408
11. The same subject—Before retreat   410
12. The same subject—After retreat   412
13. The soul's purgation   415
14. Explanation of these ordeals—Spiritual direction   419
15. The same subject   423
16. The explanation of apparent despair   426
17. The practice of self-abandonment in the midst of these ordeals   427
18. Fruit of utter death to self   429

Contents

Book VIII

SPIRITUAL COUNSELS

Counsel

1. For the attainment of perfect conformity to the will of God 432
2. Advice on the exterior conduct of a soul called to the life of self-abandonment 435
3. A method for interior direction 440
4. What we should do after committing faults 442
5. Temptations and interior sufferings 443

Father de Caussade's prayer for obtaining holy self-abandonment 449
A prayer in time of temptation 449

Part One

SELF-ABANDONMENT TO DIVINE PROVIDENCE

BOOK I

THE VIRTUE OF SELF-ABANDONMENT

CHAPTER I: SANCTITY CONSISTS IN FIDELITY TO THE ORDER ESTABLISHED BY GOD AND IN SELF-ABANDONMENT TO HIS ACTION

§ I

The sanctity of the saints of the Old Law, as likewise that of St Joseph and our Lady, consisted wholly in fidelity to the order established by God

GOD still speaks to us today as he spoke to our fathers, when there were no spiritual directors or set methods. Then, spirituality consisted in fidelity to the designs of God, for it had not yet been reduced to an art and explained in a lofty and detailed manner with many rules, maxims and instructions. Doubtless our present needs demand this, but it was not so in former ages when men were more upright and simple. Then it was enough for those who led a spiritual life to see that each moment brought with it a duty to be faithfully fulfilled. On that duty the whole of their attention was fixed at each successive moment, like the hand of a clock which marks each moment of the hour. Under God's unceasing guidance their spirit turned without conscious effort to each new duty as it was presented to them by God each hour of the day.

Such were the hidden springs of Mary's conduct, for she was of all creatures the most utterly submissive to God. Her reply to the angel when she said simply: *Fiat mihi secundum verbum tuum*, contained all the mystical theology of our ancestors. Everything was reduced, as indeed it is today, to the complete and utter self-abandonment of the soul to God's will under whatever form it was manifested.

This beautiful and lofty disposition of Mary's soul is admirably revealed in those simple words: *Fiat mihi*. Note how per-

3

fectly they agree with those words which our Lord wishes us to have always on our lips and in our hearts: *Fiat voluntas tua.* It is true that what was asked of Mary at that moment was something very glorious for her. But all the splendour of that glory would have had no effect on her had she not seen in it the will of God which alone was able to move her.

It was this divine will which ruled her every act. Whatever her occupations, commonplace or lofty, they were in her eyes but external signs, sometimes clear, sometimes obscure, under which she saw the means both of glorifying God and of acknowledging the action of the Almighty. Her spirit, transported with joy, looked on everything she had to do or to suffer at each moment as a gift from him who fills with good things the hearts which hunger for him alone and not for created things.

§ 2

*The duties of each moment are shadows beneath which
the divine action lies concealed*

"The power of the Most High shall overshadow thee," said the angel to Mary. This shadow beneath which the power of God conceals itself in order to bring Jesus Christ to souls, is the duty, attraction or cross which every moment brings. These are in fact but shadows similar to those in nature which spread themselves like a veil over visible objects and hide them from us. Thus in the moral and supernatural order the duties of each moment conceal under their outward appearances the true reality of the divine will which alone is worthy of our attention. It was in this light that Mary regarded them. As these shadows spread over her faculties, far from causing her any illusion, they filled her with faith in him who is unchanging. Draw back, archangel, you are only a shadow; your moment passes and you disappear. Mary moves beyond you; Mary goes forward unceasingly. From now on you are left far behind her. But the Holy Spirit, who under the visible form of this mission has entered into her, will never leave her.

There are few extraordinary features in the external life of the Blessed Virgin. At least Holy Scripture does not record any.

4

Her life is represented as externally very simple and ordinary. She does and experiences the same things as other people in her state of life. She goes to visit her cousin Elizabeth, as her other relations do. She takes shelter in a stable: a natural consequence of her poverty. She returns to Nazareth after having fled from the persecution of Herod; Jesus and Joseph live there with her, supporting themselves by the work of their hands. This provides their daily bread, but what is the divine food with which this material bread feeds the faith of Mary and Joseph? What is the sacrament of each of their sacred moments? What treasures of grace are contained in each of these moments underneath the commonplace appearance of the events that fill them? Outwardly these events are no different from those which happen to everyone, but the interior invisible element discerned by faith is nothing less than God himself performing great works. O bread of angels, heavenly manna, the pearl of the Gospels, the sacrament of the present moment! You present God in such lowly forms as the manger, the hay and straw! But to whom do you give him? *Esurientes reples bonis.* "You fill the hungry with good things." God reveals himself to the humble in the humblest things, while the great who never penetrate beneath the surface do not discover him even in great events.

§ 3

How much easier holiness would become if it were regarded
from this point of view

If the work of our sanctification presents us with difficulties apparently so insurmountable, it is because we do not look at it in the right way. In reality holiness consists in one thing alone, namely, fidelity to God's plan. And this fidelity is equally within everyone's capacity in both its active and passive practice.

The active practice of fidelity consists in accomplishing the duties imposed on us by the general laws of God and the Church, and by the particular state of life which we have embraced. Passive fidelity consists in the loving acceptance of all that God sends us at every moment.

Which of these two requirements of holiness is beyond our

strength? Not active fidelity, since the duties imposed by it cease to be such when they are really beyond our powers. If the state of your health does not allow you to hear Mass, you are under no obligation to do so. It is the same with all positive precepts, namely, those which prescribe duties to be done. The only precepts to which no exceptions can be permitted are those which forbid the doing of things that are evil in themselves, for it is never permissible to do evil.

Can anything be easier or more reasonable? What excuse can we plead? Yet this is all that God demands of the soul in the work of its sanctification. He demands it from the high and the low, from the strong and the weak; in a word, from all, always and everywhere. It is true then that he asks from us only what is simple and easy, for it is sufficient to possess this simple fund of goodwill in order to attain to eminent holiness.

If over and above the commandments he puts before us the counsels as a more perfect goal of our endeavour, he is always careful to accommodate the practice of the counsels to our position and character. The attractions of grace which facilitate the practice of the counsels are the chief sign that he is calling us to follow them. He never presses anyone beyond his strength or aptitudes. Once more, what could be more just?

All you who aim at perfection and are tempted to discouragement by what you read in the lives of the saints and by what is prescribed in certain books of piety; you who are appalled by the terrible ideas which you form of perfection, it is for your consolation that God wills me to write this. Learn now what you seemingly do not know.

This God of goodness has put within easy reach all the things which are necessary and common in the natural order, such as earth, air and water. Nothing is more necessary than breathing, sleeping and eating; and nothing is easier. Love and fidelity are no less necessary in the supernatural order; therefore they cannot be so difficult to acquire as is imagined. Look at your life. What is it made up of? Of innumerable unimportant actions. It is just with these very things, so trifling in themselves, that God is pleased to be satisfied. They are the share that falls to the soul in the work of its perfection. God himself makes his meaning too clear for us to doubt this. "Fear God and keep his commandments, for this is the whole duty of man." Here is all that a man has to do on his side, here is what active fidelity consists in. If man fulfils his part, God will do the rest. Grace will take full control of him, and the wonders that it will work in him surpass all man's understanding. For the ear has not heard, nor the eye seen, nor the heart felt what God plans in his mind, resolves upon in his will, and executes by his power in souls that abandon themselves to him.

The passive part of holiness is even more easy, for it consists merely in accepting what most frequently cannot be avoided, and in suffering with love, that is to say with resignation and sweetness what is too often endured with weariness and discontent.

Here then once more is the whole of sanctity. Here is the grain of mustard seed of which the fruits are lost because we cannot recognize it on account of its smallness. Here is the drachma of the Gospel parable, the treasure which we never find because we imagine it to be too far away to be sought.

Do not ask me what is the secret of finding this treasure. There is no secret. This treasure is everywhere. It is offered to us at every moment and in every place. All creatures, both friendly and hostile, pour it out with prodigality and make it pervade every faculty of our body and soul, right to the depths of our heart. We have only to open our mouths and they will be filled. Divine activity floods the whole universe; it pervades all creatures; it flows over them. Wherever they are, it is there; it precedes, accompanies and follows them. We have but to allow ourselves to be carried forward on the crest of its waves.

Would to God that kings and their ministers, princes of the Church and of the world, priests, soldiers, tradesmen and labourers, in a word all men, understood how easy it is for them to attain great holiness! They have only to fulfil the simple duties of the Catholic faith and of their state of life, to accept with submission the crosses that go with those duties, and to submit with faith and love to the designs of Providence in everything that is constantly being presented to them to do and to endure, without searching for anything themselves. This is the spirituality that sanctified the patriarchs and prophets before so many different methods and masters of the spiritual life were introduced. This is the spirituality of all ages and states of life which assuredly cannot be made holy in a nobler, more wonderful and easier manner than by simply making use of what God, the sovereign director of souls, gives them to do or suffer at each moment.[1]

§ 4

Perfection does not consist in understanding God's designs but in submitting to them

God's designs, God's good pleasure, the will of God, the action of God and his grace are all one and the same thing in this life. They are God working in the soul to make it like himself. Perfection is nothing else than the faithful co-operation of the soul with the work of God, and it begins, grows and is consummated in our souls secretly and without our being aware of it.

Theology is full of ideas and expressions explaining the marvels of this ultimate state in each soul in accordance with its capacity. A man may know all the theory of it, may speak and write admirably on the subject, and instruct and direct souls, but if his knowledge remains merely theoretical, then compared with those who attain the goal of God's design without knowing the theory of it in whole or in part, or without being able to discourse on it, he is like a sick doctor in comparison with simple people who are in perfect health.

When God's designs and will are embraced with simplicity by a faithful soul, they produce this divine state in it without its knowing it, just as medicine taken obediently by a sick man effects his cure even though he neither knows nor is capable of

[1] It would be a misunderstanding of the author's thought to suppose that he wishes to urge anyone to embark on the spiritual life without a director. He himself elsewhere says expressly that in order to be capable of doing without a director, one must already have had long and skilful direction. Still less does he seek to turn anyone away from the practices in use in the Church for ridding oneself of vices and acquiring virtues. What he means, and what cannot be too frequently said, is that the direction given by divine Providence is the first and best of all, and that the most necessary and sanctifying of all spiritual practices is the faithful carrying out and the loving acceptance of everything that this fatherly Providence ordains us to do and to suffer.

knowing anything about medicine. Similarly, as it is fire and not the philosophy or scientific knowledge of fire that warms us, so it is the will and designs of God that produce sanctity in our souls and not intellectual speculation about this principle and its effects. If we wish to quench our thirst, we must lay aside books which explain thirst, and take a drink. By itself, curiosity for knowledge can only make one thirstier. Thus, when we thirst for holiness, curiosity for theoretical knowledge of it can only drive it further from us. We must put speculation on one side, and with simplicity drink everything that God's designs present to us in actions and sufferings. What happens to us each moment by God's design is for us the holiest, best and most divine thing.

§ 5

Spiritual reading and other exercises of piety sanctify us only in so far as they are the channels of God's action

The whole essence of the spiritual life consists in recognizing the designs of God for us at the present moment. All reading that is chosen by us apart from God's designs is harmful to us; the designs and will of God are the grace which works in the depths of our hearts through the books we read as through everything else we do. Apart from God, books are merely useless externals, and being devoid for us of the life-giving power of God's plan, they succeed only in emptying the heart by the very satisfaction which they give to the mind.

This divine will, working in the soul of a simple ignorant girl by means of a few ordinary sufferings and actions, produces in the depths of her heart this mysterious fulfilment of supernatural life without putting into her mind ideas which might make her conceited. While on the contrary, a proud man who reads spiritual books only from curiosity and without any regard for the will of God receives only the dead letter into his mind, and his heart grows ever drier and harder.

The will and designs of God are the life of the soul no matter what the appearance under which the soul receives them or applies them to itself.

In whatever manner this divine will touches the mind, it

9

nourishes the soul and continually enlarges it by giving it what is best for it at every moment. These happy effects are produced not by any particular event as such, but by God's design for each individual moment. What was best for the moment which has just passed, is so no longer because it is no longer the will of God; this now presents itself under other appearances and forms the duty of the present moment. It is this duty which, in whatever guise it may appear, is the most sanctifying for the soul.

If the duty of the present moment is to read, then reading will produce this mysterious fulfilment in the depths of the soul. If the divine will bids us turn from reading to the duty of contemplation, this duty develops the "new man" in the depths of the heart, whereas to continue reading would be harmful and useless. If the divine will withdraws us from contemplation in order to hear confessions etc., even for a long time, this duty is the means of forming Jesus Christ in the depths of the heart, and all the sweetness of contemplation would only serve to drive him out.

It is the designs of God that are the fulfilment of all our moments. They manifest themselves in a thousand different ways which thus become our successive duties, and form, increase and perfect the "new man" in us until we attain the full stature destined for us by divine wisdom. This mysterious growth in age of Jesus Christ in our hearts is the end and fulfilment produced by the designs of God; it is the fruit of his grace and his divine goodness.

This fruit, as we have said, is produced, fed and increased by the duties which are successively presented to us and are filled with the will of God. In performing these duties we are always sure of possessing the "better part", for this holy will is itself the "better part". We have only to allow it freedom to work in us and abandon ourselves blindly to it in perfect confidence. It is infinitely wise, infinitely powerful, infinitely beneficent towards souls who place their hope in it utterly without reserve, who love and seek nothing but it alone, and who believe with unshakeable faith and confidence that what it does at each moment is the best, without looking elsewhere for something more or something less, and without pausing to consider the connection between God's designs and external things, for this is the mere seeking of self-love.

The will of God is the essential and real element and the power in all things; it is the will of God that adjusts and adapts them to the soul. Without it, all is nothingness, emptiness, lies and vanity, the mere letter without the spirit, empty husks and death. The will of God is the salvation, health and life of body and soul no matter what the external appearance of the thing to which it is applied. We must not therefore examine the suitability of things to mind and body in order to assess their value, for this is of little importance; it is the will of God which gives to things, whatever they may be, the power to form Jesus Christ in the depths of our hearts. We must not dictate to God's will nor set limits to its action, for it is all-powerful.

Whatever ideas the mind may choose to be filled with, whatever the feelings of the body; even if the mind be afflicted with distractions and worries, and the body with sickness and death, nevertheless the divine will is always for the present moment the life of the body and the soul, for in whatever state they are, both are ultimately sustained only by the divine will. Without it bread is poison; with it poison is a salutary remedy. Without it books do nothing but darken the mind, and with it darkness becomes light. It is everything that is good and true in all things. And in all things it gives us God, and God is the infinite being who takes the place of all things for the soul that possesses him.

§6

The mind and other human means are useful only in so far as they serve as instruments of the divine action

The mind, together with everything that depends on it, is bent upon holding first place among the means of divine action, and it has to be reduced to the last place like a dangerous slave. A man wholly devoted to God can draw from it great advantages if he knows how to use it; but it can also do great harm if it is not kept under control. When the soul longs for the use of creatures, grace makes it understand that divine action is sufficient for it; when the soul wishes to abandon created means at the wrong time, divine action shows it that these things are instruments which must not be taken up or abandoned on its own judgement, but must be accepted and adapted with simplicity to God's designs, making use of all things with detachment as one not using them, and as being deprived of everything yet lacking nothing.

Divine action, being limitless in its plenitude, can take possession of a soul only to the extent to which that soul is emptied of all trust in its own action, for such self-confidence is a spurious fullness that excludes divine action.

This is the obstacle most likely to impede divine action, namely that which is found in the soul itself, for in the case of external obstacles the divine action can, when it chooses, convert them into useful means. Everything is equally useful and useless to it. Without it everything is as nothing, and with it nothing becomes everything. Meditation, contemplation, vocal prayers, interior silence, acts of the faculties of the soul, whether accompanied by emotional feelings, and whether distinctly or less clearly perceived, a life of retirement or an active one, all these things may be valuable in themselves, but the best of all for the soul is what God wills at this particular moment, and all else must be regarded by the soul with perfect indifference as being nothing at all.

Thus, seeing only God in all things, the soul must take or leave them all at his will so as to live, to grow and to hope only in his designs, and not in things which have no power or value except through him. It must say like St Paul always and of everything: "Lord, what wilt thou have me do?" Not this thing or that, but: "All that thou wishest!" The mind likes one thing, the body another, but, Lord, I desire nothing but your holy will. Prayer or action, vocal or mental prayer, whether active or passive, in the darkness of faith or in the light of understanding, with a special gift of grace or by ordinary grace, all these things are as nothing, Lord, for it is your will that gives them all their real and sole value. Your will alone is the object of my devotion, and not created things, however elevated and sublime they may be; for the fulfilment of grace is the perfection of the heart and not of the mind.

The presence of God which sanctifies our souls is the indwelling of the Blessed Trinity, who take up their abode in the depths of our hearts when we submit to the divine will; for the presence of God that results from contemplation effects this intimate union in us only in the same way as other things which are part of God's design. Contemplation however ranks first among these things because it is the greatest means of uniting ourselves to God when the divine will bids us make use of it.

We are perfectly right therefore to esteem and love contemplation and other practices of piety, provided that our esteem and attraction to them are directed wholly to God who in his infinite goodness wills to use these means in order to give himself to our souls. In entertaining a prince's suite, one entertains the prince himself. It would be an insult to him to show no regard for his officers on the plea of wanting him alone.

§ 7

*Genuine and stable peace is to be found only in submission
to divine action*

The soul that is not attached to the will of God alone, will find neither contentment nor sanctification in the various means which it may try nor in even the most excellent practices of piety. If what God himself selects for you does not satisfy you, what other hand than his can serve you as you desire? If you are disgusted with the food prepared for you by the divine will itself, what other food will not seem insipid to so depraved a taste? A soul can be truly nourished, strengthened, purified, enriched and sanctified only by the divine plenitude of the present moment. What more do you want? Since all that is good is here, why seek it elsewhere? Do you know better than God? He ordains it thus, why therefore desire it otherwise? Can his wisdom and goodness be mistaken? Ought you not to be convinced of the excellence of whatever accords with this divine wisdom and goodness? Do you think you will find peace by struggling against the Almighty? Is it not rather this very resistance which we too often make almost without admitting the fact to ourselves, that is the cause of all our agitation?

It is indeed right that the soul that is not satisfied with the fullness of divine action in the present moment, should be punished by being unable to find contentment in anything else. If books, the example of the saints and spiritual discourses disturb our peace of soul, or if they fill the soul without satisfying it, this is a sign that we have strayed from the path of pure self-abandonment to divine action and that we are filling ourselves with these things in a spirit of self-seeking; there is then no room for God. We must get rid of these things for they are an obstacle to grace. But when divine action prescribes these things, the soul accepts them like everything else, that is to say, as God's plan for us. The soul takes them just as they are, accepting merely the use of them in order to remain faithful to God's design; and as soon as their moment is past it abandons them and turns contentedly to the duties of the next moment. Nothing in truth is really good for me but the action which agrees with God's design. I cannot find elsewhere any means, however good in itself, that is better adapted for my sanctification or capable of giving me peace.

§ 8

The perfection of souls and the excellence of various states of life are measured by their fidelity to God's designs

God's design imparts a supernatural and divine value to everything for the soul that conforms to that design. All it imposes, all it contains, and every object to which it extends becomes holy and perfect, for its power has no limits; everything it touches, it makes divine.

But in order not to stray either to right or left, the soul must not follow any inspiration, which it believes it has received from God, before making certain that this inspiration is not diverting it from the duties of its state. These duties are the surest manifestation of God's design, and nothing must be preferred to them. In them there is nothing to be feared, nothing to be excluded or preferred. The moments employed in fulfilling these duties are most precious and salutary for the soul by the very fact that they give it the undoubted assurance that it is accomplishing the good pleasure of its God.

The whole virtue of what is called holiness lies in these designs of God; nothing therefore must be rejected, nothing sought after, but everything must be accepted from his hand and nothing without him. Books, the counsels of the wise, vocal prayers and interior affections, all these things instruct us, direct us and unite us with him provided that God's will prescribes them. Quietism is in error when it despises these means and all use of the senses, for there are souls whom God wishes to go by this road always; and this is shown clearly enough by their state of life and spiritual leanings. It is useless to imagine methods of self-abandonment from which all personal activity is excluded; when the divine plan prescribes action, holiness for us lies in activity.

Beyond the duties imposed on each one by his state of life, God may require certain actions which are not included among these duties, although in no way contrary to them. In such cases spiritual attraction and inspiration are the indication of the designs of God, and the most perfect course for souls whom God is leading in this way is to add what is inspired to what is commanded, observing however the precautions which inspiration requires, so as not to interfere with the duties of one's state or with what belongs purely to Providence.

God makes saints as he pleases, but they are all made according to his plan, and all must be submissive to this plan. This submission is true self-abandonment, and it is the most perfect of all ways.

The duties imposed by their state of life and by God's Providence are common to all the saints and are God's mark on them all in general. They live hidden in obscurity, for the world is so deadly that they steer clear of its dangers; but this does not constitute their sanctity; it consists entirely in their submission to God's designs. The more absolute this submission becomes, the greater is their sanctity. We must not think that those in whom God causes virtues to be displayed in unusual and extraordinary ways and by unquestionable spiritual attractions and inspirations follow the path of self-abandonment any the less on that account. Once God's design imposes these extraordinary acts on them as a duty, they must not be content merely with the duties of their state and of ordinary Providence, for then they would not be abandoning themselves to God and his will; his will would no longer rule all their moments, and their moments would not be the will of God. They must reach out and extend themselves to the further measure of God's designs along this way which is traced out for them by spiritual attraction. The inspiration of grace must become for them a duty, and they must be faithful to it. As there are souls whose whole duty is defined for them by external laws and who must confine themselves to these because it is God's design to restrict them within these bounds, so there are others who beside their external duties should also be faithful to the interior law which the Holy Spirit imprints on their hearts.

But which are the holiest? It is mere vain curiosity to try to find out. Each must follow the way that is marked out for him. Perfection consists in complete submission to God's designs and in carrying out unfailingly what is most perfect in them.

To compare the different states in themselves takes us no further, for it is not in the quantity or quality of what is commanded that holiness is to be sought. If self-love is the motive on which we act, or if it is not corrected when we become aware of it, we shall always be poor in the midst of an abundance that is not of God's design. However, to give some answer to the question, it is my opinion that holiness corresponds to the love we have for God's good pleasure; the more his will and designs are loved, no matter what the means they ordain, the greater is the sanctity. This is seen in Jesus, Mary and Joseph; for in their personal lives there was more love than grandeur, more form than matter; and we are not told that these holy persons sought out holy things and circumstances, but only holiness in all their circumstances.

It must therefore be concluded that there is no particular path which is the most perfect one; the most perfect in general is submission to God's designs whether in the performance of external duties or in interior dispositions.

§ 9

Conclusion of the first chapter. How easy holiness becomes when this doctrine is well understood

I believe that if souls aiming seriously at holiness were taught to follow this way, they would be spared a great deal of trouble. I say this for people in the world as well as for souls specially privileged by Providence. If the former knew the merit hidden in what each moment of the day brings them, I mean their daily duties and the actions proper to their state of life; if the latter could only persuade themselves that the essence of sanctity consists in things which seem of no importance to them and which they even consider alien to it; if both these classes of souls understood that in order to rise to the highest degree of perfection the crosses, which by divine Providence are furnished them at every instant by their state of life, open to them a far surer and shorter road than extraordinary states and actions, and that the true philosopher's stone is submission to the designs of God which transmutes into divine gold all their occupations, their worries and sufferings, how happy they would be! What consolation and courage they would draw from the thought that in order to gain God's friendship and all the glories of heaven, they need neither do nor suffer anything more than what they are already doing and suffering, and that what they waste and reckon worthless would be enough to purchase eminent holiness!

O my God, how I should wish to be the missionary of your holy will and teach everyone that there is nothing so easy, so ordinary and so ready to everyone's hand as holiness! How I should like to be able to make them understand that just as the good thief and the bad thief had not different things to do and suffer in order to be saints, so two people, one of whom is worldly and the other leading an interior and spiritual life, have, neither of them, more to do or suffer than the other. The one who sanctifies himself acquires eternal happiness in doing with submission to your holy will the same things that the other who damns himself does through self-will; and the latter damns himself in suffering unwillingly and rebelliously the very same things that the other who saves his soul endures with resignation. The heart alone makes the difference.

O beloved souls who read this, the cost will be no greater for you. Do what you are doing now, suffer what you are suffering now; to do all this with holiness, nothing need be changed but your hearts. By the heart is meant the will, and sanctity therefore consists in willing what happens to us by God's design. Yes, holiness of heart is a simple *fiat*, a simple conformity of the will to God's will. What can be easier? For who can fail to love a will so lovable and good? Let us love it then, and through this love alone everything in us will be made divine.

CHAPTER 2: THE DIVINE ACTION WORKS UNCEASINGLY AT THE SANCTIFICATION OF SOULS

§ I

The divine action is present everywhere and always, although it is only visible to the eye of faith

ALL creatures are living in the hand of God; the senses perceive only the action of the creature, but faith sees the action of God in everything—faith believes that Jesus Christ is alive in everything and operates throughout the whole course of the centuries; faith believes that the briefest moment and the tiniest atom contain a portion of Christ's hidden life and his mysterious action. The action of creatures is a veil concealing the profound mysteries of the divine action. Jesus Christ after his resurrection took his disciples by surprise in his apparitions, he presented himself to them under appearances which disguised him; and as soon as he had revealed himself, he disappeared. This very same Jesus, always living and active, still takes by surprise souls whose faith is not sufficiently pure and penetrating.

There is no moment at which God does not present himself under the guise of some suffering, some consolation or some duty. All that occurs within us, around us and by our means covers and hides his divine action. His action is there, most really and certainly present, but in an invisible manner, the result of which is that we are always being taken by surprise and that we only recognize his operation after it has passed. Could we pierce the veil and were we vigilant and attentive, God would reveal himself continuously to us and we should rejoice in his action in everything that happens to us. At every occurrence we should say: *Dominus est.* It is the Lord; and in all circumstances we should find a gift from God: we should consider creatures as very feeble instruments in the hands of an almighty worker, and we should recognize without difficulty that nothing is lacking to us and that God's constant care leads him to give us each instant what is suited to us. If we had faith, we should welcome all creatures; we should, as it were, caress them and thank them interiorly for contributing so favourably to our perfection when applied by the hand of God.

If we lived uninterruptedly by the life of faith, we should be in continual contact with God, we should speak with him face to face. As the air is the medium for transmitting our thoughts and words to others, so all our deeds or sufferings would transmit to us the thoughts and words of God; they would be but the embodiment of his words giving them their external expression; for us, all would be holy and excellent. This union with God will be established in heaven by glory; faith will establish it on earth and the only difference is in our mode of reception.

Faith is the interpreter of God; without the illumination which it brings, nothing can be understood of the language in which creatures speak to us. That language is a cypher in which nothing is apparent but confusion; it is a thorn-bush from which no one could imagine God speaking. But faith makes us see, as in the case of Moses, the fire of divine charity burning in the midst of the thorns; faith gives us the key to the cypher and enables us to discover in that confusion the marvels of heavenly wisdom. Faith gives a face as of heaven to the whole earth, and by it our hearts are ravished and transported to converse in heaven.

Faith is the light of time: alone it attains truth without seeing it; it touches what it does not feel, it beholds this world as if it were not there, seeing something quite different to what appears on the surface. Faith is the key of the treasury, the key of the abyss of divine wisdom, the key of the science of God. It is faith that gives the lie to all creatures, it is by faith that God reveals and manifests himself in all things. It is faith that divinizes things, which lifts the veil and reveals to us eternal truth.

All that we see is lies and vanity; the truth of things is in God. What a difference between the ideas of God and our illusions! How can it be that though we are continually warned that every passing event in the world is but a shadow, a figure, a mystery of faith, we always behave in a merely human way and judge events by our natural understanding of them with the result that they remain an enigma? We fall into the snare like fools instead of lifting our eyes and ascending to the principle, the source, the origin of things, where everything has another name and other qualities, where everything is supernatural, divine and sanctifying; where everything is part of the plenitude of Jesus Christ; where each occurrence is a stone of the heavenly Jerusalem, where everything is a means of entrance into that marvellous city. We live as we see and as we feel; and we render useless that light of faith which would lead us so surely through the labyrinth of clouds and images among which we lose our way like idiots, because we do not walk by the light of faith which desires nothing but God and what is his and which lives for ever by him, passing beyond and abandoning what is but an image.

§ 2

The more repugnant the appearances under which it is concealed, the more clearly is the divine action visible to the eye of faith

The soul illuminated by faith is very far from judging things as do those who measure them by their senses, being ignorant of the inestimable treasure they conceal. He who knows that a certain person in disguise is the King welcomes him in a very different manner from one who seeing the exterior aspect of an ordinary man treats him according to his appearance. Similarly, the soul that sees the will of God in the smallest things or in the most distressing and fatal events, accepts them all with equal joy, gladness and respect. What other people fear and fly from in horror is received by this soul with honour. It throws its gates wide open in welcome. Though the guest's equipage may be small and the senses despise it, yet the heart none the less reveres the royal majesty beneath the mean trappings; and the more his royal majesty abases himself to come in this hidden and humble way, the more deeply is the heart penetrated with love.

I cannot express the feelings of the heart when it welcomes the divine will, so diminished in glory, so poor, so annihilated. How the beautiful heart of Mary was penetrated by this poverty of a God, this annihilation to the point of dwelling in a stable, sleeping on a little straw, to the point of weeping and trembling! Ask the inhabitants of Bethlehem, see what they think of this child: if he were lodged in a palace surrounded with the state of a prince, they would pay their court to him. But ask the same question of Mary, Joseph, the Magi, the shepherds: they will tell you that they find in this extreme poverty something which makes God greater and more lovable. The very deficiency of material things enhances, increases and enriches faith: the less for the eyes, the more for the soul. To adore Jesus on Thabor, to love the will of God in extraordinary things, does not indicate as excellent a life of faith as to love the will of God in ordinary circumstances and to love Jesus on the Cross, for faith is only living at its best when sensible appearances contradict and attempt to destroy it. This war of the senses renders faith more gloriously triumphant. To find God as good in the tiniest and most ordinary events as in the greatest is to have not an ordinary but a great and extraordinary faith. To be content with the present moment is to appreciate and adore the divine will in all we have to do and suffer in the events which reveal it to us. Souls in these dispositions adore God with redoubled love and respect in the most humiliating circumstances; nothing hides him from the piercing eye of their faith. The more the senses declare: there can be no God there, the more these souls hug to their breast the myrrh of their suffering; nothing astonishes them, nothing disgusts them.

Mary will witness the flight of the Apostles; but she will remain herself constant at the foot of the Cross. She will recognize her Son, no matter how disfigured he may be by spittle and wounds, for, contrariwise, his disfiguring wounds make him the more adorable and lovable to his tender mother; the more he is blasphemed, the greater will be her veneration. The life of faith is nothing else than a continual pursuit of God through everything that disguises, misrepresents and, so to speak, destroys and annihilates him. It is, indeed, the reproduction of the life of Mary who from the stable to Calvary remains attached to a God whom everyone fails to recognize, abandons and persecutes. In the same way men of faith pass through and beyond a continual succession of veils, shadows, appearances and, as it were, deaths, all of which do their best to make the will of God unrecognizable, but they pursue and love the divine will unto the death of the Cross. They know that shadows must always be abandoned in order to follow this divine Sun who from his rising unto his going down, however dark or heavy may be the clouds that hide him, enlightens, warms and makes to glow with love the faithful hearts who bless, praise and contemplate him at all points of his mysterious orbit.

Hasten then always, faithful souls, happy and tireless after your beloved Spouse who walks with giant's steps from one end of the heavens to the other; nothing is hidden from his sight. He walks over the tiniest blades of grass as well as over cedars. He passes over grains of sand as well as over mountains. Wherever you can step, he has passed, and in order to find him wherever you may be, you have but to pursue him incessantly.

How delightful the peace one enjoys when one has learned by faith to see God in this way through all creatures as through a transparent veil! Darkness becomes light and bitterness sweet. Faith by showing us the truth of things changes their ugliness into beauty and their malice into goodness: faith is the mother of gentleness, confidence and joy; she can have only tenderness and compassion towards her enemies who enrich her so greatly at their own cost. The more cruel the action of the creature, the more profitable does the action of God make it for the soul who endures it. While the human tool does its best to injure, the divine artificer, in whose hands it does its work, makes use of that very malice to remove from the soul what is injurious. The will of God has nothing but sweetness, favours and treasures for souls submissive to it; we cannot have too much confidence in that will, we cannot abandon ourselves too much to it. God's will desires and can always accomplish what will contribute most to our perfection on condition that we allow God to act. Faith does not doubt this. The more our senses are faithless, revolted, uncertain and in despair, the more surely faith says: "This is God; all is well."

There is nothing that faith does not penetrate and surmount. It passes beyond all darkness, and no matter how deep the shadows, it passes through them to the truth which it always firmly embraces and from which it is never separated.

§ 3
The divine action offers us at each moment infinite benefits in the measure of our faith and our love

If we are able to envisage each moment as the manifestation of the will of God, we shall find in it all that our heart can desire. For what can there be more reasonable, more perfect, more divine than the will of God? Can its infinite value increase through differences of time, place and circumstance? If you are given the secret of finding it at every moment in every event, you possess all that is most precious and worthy in your desires. What do you desire, holy souls? Do not hold back, carry your longings beyond all measures and limits, dilate your hearts to an infinite extent, I have enough to fill them: there is no moment at which I cannot make you find all that you can desire.

The present moment is always full of infinite treasures, it contains far more than you have the capacity to hold. Faith is the measure; what you find in the present moment will be according to the measure of your faith. Love also is the measure: the more your heart loves, the more it desires, and the more it desires the more it finds. The will of God presents itself at each instant like an immense ocean which the desire of your heart cannot empty, although it will receive of that ocean the measure to which it can expand itself by faith, confidence and love. The whole of the created universe cannot fill your heart which has a greater capacity than everything else that is not God. The mountains which affright your eyes are tiny as atoms to the heart. The divine will is an abyss, the opening of which is the present moment. Plunge into this abyss and you will find it ever deeper than your desires. Pay court to no one, do not worship illusions, they can neither enrich you nor deprive you of anything. The sole will of God will wholly fill you and leave you with no void; adore that will, go straight towards it, pierce through and abandon all external appearances. The stripping, death and destruction of the senses establish the reign of faith: the senses adore creatures, faith adores the divine will. Take away their idols from the senses, they weep like children in despair; but faith triumphs, for faith cannot be deprived of the will of God. When the event of the present moment terrifies, starves, strips and attacks all the senses, it is just at that moment that it nourishes, enriches and vitalizes faith, which laughs at the losses of the senses as the governor of an impregnable town laughs at useless attacks.

When the will of God has been revealed to a soul and has made it feel that God is ready to give himself completely if the soul for its part will also give itself, the soul experiences in all circumstances a powerful assistance. From now on it tastes by experience the joy of the coming of God, and it enjoys it the more the better it understands in practice the self-abandonment in which it should remain at every moment to that all-adorable will.

§4

God reveals himself to us in the commonest events, in a manner as mysterious but as real and adorable as in the great events of history and the Sacred Scriptures

The written word of God is full of mysteries; his word executed in action in the events of the world is no less so. These two books are truly sealed, the letter of them both kills. God is the centre of faith, and faith is an abyss of darkness which from that centre spreads itself over all the operations which proceed from it. All these words and works are, as it were, but the dark rays of a still darker sun. In vain do we open the eyes of the body to see this sun and its rays; even the eyes of our soul by which we see God and his works are but closed eyes. Here darkness takes the place of light, knowledge is ignorance, and we see without seeing. Holy Scripture is the language of a still more mysterious God; the events of the world are the obscure sayings of this same God, so hidden and so unknown. They are the drops of a great sea but of a sea of darkness. All drops, all brooks of water have the savour of their source. The fall of the angels, the fall of Adam, the impiety and idolatry of men before and after the Flood in the lifetime of the patriarchs, who knew and related to their children the story of the Creation and the then still recent preservation of the world: here are some of the dark words of Holy Scripture! A handful of men preserved from idolatry up to the arrival of the Messiah, in spite of the general loss of faith of the whole world; impiety always reigning and powerful; this little band of defenders of truth always persecuted and ill-treated; the way Jesus Christ was treated; the plagues of the Apocalypse! What! Are these the words of God? . . . Is this what he has revealed? . . . And are the effects of these terrible mysteries which last until the end of the world also the living word which teaches us his wisdom, his power, his goodness? All the events that form the history of the world express these divine attributes. All preach the same adorable word. Alas! we do not see it; we must believe it.

What does God mean by permitting the existence of Turks, protestants, all the enemies of his Church? It is all a striking lesson: it signifies the infinite perfections of God. Pharaoh and all the evil men who have followed and will follow him exist only for that purpose. Yet if we look at it, the letter of their history says the contrary; we must blind ourselves and cease to reason in order to see the divine mysteries.

Thou speakest, Lord, to all men in general by general events. Revolutions are but the tides of thy Providence which stir up storms and tempests in the minds of the inquisitive. Thou speakest in particular to all men in the events which happen to each of them from moment to moment. But instead of hearing thy voice, instead of respecting the mysterious obscurity of thy word, men see nothing but the movements of matter, blind chance and the human element; they find objections to everything; they wish to add to and subtract from thy word; they wish to reform it; they give themselves complete licence to commit excesses, the least of which would be considered by them an unheard-of crime if it were a matter of a single comma in the Holy Scriptures. For they respect the Holy Scriptures. These are the Word of God, they say, and everything contained in them is holy and true. If they do not understand their meaning they venerate them the more; they glorify and justly adore the depths of the wisdom of God. This is quite right. But what God says to you, dear souls, the words he pronounces from moment to moment, the substance of which is not paper and ink but what you suffer and what you have to do from moment to moment, does this deserve no attention from you? Why in all this do you not respect the truth and the will of God? Nothing pleases you, you criticize everything that happens. Do you not see that you are measuring by the standard of the senses and the reason what can only be measured by faith, and that reading, as you do, with the eyes of faith the word of God in Holy Scripture, you are greatly in the wrong to read it with any other eyes in his actions

§ 5

Divine action continues in our hearts the revelation commenced in Holy Scripture; but the characters in which it is written will be visible only on the Great Day

"Jesus Christ," says the Apostle, "the same yesterday, today and for ever." From the origins of the world he was, as God, the principle of the life of the just; from the first instant of his incarnation his humanity participated in this prerogative of his divinity. He works in us all through our life; the time which will elapse before the end of the world is but a day and this day is filled with him. Jesus Christ has lived in the past and still lives in the present; he began in himself and continues in his saints a life that will never finish. O life of Jesus which includes and exceeds all the ages of time, O life which is initiating new operations at every moment! . . . If the whole world is so incapable of understanding all that could be written of the individual life of Jesus, of his words and actions when he was on earth, if the Gospel gives us only the rough sketch of a few little details of it, if that first hour of his life is so unknown and so fertile, how many gospels would have to be written to recount the history of all the moments of this mystical life of Jesus Christ which multiplies wonders infinitely and eternally, since all the æons of time are, properly speaking, but the history of the divine action?

The Holy Spirit has set out for us in infallible and incontestable characters certain moments of this vast space of time. He has collected in the Scriptures certain drops, as it were, of this ocean. We see there the secret and unknown ways by which he caused Jesus Christ to appear in the world. We can follow the channels and veins of communication which in the midst of the confusion of the sons of men distinguish the origin, the race, the genealogy of this first-born child. The whole of the Old Testament is but a sketch of the inscrutable depths of this divine work; it contains only what is necessary to find Jesus Christ. The Divine Spirit has kept all the rest hidden among the treasures of his wisdom. Of all this ocean of divine action he reveals to us but a tiny stream of water which, having reached Jesus, loses itself in the Apostles and disappears in the Apocalypse, so that the history of the divine operations, in which consists the life of Jesus in holy souls until the consummation of the ages, can only be divined by our faith.

To the manifestation of the truth of God by word has succeeded the manifestation of his charity by action. The Holy Spirit carries on the work of the Saviour. While he assists the Church in the preaching of the gospel of Jesus Christ, he writes his own gospel, and he writes it in the hearts of the faithful. All the actions, all the moments of the saints make up the gospel of the Holy Spirit. Their holy souls are the paper, their sufferings and their actions are the ink. The Holy Spirit, with his own action for pen, writes a living gospel, but it will not be readable until the day of glory when it will be taken out of the printing press of this life and published.

What a beautiful history! What a fine book the Holy Spirit is writing now! The book is in the press, there is no day on which the letters which make it up are not being composed, on which the ink is not applied and the sheets printed. But we dwell in the night of faith; the paper is blacker than the ink, the characters are all in confusion, the language is not of this world, nothing can be understood of it. You will be able to read this book only in heaven. If we could see the life of God and could contemplate all creatures, not in themselves, but in their principle, if we could also see the life of God in all objects, how his divine action moves them, mingles them, assembles them, opposes them to each other, pushes them all to the same point by diverse means, we should recognize that all things in this divine work have their reasons, their scale of measurement, their mutual relations. But how read this book the characters of which are unknown, vast in number, upside down and blotted with ink? If the blending of twenty-six letters results in such incomprehensible diversity that they suffice to compose an infinite number of different volumes, all admirable, who can express what God is doing in the universe? Who can read and comprehend the meaning of so vast a book in which there is no letter which has not its particular symbolism and does not contain profound mysteries in its tiny bulk? Mysteries cannot be seen or felt, they are objects of faith. Faith only judges of their truth and goodness by the principle on which they are delivered, for in themselves they are so obscure that their appearance does but conceal them, and blind those who would judge of them by reason alone.

Teach me, Divine Spirit, to read in this book of life! I wish to become thy disciple and like a simple child believe what I cannot see. Enough for me that my master speaks. He says so-and-so, he groups the letters of the book like this, he makes himself understood in that way; it is enough, I judge according to what he says. I do not see why, but he is the infallible truth, all that he says or does is truthful. He wills that this word should be composed of so many letters, that that word should need another number. Three, six, are enough, no others are required, one more or less would be nonsense. He alone who understands the thought can put together the letters to express it. Everything is significant; there is a perfect meaning everywhere. This line stops here because it is necessary that it should, there is not a comma missing, not a stop too many. I believe this now, and when the day of glory reveals so many mysteries to me, I shall see what at present I can only understand confusedly, and what now seems to me so complicated, so haphazard and imaginary will entrance and charm me eternally by its beauty, by the order, reason, wisdom and incomprehensible wonders that I shall find in it.

§ 6

The divine action is as unworthily treated by many Christians in its daily manifestations as Jesus Christ was treated by the Jews in the days of his flesh

What infidelity there is in the world! How unworthily do men think of God! Unceasingly we find occasions of criticizing the divine action in a way that we should not dare to criticize the least artisan in his craft. We wish to reduce God's action to the limits and rules that our feeble reason can imagine. We propose to reform it. We do nothing but complain and murmur.

We are surprised at the way the Jews treated Jesus. Ah! divine love, adorable will of God, infallible action of God, how art thou looked upon! Can the divine will intrude, can it be mistaken? But (you will say) I have this piece of business on hand, such-and-such a thing is needful to me, the necessary means for my purpose have been taken away, this man opposes me in good works. Is not this quite unreasonable? I am attacked by this illness at the moment when I cannot get on without my health.—And I tell you that the will of God is the only thing necessary and that therefore all that it does not grant is useless. No, dear souls, nothing is lacking to you; if you knew what these events which you call misfortunes, mishaps and contrarieties in which you see nothing that is not out of place and senseless, really are, you would be in extreme confusion. You would blame yourselves for your murmurings as for real blasphemies—but that does not occur to you. All that happens is nothing else than the will of God, and his adorable will is blasphemed by his children who do not recognize it.

When thou wast on earth, my Jesus, the Jews treated thee as one possessed of a devil, called thee a Samaritan, and today, although we know that thou livest for ever and ever, how do we look on thy adorable will that is always worthy of blessing and praise? Has a moment passed from the Creation till now, and will there be one from now until the day of judgement, in which the holy name of God is not worthy of praise—that name which fills all ages and all events and makes all things salutary! What, can the will of God do me harm? Shall I fear, shall I fly from the name of God; where then shall I go to find something better, if I fear God's action on me and repulse the effect of his divine will?

How ought we to listen to the word which is spoken to us in the depth of our hearts at every moment? If our senses and our reason do not understand or penetrate the truth and goodness of that word, is it not on account of their incapacity for divine truths? Should I be astonished because a mystery disconcerts my reason? God speaks: it is a mystery, i.e. it is the death of my senses and my reason, for it is the nature of mysteries to immolate them. A mystery is life to the heart through faith, but for the rest of our faculties a contradiction. The divine action kills and vitalizes with the same stroke; the more lethal it appears, the more we believe it to give life; the darker the mystery, the more light it contains. This is why a simple soul finds nothing more divine than that which in appearance is least divine. The life of faith consists entirely in this incessant battle with the senses.

§ 7

Divine love gives itself to us through the medium of all creatures which communicate it to us under veils, like the Eucharistic species

What great truths are hidden from the eyes even of Christians who think themselves very enlightened! How few among them understand that all crosses, all actions, all spiritual impulses that are in the divine design give us God in a way that can be best explained by comparison with the most august mystery of all! Yet, what is more certain? Does not reason, as well as faith, reveal to us the real presence of the divine love in all creatures and in all the events of life as indubitably as the word of Jesus Christ and the Church reveal to us the presence of the sacred flesh of our Saviour under the Eucharistic species? Do we not know that by all these creatures and all these events, the divine Love desires to unite himself to us, that he has produced, ordained or permitted everything that surrounds us or happens to us in view of this union, the sole end of all his designs; that he uses, to attain this end, the worst as well as the best of creatures and the most disagreeable as well as the pleasantest events, and that the more naturally repellent the means of that union, the more meritorious it becomes? But if all this is true, why should not every moment of our lives be a sort of communion with divine love continuously producing in our souls the fruits of that communion in which we receive the body and blood of the Son of God? The latter, truly, has a sacramental efficacy lacking to the former, but on the other hand how much more frequently the former can be renewed and how greatly can its merit grow through the perfection of the dispositions in which it is performed. How true that the holiest life is mysterious in its simplicity and its apparently humble state. Divine banquet, perpetual festival. . . God ever given and received under appearances of the greatest weakness and nothingness! . . . God chooses what is blameworthy to the natural judgement and what human prudence leaves on one side. Of such things God makes mysteries and sacraments of love, and gives himself to souls to the full extent of their faith through the very medium which might appear to injure them.

§ 8

The revelation of the present moment is more useful because it is addressed personally to us

We are well instructed only by the words that God speaks to us personally. It is not by reading or historical study that we become wise in the science of God; such methods alone produce but a vain, confused and self-inflating science. What instructs us is what happens to us from moment to moment; that is what forms in us that experimental knowledge which Jesus Christ willed to acquire before he taught it. This was indeed the only knowledge in which, according to the expression in the gospel, he could grow, because being God there was no degree of speculative science that he did not possess. But if this knowledge was useful to the Incarnate Word himself, for us it is absolutely necessary if we wish to speak to the heart of the persons whom God sends to us. We only know perfectly what experience has taught us through suffering and action. Experience is the school of the Holy Spirit who speaks to the heart words of life, and all that we say to others should come from this source. What we read and see only becomes divine knowledge by that fecundity, virtue and light which experience gives it. All that is the dough; leaven is needed and the salt of experience must season it. When lacking this salt we have only vague ideas, we are like dreamers who know the way to all cities and lose themselves on their road home.

We must then listen to God from moment to moment in order to be learned in the theology of virtue which is wholly practical and experimental. Set aside what is said to others, listen to what is said to you for your own use: you will find enough to exercise your faith, for this interior language of God by its very obscurity exercises, purifies and increases faith.

§ 9

The revelation of the present moment is an ever freshly springing source of sanctity

O, you who thirst, know that you have not far to go to find the source of living waters: that source springs up close to you, in the present moment; hasten, then, to approach it. These little brooks only tease our thirst, they measure parsimoniously the water they give us, it is the spring itself which is inexhaustible. If you wish to think, write and talk like apostles, prophets and saints, abandon yourselves as they did to divine inspiration.

O Unknown Love! it would seem that thy marvels are over, and that all we can do is to copy thy ancient volumes and quote thy words of the past! And we do not see that thy inexhaustible action is an infinite source of new thoughts, new sufferings, new actions, new patriarchs, new prophets, new apostles, new saints, who have no need to copy each other's lives and writings, but simply to live in a perpetual self-abandonment to thy secret operations. We hear perpetually of the "early centuries", "the times of the saints": what a way to talk! ... Are not all times the successive effects of the divine operation which pours itself forth on all the instants of time, filling them, sanctifying them, super-naturalizing them all. Was there of old some now out of date way of abandoning oneself to this divine operation? Had the saints of the first days any other secret than that of becoming moment by moment what the divine action wished to make of them? And will that divine action not continue to shed its glory until the end of the world on those souls who abandon themselves to it without reserve?

Yes, dear Love, adorable, eternal, eternally fruitful and ever marvellous! Action of my God, you are my book, my doctrine, my science; in you are my thoughts, my words, my actions, my crosses. It is not by consulting your other works that I shall become what you wish to make of me, it is by accepting you in all things, in the one, ancient, royal way of my fathers. I will think, I will be enlightened and speak as they did: it is in this way that I wish to imitate, quote and copy them all.

§ 10

The present moment is the manifestation of the name of God and the coming of his kingdom

The present moment is always the ambassador who declares the order of God. The heart always pronounces its *fiat*. The soul pours itself forth by all these means into its centre and goal; it never stops, it travels by all winds; all routes and methods advance it equally on its journey to the high sea of the Infinite. Everything is a means and an instrument of holiness; everything without any exception. The "one thing necessary" is always to be found by the soul in the present moment. There is no need to choose between prayer and silence, privacy or conversation, reading or writing, reflection or the abandonment of thought, the frequentation or avoidance of spiritual people, abundance or famine, illness or health, life or death; the "one thing necessary" is what each moment produces by God's design. In this consists the stripping, the self-abnegation, the renunciation of the creature in order to be nothing by or for oneself, in order to remain as regards everything in God's order at his pleasure, finding one's only contentment in bearing the present moment, as if there were nothing else in the world to expect.

33

If everything that happens to a self-abandoned soul is "the one thing necessary", it is evident that nothing is lacking to it and that it should never complain. If it does complain, it is wanting in faith and living by its reason or its senses, which, not seeing the sufficiency of grace, are discontented. To sanctify the name of God is, in the language of the Scriptures, to recognize his holiness, to love and adore it in all things. Things indeed proceed like words out of the mouth of God. God creates at each moment a divine thought which is signified by a created thing; thus, all those things by which he makes his will known to us are so many names and words under cover of which he shows us his desire. In itself this will is one, its name is unknown and ineffable, but it becomes multiplied to the infinite in its effects, which are, as it were, so many names that it takes. To sanctify the name of God is to know, adore and love the ineffable Being which this name expresses. It is also to know, adore and love his adorable will at every moment and in all its effects, looking at all events as so many veils, or shadows, or names of that eternally holy will. For that will is holy in all its works, in all its words, in all its appearances, in all the names it bears.

This was how Job blessed the name of God. That complete desolation which signified for him the will of God was blessed by this holy man; he did not consider it to be ruin but one of God's names, and in blessing it, he protested that the divine will expressed under the most terrible appearances was holy, no matter what its name or form. David also blessed it in all times and places. It is then by this continual discovery, by this manifestation, this revelation of God's will in all things that his kingdom dwells in us, that he does on earth what he does in heaven, that he nourishes us without ceasing. Self-abandonment to his will includes and contains the whole substance of that incomparable prayer dictated to us by Jesus Christ. We recite it several times a day according to the orders of God and Holy Church, but we say it constantly in the depths of our heart when we love to suffer and do what is ordained for us by his adorable will. What the mouth can only pronounce syllable by syllable, word by word, taking time to do so, the heart truly pronounces at every instant, and it is thus that simple men are called to bless God in the depth of their souls. Yet they bewail their inability to praise him as they would wish, so true is it that God gives to these souls of faith his favours and graces through that very circumstance which seems to indicate their privation. It is the secret method of divine wisdom to impoverish the senses while enriching the heart, so that the latter is filled in proportion to the painful emptiness that the former experience.

What happens at each moment bears the imprint of the will of God and of his adorable name. How holy is that name! How just, then, to bless it, to treat it as a sacrament which hallows by its own power souls which place no obstacle to its action! Can we see what bears this august name without esteeming it infinitely? It is a divine manna which falls from heaven in order to give us a constant increase in grace. It is the kingdom of holiness which comes into the soul. It is the bread of angels which is eaten on earth as in heaven. There is nothing petty about our moments if they contain the kingdom of holiness and the food of angels.

Yes, Lord, may this kingdom come in my heart for my sanctification, my nourishment, my purification, to render me victorious over my enemies! How small is that precious passing moment to the eye of the common man, how great to the eye illuminated by faith! How indeed can we deem little that which is great in the eyes of our Father who reigns in heaven? All that comes from there is most excellent, for all that comes from there bears the character of its origin.

§ 11

Divine action brings to all souls the most eminent sanctity: to
sanctify oneself it is sufficient to abandon oneself to it

It is from not knowing how to make use of divine action that so many Christians pass their lives anxiously pursuing a multitude of means to perfection which may be useful when ordered by the divine will but which become injurious when they interfere with the soul's simple union with God. All this multiplicity cannot give us what is to be found in the principle of every life, which is constantly present to us and which impresses on every means it employs its own individual movement and causes its unique incomparable action.

Jesus has given us a master to whom we do not listen enough. That master speaks to all hearts, and to each he speaks a word of life, the unique word for each soul; but we do not hear him well enough. We would like to know what he says to others, and we do not listen to what he says to ourselves. We do not look at things sufficiently in that supernatural mode of being which divine action gives them. We should always welcome that divine action and reply to it (as it deserves) open-heartedly, with confidence and generosity: God's action can do no harm to those who receive it thus. This immense action of God, always the same in itself from the commencement of the ages until the end, pours itself forth at every moment and gives itself in its immensity and power to the sincere soul that adores, loves it and makes it its one source of joy. You would be delighted, you say, to find an opportunity of dying for God's sake; such an action, a life passed in such a way, would please you. To lose everything, to die abandoned, to sacrifice yourself for others; you find such ideas attractive.

As for me, Lord, in everything I glorify thy action, in which I find all the happiness of martyrdom, austerities and the service of my neighbour. Thy action is sufficient for me; in whatever manner it causes me to live and die I am content. It pleases me for its own sake apart from the means it employs and the effects it produces, because it extends to everything, it makes everything divine. Everything is heaven to me, all my moments are pure divine action, and in life as in death I wish to remain content with that.

I shall not count the hours nor the ways of thy approach, dear Love: thou wilt always be welcome. The divine action seems to have unveiled to me its immensity. I no longer move but in its infinite bosom. All that flows from it today flowed also yesterday. In reality it is the bed of the torrent of graces which flow unceasingly, it sustains them and moves them hither and thither. No longer therefore will I seek it within the narrow covers of a book, in some saint's life or some sublime idea. These are but drops of that ocean that I see pouring itself over all creatures, which are all inundated by it. They are but tiny atoms which disappear in this abyss. Nor will I seek it in spiritual writers. No longer will I beg my bread from door to door; no longer will I pay court to creatures.

Yes, Lord, I wish to live in a way that will honour thee, as the true child of an infinitely good, wise and powerful father. I wish to live as I believe, and inasmuch as this divine action is applied in all circumstances and at all times to my perfection, I wish to live on my immense revenue which cannot fail and is always present and available in the most profitable way. Can any creature's action equal that of God? And since his uncreated hand moulds everything that happens to me, shall I go and seek help from creatures who are powerless, ignorant and without affection? I should die of thirst running from fountain to fountain, from stream to stream, while here is an engulfing sea which surrounds me on all sides with its waters! Everything becomes bread to nourish me, soap to cleanse me, fire to purify me. Everything is a means of grace for my necessities. The very thing that I seek everywhere else seeks me incessantly and gives itself to me by the hand of all creatures.

O Love, must it be that this should be unknown, that thou shouldst throw thyself, as it were, at everyone's head with all thy favours, and that men should go on seeking thee in corners where they cannot find thee! What folly on their part not to breathe the open air, not to walk about the countryside, not to find water where it abounds, not to take hold of God and taste him and find his action present in everything.

You are seeking the secret of belonging to God, dear souls? There is no other than to make use of everything which God gives you. Everything leads to union with God, everything perfects you, except sin and what is outside your duty; all you have to do is to accept everything and let God act. Everything directs you, keeps you straight and carries you along. Everything is the hand of God. Earth, air and water are God's. His action is more widely extended, more present to you than the elements. It enters you by all your senses, provided you only make use of them according to his design, for you must close them in resistance to all that is not his will. There is no atom which, in penetrating you, does not make the divine action penetrate you to the marrow of your bones. All is from it and by it. These vital liquids which pour through your veins do so only by the movement which it gives them; all the variations to be found in your movements, their strength or weakness, their languor or vivacity, their life or death, are divine instruments put into operation to effect your sanctification. All your states of body become under its operation the workings of grace. All your feelings, all your thoughts, however they may arise, all come from the invisible hand of God. No created heart or spirit can teach you what this action will bring about; you will learn it by progressive experience. Your life flows ceaselessly in this unknown abyss where all you have to do is ever to love and esteem as best what is present to you, with perfect confidence in God's action which cannot of itself do you anything but good.

Yes, dear Love, all souls would reach supernatural, sublime, wonderful, inconceivable heights, if they would all be content with thy action! Yes, indeed, if we could only allow this divine hand to act, we should reach the most eminent perfection! All would reach it, for it is offered to all. All we have to do is to open our mouths, as it were, and perfection will enter of itself, for there is no soul but has in thee its infinitely perfect model and the advantage of thy ceaseless working in it. If souls were faithful to it, they would all live, act and speak divinely; it would not be necessary for them to copy each other; the divine action would individualize each one of them by the most ordinary methods.

What means have I, my God, to make thy creatures appreciate what I am saying? . . . Must I resign myself to possessing so great a treasure and to seeing souls perish meanwhile in their poverty? Must I see them drying up like desert plants while I am showing them the source of living waters? Come, simple souls, you who know nothing of devotion, who have no talent, not even the elements of primary instruction, who are ignorant of the language of spirituality, who admire and wonder at the eloquence of the wise; come and I will teach you a secret way to surpass all these brilliant people, and I will place you in such easy circumstances for the attainment of perfection that you will always find it under your feet, over your head and all around you; I will unite you to God, you shall hold him by the hand while you practise the instructions which I give you. Come, then, not to *know* the map of the land of the spirit, but to *possess* it and be at home in it without fear of losing your way. Come, not to study the theory of divine grace, not to learn what it has done through the ages and is doing today, but in order to be the simple subjects of its operations. You have no need to know the words it has taught others and to repeat them cleverly; grace will give you words which will be your own.

§ 12

Divine action alone can sanctify us, for God alone knows the divine exemplar of our perfection

The divine action executes in time the ideas which the eternal wisdom has formed of all things. All things have in God their own ideas, his wisdom alone knows them. Supposing you knew all those which have nothing to do with you personally, that knowledge would be useless for your own direction. The divine action sees in the Word the idea in accordance with which you have to be formed; this idea is your exemplar. The divine action sees in the Word all that is needed by all holy souls. Holy Scripture contains a part of it and the workings of the Holy Spirit complete it according to the exemplar contained in the Word. Is it not evident that the one and only way to receive the character of this eternal idea is to make oneself a simple subject in the hands of God, and that our own efforts and intellectual speculations will be perfectly useless for the purpose? Is it not manifest that this working cannot result from our own cleverness, intelligence or subtlety, but can only follow on our passive self-abandonment to receive all from God, placing ourselves in his hand, like the liquid metal in a mould, or a canvas before the painter's brush, or the stone before the sculptor? Is it not evident that it is not the knowledge of all these divine mysteries which the will of God works throughout the ages that is the means by which God conforms us to the image conceived of us by the Word, and that our resemblance to the divine archetype can only come to us by the impression of that mysterious seal which is not made on our intelligence by the medium of our ideas, but on our will by our abandonment of it to God.

The wisdom of the simple soul consists in contenting itself with its own business, in keeping to the limits of its own path, in not overstepping its bounds. It is not curious to know God's ways of acting, being content to know his will in its own regard; it makes no effort to guess what his will may be by comparisons and conjectures, only wishing to know what each moment reveals to it by the voice of the Word heard in the depth of its own heart without asking the Bridegroom what he says to others, in such a way that from moment to moment it is unconsciously divinized by everything. That is how the Bridegroom speaks to his bride, by the very real effects of his action not scrutinized curiously but accepted with loving gratitude. Thus the spirituality of such a soul is simple, substantial, intimately informing its whole being. It is not determined to action by ideas or tumults of words which by themselves merely inflate it. People make a great use of the intellect for purposes of piety; but the intellect is hardly necessary for such purposes; it is even contrary to them. We should only make use of what God gives us to do and suffer. People abandon this divine substance (of their life) to fill their minds with the marvels wrought by God in history instead of increasing them by their own fidelity.

The marvels of these workings of God which satisfy our curiosity in our reading serve often merely to disgust us with things small in appearance, by means of which divine love would work great things in us, if we did not despise them. What fools we are! We admire and glorify God's action in the books which describe his works, and when he is ready to continue them by writing them in our hearts, we cannot keep the paper still on which he is to write, and we prevent his action by being curious to see what he is doing in us and in others.

I ask forgiveness, divine Love, for I am setting down here my own faults, and I have not yet discovered what it is to leave thee to act in me. I have not yet yielded myself up to be placed in the mould. I have frequented thy studios, I have admired thy creations, but I have not yet attained the necessary self-abandonment to receive the strokes of thy brush. But at last I have found thee, Master, Teacher, Father and my dear Love, now I will be thy disciple; I will no more frequent any school but thine. I come home like the prodigal son hungry for thy bread. I abandon the ideas which merely tend to satisfy my intellectual curiosity; I will no longer run after various masters and books; such means I will only make use of in dependence on thy divine action, not for my own satisfaction but in order to obey thee in this as in everything else that happens. I wish to confine myself to the one and only business of the present moment, to love thee, to acquit myself of my obligations and to allow thee to act.

BOOK II

THE STATE OF SELF-ABANDONMENT

CHAPTER I : THE NATURE AND EXCELLENCE OF THE STATE OF SELF-ABANDONMENT

§1

The designs of God for the souls whom he places in this state

THERE is a time when the soul lives in God and a time when God lives in the soul. What belongs to one of these periods is unsuitable for the other. When God lives in a soul, it should abandon itself completely to his Providence. When the soul lives in God, it takes trouble regularly to furnish itself with all the means that it can think of in order to attain to union with him. All its paths are marked out, its reading, its examinations of conscience; its guide is ever at its side—everything is regulated, even its times for talking. When God lives in the soul, it has nothing more of its own, it has nothing but what he gives it, who is the principle which animates it at each moment. No provisions, no route traced in advance; the soul is like a child whom one leads where one wishes, and who has nothing but feeling to distinguish what is presented to it. No books are appointed for such a soul, often enough it is deprived of a director; God leaves it without any other support than himself alone. Its dwelling-place is in darkness, forgotten and abandoned by creatures, in death and nothingness. It feels its necessities and miseries without knowing how or when it will be helped. It waits in peace and without anxiety for someone to come and help it; its eyes gaze only heavenwards. God, who can find no purer disposition in his spouse than this laying on one side of all that it is, in order to exist only by his grace and divine operation, furnishes it at the appropriate moment with books, thoughts, advice, counsels, examples and insight into its own condition. All that others find by their labours, this soul finds in its self-abandonment; and

what others carefully put aside so as to find it again when necessary, a self-abandoned soul receives at the moment of need and
then relinquishes it, accepting precisely from it just what God
wishes to give, so as to live only by him. Others undertake an
infinity of things for the glory of God; this soul often remains
quietly lost in some corner like the remains of a broken pot of
which no one can make any further use. There this soul remains
deserted by all creatures but in the enjoyment of God through a
very real, authentic and active love, although this is infused
while it remains in repose. It proceeds to nothing by its own
movement, all it can do is to abandon itself into God's hands, to
serve him in the way that he wishes. Often it does not know what
use it is, but God knows. Men think it useless and appearances
are in favour of this judgement; it is, however, none the less true
that from its secret resources and by hidden channels it pours an
infinite number of graces on persons who are not thinking of it
and of whom it does not think.

Everything in these self-abandoned souls preaches apostolic-
ally and efficaciously. God gives to their silence, their self-
forgetfulness, their repose, their detachment, their words, their
actions a certain virtue which works in hearts without their
being conscious of it, and directed as they are by the haphazard
actions of innumerable creatures of whom grace makes use for
their instruction without their knowing it, they also serve others
with support and guidance, without any explicit connection or
intention. God works in them often by unforeseen and secret
movements, so that these souls are like Jesus from whom a secret
healing virtue went out to others. There is this difference, that
in their case they often do not feel this virtue going out from them
and even do not themselves consciously contribute to the fact. It
is like a hidden balm which men do not see but of which they
perceive the fragrance: a balm unconscious of its own power.

§ 2

The soul in this state is led by the divine action through all obscurities

When the soul has discovered this divine influence it leaves all
its good works, its practices of devotion, its methods of prayer, its

43

books, its ideas and consultations with spiritual people in order to be under the guidance of God alone by abandoning itself to this influence which becomes the one and only principle of its perfection. It is in his hand, as all the saints have always been, it knows that God alone knows the way that is right for it, and that if it sought for created means of action, it could do nothing but lose its way in this unknown land where God makes it walk. It is therefore his unknown action that directs and leads these souls by ways known only to him. These souls are something like the movements of the air. They can only be known in the actual present moment; what is to follow has its causes in the will of God, and his action can only be explained by its effects, by what it does in these souls and what it actually causes them to do, whether by secret, unsuspected instincts or by the duties of the state of life in which they live. This is all they know of spirituality, here are all their visions and revelations, this is all the wisdom and counsel they have, and it is of such a kind that they never lack anything. Faith assures them of the excellence of what they do: if they read, if they talk, if they ask advice, it is only to find the means of discerning the divine action. All this belongs to the order of divine action and they accept it as part of the whole, apprehending underneath these things the divine influence, while leaving on one side the things themselves. They make use of what happens to be there or what happens to be lacking, supported through faith by this infallible, even, immutable and always efficacious divine action at every moment. This action they see and enjoy in everything, in the humblest as in the greatest objects; every moment gives it them entire. Thus they make use of things with confidence, but also in submission to God's orders and his divine operation which they find with equal facility and certitude under the most contradictory appearances. Thus their lives are passed not in investigations, in desires, in disgust and in sighs, but in the continual assurance of the possession of the most perfect.

All the states that body and soul endure, all that happens to them internally and externally and that each moment reveals to them, is for them the plenitude of divine action, it is their happiness. The whole of creation is for them nothing but misery and starvation; what God's action does is the true and real measure of things. So that if his action removes their thoughts, their words, their books, their food, their friends, their health, their life itself, it is just the same as if it did the contrary. The soul loves the divine action and believes it to be equally sanctifying under all its forms. It does not reason about the way it is led, it is enough that things should come to it from this source in order to win its approval.

§ 3

The state of self-abandonment includes the states of pure faith,
pure hope and pure love

The state of self-abandonment consists of a certain mingling of faith, hope and charity in one single act which unites the heart to God and his action. These three virtues united are but one virtue, they produce one single act, one single elevation of the heart to God and a simple self-abandonment to his action. How express this divine blend, this spiritual essence? How find a name which will rightly describe its nature and idea, that will enable us to conceive the unity of this trinity? It consists, in its three virtues, in one single possession and enjoyment of God and of his will. The soul sees this adorable object, it loves it and it hopes everything from it. This state might be called with equal justice pure love, pure hope and pure faith, and if the state of which we speak is usually designated by the last-mentioned name, it is not meant to exclude the other theological virtues, it is rather to make us understand that in this state those other virtues are exercised in an obscure manner.

On God's side nothing is more assured than this state; on the side of the human heart nothing is more disinterested. On God's side there is the absolute certitude of faith, and on the side of the heart certitude seasoned with fear and hope. O lovable unity in trinity of these holy virtues! Believe then, holy souls, hope and love; but do so as a result of a simple touch of your heart by the Divine Spirit which God grants you. That is the unction of the name of God with which the Holy Spirit anoints you in the depth of your heart. Behold this word and this mystical revelation, this earnest of predestination and all its happy consequences: *Quam bonus Israël Deus his qui recto sunt corde!*

This touch of the Holy Spirit in souls on fire is called pure love on account of the torrent of pleasure that pours over all their faculties with a plenitude of confidence and illumination; but in the case of souls fed on bitter herbs this touch is called pure faith, for they contain nothing but darkness and the shadows of the night. Pure love sees, feels and believes. Pure faith believes without seeing or feeling. That is the meaning of the difference in definition. It is only founded on appearances which are not identical in all cases, for in reality just as the state of pure faith is not without love, neither is the state of pure love without faith or self-abandonment; these terms are "appropriated" to each state in virtue of their dominant factor. The different blending of these virtues under the divine touch causes the variety of all supernatural and exalted states. And inasmuch as God can blend them with infinite variety, there is no soul that does not receive his touch with personal individualizing characteristics. But what matter? The ingredients are always faith, hope and charity.

Self-abandonment is a general means for the reception of special virtues in all these various divine touches. Not all souls can aspire to receive the same kind of virtue or the same state from these divine impressions, but all can unite themselves to God, all can abandon themselves to his action, and thus all can receive the touch belonging to that state which is appropriate for them, and, finally, all can find the kingdom of God and share in its justice and its benefits. In this empire every soul can aspire to a crown, and whether it be a crown of love or a crown of faith it is always a crown, and a crown in the kingdom of God. The difference, indeed, remains that some dwell in light and some in darkness, but what does this matter so long as they are controlled by God and his action? Is it the name of the state, its specific distinction or excellence that the soul seeks? Not at all; it is God himself and his action. The *manner* of his reception should be indifferent to the soul.

Let us then preach to all souls the gospel—not of the state of pure faith or of pure love, not of the cross or of the caress; all cannot receive these in the same degree or manner—but let us preach to all simple hearts that fear God the gospel of self-abandonment to the divine action in general, and let us make them all understand that they will receive by that means the special state which has been chosen for them from all eternity. Let us not distress or reject souls or keep any away from eminent perfection. Jesus calls all the world to it since he demands that all should submit to the will of his Father and form his mystical body, the members of which cannot truthfully call him their head except in so far as their wills are perfectly attuned to his. Let us repeat unceasingly to all souls that the invitation of their sweet and loving Saviour exacts nothing of them that is difficult or extraordinary. He does not demand their labour; he desires that their goodwill should be united to him that he may lead and direct them, and favour them in proportion to the intensity of that union.

§ 4

The state of self-abandonment comprises the most heroic generosity

There is nothing more generous than a believing heart that sees only the divine life in labours and mortal dangers. If it be necessary to swallow poison, to march to the breach, to devote oneself to the service of the plague-stricken, such duties are seen to contain a plenitude of divine life, not distilled drop by drop, but in an instant inundation which swallows up the soul. An army animated by such views would be invincible. For the instinct of faith elevates and dilates the heart beyond and above all that is presented to the senses.

The life of faith is one and the same thing as the instinct of faith. It consists of joy in God's gift and a confidence founded on the expectation of his protection which makes everything harmonize and makes us receive everything with a good grace. It produces a certain indifference of soul and prepares us for all situations, all states and all persons we may meet. Faith is never unhappy, even when the senses are in a state of desolation. The soul ever maintains a living faith in God and in his action beyond the contrary appearances that darken the perceptions of the senses.

47

The senses suddenly cry out in terror to the soul: "Unhappy one, now you are lost, you have no resource left!" and faith with a stronger voice replies at once: "Keep firm, advance and fear nothing."

§ 5

The state of self-abandonment and pure faith gives the soul more merit than the most striking good works

All the extraordinary things we see in the saints, visions, revelations, interior locutions are but external rays of the excellence of their state contained and hidden in the exercise of faith. Faith possesses all that, for it knows how to see and hear God in all that happens from moment to moment. When the state of a saint's soul bursts forth visibly, it is not to say that his faith had not already that beauty, but it is in order to show forth his virtue and draw souls to the practice of it, just as the glories of Thabor and the miracles of Jesus Christ were not, as it were, "extras", but rather flashes of his glory which from time to time pierced the dark cloud of his humanity in order to render it venerable and lovable to others.

The true marvel of a saint is his life of continual faith through everything. If he had not that, the rest of his gifts would not make him holy. His holiness based on the loving faith which causes him to enjoy God in everything needs no exterior wonders; if such have their use it is for the sake of others who may need this testimony. As for the soul of faith contented in its obscurity, it does not rest on these brilliant manifestations; it lets them appear externally for the benefit of its neighbour, keeping for itself the most ordinary elements it can find, the order of God and his good pleasure which exercise its faith in obscurity rather than in manifestation. Faith asks for no proofs, and those who need them have less faith than those who do not. Those who live by faith do indeed receive proof, not as such but in the course of the divine order, and in this sense there is no contradiction between these extraordinary events and the state of pure faith. For there are many saints whom God raises up for the salvation of souls and from whose countenance he causes rays to proceed which enlighten the feeblest souls. Such were the Prophets and

Apostles, and, indeed, such are all the saints when God chooses to place them, as it were, in a candlestick. There always will be, as there always have been, saints like these as well as an infinite number of others in the Church who are hidden, who, being intended to shine only in heaven, send forth no light in this life, but live and die in profound obscurity.

§ 6

The state of self-abandonment contains the merit of all other particular spiritual operations

Self-abandonment in the heart includes all possible ways of serving God: for one's own being is given up to the good pleasure of God, and the transport caused by pure love covers the whole field of operations of God's good pleasure. Thus the soul at every moment exercises an infinite self-abandonment and all possible qualities and manners of serving God are included in its virtue. It is not the business of the soul to determine the particular matter of the submission it owes to God, its sole business is to be ready for everything and to submit to everything. There lies the essence of self-abandonment; that is what God demands of the soul. The free self-offering that he asks of the heart consists of abnegation, obedience and love: the rest is his business. Whether the soul takes pains to fulfil the duty of its state of life, or follows with sweetness an attraction inspired by God, or peacefully submits to the impressions of grace on its body and soul is no matter: in all this it exercises in the depth of the heart one and the same general act of self-abandonment. This act is not in the least limited by the term of the soul's activity and by the special divine order which appear at the moment, but has in its depths all the merit and all the efficacy that a sincerely good will always has when the effect is outside its control. What the soul has wished to do is taken as done before God.

If the good pleasure of God sets limits to our exercise of our particular faculties, he puts none on the exercise of the will. The good pleasure of God, the being and essence of God are the object of the will, and through the soul's exercise of love God unites himself to it without limit of mode or measure. If in a par-

49

ticular case this love is directed in the concrete to the exercise of this or that particular faculty, it means that the will of God also directs itself to that particular object, and that God's will, as it were, foreshortens itself in the present moment, thus passing into the faculties and thence into the heart. Finding the heart pure and resigned without limit or reserve, God's will communicates itself fully on account of the heart's infinite capacity actuated by the virtue of love, which having emptied it of everything else has made it capable of receiving God.

O holy detachment! It is this that makes room for God. O purity, O blessed annihilation, O submission without reserve! This is what attracts God into the depth of the heart. Let my faculties be what they will, thou, Lord, art all my good. Do what thou wilt with this little creature: that he should act, that he should be inspired, that he should be the subject of thy impressions is all one, for all belongs to thee; all, indeed, is thee, from and for thee. I have nothing more to say to it or to do. Not a single moment of my life is of my own ordering; all belongs to thee, I have neither to add nor subtract, to inquire or reflect: sanctity, perfection, salvation, direction, mortification, is all thy affair, Lord. Mine to be content with thee and to choose for myself no action or condition, but to leave all to thy good pleasure.

§7

All souls are called to the enjoyment of the infinite benefits of this state

It is then self-abandonment that I preach, O God, and no particular state of life. I love all the states in which thy grace places souls without any personal preference for one over another. I teach all souls a general means of arriving at that state which thou wilt assign to them; all that I ask from them, is the will to abandon themselves to thy leading; thou wilt make them arrive infallibly at what is best for them. I preach faith to them: self-abandonment, confidence and faith; the will to be the subject and instrument of the divine action and to believe that at every moment and in all things this action is simultaneously applied according to the state of the soul's goodwill; that is the faith I preach. It is not a special state of faith and pure love, but a general state by which all souls can find God under the different ways in which he clothes himself, and can receive the divine form which his grace has prepared for them. I have already spoken to souls in distress, I am speaking now to all kinds of souls. My heart's true instinct is to belong to everyone, to announce to all the secret of the Gospel and make myself all things to all men. In this disposition of mind I consider it a duty (which I obey without difficulty) to weep with those who weep, to rejoice with those who are in joy, to talk with the simple in their own language and to make use of more learned and careful terms with *savants*. I wish to make all men see that they can aspire, not indeed to the same special favours of certain others, but to the same love, the same self-abandonment, the same God, the same work for him and consequently, all without distinction, to an eminent sanctity. What are called extraordinary and privileged graces are so called solely because there are few souls faithful enough to be worthy to receive them. This will be seen clearly on the day of judgement. It will, alas, be seen on that day that it was not in consequence of any reserve on God's part that the majority of souls were deprived of this divine largesse, but solely through their own fault. What an abundance of good would have been poured into their bosoms had they made a complete and constant submission of their goodwill to God. The same reasoning applies to the divine action as to Jesus. If those who had neither confidence in him nor respect for him did not receive the favours which he offered to everyone, they had only their own evil dispositions to thank. All, it is true, cannot aspire to the same sublime states, to the same gifts or degrees of excellence, but if all, faithful to grace, corresponded each according to his measure, all would be content because all would arrive at a point of excellence and of God's favour that would fully satisfy their desires. They would be content both in the realm of nature and that of grace, for nature and grace are indistinguishable in the sighs which the desire of this precious union with God causes to rise from the depth of the heart.

§ 8

*All the riches of grace are the fruit of purity of heart and of perfect
self-abandonment*

He, therefore, who wishes to enjoy the abundance of all goods
has but one thing to do: to purify his heart, to detach himself
from creatures and abandon himself entirely to God. In this
purity and this abandonment he will find everything. Let others,
Lord, ask all sorts of gifts from thee, multiplying their words and
their prayers; as for me, I will ask one gift only, and I have only
this one prayer to make to thee. Give me a pure heart! O man of
pure heart! how happy you are. You see God in your heart
through the liveliness of your faith. You see him in everything
and at every moment working within you and without. You are
in all things his subject and his instrument. He leads you in
everything and to everything. Often you do not think about it,
but he thinks for you. It is sufficient that you should desire what
happens, and ought to happen to you, by his command; he
knows how to prepare you for it. In your salutary blindness, you
hunt about to discover this desire in yourself and you cannot see
it. He sees it well enough. But how simple you are! Do you not
know what a well-disposed heart is? It is nothing but a heart
where God is found. Seeing his own intentions in such a heart,
God knows that it will always remain submissive to his orders.
At the same time he knows that you do not know what is good
for you and he makes it his business to give it you. He does not
mind disappointing you. You thought you were going east-
wards, he takes you to the west. You were on the point of
striking something dangerous, he turns the rudder and brings
you safe to port. Without chart or course, knowing nothing of
wind or tide, all your voyages are successful. If pirates cross
your bow, an unexpected puff of wind takes you out of their
reach.

A good will, a pure heart! How rightly did Jesus place them
among the beatitudes. What greater happiness than to possess
God and be possessed by him! The soul sleeps peacefully on the
breast of Providence playing with the divine wisdom like an
innocent child without anxiety about the journey which con-

tinues without interruption, and in spite of rocks and pirates and continual storms pursues its even way!

The pure heart, the good will: this is the sole foundation of all spiritual states! It is to it that are given the gifts of pure faith, pure hope, pure confidence and pure love. It is on this trunk that are grafted the flowers of the desert, by which I mean those precious graces which one sees blooming only in those wholly detached souls in whom God makes his habitation as in a deserted place to the exclusion of every other object. It is the fertilizing spring where rise all the streams that water the flowers of the Bridegroom and the garden of the Bride. We may imagine the pure heart addressing all souls in these terms: "Look at me well. I am the producer of fair love, that love which discerns the better part and fixes on it; it is I who bring to birth that sweet and efficacious fear which gives the soul a horror of evil and renders it easy to avoid; to me is due the knowledge which reveals to us the greatness of God and the value of virtue; it is from me that ardent desires full of holy hope are ceaselessly springing; it is I who cause the soul to be constant in the practice of virtue in the expectation of that divine object, the enjoyment of which will one day, as now, but more perfectly, make the happiness of faithful souls."

The pure heart can invite all souls to enrich themselves out of its inexhaustible treasures, for to the pure heart all spiritual states and methods lead back. It is from purity of heart that they draw all their beauty and charm. The wonderful fruits of grace and all sorts of virtues, so nutritious for the soul and bursting into blossom on all sides, are the results of purity of heart. This is the land flowing with milk and honey.

Come then, beloved souls, let us run, let us fly to this ocean of love that calls us. What are we waiting for? Let us start at once; let us go and lose ourselves in God, in his very heart, so as to be intoxicated with his love. We shall find in his heart the key to all heavenly treasures. Let us then take the road for heaven. There will be no secret places into which we cannot penetrate. No door will be shut against us, not the door of the garden, or of the cellar, or of the vineyard. If we wish to enjoy the air of the country, all we need do is to go there; we shall come and go, in and out, as we will, with this key of David, this key of knowledge, this key of the abyss in which are contained the hidden and deep treasures of divine wisdom. It is also with this key that the doors of mystical death, and its sacred darkness, are opened. With it we can descend into the lakes below and the den of lions. With it souls penetrate into these obscure dungeons and return from them in safety. This key introduces us into that blessed abode where intelligence and light have their dwelling, where the Bridegroom takes his noontide repose and reveals to his faithful spouses the secrets of his love. O divine secrets which it is not lawful to reveal and which no mortal tongue can express!

Let us love then, dear souls. We need nothing but love in order to be enriched with all good things. Love gives us holiness with all its accompaniments, with both hands, so that it may flow from both sides into hearts open to these divine effusions. O divine seed of eternity, never can we sufficiently praise it. But why should we speak of it? It is better to possess it in silence than to praise it in mere words. What do I say? We must praise love, but only as a consequence of being possessed by it. For from the moment that love possesses a heart, reading, writing, talking, acting or their contraries are the same thing to it. One prefers nothing, one avoids nothing, one is a solitary, or an apostle, one is well or ill, one is rustic or eloquent—as you please. What love dictates to the heart, the heart its faithful echo repeats to the soul's other faculties. It is the heart that reigns under love's auspices over this material and spiritual composite which it is willing to take for its kingdom; since the heart has no other instincts than those with which love inspires it, every object pleases it in the light in which love presents it. Such objects as nature or the evil spirit would fain substitute, merely disgust and horrify the heart; if God permits that it should sometimes be taken by surprise this is but to render it wiser and more humble; as soon as it recognizes its illusion, it returns to God with more love and clings to him more faithfully.

54

CHAPTER 2: THE DUTIES OF SOULS WHOM GOD CALLS
TO THE STATE OF SELF-ABANDONMENT

§ I

*The great duty of souls whom God calls to this state is to give themselves
completely and absolutely to him*

Sacrificate sacrificium justitiae et sperate in Domino : "Offer a sacrifice
of justice," says the Prophet, "and hope in the Lord." This
means that the great and solid foundation of the spiritual life is
to give oneself to God in order to be the subject of his good
pleasure in everything internal and external, and afterwards
to forget oneself so completely, that one considers oneself as a
thing sold and delivered to the purchaser to which one has no
longer any right, in such a way that the good pleasure of God
makes all our joy and that his happiness, glory and being become
our sole good.

This foundation being laid, the soul has nothing to do save
to pass all its life in rejoicing that God is God, abandoning itself
so completely to his good pleasure, that it is equally content to do
this or that, or the contrary, according to his divine will, without reflecting on the use which his good pleasure makes of it.

To abandon oneself! This then is the great duty which remains to be fulfilled after we have acquitted ourselves faithfully
of the duties of our state. The perfection with which this duty is
accomplished will be the measure of our sanctity.

A holy soul is but a soul freely submitted to the divine will
with the help of grace. All that follows this simple acquiescence
is the work of God and not of man. The soul should blindly resign itself in self-abandonment and universal indifference. This
is the only disposition asked of it by God; the rest belongs to him
to choose and determine according to his designs, as an architect selects and marks the stones of the building he proposes to
construct.

We should then love God and his plan in everything, and we
should love it as it presents itself, desiring nothing more. That
these or those objects should be presented is no concern of the

55

soul, but of God, and what he gives is best. The whole of spirituality can be expressed in abridged form in this maxim: we should abandon ourselves purely and entirely to God's design, and thus, with a complete self-forgetfulness, be eternally busied with loving and obeying him, without all these fears, reflections, twistings and turnings and disquietudes which sometimes result from the care of our own salvation and perfection. Since God offers to manage our affairs for us, let us once for all hand them over to his infinite wisdom, in order to occupy ourselves only with himself and what belongs to him.

Come, my soul, let us pass with head erect over all that happens within us or outside us, remaining always content with God, content with what he does with us and with what he makes us do. Let us be very careful not to engage imprudently in that multitude of restless reflections which like so many paths leading nowhere present themselves to our mind to make it wander and stray endlessly to our sheer loss: let us pass this labyrinth of our own self-love by vaulting over it and not by following it out in all its interminable details.

Come, my soul, let us pass beyond our languors, our illnesses, our aridities, our inequalities of humour, our weaknesses of mind, the snares of the devil and of men with their suspicions, jealousies, sinister ideas and prejudices. Let us fly like the eagle above all these clouds, our gaze ever fixed on the sun and on its rays, which are our duties. We feel all these miseries, and it is not in our power to be insensible to them, but let us remember that our life is not a life of feeling. Let us live in that higher region of the soul where the will of God produces his eternal operation, ever equal, ever uniform, ever immutable. In that spiritual home where the Uncreated, the Formless, the Ineffable, keeps the soul infinitely removed from all the shadows and dust of earth, we remain calm even when our senses are the prey of the tempest. We have become independent of the senses; their agitations and disquietudes, their comings and goings and the hundreds of metamorphoses they pass through do not trouble us any more than the clouds that darken the sky for a moment and disappear. We know that everything happens in the senses as in the air where all is without sequence or order, in a state of perpetual change. God and his will is the eternal object which charms the heart in the state of faith, as in the state of glory he will be its true felicity; and the state of the heart in glory will have its effect on the whole of our material being, at present the prey of monsters, owls and wild beasts. Under these appearances, however terrible they may be, the divine action will give to our being a heavenly power and make it as shining as the sun; for the faculties of the sensitive soul and of the body are prepared here below like gold, iron, fine linen and precious stones. Like the material substrate of those various things, they will only enjoy the splendour and purity of their form after much manipulation and when much has been destroyed and cut away. All that souls endure here below under the hand of God has no other purpose than to prepare them for this.

The soul of faith, knowing God's secret, remains ever in peace. All that happens to it, far from frightening it, reassures it. So intimately persuaded is it of God's guidance that it takes everything as a grace and forgets the instrument with which God works in order to think only of the task committed to its care. Its love stimulates it ceaselessly to fulfil faithfully and exactly its obligations. All that is distinctly perceived by a self-abandoned soul is the action of grace, with the exception of the sins which are trifling and which the action of grace turns to its advantage. I call "distinctly perceived" all the afflicting or consoling impressions which the sensitive soul receives from the objects with which the divine will ceaselessly places it in contact for its good —"distinctly" because that is what is most clearly discerned in all that occurs to it. In all these things, faith sees only God and applies itself solely to conformity with his will.

§ 2

To arrive at the state of self-abandonment, the soul must strip itself
of all created things

This state presents nothing but sweetness when attained, but many agonies have to be passed through on the road. The doctrine of pure love can only be learnt by God's action, not by any effort of our own spirit. God instructs the heart not by means of ideas, but by pains and contradictions. The science of this state is a practical knowledge by which one tastes God as the sole good. In order to possess it, we have to be disentangled from all particular goods, and to reach that state of disentanglement we have to be really deprived of them. Thus, it is only through a continual self-contradiction and a long series of all kinds of mortifications, trials and strippings that one can be established in the state of pure love. We have to arrive at the point at which the whole created universe no longer exists for us, and God is everything. For that purpose it is necessary that God should oppose himself to all the particular affections of the soul, so that when it is led to some particular form of prayer or idea of piety or method of devotion, when it proposes to attain perfection by such and such plans or ways or by the direction of such and such people, in fact, when it attaches itself to anything whatever, God upsets its ideas and permits that instead of what it thought it would do, it finds in it all nothing but confusion, trouble, emptiness, folly. No sooner has it said: that is my path, there is the person I ought to consult, that is how I should act, than God immediately says the contrary and withdraws his power from the means chosen by the soul. So, finding in everything only deception and nothingness, the soul is constrained to have recourse to God himself and be content with him.

Happy the soul that understands this loving severity of its God and corresponds to it faithfully! It rises above all that is transitory to rest in the unchangeable and infinite. It no longer lets itself go forth by love and confidence to created things, it admits them only by duty, by the command of God and a special application of his will. It lives above the alternations of abundance and deprivation in the plenitude of God who is its permanent good. God finds such a soul quite empty of individual inclinations, movements or choice. It is dead and buried in a universal indifference. The Allness of the Divine Being thus appearing in the depth of the heart spreads over the surface of creatures a tint of nothingness which absorbs all their distinctions and variety. Creatures by themselves are without power or efficacy and the heart lacks any tendency or inclination towards them because the majesty of God fills all its capacity. A heart

that thus lives for God is dead to everything else and everything
is dead to it. It is for God who gives life to everything to
vivify the soul and other creatures in regard to it. This life
is God's design. By this design the heart is moved towards
creatures in so far as that is necessary or useful, and by the same
design creatures are presented to the soul and accepted by it.
Without this divine power of the good pleasure of God, creatures
are not admitted by the soul, and the soul does not move towards them. This reduction of all creatures, first into nothing
and then into the particular point of God's design, results in
God being God as well as all things to the soul at each moment.
For each moment is for the soul a contentment with God alone
in the depth of the heart and a self-abandonment without
reserve to all possible creatures, or rather to the whole created
or possible universe according to the order of God. Thus each
moment contains the whole.

§ 3
*The active exercise of self-abandonment with reference to the precepts
and inspiration*

Although souls raised by God to the state of self-abandonment
are much more passive than active, they cannot be dispensed
from all action. This state, being nothing else than the virtue of
self-abandonment practised more habitually and with greater
perfection, should consist, like that virtue, of two orders of
duties: the active accomplishment of the divine will and the passive acceptance of all that it pleases God to send us.

It consists essentially, we have said, in the complete donation
of our being to God to be used according to his good pleasure.
Now the good pleasure of God makes use of our being in two
ways: he either obliges us to perform certain actions, or he
simply acts himself in us. We thus have two ways of submitting
to him; the faithful execution of his clearly manifested commands, and the simple and passive submission to the effects he
produces in the soul, whether agreeable or painful. Self-abandonment includes all that, for it is nothing but a perfect submission to God's design according to the disposition of the pre-

sent moment. It is of small importance to the soul to know in what it has to abandon itself and what the present moment may present, but it is absolutely important that it should abandon itself.

There are therefore duties of precept that must be accomplished and duties of necessity that must be accepted; and there is also a third kind of duty which also belongs to active fidelity though not concerned with actual precepts: the duties of inspiration to which the spirit of God inclines hearts that are submissive to him.

The accomplishment of this class of duties demands a great deal of simplicity, of gentle and cordial facility, of a certain sensitive mobility of the soul under the breath of grace directing it, for nothing is actually performed; one merely lets oneself go, and freely and simply obeys one's impressions. That souls may not be deceived in this way, God never fails to give them wise directors who point out the degree of liberty or reserve with which these inspirations should be utilized. This third class of duties is quite beyond and outside any law, form, or determined matter. Hence comes the individual and extraordinary element in the lives of the saints, regulating their vocal prayer, their interior communications, their feelings and the astounding quality of their life, their austerities, their zeal, their prodigality of self-sacrifice for their neighbour. Since the whole of this domain is under the interior law of the Holy Spirit, no one should advance to it or take its duties upon themselves or desire it or repine because they do not receive the graces which would make them undertake this kind of good work and practise these uncommon virtues, for their real merit comes from their being in God's design. Unless we practise this reserve we shall fall under the influence of our own will and be exposed to illusion.

We should note that there are souls whom God wishes to keep hidden, little in their own eyes and those of others. Far from bestowing striking qualities on them, his design for them prescribes obscurity. They would deceive themselves if they tried to walk by any other path. If they are sufficiently instructed, they will know that their part is fidelity in their own nothingness, and their lowliness will be their peace. The only real difference between their path and the path of those who seem to be more favoured is whatever difference there may be in their love and their submission to the will of God, for if they surpass in this respect souls who seem to accomplish more in exterior works, no doubt their holiness will be greater.

This shows that every soul should content itself with the duties of its state and the commands of Providence; it is evident that God demands this equally of all. As for the attractions and the impressions the soul may receive in itself, it belongs to God alone to give them. One should not oneself try to produce them or make efforts to increase them. The effort of nature is here directly opposed and contrary to the infusion of grace. The latter comes in peace. It is the voice of the Bridegroom that should awaken the spouse, who should act only in so far as she is animated by the Holy Spirit, for in acting apart from that influence the soul accomplishes nothing. When then it feels no inclination or power of grace to imitate the marvels that make the saints so wonderful, it must judge itself and say: That is what God wants from the saints; he does not want it from me.

§ 4

The conduct of the soul that is raised to the state of self-abandonment in relation to this double manifestation of the good pleasure of God

The souls who are called by God to live in the state of perfect self-abandonment lead on earth a life like to that of Jesus, the Blessed Virgin and St Joseph. This life is entirely filled with the will of God. These souls fully submissive to the divine will as soon as it is manifested in precept or inspiration, are in continual dependence on what we may call the will of pure Providence. It follows from this that their life, though most extraordinary in its perfection, shows nothing exteriorly except what is quite ordinary and common: they fulfil the duties of religion and of their state; others apparently do the same. Examine them in other matters; there is nothing striking or peculiar; only ordinary things happen to them. What distinguishes them is not perceptible to the senses; it is the dependence on the supreme will in which they live which seems to arrange everything for them.

This will keeps them always masters of themselves through the habitual submission of their hearts.

Thus the souls of whom we speak are by their state solitary and free, disengaged from everything in order to content themselves in peacefully loving the God who possesses them and faithfully fulfilling the duty of the moment according as his will is signified to them without permitting any reflection on themselves or any scrutiny of consequences, causes or reasons; it must suffice them to walk simply in pure duty as if there were nothing in the world but God and the particular duty of the moment.

The present moment is, as it were, a desert in which the simple soul sees nothing but God only, whom it enjoys, being solely occupied with his will for it; all else is left aside, forgotten, abandoned to Providence. The soul like an instrument in God's hand only accepts or does things in so far as it is passively occupied with God or directed by him to some external purpose.

This interior application of the soul is accompanied by a co-operation, free and active, indeed, but infused and mystical, which means that God, finding everything in the soul ready for action, should he ordain it, spares it the trouble, enriching it with what would have otherwise been the fruits of its own efforts and goodwill. As if someone, seeing a friend ready to make a journey for his service, were promptly to insinuate himself into his friend's person and under his friend's appearance make the journey by his own activity, so that nothing was left to the friend but his will to go, while in fact he would be walking by the other's power. His action would be free because it would be a result of a free decision taken beforehand through love for the friend who would actually perform the task; it would be active, for the journey would really be taken; it would be infused because it would take place without the friend's own action; finally, it would be mystical, for the source of the movement would be hidden.

But to return to this kind of co-operation which we have explained by this imaginary journey, it should be noted that it is totally different from the fidelity with which one fulfils one's ordinary duties. The action with which one fulfils these is neither mystical nor infused but free and active in the ordinary meaning of the words. Thus self-abandonment to God's good pleasure has in it both passivity and activity; the subject of the act makes no contribution of his own beyond the habit of general goodwill ready for anything and wishing for nothing in particular, like an instrument without any action of its own. Once it is in the workman's hands, it serves for all the uses for which its nature and quality adapt it. Contrariwise, the obedience paid to the signified and declared will of God is part of the common order of vigilance, care, attention, prudence and discretion, according as grace helps or stimulates our ordinary spiritual efforts. We leave everything else then to God's action, retaining in our own power nothing but our acts of love and obedience to the present duty, for the soul will practise these acts eternally. This love of the soul silently infused is a true action of which it makes a perpetual obligation; it must constantly preserve it, which it cannot do without action. Such action, however, is altogether different from the obedience to the duty of the present moment by which the soul disposes its external faculties to execute completely the external will of God without expecting any extraordinary call.

The will of God is in all things the rule, the method, the law, the simple and certain way for this soul. It is the invariable law, belonging to all times, all places, all states. It is a straight line which the soul follows with courage and fidelity, straying neither to the right nor to the left and unconcerned with what exceeds its grasp: all that is beyond, is received and performed in self-abandonment. In one word, the soul is active as far as it is concerned with its present duty, but passive and abandoned as regards all the rest, where its only action is to await in peace the divine motion.

§ 5

The soul that wishes to be united to God should esteem all the operations
of his grace but should attach itself, for its part, to the duty
of the present moment only

It is by union with his will that one enjoys and possesses God, and it is an illusion to seek for that enjoyment by any other means. The will of God is the universal means. This means does

not belong to this or that method, but it has the virtue of sanctifying all methods and special calls.

The divine will unites itself with our souls in a thousand different ways, and the method that it adopts in our regard is always
the best for us. We should esteem and love them all, for in all we
should see the divine design accommodating itself to each soul
and choosing the best way to effect the divine union in it. The
duty of the soul is to be faithful to that choice, but nevertheless
to love and esteem the adorable will of God as indicated for
others. For example, if the divine will prescribes for me vocal
prayers, affective sentiments, illuminations on the mysteries, I
shall love and esteem the silence and spiritual nudity which the
view of sheer faith brings about in others, while for my own part
I shall make use of this present duty and unite myself to God by
means of it. I shall not reduce all religion (as the Quietists do) to
complete inactivity, for what makes perfection is the order of
God which renders useful to a soul any means that he chooses to
apply to it. No, I will not confine the will of God to any limits
or figures, but I will receive his will under the forms it may
choose to adopt, and I shall think highly of those which God
adopts for union with others.

Thus all simple souls have one general way differentiated and
particularized in each of them so as to make up the variety of the
mystical robe of the Church. All simple souls approve and esteem each other, saying: let us go each by our own path to the
common goal, united in that same purpose and by the same
means according to the designs of God so variously expressed in
us all. This is the spirit in which we should read lives of saints and
spiritual books without giving way to delusions and leaving our
appointed path. This is why it is so necessary only to read and
have spiritual conversations in conformity with God's design,
for if they come to us as our present duty in that design, the soul
far from being deceived will be confirmed in its own way both
by what resembles that design and by what differs from it. But
if our spiritual reading or conversation is not our present duty in
the order of God for us, we shall always be troubled afterwards
with a confusion of continually varying ideas, because, apart
from the order of God, there can be no order anywhere.

How long shall we go on filling our receptive souls with troubles and anxieties which have nothing to do with our present duties? When will God be to us everything in all things? Let us leave creatures to produce on us impressions according to their nature, but let nothing make us halt; let us go beyond the whole of creation, and live purely on God himself.

§ 6

God exacts from souls whom he places in this state the most perfect docility to the action of his grace

How detached from everything that one feels or does must one be in order to walk by this path in which one lives on God only and one's present duty. We must cut off all more distant views, we must confine ourselves to the duty of the present moment without thinking of what preceded it or what will follow it.

I assume, of course, that the law of God is well kept and that the practice of self-abandonment has made your soul docile to divine action. You will have a feeling that will cause you to say: I feel at present an affection for this person or book, I would like to give or receive this piece of advice, to make such or such a complaint, to open myself to this soul or receive confidences, to give or do this thing or the other. You should follow this impulse under the motion of grace without relying an instant on your own reflections, reasonings or efforts. We must apply ourselves to things for the time that God wishes without mixing ourselves up in them personally. The will of God is applied to us in the state of which we are speaking; it should completely take the place of all our ordinary supports.

Each moment has its obligatory virtue to which the self-abandoned soul is faithful, yet it misses nothing of what it reads or hears; the most mortified novice does not fulfil her duties better; that is why these souls are now led to one book and now to another, or to make this or that remark on some trifling event. God gives them at one moment the desire to instruct themselves in what at another moment will help their practice of virtue.

In all that they do, they feel only the attraction of the act without knowing why. All they can say reduces to this: I feel drawn to write, to read, to ask this question, to look at that object; I follow this inclination, and God who gives it me makes in my soul a reserve-fund of such things to be in the future the means of further attractions which will enable me to make use of them in my own interest and that of others. This is what obliges such souls to be simple, gentle, flexible and mobile under the slightest, almost imperceptible, impressions of the divine will.

In the state of self-abandonment the sole rule is the present moment. The soul is as light as a feather, as fluid as water, simple as a child, as easily moved as a ball, so as to receive and follow all the impressions of grace. Self-abandoned souls have no more hardness or resistance than molten metal. For just as metal takes all the shapes of the mould into which it is poured, these souls adapt and adjust themselves as easily to all the forms which God wishes to give them. In a word, their disposition resembles that of the air which is at the service of all who breathe it and of water which takes the form of every container.

They present themselves to God like a perfectly plain and simple canvas, without concerning themselves to know the subject which it may please God to paint in their souls, for they trust themselves to him; they surrender themselves and, wholly occupied with their duty, think neither of themselves nor of what is necessary for them, nor of how they are to procure it.

The more, however, they apply themselves to their little job, so simple, so hidden, so contemptible (as its outward appearance may be), the more God diversifies and beautifies it. On the background of simple love and obedience, his hands love to trace the most beautiful details, the most delicate and exquisite drawings, the most divine figures: *Mirificavit Dominus Sanctum suum*. A canvas which is simply blindly abandoned to the painter's brush merely feels each moment the touch of the brush. Similarly if a stone could feel, it would feel nothing but the cruel edge of the chisel cutting it away and destroying it, for the stone being chipped by repeated blows is totally unaware of the figure which is being carved out of it by these blows. It feels only a chisel which is reducing it in size, is beating it, cutting it and changing its shape. Take for instance a poor bit of stone which you wish to make into a crucifix or a statue, although the stone does not know it. Suppose you ask it, "What is happening to you?" It might answer, "Don't ask me. As far as I am concerned there is nothing for me to know or do except to remain steady under the hand of my master, to love this master and to put up with his treatment. As for what I am destined to be, it is his business to know how to manage that. I do not know what he is doing or what I am being turned into by his work; I only know that whatever he is doing is best and most perfect, and I accept each blow of the chisel as the most excellent thing for me, although to speak the truth every blow makes me feel that I am being ruined, defaced and destroyed. But I leave all this to him and content myself with the present moment, thinking only of my duty; and I accept this skilful master's treatment of me without knowing or troubling myself about it."

Yes, dear souls, simple souls, leave to God what belongs to him and remain loving and passive under his action. Hold for certain that what happens to you internally and externally is for the best. Leave God to act and abandon yourselves to him. Let the point of the knife and the needle work. Let the brush of the master cover you with a variety of colours which seem only to disfigure the canvas of your soul. Correspond with all these divine operations by the uniform and simple disposition of a complete self-abandonment, self-forgetfulness and application to your duty. Keep to the line of your own advance and, without knowing the map of the country or the details, names and directions of the land you are passing through, walk blindly along that line and everything will be indicated to you if you remain passive. Seek only the kingdom of God and his justice in love and obedience and all the rest will be given you.

One sees many souls who are disturbed and ask: Who will give us holiness, perfection, mortification, direction? Let them hunt up in books the precise terms and qualities of this wonderful business, its nature and parts; as for you, remain in peace in the unity of God by your love and walk blindly in the clear straight path of your obligations. The angels are at your side in this night and their hands make a barrier for you. If God wishes more from you, his inspiration will make it known to you.

§ 7

The docility of the soul in this state should make it close its
eyes on the road by which God leads it

When God becomes the guide of a soul he demands with justice
that it should confide absolutely in him and be not at all disturbed by the way in which he leads it. The soul is pushed along
without seeing the road over which it is passing. What it has
seen or read is no guide to it now. In the case of its own action,
it must walk guided by experience; it cannot do otherwise; it
cannot take risks. But divine action is always novel, it does not
return on its steps, it always finds new paths. Souls led by divine
action know not where they go, the paths they follow are not to
be found in books or in their own reflections, divine action continually shows them the forward path; they follow it by a divine
impulse.

When one is being led by night across fields, through an unknown roadless country by a guide who follows his own ideas
without asking the way of anyone and without revealing his
plans, what can one do but abandon oneself to his care? What
is the use of trying to find out where one is, of asking the passers-
by or of looking at the map? The intentions and the caprice, so
to speak, of a guide who insists on our trusting him will be contrary to all that. He will take pleasure in confounding the soul's
anxiety and suspicions. He demands a complete confidence in
himself. If one had proof that his guidance was right there
would be neither faith nor self-abandonment.

The divine action is essentially good, it needs neither reform
nor control. It commenced at the moment of the Creation and
up to this moment it has brought forth novelties, its operations
have no limits, its fecundity is never exhausted. This was done
yesterday, something else is done today; the same action which
is applied at all moments produces constantly new effects, and
its manifestations will go on eternally. Divine action made an
Abel, a Noah, an Abraham on different patterns; Isaac is an
original figure, Jacob is not a copy of him, nor is Joseph a copy of
Jacob. Moses is like none of his forebears. David and the prophets are quite different to the patriarchs. John the Baptist
surpasses them all. Jesus Christ is the First-born; the Apostles

act more by the influence of his spirit than by a literal imitation of his works.

Jesus Christ did not limit his own action, he did not obey literally all his own maxims. The Divine Spirit perpetually inspired his holy soul; having always been abandoned to that divine Breath there was no need to consult the preceding moment in order to determine the following one. The breath of grace formed all his moments on the model of the eternal truths which the invisible and impenetrable wisdom of the Holy Trinity preserved. The soul of Jesus Christ received the divine orders at each instant and reproduced them in his conduct. The Gospel shows us the result of these truths in the life of Jesus Christ, and the very same Jesus always living and working produces new wonders in holy souls.

Do you wish to live according to the Gospel? Live in a pure and complete self-abandonment to the action of God. Jesus Christ is the sovereign organ of that action. He was yesterday, he still is today, continuing his life, not beginning it over again. What has been done is done, what remains to be done is being done at every moment. Each saint receives a part of that divine life; Jesus Christ, though the same, is different in all. The life of every saint is the life of Jesus Christ, it is a new gospel. The cheeks of the Spouse are compared to a bed of sweet-smelling flowers. The divine action is the gardener who admirably diversifies their arrangement. This flower-bed is unlike that one; among all the flowers there are not two that resemble each other, except by the fidelity with which they receive the action of the Creator, leaving him to do what he wills as master and for their part obeying the laws he has imposed on their nature. To let God do what he wills and to do what he demands of us, that is the gospel, the whole of Scripture and the ordinary law.

§ 8

This complete self-abandonment is as simple a thing as its effects are
wonderful

Such then is the straight highroad of sanctity, such is the state of perfection, such are the duties it imposes, such is the great, the incomparable secret of self-abandonment, but it is a secret without a secret, an art without art. God who demands it of everyone has explained it very clearly and made it very intelligible and simple. The obscurity of the road of pure faith is not in anything that the soul has to practise, for nothing is easier and clearer to understand; the mystery resides entirely in God's action.

See what happens in the Eucharist. What is necessary in order to change the bread into the body of Jesus Christ is so simple and easy that the most ignorant priest can do it, and yet it is the mystery of mysteries in which everything is so hidden, obscure and incomprehensible, that the more spiritual and enlightened one is, the more faith one requires to believe it. The road of pure faith shows us something similar. Its effect is to make us find God at every moment; what can be more marvellous, more mystical, more beatifying! It is indeed an inexhaustible fount of thoughts, discourses and writings. It is an assemblage and a source of all marvels. And yet what is necessary for the production of this prodigious effect? One thing only. To allow God to act and to do what he wishes according to one's state of life. Nothing easier in the spiritual life or better adapted to the powers of all and yet nothing more wonderful, no path more dark. To walk in it, the soul needs a great faith; everything is suspect, reason finds difficulties everywhere. All the soul's ideas are confounded, here is nothing that it has seen or read about, nothing of what it has been accustomed to admire. The prophets were saints; this Jesus is an enchanter, said the Jews. How little faith has the soul that, following their example, is scandalized, and how it deserves to be deprived of the wonders God is ready to work in it!

CHAPTER 3: TRIALS ACCOMPANYING THE STATE OF
SELF-ABANDONMENT

§ 1

*First trial: The blame and criticism of persons who are
reputed wise and pious*

NOTHING is more secure than the way of self-abandonment, just
as nothing is clearer, easier or more pleasant and less exposed to
possible error and illusion. Travelling on this road, we love God,
we fulfil our Christian duties, we frequent the sacraments,
we produce the external religious acts obligatory for everyone,
we obey our superiors, we continually resist the movements of
the flesh and the devil, for no one is more attentive or vigilant
in fulfilling all their obligations than those who walk in this
way.

If this be so, how then comes it that these souls are so often
exposed to contradictions? One of their most ordinary trials is
that when they have performed like other Christians the duties
laid down by the strictest doctors, people try to oblige them in
addition to wearisome practices which the Church does not impose, and if they make no use of them they are taxed with illusion. But tell me, is a Christian who confines himself to the observance of the commandments of God and the Church, and
who without meditation or contemplation, without spiritual
reading or any particular private devotion spends his time in
worldly business, in error? No one thinks of charging him with
it or suspecting him of it. Let us be consistent. If we leave un-
disturbed the Christian of whom I have just spoken it is only
justice not to disquiet a soul who not only fulfils the precepts at
least as well as he does, but who in addition practises external
works of piety of which the former knows nothing or towards
which, if he does know them, he shows nothing but indifference.

Prejudice reaches the point of assuring us that such a soul is
deluded because after having submitted to all that the Church
prescribes, it keeps itself at liberty to give itself up without
obstacle to the intimate operations of God and follow the im-

pressions of his grace at all moments when it has no express obligation to fulfil. It is condemned, in a word, because it spends in loving God the time that others give to recreation or worldly affairs: is not this a crying injustice? One cannot insist too strongly on this point. In the case of one who remains in the ranks and confesses once a year, nothing is said about him, he is left in peace, being perhaps occasionally exhorted to do something more but without being strongly pressed and certainly without its being put to him as an obligation. If he changes his life and comes out of the indevout multitude, at once he is attacked with maxims, methods of direction, methods of prayer, and unless he binds himself to what has been established by the art of piety and constantly follows it, he is done for, people are anxious about him and his way of life becomes suspect. Are these critics ignorant that these practices, however good and holy they may be, are, after all, only the road leading to divine union? Do they wish those who have reached the goal to stay in the road?

That, however, is what is demanded of this soul on behalf of whom these critics are so afraid of illusion. This soul has accomplished its journey like others; at the beginning it learned these practices of devotion and followed them faithfully; it would be in vain to try and keep it subject to them today. Since God, touched by the efforts that it has made to advance by means of such help, has come to meet it and has led it to this blessed union; since it has arrived in that fair region of which the atmosphere is self-abandonment and where the possession of God in love is initiated; since finally this God of goodness has substituted for its care and labour *himself* as the principle of its operations, these methods have lost their utility for it, they do but indicate the road it has passed over and left behind it. To demand that it should take up these methods again or continue to follow them would be to make it abandon the goal at which it has arrived in order to return to the road which brought it there.

Moreover, it would be a loss of time and trouble, for if this soul has any experience it will remain untroubled and unshaken in that intimate peace in which it exercises its love so advantageously. That is the centre where it will repose, or, if you wish, that is the straight line traced by God himself which it will always follow. It will walk with constancy along that line and all its duties will be marked out for it moment by moment. Following the order of that line, it will fulfil its duties without hurry or confusion as they are presented to it. For all the rest, it will remain in perfect liberty of mind, always ready to obey the movements of grace as soon as they make themselves felt, and to abandon itself to the care of Providence.

God tells it that he intends to be its master and to direct it in his own way, and he makes it understand that it cannot without infringing the sovereign rights of its Creator allow its own liberty to be enchained. It sees that if it were to confine itself within the regulations of souls who live under a regime of effort and industry, far from following the invitation of grace, it would deprive itself of a thousand things necessary for its future duties. But as people are ignorant of that, they judge it and blame its simplicity, and it who blames no one, who approves all states of life, who knows so well how to judge different degrees of progress, sees itself despised by these false sages who cannot appreciate this gentle and cordial submission to Providence.

The wisdom of the world does not approve the constant instability of the Apostles who could not fix themselves anywhere. No more can the common run of religious people endure souls who depend upon Providence in this way for their principle of movement; only a few souls of that order will approve them, and God who uses men for the instruction of men will not fail to make souls that are simple and faithful to their self-abandonment come across them.

Moreover, these souls have less need of direction than others, for they have only reached this stage with the aid of very great and excellent directors. If they find themselves momentarily left to themselves, it is but by the disposition of Providence when death takes, or some event places at a distance, the guides who had introduced them into this state. Even in these circumstances they are always disposed to accept direction, only they peacefully await the moment of Providence. And then without fussing about it, from time to time they will meet persons in whom, without knowing them or where they come from, they will feel a

 Self-abandonment to Divine Providence

secret confidence at such times of privation. Such a feeling is a sign that God wishes to make use of them at the moment to communicate some lights. These souls then consult and follow with complete docility the advice they receive, but if this help does not present itself they cling to the maxims given them by their first directors. They are thus always being truly directed either by the original principles which they imbibed heretofore or by these chance counsellors, and they make use of them until God sends them persons in whom they can confide and who reveal his will to them.

§ 2

Second trial in the state of self-abandonment: The apparent uselessness and external defects which are the portion of souls whom God wishes to raise to this state

A second trial of souls whom God leads by this way results from their apparent uselessness and their external defects. As a rule, neither honours nor revenues come their way, but rather a state of life abject and useless from the world's point of view. No doubt, those who occupy important posts are not on that account necessarily excluded from the state of self-abandonment, and even less is this state incompatible with the shining virtues of a sanctity which imposes universal veneration. But how much more numerous are the souls raised to this sublime state whose virtues are known to God only. Such souls are by their state freed from almost all exterior obligations. They are hardly fitted for the world, for business or for industrial occupations, for complicated situations or for study. They seem useless for anything, the only noticeable thing about them is their weakness of body, mind, imagination and passions. They pay attention to nothing. Their life is, so to speak, a brute-life; one sees in them none of the advantages which culture, study and reflection bring to men. Their nature seems like that of children before they are placed in the hands of educators to be formed. Their defects are obvious, and, though these do not make them more guilty than children, they are more shocking in them. God takes everything from these souls but innocence, so that they may possess nothing but himself alone.

74

The world, which does not understand this mystery, judges by appearances only and finds nothing to appreciate or esteem. So the world rebuffs and despises them, they are indeed butts for everyone's censure. The nearer one sees them the less one likes them, in fact the more one dislikes them: one does not know what to say or think of them. Nevertheless, something or other seems to speak in their favour, but instead of following that instinctive feeling, or at least of suspending one's judgement, we prefer to follow the leading of our malignity. People spy on their actions so as to confirm their own opinion, and like the Pharisees who could not endure the conversation of Jesus, scrutinize them with such prejudiced eyes that all they do seems ridiculous or criminal.

§ 3
Third trial: Interior humiliations

Contemptible in the eyes of others, the souls whom God raises to this state are still more so in their own. There is nothing about their sufferings or actions but what is very trivial and humiliating, there is nothing striking about their manner of life, all about them is commonplace. Within are nothing but troubles, without nothing but contradictions and plans that fail, and a sickly body needing care and comforts which seem to be the opposite of the excesses of poverty and austerity which have made us admire the saints. In the case of these souls we see neither heroic enterprises nor excessive fasts or alms-giving, nor ardent and heroic zeal.

Simply united to God by faith and love, they see all their interior feelings in disorder. They despise themselves still more when they compare themselves with those who pass for saints, and who, capable as they are of subjection to rules and methods, show nothing but what is correct in public opinion in all their person and actions. Then the sight of themselves is insupportable and covers them with confusion. This is what draws from their hearts those sighs and bitter groanings which mark the excess of grief and affliction with which they are filled. Let us remember that Jesus Christ was at once God and Man. As Man he was reduced to nothingness and as God was filled with glory.

These souls without sharing his glory feel nothing but the death and annihilation caused in them by their sad and grievous appearance. They appear, to the eyes of men, as Jesus did to Herod and his court.

As regards their senses and judgement, these poor souls are thus led in a way that is altogether disgusting to them, for none of all this is pleasant to them; they long for something quite different, but all the roads leading to that sanctity they so desire are closed to them. They have to live on this bread of ashes and anguish under continual external and internal constraint. It is their lot to perceive an ideal of sanctity which causes them constant and irremediable torments. Their will is famished for it, but they have no means of effectively attaining it. Why all this, if not in order that the soul should be mortified in its most intimate and spiritual part, and finding no satisfaction or happiness in anything that happens to it should place all its happiness in God who is leading it expressly by that way, so that there should be none but himself who can be its pleasure?

I think that the conclusion from all this is easy, that these abandoned souls cannot, like others, occupy themselves with desires, pursuits, and matters of detail, that they cannot combine with other people, enter into plans or prescribe for themselves methodical ways or detailed plans for action or reading. If they could, it would imply that they were still in a position to dispose of themselves and this is excluded by the state of self-abandonment in which they are. In that state one belongs to God by a full and complete cession of all one's rights over oneself, over one's actions, one's thoughts, one's movements, over the employment of one's time and over all one's relationships. One only desire remains to be fulfilled; to keep one's eye on the Master to whom one has given oneself and to be constantly on the alert to divine his will and execute it immediately. No condition better represents this state than that of a servant who is in his master's presence only to obey at each instant the orders he may please to give him and not to conduct his own affairs, which he should abandon in order to belong to his master at every moment. Let not, however, these souls be distressed by their helplessness: it is already a great deal to be able to give oneself over completely into the hands of an almighty Master capable of performing the greatest things by means of the weakest instruments, if they do not resist him.

Let us then without anxiety suffer the outer shell of our life to humiliate us in our own eyes and those of others, or rather let us hide ourselves under this shell and enjoy God who alone is all our good. Let us make profit of this infirmity, of our needs, of our necessities in the matter of food and comforts, of our failures, of the contempt of others, of our fears, doubts, troubles and the rest, so as to find all our good in the enjoyment of God who by these things gives himself entirely to us as our sole good.

God wishes to dwell in us in poverty and without all those accessories of sanctity which cause souls to be admired: it is because he wishes to be alone the food of our hearts, the sole object of our complacency. We are so weak that if the splendour of austerity, zeal, almsgiving or poverty were to shine out in us, it would become a part of our joy. But in our way there is nothing but what is disagreeable, and by this means God is the whole of our sanctification, the whole of our support, while the world can only despise us and leave us to enjoy our treasure in peace.

God wishes to be the principle of the whole of our sanctity, and for that reason all that depends on us and our active fidelity is very trifling and in appearance the opposite of sanctity. There can be nothing great in us in the eyes of God except by the way of passivity. Let us then think no more about our sanctity but leave the care of it to God who knows the means to produce it. These all depend on a special protection and operation of Providence; they usually occur unknown to us and through those very things which we dislike most and expect least. Let us walk peacefully in the small duties of our active fidelity without aspiring to great ones, for God will not give himself to us for the sake of any trouble that we can take in the matter. We will be saints of God, of his grace and of his special Providence. He knows the rank he wishes to give us, let us leave it to him to do as he pleases, and without forming henceforward false ideas and vain systems of sanctity, let us be content to love him without ceasing, walking with simplicity in the road which he has traced for us where everything is so little in our eyes and those of the world.

§ 4

Fourth trial of souls in the state of self-abandonment: the obscurity of their state and its apparent opposition to the will of God

But a much more distressing trial for a soul who desires nothing but to love God is the impossibility of feeling sure that it loves him. Formerly by the ideas it formed and the lights it received, it saw what made up the plan of its perfection; but now no longer so. Perfection is given to it contrary to all its ideas and lights and feelings, by all the crosses sent by Providence, by the actions demanded by the duty of the moment, by various inclinations which have nothing good in them except that they do not lead to sin, but which seem far distant from the sublime and extraordinary splendour of virtue.

God hidden in his veils gives himself with his grace in an altogether unknown way, for the soul feels nothing but feebleness under its crosses, disgust with its obligations, while its attractions are only to very commonplace exercises. The idea which it has formed of sanctity reproaches it internally with these low and contemptible dispositions. All the saints' lives condemn it. It knows nothing with which to defend itself; it has light to see a sanctity which, however, brings it desolation, for it has no strength to rise to it, and it does not recognize its weakness as divine order, but as its own cowardice. All the people it knows distinguished by the splendour of their virtues or the sublimity of their speculations look at it with contempt. What an odd saint, they say. And the soul believing them and confused by so many useless efforts that it has made to rise from this degradation is surfeited with obloquy and finds nothing to reply either to itself or others.

It feels itself lost in this dreadful state; it has no support, neither that of the thoughts which used to guide and animate its actions nor that of grace no longer perceptible; but in this loss of everything it finds everything restored, for that very grace that it cannot perceive in, so to say, a new form, gives the soul the hundredfold of what it has taken away, by the purity of its secret effects.

It is no doubt a great blow, like death, to the soul, this loss of the sight of the divine will which retires from its sight to take up a position behind it, as it were, and impels it forward, being no longer its clearly conceived object but becoming its invisible principle.

Experience shows us that nothing so much as this apparent loss inflames the desire of the soul for union with the divine will. What profound sorrow for the soul! . . . No consolation is possible.

To ravish God from a heart longing for nothing but God, what a secret of love! It is indeed a great secret, for by this way and by this way only are pure faith and pure hope established in a soul. Then, indeed, one believes what one does not see and one hopes for what one does not sensibly possess. Oh! how we are perfected by this unknown effect of an action of which we are at once, though invisibly to ourselves, the subject and the instrument. Everything one does seems the fruit of chance and natural inclination. Everything that happens humiliates the soul. When one is really speaking from inspiration, one seems to be speaking from nature. We can never see by what spirit we are moved, the divinest inspiration frightens us, and whatever we may do or feel, we feel incessant contempt for ourselves as if all were faulty. Others are always admired, but we feel miles below them and put to confusion by their every action. We suspect all our lights, we cannot feel sure of any of our thoughts, and we submit, even in excess, to any advice that seems true to us. The divine action seems to keep us far from virtue only to plunge the soul into a profound humility. But this humility does not seem to be such to the soul, it thinks it is suffering from the rigours of pure justice.

The most remarkable thing about this is that in the eyes of those whom God does not enlighten concerning its path, the soul seems animated by quite contrary feelings such as obstinacy, disobedience, contempt and indignation that cannot be cured, and the more the soul tries to reform these disorders, the worse they become, for they are the most proper means to detach it from itself and fit it for divine union.

From this painful trial comes the principal merit of the state

79

of self-abandonment. In the duty of the present moment every-thing is of a nature to draw the soul away from its path of love and simple obedience. It needs heroic courage and love to stand firm in its simple, active fidelity and sing its part with assurance, while grace sings its own with different melodies and in different keys which do nothing but convince the soul that it is deceived and lost. That is all it hears, and if it has the courage to endure the pealing of the thunder, the flashing of the lightning and the roaring of the tempest and walk firmly in the path of love and obedience to duty and the immediate inspiration given by God, we may say that it resembles the soul of Jesus, and shares the state of his Passion, during which our divine Saviour walked with even step in the path of love for his Father and submission to his will, a path which made him do things in appearance most contrary to the dignity of so holy a soul as his.

The hearts of Jesus and Mary, braving the uproar of this dark night, let the clouds burst asunder and the storm pour down. A deluge of events in appearance most opposed to the designs of God and his commands overwhelm their faculties, but deprived of all support from the senses, they walk on unshaken, on the tip-toe of the heart, so to say, in the path of love and obedience. They fix their eyes solely on what they have to do, and leaving God to act as he pleases in their regard, they endure the whole weight of his divine action. They groan under the burden, but they do not stagger or stop for one single instant. They believe that all will go well, provided the heart keeps to God's path and does not interfere with his action.

§ 5
The fruit of these trials. Conduct of a soul undergoing them

It follows from all that has been said, that in this path of pure faith all that happens in soul and body and the circumstances and events of one's life wears an appearance of death. We should not be surprised at this, for it is precisely the nature of this state. God carries out very successfully his designs on souls under these obscuring veils. Under the name of veils I include mis-fortune, bodily infirmities and spiritual weakness. All succeeds in the hands of God. He arranges and prepares his highest designs by means of these things so distressing to nature: *Omnia cooperantur in bonum iis qui secundum propositum vocati sunt sancti.* In the shadow of death he produces life, and though the senses are terrified, faith, taking all for the best, is full of courage and assurance.

Since we know that the divine action embraces everything, directs everything, indeed does everything, apart from sin, faith has the duty of adoring, loving and welcoming it in everything. We should do so full of joy and confidence, rising in everything above appearances, the very obscurity of which provokes the triumph of faith. This is the way to honour God and to treat him as God.

To live by faith is then to live in joy, assurance, certitude, confidence in what one must do and suffer at each moment at God's command. It is to animate and sustain this life of faith that God permits the soul to be overwhelmed and carried away on the tumultuous waters of so many pains, troubles, embarrassments, weaknesses and defeats, for faith is needed to find God in all that. The divine life presents itself at every moment in an unknown but very certain manner under such appearances as physical death, damnation in the soul, ruin in temporal affairs. In all this faith finds its nourishment and support. Faith pierces through these appearances and comes to rest on the support of God who keeps it alive. A faithful soul should walk on in confidence, where there is no prospect of sin, taking all these things as the veils of disguise of God, whose intimate presence at once alarms and reassures its faculties.

Indeed, the great God who consoles the humble gives the soul in the midst of its greatest desolation an intimate assurance that it has nothing to fear provided it allows him to act and abandons itself completely to him. In the midst of its affliction at the loss of its Beloved, something tells it that it is in possession of him. It is troubled and upset, and yet in its depths there is a sort of fundamental weight which keeps it unchangeably attached to God.

"Truly," said Jacob, "God is in this place and I knew it not." You are seeking God, dear soul, and he is everywhere, everything cries his name to you, everything gives him to you, he is at your side, around you, within you, and astride your path; he remains with you and you still seek him! . . . Ah, you are seeking the idea of God, while you possess his substance, you are pursuing perfection and it is there all the while in everything that comes to meet you. Your sufferings, your actions, your inclinations are, as it were, the sacramental species under which God gives himself to you, while you are off chasing your sublime ideas. But God will not come to your house clothed in their splendour.

Martha tries to please Jesus by good cooking and Magdalen is content to receive him as it pleases him to come to her. He even deceives her and presents himself under the appearance of a gardener when she seeks him according to her own idea of him. The Apostles see Jesus and take him for a phantom.

God then disguises himself to raise the soul to pure faith, thus teaching it to find him under all sorts of disguises; for once it has learned the secret of God, he may disguise himself as he pleases; it says: "He is there behind the wall, he is looking through the lattice, he is looking through the windows." Hide thyself, divine love, try test after test, bind the soul with your attractions and duties, blend, mingle, confuse, break up like spiders' webs all the soul's ideas and standards. Let it lose its foothold and feel no roads or paths nor see any light. After having found thee in solitude and in prayer, in its religious exercises, in sufferings, in services to its neighbour, in the avoidance of society and worldly affairs, and after having tried every known method of pleasing thee, let it no longer be able to find thee in any of these things as heretofore. But grant that the uselessness of its efforts may lead it to abandon them all in order to find thee in thyself, and then in everything, everywhere, without distinction or reflection.

For what an error not to see thee in all that is good, indeed in all creatures! Why seek thee in others than those through which thou wishest to give thyself? Why seek thee under other species than those chosen by thee for thy sacrament? And does not the insignificance of their appearance subserve the merit of our obedience in believing? Dost thou not give fecundity to the root trodden in the earth, and canst thou not render fruitful this darkness in which it is thy will to keep me?

Live on then, little root of my heart, in the hidden bosom of God. Push forth, vitalized by his secret power, the branches, foliage, flowers and fruit which you will be unable to see yourself but which will nourish and rejoice the hearts of others. Give to all who approach you your flowers and your fruit according to their taste rather than your own. May all the slips grafted on you receive an undetermined sap that will only be specified in their own form. Become everything in all souls, in your own be nothing but self-abandonment and indifference.

Dwell then, little silkworm, in the dark and narrow prison of your cocoon until the warmth of grace forms you and hatches you out. Eat all the leaves which grace presents to you and do not regret in the activity of your self-abandonment the peace you have lost. Stop what you are doing when the divine action gives the signal. In your alternating periods of repose and action and your incomprehensible metamorphoses, you must shed your old forms and methods 'and habits, and in your recurring death and resurrection take on those which the divine action points out to you. Then go on spinning your silk in secret, doing what you can neither feel nor see. Feel throughout your whole being a secret agitation which you will yourself condemn, while you envy your companions in their death-like repose who have not yet reached the point where you are. You still admire them though you have surpassed them. Abandon yourself to this agitation in order to spin a silk in which princes of the Church and the world will be proud to be clothed. After that, what will you become, little worm? . . . What will be the issue for you? . . . What a wonder of grace that a soul can assume so many forms! Who can guess where grace will lead it? Indeed, who could guess the designs of nature on a silkworm, if he had not observed them? All it needs is leaves, that is all. Nature does the rest.

So it is, dear souls, that you cannot know where you come from or where you are going, from what divine idea God's wisdom produced you, or to what end it is bringing you. Nothing remains to you but a completely passive self-abandonment, to let yourself go without deliberation, without following any model or example or method; acting when it is the moment for action, keeping quiet when you should do so, enduring loss when you ought to. In this way, moved by spiritual attraction and self-abandonment, one acts or ceases to act, one reads or not, one puts books and friends on one side, one is silent, one writes, one stops writing without ever knowing what will follow. But after several transformations, the consummated soul receives wings with which to fly up to heaven, leaving on earth a fertile seed to perpetuate its state in other souls.

CHAPTER 4: OF THE PATERNAL ASSISTANCE WITH
WHICH GOD SURROUNDS THE SOULS WHO
ABANDON THEMSELVES TO HIM

§ I

The less the self-abandoned soul feels the support of God, the more efficaciously is he in reality sustaining it

THERE is a sort of sanctity in which all the divine communications are luminous and clear. In the passive way of faith, all that God communicates shares his nature and the inaccessible darkness that surrounds his throne: the sentiments the soul feels are confused and cloudy. The soul in this condition, like the prophet, is often afraid of running headlong into snares while crossing this obscure region. Do not be afraid, faithful soul, for this is precisely your path and the way God wishes you to go. Nothing is surer and more infallible than the darkness of faith. But you wish to know what direction to take in such obscurity of faith? Go wherever you like; you cannot lose your way when there is no longer any road to find, all roads being the same in this darkness—you cannot aim at any point, no object is visible. But everything alarms me (says the soul), I seem at each moment to be falling over a precipice. Everything wearies me. I know well enough that I am acting on the principle of self-abandonment, but it seems to me that in everything I can only act by going contrary to virtue. I seem to hear all the virtues complaining that I am abandoning them. The more attractive and pleasing they seem to be, the further the obscure influence under which I act seems to take me from them. I love virtue, but I yield to that obscure impulse; I cannot see that it is leading me aright, but I cannot help believing that it does so. The spirit flies to the light, but the heart is content with darkness. Intellectual people please my mind, but my heart cares only for conversations and sermons in which I understand nothing and my whole state is nothing but an expression of the gift of faith which makes me love and relish principles and truths in which my mind finds neither objects nor ideas, in which it trembles and totters. I know not how, but assurance dwells in the depths of my heart which acts as it is moved, convinced of the goodness of the impression which governs it, not indeed through evidence but through the conviction of faith. And this certitude is victorious over all censures, all fears, all the efforts and ideas of the mind. The spirit may cry out and criticize as much as it likes, the bride feels the presence of the Bridegroom without feeling himself, for when she tries to touch him, he is no longer there. She feels the right hand of the Spouse who is on every side of her, and she would rather stray in self-abandonment to his guidance though it leads her without reason or order, than assure herself of her road by laboriously following the familiar and well-marked paths of virtue. Come then, my soul, let us go to God by the road of self-abandonment; let us confess our inability to produce virtue by our own efforts and industry. But do not let this lack of virtue of our own manufacture diminish in any way our confidence. Our divine guide would not reduce us to the state of being unable to walk, if his divine goodness were not carrying us in his arms. What need have we of lights, assurance, ideas, reflections? What advantage would it be to us, O Lord, to see, to know, to feel, since we are not walking on our feet but are being carried in the bosom of Providence? The darker it grows, the more numerous the chasms, the snares, the fears, the persecutions, the famines, the troubles, the despairs, the purgatories and hells that line our path, the greater shall our faith and confidence be. It is enough to cast our eyes on thee to be safe in the greatest dangers. We will forget all about the road and its condition, good or bad; we will forget ourselves and completely abandoned to the wisdom, goodness and power of our guide, we will remember nothing but to love thee, to fly not only obvious sin, however slight it may appear, but everything that wears any semblance of sin and to fulfil our ordinary duties. This is the only responsibility, dear Love, that thou leavest to thy children; all the rest is thy affair. The more terrible the rest becomes, the more thy children wait upon and see thy presence; they think of nothing but loving thee without bothering about the rest, and they go on fulfilling their little duties like a child in his mother's arms absorbed in his play as if there were nothing in the world but his mother and his games. The soul must pass beyond all this shadow; the night is not the time for action but for repose. The light of its reason can only augment the darkness of faith: the ray which will pierce it must come from the same height from which that darkness proceeds.

God communicates himself to the soul in this state as *life*, but he no longer presents himself to its vision as the *way* and the *truth*. The bride seeks the Bridegroom in the night: but he is behind her, he holds her in his hands, he moves her in front of him. He is no longer there as object and idea, but as principle and source. There are in the divine action marvellous, unknown and secret sources of inspiration sufficient to deal with all the needs, embarrassments, troubles, upsets, persecutions, incertitudes and doubts of souls who have no longer confidence in their own actions. The more complicated the play, the more delight we anticipate in the *dénouement*. The heart says: All will go well, God has the work in hand; there is nothing to frighten us. Fear itself, the suspension of the faculties and desolation are the stanzas of this canticle of darkness. It is our joy to omit no syllable of them. We know that all ends with *Gloria Patri*. So each one follows the path of his own wanderings, the very darkness serves for his direction, and doubts do but imply assurance. The more trouble Isaac has to find a victim for the sacrifice, the more completely Abraham places his lot in the hands of Providence.

§ 2

*The desolation with which God afflicts such a soul is but a loving
artifice which will one day make it rejoice*

Souls who walk in light sing the hymns of light, those who walk
in darkness, the hymns of darkness. They must both be left to
sing to the end the part and the motet which God allots to each.
Nothing must be added to what he has made complete; and
every drop of this divine bitterness must be allowed to flow, even
when it overwhelms and intoxicates the singers. Thus did
Jeremias and Ezechiel act; their only words were sighs and sobs
and their only consolation was in the continuation of their
lamentations. If their tears had been wiped away, we should
have lost the most beautiful passages in Scripture. The Spirit
who makes them desolate is the only one that can console them;
these different waters spring from the same source.

When God appears to be angry, the soul trembles, when he
threatens it, it is afraid; there is nothing to be done but allow the
divine operation to develop; in its full expansion it brings both
the illness and the remedy. Weep and tremble, dear souls,
agonize in your anxiety, do not make efforts to get rid of these
divine terrors, these heavenly groanings. Receive in the depths
of your being these streams from the ocean of suffering which
God carried in his holy soul. Go on your way, casting your seed
of tears as long as the influence of grace makes them fall; that
same influence of grace will dry them unbeknown to you. The
clouds will be dissipated, the sun will shine, the spring will cover
you with its flowers and the full course of your self-abandonment
will reveal to you the admirable variety of the divine action
when it is seen in its full extent.

It is truly in vain that man troubles himself, all that happens
to him is, as it were, a dream. The shadows in passing efface
each other. Afflicting and consoling imaginations follow each
other in the sleeper's mind. The soul is the plaything of these
appearances which devour each other, and the moment of
awakening shows their lack of anything substantial enough to
arrest the soul's attention. That moment dissipates all these im-

pressions and one takes no heed either of the dangers or the joys of sleep.

Lord, may I not likewise say that thou holdest asleep on thy bosom all thy children during the night of faith, that thou takest pleasure in causing an infinite number of infinitely various sentiments to pass through their souls, sentiments which at bottom are but holy and mysterious dreamings? In the state in which the night and their sleep place them, they experience authentic and painful terrors, anguish and worries which thou wilt dissipate and transform on the day of glory into true and solid joys.

After this moment of awakening, holy souls, restored to themselves and their full liberty of judgement, will never grow weary of admiring the skill, the finesse, the loving inventions and deceptions of the Bridegroom. Then they will understand how impenetrable are his ways, how impossible it was to guess his riddles, to detect him under his disguises or to admit any consolation when he wished to spread fear and alarm in the soul. At that moment of awakening, a Jeremias and a Daniel will see that those very things which had caused them inconsolable desolation were to God and the angels a subject of joy.

Do not awaken the bride with the clamour of human wit and action, leave her to her groanings and her trembling pursuit of her Spouse. It is true that he deceives her, he is disguised, she is dreaming. But let her sleep. Leave the Bridegroom to work in the beloved soul and reproduce in it those traits which he alone can paint and express; let him develop them to the full. He will awaken it when the time comes. Joseph is making Benjamin weep. Servants of Joseph, do not reveal his secret to his beloved brother! Joseph is deceiving him, his trick will never be found out, Benjamin and his brothers are plunged into irremediable sorrow. It is only a game of Joseph's; his poor brothers see nothing in his action but a woe without remedy; say not a word. He will put everything right; when the time comes, he will awaken them from their sleep himself, and they will admire his wisdom in causing them to see so much misery in what was in truth the most real subject of joy that they have ever had in the world.

§ 3

*The more God seems to strip the soul in the state of self-abandonment,
the more generously is he really giving to it*

Let us proceed further in the knowledge of the divine action and
its loving deceptions. What God seems to take away from a soul
of goodwill he really gives, as it were, incognito. Never does he
allow it to lack anything: he acts like one who at first maintains
a friend by gifts of which he is openly the source but who sub-
sequently, in the interest of his friend, appears no longer willing
to oblige him, while continuing his assistance at the same rate
anonymously. If the friend did not suspect this mysterious ruse
of love, he might well feel hurt. What reflections would he not
make on the behaviour of his benefactor? But as soon as the
mystery began to unveil itself, God knows what sentiments of
tender joy, of gratitude and love, of confusion and admiration
would arise in his soul. Would he not burn still more with
zealous affection for his friend, and would not this trial confirm
him in his attachment, fortifying him for the future against
similar surprises?

The application of this parable is simple. The more we seem
to lose with God, the more we gain; the more he deprives us of
the natural, the more he gives of the supernatural. We loved him
a little for his gifts; when we no longer see them, we begin to
love him for himself only. It is by the apparent subtraction of
those sensible gifts that he prepares this great gift for us, the
vastest and most precious of all, for it contains all the rest.

Souls who have once totally submitted themselves to God's
action should always interpret everything favourably; yes,
everything, whether it be the loss of the most excellent directors,
or the suspicion which one entertains in spite of oneself for those
who put themselves forward more than one wishes. For, in a
general way, the guides who run after souls deserve to incur a
little suspicion. Those who are truly animated by the Spirit of
God do not, as a rule, display so much hurry and self-sufficiency;
they do not propose themselves unless they are called in, and
even so they always advance with a certain timidity.

Let the soul that has given itself wholly to God go through

these trials without fear, let it not allow its liberty to be snatched from it. Provided that it is faithful to the divine action, that action will work marvels in it in spite of all obstacles. God and the soul perform in common a work the success of which, though it depends entirely on the action of the divine workman, can be compromised only by the infidelity of the soul.

When the soul is well, all goes well, for what comes from God, i.e. the share his action takes in the work, corresponds to the precise degree of the soul's fidelity. God's share is like the upper side of those magnificent pieces of tapestry which are woven point by point from the reverse side. The workman employed on them sees nothing but the point on which he is working and his needle, and these points successively filled make up those magnificent figures which only appear when, at the completion of all the parts, the right side is displayed, although during the time of the work all this marvellous beauty is in obscurity.

So is it with the self-abandoned soul; it sees nothing but God and its duty. The accomplishment of this duty is at each moment but an imperceptible point added to the work, and yet it is with these points that God works his wonders of which we have now and then a presentiment in the time of our pilgrimage, but which will only be known in the great day of eternity.

How full of goodness and wisdom is the conduct of God! He has in such a way reserved to his grace and action alone the sublime, elevated and admirable part of perfection and holiness, and he has so completely left it to our souls to perform with the help of his grace what is small, plain and easy, that there is no one in the world who cannot arrive without difficulty at the most eminent perfection by fulfilling with love lowly and common duties.

§ 4

The more God seems to blind the soul in the state of self-abandonment, the more surely is he leading it

It is principally in the case of those souls who completely abandon themselves to God that the word of St John is fulfilled: *You have no need to be taught, for the divine unction teaches you all things*. To know what God asks of them, they have but to consult this spirit, sound their hearts and listen to what they hear, for the heart is the interpreter of God's will according to circumstances. For the disguised divine action reveals its designs not by ideas but by instinct. God's action reveals them to the soul either by the compulsion of necessity preventing it from taking any other line than the one presented, or by an original movement and a sort of supernatural transport which causes the soul to act without reflection, or, again, by communicating to it an inclination or disinclination which, while leaving the soul all its liberty, yet brings it to the point of approaching or avoiding objects. Judging by appearances, a great lack of virtue is shown by this uncertainty. Judging by ordinary rules, there is nothing fixed, uniform or harmonious in this action of God. Nevertheless, fundamentally speaking it is the highest point of virtue to have reached this state, and it is, as a rule, only after long exercise that one attains to it. The virtue of this state is *pure* virtue, perfection itself. The soul that has attained to it is like a musician who combines with a long practice of the art, a perfect theoretical knowledge of music. He is so penetrated by his knowledge that all that he produces has, even unconsciously to himself, the perfection of music, and his compositions, on examination, manifest perfect conformity with the rules of his art. It is evident that his success will never be greater than on those occasions when freeing himself from the rules which, followed too scrupulously, hold genius in bonds, he acts without constraint, and his impromptus, so many masterpieces, will be the admiration of connoisseurs.

So the soul, exercised for years in the science and practice of perfection, forms for itself insensibly, under the influence of those methods and reasonings with which it used to help itself to correspond with grace, a habit of acting in all things by an instinct for God. It seems to it that the best course for it to follow is the first one that presents itself, without the necessity of that string of reasonings that heretofore preceded its decisions. All it can do is to act at random; it can only give itself up to the genius of the grace that cannot but keep it straight. What it does in this state of simplicity is marvellous to enlightened eyes and intelligent minds. It has no rule, yet nothing is more exact than its conduct; no sense of proportion, yet nothing more exquisitely harmonized; it uses no reflection, yet nothing is deeper; it takes no trouble, yet nothing is better arranged; it makes no effort, yet no one is more efficient; it has no foresight, yet its behaviour is always perfectly adapted to every new situation.

Spiritual reading engaged in as the result of divine action frequently has a meaning that never occurred to the author of the book. God makes use of the words and writings of others to convey hidden truths. If it is his will to enlighten us by these means, self-abandoned souls should make use of the opportunity, and any means resulting from divine action has an efficacy always transcending its natural power.

It is characteristic of the state of self-abandonment that, while the soul always leads a mysterious life, it should receive extraordinary and miraculous gifts of God through contact with natural, fortuitous events where nothing is apparent but what is in the normal order of the world and the natural elements. Thus the simplest sermons, the most ordinary conversations and the least remarkable books become for such souls by virtue of the divine design sources of intelligence and wisdom. This is why they gather up with care the crumbs that the self-sufficient man tramples underfoot. All is precious to them, all enriches them. They remain absolutely indifferent to all things, but while they neglect nothing they respect and derive what advantage they can from everything.

Since God is in all things, the use we make of them by his design is not use of creatures but rather enjoyment of the divine action which dispenses its gifts through different channels. These channels do not sanctify by themselves but only as instruments of the divine action which can and frequently does communicate its gifts to simple souls by means of things which appear opposed to the end proposed. In the hands of God, mud is as transparent as light and the instrument he selects is always the unique means to his purpose. Everything is the same to him. Faith believes always that nothing is wanting; the faithful soul does not complain of the lack of means that it may think useful for its advancement, for the Workman who makes use of them supplies by his will for their shortcomings; and this holy will is the whole virtue of creatures.

§ 5

The less the soul is capable of defending itself in the state of self-abandonment, the more powerfully does God defend it

The unique and infallible movement of the divine action always applies the simple soul to the right object at the right time; and it corresponds wisely in everything to God's intimate direction. Sometimes this happens consciously and sometimes unconsciously, the soul being moved by obscure instincts to speech, action or abstention without other motives.

Frequently the determining occasion and reason are only of the natural order; the simple soul sees no mystery here: to it all this is a matter of chance, or necessity, or some convention, nothing at all in its eyes or anyone else's. And yet God's action, which is intelligence, wisdom and counsel for his friends, makes use of all these simple things for their benefit. God, as it were, appropriates them, places them so carefully in the path of those who are planning to harm his friends, that they are unable to achieve their ends.

To deal with a simple soul is in a certain sense to deal with God. What measures can we take against the Almighty whose ways are inscrutable? God takes in hand the cause of the simple soul: it has no need to scrutinize your intrigues, or to match your anxiety with its own in carefully watching all your proceedings; its Bridegroom dispenses it from all these cares; it takes shelter with him and rests on his heart peaceful and secure.

The divine action sets free the soul and delivers it from all those low and feverish methods so necessary to human prudence. All this is necessary for Herod and the Pharisees, but the Magi have only to follow peacefully their star; the child need only rest in the arms of his mother, his enemies do him more good than harm; the more they try to oppose and trap him the more tranquil and free will his activity be. He will do nothing to win them over, he will not pay court to them to escape their blows;

their jealousies, suspicions and persecutions are necessary for him. Thus lived Jesus Christ in Judea, thus he still lives in simple souls; he lives in their hearts generous, gentle, free, peaceful, without fear or need of anyone, seeing all creatures in his Father's hands anxious to serve him, some by their criminal passions, some by their holy actions, these by their opposition to him, those by their obedience and submission. The divine action adjusts it all marvellously. There is no lack of anything, there is nothing too much, only just what is needed of both good and evil.

The divine order supplies for the task of each moment the proper instrument, and the simple soul brought up on faith finds everything right and wants neither more nor less than what it has. It blesses on every occasion the divine hand which provides it so perfectly with the means necessary for its task and delivers it from the obstacles to its fulfilment. It accepts its friends and its enemies with equal gentleness, for it was Jesus' way to treat everyone as an instrument in God's hand. We need no one, and yet we also need every one; the divine action renders everything it selects necessary, and everything must be accepted from God's hand, taking everything according to its quality and nature with a certain gentle and humble correspondence, treating the simple simply and the gross with kindness. This was the teaching of St Paul, and what Jesus Christ practised even better.

To grace alone does it belong to give that supernatural stamp to the soul which particularizes and fits itself so appropriately to the nature of each person. This cannot be learned in books, it is a true spirit of prophecy, the effect of an intimate revelation, the teaching of the Holy Ghost. To understand it, the soul must be in the last stage of self-abandonment, in a condition of the most complete detachment from every plan or interest, however holy. The soul must have before its eyes nothing but its one solitary task: to let itself go passively under the influence of the divine action, in order to give itself to what concerns the duties of its state; leaving the Holy Spirit to work in it interiorly without watching what he does, being indeed glad not to know it. Then one is safe, because all that happens in the world exists for no other purpose than the good of souls perfectly submissive to the will of God.

§ 6

A soul in the state of self-abandonment, instead of fearing its enemies, finds in them useful auxiliaries

I am more afraid of my own action and that of my friends than of that of my enemies. No prudence equals that of not resisting one's enemies and of merely opposing to them a state of simple self-abandonment; this is to have the wind at one's back and one can remain at peace. No opposition to the prudence of the flesh is surer than the simplicity which eludes all the traps of worldly wisdom without thinking or even being aware of them. The divine action causes the soul to take such wise measures that it surprises those who are trying to make it stumble. It profits by all their efforts, it rises by means of what is intended to bring it down. Their efforts really bring it to port like galley-slaves rowing at top speed. All the contradictions it meets turn out to its advantage, and by letting its enemies do as they will, it receives from them a service which is continual and so sufficient that its only fear should be lest it mix itself up in the business and take a hand in a work of which God wishes to be the principle, of which his enemies are the instruments and in which it has nothing to do except to watch peacefully what God does and follow with simplicity the inspirations which he gives it. The supernatural prudence of the Divine Spirit, the source of these inspirations, strikes infallibly the centre and precise circumstances of every situation, and applies the soul thereto with such exquisite precision that all who oppose it never fail to be broken to pieces.

§ 7

A soul in the state of self-abandonment can abstain from saying or doing anything in its own justification: the divine action justifies it

The large, solid, steady rock on which the self-abandoned soul reposes, safe from waves and tempests, is this design of the divine will continuously present under the veil of crosses and the most ordinary actions. God hides his hand in these shadows

95

to sustain and carry those who abandon themselves to him. From the moment that the soul is firmly established in this perfect self-abandonment, it is fully protected against the contradiction of tongues, for it has nothing further to say or do for its own protection. Since the work is of God, its justification must not be sought elsewhere. Its effects and consequences will justify it sufficiently. All that is needed is to allow it to develop. *Dies diei eructat verbum.* One who does not follow his own ideas should not defend himself with words. All our words can do is to express our ideas; where there are no ideas, there should be no words. What end would they serve? To explain our conduct? But the soul is ignorant of the reason for its conduct, which is hidden in the principle causing it to act and of which it has only felt the impression in an ineffable way.

We must then leave to consequences the task of justifying principles. All holds together in this divine chain; each link is firm and solid, and the explanation of the antecedent is found as effect in the consequence. The soul is no longer occupied, fed or sustained by a life of thoughts, imaginations, many words; this is not the strength in which it walks. It sees no longer where it walks or will walk, it no longer helps itself with thought to support the fatigue and inconveniences of the journey; its experience is penetrated by the most intimate sense of its own weakness. The road opens before its feet, it proceeds on it without hesitation. It is pure, simple and true; it walks in the straight line of God's commandments, gently, leaning on God himself, whom it meets continuously at all the points of that straight line, and the God who is its only quest undertakes himself to manifest his presence in such a way as to avenge it of its unjust detractors.

§ 8

God keeps a soul alive in the state of self-abandonment by methods seemingly more adapted to bring it to death

There is a time when God wishes to be the life of the soul and achieve its perfection himself in a secret and unknown way. When this time comes, all the soul's own ideas, lights, labours, inquiries and reasonings are sources of illusion. And when the soul after several experiences of the sad consequences of its own self-direction at length recognizes its uselessness, it finds that God has hidden and mixed up all the channels of his grace in order to make it find its principle of life in him. Then, convinced of its own nothingness and that all that it can draw from that nothingness is injurious to it, it abandons itself to God so as to have nothing but him. So that God becomes in a sense its life, not through its ideas, illuminations or reflections—all that for it is but a source of illusion—but in his effects and the reality of his graces concealed under the most improbable appearances. The divine operation in itself being unknown to the soul, it receives the virtue and substance of it through thousands of circumstances that to its belief spell its ruin. There is no remedy for this obscurity, we must allow ourselves to be plunged in it. God gives himself in that obscurity and with himself all things in the obscurity of faith; the soul is now but a blind subject, or, if you like, it is as an invalid who, being ignorant of their virtue, experiences only the bitterness of its remedies. The poor patient often thinks that they will kill him; the crises and relapses that follow them seem to justify his fears; nevertheless under this appearance of death he is really gaining health, and he takes them on the word of the doctor who prescribes them.

Thus self-abandoned souls do not bother about their infirmities, except such obvious illnesses as, by their nature, oblige them to stay in bed and take suitable medicaments. The languors and weaknesses of these souls are but illusions and phantasms which they should defy with confidence. God sends them and permits them in order to give exercise to their faith and their self-abandonment, which is the real remedy. Without paying any attention to them, they should bravely pursue their way through the actions and sufferings of God's order, making use of their bodies as hacks whose lives are valueless and serve for any job. So to act is better than to indulge in those delicacies which injure the vigour of the spirit. Such energy of spirit has the power to sustain a feeble body, and a year of a noble and generous life is worth more than a century of care and fears.

We should try to preserve habitually the air and bearing of a child of grace and goodwill. What, after all, have we to fear if we follow the divine fortune? Led, sustained, protected by it, its children should manifest nothing short of the heroic in their exterior. The terrifying objects which they meet on their way are nothing; these are only designed to embellish their lives with more glorious actions. Their vocation engages them in all sorts of predicaments in which human prudence, unable to see any issue, is made to feel all its weakness and proved to be short-sighted and confounded. It is at this point that the divine fortune appears in all its beauty what in truth it is to all who follow it. It frees them from their troubles more wonderfully than the novelists, aided by their fertile imaginations in the leisure and privacy of their studies, resolve the intrigues and perils of their imaginary heroes who always reach happily the end of their tale. The divine action leads them, by much more admirable devices, through dangers of death and of monsters, of hell and its demons with their snares. God raises these souls to heaven, and makes them the subjects of histories at once real and mystical, more beautiful and strange than any invented by the shallow imaginations of men.

Come then, my soul, let us cross this dangerous territory directed and sustained by the sure, invisible, all-powerful and infallible hand of divine Providence. Let us proceed without fear to the end of our journey in peace and joy: let all that presents itself be matter for our victories. It is to fight and conquer that we march under God's standards: *exivit vincens ut vinceret*. Every step we take under his auspices is a victory, my soul! ... The Spirit of God has the pen in his hand; he holds his book open in order to continue the unfinished sacred history, the matter of which will only be exhausted at the end of the world.

This history is no other than the account of the actions and designs of God on men. All we have to do so as to figure in this history, is to weave into its web by our union with God's will our sufferings and our actions. Everything that happens to us in the way of action or suffering is not sent us for our loss—no, indeed; it comes to us as the rough material of that Holy Scripture which is growing every day.

§9

Divine love takes the place of everything else for the souls walking in this way

While depriving of everything the souls who give themselves absolutely to him, God gives them something that takes the place of all else, whether it be light, wisdom, life or strength; it is his love. Divine love dwells in these souls like a supernatural instinct. Everything in nature has what belongs to its species, every flower has what it needs, every animal follows successfully its instinct, and every creature has its own perfection. Just so is it in the various states of grace: each has its specific gifts, and there is a recompense for each of those whose goodwill fits itself into the state where Providence has placed it.

A soul comes under the divine action as soon as goodwill springs up in its heart, and God's action has more or less influence on it according to the degree of its self-abandonment. The art of self-abandonment is nothing but the art of loving, and divine action is the action of divine love. How can these two loves which seek each other fail to agree when they meet? How could divine love refuse anything to the soul whose every desire it directs? And how could God meet with a refusal from a soul that lives only by him? . . . Love can but ask for what love wishes, and is it possible for love not to desire what it desires?

God pays attention to nothing but a good will. It is not the capacity of the other faculties which attract him, nor their incapacity which repels him. All he demands is a good, pure, upright, simple, submissive, filial and respectful heart. If he finds such a heart, he takes possession of it and of all its faculties and disposes so well all things for its good that it will find materials for its sanctification in everything. If what gives death to others enters the soul, the antidote of its goodwill will not fail to prevent the effects. Should it come to the edge of a precipice, the divine action will steer it away, or prevent it from falling as long as it remains there; should it actually fall, the divine action will raise it up. After all, the faults of such souls are faults of frailty and scarcely perceptible; love can always turn them to their advantage. By his secret inspirations God makes them understand what they are to say or do according to circumstances.

These souls receive in themselves, as it were, flashes of the divine intelligence: *intellectus bonus omnibus facientibus eum*. For the divine intelligence accompanies them in all their steps and withdraws them from the awkward situations in which their simplicity lands them. If they move to some compromising position, Providence arranges some fortunate contacts which repair everything. Multiple intrigues are woven round them, Providence cuts the knots, confounds the authors of these plots and sends on them a spirit of vertigo which causes them to fall into their own snares. Under God's direction, the souls whom it was desired to trap do certain apparently useless things, without thinking, which serve afterwards to deliver them from all the embarrassments into which their own uprightness and the malice of their enemies had thrown them.

Ah! what a fine policy is this goodwill! What prudence in its simplicity, what deliberation in its innocence and its frankness; what mysteries and secrecy in its uprightness! See young Tobias: he is a mere child, but Raphael is at his side; with such a guide he walks surely; nothing frightens him, he lacks nothing. The very monsters in his path give him nourishment and remedies; the one that attacks him in order to devour him becomes his food. He is occupied with nothing but weddings and banquets, these being, in the order of Providence, his present concern. Not that he has no other affairs, but they are abandoned to the skill of him who has the charge of helping him in everything; they are so well managed that he could never have done so well by himself, for they produce nothing but blessing and prosperity. Yet his mother weeps in utmost bitterness, though his father is full of faith. The child so keenly regretted returns joyfully and enters into the happiness of all his family.

Divine love is, then, for the souls who give themselves wholly to it, the principle of all good. And in order to acquire this inestimable good it is sufficient to will it firmly.

Yes, dear souls, God asks for your heart only; if you are seeking this treasure, this Kingdom in which God reigns alone, you will find it. For if your heart is wholly devoted to God, it forthwith becomes this treasure, this very kingdom that you are desiring and seeking. From the moment that we desire God and his will, we enjoy God and his will, and our enjoyment corresponds to the ardour of our desire. To love God is to desire sincerely to love him; because we love him, we wish to be the instrument of his action, so that his love may exercise itself in and through us.

It is not to the cleverness of the simple and holy soul that the degree of the divine action corresponds; it corresponds to the purity of its intention and not to the wisdom of the measures it adopts, or the projects that it forms or the means it chooses. The soul may be deceived in these, and it not infrequently happens that it is so deceived, but its upright and good intention never deludes it. Provided that God sees this good disposition, he forgives all the rest, and he accepts as done what it would be certain to do, if sounder views were at the service of its goodwill.

Goodwill has therefore nothing to fear; if it fall it can only fall under that all-powerful hand which guides and sustains it in all its wanderings. It is this divine hand that brings it nearer its goal when it is moving away from it, that replaces it on the road when it wanders off it; in that hand the soul finds its resource when the action of its blind faculties makes it stray; it is the pressure of that hand that makes it feel how completely it should despise them, to count only on God and abandon itself wholly to his infallible direction. The errors into which these good souls fall are then resolved in self-abandonment and never does a good heart find itself at a loss; for it is a dogma of faith that all things co-operate for its good.

§ 10

The soul in the state of self-abandonment finds more light and strength
in its submission to the divine action than is possessed by
the proud souls who resist God

Of what use are the sublimest lights or divine revelations when one does not love the will of God? That way Lucifer was lost. The course of Providence which God revealed to him in manifesting the mystery of the Incarnation caused him nothing but envy. On the other hand, a simple soul enlightened by faith alone is never wearied of admiring, praising and loving God's order; finding it not only in holy creatures but also in the wildest confusion and disorder. A simple soul is more fully enlightened by a grain of pure faith than Lucifer by all his intelligence.

The knowledge possessed by a soul faithful to its obligations, quietly submissive to the intimate orders of grace, gentle and humble towards all, is worth more than the most profound penetration of mysteries. If only one saw nothing but divine action in all this pride and harshness of human action one would always accept it with humility and respect, and the disorder of creatures would not make us leave the path of order ourselves, how great soever they might be. We should see in them only the divine action which they bear and which they hand on to those who faithfully practise gentleness and humility. We must not look at the path they themselves follow, but walk on firmly in our own, and in this way our gentle pressure will break down cedars and overturn mountains.

What is there among creatures that can resist the force of a faithful, gentle and humble soul? If we would infallibly conquer our enemies we must oppose them with no other arms than fidelity, gentleness and humility. Jesus Christ has put these in our hands for our defence; there is nothing to fear when we know how to use them. We should not be cowardly but generous, for this is the only disposition in which we can use these divine instruments. All that God does is sublime and marvellous and never can individual action at war with God resist one who is united to the divine action by gentleness and humility.

What is Lucifer? He is a brilliant intelligence, the most enlightened of all, but an intelligence discontented with God and his order. The mystery of iniquity is nothing but the result of this discontent manifested in as many ways as possible. Lucifer, as far as lies in his power, wishes to leave nothing in the state in which God has ordained and placed it. Wherever he penetrates, you will always find the work of God disfigured. The more lights, knowledge and general capacity a person has the more he is to be feared, if he has not the foundation of piety which consists in contentment with God and his will. It is the regulation of the heart that places us in union with the divine will; without that union, everything is but pure nature and, usually, pure opposition to the divine order; God has not, properly speaking, any instruments but humble souls: though he is always contradicted by the proud, he does not fail to make them serve, like slaves, the accomplishment of his designs. When I see a soul who makes God and submission to his orders its all, however deficient it may be in other things, I say: There is a soul who has great talents for serving God. The Holy Virgin and St Joseph were like that. The rest, without that, frightens me and I fear to find there the action of Lucifer; I keep on my guard and I fortify myself in my stronghold of simplicity in order to oppose it to the whole of this life of the senses which, by itself, is for me nothing but brittle glass.

§ 11

The soul in the state of self-abandonment can see God in the proud
soul who fights against his action. All creatures, good or evil,
reveal God to it

The simple soul practises no other devotion than the order of God. It respects this order in the irregular actions which the proud man performs to insult it. The proud man despises a soul in whose eyes he is nothing; for it sees nothing but God in him and his actions. Often he thinks that its humility means that it fears him, although it is but the sign of the loving fear it has of God and his will which it perceives in the proud man.

No, poor fool, the simple soul is not afraid of you. You awaken its compassion. It is to God it is replying when you think it is speaking to you; it looks on you as one of his slaves or rather as a shadow under which he is disguised. So the higher the tone you take, the lower is its answer. All your tricks and acts of violence are for it favours of Providence.

The proud man is an incomprehensible enigma to himself but very intelligible to a simple soul enlightened by faith.

This discovery of the divine action in all that passes within us and around us is the true knowledge of things. It is a continual revelation of things; it is a ceaselessly renewed commerce with God; it is the enjoyment of the Bridegroom, not in secret in the wine-cellar or the vineyard, but openly and in public, without fear of any creature. In its depths, it is peace, joy, love and contentment in God, seen, known (or rather believed) to be living and always working in the most perfect way in everything that happens. It is the eternal paradise which is, indeed, only known and savoured in dark and shapeless forms; but the Spirit of God who is the stage-manager of this life by his continual and fecundating action, will say at the moment of our death: let there be light: *Fiat lux*; and then we shall see the treasures concealed by faith in that abyss of peace and contentment with God who is present at every moment in all we have to do and suffer.

When God gives himself in this way, the ordinary becomes extraordinary, and this is why nothing seems extraordinary. For this path in itself is extraordinary and it is quite unnecessary to adorn it with irrelevant marvels. It is itself a miracle, a revelation, a continuous joy, apart from our trifling venial faults, but it is a miracle which, while it renders marvellous all our everyday life of the senses, has nothing in itself that is marvellous *to* the senses.

§ 12

God assures to the souls who are faithful to him a glorious victory over the powers of the world and of hell

It is in order to augment the merits of faithful souls that the divine action hides itself here below under the appearance of weakness, but its triumph is none the less certain for that.

The history of the world is nothing but the history of the war waged by the powers of the world and of hell since the beginning against the souls humbly devoted to the divine action. In this war, the advantages seem all on the side of pride, and yet humility always wins the day. The figure of this world is presented to us under the image of a statue of gold, bronze, iron and clay. This mystery of iniquity, shown in a dream to Nabuchodonosor, is but a confused assemblage of all the interior and exterior actions of the children of darkness, who are also represented by the Beast that comes out of the bottomless pit to make war from the beginning on the interior and spiritual man; all that happens today is nothing but the continuation of this war.

The monsters follow each other, the abyss devours and regurgitates them in incessantly renewed jets of smoke. The battle begun in heaven between Michael and Lucifer is still going on. The heart of that proud and envious angel has become an inexhaustible abyss of all sorts of evils. He caused the revolt of the angels in heaven; and his entire occupation since the creation of the world is to keep constantly renewed the supply of evil men who take the place of those swallowed by the abyss. Lucifer is the leader of those who will not obey the Almighty. This mystery of iniquity is the inversion of the order of God; it is the order or rather the disorder of the devil. This disorder is a mystery, for it conceals under beautiful appearances irremediable evils. All the evil men from Cain to those who ravage the world today have had the appearance of great and powerful princes who have produced a great effect in the world and whom men have worshipped. This appearance of pomp is also a mystery; in reality these princes are the beasts who have come up out of the abyss, one after the other, to overturn God's order. This order (which is another mystery) has always opposed to them truly great and powerful men who have slain these monsters, and as hell vomits forth new ones, heaven has brought to birth its heroes who have combated them. Ancient history, sacred and profane, is nothing but the history of this war. The order of God has always remained victorious; those who have been on his side have triumphed with him and are happy for eternity; injustice has never been able to protect the deserters, but has paid them with death, and that an eternal death!

The man who has wickedness in his mind always believes himself invincible. But, O God! how can we resist thee? A single soul with hell and the world against it can fear nothing if it be on the side of self-abandonment to God's order. This monstrous show of impiety armed with so much power, this golden head, this body of silver, bronze and iron is but a phantom of iridescent dust. A tiny pebble scatters it to the winds.

How admirable is the Holy Spirit in this dramatic representation of all the ages! So many revolutions which create such havoc among men, such heroes who come in such splendour like so many constellations moving in the sky over our heads; so many wonderful events—all this is but a dream which Nabu-chodonosor forgets when he wakes, however terrible the impression it has made on his mind.

All these monsters come into the world only to exercise the courage of the children of God, and when these have learned enough, God rewards them with the pleasure of killing the monster, and calls new athletes to the arena. And so this life is a continual spectacle which is the joy of heaven, the training of the saints on earth and the confusion of hell.

Thus, all that is opposed to God's order does but result in making it more adorable. All who freely serve iniquity become the slaves of justice, and the divine action builds the Heavenly Jerusalem with the ruins of Babylon.

PART TWO

LETTERS ON THE PRACTICE OF
SELF-ABANDONMENT

BOOK I

THE ESTEEM AND LOVE OF
SELF-ABANDONMENT

LETTER I : TO SISTER CHARLOTTE-ELIZABETH
DE MONTHUREUX

*The happiness and unalterable peace of the soul that abandons itself
entirely to God*

PERPIGNAN, 1732

MADAME and very dear Sister,—You do well to devote yourself
vigorously and, as it were, uniquely to the excellent practice of
a complete self-abandonment to the will of God. Therein lies for
you the whole of perfection; it is the easiest road and leads
soonest and most surely to a deep and unalterable peace; it is
also a sure guarantee of the preservation of that peace in the
depth of our soul through the most furious tempests. The soul
that truly abandons itself to God has nothing to fear from the
most violent storms. Far from doing it any hurt, they will infallibly serve not only to increase its merits, but also to establish
it more and more firmly in that union of its own will with the
divine will which renders the tranquillity of the soul invariable.

What happiness, what grace, what confidence for the next
life, and what unalterable peace for the present one is to be
found in having our being in God only, in possessing nothing
more than God alone, no other support, no other help, no other
hope! What a beautiful letter one of your sisters has just written
me on this point! For a month, she says, she has had but one
thought: God only; I have nothing left but God; and that
thought alone consoled, sustained and encouraged her so
powerfully that, instead of regrets, she felt within her a deep
peace and inexplicable joy. It seemed to her that God took the
place of director and friend and that he wished himself to be
everything to her.

The more deeply these sentiments penetrate us, the more solid will be our peace; for the decision definitely taken to seek nothing but God and to will only what he wills is above all else that *goodwill* to which the reward of peace has been promised. How can creatures trouble a soul who has neither desire nor fear in their regard? Let us force ourselves to reach that point and our peace will be truly imperturbable. Let us imitate the holy Archbishop of Cambrai who said of himself: "If the worst comes to the worst, I put up with it all; and in the depths of the worst I find my peace in an entire self-abandonment."

LETTER 2

Self-abandonment is the quickest way to reach pure love and perfection

YOUR letter, my dear Sister, reminds me of that passage in the Gospel which shows us a young man approaching our Lord in order to ask him the way to reach eternal life. The good Master makes the immediate reply that he must keep the commandments, and when the young man answers that he has observed them faithfully up to that day, the Saviour says to him: "If thou wilt be perfect, go, sell all that thou hast and give it to the poor and follow me."

The question you ask me is the same as the question of this young man. You wish me to point out to you the shortest and surest way to reach the perfection which is the plenitude of eternal life. If I did not know you as well as I do, I should reply that above everything you must keep your rule, since for all religious, their rule is the only assured path to perfection. But I know that you have been observing it for a long time with the most scrupulous exactitude, and that what you wish to learn from me at this moment is the most suitable practice to raise to high sanctity a religious who is in the habit of accomplishing faithfully all her duties. And to that question, my dear Sister, I shall give the same reply as the good Master. If you wish to be perfect, strip yourself of all your own views, of all pretensions, of all self-seeking, of all thought of yourself, of all that you can call *yours*, and abandon yourself without reserve and once and for all to the direction and good pleasure of God. Self-abandonment;

yes, complete self-abandonment, blind and absolute, is for souls who are walking in your path the height and sum of perfection, for perfection consists in pure love and for you the exercise of pure love consists in self-abandonment.

It is true that even the purest love does not exclude from the soul the desire of its salvation and perfection, but it is equally incontestable that the nearer a soul approaches to perfect purity of love the more it turns its thoughts away from itself in order to fix them on the infinite goodness of God. The divine goodness does not oblige us to repudiate the reward that it destines for us, but it has surely the right to be loved for itself without any backward glances at our own interests. Such a love which does not exclude, but is independent of, the love of ourselves is what all theologians call pure love, and they all agree that the soul is more perfect in proportion as it habitually governs itself by the motive of that love, stripping itself entirely of all self-seeking, except in so far as its own interests are subordinated to those of God. Moreover, total self-abandonment, without reserves or limits, has no thought for its own personal interests: it thinks only of God, his good pleasure, his will, his glory; it knows and it desires to know nothing else. Far from making self-interest the motive of its love, a truly abandoned soul accepts and generously embraces all that seems to tend to its own annihilation: obscurity, incertitude, weaknesses, humiliations. All this is pleasant to it as soon as it knows that it pleases its Beloved, because the pleasure and contentment of its Beloved make its own pleasure and contentment. It has no longer any will, any desire, any life of its own, but is altogether lost, engulfed and, as it were, annihilated in the dark and deep abyss of the will of him whom it loves.

I can tell you of souls that I have known who after having crossed hundreds of times this apparently terrifying pass of complete, unqualified, and limitless self-abandonment into the depths of the impenetrable designs of God could not prevent themselves from crying out in transports of joy and holy confidence: O will of my God, thou art infinitely holy, just and adorable, but to me yet more lovable and beneficent. If thou art fully accomplished in me, I must infallibly find in thee my true contentment in this life and my eternal happiness in the next. How could thy infinite mercy permit thee to will anything but what tends to the greater good of thy poor creatures? They alone can destroy themselves through the perversity of their own will which can prevent, and too often does prevent, the accomplishment of thy holiest and most beneficent dispositions. Give me then, my God, the grace to destroy by my entire self-abandonment these foolish obstructions and when that is done, assured of the fulfilment in me of thy divine intentions, I shall be equally assured of my salvation and perfection.

LETTER 3: TO SISTER MARIE-THÉRÈSE DE VIOMÉNIL

His doctrine applied to himself. The profound peace which he enjoys through self-abandonment in the midst of business worries

PERPIGNAN, 1740

WHAT I have always most dreaded has just happened to me. I have not been able to get out of accepting an office contrary to all my likings and for which I believe myself to have no aptitude. In vain I groaned, prayed, offered to spend the rest of my life in the novitiate-house of Toulouse; the sacrifice, one of the greatest of my life, had to be made. But see how visibly the action of divine Providence appears. When I had made, and repeated, my sacrifice a hundred times, God removed from my heart all my old repugnance so that I left the professed house—and you know how much I loved it—with a certain peace and liberty of spirit at which I was myself astonished. But there is more. On my arrival at Perpignan, I found a quantity of business of which I understand nothing, and many people to see and conciliate: the Bishop, the Intendant, the King's Lieutenant, Parliament, and Army Staff. You know my horror of all sorts of formal visits and above all of visiting the great, yet I find that none of this frightens me; I hope that God will supply for everything and I feel a confidence in his divine Providence which keeps me above all these troubles. So I remain calm and in peace in the midst of a thousand worries and complications in which I should have expected, naturally speaking, to be overwhelmed.

It is true that what contributes most to this great peace is the disposition in which it has pleased God to place me of fearing and desiring nothing during the course of this short and miserable life. Thus, when I have done what I think before God I ought to do, the success of the enterprise will be what he chooses: I abandon that question entirely to him and with my whole heart, thanking him for everything in advance, desiring only in everything and everywhere his holy will, because I am convinced by faith and by many personal experiences that everything comes from God, and that he is powerful enough and a good enough Father to bring all issues to the best advantage of his dear children. Did he not prove that he loved us better than his life when he laid it down for love of us? And can we not be assured that having done so much for us he will not forget us? I beg of you, do not distress yourself about me or what I am doing. Do what I strive to do myself. As soon as I have taken a decision before God and according to his will, I leave all the care of it to him and entrust him with its success. I expect success with confidence, but also with calm and I am willing for it to occur, not in accordance with my own impatient desires, but at the time of divine Providence which regulates and arranges everything for our greater good, although we usually understand nothing of what it is doing. How can we judge it, poor ignorant creatures that we are, as blind as moles living underground?

Let us accept everything from the hand of our good Father, and he will keep us in peace in the midst of the greatest disasters of this world the fashion of which passes away in a flash. Our life will be holy and tranquil in proportion as we trust in God and abandon ourselves to him. Without that self-abandonment, there is no solid virtue, no sure repose.

You were wrong to be surprised that I was not so at the views and plans of *N.*, for apart from the fact that nothing surprises me in this life, you ought to know my habit of always looking at the good side and most favourable aspect of everything, as St Francis de Sales says. This fortunate habit keeps me out of danger and, in a certain way, prevents me thinking, judging or speaking evil of anyone. I strongly advise you to adopt this method. It will contribute greatly to the preservation of the peace of your soul and the purity of your conscience. Believe me: let us sacrifice all human sentiments and let us console ourselves for everything by self-abandonment and confidence in God only, for he alone can and should take the place of everything else.

LETTER 4: TO THE SAME

The same subject

MY DEAR SISTER,—I am touched by your sympathy in my trials, but I am glad to be able to reassure you. It is true that at first I suffered acutely on seeing myself burdened with a quantity of business and anxieties contrary to my liking for solitude and silence, but see how divine Providence has come to my aid. God gives me the grace to remain unattached to all these affairs, so that my spirit remains always free. I leave their successful issue to his paternal care, so that nothing distresses me. Often things go all right and I give thanks to God; sometimes everything goes wrong, I again bless his holy name and offer him the sacrifice of my efforts. Once this sacrifice has been made, God arranges everything. Already our good Master has prepared several of these agreeable surprises for me. As for leisure, I have more than anywhere else. At the moment visits are rare, because I only pay them out of duty and pure necessity. Our Fathers themselves, who know my tastes, soon finish their business with me and as they are convinced that I do not act as I do out of pride or misanthropy no one disapproves of my behaviour and several are edified by it.

Moreover, I am not as dead as you think; but God gives me the grace not to bother about disapproval when I am following the path on which he calls me. Our concern is to please him only; if he is content, that is enough for us, all the rest is a mere nothing. In a few days we shall make our appearance before this great God, this sovereign Master, this infinite Being. Of what use then (and for all eternity) will anything be that was not done for his sake and animated by his grace and Spirit?

If these simple truths were a little more familiar to us, what peace of heart and mind should we not enjoy already in our present life! From how many vain fears, desires and anxieties, both for this life and the next, should we not be delivered! I will confess to you that since my return to France I begin to envisage more closely than ever the end of this sad life of ours, and I do so with much peace and tranquillity. How could I feel anything but joy, when I see the end of my exile approaching?

LETTER 5 : TO THE SAME

On the same subject

PERPIGNAN, 1741

I AM experiencing here the constant care of divine Providence, for no sooner have I sacrificed everything to God than he discovers a remedy for everything and causes me to find whatever I need. When I find myself without resource, I place all my affairs in the hands of Providence, I hope everything from it, I have recourse to it in everything and for everything; I thank God ceaselessly for everything, receiving everything from his divine hand. And never does he fail us, so long as we put all our confidence in his protection. But what do people do as a rule? They try to substitute their own blind and impotent providence for the infinitely wise and good providence of God; they base themselves on their own efforts, and by doing so they place themselves outside the order of divine love and lose all the support they would have had in carrying out that order. What folly! How can we doubt that God understands our interests much better than we do and that his dispositions of events in regard to us are advantageous even when we do not understand them? Would not a little wisdom be enough to determine us to allow ourselves to be led with docility by his Providence, though we cannot understand all the secret springs which God brings into play, or the particular ends that he has in mind?

But, you will say, if it is enough to let us be passively guided what becomes of the proverb: "Help yourself and God will help you"? I do not say that we must not act: no doubt we must help ourselves; to fold our arms and expect everything from heaven, whether in the order of nature or that of grace, would be an

115

absurd and sinful quietism. But while we are co-operating with God we must never cease to follow his direction and lean upon him. To act in this way is to act with assurance and consequently with calm. When one looks upon oneself in all one's actions as the instrument of divine Providence and aims at nothing but fulfilling God's designs, one acts gently, without trouble or hurry, without disquiet about the future or regret for the past, abandoning oneself to God's fatherly Providence and counting on it more than on all possible human means. In that way, one is always at peace, and God unfailingly directs everything for our good, either temporal or eternal, and sometimes for both.

LETTER 6: TO THE SAME

Self-abandonment softens the hardship of loneliness

MY DEAR SISTER,—You are distressing yourself quite unnecessarily over my affairs; you are persuaded that I regard the isolation in which I live as a misfortune; but I think quite differently. I bless God daily for this fortunate disposition of Providence. By means of it I learn to die to all things in order to live for God only. I was not so completely buried at——, there many things internal and external supported me and made me feel I was alive; here and now there is nothing of all that. It is as if I was in a veritable desert, alone with God alone. How good that is! This exterior solitude is combined in my case with a great interior emptiness. Though this state is painful, I thank God for it because I have no doubt that it is salutary for me. It is a death in general to the whole world of the senses, even in spiritual matters; it is a sort of annihilation through which it is necessary to pass in order to rise with Jesus Christ to a new life, a life wholly in God, stripped of everything, deprived of all consolation in which the senses could take part. God wishes me to be deprived of all exterior help and dead to everything so as to live no longer except in him; his holy will be done, may it be fulfilled in all things and at all times. That is the firm pillar to which we should always remain immovably attached, for it is the solid and unshakeable foundation of all our perfection.

You see, my dear Sister, how little I deserve your compassion, since the cause of your pity is the precise object of my joy. I will confess to you, however, that the great solitude in which I have suddenly found myself here appeared at first agreeable only to the superior part of my soul, but after a short time my whole soul was penetrated by its sweetness. Once more have I learned by experience that we cannot do better, even from the point of view of our temporal interests, than let things go as they will in step with divine Providence. That is my great inclination; and more than ever I am determined to let myself follow it blindly and without reservations in everything, in my dwelling-place, my occupations, my time, in fact, everything. For a long time I have asked of God one grace alone which is to have in this world only the desire to please him, and only the fear of offending him. If he grants me this grace, I am rich for time and for eternity. I wish nothing for you, as for myself, but this self-abandonment.

What has one to fear in abandoning oneself entirely to God? Apart from the peace of heart attached to that state, we also find in it our perfection. If merit consists principally in sacrifice, what can be more meritorious than the complete sacrifice of all the objects of our will, even of those which seem to us the most reasonable and holy for the sake of God's will alone? Let us then have no other care, no other ambition than to unite ourselves to that infinitely merciful will, confident that it will save us, even when we may think that all is lost.

LETTER 7

The happiness gained from self-abandonment by a community of Poor Clares

MY DEAR SISTER,—I have discovered something here which gives me more satisfaction than all imaginable delights. There is in this town of Albi a convent of Poor Clares of the Great Reform totally cut off from the world who enter religion without any dowry and live on alms from day to day. The superior is one of the holiest persons I have known in my life. I felt at once a great interior attraction to be in holy relations with them and most of them have admitted that they had the same attraction towards me. I believe that God is preparing some great graces for me by means of their prayers. They are very interior souls and practise self-abandonment to God in admirable perfection. When I said to them that on every occasion that offers, I would endeavour to procure alms for them, they seemed to me almost scandalized and begged me to think only of making them more spiritual, more detached and more holy by my instructions and my prayers. Nothing can be imagined more admirable than their sisterly union, their candour and their simplicity. Struck by their great austerities I asked them one day whether the hardship of their life did not greatly damage their health, and shorten their days: they replied that they hardly ever had invalids among them, that very few died young, and that most of them lived till past eighty. They added that their austerities and fasts contributed to fortify their health and to prolong their lives which a too plentiful regime would shorten. Never have I seen more gaiety and holy joy than among these saintly women. But in order to content them, one must speak only of the things of God, for they cannot endure listening to trivial gossip and news of the world. What, they say, does that matter to us? I feel sure that you will be edified and glad for my sake of this happy discovery, for though I have often lived here, I knew but the name of the community and looked upon these holy souls as persons dead to everything, buried and completely invisible.

What a grace and consolation for me! I may add; what a piece of instruction for my own sanctification! This is indeed an occasion to praise and bless God for his wonders in the souls of his servants.

LETTER 8: TO SISTER MARIE-ANNE-THÉRÈSE DE ROSEN (1734)

Motives for our self-abandonment on God's side—The divine grandeur and goodness

MY DEAR SISTER,—Do not ask of me any new secret recipes for winning the friendship of God and making rapid progress in virtue; I only know one which I have put before you several times, the truly infallible efficacy of which my daily renewed experience proves more and more surely: it is self-abandonment to divine Providence. Allow me once more to recommend it to you and do not grow weary of learning it any more than I shall grow weary of teaching it. I would gladly shout out everywhere: Self-abandonment! self-abandonment! and again self-abandonment. A self-abandonment without limits or reservations, and that for two real reasons.

First because the greatness of God and his sovereign dominion over us demand that all should bow, should be as it were beaten down and annihilated before his supreme majesty. His infinite greatness is wholly out of proportion to our littleness. It dominates everything, contains everything, swallows up everything in its immensity, or, rather, it is everything: for whatever exists and is not God, has received its being from him by creation, receives it indeed at each instant by conservation (which is an incessantly renewed creation), since the being thus received always remains plunged and lost in his bosom. It follows that God is the Being of all beings; nothing is or lives or subsists except by him and in him. He is He-Who-Is, by whom everything is, in whom everything is and who is All in all things. Other beings compared with nothingness appear to be something, but compared with God they appear to be nothing. Their being and substance are borrowed, while God exists solely of himself and is no one's debtor but his own. It is, therefore, necessary that since everything necessarily belongs to him, all should return to him, and that his sovereign dominion should be glorified by all the creatures that his hands have made. Creatures deprived of reason glorify him in their way by following with inviolable exactitude and unwearying docility the movement that he communicates to them, but he rightly expects from his reasonable creatures a glory more worthy of himself, which results from their voluntary self-abandonment. How indeed can they make a more just and worthy use of their liberty than in giving back to God all they have received from him and offering him in advance all they may receive from him in the future?

Let us, however, be careful to understand the situation aright. This homage which God expects from us, he alone can give us the power to pay it by communicating to us the thought, the desire, the movement and the will of doing so. If he should accord us this grace and we profit by it, far from applauding ourselves we should thank him as for a benefit which crowns the other benefits we have received from him. The very movement which induces us to pay him this last thanksgiving is again as much a new grace as the reflection which gives birth to it. Thus, each instant of our lives, and each one of our actions, while increasing our debt towards him, form new bonds which make us yet more dependent on his divine goodness. At this thought, the spirit, heart and soul with all its powers remain lost, swallowed up and annihilated in the profound depth of this sovereign dominion. Our merits, looked at in this light, far from filling us with pride, fill us with a realization of our sovereign dependence which becomes more clearly understood in proportion as our minds grow more enlightened, and which finally attains to the annihilation of our whole being before God. This is the point at which we reach the truth and place ourselves before God in our natural state which is nothingness; and it is here also that we practise perfect self-abandonment. To maintain oneself constantly in this interior disposition is what Scripture calls walking in justice, in the truth; apart from that state there is nothing but injustice and lies towards God. Injustice, since he is robbed of part of the glory which belongs to him; lies because we are flattering ourselves and appropriating what can never belong to us.

The second motive of this unreserved self-abandonment is that God has no sooner obtained from his creature the homage due to his infinite majesty, than he gives free course to his infinite goodness. He wishes his creature to recover by the free gift of his mercy all that it has resigned to him through its entire self-abandonment, or, rather, he repays it infinitely more than it gave him, for he answers the gift it made him of its limited being by the gift of his infinite riches. So that in the depths of this act of self-abandonment where it was to find pure nothingness, it finds the infinite. What a bargain from the hands of the divine liberality! What ingenuity on the part of divine wisdom! What a surprising trick of divine goodness!

LETTER 9: TO SISTER MARIE-THÉRÈSE DE VIOMÉNIL

A further motive for self-abandonment to God: his paternal Providence

I DO not understand your anxieties, my dear Sister; why do you take pleasure in tormenting yourself, as you do, over the future, when your faith teaches you that the future is in the hands of a Father who is infinitely good, who loves you more than you love yourself and who understands your interests far better than you? Have you forgotten that everything that happens is directed by the orders of divine Providence? But if we know this how can we hesitate to remain in a state of humble submission, in the most trifling as in the greatest events, to all that God wishes or permits? How blind we are when we desire anything other than what God wishes. He alone knows the dangers which threaten us in the future and the help which we shall need. I am firmly convinced that we should all be lost if God gave us all our desires, and that is why, as St Augustine says, God, in his mercy and compassion for our blindness, does not always grant our prayers, and sometimes gives us the contrary of what we ask as being in reality better for us. In truth, I often think that nearly all of us are in this world in the position of poor sick people who in their frenzy or delirium ask for the very thing that would cause their death and who have to be refused out of pure charity and an enlightened pity.

My God, if this truth were once for all well known, with what blind self-abandonment should we not submit ourselves to thy divine Providence. What peace and tranquillity of heart we should enjoy in every circumstance, not only regarding external events, but also with reference to our interior states of soul. Even in cases where the painful vicissitudes through which God makes us pass are a punishment for our infidelities, we should say to ourselves that God has willed it thus by his permissive will, and we must humbly submit; we should detest our fault and accept its painful and humiliating consequences, as St Francis de Sales so often advises us.

How many troubles and useless anxieties injurious to our peace of heart and spiritual advancement would not this one principle, rightly understood, dispel! Shall I never succeed with the help of grace in instilling into your mind and still more into your heart this great principle of faith, so sweet, so consoling, so loving and so pacifying? We ought often to pray: My God, may all thy most holy intentions be accomplished in me and never my own; may they be accomplished because while infinitely just in themselves, they are also infinitely advantageous for me. I know that thou canst will only the greatest good of thy creatures so long as they remain submissive to thy orders. May my own will never be accomplished except when it is in perfect agreement with thine, because otherwise it can only be harmful to me. If ever, my God, it should happen through ignorance or passion that I persist in desires contrary to thine, may I be disappointed and punished, not by thy justice, but by thy pity and great mercy.

Come what may, as St Francis de Sales used to say, Long live Jesus! I shall take sides with divine Providence even if human wisdom tear out her hair with rage. When one is illuminated by heavenly light, one thinks very differently from most men, but what a source of peace, what power one finds in this way of thinking and looking at things! How happy are the saints, how peacefully they live, and what miserable blind fools we are not to be willing to train ourselves to think as they do, preferring to be entombed in the thick darkness of this accursed human wisdom which makes us so wretched, blind and guilty. Let us study how to give all our care and attention to the task of conforming ourselves in all things to the holy will of God in spite of interior revolt. That revolt itself must be accepted in obedience to the will of God which permits it in order to accustom us to remain at all times and in all circumstances before him in a state of sacrifice by even an interior silence of respect, adoration, self-annihilation, submission and love, and with a self-abandonment full of confidence.

LETTER 10
The same subject

MY DEAR SISTER,—I sympathize with you on the continuation of your cross, but I should do so much more if you were not able to profit by it, at least by making, as they say, a virtue of necessity. Remember our great principles: (1) That there is nothing so small or apparently trifling, even the fall of a leaf, that is not ordained or permitted by God; (2) that God is sufficiently wise, good, powerful and merciful to turn the most seemingly disastrous events to the good and profit of those who are capable of adoring and humbly accepting all these manifestations of his divine and adorable will.

Is there anything more consoling in religion than these two principles? Particularly when one knows that the repugnances and revolts of nature, far from depriving our submission of merit, merely increase it when we sincerely submit with the higher part of our soul, and further that our half-voluntary fits of impatience and gloom are but imperfections and faults of pure frailty which do not destroy our submission, but only slightly diminish its merit.

Often, indeed, these imperfections are useful to us, by keeping us humble and preserving us from the danger of losing all through a vain complacency. Remember that great word of Fénelon: "It is a great grace from God to be able to suffer, not courageously on the grand scale, but in a small and humble manner, for thus we become patient, small and humble all at once."

As to the grave trouble of which you speak, hang it on your cross like an extra weight with which divine Providence permits you to burden yourself, and say two *fiats* instead of one. After this, remain in peace in the higher part of your soul whatever the storms and tempests devastating your lower nature. It is as if you were at the bottom of some great mountain where torrents of rain and hail are pouring down, while on the summit the weather is beautiful. Remain on those safe heights so as to be protected from lightning and other disagreeable mishaps.

I think that you look too much on the creaturely side of events; as for me, thanks to God, I wish to see nothing but him in all that happens. I rise from everything to him, so as to depend on him only. Since it is he who places us in the power of those who crucify us, it is on him only that we really depend. It is to him alone, I know, that all the actions of men are due, I will receive all from his hand, have no obligation but to him, address my thanksgivings to him alone. If you would remember how little men contribute to events, you would see that divine Providence itself arranges everything in a singular way in favour of its servants and disposes everything for the best. God brings into being circumstances and necessities as he pleases. May he be blessed for all, in all and for ever!

I know that my behaviour is thought too simple; but what does it matter! I find this holy simplicity that is so abhorred by the world, so delightful that I shall not even dream of correcting myself in the matter. To every one his path: I respect the wise and prudent, but am content myself to be one of those poor simple little ones of whom Jesus Christ and following after him St Francis de Sales speak. Let us be perfectly persuaded that God arranges everything for the best. Our fears, our fussiness and our tendency to worry often make us imagine trials where there are none. Let us follow the leadings of divine Providence one step at a time; as soon as we see what is asked of us, we also will desire it and nothing further. God knows far better than we, poor blind creatures that we are, what is good for us. Our pains and troubles often come from the granting of our wishes. Let us leave everything to God, and all will go well. Let us abandon everything to him *in toto;* that is the only way to provide surely and infallibly for our true interests; I say: our *true* interests, for we have also false interests leading to our ruin.

My self-abandonment to divine Providence, as I conceive and recommend it, is not so heroic or so difficult as you think. It is the centre of the solid peace of the soul and there only is found unchangeable repose which the most trying events cannot ruffle. Ah! how well God pays us for the wretched little sacrifices we make for him! Moreover, by the mere habit of making them, one finds that one has no more to make, for one ceases to desire anything at all of one's own accord, one desires everything that is in the will of the sovereign Master and according to his divine permission. A blessed condition for this life and the next!

LETTER II: TO THE SISTERS OF THE VISITATION
AT NANCY (1732)

The mutual good wishes of souls who seek nothing but God

MY VERY DEAR SISTERS,—Your good wishes for me are all heavenly. It is evident indeed that they are dictated by your hearts, but what hearts! Hearts wholly spiritual and interior which esteem only divine things and are moved only by the interests of eternity.

Profiting by your example I make thousands of wishes for you, all of them of the same kind, and in particular that it may please God to preserve and increase more and more in you: firstly, that love of exterior solitude and silence which forms the spirit of recollection so necessary for the interior life; secondly, that spirit of peace and charity, of unity, detachment and interior abnegation which preserves in the depths of the heart that sweet tranquillity which is the true happiness of our present life and the basis of the interior life; thirdly, a taste for the presence of God and the prayer of the heart, the two main springs of the interior life; fourthly, that sincere wish to belong to God without reserve which ceaselessly renews a spirit of fervour; fifthly, that entire and perfect union of our will with the will of God which goes so far as to make us find contentment in our spiritual poverty because God wishes it; in this way we sacrifice the most intimate and delicate part of our self-love. This is an indispensable condition for peace of mind in the case of certain souls who, indifferent to the rest, still suffer too much from their own interior miseries; here is the means of supplying all that is lacking to us, the great remedy for all our miseries, the treasure of our poverty; for we cannot be richer than to keep always in our hearts the will of God as the norm of our own in spite of our dearest and most desirable interests. Since we should only desire virtues in so far as they please God, for it is only in so far as they please God that they are virtues, is it not to wish them all for you to wish you this conformity to the divine pleasure, so generous, universal and perfect as to cover everything except offending God? I congratulate you with all my heart on your delight in celebrating the centenary of the foundation of your house, but still more that it was founded on the poverty of our Lord in his Crib and on confidence in divine Providence.

The virtues of your first holy sisters have built on this rich foundation, and with this help have raised the walls of the house; your virtues will preserve and perfect it to the honour and glory of the divine Master, its only true proprietor.

BOOK II

THE PRACTICE OF THE VIRTUE OF
SELF-ABANDONMENT

LETTER I : TO SISTER MARY-ANTOINETTE DE MAHUET (1731)

Principles and practices of self-abandonment

MY DEAR SISTER,—The Lord has given me for you something better than you asked for, and which did not occur to you: some general principles of conduct for your whole life and the most simple method of putting them into practice.

1st principle. The mainspring of the whole spiritual life is good-will, that is a sincere desire to be God's, fully and without reserve: you cannot, therefore, renew this holy desire too frequently in order to strengthen it and make it constant and efficacious in you.

2nd principle. This firm desire to belong to God should bring to birth in us a resolution to think of nothing but him, which may be practised in two ways: firstly, we must try and accustom ourselves not to entertain voluntarily and deliberately thoughts which do not concern God, either directly or indirectly, such as general or particular duties of our state. The best way to drive off useless thoughts is not to combat them openly and still less to allow oneself to be troubled and disquieted by them, but just to let them drop, like a stone into the sea; little by little the habit of letting them drop makes this salutary practice quite easy.

The second way of thinking of nothing but God consists in a sort of general forgetfulness of everything at which one arrives through the habit of letting drop our useless thoughts, so that, for some time, one may pass whole days without thinking, as it seems, of anything at all, as if one had become stupid. Often indeed God places certain souls in this state, which is called emptiness of the spirit and of the intelligence; it is also called being in nothingness. This annihilation of our own spirit disposes us wonderfully to receive that of Jesus Christ. This mystical death of our own activity renders our soul apt for the reception of divine operations.

This great emptiness of spirit sometimes produces another emptiness which is more painful, namely emptiness of the will, so that one seems to have no feeling at all for the things of the world or even for God, being equally insensible to everything. Often indeed it is God who produces this second emptiness in certain souls, so that one should not try to get out of this state which disposes us for the reception of the most precious workings of God in us. It is a second mystical death which must precede our happy resurrection to an entirely new life. We must then esteem and cherish this double void, this double self-annihilation so hard to self-love and the spirit of pride, and accustom ourselves to this state in an interior spirit of holy joy.

3rd principle. We must limit our attention to the complete fulfilment of all that is imposed by the holy will of God, abandoning everything else to him, i.e. the care of all temporal and even of our spiritual interests such as our advancement in virtue. This is how this double self-abandonment should be practised.

As for the first point, whenever we feel in our hearts a desire, a fear, or views or ideas concerning our interests or those of our relations and friends, we should say to God: Lord, I offer all that to thee, I abandon to thee all these wretched anxieties. May all that pleases thee, all that thou wishest, happen. Nevertheless, since occasions do arise on which reason demands that we should think and act either for ourselves or for others, for we must never tempt Providence, this is what we should say in such circumstances: "Lord, if it is expedient that I should act in such or such a way in such or such a situation, I beseech thee to give me the thought of doing so when the time comes; in this case I shall do nothing but what thou deignest to inspire me to do, and I accept in advance the good or bad result of my action." Having made this interior act, we must let drop like a stone all our desires, fears, etc., without bothering ourselves about them, with the conviction that God will give us, at the right time and place, the thought and inspiration to act according to his holy will and his divine impulse.

As regards the practice of the second kind of self-abandonment, that is, the abandonment of our own advance in perfection, it is the most delicate point [of the process], the point least well practised by spiritual persons, the point at which most faults are committed which trouble and delay us on the road to God. Here is a very simple way of practising it which Jesus Christ himself communicated to St Teresa in one of his appearances to her: "My daughter," said he, "think of nothing but pleasing me, loving me and doing my will and I will take care of all that concerns you either for body or soul." In order thoroughly to understand this maxim, we should look on ourself as a man entering the service of a king, a Solomon for example, the greatest, best and wisest of all kings. If such a man had any nobility of sentiment or refinement of heart, or, for the matter of that, any good sense and real ability, this is what he would say to his master: "My Lord, I know you to be a generous and magnificent Prince, as powerful as you are good; I therefore give myself to you without reserve; I wish to serve you without knowing what I am to gain by it each day or year or even at the end of my career. I promise to think of nothing but your interests, and, as for my own, I abandon them entirely to your discretion or rather to your goodness and liberality." Think often of this very imperfect and humble comparison with the great Master whom we serve, and be fully convinced that just as the great king could not bear to see himself surpassed in liberality by one of his servants, our all-powerful and infinitely good God will never allow himself to be so surpassed by his miserable creatures.

Here is a method of practising this principle and the consequence to be drawn from the conviction of its truth.

1. I experience impetuous desires of acquiring the gift of prayer, humility, gentleness, the love of God; to this I reply: Let us not think so much about our own interests: my duty is to occupy myself simply and quietly with God, to accomplish his will in all that he asks of me at the moment. That is my task; everything else I leave in the care of God, my advancement is his business, as mine is to occupy myself ceaselessly with him and to execute his orders.

2. It occurs to me that I am still so imperfect, so full of defects and meannesses, of infidelities and weaknesses; how long will it be before I am delivered from these things? I reply at once: By the grace of God I do not love my faults, I am resolved to combat them; but I shall only be delivered from them when it may please God to deliver me. That is his affair, mine is to hate these faults and to fight them with patience, penitence and humility until it pleases God to give me the victory over them.

3. The thought occurs to me: But I am so blind that I do not even know my faults, yet my duty is to lament them before God and confess them; I at once reply: I wish to know my faults, I no longer live in voluntary dissipation of mind, I spend a certain time quietly examining my conscience. This is what God demands of me; he will give me more light and knowledge when he thinks it well to do so; that is his affair; I have placed all my spiritual progress in his hands; it is, therefore, enough for the present, for me to accuse myself of a few daily faults, as God gives me to know them, adding to them a sin of my past life.

4. Again, it will occur to me: Have I ever in my life made a good confession? Has God pardoned me? Am I in a good or a bad state? What progress have I made in prayer and in the ways of God? I at once reply: God wishes to conceal all that from me, so that I may blindly abandon myself to his mercies; I submit, and adore his judgements; I do not wish to know what he does not wish to show me and I wish to go on in the midst of whatever darkness he may plunge me into. It is his business to know the state of my progress, mine to occupy myself with him alone, to serve him and love him as little faultily as I can; he will take care of all the rest; I leave it to him.

5. But I have asked him so long for certain graces; I make use for that purpose of the intercession of the most powerful protectors, the Blessed Virgin, St Joseph, the holy Apostles, the whole court of heaven; nothing moves him. He is the Master, may all that he wills be accomplished in me, I only wish for grace, or merits, or perfection in the degree in which he is pleased to give them to me; his will alone suffices me, it will be the constant rule of my desires for ever.

LETTER 2: TO SISTER MARIE-THÉRÈSE DE VIOMÉNIL
(1731)

A general plan of the spiritual combat

"GOD has left man to his own judgement; life or death, good or evil, are in front of him; as he chooses, so shall it be done unto him." In these words Scripture gives us to understand that man is free and that his salvation depends on the good use he makes of his liberty. It is true that since the Fall, his liberty for good is greatly weakened and his freedom to commit evil is greatly strengthened. Nevertheless, with the help of grace which never fails him, it is always in his power to fortify his naturally weak liberty for good and to diminish his unfortunate and too strong liberty for evil.

There are three sorts of goods towards which our enfeebled liberty moves with great pain and difficulty.

1. The good essential to our salvation, the omission of which constitutes a mortal sin.

2. The good commanded by a less grave precept, the omission of which would be a venial fault.

3. The perfect good, the neglect of which involves the diminution of our merits.

All the inclinations which weaken in us the resolution of accomplishing our essential obligations, hatred, desire of vengeance, anger, irregular attachments, avarice, envy, etc., are so many principles of spiritual ruin. The same must be said, due proportion being observed, of inclinations which lead us to venial sin and voluntary imperfection for, as the Holy Spirit says, the man who despises little faults will fall by degrees into grave ones; and cowardice on a single point of perfection will prevent us ever attaining it.

But it is also true that all the victories that strengthen our will towards good are principles of predestination and salvation.

Our constant care should, then, be ceaselessly to fortify our feeble liberty for good, and to conquer our inclination to evil. We have three means for assuring and hastening the success of this enterprise:

The first is to make great sacrifices for God, generously surmounting our repugnances in what costs us most.

The second is to make all the little daily sacrifices, the occasions of which are frequent and continuous, with a constant, generous and universal fidelity.

The third and great means is prayer; but humble simple prayer formed in us by the operation of the Holy Spirit; for he it is who teaches us to pray, as St Paul said, who groans and prays in us with cries and ineffable groanings. The Publican is an excellent model: he prayed in silence and in a state of humble compunction. The greatest sinners and the most imperfect souls can pray in this way and thus they will raise themselves by degrees, if they are faithful, from the depth of their unworthiness to the highest sanctity.

LETTER 3: TO MADAME DE LESEN (1731)

The first work of God in the soul

I AM not at all surprised at the first effect of your meditating on the great truths; I congratulate you and give thanks to the Lord. You were in need of these acute feelings, and I believe that they will last so as to produce in you that spirit of compunction and humiliation which should be the foundation of your spiritual edifice and the commencement of your spiritual childhood. The agitation accompanying these feelings was superfluous, but, unless I am mistaken, it was involuntary and perhaps necessary and an effect of divine justice. These same feelings, when they return, will in future be gentler and more peaceful.

I had already understood, independently of your letter, that God had bestowed great graces on you; I had already divined that you had not corresponded sufficiently with them and I understand more clearly than ever:

1. That your soul is like a great hall, unfurnished or insufficiently furnished.

2. That it will never be fit for the reception of our sovereign Lord unless he himself furnishes it and arranges in it the precious furniture suitable for such a guest.

3. That the only way in which he will do this and enrich your soul with his gifts will be during the silence and peace of prayer.

Your duty is, therefore, to keep the hall well swept and clean with the help of grace, and, then, give place to him who will make it his own business to supply the beautiful furniture with which it is to be enriched, and who wishes to arrange it according to his own taste.

Do not go and upset yourself for nothing in a matter in which you would spoil everything by interference. Let him do as he likes; consider yourself as a picture which a great master is proposing to paint; but take courage, for I foresee that it will take some time to grind and powder the colours, and then to lay them on, combine them and shade them. All you have to do is to keep the canvas ready, well-cleaned and fastened on its two motionless pivots, the one being self-humiliation pushed to the point of self-annihilation, the other a complete self-abandonment pushed to the point of losing your will altogether in the will of God.

LETTER 4: TO SISTER MARIE-HENRIETTE DE BOUSMARD

The practice of self-abandonment in general

ALBI, 1733

You are quite right in what you say, my dear daughter, and indeed the great maxim of Blessed Mother de Chantal was: "Not so many opinions, so much learning and writing, but sound practice." As regards souls which have acquired the habit of avoiding deliberate faults and faithfully fulfilling the duties of their state of life, all practical perfection may be reduced to this one principle: the exercise of a continual resignation to all the manifestations of the will of God, a complete self-abandonment to all the exterior or interior dispositions of his Providence, whether in the present or in the future; one single *fiat*, or in St Francis de Sales' words: "Yes, heavenly Father, I accept everything; yes, and always yes." This phrase said and repeated, without its being necessary that it should be pronounced interiorly, represents in a few words the great and short road of the highest perfection because it tells of a continual union with the holy and adorable will of God.

There is no mystery about the way to reach that point; only two things are necessary: firstly, the profound conviction that nothing happens in this world, in our souls or outside them, without the design or permission of God; now, we ought to submit ourselves no less to what God permits than to what he directly wills; secondly, the firm belief that through the all-powerful and paternal Providence of God, all that he wills or permits invariably turns to the advantage of those who practise this submission to his orders. Supported by this double assurance, let us remain firm and unshakeable in our adhesion to all that it may please God to ordain with regard to us, let us acquiesce in advance, in a spirit of humility, love and sacrifice in all imaginable dispositions of his Providence, let us protest that we wish to be content with whatever satisfies him. We shall not always be able, no doubt, to feel this contentment in the lower (the sensitive) part of our soul, but we shall at least preserve it on the heights of our spirit, on the fine point of our will, as St Francis de Sales says, and in those circumstances it will be even more meritorious.

LETTER 5

On the means of acquiring self-abandonment

You say truly, my dear Sister, and it is indeed the Spirit of God who inspired you to make the remark, that one of the greatest obstacles to the reign of the divine Spirit in our hearts is our miserable nature which shrinks from captivity and death, in exchange for which the holy virtue of self-abandonment gives us liberty and the life of God.

But this very Spirit who has made you perceive so clearly what the evil is, will help you to apply the remedy. Here, in a few words, is what you ought to do in order to attain promptly to pure love and perfect self-abandonment. You must, first of all, ardently desire and energetically will it whatever the price you may have to pay. Secondly, you must firmly believe and say repeatedly to God, that it is absolutely impossible for you to acquire by your own strength such perfect dispositions, but, also, that grace makes everything easy, that you hope to receive this grace from his mercy, and you must beg it of him in and through Jesus Christ; thirdly, you must gently and quietly humble yourself, whenever you have withdrawn yourself from the holy bondage of his will, without discouragement, but on the contrary protesting to God that you will await with confidence the moment at which it will please him to give you that decisive grace that will make you wholly die to yourself and live in him by a new life wholly hidden with Jesus Christ our Lord; fourthly, if you are docile to the inspirations of God's Spirit, you will take care not to make your advancement depend on the warmth and sensible sweetness of your interior impressions. The divine Spirit will, on the contrary, make you esteem rather his almost imperceptible operations, for the more delicate and profound they are, the more divine they are and so much the more removed from the impressions of the senses. One belongs more totally to God then, because one tends to him and to union with him with all one's powers, and the whole extent of one's being, without particularizing any special point. For every being seeks its centre.

Be sure, however, that you have an enormous journey to make. There are centuries of work and growth in front of you, but on this point as on all others you should say: My God, thy holy and lovable intentions shall always be the measure of my desires, even the holiest, the justest and the most apparently perfect. I wish for neither graces nor holiness except at the time determined by and in the precise measure fixed by thy most holy will, no less, no more. Even if all the saints and blessed spirits were to prostrate themselves before thy throne to beseech from thee one single degree of grace or glory beyond what thou hast destined for me, I would sacrifice it, because I prefer to confine myself precisely and simply to what thou hast been pleased to ordain for me.

I adjure you, and it is my last piece of advice, to keep before you as the rule of your actions no other motive than a most pure love of God and his greater glory. Do not exclude, however, motives of hope and fear, and when inspired to do so by the Spirit within you, do not hesitate to abandon yourself to them, but pure love should dominate all other feelings in your heart. You should desire most ardently your salvation and perfection, but in this very desire you should look rather at the glory of God than at your own happiness. Nothing is more adapted to cause you to make rapid progress in virtue and amass great merits than this sentiment habitually entertained in your heart. The smallest actions animated by pure love are worth more than the greatest performed from other good motives. But do not forget that your progress will be more assured if pure love urges you to renounce yourself in the smallest things. If it did not produce this effect it would not be a true love.

Remain carefully on your guard against the snares which the enemy will lay for you in order to make you abandon this blessed disposition. Seek, and expect, nothing from creatures but forgetfulness and contempt and may the joy of resembling your divine Model Jesus Christ make this contempt dearer to you than all the glories of the world. Do not let slip any occasion, however trifling, of perfecting this divine resemblance and while faithfully profiting by these light trials, humble yourself because you are not judged worthy to endure something more serious.

LETTER 6: TO SISTER MARIE-THÉRÈSE DE VIOMÉNIL

General directions

MY DEAR SISTER,—1. Do not overload yourself with vocal prayers beyond those of obligation and apply yourself rather to interior perfection and mental prayer.

2. It is very useful to anticipate possible faults by penances, but it is more fitting to be faithful in expiating them when they have been committed than in multiplying penances beforehand without real necessity.

3. Moderate and supernaturalize your affection for persons who are dear to you.

4. Take profit, in order to excite yourself to fervour, from the

good examples of others and from conversations with spiritual persons, but without showing any disdain for others or abandoning yourself to any feeling of disgust towards them.

5. Do not distress yourself so much at being so frequently at war with your wretched nature; heaven is worth all these battles. Perhaps they will shortly come to an end and you will achieve a complete victory. After all they will pass, and rest will be eternal. Be at peace and let your humility always be mingled with confidence.

6. You should profit by the infirmities of the body to fortify your soul by a spirit of self-abandonment to the will of God and of union with Jesus Christ.

7. Take pains to die to yourself, to renounce natural inclinations, to smother, on all occasions, human hastiness and touchiness. This is the most necessary kind of mortification; it does no harm to the health and it has more power than corporal mortification to increase merit and realize the designs of God, who wishes us to belong solely to him without reserve.

8. Try with peaceful fidelity to profit by all the various states through which our Lord may wish you to pass for his glory and your own perfection. Turn all that happens in the direction of divine love and a simple self-abandonment to the paternal guidance of God's adorable Providence.

9. Our zeal for our own advancement and for that of those committed to our charge should be ardent and active, but never restless, anxious and without confidence.

10. Endeavour to become more and more interior, aspiring to the full perfection of your holy state by your perfect regularity. Humble yourself ceaselessly before God that he may make you victorious over yourself. You need very great help so that your touchiness and too human and natural fastidiousness of feeling may be completely extinguished in your heart before death, for these defects are born of your character and temperament. It is true that this fact is some excuse for your faults and excites the compassion of God for his poor spouse; nevertheless, you must always go on fighting so that if your miserable pride and self-love are not completely destroyed before your last hour comes, death should at least find you fighting them in the en-

deavour to destroy them. Your chief arms in this combat should be divine love, an infinite gratitude for the graces of God with complete confidence and profound mistrust of yourself—all this peacefully and without discouragement. You will find ever-increasing strength in Holy Communion, in prayer, patience, obedience, mortification, and principally in interior self-renunciation.

11. Illnesses and infirmities accepted in complete submission to the will of God with humble thanksgiving and in union with Jesus Christ are very useful to expiate the past and to weaken the "old man" in us; they help us to die spiritually to everything before our natural death, which by finishing off our transitory troubles will make us enter (we must hope) into the enjoyment of eternal goods. When God himself sends us this sort of penance, being at the time unable to mortify ourselves externally, we must make up for this by interior mortification, applying ourselves more and more to the destruction of self-love and the pride, sensitiveness and tendency to criticize which are its evil fruits. Try, in fine, to become humble and simple like a little child, from love and so as to imitate our Lord in a spirit of peace and recollection. If God finds this humility in us, he will himself cause his work in us to advance. Let us persevere and be faithful to grace for the greater glory of God and for his pure love. Everything depends on truly loving, in heart and deed, the God of goodness.

12. As this earthly pilgrimage advances, let us force ourselves to grow in solid fervour according to the perfection of our holy state and the particular designs of God on our souls. When he gives us special tastes in devotion, special sensibilities, let us profit by them to attach ourselves more firmly to him beyond all his gifts. But in times of dryness, let us always keep the same gait, humbly recalling our indulgence, and considering also that perhaps God wishes to prove the solidity of our love for him by these salutary trials.

13. Let us be truly humble and occupied in the correction of our faults, and we shall not think much about those of other people. Let us see Jesus Christ in all our neighbours, and we shall not find it hard to excuse them, to endure and cherish them. His

example engages us to this: what patience he had with his coarse, ignorant disciples! Let us turn our quick temper on to the task of glorifying God in ourselves and in those whose confidence he gives us. Let us live hidden in Jesus Christ, dead to all creatures and to ourselves; unless we do so, Jesus Christ will not deign to live in us in the sense of absorbing all our human life into his own, as he desires to do. For the rest, let us charitably endure ourselves as it is our duty to endure others, humbling and punishing ourselves as promptly as possible for our faults. And when we pray for ourselves, let us also pray for our brother sinners.

LETTER 7: TO SISTER MARIE-THÉRÈSE DE VIOMÉNIL
(1731)

The same subject

MY DEAR SISTER and daughter in our Lord, the peace of Jesus Christ be ever with you.

1. I thank God for all the good sentiments with which he continues to inspire you. As long as you preserve your good intention of belonging to God without reserve in complete and total self-abandonment to his good pleasure, fear neither dryness, darkness, temptation nor desolation: all will turn to your greater spiritual advancement.

2. Your fear of deception as to the peace which you enjoy in the midst of your interior troubles is very unreal. From what you tell me unconsciously, I understand that this peace is very real; it is the basis of everything and a great grace that you must try to preserve at any cost. The devil will direct all his attacks and tricks towards making you lose it or at least weaken or disturb it; but do you remain firm in faith and confidence in your self-abandonment. Take care not to engage yourself by vow to anything. . . .

3. A complete separation from creatures in your mind and heart is a great favour which leads infallibly to pure love and divine union.

4. The secret presentiment of death being near may come

from God or the devil. If this presentiment merely detaches you more effectively from everything without troubling you or leading you to discouragement and mistrust it comes from God and you should preserve it: if not, reject it; for everything that comes from God has good effects, and it is solely by these effects that the different spirits can be discerned with certainty.

All the repugnances of which you tell me are intended to detach you absolutely from all human support so that you should rest on God only; your interior exercises on that point are very good. But I am surprised that you have not yet learned that when God permits this darkness every good sentiment disappears like the sun at night. All you have to do is to remain firm and in repose, awaiting the return of the sun and the breaking of day, when everything will be as visible as before.

I permit you to write to me four times a year, and whenever, after having implored the assistance of God, you judge it to be necessary. And if I think the same I will be very prompt in replying.

LETTER 8: TO SISTER MARIE-ANNE-THÉRÈSE
DE ROSEN (1731)

The prayer of souls called to a life of self-abandonment—Some wise advice on prayer

1. Apply yourself to prayer with a simple gaze at your subject, i.e. apprehending the object by faith without using any reasoning.

2. I advise you to dwell as long as you can on what humiliates and annihilates you; the more you feel yourself penetrated by your misery and reduced to nothing by it when you come out of prayer, the more will you be disposed to receive God's gifts.

3. You should pay no attention to distractions, but when you become aware of them, recall very gently your mind and above all your heart to faith in the presence of God and to the enjoyment of your holy repose in his presence. If you cannot succeed in doing this, you have only to resign yourself. This cross of distractions is often more meritorious than prayer itself,

for it unites our will with God's will, in which lies all our good.

4. The dispositions in which one leaves prayer are the mark of its efficacy. A solid faith is worth incomparably more than a sentimental faith. Guided by the former the soul makes more rapid progress, and walks more surely.

5. Assist at Holy Mass with great recollection, and abandon yourself to a boundless confidence in the divine goodness, resting on the merits of Jesus Christ as Victim.

The simpler and the clearer your feelings are of all thought and reasoning, the better they will be.

6. The path of dryness and aridity is far preferable to the path of consolation, though much more painful. This is the only path on which you can acquire the solidity of virtue; on the other the most apparently perfect dispositions are liable to give way at the slightest breath or aridity or temptation. And it is God's custom to place souls in this state of trial after a certain period of sweetness and consolation.

7. When it pleases the divine goodness to make a soul walk by the path of pure love, fear does not make the slightest impression on it. Just as fear brings love, so love drives away fear, says St Augustine, commenting on St John. The director of a soul in this state should second this design of God and lead it only by love and confidence. Should some circumstance present itself in which fear is necessary in order to avoid evil, God will take care to give it the necessary inspiration. Let it continue always to love without bothering about anything else, and above all let it avoid disquiet and trouble. This temptation is more to be feared than any other for souls who walk in this way. They should always be counselled to preserve their interior peace at all costs, and to reject as a messenger from hell anything that tends to trouble or disturb it.

For the rest, the most perfect prayer is the simplest, and the simplest is the prayer into which less of our own enters, fewer ideas, less imagination or reasoning—the prayer that is formed of a single sentiment long drawn out.

The more the sentiments inspired by grace persist in the soul, the more it will be penetrated by them and the easier it will be for it to act under their influence. The sentiment of divine love

141

which super-eminently contains all the others should form its most habitual food. When that sentiment dominates all its affections, it will experience an ardour and a sort of enchantment which will make it run fast along the road of sanctity.

LETTER 9: TO SISTER MARIE-ANNE-THÉRÈSE DE ROSEN (1731)

The same subject: The danger of illusion in the prayer of recollection

MY DEAR SISTER,—Keep ever close to the great interior Director who alone can give light and strength in all our needs. Pay no heed to books when he is speaking in your soul. Give yourself principally to holy repose in his divine presence and never leave it. Do not break this sacred silence save when God sends you an inclination for holy and profitable colloquy. When it is over, return to your fortress and sanctuary which is no other than recollection and interior silence, in the presence and sight of the Beloved. In him alone, in this simple and sweet repose in God, you will find all light, courage, strength, sweetness, patience, humility, resignation, peace and repose of heart.

I wish you all of this in the highest perfection.

Do not be afraid of darkness and aridity in prayer. When one can unite oneself to God and his holy will, accepting all that he wishes, one is in comfort, one has everything. This is the most perfect prayer and the purest love, according to St Teresa.

You have done wisely to ask the Reverend Father . . . for some explanations on the subject to which you refer. I have such respect for his views that I should think myself in error if I held opinions opposed to his. I have always thought, as he does, that no one can or ought to push themselves forward into the prayer of recollection without being called to it: and that the soul cannot merit this grace by its good works, or attain to it by all its efforts. I have merely added, with Father Surin and the authors who treat of it, that one can indirectly and from a distance dispose oneself to receive this great gift from heaven, by removing the obstacles to its reception by a great purity of heart, of spirit, of intention, which alone carries the soul a great distance; after that, one can and should dispose oneself proximately for its reception by recollecting oneself frequently for a moment as though keeping oneself on the watch for its approach and making way for the interior spirit.

When you have read this to the Reverend Father, or sent him this letter if you cannot see him immediately, I beg you to tell him that I think he is obliged in conscience to disabuse, as on my part, people whom he judges to be deceived, and that in my ignorance of where the blow should fall, I discharge this duty on to his shoulders.

But in order to proceed with all the necessary discretion and prudence, I beg him before taking action to reflect on two points: (1) He should assure himself of the existence of the abuse by personal knowledge of the interior state of the people in question, for a mere report by a third person does not throw much light on so secret and interior a condition. It may be said that we know these people to be very imperfect, we see them commit many faults which scandalize us. I reply to that, and my reply comprises the second reflection I would beg him to make, that the experience of direction teaches us that God frequently hides great interior virtues known to him alone under very imperfect exteriors. Consequently, I do not think that one can make a definite judgement that such persons are deceived with regard to this sort of prayer, the more so that it frequently happens that their imperfections and faults are considerably magnified and exaggerated by the want of charity of others, and sometimes from even worse motives. I remember here what St Teresa said, speaking of herself, that in her own case this sort of prayer was for long considered suspicious by the enlightened people whom she consulted, and liable to be a diabolical illusion, because they could not reconcile in their minds such a gift of prayer with her conduct at that time, i.e. her eagerness to visit the parlour, to know people, to see and be seen, and keep up worldly connections and relations, thus wasting much time and neglecting her soul, for such according to her own account was the way she was living at that time. "And this," she adds, "was the reason why all who knew me thought that my prayer was nothing but illusion. But afterwards I found certain directors who had learned by experience (they said) that God sometimes gives this prayer: (1) to great sinners from the first moment of their conversion so that they may be more promptly and completely converted; (2) to very imperfect people so as to correct the better and more quickly their defects. But they add, and I think very soundly and justly, that the preservation of this gift of prayer compatibly with considerable defects or imperfections, habitual or constant and known to be such, unless the soul makes efforts to correct itself, is very difficult and of infinitely rare occurrence."

LETTER 10

The same subject

THIS is what I should reply with regard to the person in question: her prayer of recollection seems to me to proceed rather from her head than her heart. This is the inverse of what ought to be, for in order that this kind of prayer should bear fruit, it is necessary that the heart should be more applied to it than the intelligence. It is, in fact, a prayer wholly of love: the heart, reposing sweetly in God, loves him without distinguishing clearly the object of its love, or how this love is produced in it. The reality of the prayer is clearly shown by a certain ardour which is continually experienced in the heart, by a constant tendency towards the divine centre of our being which continues without any clear intellectual perception, and by the overpowering attraction to which the soul yields without possibility of distraction. From this comes the great facility of this kind of prayer, which is a sweet repose for the heart and which continues without effort almost as long as one wishes.

If, therefore, the person of whom you speak feels in the course of her prayer a very great application of mind, it is a sign that her recollection is not yet what it should be. What is the remedy? This, I think:

1. When one feels oneself seized by this profound recollection, one should turn one's interior gaze, i.e. one's reflection and action on the heart, so as, as it were, to taste and feel this sweet repose (this sweetness is a charm which turns almost all the

soul's attention on to the heart and at the moment causes one to *feel* that one loves): while the mind without effort and almost without any voluntary application is entranced by the sentiment with which the heart is filled.

2. If, in spite of this, this excessive application of mind should continue, you should forbid the subject to give more than two hours in all to her prayer daily, and you should instruct her not deliberately to seek recollection during her reading and at other times, but only to give herself to it when God draws her to it, always remembering to turn her interior attention on her heart, in order to enjoy at leisure the sweetness of interior calm and repose.

3. You should tell her always to give a short time to the examination of her prayer, its beginning, progress and completion. She should inquire (1) how her recollection began; (2) whether it produced distinct feelings and thoughts in her, or whether this gentle sleep was so deep that she remembers nothing about it (which is the best); (3) in what state she is on emerging from this condition; perhaps in a state of great recollection with a great desire to do good, to attach herself to God alone and to please only this great Master.

Let us thoroughly persuade ourselves that God can be found everywhere without effort, because he is always present to those who seek him with their whole heart, though he may not always cause his divine presence to be felt. For instance, when you happen to be entirely unoccupied with created things so that you seem to be thinking of nothing and desiring nothing, you should know that then your soul is unconsciously occupied with God and in God. Here is the explanation of this. God being that hidden and invisible object towards which all the desires of a pure heart unconsciously tend, the moment that these desires cease to be turned upon creatures, they revert to their natural centre which is God, and by being fixed there, they increase little by little so as sometimes to make their presence felt very keenly, producing, as it were, bright flames of love. Thus, the true presence of God is, to speak exactly, nothing but a sort of forgetfulness of creatures with a secret desire of finding God. It is in this that interior and exterior divine silence consists, so precious, so desirable and so profitable: the true earthly paradise, where souls who love God enjoy already a foretaste of heavenly joy.

LETTER 11: TO MOTHER LOUISE-FRANÇOISE DE ROSEN
(1735)

The practice of self-abandonment in different states of the soul

MY DEAR SISTER,—The peace of our Lord Jesus Christ! If we are attentive and docile to the interior spirit, we shall be so surely guarded that we shall rarely make a false step. I approve, however, the wise precaution of sometimes explaining one's state to the ministers of Jesus Christ, through a holy distrust of oneself. God has so blessed such humility in you that I feel almost inclined to reply to you in one word: All is well, continue. Nevertheless, for your consolation I shall add what God inspires me to add as I re-read your letter.

"I do not care," you say, "to talk or write or read much." What a beautiful confession! It alone indicates a soul which is ordinarily well occupied within itself; a great spiritual writer has said of such persons that they have immense occupations without labour. Another calls this happy disposition by the name of holy leisure or holy unemployment, for it seems that doing nothing means doing all things, and saying nothing, saying everything.

1. I find nothing but good in the three dispositions of soul which you experience in turn: firstly, your disposition of faith, secondly, the disposition of your tastes and sentiments, thirdly, your disposition in the midst of disturbances and troubles; but the degrees of their goodness are different. The first is the simplest and surest, and favours self-love least. The second is more agreeable and demands a great detachment from all personal tastes and feelings, even divine, so as to attach yourself to God purely and solely, as Fénelon says. The third is painful and often excruciating, but it is also the best, because all that mortifies the soul makes it purer and disposes it for a closer union with the God of all purity and holiness.

2. Thanks to his goodness, you behave very well in all these three dispositions of soul; you have only to go on as you are doing, but you explain yourself in a way that would distress those without experience of this state of prayer. You say that you do nothing, and yet you are always doing something or you would be in a state of pure idleness; but your soul acts so gently that you do not perceive your interior acts of consent and adherence to the inspirations of the Holy Spirit. The stronger these inspirations are, the less you should act; you should merely follow what is drawing you and allow yourself to be drawn gently on, as you rightly say.

3. Your manner of behaving in times of storm and upset, enchants me. Submission, total self-abandonment without reserve, being content with lack of contentment when God wills it. In those conditions one advances more in one day than in a hundred filled with sweetness and consolations. O my good God! This is indeed the right and solid line to take. Teach it to every one and repeat it often to poor Sister *N*. Properly speaking, this is all she needs at present: the constant practice of this maxim would make a saint of her and sweeten all her interior sufferings; a little more and with the practice of this point alone, you would see her shortly quite different, as if she had been made over again and transformed.

4. Your total, continual and universal self-abandonment to God through a sentiment of confidence and union with Jesus Christ, always doing the will of his Father, is the most divine and surest method of success in everything; try to communicate it to every one, particularly to the dear Sister of whom I have just spoken.

5. The grace and the light which make you fight and smother the feelings of nature on all the occasions of which you speak deserve to be carefully preserved. Your attention and fidelity in corresponding with these graces, even on the most trifling occasions, are able to increase them still more; but do not wish ever to be delivered from your sensitiveness to your first impulses; they are useful for the preservation of interior humility which is the foundation and guardian of all virtues.

6. As for your habitual faults, you should know that from the

moment that our imperfections sincerely displease us and that we are sincerely resolved to combat them without reserve, there is no affection towards them in our heart and consequently nothing that can oppose our union with God. What we have to do then is first of all to work with all our strength at diminishing the number of these faults and imperfections, and when we fall into them by frailty, surprise or otherwise, to rise immediately with courage and to return to God with the same confidence as if nothing had happened, after having humbled ourselves in his presence and begged his pardon, without any spite against ourselves, or trouble or disquiet. In such a case humility supplies for the lack of fidelity and often repairs our fault with advantage to ourselves. Finally, if there is some little reparation to be made to our neighbour, let us never fail in this duty, but take the opportunity to conquer generously our pride and human respect.

7. When you experience involuntary disorderly impulses, give yourself time, before grace extinguishes them, to realize clearly to what excesses pride and passion would carry you without its help. In this way, you will be able to acquire by personal experience the complete knowledge of that depth of perversity into which we should fall, if God did not keep us back. It is by this practical knowledge, these reiterated feelings, these frequent personal experiences that all the saints have acquired that profound humility of heart, that complete contempt and holy hatred of themselves of which we find so many proofs in the history of their lives and which were the most solid supports of their perfection.

8. As for the feeling of external trouble and temptation, all that you tell me shows me that the Holy Spirit has in this respect regulated so well your thoughts, your feelings, your interior and exterior behaviour, that I have nothing to add. Evidently, if it is certain that the unsought signs of esteem and friendship which we receive are a cross to us instead of a matter of complacency, the distress and disgust that they cause us is an antidote to their poison. There can be nothing but great merit in suffering patiently in conformity with the orders of God and the arrangements of Providence, and in accordance with the

example of Jesus Christ, suspicions, false judgements, envy and jealousy without explaining matters or defending oneself further than is required for the edification of our neighbour. If when we see ourselves exposed to various criticisms and unjust prejudices, we persevere in our line of conduct without change, following the guidance of Providence step by step, we are truly living by faith alone, with God alone in the midst of the quarrels and confusion of creatures. In such a disposition of soul, external things cannot reach our interior life, and the peace which we enjoy can be troubled neither by their favours nor their contempt. This is what is called living the interior life, and a very interior life it is. Until this independence of soul has been acquired the most apparently brilliant virtues are in reality very fragile, superficial and liable to corruption by self-love, or to be upset by the slightest breath of inconstancy and contradiction.

9. Be well on your guard against all illusions, which however specious they may be incline you to follow your own ideas and prefer yourself before others. A self-sufficient and critical spirit seems to many but a trifle, but we cannot deny that such a spirit is greatly opposed to religious simplicity and that it prevents many souls from entering on the interior life. For, indeed, we cannot enter the path of that life unless the Holy Spirit who never gives himself save to the humble-minded and the simple, introduce us to it.

10. Your profound, delicate, simple and almost imperceptible method of resisting all sorts of temptations is a pure grace of God; attempt no other. That simple turning to God is worth infinitely more than all other kinds of acts. It cannot very well be explained, God alone teaches it and gives it to the soul in the school of the Holy Spirit, which is carried on in the depths of the heart. The peaceful doubts that we experience after temptation are the fruit of chaste fear which should never be eliminated; as for the restless sort of doubt which is born of self-love it should be expelled and despised.

Moreover, nothing in the world is easier to recognize and uncover than the abuses and illusions to which the prayer of faith and simple recollection is liable; we have but to apply the infallible test of Jesus Christ: the tree is known by its fruits. All prayer, then, which produces reformation of the heart and of conduct, flight from vice, the practice of the evangelical virtues and the duties of one's state, is a good prayer. Contrariwise, any prayer which does not give these fruits or produces opposite fruits, is a bad tree and a bad prayer, even if accompanied by raptures, ecstasies and miracles. Faith, charity and humility are the roads that lead to God; whatever causes us to walk in those paths is profitable to us, whatever makes us stray from them is hurtful. There is the sure, infallible rule, and one that can be brought home to all, for the prevention and reformation of every abuse or illusion.

I cordially salute your dear sister; tell her, please, from me that she is always to continue to allow herself to be led by the interior spirit and to remain, as she is, in complete self-abandonment in the hands of God, equally pleased with his gifts and his deprivations, and with the apparent nothingness in which he leaves her when he pleases. There lies all the perfection and the true progress of a faithful soul. Ah! How pleased God is to speak unceasingly to his spouses of that holy self-abandonment which can alone unite them solidly to him.

LETTER 12 : TO SISTER CATHERINE-ANGÉLIQUE DE SERRE

The practice of self-abandonment through peace of soul

MY VERY DEAR SISTER,—The peace of Jesus Christ be always with us and within us, since God dwells and works freely only in peaceful hearts.

I rejoice in and I congratulate you on the peace which the Lord makes you find in an entire conformity to all the commands and arrangements of his amiable providence. This peace, as you know, is the basis of the interior life, and that for several reasons: firstly, because it is the health and strength of the soul, trouble being to the soul what fever is to the body, a source of languor and weakness. Secondly, because agitation and trouble in our soul prevent us from hearing the gentle voice and delicate inspirations of the Holy Spirit.

Nothing is necessary in order to remain in this peace, which will, I trust, ever increase, except never to depart from the total self-abandonment and absolute resignation of which I have just spoken. You will arrive at this state of mind without difficulty if you never lose sight of the great and consoling truth that nothing happens in this world but by the order of God or at least by his divine permission, and that all that he wills or permits turns infallibly to the advantage of submissive and resigned souls. Even that which most upsets our spiritual plans turns into something which is better for us. Remain firmly attached to this great principle and the most violent storms will be unable to disturb the depths of your soul, although they may agitate your emotions which are, as it were, its surface.

When, in the course of prayer, you experience certain attractions, such as a sweet repose of soul and heart in God, receive these gifts with humility and thanksgiving, but without becoming attached to them. If you loved these consolations for their own sake, you would oblige God to deprive you of them, for when he calls us to prayer, it is not in order to flatter our self-love and give us an occasion for self-complacency, but to dispose us to do his holy will and to teach us an ever-increasing conformity to that will in all things.

When distractions and dryness follow these consolations, you know how you should endure them: that is, in peace, submission and self-abandonment according to God's good pleasure in permitting them. You know also that the only harmful distractions are those of the will; it follows that those which displease you do not impede the prayer of the heart and the desire. Never force yourself to fight obstinate distractions, it is a safer and better policy to let them drop, as one lets drop the various absurdities and extravagances that in spite of ourselves pass through our mind or imagination.

What has already happened will often happen again. What God may have refused you during prayer, he will give you when it is over, so as to make you realize that it is the pure effect of his grace and not the fruit of your own labour and industry. Nothing is more useful for keeping us in a sense of our dependence on grace and of abjection in our own eyes; this is the source of true humility of heart and mind.

The Practice of Self-abandonment

During the course of the day, try to keep yourself united to God either by frequent aspirations and raising of the mind towards him, or by the simple gaze of pure faith, or, still better, by a certain repose of the depth of your soul and of all your being in God accompanied by a complete disengagement from all the exterior objects of this world. It belongs to God himself to show you which of these three methods you should adopt to unite yourself with him by the movement, the attraction and the facility which he will give you; for this union with God depends on the various states of prayer to which grace raises souls. Each of these states has its particular attraction; one must recognize one's own and follow it simply and faithfully; without trouble, disquiet or excitement, always gently, sweetly and peacefully, as St Francis de Sales says.

LETTER 13: TO SISTER CHARLOTTE-ELIZABETH BOURCIER DE MONTHUREUX (1731)

The same subject

WHAT you tell me about your peace and tranquillity of soul has given me much pleasure. You should remember all your life that one of the principal causes of the small progress made by certain good people is that the devil continually fills their souls with disquiet, perplexities and troubles, which render them incapable of serious, gentle and constant application to the practice of virtue. The great principle of the interior life lies in peace of the heart: it must be preserved with such care that the moment it is in danger everything else should be abandoned for its re-establishment, just as when the house is on fire, one leaves everything in order to extinguish it. Read from time to time, on this important subject, the treatise on peace of soul which is at the end of the little book called *The Spiritual Combat*, which ancient writers truly called "The Path of Paradise", to make us understand that this blessed peace of soul is the high road to heaven. And the reason of this is that peace and tranquillity of spirit alone give the soul great strength to achieve all that

God wills while trouble and disquiet turn the soul into a weak languishing invalid. In that state, one feels neither zest nor attraction for virtue, but, contrariwise, disgust and discouragement by which the devil never fails to profit. This is why he makes use of all his ruses to rob us of this peace on a thousand specious pretexts: at one time on pretence of examination of conscience or of sorrow for our sins, at another time on the ground that we are abusing grace and that our total lack of progress is our own fault, in short that God is about to abandon us; and by means of a hundred other dodges against which few are able to defend themselves. This is why the masters of the spiritual life give this great principle for distinguishing the true inspirations of God from those which come from the devil, namely, that the former are always gentle and peaceful and lead us to confidence and humility while the latter are agitating, unquiet and turbulent, leading to discouragement and suspicion, or even to presumption and the following of our own will. We must, therefore, firmly reject all that does not bear this mark of peace, submission, gentleness and confidence, the impressions as it were of God's seal; this point is of great importance for the whole of our life.

You ask me for some principles for the fixation of our thoughts during the day; to this I reply as follows:

1. That it is better to advance towards God and virtue by the sentiments of the heart than by the thoughts of the mind, and it is important to feed the heart and starve the mind: i.e. to desire God, to sigh after him and aspire to his holy love, to an intimate union with him without the diversion of so many thoughts and mental reflections which often dry up the heart and become a sort of dissipation, a pure amusement of the intelligence, a series of vain complacencies in our own thoughts and speculations. It is far better to be occupied with the care to belong to God without reserve, with the desire of interior life, of a profound humility, of fervour, of the gift of prayer, of the love of God, of the true spirit of Jesus Christ and of the practice of the virtues that he taught by his virtues and his divine example, etc., than to make a thousand useless reflections on these very

subjects. When one feels none of these desires, the sole desire to possess them, the affection of the heart alone suffices to keep a soul recollected and united to God.

Once more: the simple tendency of the heart towards God, or towards certain virtues, in order to please him, causes us to advance more than all our grand thoughts and reflections.

This is called tending towards God by inclination, attraction or feeling; and this method is sweeter, surer and more efficacious than all the most beautiful inward illuminations in the world, unless these illuminations are given by a special favour of God and through a pure effusion of his grace, and even so they are combined with a certain zest and interior attraction which touches and charms the heart, for otherwise no advance can usually be made.

2. God often causes in souls a certain emptiness of mind of which we have spoken; in these circumstances, it would indeed be useless to attempt distinct thoughts, since it is God who removes them; it would even be injurious to make efforts to think or reflect much in such a case, from which I conclude that the best for all is to remain in peace before God, cordially acquiescing in what he does at his good pleasure, whether he bestows or takes away, confining ourselves to preserving in the depth of the soul the sincere desire of belonging to God without reserve, of loving him ardently, and of being intimately united to him, or, as we have said, desiring to have these desires.

3. Since God gives lights or thoughts when he pleases, during or outside the time of prayer, when we feel that such lights or thoughts are sweetly and gently coming to us, we pause as long as we experience attraction or repose, prepared to see them disappear at God's pleasure without ever making any effort to retain them; to do so would be to wish to make them our own property and would be in contradiction to that continual dependence in which God wishes to keep the souls he calls to the interior life. And it is precisely in order to keep them in that perpetual dependence, that at certain times he bestows and takes away such favours, in an almost continuous alternation, causing in the interior of such souls perpetual variations. It is by such continual changes and vicissitudes that God exercises

them himself in that perfect submission of mind and heart in which true perfection consists; more or less like a wise and strong-minded mother, who in order to break a child's self-will and make him perfectly supple and docile, alternately gives and deprives him of what he likes best, caresses him, scolds him, flatters him, threatens him, and in less than an hour will make him do, or abstain from doing, a hundred different things. That is exactly the interior guidance that God gives these beloved souls whom he wishes himself to train to pure and solid virtue.

Oh, if we only understood this loving guidance of God, how submissive we should be, what peace we should enjoy in the midst of all the spiritual vicissitudes and changes of our interior state! From this follows the consequence of which I have often spoken, that in certain situations the most efficacious method of interior advance is a simple acquiescence in all that God wills. I cling to all thou givest me, Lord, I will all that thou willest, I resign myself to all.

This is what we call willing all and willing nothing, nothing of our own initiative and everything by resignation; it may be also called walking before God in the greatest simplicity. This path in a certain sense is not wearisome, because this simple adhesion to all that is willed by God comes of itself through liking and attraction and at length by the habit we have formed of it.

You are surprised to find that after having generously made certain sacrifices to God, temptation on that very point comes back more violently, so much so as to distress you. It is expedient that this should happen in order to forestall the vain complacencies of self-love, which would spoil everything. Be content that God has induced you by his grace to make these sacrifices to him, and resist the temptation to retract what you have already offered him. In this way God wishes to keep you humble: for the mind is naturally so disposed to swell with pride on every occasion, to praise itself in reference to everything, and to appropriate to itself all good and all virtue by its vain complacency, that without the help of these repeated trials to our misery and weakness we should flatter ourselves that we had a great share in the victory and should thus lose all the fruit that we might have gained. For by thus abandoning truth and our own nothingness, we should be walking in the path of vanity and falsehood so opposed to God who is essential Truth.

Thus the actual and almost continual experience of our weakness becomes the guardian of the virtues that grace makes us practise. From this it follows that in proportion as we advance God enlightens us with more and more vivid sentiments of our own misery and poverty, to preserve in us, in that way, the treasure of graces and virtues which our enemies would snatch from us, if God did not bury it in the abyss of our clear knowledge and vivid experience of our own misery. This will make you understand why it is that the holiest people are always the humblest and have the lowest opinion of themselves. It is because by our quick tendency to vanity we force God to hide from us the small amount of good that we do by his grace, and all the spiritual advancement and the virtue with which, unbeknown to us, he enriches us. This is a very touching proof both of the excess of our misery and of the wisdom and goodness of our God, reduced, as it were, to hiding from us his greatest benefits, for fear that we should love them by appropriating them to ourselves in our vain and barely perceptible complacency. On this is based that great maxim that our own misery rightly known and felt is worth more than an angelic virtue of which we unjustly take the credit to ourselves. If this principle is deeply engraved in the soul, it keeps us ever at peace in the midst of the keenest realization of our own misery, for we look on such realization as a great grace from God, as indeed it is.

LETTER 14: TO SISTER ANNE-MARGUERITE BOUDET DE LA BELLIÈRE (1734)

The practice of self-abandonment in time of consolation

MY DEAR SISTER,—What you tell me about the extraordinary circumstances which accompanied your vocation is more useful than you think: for a director, who sees in a vocation an act of Providence, has the right to judge that when God calls a soul in a special way he has particular designs on it and desires to find in it a devotion proportionate to the predilection which he has shown it.

I thank God for this first grace, and still more for the second which consists in making you recognize and feel this singular favour. I conclude from both that you belong to the fortunate band of those from whom God expects a special fidelity, and who would risk much if they did not respond to the advances of the heavenly Bridegroom, thus wounding the jealousy of his divine love.

It is certain that we must expect constant vicissitudes in the interior life. Such is the law to which God has subjected all transitory things in this life, and so universal is this law that a permanent state by that very fact would become suspicious. What then must you do now that it pleases God to overwhelm you with lights and graces?

1. You must expect and prepare yourself for brusque absences of the Spouse, as during his absence you will have to sustain yourself by the hope of his return.

2. You must not surrender too much to this zest and sweetness for fear of becoming attached to it. You should adopt the same moderation and sobriety in regard to this heavenly banquet as a mortified person at an earthly feast.

3. Your present method of prayer comes much more from grace than from yourself. You should, therefore, let grace act, and remain in an attitude of humble docility, calmly and simply keeping your interior gaze fixed on God and your own nothingness. God will then work great things in your soul without your knowing what is happening or the method of his operations. Beware of all curiosity on the subject, be content to know and feel the divine operation; trust yourself to him who is working in you and abandon yourself totally to him, that he may form you and shape you interiorly as he pleases. Is it not enough for you that you should be according to his taste and liking?

4. Have no other fear in these happy moments but that of attaching yourself rather to his gifts and graces than to the Giver. Do not esteem or savour these graces except in so far as they inflame you with divine love and help you to acquire the solid virtues that please the divine Lover: self-abnegation,

humility, patience, gentleness, obedience, charity and the endurance of your neighbour. Be sure that the devil is not the author of these favours, and that he will never be able to deceive you so long as you make your zest and sweetness serve towards the acquisition of the solid virtues which the Faith and the Gospel teach and prescribe to us. Let God act; place no obstacles through your natural activity to his holy operation, and be faithful to him in the slightest things, on pain of exciting and even irritating his divine jealousy.

5. The simplest ideas and those which lead to a spirit of holy childhood and filial confidence are always the best in prayer. How agreeable to God and how all-powerful with him are prayers that are at the same time simple, familiar and respectful. How I wish for you the continuation of this simple and humble gift of prayer, which is the great treasure of the spiritual life!

6. You say that you do not understand how you have passed from dislike of your state to so perfect a love for it. The explanation of this, my dear Sister, is that, by various interior operations, your soul has been, so to say, recast in the same way as an old tin or silver pot is recast, so as to become new, beautiful and shining. There will be much more recast in your soul, if you are well detached from consolation, faithful to grace and wholly resigned to the good pleasure of God, in aridity, pain and desolation.

7. I agree with you in thinking that God wishes you little by little to die to everything, to live only in him, for him and by him: i.e. to have neither thoughts, desires, designs, pretensions, affections, joys, fears, hopes nor love save for God alone. But you will have to suffer cruel agonies before arriving at this entire detachment, which is called, and truly is, a mystical death. You must commence your preparation from now on as virgins and the rest of the faithful used to prepare themselves for martyrdom; for it is indeed a martyrdom which is born of love and tends to its consummation. But be of good cheer. God will support you, and in order to do so he will give you from time to time a breathing space by foretastes of heaven and delicious sweetness which he will cast into your soul like a heavenly manna to feed and strengthen it while crossing the desert.

8. Oh, blessed attraction that ceaselessly calls you within your soul! How holy is the home and blessed the retreat which the heavenly Spouse has built for himself there, whither he often calls you and where lovers can speak heart to heart in the deepest silence, without noise of words and confusion of distracting thoughts! There, happy soul, should be your continual abode; and when you feel that you have strayed a little from it, try gently to return and keep as speedily as possible your divine rendezvous. On this point fidelity is specially necessary for you.

9. As regards your extreme weakness and misery in times of aridity and of the heavenly Spouse's absence, do not be surprised at it, or beyond measure troubled or afflicted by it. That happens to all good souls; and God acts thus in order to make us feel by a hundred personal experiences what we are without him, so that we may refer to him alone all the glory for the good that we do by his grace, without attributing to ourselves anything but the evil we do.

10. You would hardly believe how important it is, during the beginning of a soul's entrance on the path of holy recollection, to deny oneself not only all vain joy and natural satisfaction, curiosity and useless words, but also long conversations even on pious subjects. Such are frequently a ruse of the devil intended to feed our pride, self-love and vain self-esteem, to draw us out of ourselves little by little and lead us to forget God, even when we are speaking of him and of our spiritual state. The danger involved can only be escaped when we have acquired by constant effort the habit of the true interior life and are accustomed to speak rather from the heart than from the head.

11. Preserve carefully, then, this zest for solitude and silence. The desire thereof is sufficient for you at present, the time will come for you to put it into practice.

12. It is certain also that the habit of writing even the most innocent letters is an obstacle to perfection particularly in youth. One of your preceding directors has already given you this advice, and you have profited by obedience to him. This little sacrifice was very pleasing to God and surely has obtained for you the grace to make another which I judge to be necessary.

Not that I see in the relations which you have preserved the faintest shadow of sin; what I do see is, firstly, that we should always be trying to make continual progress on the path of detachment, and, secondly, that the special graces given you by God give him the right to expect a quite special fidelity. This is my advice after having considered everything before God and in the interests of your soul: I would like you simply to lay the situation before this person: say that you have a director whose advice you wish to follow and who maintains that you should make a little sacrifice of even the most innocent correspondence; that this is his definite wish and decision, although he knows perfectly well that no danger exists on either side, although you have told him that the particular correspondence is carried on with a good man, a good religious, a relative of your own; that in spite of all this, the director is inflexible and maintains his veto, under pain of refusing you his direction, and that you neither dare nor wish to disobey him. I think that such a declaration made with gentle firmness will suffice to give your soul complete liberty.

13. I know well that wretched self-love of which you speak, the natural fruit of which is the instinctive and indeliberate seeking of our little comforts and convenience. This love is so profoundly rooted in us, that only the operation of divine love (its contrary) is able to make it less sensitive. For the present it will be enough for you to suffer it and humiliate yourself on account of it before God.

The prayer which he gives you is a divine fire which insensibly burns up all your bad inclinations as if they were straw. So, have confidence in God and wait patiently till the poor straw is wholly consumed.

LETTER 15: TO MOTHER LOUISE-FRANÇOISE DE ROSEN

The same subject

MY DEAR SISTER,—I see nothing in your state of soul as you manifest it to me in your letter to cause you any anxiety.

1. That feeling of gratitude, of joy, of self-annihilation which

keeps you united to God without dissipation of mind for several days at a time is an operation of God similar to many others that you have experienced. You have only to accept this gift with humble thanksgiving and I have but to congratulate you on the grace which God has given you.

2. It is certain that there is a language of the heart which God alone understands in which we speak to him by our desires only and other interior acts just as we speak to men in articulate language with our voices. This language is what is called the prayer of the heart, all interior and purely spiritual. The Holy Spirit is then teaching us from within, in the depths of the soul; he listens to it, speaks to it, instructs it, moves it this way and that, and shapes it to his taste. These are operations of Spirit on spirit in which the subject itself understands, it seems, hardly anything, but from which it issues with certain impressions which have totally renovated it. Here again we have but to receive the gift of God with simplicity, and since it pleases him to communicate with the soul secretly and as it were incognito, the soul on its part must scrupulously abstain from counteracting his designs by fussy inquiries and indiscreet curiosity.

3. Your impression and opinion about the happiness of the saints are founded on truth, since it is of faith that the essence of their supreme joy is but the tide of the very happiness of God ebbing and flowing into their souls, according to the capacity of their hearts and proportionally to their merits. When God pleases, he causes us to experience a tiny sample of this joy on earth in order to draw the soul to himself by giving it a disgust for everything else; for this is the good effect produced by these transitory impressions and why we are permitted to esteem and savour them with modesty and interior sobriety.

4. The comparison of the stone which is carved and polished by hammer and chisel is quite right. We have but to let ourselves be carved and shaped and take care not to destroy by contrary sentiments and actions the form and shape impressed on his work by the divine Mason.

LETTER 16: TO SISTER MARIE-ANNE-THÉRÈSE
DE ROSEN (1734)
The same subject

My DEAR SISTER,—I have read your letter with much consolation and spiritual joy. I have blessed God from the bottom of my
heart for being willing to glorify himself in your weakness and
poverty of spirit. We celebrate today the feast of St Agatha, in
whose "prayer" we say to God that it pleases him to choose the
feeblest material so as to make his power shine forth. I applied
this thought to you.

1. Your great liking for simplicity is a grace the effect of
which can only be to make closer your union with God, for simplicity tends to unity. You must preserve this, firstly, by a simple
and loving gaze at God in pure faith, whether this gaze is perceptible to you by its sweetness as at present or becomes almost
imperceptible, remaining only in the depth of the soul or at the
summit and fine point of the spirit, secondly, by keeping your interior senses in a profound silence, thirdly, by only repeating
sensible acts based on reflection in so far as God gives you the
thought, attraction and movement necessary to do so.

2. This indistinct knowledge or rather this vivid awareness of
the immensity of God is an enriching operation of grace. It produces and leaves in the soul very salutary effects which no one
can explain in detail and on which we should not speculate too
much, or even dwell too much, unless God himself inclines us
to do so. Let these impressions pass through your mind, and do
not be disturbed when, in accordance with God's pleasure, they
disappear. Thus is the soul preserved from the danger of becoming attached to the gifts of God rather than to God himself, in
this way ruining all the operations of grace by referring to itself
the happy effects they produce.

3. God dwells, says Scripture, in darkness inaccessible to
every human spirit, but when he transports a soul into that darkness, it becomes luminous. So the soul sees all while seeing nothing, it hears all while hearing nothing, it knows all while
knowing nothing. This is called learned ignorance and in St

Denis' words the darkness of the rays of faith. All we need to know about this is that it is an operation of grace and that we should allow ourselves to be put into that state with joy, and plunge into it and lose ourselves in it for as long as it pleases God.

4. This liking and zest for prayer, this deep calm, this silence of wonder and love which says everything without saying anything, is merely a more marked effect of the prayer of recollection. But to find oneself in a certain state of inaction, as if one were a pure potentiality or a humble tool awaiting the hand of the Master-builder, is another operation of grace. In this state you have only to act as you are inspired by the Holy Spirit, either to remain in a state of peaceful, silent and resigned waiting, or, as says the holy King David, like a maid-servant keeping your eyes fixed on your mistress to see and accomplish her orders at the slightest sign; if she says nothing, remain in that position and interior sentiment of submission and self-abandonment; if grace demands from you express and formal acts, perform them gently, following step by step the prompting which is given you, and cease as soon as prompting ceases, returning to your state of silent expectation.

5. This spirit of total self-abandonment, accompanied by a fervent and reiterated prayer to fulfil all the demands of the holy will of God, frequently announces a coming transition to painful and crucifying interior states. You can only prepare yourself for these in a general way before God, by a complete mistrust of yourself and a great confidence in him and a universal self-abandonment to all that he may send you without entering into detail, unless by a particular manifestation of God. I will merely say in passing that if owing to the lack of tyrants, there are no more martyrs who shed their blood for the faith, Jesus Christ does not fail to have plenty of martyrs of grace. Bodily torments are advantageously replaced by the various interior crucifixions which occur in souls to purify them more and more, so that they may be made capable of an ever greater and more intimate union with the God of all purity and holiness. The sentiment of confusion and self-annihilation is a solid effect of the Spirit of God: all the graces which he gives us should always bring with them humility, and one should regard as sus-

picious all impressions which do not tend in that direction or which leave behind them the slightest smoke of pride, presumption and vain self-esteem.

6. I am not surprised that when one has once thoroughly experienced the sweetness, efficacy and purity of divine operations, one feels a kind of horror for one's own acts which are almost always hurried, turbulent, unquiet and followed by a thousand vain reflections on oneself. It is no evil to remain in inaction when one does not believe oneself to be moved by the Spirit of God, granted the presence of one of these two conditions: that such inaction should not last long or that it should take the form of a peaceful expectation which is no idleness, for it consists in an interior and loving gaze on God with faith, hope and desire for his holy operation, all of which dispositions are so many acts and movements of the spirit and heart which are the essence of true interior prayer. We must not be for ever probing spiritual matters; we should deal trustingly with God, as St Francis de Sales says. To do otherwise is to act contrary to the holy simplicity of fresh and innocent souls. All that happens or is done from love of God, says your blessed Father in another passage, is gentle and sweet like his holy love; whereas trouble, disquietude and hurry are the signs of self-seeking nature and a restless, breathless and turbulent self-love.

7. I understand that you have always had an attraction for the knowledge and love of God in and through Jesus Christ. A simple view or consideration of his mysteries accompanied by holy reflections is already a good way of prayer. When all the thoughts of the mind and affections of the heart unite in one all-containing centre, I mean his Divinity, the prayer becomes still simpler, better and more divine; but you must not imagine that your prayer will always be like that; it is not a permanent state, but a passing grace. When it leaves us we should return to the simple contemplation of the mystery, accompanying it with a few movements of the heart, gentle and peaceful, effortless and without too much curiosity.

8. Guard yourself in the time of prayer against reflections on yourself and your way of praying; for unless one watches oneself closely one often abandons a simple gaze at God for the contemplation of oneself, entering into and reflecting on oneself by

a pure movement of self-love, which never willing wholly to abandon itself naturally falls back on itself. When you feel the divine repose approaching, do not think about its sweetness, but of God alone in whose bosom your soul should seek love and the virtues which are infused into it during this blessed slumber rather than its own comfort. Moreover, these are the worthiest dispositions for the recitation of the Divine Office or hearing Mass, but you must be ready to be weaned from them so that you may eat the bread of the strong after the milk of spiritual childhood. Let us bless God in anticipation.

9. It is certain that the emptier of all creatures the self-annihilated soul becomes, the greater the capacity it acquires for divine love and the more abundant will be the infusion it will receive. At such times one seems to drink long draughts of love, with an insatiable thirst and delicious satisfaction. Let us, in such moments, be content to drink at the source without importunate agitation. Formal acts of love would be greatly out of place when the heart is felt to be wholly plunged in love. God grant that by means of this repeated plunging into love, your heart may become intoxicated, and all on fire with its pure and divine flames. In order to attain to this, you should, for your part, think only of two things; first, to separate yourself more and more in heart and mind from all creation, and secondly, to allow God, who alone can effect such results in souls, to do his part. You may, however, and indeed you ought when you feel moved and urged to it, always desire and ask more love for God; but this will come about almost without thought, indeed, you will scarcely be able to prevent yourself doing so.

10. God does his work as he pleases, and often produces marvels through the feeblest instruments. Do not, then, keep aloof from souls whom he inspires to address themselves to you: say simply what you think, saying what God gives you to say, and be sure that he will bless your simplicity and the humility of these dear souls. To help others, when God sends them to us, whatever means he may take of doing so, is not to push in where one is not wanted, but is to show to God our love and gratitude. Even if you appear to meet with opposition, remain firm and accept everything for the glory of the great Master.

LETTER 17: TO MOTHER MARIE-ANNE-SOPHIE DE
ROTTEMBOURG (1738)

*Docility to interior inspirations of the Holy Spirit;
Peaceful waiting*

REVEREND MOTHER,—What you tell me of the interior inclination of many of your daughters for holy recollection and the
manner that you adopt in order to remove the specious and well-
disguised obstacles by means of which the devil tries to turn
them from their purpose, can only come from the Holy Spirit. I
have nothing to add. Follow gently and little by little the lights
which God gives you. What a consolation and joy it is for me to
learn that all those good Sisters whom I know best and in whom
I take a special interest, are precisely those who have most
inclination and desire for the interior life. I beg you to congratulate them from me on the gift of God and salute them all
and particularly your dear Sister, Marie-Anne-Thérèse de
Vioménil. How delighted I am that she has been confirmed in
her office. The seven whom you name and with whom you have
formed a holy league for the renewal of the interior spirit in your
community will little by little make proselytes and the spirit of
the whole house will soon be renewed.

As for yourself, profit by your experiences never to abandon
on any personal ground the simple way of pure faith, to which
God has introduced you. Do not forget that in this way the
operations of God are almost imperceptible. The work of grace
is accomplished in the most intimate part of your soul, in the
part of the soul's depths which is furthest from the senses and
consequently from sensible experience. To strengthen your steps
in this way remember (1) that this way is what Jesus Christ was
referring to, when he said that we should adore the heavenly
Father in spirit and in truth, (2) that in Louis Lallemant's
words, the sensible side of grace is but the dregs and (3) that
Mother de Chantal has well said that the simpler, deeper and
more imperceptible the operations of God, the more spiritual,
solid, pure and perfect they are.

A *peaceful spirit* with oneself and others is one of the greatest gifts of God. Follow that spirit and all his inspirations: he will work wonders in your neighbour and yourself. When one has learnt how to remain in peace in one's soul, God holds his divine school in the soul where he teaches everything without noise of words to attentive, peaceful and docile souls in such a way that directors have nothing to say but: Listen attentively to the voice of God's Spirit, or better still: follow faithfully the interior impulse of his grace. This is what St John said to the first Christians: "You need not any man to teach you, for you have a divine unction from the Holy Spirit which dwelleth in you and teacheth you of all things." The great means of advance, rapid and safe, in the way of perfection is to follow with perfect docility this divine unction when we perceive it; to wait peacefully and confidently for it when its impression is less distinct.

Why will we always substitute our own action for that of the divine Worker, who labours ceaselessly in us at the work of our perfection? How much more progress would we make if we made it our principal study not to get in the way of his action, to abandon ourselves to him and wait. Scripture often recommends us to *wait for the Lord*, and there is no more useful secret for our sanctification. There is nothing to which souls sufficiently exercised in the active life and the accomplishment of the divine precepts should more carefully apply themselves than to these occasions of peaceful waiting. Such application is the means of acquiring the spirit of prayer, holy recollection and the most intimate union with God. The hands of God, who is infinitely liberal, are always full of graces, and he longs to pour them upon us. All we have to do to receive these graces abundantly is to keep our heart ready and remain continually in an attitude of waiting. But the aridity and boredom of doing so fatigue impatient and hurried souls. These trials repel those who merely have an eye on their own interests instead of letting themselves be led by that pure love which consists in the conformation of our will to the will of God always and in everything. There is no treasure on earth comparable to that conformity. But souls pursue some chimerical perfection or other, and lose sight of the unique standard of true perfection which is the divine will: that infinitely wise and gentle will, which if we take it for our guide will cause us to find close at hand and at every moment what we are seeking everywhere else laboriously and in vain.

LETTER 18: TO SISTER MARIE-THÉRÈSE DE VIOMÉNIL

We should moderate our desires and fears

A HEALTHY fear is one that causes neither trouble, disquietude nor discouragement. When it produces contrary effects we should drive it away, for in that case it surely comes from the devil or our self-love. With regard to our most legitimate desires and holiest plans, we should always remain before God in an attitude of peaceful expectation, submissive and resigned to all that he may will. Why is this? (1) Because the desires of God should be the only standard of our own desires. To submit ourselves and continually to adhere to all the interior or exterior circumstances in which one may find oneself by the dispositions of the divine Providence which extends to everything, which regulates all down to the fall of a leaf from a tree or a hair from our head; this is the surest way of arriving at perfection. (2) Because the renunciation of our own will is a very important condition of our sanctification.

Nothing is more calculated to make us acquire this renunciation than the delays which prevent the execution of our good designs, and this is why God sometimes postpones their accomplishment for whole years. Faith, self-abandonment, confidence are then indeed necessary. An experience which occurs sometimes, makes the trial much more painful: it is the failure to find any of these virtues we aim at in ourselves because we are deprived of the power of making sensible acts of them. What can we do in this case? We must sustain ourselves by the simple light of pure faith and by having frequent interior recourse to God to implore his assistance, humbly confessing our impotence and misery. In that way we shall enter into the designs of God who only appears to abandon us to ourselves in order to make us well understand what we really are. What a great favour (and important virtue) it is to have learnt by our personal and frequent experience the full extent of our weakness, our misery, our poverty and our constant need that God should sustain us, should animate, influence and hold us up by the interior effects of his grace.

The intimate impression that God has given you of a great desire to be stripped of your own will so as no longer to have any will but his is one of the most precious graces; in order to preserve and increase it, you must give your heart and soul up to it for as long and as often as you can, particularly during prayer. I wish you could pass your whole life in this sentiment alone, adhering in a deep interior silence to the operation of the Spirit of God; this whole state should be without violence or effort, gentle, tranquil, peaceful, for God dwells only in peace and his pleasure is only in peaceful hearts.

LETTER 19: TO SISTER MARIE-ANNE-THÉRÈSE DE ROSEN
To tend towards simplicity

MY DEAR SISTER,—It is only a few days since I replied at some length to your last letter but one. If you find that God does not give me much that is useful to you, you should conclude that he does not consider my assistance necessary for you or that he wishes to provide himself for your needs. How well he can do without us when he chooses! One word that he whispers in the ear of the soul instructs it better than all the discourses of men. The slightest breath of grace pushes along our little boat more vigorously and brings it more quickly and safely to port than all our oars and sails and rudders. I am delighted that you are beginning to find proof of this, and I hope that every day you will discover new and far more touching proofs of it. Remain as you are; an interior silence based on respect and submission humbly preserved in the presence of God when he does not bid us act, sanctifies our activity, mitigates our restlessness, pacifies our troubles, and that almost instantaneously. Cling to this unity and simplicity: a multiplicity [of thoughts] brings trouble and confusion into the mind, dissipates our powers which go off wandering without our perceiving it. The multiplication of desires afflicts the soul, says the Holy Spirit. Here is a method which I recommend to you for the unification of all your desires. Soak yourself well in this truth: I have been created and put into this world only to serve God, to love him and please him; that is my task here below; what will he do with me in this world and the next? To what grade of perfection and glory will he raise me? That is for him to see to. It is his affair; so to say, his task. Each to his own task with his thoughts on nothing else; please God that I may think as gladly and well about mine, as he does about his! I am, in him and through him, all yours, my dear Sister.

LETTER 20: TO SISTER ANNE-MARGUERITE BOUDET DE LA BELLIÈRE

The same subject

MY DEAR SISTER,—The manner in which you accept little trials is infinitely pleasing to God, and I do not hesitate to give you the assurance that by the generous renunciation, which you make for the love of God, of sweetness and interior consolation, you abundantly merit them, when the time of consolation comes. The little that you tell me you have remembered of what I said to you is the essential; that suffices you. God sees the heart and asks nothing but that. Perfection does not consist in a multitude of acts, even interior acts; on the contrary, the further we advance the more it pleases God to place us in a state in which we cannot produce a great number, inviting us to remain before him in silence and a humble recollection. Follow this impulse of grace. Be content to renew from time to time a simple act of faith and love, accompanied by complete self-abandonment and filial confidence. In all the various changes you go through say constantly to him from the bottom of your heart: My God, you wish this, I wish it also. . . . I refuse nothing from your fatherly hand; I accept all, I submit to everything. In this sole act continued or rather made habitual consists the whole of our perfection. This is what maintains peace in the depth of the heart and the centre of the soul, even when one is agitated by various troubles and contrary movements. The more you can maintain yourself in this holy interior simplicity, the more will you advance, or to speak more correctly, the more will God himself make you advance.

Do not, however, expect to be able to measure your rate of progress; it is impossible to do so for the reason that it depends far less on your own acts than on God's operations in your soul, and since these are wholly spiritual they are for that very reason almost imperceptible.

Here, however, are some indications by which you will be able to recognize in the long run the results of the divine action and the changes produced in your heart. (1) A holy indifference like a sort of stupidity in reference to the things of this world; (2) a depth of peace such that you no longer worry about anything at the bottom of your soul, not even over your own imperfections and faults, and still less over those of others; (3) a certain zest for God and the things of God, a sort of hunger and thirst for justice, i.e. for virtue, piety and all perfection. This hunger which is very keenly felt is, however, exempt from hurry and anxiety; it leads us to wish all that God wishes and nothing more, to bless him in our spiritual poverty as in our spiritual abundance.

Always remember that great word of Jesus Christ: "Unless you become as little children, you shall not enter into the kingdom of heaven." Take the greatest care never to injure in the slightest way this holy simplicity, so little known, so little esteemed, and yet so precious in the eyes of God. Grow more and more upright and simple in your thoughts, words and feelings, in all your actions and behaviour. There are some who aim at the opposite of this, and even affect it through vanity. How far are these from the kingdom of God, lacking indeed its very foundation, humility!

As long as you approach and leave the time of prayer with your spirit tranquil, recollected and well-disposed, you will always retain some fruit, one way or another; moreover, it is just when you think God furthest from you that he is nearest. Do not multiply your acts in prayer; make few, very gently, in the greatest repose of mind and heart, and the greatest peace that you can.

The Practice of Self-abandonment

During the day, do not force yourself to make so many different acts and still less to feel fervour and devotion in them; remain courageously, humbly and gently at peace, tranquil and fully resigned in your emptiness of spirit and will. It is just this emptiness of spirit which leads to pure love and union with God.

LETTER 21: TO MOTHER LOUISE-FRANÇOISE DE ROSEN
Diverse attractions of grace

MY DEAR SISTER,—The dispositions about which you consult me are not rare among the souls whom God calls, as he does you, to union with himself by a loving self-abandonment. Sometimes, you tell me, you feel yourself drawn to adore the divine Majesty with a humility mingled with love and with very distinct acts full of fervour which occur somehow of themselves, and produce a contentment completely filling the soul. At other times, you are drawn to remain in a great repose, with a very simple view of God as present, without being able to form distinct acts except with a great effort, even during Holy Mass; and that you then feel yourself obliged to take a book and do violence to yourself in order to come out of this state of apparent inaction which disturbs you; such are the principal features of the two states which you describe in your letter and on which you wish me to give you my opinion. This is what I think:

First of all, it is certain that both these dispositions are a gift from heaven, but the second seems to me the better. Primarily, because it is the simpler, the more profound, the more spiritual, the more removed from the senses and consequently the more worthy of God, who is a pure spirit and is to be adored in spirit and in truth. In the second place, because it is an exercise of pure faith, which gives less contentment and reassurance to the soul and which contains, therefore, more sacrifice and pure self-abandonment to God. Thirdly, because in the second case it is the Holy Spirit who is acting with the goodwill and consent of the soul, whereas in the first case, which belongs rather to ordinary affective prayer, it is the soul which is acting together with the grace of God. You well understand that where there is more of God's action and less of the creature's, the operations are necessarily more perfect.

It follows from this that there is in the second state no serious danger of your losing your time nor any reason to think that you do not fulfil the precept of hearing Mass. You may accept this decision without the slightest scruple. If you care to hear my advice on the way to behave when experiencing these diverse impulses, I will give it you. Firstly, whenever the second disposition makes itself felt strongly and absorbs you as it were in spite of yourself, you should gently let yourself go; to do otherwise would be to reject the inspiration and the secret operations which the Holy Spirit wishes to accomplish in you, and this in order to act on your own judgement through self-love in order to feel more content and reassured. But we should seek in everything, not our own contentment however spiritual, but purely the contentment of God.

When this disposition is not so strong nor so pressing, you should nevertheless encourage it, keeping yourself in a profound silence, so as to leave more room for the operations of the Holy Spirit. I advise this at least during a long period of prayer. For when you have very little time as at the short morning and evening visits to the Blessed Sacrament, it would be better to encourage and cultivate the first disposition of which you speak. You may then make your formal and conscious acts of adoration and love of God. But I would remind you of the counsel given by St Francis de Sales to a person walking in your path: I would prefer that these express and conscious acts should be performed without much sensible feeling or effort, so that they should flow, strained, as it were distilled, through the apex of the spirit, as the same saint says; for it is an accepted principle that our simplest operations, those most elevated above the senses and the most profound, are the most spiritual and consequently the most perfect.

To pray according to your first disposition is to pray by formal successive and conscious acts; to pray according to the second is to pray by acts which are practical, although in no way indicated or perceived, except confusedly. Or to put it another way, it is to pray by a simple though actual disposition: now this simple and actual disposition of the heart contains everything and says everything to God, without doing so expressly. The various names given to this way of prayer will make you understand this perfectly: it is called the prayer of loving attention to God; the prayer of a simple looking at God; the prayer of pure faith and simplicity which stretches out to God; the prayer of loving recollection in God; the prayer of self-surrender and self-abandonment to God, which is born of the love of God and always causes a still greater love of God to be born in the soul. You see by this that this second disposition is worth more than the first; you must, therefore, make it your principal exercise, without, however, neglecting the former at certain times as I have said above. Entirely yours in our Lord.

LETTER 22: TO SISTER CATHERINE-ANGÉLIQUE DE SERRE (WHEN A POSTULANT), 1731

Self-abandonment in the trials to which a vocation is subjected

ALL that you have said and written shows me that God is truly calling you to religion and in particular to the Order of the Visitation. Your interior attraction for this institute and the reasons you give leave me no doubt of this double vocation: for just as there is a vocation to religion in general, so there is a vocation to this or that community. All you have to do is to be faithful to God, and thus assure your predestination.

Now, fidelity demands three things of you. Before everything you must endeavour in spite of all interior or exterior opposition to preserve in your heart this divine attraction, with the sincere desire to follow it at such time as he who gives it you shall provide the means of consecrating yourself to his service in reality, as you do in advance in heart and spirit.

Your second duty is to hope against hope, as was said of Abraham: i.e. to believe firmly that since God is all-powerful and nothing can resist him, he will be able in his own time to conquer all the obstacles and opposition set up by men. All spirits and hearts are in his hands and he inclines them as he wills without it costing him more than the single word: I wish it.

By that word alone: *fiat*, did he bring creation out of nothing. So when the time comes, he will only have to say: *fiat*, and all the obstacles to your vocation will be annihilated. Meanwhile he permits these obstacles, to try your patience and your faith in him and your firm hope in his powerful help. Do not distress yourself, but continue to hope strongly in God, accept all the trials he sends, repeating ceaselessly to him: I accept everything, I sacrifice my own interests, my wishes and all the desires of my heart so as to have none other than to obey you and please you in all things.

Your third duty is a great fidelity to all your ordinary duties of piety: prayers, reading, meditations, Masses, confessions, communions, examinations of conscience, interior recollection, frequent elevations of the heart to God, without ever giving up the smallest of these exercises through chagrin, trouble, disgust, boredom or aridity, or for any other reason whatever. These troubles are necessary in order to accustom you to detach yourself from everything and keep yourself united to God, who alone should be your light, support, consolation and strength. It is apparently in order to make you practise this meritorious self-abandonment, that God has permitted that you should be forbidden to go to the Visitation, so that receiving no consolation except immediately from him, you should attach yourself purely and solely to him. You must then obey his orders by obeying the persons who have a right to command you on his behalf. If this order were to do serious injury to your soul, be assured that God would not allow it to subsist long. He will be able to remove the obstacle when he wills to do so; so continue gently to repose without the least anxiety in the arms of his Providence, like a little child on its mother's bosom.

LETTER 23: TO THE SAME

The same subject

THE increase of your desire to consecrate yourself to God is a new grace from his mercy. To suffer with resignation all the anguish of not being able to accomplish these ardent desires is to correspond well with grace and to merit its increase. The interior suffering that one endures in order to maintain this state of resignation is a sort of martyrdom which will have its reward sooner or later. God will accomplish the pious design with which he inspires you; these delays occur in order to test your fidelity. If, in the meanwhile, you are advancing in age, you should not grieve over this, since you already have the better part of what you wish for, which is the lively desire of consecrating yourself to God. This desire is worth more before God than the actual sacrifice [of yourself]; it is indeed a double sacrifice, since you are already offered to him in spirit and in heart, and are offering to him in addition your most ardent desires by patiently waiting the time destined by his Providence for their fulfilment. Perhaps the latter sacrifice has a greater value than the former, inasmuch as in the latter there is the greater abnegation of your own will. So remain in great peace and tranquillity in the presence of him who sees the depths of the heart, and who accepts all your good desires as their accomplishment. He needs none of the gifts that you can offer him, but he loves the heart which is prepared for all sacrifices.

The fear of death and the judgement is good, provided it does not go so far as to trouble and disturb you; if it did so it would be an illusion of the devil. After all, why should you be troubled? Because you have not yet done what you have not been able to do? Does God demand the impossible? Because you have not yet done anything for heaven? Beware here; the point is a very delicate one, for it looks as if there were a desire to acquire merits in order to trust in them. That is not true confidence which can only be founded on the mercy of God and the infinite merits of Jesus Christ. Any other confidence would be vain and presumptuous, being based on our own nothingness and I know not what wretched good works that are worthless in the eyes of God. Without counting in any way on ourselves, we must try to accomplish all that he asks of us and hope only in his goodness and the merits of Jesus Christ his Son.

You are right in saying that more virtue is required to save one's soul in the world than in religion, from which I draw the obvious conclusion that one needs a stronger, a more clearly

marked vocation to remain in the world than to consecrate oneself to God in the religious state; nevertheless there are special
graces for the time during which in spite of oneself one remains
in the world. In that case God is as it were obliged to sustain us.
Try to conform your thoughts, sentiments and exercises to those
of that holy state, but let all be done in peace and tranquillity of
spirit, with humble resignation and perfect confidence in the
paternal goodness and power of the heavenly bridegroom you
have chosen and who looks on you as his beloved spouse.

LETTER 24: TO THE SAME

The same subject

You are right to consider the design with which God has inspired you as one of the greatest of graces. The attraction to his
service is one of the surest marks of God's predestination of a
soul. On that depends not only its eternal salvation, but also its
temporal happiness, for experience teaches us that it is only in
the service of God that we can find happiness in this world.
Moreover, the malignity of the world is so great that it is very
difficult to serve God perfectly outside the religious state. In the
world it costs so much to belong truly to God, that one often
loses courage and gives up one's best intentions. We should,
therefore, ceaselessly thank the Lord for such a grace as he has
gratuitously granted you in preference to so many other souls
who lose themselves in the world, while living a life of crosses and
miseries.

In the second place, you must trust in the goodness of God,
and firmly hope that in his own good time he will bring to success that with which he inspires you. His Providence has secret
and infallible methods to bring about successfully, in spite of all
obstacles, things which appear altogether impossible. God often
permits that his designs should be crossed, so as to show the
better his power and convince us utterly that he is the absolute
master of all events, and that just as without him we can do
nothing, so with his help we can accomplish what appears impossible in our eyes.

The Practice of Self-abandonment

Thirdly, you must resign yourself entirely to all that God wills, often saying that you wish to depend entirely on him and have no other will than his. Thus, when something happens which seems contrary to your holiest desires, make first of all the sacrifice of them and remain in peace. For nothing is so contrary to the Spirit of God and the influence of grace as interior troubles which produce a hurried aspiration for even the best and holiest things. This indiscreet ardour, this too great eagerness, must be moderated by making all possible efforts to attach yourself in everything to the unchangeable will of God alone, renouncing your own will however holy and reasonable it may seem.

There is, indeed, no solid virtue or true sanctity save in a full acquiescence in God's will. If you sometimes feel a repugnance to submit to what God wishes, you should at once have recourse to him by interior prayer, and beg him to conform your will to his in everything, by giving you the strength to surmount your repugnance and the self-love which seeks its own satisfaction in the holiest things. Nevertheless, as the divine order demands that we should do all that we can for the success of the good desires with which he inspires us, you should act as follows: (1) frequent the sacraments as often and as well as you can; (2) live in a great purity of conscience, so as to avoid the slightest faults which might drive God from you; (3) do some spiritual reading every day at your leisure and with serious attention to take the place of your meditation when you cannot make it; (4) in the course of the day raise as often as you can your heart and mind to God, particularly when you are experiencing pain, weariness, sadness and vexation in order to offer these sufferings to him as continual sacrifices. In this way, you will constantly obtain new graces and inspirations from heaven to which it is infinitely important for you to be faithful, for to such fidelity God usually attaches great gifts and in particular the gift of perseverance.

LETTER 25: TO THE SAME

The same subject

THIS sort of martyrdom which you are enduring will be very agreeable to God if you suffer it with patience and a great resignation; for all perfection consists in a complete conformity to the will of God in everything; that is to say that we must never will anything but what God wills. It is of faith that God wills everything that happens to us except sin, for, apart from sin, nothing happens in this world but by the secret orders of his Providence. Taking that for granted I do not understand how you can be suffering so much from the postponement of your sacrifice, since God, who puts these obstacles in your way, actually only demands of you the desire of making this sacrifice to him at the time and place which he will indicate, by himself giving you the means to accomplish it easily. But note that, since in everything we try to content our self-will, the impossibility of achieving our desires may distress our self-love, destroy our interior peace, and cause all manner of troubles. Such an experience is an evident sign that we are seeking rather to satisfy our self-love than God, to do our own will rather than that of God. For if we were seeking only that divine will, we should be rendered always content and tranquil by this sole thought: God actually desires from me only what depends on myself, i.e. to be willing to make my sacrifice to him; and to be in conformity with his will, this desire should be peaceful, tranquil and submissive to all the orders of his divine Providence. But suppose I never arrive at accomplishing my holy desires? Well, that very fact will convince me that God does not wish me to and I shall be content with doing his holy will, for it will then be evident that God has only asked the desire of making my sacrifice and not the sacrifice itself. Thus he acted in the case of Abraham, whose resolution to obey God was as generously recompensed as if he had really sacrificed his son Isaac. It has been the same with so many holy men and women who have had a most true and burning desire to give up their lives by martyrdom without ever finding the means to do so. God has not permitted or willed it and he is content with the sacrifice of desire which for him has the same value as the actual concrete sacrifice. But if I am thus obliged to stay in the world what will happen to me? These are vain fears and alarms which the devil injects into your mind so as to destroy your peace of heart. You must abandon yourself entirely to God and trust in him. He is powerful enough to sustain us in the world and good enough to be willing to do so, when he destines us by his Providence to remain there.

You cannot then practise better recollection and abnegation than by renouncing your own will in everything, and particularly in the matter of your too ardent and lively desires, however holy they may be; for this immoderate ardour and feeling of disturbance and hurry indicate much imperfection and self-love. These defects are even more clearly manifested in the disturbance of soul to which one abandons oneself, after having fallen into some fault or other, impatience or chagrin—for these disturbances and troubles do not come from the love of God, which always produces peace, but from a rebellious self-love and a secret pride mortified at the soul's imperfection. A soul that has a little humility, instead of troubling itself uselessly and even dangerously after its faults, humbles itself gently and quietly and without disquietude before God; it conceives sorrow for its faults without anxiety and asks their pardon of God without disquietude; it even thanks God for saving it from falling into graver ones.

LETTER 26: TO SISTER MARIE-THÉRÈSE DE VIOMÉNIL

Self-abandonment in regard to one's occupations and undertakings

MY DEAR SISTER,—How is it that you cannot understand once for all that everything succeeds if God wishes it, because he can make the opposition and difficulties raised by men against it subserve his own designs? Believe me, if the thing is really for your greater advantage, men may do what they choose, it will succeed; but on the other hand can God do better than prevent its success, if it is disadvantageous to you? God alone knows the future and all the consequences which will flow from it; as for

us we are poor blind creatures who may well be afraid of all
sorts of dangers in those very events which appear to us in the
most favourable light. Can we then do more wisely than refer
everything to God's care? Can our future be in greater safety
than in the almighty hands of that adorable Master, that good
and tender Father who loves us much more than we love ourselves? Where shall we find a safer refuge than in the maternal
bosom of his loving Providence? That is where one's heart
should rest as in its beatific centre. Outside that centre, there
is neither peace nor real repose, nothing but excitement, bitterness, anxieties of heart, sorrows in our present life and dangers
for our eternal salvation.

LETTER 27: TO MOTHER MARIE-ANNE-SOPHIE DE ROTTEMBOURG (1738)

Self-abandonment in the acceptance of offices

MAY the peace of Jesus Christ reign always in your heart and
may the most holy will of God be ever accomplished in you and
by you.

I was already aware, Reverend Mother, of your election, and
I at once rejoiced in God, because I have no doubt that it will be
for the contentment of all your community and for its spiritual
profit.

As long as you maintain your present dispositions, your office,
however apt it may seem to you to lead to dissipation of spirit,
will do you no harm, for I remember having read that what is
dissipating is not our employments or offices, but the excitement,
disturbance and trouble which arise from our natural activity
and our desire to succeed in everything before the eyes of men.
The celebrated M. de Renti used to say that it was long since he
had found any difficulty or difference between being in prayer
in his oratory or actively working and moving about for the love
of God and the service of his neighbour. We might say the same if
we were as detached as he was from all the seekings of self-love.

You did wrong, then, to resist so much the employment
which Providence intended for you. May God forgive you, but

do not repeat that line of conduct. To desire nothing and to refuse nothing was the maxim of St Francis de Sales: I order you to make it your own. The new experience which you are certainly going to have of the visible help of heaven will make you inexcusable if in the future you are not settled in a self-abandonment and confidence without reservations or limits.

Sister *N.* has been unfaithful in the same way, but she has less excuse than you for she did not give way to the requests made to her. Kindly tell her that I was but little edified by her conduct. The hope of preserving her recollection caused her to lose the opportunity of practising many virtues. If she had submitted [to the will of the community] with more simplicity, she could have exercised simultaneously her obedience, her charity and her zeal. Not to speak of renunciation which she would have practised in a high degree in surmounting her repugnance and offering herself to the service of the community in the post offered her. The incapacity that she believed she saw in herself should have decided her acceptance, for the community's loss through that incapacity was no business of hers since she had in no way sought the post, while for herself nothing but merit could have resulted. How many little acts of humility, patience, endurance, self-denial, constraint, vigilance and charity might not have been the result of her incapacity! But she lacked the courage to face these sacrifices and yielded to self-love believing herself to be following the counsels of humility. Let her now at least profoundly humble herself before God: may she learn how to become very small in her own eyes, and omit nothing in order to repair the disedification she has given to her sisters.

LETTER 28: TO SISTER MARIE-THÉRÈSE DE VIOMÉNIL

The same subject

ANYTHING and everything that curbs the urgency of our passions and keeps them in abeyance is a notable grace of God. Surrender yourself, therefore, to those influences which guide you to that blessed peace. Allow nothing that comes in the guise of desire or hope or fear or sadness or joy or voluntary dejection to have easy access either to your mind or your heart. So shall the peace of God gradually make your secret soul its dwelling place. The less perceptible that peace is, the more precious it will be, coming, as it does, from God alone.

When we have no wish to meddle in an affair that is none of ours, a delightful solitude is always at hand. But when we are prompted by divine Providence, difficulty and anxiety are to be preferred to that solitude. Certainly the former position is pleasanter and more comforting; yet the latter, since it is harder, is more meritorious, assuming it to be God's command that drives us to it, against our inclination.

To conclude: while there are various ways that lead to God each of us must keep strictly to his own, unenvious of the rest. Have no will but God's will: all earthly delights and all hope of eternal happiness are compressed into that brief phrase. In every case let us regard our eagerness, especially in our good works, with distrust. Let us endure patiently all God sends. Finally, having done all that within reason we can, and should, do according to the light God has given us, let us live in tranquil peace, wholly surrendered to his adorable will.

LETTER 29: TO THE SAME

The same subject applied to the writer himself

DEAR SISTER,—So you want to know when I am coming back? That I do not know myself. I cannot know it nor do I wish to know it. Each day and every day I surrender myself utterly and in all things to divine Providence. So far as you are able, do the same. There is no better thing than this.

How I wish, dear Sister, that you might taste of that secret manna which with the truly faithful serves instead of more elaborate fare. Let us desire none but God: then will he grant us all our desires. Let us abandon ourselves wholly and blindly to his will: so shall we be freed from all our burdens. Plainly then, when all is said and done, there are few things we need do in order to walk steadily in the ways of salvation and perfection. Plainly, too, it is enough if without taking overmuch thought either as to the past or to the future, in the present we look trustfully upon God as a kind Father who leads us by the hand.

God forbid me to take even the slightest step to emerge from my present utter ignorance of my future. I much prefer to remain in this ignorance, surrendered to God, with neither burdens nor cares, like a little child in the bosom of its good and tender-hearted mother, wanting everything and yet wanting nothing—everything that God wills, nothing that he does not will. In this self-abandonment I find peace and a profound tranquillity—both of heart and mind that rids me alike of vain thoughts, restless cravings and all anxiety for the future.

Every circumstance, every place and every post in which God has set me have had so much mingled good and evil attendant upon them that even though I were to repeat these experiences, I should not be able to choose anything for myself. God alone knows what is best for us: he loves us more than we love ourselves: can we then do better than leave all our desires and all our decisions to him? Can we then forget that for us the great and important matter in this world is eternal salvation? Granted success in this one fundamental, we have achieved everything, and there is nothing about which we need be apprehensive.

Lastly, as to any pleasure I may wish to make mine: there is surely none sweeter than to be like the bird on the bough and to know as little security in my life. Such uncertainty leads to a greater self-abandonment and in that abandonment lies my tranquillity. Relieved of the need to direct myself I am left convinced that I shall unerringly reach my journey's end. For God's arm shall support me as I keep step with his divine Providence. In which of his creatures is to be found the perfection and the friendship that could give me as comforting a conviction?

LETTER 30: TO THE SAME

Self-abandonment in illness

YOUR incurable sickness would make me compassionate indeed, did I not realize so clearly that it is storing up a great treasure for you in eternity. Whether it be regarded as martyr-dom or as purgatory, it is the inexhaustible source of every kind of sacrifice and of unceasing acts of self-abandonment. I assure you that all such sufferings, borne as you bear them with neither murmuring nor complaint, are calculated to sanctify you. Had you been content to show the patience of all good Christians, there would have been much merit in it. Yet, in spite of what you say, you are doing more than that. Neither the involuntary revolt of the flesh nor those passing moments of impatience that have escaped despite yourself, hinder you in your secret heart from living in union with God. As your life can fairly be called one of wearisome hardship and of painful crucifixion, equally it follows that it can serve as your purgatory in this world and can deliver you from the purgatory to come, or at least shorten your term there.

Here you have the reason why I dare not beseech God for your deliverance from an evil of which the end must swiftly come and for which through all eternity you will need to give him thanks as for a notable gift of his grace.

One thing only I can ask of him on your behalf: that his love shall be made even more abounding and with it those virtues of submission, of patience and of complete self-abandonment which add to the merit of your sufferings.

To dwell but little on the thought of death is one of God's graces. As for your sufferings and your external trials, endure them as you have endured your physical ills. God asks no more of you than that: a *fiat* said once each day in regard to your ex-terior sufferings, must effect your salvation and even your per-fection. Everything that books and spiritual directors have to tell you can be condensed into one short word: *fiat.* At every season and in every circumstance just—*fiat!* In respect to that penitent and crucified life to which it has pleased Providence to reduce you, an especial—*fiat!* Tobias in his blindness, Job on his dunghill and many other saints, both men and women, who too have known the racking of anguish—all these have achieved no more. Admittedly they achieved it with fewer faults as well as more perfection and more love. Let us strive to emu-late their virtues, even as we share their tribulations: then most surely a day shall come when we shall share also their triumph.

LETTER 31: TO SISTER MARIE-ANTOINETTE DE MAHUET (1735)

The same subject

DEAR SISTER,—Although your illness may not be very serious, I feel sure that you behave like many generous souls who, in their least infirmities, carry on to the last, that they may have the opportunity of making God still greater sacrifices.

A very usual question is this: before you can make an offering of your life to God, must you not feel prepared for it, whereas you feel so unprepared. To such fears I urge you to make the answer of those generous souls I have mentioned.

Ready, or unready, prepared, or unprepared, I am always ready, always prepared to do the will of God. On this subject your blessed Father St Francis de Sales made a remark that was as notable as it is comforting to all manner of men: take the case, he said, of the worst sinner in the world who with his dying breath makes ungrudging offering of his life to God by the complete surrender of himself to God's divine purpose and his beneficent Providence. No matter how great that sinner's crimes, God would in no case condemn him. I, too, believe this, since such an offering is a perfect act of love, able, like baptism or martyrdom, of itself to wipe away all sins. Let us then frequently perform these acts of love by restoring to God's custody all that he has lent us since he could not give it to us in our own right. And since in the language of Jesus Christ we must once more become as children, let us emulate those little ones whose father, as part of their training, asks them to return one or more of the toys and the sweets which he has given them. Only silliness or selfishness will prevent us from saying to him: dear Father, take what you want—they're all yours. Actually the child gives what is not his to give. Yet his father's heart is moved by these small indications of a lovable disposition. He calls the little one his dear and beloved child, he kisses it; from that time onward, towards that child he is even more generous than before. When God gives us the opportunity of making an offering to himself, this is the attitude he in his kindness adopts towards us.

LETTER 32: TO SISTER MARIE-THÉRÈSE DE VIOMÉNIL

Bearing with one's neighbour and oneself

DEAR SISTER,—There is a great grace in witnessing the ill-behaviour of others with neither harshness, nor indignation, nor impatience, nor even with annoyance. If for some good reason you comment on it, curb both your emotion and your tongue that nothing displeasing to God escape you. Further, say nothing at all except your motive be good. On all occasions bear yourself with meek humility, and, when alone, regret those faults that tend to creep into such conversations. Beseech God constantly to give you abundance both of charity and circumspection, and so be at peace. Make yours the blessedness of desiring to be wholly God's; in your prayers let there be faith, trust and self-abandonment. Above all abase yourself humbly before his divine Majesty. It is for him to finish the work he has begun in you: there is none other that can accomplish it. Yet remember that many sacrifices are necessary before God possesses our hearts with his pure love. Let us long for that happiness, let us beg for it unweariedly; let us buy it with unstinted sacrifice; nor count its cost too dear, however high it be. As it is love alone that can keep our hearts alive, so it is only in God's that the heart can find the nourishment to satisfy its hungry need. Let then this divine love come to us; let it possess our hearts; let it uphold them; let it wrap them round; let it transform them into itself! Let us abandon ourselves unreservedly to God; let our thought concern itself only with following the way which God through all eternity has marked out for us and which we now are treading. Argument about predestination can be endless, and such argument merely serves to make our salvation the more remote. This one thing is certain: there is no better means of making the predestination of our salvation sure than the ceaseless performance of God's will in the present.

LETTER 33: TO THE SAME

Bearing with oneself

DEAR SISTER,—We have to submit ourselves to God in all things and for all things, whether it be the station and the circumstances in which he has placed us, the good and ill fortune which he has allotted us, even the character, intelligence, disposition, temperament and tendencies with which he has equipped us. Practise patience in your own affairs and perfect submission to the will of God. When you have made such patience yours, you will enjoy that great peace which nothing can disturb, into which no self-recrimination can enter, and you will put up with yourself with the same gentleness as you must show to others. This matter is more important than you think: just now there is nothing, possibly, more essential to your sanctification. Never lose sight of it, then, but constantly perform acts of submission to God's blessed will, and acts of charity, forbearance and sweetness for yourself even more than for others.

Before this is possible you will need to put great constraint upon yourself.

A soul to which God has revealed its shortcomings is far more of a burden to itself than its neighbour can be. For, however near he be, that neighbour is not always by our side, while in no case is he within us. We are our own burden, on the other hand; we cannot escape ourselves for a single moment, nor lose ourselves from sight and feeling, nor cease from trailing everywhere we go our imperfections and our failings. The supreme manifestation of God's infinite goodness lies in the fact that the sorrow and the shame these failings cause us, cure us of them, always provided that the shame does not become vexation and that the sorrow is inspired by love of God and not by self-love. Sorrow born of self-love is full of perturbation and bitterness: far from healing our soul's wounds it serves only to pour poison into them. On the contrary, sorrow springing from love of God is serene and full of abandonment. While it abhors the fault, it delights in the humiliation which is its sequel: as a consequence it gives all the credit to the humiliation, thus making loss itself an opportunity for gain.

No longer, then, torment yourself on account of your failings and of the imperfection of your works. Make God an offering of the sorrow that imperfection brings you, and allow his merciful Providence to redeem these small infidelities by small afflictions and troubles of every kind. Let patience be your one weapon; after a fall pick yourself up as speedily as possible, lamenting the tumble only with meek and tranquil humility. God wills it thus. Moreover, by such unwearied patience, you render him more glory and yourself make more progress than you could ever do by the most violent effort.

LETTER 34: TO THE SAME

Preparation for the sacraments, prayers, reading; instruction on behaviour

THE best and most useful preparation for the sacraments—believe me, dear Sister—is peace of soul, trust and surrender to God combined with the desire for union with Jesus Christ. The devil, however, seeks to put you on the wrong scent; he omits nothing that may disturb your interior peace, since he is well aware that this divine peace, once established in the soul, will make everything easy for us and, metaphorically, we shall fly rather than walk the ways of perfection. So let us not be disconcerted by the pretexts he will make use of, however plausible these be. Rather, let us go to God humbly yet, as St Francis de Sales says, with the simplicity and confidence of an upright heart that sincerely seeks God.

As for prayer, you will not have forgotten what I have so often enjoined on you: never allow yourself to be discouraged or troubled by your distractions. Only endeavour that your moments of recollection and raising your heart to God shall be so constant throughout the day that, if need be, these alone shall serve you instead of prayer. But never omit to pray whenever prayer is possible.

Apply yourself particularly to reading the letters of St Francis de Sales: you will find them so appropriate to your case and your present circumstances that, reading them, it will seem to you that the great saint had written them from heaven and that the Holy Spirit had dictated them especially for yourself.

Would you like to know what I in particular am asking of God for you? They are things so easily achieved that their very easiness will delight you:

1. Outward restraint that shall notably assist you in subduing step by step the impetuosity of your passions with the result that your words and your deeds shall be neither headstrong nor hasty, but gentle as they would be were you of a placid disposition.

2. Interior gentleness, both towards yourself and others in a degree that shall forbid the manifestation exteriorly of anything the reverse of that quality, or that, should you forget yourself momentarily, will enable you to make amends and at once to retrieve the ground lost.

3. Complete self-abandonment to divine Providence for success in all your aims, not excepting that of your advancement in virtue—such success to be desired only to the extent that God wills it for you and with the constant declaration: I desire only what God desires.

4. A peace of soul that nothing—not even your shortcomings or your sins—may perturb and that shall constrain you to go back to God in a state of humiliation at once tranquil and sweet, as though you had not had the misfortune to offend against his divine goodness, or as though you were certain of forgiveness. Act simply on this advice, and you will see how God will help you.

LETTER 35: TO A WOMAN IN THE WORLD

Programme for a time of rest in the country

This is what you must do throughout your stay in the country. The obedience you give to my directions will bless this time of rest and ensure you all its benefits.

1. Go to the sacraments as often as it is thought fit for you to go.

2. Each morning offer up to God with the pleasures of the day the trials both exterior and interior with which it shall please his goodness to season them, and at intervals repeat the words: "For all things and in all things may God be blessed. Lord, may your holy will be done!"

3. Now that you are less busied with others, spend more time in nourishing your soul with good reading. To make this nourishment the more beneficial, let this be your method of taking it. Begin by entering the presence of God and by begging his help. Read softly and slowly, a word at a time, that you may interpret your subject with your soul rather than with your intelligence. At the end of each paragraph containing a finished thought, pause for as long as it would take you to say an *Our Father*, or for even a little longer, to appreciate what you have read or to rest yourself and to gain interior tranquillity before God. Should this rest and tranquillity last longer, so much the better; but when you notice that your attention is wandering, go back to your reading, constantly making similar pauses as you continue.

4. If you find the above method useful to your soul, there is nothing to prevent you adopting it during the time set aside for meditation.

5. Busy yourself during the day with such useful work as obedience has entrusted to you and as is in the plan of divine Providence.

6. Be at pains to cast out all vain and useless thoughts, as soon as you are aware of them; yet do this peacefully, without effort or violence.

7. Cast out in particular all unquiet thoughts, relinquishing to divine Providence everything tending to preoccupy you.

8. When you lift your heart to God say not once but many times: "Lord, deliver me from those many seemingly good reflections that encourage my intellectual conceit and the pernicious trust I have in myself. Fill my mind with your divine Spirit; transform and renew all my soul's resources with your holy Spirit and its blessed operations." Repeat on other occasions: "When will it please you, O God, to teach me the great secret of remaining interiorly at rest and in silence, that in my

soul you may effect those many changes of which you know I stand in need? Lord, I long for them with all my heart, and I implore you for them most urgently, through Jesus Christ your Son, in order that gradually you may establish within me the kingdom of your ineffable peace, of your grace, and of your blessed love. Since in this you desire the co-operation of your poor and unworthy creatures, helped by you I wish to prepare myself for it, by faithfulness in all the little exercises to which I have been directed. I hope that you will bless me and will assist my blind submission; and I offer you in advance the intellectual difficulties and the emotional rebelliousness permitted by you in order to test me. To this test I resign myself and of those difficulties and rebelliousness I henceforth make you a sacrifice."

LETTER 36: TO SISTER MARIE-ANTOINETTE DE MAHUET
(1742)

Life and death—Consolations and ordeals

I AM back again at Albi with its mild climate and its friendly folk whose only fault from the point of view of a lover of solitude like myself is that they are too friendly. The many invitations which I receive will become a real cross to me while God will doubtless send me others to moderate the delight I take in seeing for the fourth time a countryside I have always greatly loved. God be blessed for all things! He scatters his crosses on every side; I, however, have made all my sacrifices—have accepted and made offering in advance of all the trials it shall please him to send me. This attitude adopted well beforehand makes such trials far milder when they materialize and much less considerable than the imagination pictured them. Nevertheless I am delighted to be where God would have me as the direct result of his loving Providence that for ever leads me by the hand. His fatherly care, of which I perceive myself to be the constant subject, still further strengthens my trust.

Though my health is consistently good, I am conscious that the swiftly passing years bring us nearer to that eternity to which we all must come. Admittedly this reflection is distasteful to our humanity. Yet, if we but regard it as beneficial, it becomes pleasant rather than otherwise, much as a disagreeable medicine gradually loses its repulsiveness as we grow aware of its efficacy. A few days back one of my friends remarked to me that in growing old like myself he found that time seemed to pass incredibly fast, that weeks appeared to him now as short as days in the past, and months as weeks, and years as months.

In point of fact, alas! what do a few years more or a few years less amount to when we are to exist as long as God himself? Those who have preceded us by twenty or thirty or even a hundred years and those who in twenty or thirty years must come to join us will neither have lost nor have gained ground in that vast eternity; to all of us it will seem that we are equally upon its brink. How greatly this thought mitigates the tribulations of this short and miserable life, turning them to account by reason of the patience with which we bear them! What is a little longer or a little shorter stretch of life, a few more or a few less tribulations, in comparison with the eternal life awaiting us to which we walk—we run—without a pause and which already is within hand's reach? Particularly in my own case for I perceive myself so to say upon the bank, with embarkation immediately ahead of me. It is time, then, I must say with St Francis de Sales and Fr Surin, to make ready my little provisions for eternity. Now, crosses lovingly borne and great sacrifices made to God's will are the best such provisions. Nothing will comfort us so much in death as our humble submission to the various plans of divine Providence, despite the insidious promptings of self-love that so often come under the most spiritual guises and with most plausible pretexts.

Be not then surprised, dear Sister, at the compulsion God puts upon you to practise this self-abandonment. The vicissitudes that he allots you of good fortune and of bad, of health and of sickness, are well calculated to keep you wholly dependent upon him and to constrain you to perform the most meritorious acts of trust. Our troubles, rightly used, become greatly lessened and proportionately profitable. Worthy endurance of them is a great sacrifice comparable to that of those noble Christianswho of old confessed their faith at the stake, since life's sufferings and the sorrows of circumstance provide the martyrdoms of Providence, even as the tortures of tyrants provided martyrdoms for faith and religion. No less true, I agree, is your own comparison: our life is like the wanderings of the Israelites through the desert with their countless tribulations and well-merited punishments at the hands of divine justice. Let us emulate the righteous Jews in recognizing God's equity in the punishment he imposes upon us; let us look upon our afflictions, whether general or particular, as God's work and not man's injustice. God, St Augustine said, would permit no evil that his power and his goodness could not avail to turn to the great advantage of his elect. Let us, then, make use of present ills to avoid those that are everlasting and to deserve the rewards promised to faith and to patience. The time will come and that shortly, when we shall say with David: "We have rejoiced for the days in which thou hast humbled us: for the years in which we have seen evils."

LETTER 37: TO THE SAME

The same subject

Nancy, 21 *February*, 1735

Dear Sister,—In the sacristy I saw a notice of the death of dear Sister Anne-Catherine de Preudhomme.[1] I have not the smallest regret for the death of one whose lot is rather a matter for envy.

[1] This Sister came of a noble Lorraine family, and took her vows in the convent of the Visitation, Sainte-Marie de Nancy, in 1666, at the age of twenty-one. Her most notable quality was self-abandonment to divine Providence: her submission to the will of God was perfect, her *fiat* constant whatever befell. In every circumstance she would say: "My divine king, my great sovereign, it is you who will, or do not will, this thing. For me that is enough: bless you for all things and in all things." Her great trust in God endowed her with many graces. She made her last illness one long act of faith and adoration, of trust and contrition, of union with Jesus Christ crucified, of love for God and surrender to his paternal goodness. Throughout, she appeared peaceful and joyous and full of thanksgiving. This union with God she maintained until she drew her last breath, dying tranquilly at last from sheer weakness. Ninety when she died, to her end she kept the mental faculties she had always cultivated in life. (Extract from the life of this dear Sister, by Mother L. F. de Rosen.)

In the presence of death terror and trust must mingle, though the latter should predominate. Sister ——'s need is self-abandonment. On this subject I refer her to B. Paula's letter. The latter no longer worries, she tells me, as she used to do, over graces needful in life and still more needful at death, because she has found reassurance in God: the very word father gives her both trust and self-abandonment. Even though you have no sense of it, still you must make that fact itself a reason for self-abandonment to God. Such unfelt abandonment is the more worth while in so far as it embraces a greater sacrifice.

B. Paula's letter provides me with spiritual reading. When I had answered it, it seemed to me that I had more clearly understood and appreciated a number of interior things that are essentially delicate and profound. I am no more in love with the restless pursuit of alleviations of spiritual than of physical poverty and wretchedness. This arises from overmuch tenderness towards oneself. I long for strong and courageous souls able to endure the apparent absences of the heavenly Spouse—those absences that are never more than apparent and that are designed to detach us from mere feelings, even from spiritual consolation. For God's gifts are not God. He alone is all; he alone is worth all; he alone must be all for us.

Excessive fears spring only from lack of trust and self-abandonment. That is why I have referred Sister *N.* to the case of B. Paula. Like yourself, God is so intent upon her in her poverty that he gives me nothing for the rest of you. Yet I hope that you will draw some profit from a long letter written this morning to a certain correspondent whom I asked to copy it and return the original to me for someone else—it was none other than Sister —— whom God put into my mind. My warm greetings in God to all the Sisters and to Sister Marie-Anne-Thérèse in particular; my especial respects to your honoured Mother L. F. de Rosen.

BOOK III

OBSTACLES TO SELF-ABANDONMENT

LETTER I: TO SISTER MARIE-THÉRÈSE DE VIOMÉNIL

Feelings of vanity—Recurring infidelities

DEAR SISTER and beloved daughter in our Lord, the peace of Jesus Christ be for ever with you.

You should know that before he cures you of vanity, God wishes you to realize the utter repulsiveness of this accursed passion and to be altogether convinced of your own helplessness to cure it, to the end that all the glory of that cure shall be his alone. In this matter you have but two things to do:

1. To look peacefully at this hideous interior ugliness.

2. As peacefully to hope and expect of God alone the moment ordained for your cure. You will be tranquil only when you learn how to distinguish what is God's from what is the self's, and to separate what belongs to him and what is your own.

You ask: Why cannot you teach me that secret? As to that, you do not know what you are asking. Certainly I can teach it to you forthwith; yet you can practise it interiorly only on condition that you are peacefully conscious of your own pitifulness. I specify *peacefully* so that grace may have its opportunity of working.

Bear in mind the saying of St Francis de Sales: You do not put on perfection as you put on a dress. In this the secret you ask of me is to be found for the seeking. Impress it thoroughly upon yourself that your longing may sink slowly into your soul. Everything good in you originates in God; everything evil, spoilt, and corrupt originates in yourself. Set aside, then, nothingness and sin, evil habits and inclinations, abysmal weakness and wretchedness. These are your portion; these originate in, and unquestionably belong to, you. Everything else—the body and its senses, the soul and its energies, the modicum of good you have performed—are God's portion. It so manifestly belongs to him that you realize you cannot claim one whit of it as yours, nor feel one grain of complacency, without being guilty of theft and larceny against God.

At frequent intervals repeat interiorly: "Lord, have pity upon me; with you all things are possible." There is nothing better or more simple than this; nothing more is needed to call forth his powerful help. Hold steadily to these practices and interior inclinations. God will do the rest without your perceiving it.

I am inwardly convinced that, failing some great unfaithfulness on your part, by his blessed works God will effect many things in you. Regard this as certain; do nothing willingly to obstruct it. Should you perceive that unhappily you have done so, humble yourself without delay; return to God and to your true self, showing always complete trust in divine goodness.

3. A keen consciousness of your pitifulness and of your unending need of God's help is a great grace that tends to every kind of good and especially to the prayer of humility and the self-obliteration before God in which he rejoices.

4. You do not understand as I do the effects and the workings of grace in your soul. If you were aware of them you would be greatly content. Your weakness and lack of virtue as yet leave you in no state to endure such knowledge. This fruit of grace needs to remain hidden, as if buried in the deep pit of your wretchedness and beneath the keenest comprehension of your weakness. It is beneath this dung-heap that God keeps the fruits of his grace. For our own wretchedness is so abysmal that we compel God to conceal his gifts from us and the interior riches with which he adorns us. Otherwise, the smallest breath of vanity or complacency, however imperceptible, would rot and destroy these flowers and fruits. Once you are in a state to wear and enjoy them without danger, God will cause your eyes to open. Your only endeavour, then, will be to praise and bless him, forgetting yourself and rendering all the glory of your deliverance to your divine Liberator. Meantime, follow the present guidance of his holy Spirit, and do not terrify your heart. Be sure that there is no sin in all you are experiencing at this time, since you endure it with so much grief and you would

know such happiness could you extirpate these wretched results of your sensitiveness. Uphold yourself in this blessed longing; offer up your prayers; be patient in your petitions; above all humiliate yourself before God: he it is who will complete the work he has begun in you; there is none other able to perform it. Recognize that this is the delicate sacrifice God asks of you before filling your heart with the ineffable delight of his pure love. You will know peace only when his merciful purpose has been fulfilled; for without love your heart cannot live. Pray therefore that its hunger be satisfied by the love of God alone, and that he and only he may delight and possess, kindle and enrapture our hearts.

5. The abyss of wretchedness and corruption into which, it would seem, God takes delight in seeing you thrust deep is, believe me, a supreme grace. For it is the basis of all distrust of self and of utter trust in God. For these two are the poles of the interior life. Certainly it is the grace I myself most prefer and most often find in developed souls. However horrifying, therefore, the thoughts you have of yourself, they are nevertheless true and deserved; for if God left you to yourself you would be a mass of sin, a monster of iniquity. He, however, reveals this great truth only to a very few, since there are not many capable of sustaining it as they ought—in peace, that is, in trust in God alone, and with neither perturbation nor discouragement.

6. The one cure for repeated unfaithfulness is to lament it, to be peacefully humble over it, and to turn again to God as soon as may be. Until we die life's difficulties and humiliations will be with us because of our besetting ingratitude and unfaithfulness. Yet provided that this is the result of our weakness of nature without affection of the heart, all is well. For God recognizes our weakness; he is aware of our wretchedness and our powerlessness to shun all unfaithfulness. He perceives, further, that it is for our good to be reduced to that pitiful state since, failing it, we should be unable to resist the assaults of presumptuous pride and of secret trust in ourselves. Guard against discouragement, even though you witness the failure of your repeated resolutions to serve God. Take advantage of this recurring experience to explore ever more thoroughly the deep

pit of your nothingness and of your corruption. From it learn utter distrust of yourself and complete reliance on God. Often repeat these words: I shall do nothing, Lord, unless you cause me to do it. Enlightened by disastrous experience my sole reliance is upon your all-powerful grace. The more unworthy of it I find myself, the greater my hope, since my unworthiness makes your mercy the more apparent. Your trust in God can never be pushed too far. Infinite goodness and mercy should induce trust as infinite.

7. One of self-love's subtle and unperceived illusions is to seek to discover the stage reached in your mystical dying, under pretext of getting to know what it must do to make that death in you still more thorough. In this life you will never make this discovery, nor is it to your advantage to do so. For even in the case of a soul that has completely died to self, there is the risk of the self's revival if this discovery be made. This, because self-love's satisfaction at such an assurance would be so excessive that it would revive, and enter upon a new life more subtle and more difficult to destroy than the old. O God! how insidious is self-love! Twisting like a snake, only too often it succeeds in preserving its life in the face of mortal threats. There is no illusion more deceptive than this. Go in dread of this accursed self-love, remembering that, despite every effort of yours, it will die finally and irretrievably only in the last moment of your life.

8. That perception of God's holiness which without too great constraint upon yourself you contrive to preserve amid so much bewilderment and trouble is, believe me, a great grace, more valuable and more sure than the consolation preceding it. My only wish is that you may persist in it. Offer no resistance, therefore, but allow the self to be abased, humiliated and destroyed. There is nothing more calculated to purify the soul, nor can you bring to Holy Communion a frame of mind more harmonious with that state of obliteration to which Jesus Christ is reduced in that mystery. He will be unable to repulse you when you come into his presence with abysmal wretchedness and in humility verging on self-annihilation.

If, having asked for grace, you have neither the impulse nor the ability to look at the state of your soul, you must remain silent and at peace. Discouragement, so far from being evidence of pure intention, is a dangerous temptation; for progress is to be desired only to give pleasure to God and not to the self. Your need, then, is to be content invariably with what God wishes or allows, inasmuch as his will alone must be the standard and the definite boundary of our desires, however holy they be. Again the notion that you will reach some particular state must not be entertained, otherwise you will become self-satisfied. That would be a great misfortune. The surest sign of our advancement is the conviction of our wretchedness. Then shall we be as rich as we think ourselves poor; our interior humiliation will increase, and with it our distrust of ourselves and our readiness to depend upon God alone. God has begun to make you this gift: be not anxious, therefore, nor discouraged. Say to yourself daily: Today I am going to make a start.

I very much approve of the practice you have adopted of not defending yourself and of accepting blame and censure even in circumstances in which you believe you have good cause to excuse yourself. You offer up, you tell me, the good opinion which you wish others to have of you; you keep silent, although, until now, you would have thought it more edifying to defend yourself against unjust remarks. Here is my comment: endure in silence every kind of censure and unjust accusation, on no pretext whatsoever allowing even a single word to escape you in your defence. This accords with the spirit of the Gospel and with the example set by Jesus Christ and all the saints. Your belief in the reverse of this is simple illusion. Keep steadily then to your new and blessed line of conduct. You are right in saying that we are burdened with a mass of corruption inescapable in our humanity, that resembles a muddy and stagnant pool which, when disturbed, gives off an intolerable stench. In this there is a truth that does not vary and God has granted you a great grace in giving you so lively a perception of it. That holy hatred and complete distrust of self of which humility is largely made up will gradually spring from that perception.

LETTER 2[1]

The failings of beginners

I AM not surprised at the peacefulness of the person you mention. It comes of the humility which she has shown in overcoming her repugnance to open her heart, and as a sequel to the advice with which God then unfailingly inspires those who speak in his name. Make her realize fully that God has begun to try her thus in order to chastise and cure in her a subtle streak of hidden pride that she has long harboured unwittingly. The greater her perturbation of spirit, the more manifest is made the extent of her vanity which becomes disconcerted and rebellious at the least humiliation, interior though it be. She must seek, then, to rid herself step by step of that secret complacency which lurks in the innermost recesses of her heart, no matter whether this has to do with human qualities or with virtues she possesses or thinks she possesses. For, unless care be taken, this gives occasion for vain self-gratification; and while we do not confess it to ourselves, we imagine ourselves superior to others in many respects. A subtle self-love is nourished by these spiritual vanities even as worldly pride is fed by physical charms. Just as the proud worldling delights in giving all her thoughts to her beauty or in gazing at it in the mirror, so the spiritually vain person rejoices interiorly in all the natural or supernatural gifts she flatters herself to have received from heaven. The cure for this diabolical evil—it was the sin of the rebellious angel—lies in:

1. Imitation of those modest women who never look at themselves in the mirror or who drive from their minds every vain thought of their beauty or external attractiveness.

---

[1] This letter was addressed in 1731 by Fr de Caussade to Sister Marie-Anne-Thérèse de Rosen, in relation to a person in retreat. There are grounds for believing that its subject was Mme or Mlle de Lesen whom God had brought to himself by putting her to the test of losing her wealth. She made a vow to become a nun, but for a considerable time was kept in the world in which she led a devout life. In 1731 and 1732 she made retreats in the convent of the Visitation in Nancy, where her directress was Sister Marie-Anne-Thérèse de Rosen. Not long afterwards—in 1733—she joined the Annonciades de Saint-Mihiel.

2. Constraint constantly imposed upon self-love to scrutinize closely all its failings, weaknesses and miseries, to appreciate the abjection they induce, and to make scorn its daily fare.

3. Consideration of what we have been, are, and would become, did God withdraw his support from us. Neglect to cultivate this humiliating line of thought sees God constrained, out of his paternal goodness, to adopt other means of destroying the secret vanity of souls he wishes to lead to lofty perfection: he permits temptations or even lapses that throw them into abysmal confusion and heal them of such puffed-up pride of mind and heart. When God prepares this bitter remedy for us we must submit humbly with neither vexation nor voluntary agitation.

4. Refusal to believe that by dint of thought we can lessen our difficulties; instead we must lie restfully upon the bosom of God's mercy, allowing the storm to pass overhead without strife or interior perturbation: otherwise the evil is then accentuated instead of diminished.

5. Refusal to petition for deliverance from our difficulties, since they have been ordained by a kindly decree of Providence; rather we must become wholly resigned and patient both with ourselves and others.

6. Substitution for intellectual pride of the need to become childlike through the practice of great simplicity, frankness, ingenuousness and open-heartedness towards those who direct us.

LETTER 3: TO SISTER CHARLOTTE-ELIZABETH BOURCIER DE MONTHUREUX (1735)

Interior troubles voluntarily entertained; weakness

Dear Sister,—For some days I have had so many letters to write both in this country and to France that I have not been able to read your long report. I shall not disguise from you that to me it seemed to serve very little purpose. For God has granted me the grace of a thorough knowledge of your state without need on my part to read what you have written. Nevertheless I have read the significant paragraph specially marked by you and it merely confirms me in the conviction I have long held about you. Allow me, then, dear Sister, to stress the direction I have consistently given you. Up till now you have greatly benefited by following it; why then let yourself be diverted from it by the devil's fallacies? I do not write at a venture but from complete certainty. Please then believe me, and prove to me by your docility that the trust with which you have honoured me is not a mockery.

If your intentions are truly good, if you are sincerely and energetically resolved to belong to God, you must make every effort to live in a state of peace that the message of the angels may not be falsified—peace to men of goodwill. You must expect, however, that Satan will make every effort to prevent you from attaining that wished-for peace. I am convinced that unfortunately he has met with only too much success recently. At present your soul's greatest failing is its perturbation, inquietude and interior agitation. Thanks to God, its ills are not incurable; yet so long as they remain uncured, they can only be as disastrous to you as they have been grievous. Interior agitation deprives the soul of the ability to listen to and obey the voice of the divine Spirit; to receive the delightful impress of his grace, and to busy itself with pious exercises and exterior duties. A sick and agitated mind is in the same case as a fever-weakened body that can perform no serious work until healed of its complaint. As there is an analogy between the diseases of both, so, too, there are likenesses between the remedies to be applied.

Physical health can be restored only by a threefold prescription: rest, good food and obedience to the doctor's orders. The like threefold prescription will bring back peace and health to a soul troubled and sick almost to death. The first requirement for its cure is docility. This docility must be childlike, unquestioning, and founded upon the principle that God, who has appointed ministers in his stead for our guides, cannot permit them to lead astray those souls who, in his presence, abandon themselves blindly to their guidance. Above all base your virtue upon renunciation of your judgement and upon a humble and warm-hearted readiness to accept and perform everything your director deems pleasing to God. If you are animated by the spirit of obedience, you will never allow yourself to be set back by any thought contrary to the direction you have received. Equally you will take good care not to yield to the inclination to question and examine everything. Yet if, despite yourself, thoughts antagonistic to obedience creep into your mind, you will cast them from you; or still better, you will contemn them as dangerous temptations.

The second treatment for your spiritual sickness is tranquillity and peace of soul. For the attainment of these you must first and foremost long for them and earnestly petition God for them. Secondly, you must bend all your energies towards their acquisition. I will now answer the question you will probably put as to how you are to set about this.

In the first place take care never to harbour voluntarily in your heart any thought calculated to grieve, disquiet or dishearten it. From one point of view, such thoughts are more dangerous than impure temptations. Your need, then, is to allow them to pass you by, despising them and letting them fall like a stone into the sea. You must resist them by concentrating your attention upon contrary reflections, and especially upon aspirations designed to this end, upon interior sighs and groans with acts of humility to go with them.

Yet while we are to put energy and generosity into our struggle, mildness, tranquillity and peace are as necessary. For unquiet grieving and vexatious restlessness will make the remedy worse than the disease. In the second place you are to avoid purely human ardour, eagerness and activity in all your efforts, whether exterior or interior. On the contrary you must make it your habit to walk and talk, to pray and read, softly and slowly, putting no strain upon yourself in anything, even though it be resistance to the most frightful temptations. Remember that the best repudiation of such temptations is the grief that they bring you. As long as your free will feels only horror and detestation for the ends which those temptations hold out to the imagination, plainly it will give no consent to them. Remain, then, in peace in the midst of such temptations, no less than in spiritual ordeals.

We come now to the remedy for the weakness evinced by a

troubled soul as the result of the fever that afflicts it. For such a soul a strengthening diet is necessary: in other words:

1. Let good books be read and this reading be done in a low voice with frequent pauses, less to bring to it the reflections of the intelligence than to allow the mind to digest what it reads. This apt saying of Fénelon's should not be forgotten: "Words we read are but the leavings, while the relish we have in them is the juice upon which our soul is fed and fattened." We need to do with this spiritual food what the greedy and the sensual do with *ragouts*, sweetmeats and liqueurs, which they still taste and savour, even after they have swallowed them.

2. Talk only of useful and edifying subjects with those most capable of drawing us to God by their pious conversation.

3. At all times shun the pursuit of consolation through vain talk with fellow human beings. This is one of the essentials for those passing through spiritual ordeals. God, who sends us these for our good, wishes us to endure them without seeking consolations other than his own, and ordains that he himself shall determine the juncture at which these consolations shall be bestowed upon us.

4. Each, according to his ability and inclination, must devote himself to interior prayer, and this with neither strife nor violence, and keep himself quietly in God's holy presence, turning to him from time to time with some interior act of adoration, repentance, trust and love. If such an act cannot be performed, be content with the earnest wish to perform it; for, in good as in evil, the desire with God is equivalent to the deed. Bossuet said somewhere notably: "In God's sight desire is what the voice and spoken word is in man's. For as with the spoken word we talk with, petition, and thank our fellows, so in God's case all these are achieved by the mere desires of our hearts. These desires speak to and solicit him far more eloquently than any words or even any interior act, such as we call formal and distinct. From this it follows that to him for whom our souls are an open book, a cry retained in the depths of the soul is worth as much as a cry raised to heaven.

5. You must set yourself to pray with gentle sweetness and loving tenderness both at morning meditation and at all times

throughout the day. Pray either by a constant turning of your heart to God or by gazing interiorly upon his divine presence. To gain greater facility in prayer, in the morning you can anticipate the various situations, interior and exterior, in which you will probably find yourself during the day, and then set yourself this question: At that juncture or in this or that situation what shall I say to God, what act shall I perform? If, when the time comes, you are prevented from carrying out these good intentions, be content to cling to them as far as may be and to explain your powerlessness to God.

Finally, this good food of the soul lies in willing at all times and in all places what God wills; or, to put it otherwise, to obey every command of divine Providence in every imaginable state of soul, interior and exterior, whether in health, sickness, aridity, distraction, weariness or temptation; in all these saying with the whole heart: Truly, O God, I long for all things, I accept all things, to you I make offering of all things or at least I desire to do so. In this I beg your grace; help me and strengthen my weakness. In bitter temptation you must cry to him: O God, keep me now from all sin. This holy abjection, and interior humiliation and humbling of my pride I gladly accept as much as, and for as long as, it pleases you.

The weakest and most troubled soul adopting the methods just outlined cannot fail to make its own once more its lost peace and joy.

LETTER 4: TO THE SAME (1755)

The same subject

If my letter has grieved you, dear Sister, I shall say, like St Paul, that I am glad not of the grief but of the good effect it has had. It is good to perceive oneself blameable in many matters, not in order to reproach oneself for them with harsh bitterness and feverish anxiety, but to humble oneself sweetly and peacefully, showing neither vexation nor hardness against oneself. You appear to lack docility, you say, only because you state honestly your doubts and fears. The trouble is not that, dear Sister, but the fact that you cling too fast to these doubts and fears. You concentrate upon them too much, instead of ignoring them and casting yourself upon God in utter self-abandonment, as I have consistently exhorted you for so long past. Only through this holy and happy self-abandonment can you ever enjoy an enduring peace full of perfect trust in God through Jesus Christ.

Yet once again, what have you to fear in this self-surrender especially after so many plain signs of God's great mercy to you? You seek for conscious support in yourself and in your works and conscience, as if they provided more assurance and stronger support than God's mercy and Jesus Christ's merits, and under the assumption that these cannot lead you astray. I pray God to enlighten you and to change your heart at last in this matter so vitally important to you.

To get back to your letter. I should be surprised, you say, and disconcerted, were you able to disclose to me all you see and feel. People in your state, whom I know no better than you, are constantly saying precisely this to me. My answer to you and those others is this: A lively perception of our failings and imperfections is the grace which befits that state—a very precious grace. And the reason? (1) Because such intimate perception of our wretchedness maintains us in humility, at times it avails to inspire us with a wholesome horror and holy fear of ourselves; (2) because this state, outwardly so wretched and so hopeless, makes way for a heroic self-abandonment in the arms of God.

When we have reached the lowest depths of our nothingness, we can have no kind of trust in ourselves, nor in any way rely upon our works; for in these are to be found only wretchedness, self-love, and corruption. Such complete distrust and utter scorn of the self is the one source from which originate those delightful consolations of souls wholly surrendered to God—their unalterable peace, their blessed joy and their unshakeable trust in none but God. Ah, would that you knew the gift of God, the reward and the merit and the power and the peace, the blessed assurances of salvation that are hidden in this abandonment; then would you soon be rid of all your fears and anxieties! You imagine yourself lost as soon as you think of surrendering yourself, notwithstanding that there is no more certain path to salvation than that which leads through complete and perfect self-abandonment. I have never met a soul more obdurate than yours in refusing to make this surrender to God. Yet you will have to come to it, if only at death; for no one, unless by express revelation, can be assured of his eternal salvation or can be free of fear to his dying moment. It is utterly necessary then to abandon yourself to God's great mercy.

But, you will say, I could believe myself warranted in practising this self-abandonment and ridding myself of my fears only if, living a saintly life, I had performed many good works. You delude yourself, dear Sister. Such a remark on your part can be prompted only by your unhappy self-love that would completely rely on itself, whereas your duty is to put your trust in God alone and in the infinite merits of Jesus Christ. You have never had as firm a wish as you should have to perceive this fundamental truth. You consistently stop to examine your doubts and fears instead of disregarding them in order to cast yourself blindly into God's hands and headlong upon his bosom. In other words, you wish in every case to be given a firm guarantee to make your self-abandonment easier. Assuredly in this there is no true self-surrender to God arising from utter trust in him alone, but merely an unconfessed desire for the self to be assured before that surrender is made to his infinite goodness. So does a law-breaker act who before he throws himself upon the king's mercy requires his pardon to be guaranteed! Is this a call then to depend upon God and to base all our hope upon him? It is for you to draw your own conclusions. In any event there remains that self-abandonment through filial trust to which God has called you for so long past. Yet you turn your back on both these, preferring the crucifying tyranny of slavish fear. I am stressing this point strongly, because I have been taught by experience that it is here that souls in your state offer their last resistance to grace and the final leap that may free them from the self—a leap that is as difficult as it is necessary. I seem to have met with no one who has offered as much resistance as yourself. This arises from an extreme self-love, a great and hidden presumption and a reliance upon yourself that you may never have suspected. For make no mistake about it, as soon as this complete surrender to God is mentioned, you are aware of a certain interior upheaval, a feeling that all is lost or that you have been asked to close your eyes and hurl yourself into a deep pit. The truth is nothing of the kind; in fact it is the exact opposite. For the greatest certainty of spiritual safety in this life is to be found in this utter self-abandonment which, in the words of Fénelon, consists in being driven to breaking-point and to an utter despair of oneself so as to have no hope but in God alone. Such language may at first sight seem fantastically strong; give it your earnest consideration.

Now God has given you two kinds of grace to bring you to this full self-abandonment: (1) strong inducements to tempt you to put full confidence in his great mercy and goodness; (2) surpassing understanding and penetrating awareness of your wretchedness, weakness, perversity and general failure to achieve goodness. In effect he says to you: Know that in your present state you neither ought, nor can, in any wise help yourself, nor be helped by anything coming from that pit of corruption which is yourself. By self-abandonment, by renunciation of all recourse to self and by fixing all your thought upon me, do you then leave all your burdens to me!

What of the question of my salvation? you ask. Can it be that you still do not know the surest guarantee of that, too, is by dwelling only on God, to place the whole burden of that also upon him? Just as a man whom a great king has honoured with his confidence would trust himself entirely to him for his advancement, content to think only of his master's service and interests. Surely you can see that only by such generous methods would he advance his own cause far better than other less disinterested men who spend their time in a calculating pursuit of their own gains?

Yet is it not a duty to commune with and be watchful over the self? Why yes, upon your entrance into God's service when your need is for detachment from the world, withdrawal from exterior things and correction of bad habits previously formed. But afterwards you are to forget self and think only of God. In your case your one desire is to remain buried in yourself and in what you imagine to be your spiritual interests. To deprive you of this last wretched recourse to self-love, God ordains that you find in yourself only a hot-bed of doubts, and fears, griefs and uncertainties, disquietude and defeat. Such is God's way of saying to you: Do but forget yourself and you shall find in me peace, tranquillity, interior joy and a firm assurance of your salvation. I and I alone am the God of salvation, you by yourself can effect only your perdition.

You may argue further that in this self-forgetfulness you will not even perceive your faults and imperfections, much less correct them. Error, illusion and ignorance are never so clearly perceived as in the clear sight or presence of God. These are like a sun shining interiorly, that, freeing us from the dread of perpetual self-examination, at a stroke reveals to us all we need to know. Equally it serves to consume gradually, as a fire consumes straw, our every fault and imperfection.

What next? No other than the state to which you should have long since come, and of which God has given, and continues to give, frequent proofs to me. Because the wretchedness and corruption of the human heart is a bottomless pit, the deeper it is penetrated by God's light of wisdom, the more melancholy and humiliating discoveries are made in it. Yet these discoveries, so far from saddening the soul, by strengthening its interior humility bring it the consolation it knows to be the firm foundation of every spiritual edifice. Instead of shaking and undermining its blessed joy, these discoveries inspire it with resolute trust. A trust that the soul now feels can be placed in God alone; a trust that, to quote the Scriptures, has never been confounded. I have known, and know today, souls following this way to be astonished when they behold their trust in God increase proportionately with their increasing perception of their poverty, weakness and misery. The explanation is that the keener this consciousness of our wretchedness and corruption becomes, the greater grows the self-distrust of those souls possessing it and the greater their corresponding trust in God. Thereupon God makes them aware that such complete distrust of self combined with that utter trust in him which is born of self-abandonment are the two great props of the spiritual life. So much so that as long as you remain in this state, there is no risk whatever to your salvation.

Surrender, then, all things to God and in him you shall find all things more abundantly. So shall you rid yourself once for all of that wretched retrospection, fear, perturbation and anxiety: all the torments, to be brief, to which those calculating souls are condemned who would love God only out of love for themselves and who seek their salvation and perfection less to please God and to glorify him than to serve their own interest and eternal welfare.

Yet, you will say, God ordains that we should yearn for salvation and eternal happiness. Undoubtedly; but that yearning must accord with his desire and decree. Now—and it is important that you should know this—this is God's decree: God created us only, and could create us only, to serve his own glory and to fulfil his own purpose; for his nature and his sovereignty demanded this. Yet, since also he is infinitely merciful, he willed that his creature should gain his own ends and his eternal welfare by accomplishing God's will. Precisely the opposite is true of that unhappy self-love which seeks itself in all it does: first and foremost we think of our own spiritual and eternal interests; thus preoccupied, we relegate to second place that which has to do with the glory of God.

When this is true of souls whom he has loaded with graces and by whom he wishes to be loved with a pure and disinterested love, God's jealousy is aroused. To bring them back within the limits of his plan, he threatens them and afflicts them interiorly. He wills that such secret tribulation shall overthrow that accumulated self-love which does them so much harm. He wishes to induce them by degrees to think less of themselves and their own interests and instead, by resigning to him the care and the manner of their salvation, to come to dwell in him tranquilly. The noble words Jesus Christ has addressed to various saintly souls are relevant here: "My daughter, think of me and I will think of you: make my glory your concern and leave me to make your welfare and eternal happiness my concern."

What are we about when we are forever preoccupied with ourselves? We might well be saying: Ah, Lord, what do your words mean? I should be lost did I not constantly think of my interior needs and did I not as constantly ask how I stand with you and what is to become of me. These must be my ceaseless preoccupation. I can only think occasionally of those things that tend to your glory and gratification. Later I hope to give more time to them. That must be when I have seen the last of my faults disappear and have had it revealed to me that I run no risk in studying your interests uninterruptedly. Until then, I cannot make up my mind to do it. For I should believe myself lost and do you not wish above all things else for me to ensure the safety of my soul?—In the Holy Scriptures the divine Saviour has answered clearly and precisely brides of his who use such language: "He that loveth his life shall lose it: and he that hateth his life in this world keepeth it unto life eternal."

Indeed, I know no souls with more horror of sin, more strength to practise good and to make great sacrifices to God than those who, in order to be for ever engrossed in God, seem never to think of themselves, relying upon him for their salvation and all things else. It is precisely this spiritual state that most nearly ensures salvation. I infer from this that not merely scruples but excessive fear, grievous doubt, interior vexation and bitterness of heart derive only from that mercenary love which is concerned more with its individual interest than with God's glory or his will, or than a singlehearted wish to please him in all the things more excellent. Since God is the supreme good, love of him must take precedence of the love we owe ourselves. As too he has promised to love all who love him and to love them the more as they love him more purely, we can be sure that in exerting all our strength to love him for himself, in that pure love we shall discover again and more abundantly all that we seem to have sacrificed to him. Thus, utter self-abandonment to God in love and in trust involves not perdition, but the gain of all things.

The spectacle of this confused mass of frailty, wretchedness, unworthiness and every kind of corruption must in no way disconcert us. That is why I say emphatically that it does us good service; for no soul I have met with, gifted with this acute and humiliating perception, has failed to discover in this a singular grace of God; or, aided by true self-knowledge, to find that lasting humility of heart upon which all perfection is based. I have known, and know, many saintly souls whose only riches is a profound knowledge of their wretchedness, and whose greatest contentment is, metaphorically speaking, to see themselves engulfed. Only then are we possessed of truth and, therefore, of God who is the supreme Truth. Do you know that almost the whole of the interior life is embraced in going your ways before him with your head bowed and your mood one in which self is obliterated? It is merely a question of learning how to do this in submissive peace and trusting self-abandonment. This, then, is my word to you: Do but live so and you will have achieved everything; all the rest God will perform, though what he accomplishes you may well neither see nor feel.

You go in fear of your spiritual state. Yet I bless God for it on your behalf. There is only one change I would wish for you; that to your self-obliteration may be added, as I have said, submissive peace and trusting self-abandonment. Given that, I shall have no further fear for you despite those backslidings which you tell me of, causing you to move like a crab. God prevents serious backslidings and permits minor lapses in order to keep you humble. St Francis de Sales sees heroic courage in consistently picking oneself up again after a fall and never losing heart. God be blessed in all things and for all things!

LETTER 5: TO SISTER DE LESEN

Love of relations

NANCY, 1735

THE affection you have for your dear relative does not surprise me. I realize that you owe it to her on several counts. Nevertheless, as on your own confession this affection is also a source of grief to you and an obstacle to your complete attachment to God, some difficulties must necessarily arise. God's demands upon you if you are to sanctify it and to lift it above the merely human are: (1) that you do not dwell too much and too devotedly upon this woman you love; for there should be moderation in all things; (2) that you make to God the sacrifice and surrender of any sickness or affliction she may suffer, to the end that at all times and in all places, he may deal with both you and her according to his blessed will and adorable good pleasure. Realize that in so surrendering her to the will and the care of divine Providence you do her no less than yourself the greatest service open to you in that you entrust her to the hands of an infinitely good and infinitely mighty God.

By all means make use of your reason in your difficulties. But, as a learned and saintly Christian woman has said pertinently, no great reliance must be placed upon so thoroughly weak a thing as reason whose strength is chiefly exerted in resisting good and whose weakness is most manifest when it is a question of vanquishing evil. In religion and the grace that comes of humble prayer is our true strength. The grief, despondency and interior rebelliousness prompted by affection that we feel when life's various mischances befall those near to us can be made the occasion of great virtue and merit, if we but rise through faith above our human feelings and learn to sacrifice these and all things else to the blessed and admirable will of God. For do we not know that nothing can happen in this world without his decree, and that he has arranged everything for the greatest good of those who have submitted themselves to him or who at least yearn to acquire and practise this blessed submission? Would we were as well aware of the value and the virtue of it! When it is combined with obedience to the divine precepts, it offers the widest and most infallible way to salvation. Most men would find it all that is necessary for their sanctification and for the alleviation of all life's troubles. A wise pagan echoed Christian thought when he said: "Patience makes the inevitable tolerable."

It is no easy matter for a tender-hearted person to relinquish what the world calls delicate and generous sentiments, to rid himself of too excessive a preoccupation with his family's honour or too great a concern for its interests or too keen a sensibility concerning those near and dear. Much pondering and strife are needed as well as much prayer. (1) We must ponder upon the uselessness of our anxiety and our sensibility and upon the harm they do us, spiritually and physically alike. (2) We must strive to spend less time and less eagerness upon these, making sacrificial offerings of them to God whatever heart-break we may feel at the greatness of this sacrifice, and remembering always that it is a question of necessity and that, provided all is well in the one essential, with the rest it shall be as it pleases God. All these subordinate affairs are transitory trifles, come and gone like a flash of lightning never to return. Copy the example of people in the world who in matters of supreme importance affecting honour, life, worldly goods —their all in short—think day and night only of the one great issue, ignoring everything else because to their mind everything else is negligible. As Jesus Christ has said, let us who are the children of light be instructed how to act by the children of darkness.

Do not forget that our saving seclusion and solitude are not exterior things such as can be enjoyed even in the world; but an interior seclusion of both mind and heart: of mind in the expulsion of unnecessary thoughts and cares and in the attempt to make God its one concern; of heart in lamentation and constant humble-heartedness in God's sight as in the search for gradual self-detachment from all creatures and subsequent attachment to the Creator alone. He alone truly exists; all other things have reality only in as far as they are in contact with God's existence. It follows that purely temporal affairs—business or preferment, joys or sufferings—are no more than illusory trifles and spectral shadows of true reality.

LETTER 6: TO SISTER ANNE-MARGUERITE BOUDET DE LA BELLIÈRE

Too friendly attachments

DEAR DAUGHTER in our Lord,—I cannot bless God sufficiently for the desire he has given you to be unreservedly his, and for the courage with which he has inspired you to make him numerous small sacrifices and to show moderation in your most innocent attachments. How greatly, dear Sister, has God enlightened you in this matter: do but be faithful to that enlightenment and the dangers you will avoid will be many indeed! There are unhappily only too many to be found who hinder all advancement in the piety they profess by falling into this particular snare. Claiming that there is no sin in the attachments they have formed, they surrender themselves to these without further scruple, and thus insuperably obstruct God's graces and communications. How can his pure love fill and kindle their hearts, as it deserves to do, while those hearts are preoccupied by vain amusements and given up to the pitiable love of a mere creature? You know how this snare threatened disaster to St Teresa: after such an example, surely you cannot be too much upon your guard. Persist, then, in detaching yourself still further, and I promise you that as your detachment increases, you will feel a greater attraction to God, to prayer and recollection, and to the practice of every kind of virtue. For, when a heart is empty, God fills it and straightway all things we do are done easily and gladly, because they are done with love, which as you know, makes all hard things easy and all bitter things sweet.

LETTER 7

The same subject

DEAR SISTER,—Let me in all sincerity disclose a fear I have on the subject of yourself. In my opinion your too frequent contacts with your many relatives and others in the world are a stumbling-block to your advancement. Be careful that in wanting to do good to others you do not do harm to yourself. Though, because of my calling, I am more compelled than you to keep these contacts with the world, I must yet confess that I find it for my soul's good to limit them as much as possible. During my stay here I have paid none but necessary visits; while, so far as I am able, I discourage calls upon myself. I speak of God, salvation and eternity to all those who come to see me, this being a rule prescribed by St Ignatius as one he himself used with consistently happy results. If they appreciate this kind of talk they will profit by it, and their visit will not have been a waste of time. If they do not appreciate it, they will stop calling, or at least call less often, leaving me more time to give to my duties as priest.

Our hope to make some progress in virtue will be in vain as long as our minds are filled with worldly talk and our hearts pre-occupied with temporal interests. Recollection is the interior life's first need. I cannot urge you too strongly to limit your contacts and to adopt St Ignatius's method in those you think you should keep.

This rule befits no one better than a nun whose vocation vows her to seclusion. Far from being astonished at it people will be edified by the faithfulness with which she conforms her behaviour to it. If, on the other hand, she is seen too often in the world, people will be scandalized; while, in these vain contacts with men, she will lose every grace that could have been hers through contact with God.

LETTER 8: TO SISTER MARIE-HENRIETTE DE BOUSMARD

Active natures

I WOULD, dear Sister, that you thoroughly understood all the harm your excessively active nature can, and inevitably will, do to yourself, until you have made it wholly subordinate to the guidance and dominance of grace. This is an example of a failing that the world mistakes for a virtue and that is none the less disastrous to the advancement of a soul upon the way of holiness. Natural bustle and activity is the enemy of self-abandonment, without which, as I have so often told you, no true perfection is possible. It hinders, spoils, or prevents every operation of grace, and substitutes, in the soul possessed by it, the impulse of its own intelligence for that of the Holy Ghost. Indeed there is no doubt that the active person's impetuous pursuit of good works originates only in a secret reserve of trust in the self and in an unthinking hardihood inclining us to believe that we are doing, or are able to do, a very great deal.

How much more modest and restrained we should be if we were for ever conscious of the undoubted truth that of ourselves we are nothing, as of ourselves we are incapable of good and relatively all-powerful in evil! If we are to be cured and are to eradicate this plague-spot that breeds imperfections and even sins, much time will be needed and many means must be adopted.

I especially recommend the following: (1) Let us become convinced, as the result of past and present experience, that such activity brings us only to impotence and wretchedness, so that in the end our distrust of our own efforts is such that we view them with a kind of horror. (2) Let us restrain untoward exterior activity by performing all our actions with neither eagerness nor precipitancy but with the mildness and the gentleness advised by St Francis de Sales. (3) Let us make this true also of our spiritual exercises, on every occasion curbing the initial eagerness that prompts us to this good work or that, and undertaking it only through God's holy Spirit and at the tranquil prompting of grace. (4) Let us, in prayer and interior dealings with God, endeavour to put away from us all sense-inspired eagerness and that imaginative human fervour found in beginners. To do so, follow the precept of St Francis de Sales, behaving in such a way that every interior act be strained and filtered through the finest mesh of the soul, and that we ourselves scarcely know we pray and perform these acts. So far from being less profitable because of this, these acts, on the other hand, permeate our soul—and our interior life generally—the more thoroughly and agreeably. (5) On occasions when we perceive, however vaguely, that some interior work is in progress, we must remain the quieter and the more peaceful and the more seemingly inactive, the stronger that impression grows: thus we shall spoil nothing by our meddling. (6) On those occasions when God allows us consolations or vivid feeling, we must at all costs avoid surrendering to them with emotional eagerness, but behave with the same discretion and restraint as a mortified man invited to a great feast. (7) Let our chief interior occupation during the day be what is known as simple interior expectancy maintained in silence and tranquillizing resignation. We are not to imagine this to be mere idleness and time-wasting futility; for, just as a poor man who waits all day at a rich man's door or at the entrance to a church, is in no way idle, but wholly taken up with his poverty, his needs and ceaseless desire for alms; so the soul in such simple waiting upon God is busily and unassumingly engaged in all the following acts: of faith in God's presence; of adoration before God whose almighty and infinite mercy it recognizes; of self-distrust and utter humility in the belief of its own incapacity; of eagerness that God should work within it; of hope, since hope and expectancy go together; of self-abandonment to Providence in everything Providence would bestow or perform. Though not all these acts be precisely defined or clearly felt, they yet exist in the depths of the heart. And there God beholds them if only in the shape of wishes and a ready will. Now, as you know, our wishes and desires, even if but half-formed, are in regard to God what speech is to mankind, he hears them far more clearly than men hear our voices; he does not need even that our desires be expressed; for, to quote the Psalmist, he understands even the disposition and inclination of our hearts from the moment when they stir and incline towards him. Such words are indeed comforting to you in your present condition interiorly.

Patient endurance of obscurity, darkness, dryness, insensibility and helplessness offers a means more effectual than any other. This sorrowful state is the particular remedy God makes use of to end merely human activity, by reducing us to simple nothingness. We shall never succeed without it; for the confused activity of our faculties can lose its confusion only in proportion as, by repeated efforts, we contrive that they function neither by, nor through, themselves, but solely through the grace and the inspiration of the Holy Ghost. It should now be plain to you how blind and unjust we are when one of the greatest of God's blessings becomes for us a source of grief and grumbling. A blessing that serves not merely to weaken human activity, but to ensure that, dying to ourselves, we live only the supernatural life of grace.

LETTER 9: TO SISTER MARIE-THÉRÈSE DE VIOMÉNIL

Excessive eagerness of good desires

DEAR SISTER,—The desire about which you ask my advice, while excellent in itself, has too much eagerness in it, I fear. If you really wish that, under its show of good, it shall work you no harm, you must make it always peaceable. As you know, the best of our desires can be mixed with human passion so that they become violent, anxious and turbulently eager. To save us from the danger of this and to purify even the holiest of our desires, God often grants our petitions only after long delay. For turbulent human desires do not deserve to be granted; only those mild, calm and peaceful desires prompted by the Holy Ghost deserve that God should hearken to them. Do all you can to live in peace and holy joy that you may be the more amenable to all good inspirations. Grace, as you know, has more easy access to tranquilly expectant souls, while anxiously troubled hearts are more subject to the promptings of evil.

LETTER 10: TO THE SAME

Haste in pious reading

I send you *Espérance chrétienne,* the book I promised you. It is a real treasure for you. Yet if you are to get all the good from it I expect, you must not plunge too eagerly into it or let yourself be led away by curiosity as to what comes next. Spend the time upon it allowed to you by the Rule; fix your attention upon what you are reading and do not think upon what follows. I recommend you strongly to assimilate the enduring and consoling truths set out in this book, not so much by mental reflection as by savouring them. Pause now and then to give these glad truths time to soak more thoroughly into your soul, and to make easier the workings of the Holy Ghost who, during these peaceful pauses and silent expectancy, will imprint these heavenly truths more deeply upon your heart. Do all this without straining your attention or too violently curbing mental speculation. Let your unforced and simple endeavour be to allow them to sink into your heart rather than into your mind.

Make special note of important chapters of which you have particular need so that you can read them again when leisure permits. In general, I strongly advise you not to burden your mind with overmuch reading or over-many exterior practices.

You had far better read little and digest that little. Your soul needs, never more than now, unity and simplicity. Your reading, then, and your actions should have as their one aim the fostering in you of the spirit of recollection. God will gradually grant you this grace, do you but yearn for it with gentle trust and humble simplicity, showing neither precipitancy nor unquiet anxiety. Beseech God often to detach you completely from everything, that, in and through Jesus Christ, you may have neither liking nor love for any save him, and that, making your heart wholly his, he shall possess it fully and unreservedly. "O God, I abandon myself to you; make me desire none but you."

LETTER 11 : TO THE SAME

Indiscreet and undisciplined zeal

It is plain to me, dear Sister, that a mistaken zeal exposes you to dangers all the more formidable because their outward appearance is so specious. A desire for our neighbour's perfection is undoubtedly excellent; the interior grief we feel at sight of his failings can be equally excellent if it originates from a pure desire to see him perfect. Yet all this can be mixed with much secret self-complacency, reliance upon our own wisdom, and severity towards our neighbour. Such a zeal, make no mistake about it, cannot come from God, but is one of the devil's illusions thoroughly harmful to both yourself and others. Yet this evil can be easily remedied, assuming you are docile and sincere enough to recognize its seriousness and to undertake its cure. The latter, which I am going to prescribe for you, has already been successful with a soul suffering from the same illusion. I can only hope that it will be no less effectual in your own case.

I advise and direct you, then, in the blessed name of Jesus Christ and his divine Mother, to think no further of practising the virtue of zeal until this ban be definitely raised. I absolve you before God, and I take upon myself the responsibility for any drawbacks that may result from the omission. Should you have any scruples, or should the devil incite you to some good work of zeal to be performed or some evil to be warded off, you shall say to God: O God, charity is the queen of virtues: I must practise zeal only when you have made me fit to do so without risk to the charity I am to show both others and myself. When I am seen to be strong enough, or rather humble enough, to exercise zeal with a deep peace in my soul and with gentle compassion and kindliness for my neighbour; when I can exercise it with benevolence and a charity that nothing can irritate and which takes offence at nothing save its own faults; with, likewise, all the patience and forbearance that shall enable me to endure the defects of others as long and as calmly as you do, O God; when I am no longer grieved or anxious or surprised at the incorrigibility of my fellows: then the ban put upon me will be raised, and I shall be able to think of glorifying you in others. Until, then, O God, I must show my zeal inwardly and in the correction of my numerous failings.

Indeed, dear Sister, when humility has dug deeply the foundation of all the virtues, I shall be the first to urge you to practise zeal again. Until then, let your thoughts be only of yourself and your sole business with yourself. Remember that God has permitted men who needed correction and punishment for this indiscreet, turbulent and bitter zeal to fall into worse faults than those which had offended them in others.

In the second place I order you never to speak of God or any holy thing except in a spirit of meekness and humility, and in a manner at once loving and gracious. In such speech be always restrained and encouraging; never bitter and harsh since this is likely to chill and rebuff those who hear you. For although your talk be only of what is in the Gospel and the best kind of books, I judge that, in the state in which you now are, that talk can take so clumsy a form that nothing but evil results from it. Did not Satan make use of words from the Holy Scriptures to tempt our Lord? Truth consists in relating things exactly. It is distorted immediately it is stated extremely or applied unsuitably. Your peevish mood is like a blackened glass which, unless you make allowance for it, prevents you from seeing things and describing them to others in their true colours. Be always on your guard against this distressing tendency; cherish thoughts and sentiments that counteract such peevishness; assure yourself and make it your delight to assure others of the infinite goodness of God and the trust we should have in him; let your behaviour give them an example of virtue that is neither stiff nor embarrassing to others; take special care never to make harsh announcements to your sisters. When you can find nothing gentle to say, keep quiet, leaving the burden of such pronouncements to others who will find it easier than you to be rightly strict, avoiding too great leniency and too great severity alike. At all times severity is as blameable as strictness is laudable: it serves only to antagonize minds instead of convincing them, and to embitter hearts instead of winning them. That true gentleness which has God's approval is as calculated to frustrate evil and forward good, as excessive harshness is to make good difficult and evil obdurate. The one builds; the other destroys.

LETTER 12
Dislike of accepting privileges ordered by superiors

TAKE particular care never to deviate from obedience on the pretext of self-mortification, remembering always the words of the Holy Ghost: "Obedience is better than sacrifice"; accept without hesitation or scruple then, those little reliefs which doctors, nurses and your superiors prescribe for you. Rather have the greater scruple in refusing them. Thus you will practise abnegation more meritorious than physical mortification, since it involves the renunciation of your ideas, as of your judgement and will.

Not a few of the devout, wedded to their own ideas, headstrong in their supposed renunciation, far from mortified in their mortifications, are driven to commit many faults through ignorance or forgetfulness of this truth. What illusion they harbour not to realize that self-love spoils and corrupts the most holy of practices! Whoever, out of love of God, shall once renounce will, judgement and ideas shall make great progress in the ways of true and lasting perfection.

Henceforth use your intelligence and your reason solely to learn what is required of you, and to do it with ready cheerfulness, utter trust in God, and complete surrender to his mercy. This trust will come to you easily as soon as your one ambition is to do his holy will. And, indeed, is there anything more delightful than this? That holy will sanctifies all that it ordains for us. Follow it then in all things, be they agreeable or exacting, privileges or privations, work or leisure, mental or spoken prayers, whether at Office or at Mass, at confession or communion. Blind obedience knows no exception, but makes warm-hearted sacrifice of its own intelligence, ideas, judgement, inclinations, dislikes, aversions, and moods—in short, of every one of its desires. It follows that this sacrifice is more pleasing to God than any other open to us and that without it all else is prejudicial rather than valuable. Accordingly, the Holy Ghost tells us in the Scriptures that victory goes to the obedient.

LETTER 13

The same subject; attachment to one's own opinions

MY DEAR SISTER,—At last you find yourself free of ties and of all those engagements with which the world would keep you bound for ever. I have no doubt that you appreciate the full value of this inestimable grace and that you are bent on a generous performance of all your duties. The longer you have waited for this grace, the more grateful you must be to him who has at last accorded it to you. Nevertheless in your life you must expect to meet with difficulties unknown to those who enter earlier. Yet humility, renunciation, simplicity and spiritual childhood will considerably lessen these difficulties and will end with making them disappear. Aided by these virtues you will avoid one of pride's insidious illusions—an illusion the more dangerous that it is almost imperceptible—into which many novices fall. To show their zeal they are for ever trying to do something out of the common, or deny themselves the little privileges allowed them by the charity of their superiors. In all this, is merely disguised vanity and subtle self-love. Never make claim, my dear Sister, to do one whit more than the rest. Accept simply and humbly the little privileges and alleviations offered to the weak;

be glad to be ranked with small children and treated like them, and avoid making yourself conspicuous by a show of strength and courage. In this is an exercise of deep and meritorious humility more pleasing in God's sight than a life whose great austerity is of your own choice. Any other line of conduct is so much pride and vanity.

To be frank with you, my long experience has taught me that those who have been most devout in the world before they enter upon the religious life are usually those who give most trouble to their superiors and mistresses; for in the world these good devout women acquire various ideas of virtue that they find hard to give up. Used to the admiration of all about them and, very frequently, to the praise of their directors, they become obsessed with their own thoughts and outlook, never suspecting that the obsession is poles removed from true holiness. Consequently, it is much more difficult to induce them to practise humility and renunciation, and to discipline their ideas and wills than to persuade the young and unformed—or even converted worldlings —to make similar sacrifices. Unless, however, we become as little children we cannot enter the kingdom of heaven. My wish, then, is that you shall be treated as young girls of fifteen and sixteen are treated, since their needs of both body and mind are the same as your own. To such, one says: Sister, you are to rest tomorrow; you are excused from this or that: enjoy yourself in the garden. . . . My dear Sister, this work is too much for you: the Mother Superior says you are to be excused it. You who are mature, and have been so devout in the past, are to do all that you are told without a question or even the flicker of an eyelid. You are to do it in a spirit of humility and simplicity, content to see yourself like the weakest and least of them all. You are to look upon yourself as precisely the latter, and are to rejoice at it or as nearly rejoice as you may; you are to admire the tender charity of the Mother and the Sisters and to bless God for it. True interior insight and genuine spirituality will teach and inspire you to this. Yet it must be confessed that there is the greatest difficulty in bringing our so-called truly devout to this frame of mind. The less they, poor blind deluded souls, can humble themselves, the farther they are from true greatness. Let them go to Bethlehem and there behold the God of heaven become a little child wrapped in swaddling clothes, set in a manger, taken up, carried here, carried there, turned this way and turned that, at the caprice of all! That, my dear Sister, is the example you should set yourself throughout your novitiate. By becoming like that little child you will be worthy of entering the kingdom of heaven.

LETTER 14: TO SISTER MARIE-THÉRÈSE DE VIOMÉNIL

Dislike of self-revelation

STRIVE, my dear Sister, with all your might against the dislike you have of talking frankly of your soul. Look upon that jealous susceptibility, which leads you to imagine that your faults will be disclosed to others, as a dangerous temptation. None other than the devil inspires this excessive fear and reluctance to disclose interior wretchedness; for, from innumerable experiences, the devil knows that souls possessing sufficient courage and humility to make simple and straightforward revelation of themselves are straightway cured or at least very greatly comforted.

He is as well aware how many of the soul's wounds, which generally heal when opened, can become poisoned and more spreading when we refuse to let the doctor see them. Indeed, there is nothing plainer than that while our self-love lives (and it will die only when we do), we shall tend to delude ourselves about those things which prick and disturb our conscience. This thought is calculated to make all of us tremble, whoever we be. There is but one method of avoiding the danger: we must never rely upon our own wisdom in things concerning ourselves, but must be guided by the keepers of our consciences to whom we are to disclose with complete frankness everything likely to enlighten them. The trouble is that in these very disclosures we are liable to let our self-love delude us, and with us those whose advice we ask. What can be done to guard against this new danger? Our directors must be enlightened by others on our account, yet this is not easily tolerated. There is no lack of people ready to show zeal on behalf of others but who thoroughly dislike zeal shown in regard to themselves. This ought not to be so. True zeal should say to itself: Think of yourself and not of others for whom you are not responsible. Yet be very glad that some charitable person has enabled your director to know how you appear to others, so that he is the better able to direct you.

This twofold attitude is found only in the most perfect of souls and possibly in a few whose dispositions are unusually sincere though their virtue may be small. Normally, zeal to instruct others is accompanied by great irritability towards those who would perform the same good office by giving full information to our directors as to what is being thought and said about ourselves. Here, once more, you have the twofold illusion of every ordinary devout person living in the world and even in the cloister. Examine yourself without self-flattery upon this double question, allowing the points I have just indicated to bring light to bear upon it.

LETTER 15: TO THE SAME

Discouragement

MY DEAR SISTER,—Just now you are the victim of one of the most dangerous temptations that can assail a well-intentioned soul—the temptation of discouragement. I adjure you to offer every resistance in your power. Trust in God, and be sure that he will complete the work he has begun in you. Your vain fears for the future come from the devil. Think only of the present; leave the future to Providence. A well-employed present assures the future. At all times and in all places strive to cleave and conform to all God's wishes even in the smallest matter; for virtue and perfection consist wholly of this.

Again, God permits our everyday faults only to humiliate us! If you can profit by them and yet remain trusting and at peace, you will be in a better state than you would if you committed no obvious fault and so flattered your self-love greatly, leaving you in grave danger of self-complacency. Actually you can very easily make use of all your faults to become one degree more humble and to dig still more deeply within yourself the one foundation of all true holiness. Ought we not to admire and bless the infinite goodness of God who can thus derive our greatest good from our very faults? All we need do is to have no love for them, and humble ourselves gently because of them; after each of our falls to pick ourselves up with tireless persistency, and to go to work peacefully to correct them. Subject yourself to God's will in the work you do, but do not be too eager and restless. Do honestly what you believe you ought to do, and rely on Providence for success, knowing neither care nor anxiety and thus possessing as far as possible a tranquil heart and unshackled mind. Be faithful in this practice and you shall dwell in peace even in the midst of perplexity; while the involuntary troubles you may encounter will serve only to increase the merit of the fundamental compliance of your will with God's. May he be blessed for all things and in all things, now and for ever.

LETTER 16: TO THE SAME

Fear of failure and of making oneself conspicuous

WHEN one begins wishing to belong earnestly and unreservedly to God, the interior workings of grace develop the growth of that holy desire which he himself has inspired. Yet the more vehement this desire becomes, the more the soul is seized and possessed by the fear of failing. This fear is a new gift of God, and, provided the soul can make use of it, it will greatly profit: it will be more humble, more self-distrustful, more watchful and more eager to ask for God's help. Yet just because it is one of God's gifts, the spirit of darkness does not fail to pursue his usual tactics: unable to obstruct the gifts of God, he brings all his cunning into play to spoil and corrupt them.

He does this in the case of the salutary fear of which I am speaking, in this instance resorting to two kinds of stratagems. First, he seeks to make this fear excessive, unbridled, restless and fretful, that the soul may grow weak and disconcerted and at last be plunged into cowardice and defeat. The one remedy for this is to laugh at the tempter and answer him: He who began the work will finish it; since in his goodness he sought me even when I fled from him, he will take care not to forsake me now that I seek him with all my heart. Again, do not forget that perseverance has no better guarantee than a good beginning. It is far easier to continue on one's way than to take another. Had one paid attention to these vain fears, conversion would never have taken place. This is the first temptation novices undergo.

A second and more perilous ruse is this: the tempter looks for accomplices and too often finds them among good people. He puts in the way of our good resolutions those who lack neither a certain amount of wisdom nor good intentions. These find fault with everything souls do when inspired by grace to lift themselves from the spiritual rut. If these counsellors—who are as eager to give advice as their listeners are reluctant to take it— are to be believed, there is no more lamentable way to make oneself conspicuous than the pursuit of perfection. We must never, they say, overdo things, nor adopt a way of living at variance with our nature, since what is violent is not lasting and, in any case, exaggeration is a fault. I have no hesitation in saying that here is to be found one of the greatest obstacles divine grace encounters in souls called to perfection. It is that human respect of the cloister which is as dangerous in its way as that of the world. The souls whose conversion from imperfection to holiness the former hinders are as numerous as those whose conversion from evil to good is prevented by the latter.

What ways are open by which these dangers can be avoided? These are they: out of love for Jesus Christ we must be courageous in subduing false human respect; we must make it a frequent sacrifice to the Lord; we must beseech him to help and strengthen us that we may disregard vain arguments levelled at us. If we set Gospel teaching by the side of the captious sophistries presented to us, we shall need no more to convince us that they cannot come from the Holy Ghost, but solely from mortal reasoning and that human prudence which God rebukes. Yet it is pious people who talk like this!—possibly; but this is merely a proof that such pious folk do not always think in terms of the Gospel's pure wisdom, but sometimes allow themselves to be deceived by prejudice, human considerations, error, blindness, ignorance and the dictates of self-love. Indeed, only ignorance or blindness can be unaware that no genuine conversions and deep interior changes can take place, either in the world or in the cloister, without being known. Why should this be true of genuine conversions? Simply because they affect exterior behaviour. Even when there is no exterior irregularity to be corrected, the perfect harmony and heavenly peace established interiorly can never fail to radiate outwardly, making themselves plain by various perceptible signs which, though they make for good, may arouse jealousy in those given to self-love. Equally, it can only be blindness which fails to understand that, at the beginning of a new life, there may be an appearance of exterior disturbance and constraint, because neither the converted nor his fellows are used to his new state. In every sphere ease of manner comes with practice.

Again, can a soul wholly given up to a pursuit of recollection, to a conflict with self and the acceptance of many constraints both interior and exterior—can such a soul be expected to appear playfully gay and pleasantly amusing? Indeed, if any do appear so I gravely doubt whether any interior change has taken place. Yet are there not, you ask, those whose intense interior life goes with much exterior graciousness? True; but only after long practice that has in a measure made interior recollection natural to them. At the outset they were as you are, my dear Sister; and what is said of you was said of them. They have said nothing, but have gone their way, till God has at last brought them to that spiritual state known as the freedom of God's children. You will reach it just as they, have no doubt about that. A day will come when your recollection will be free and unforced, mild and pleasingly gentle. Then you too will make others approve of and rejoice in you because of the exterior peace which the full love of God and your neighbour make abundantly manifest in you. Yet you cannot attain this either quickly or at once. For it comes of virtue assiduously practised and of an interior life which, at the beginning, must needs seem somewhat forced and difficult. All this will come naturally in the end, however. Once you have attained this, you can resume your gaiety of manner and unreservedness, since both will then be changed and made spiritual by the blessed workings of grace, whereas at an earlier stage these would certainly do harm.

Note the ignorance of these clever pundits! Both their talk and their judgement arouse my pity; for their arguments are precisely those heard in the world, when God's grace has effected in it one of those true conversions which are plain to all. Can nuns indulge in such talk? Only the demon of error and illusion can make them speak and reason so wrongly. Blessed be God in all things. In one way or another he will derive glory. On your part, be your one thought to endure this ordeal bravely, going for help to those lessons of faith and Gospel teachings of which such fine reasoners seem to have lost sight. Be glad interiorly of the seeming foolishness and stupidity that expose you to their railings: there is no surer sign of the change which has been effected in you. Cry to the Lord like the Psalmist: "I am become as a beast of burden before you: no one will be able to separate me from you any more."

In the service of so great a Master can every rank be equally exalted? Perform gladheartedly and to the best of your ability the rôle of awkwardness and stupidity which at present he has given you to play, and patiently await the moment which is ordained to bring a change the reverse of that which has just been effected in you. Then shall your faculties, which now seem shackled, have free play; ease shall succeed constraint and the blessed liberty of God's children shall drive out excessive fear.

A perception of the faultiness of all your works is a great grace of God. By means of it he wishes to keep you in humility and give you a poor opinion of yourself. Yet the overharshness with which you are tempted to regard yourself, when you do perceive this, and the melancholy, despondency and thought of reprobation that afflict you are merely the suggestions of Satan designed to corrupt and poison God's gift in you. Reject all such thoughts, then, as coming from the devil. For a time they will return to you again and again, providing matter for your struggles, your triumphs and your merits. Yet have a little patience: perfection cannot be achieved in a day. Do not at first yearn for perfection at its highest; for in this you are asking to fly before you have wings, to quote St Teresa. Be content with what God gives you and with what he performs in the meanwhile, asking no more until he shall deem fit to grant it you. You will then avoid that interior agitation which enables the devil to succeed so thoroughly in overthrowing those souls who in the practice of virtue seek less the glory of God than the satisfaction of self-love. The raging of mortified pride is plain to be seen in the impatience with which they perceive their imperfections, and in the vexation with which they perceive themselves at the bottom of the ladder of holiness when they would prefer to think of themselves as at its top.

Be guided by me, my Sister, and let your line of conduct be precisely the reverse. Cherish your abjection, permitting God to perform peacefully his work within you. Allow him to lay the enduring foundations of humility and to cement them with repeated experiences of your wretchedness and your weakness. There would be too great a risk of *our being absorbed by our own vain notions* were God to give us from the outset all the perfection we desire. Undisciplined love of our own excellence would find us soaring, quickly to fall once more, like Lucifer, into the abyss of pride. God, who knows our frailty in this respect, allows us to grovel like worms in the mire of our imperfections, until he sees that we can be lifted up and feel neither self-complacent nor scornful of others. This design of God's, full of wisdom and of goodness as it is, is the admiration of those who direct souls. Their grief is great when souls that undergo these merciful ordeals refuse to understand them, showing exasperation when the ineffable ways of divine Providence are explained to them.

BOOK IV

FIRST ORDEAL OF SOULS CALLED TO THE STATE OF SELF-ABANDONMENT —ARIDITY, HELPLESSNESS, AVERSION

LETTER I[1]

Ordeals as a whole—General instruction

GOD, my dear Sister, has granted the prayer you made to him when you wrote to me. For, reading your letter, I seemed to be reading your soul and to be getting to know it interiorly, much as if I had confessed and directed you for a long time past. Oh! What a lot of consoling and instructive things I have to say to you! I hope that the Holy Ghost will make you understand and appreciate them, and that God will deign to give you his holy benediction because of them, through the merits of Jesus Christ, the intercession of his blessed Mother, of St Joseph, of St Francis de Sales and all his blessed daughters, your sisters, who are in heaven.

1. Your vocation appears to me to have received God's seal. There are in it plain signs of his holy will, proofs of his completely gratuitous predilection for your soul, and firm assurances of your eternal salvation: Rejoice; bless God; thank him unceasingly for his great and precious grace.

2. The inclination God gives you to surrender yourself wholly to him and to live, despite the mind's vagaries and the rebellion of the flesh, a wholly interior life, is a grace whose value I wish that God would make known to you as he has made it known to me. It is so much the more real in being so little discoverable by the senses and so well hidden beneath the unlikeliest of guises.

3. Why then, in spite of this inclination and all your pious

[1] There is reason to believe that the letter was addressed by Fr de Caussade to Sister Marie-Thérèse de Vioménil, who, to increase her director's knowledge of her, had sent him an account of her vocation and her interior states subsequent to her adoption of the religious life.

reading, are you able to get no farther than the threshold of the interior life? I see plainly that this is the reason, my dear Sister: you have frustrated this inclination by unrestrained desires, by over-eagerness and human activities which are displeasing to God and obstructive to the gentle workings of grace. Further, the reason is that in your behaviour is a secret and scarcely perceptible presumption that causes you to put too high a value on your own work and efforts. God wished to humiliate and confound you through your own experiences, and so curb that human fervour which removes you from the influence of grace. Without taking much account of it, you acted as if you claimed to do all the work yourself and even to do more than God wished. You who would have considered worldly ambition a great fault have no scruples in allowing yourself to be led astray by a more insidious ambition and a longing for your own exaltation in the ways of the spirit. Yet be comforted: thanks to the merciful sternness God has shown towards you so far, there is nothing lost. In fact, you have gained a great deal. With the tenderness of a loving father, God punishes you for these imperfections and offers you the remedy for your ill in the very punishment he awards you. To chastise you for your unfaithfulness, he makes use of the ordeals he employs for the purification and detachment of those chosen souls whom he calls to pure love and divine union.

4. Try to understand this fatherly attitude God adopts towards you, keep your trials in perspective: then all your fears will vanish of themselves. For instance, you will not be surprised that your aridity and your interior troubles have increased since you began the religious life. I certainly am not astonished; in fact, I should have been much grieved on your behalf had it been otherwise. For only since you made that beginning have you belonged more completely to God. Accordingly, your divine Spouse has worked more vigorously for your soul's purification that it may be the more ready for perfect union with him.

I agree with you that your many distractions are the result of the natural liveliness of your imagination and more especially of your former bad habits. Yet God has permitted this only to humiliate and confound you still further; while the keen grief it excites in you is by no means the least meritorious aspect of the ordeal. I am not, you see, at one with you in believing that this evil is incurable and that it springs from some secret sins.

The fears these distractions cause you at prayer time are temptations or mere fancies: God confers a great grace on you when he gives you courage to ignore them and to draw near to him trustfully in spite of these false fears.

5. I believe that your antipathy to exterior things and for the tasks you do is but one more aspect of your ordeal—an aspect well pleasing to God if only you master this antipathy instead of allowing it to master you.

Your rejection of such antipathy, and your acts of sacrifice and self-abandonment, are both good and sound. Recurrence of interior rebellion which tortures you afresh can only make them the more worth while. This is one more aspect of the ordeal.

6. The further details you give of your helplessness and apparent idleness in prayer are a sequel to the ordeal and follow naturally on what has gone before. Anything else would have greatly astonished me. Yet do not be anxious, my dear Sister; you are far from wasting time in prayer. Doubtless you could pray more tranquilly, and will do so when it pleases God. Yet your prayers will never be more availing or of more worth: for the prayer of suffering and of self-obliteration is the hardest of all and purifies the soul proportionately, causing it to die the sooner to self and to live thereafter only in God and for God.

I rejoice in those prayers in which you stand before God like a beast of the field, lost to everything and bowed down by the burdens of every kind of temptation. Nothing can better serve to humiliate, confound or prostrate a soul in God's presence. This is what God wants, and it is the purpose of all these afflictions. If only you can keep yourself respectfully and submissively in that state, so utterly surrendering yourself to the divine will that out of love for him you can delight in your abjection and your self-obliteration, your passive silence will be far more pleasing to God than the most energetic of formal acts.

This whole-hearted surrender of a broken and prostrate heart is the sacrifice of all sacrifices which God most gladly accepts.

The smoke of such a holocaust has indeed a pleasant smell. The sweetest and most fervent of prayers, the harshest of voluntary mortifications, can no more be compared with it than they can approach it.

7. Your fears relating to confession and communion provide still another aspect of your ordeal. They are but temptations and vain fancies that you must scorn and reject. If, despite your resistance, they continue to vex you, ignore them, cultivating patience in this matter as in all the rest.

Your longing to escape from this disturbed state is less a consequence of the ordeal than a prompting of your self-love and nature. These clamorously rebel when they see themselves on the brink of pitiless immolation. You must be neither astonished nor afraid because of this, but must of your free will fight these surrendered desires with courage, resolute in your constancy to wish for nothing but the performance of God's will in all things. The importance of this cannot be exaggerated both as regards getting all the profit possible from the ordeal and even more in lessening its bitterness and shortening its length. I am inclined to put down the fact that it has seemed long to you, to your insufficient courage in making the full sacrifice God asks of you. Make it, then, without delay, saying to him: O God, I accept all things, wholly and unreservedly submitting myself for as long as it shall please you.

You will conclude from all I have just been saying that the one thing you need to do is to let God do with you as he wills, yourself remaining in peace and interior tranquillity as long as you are able, but without straining.

At the moment, then, your sole need is self-abandonment. This is what you must do to attain it:

1. In praying you must be resigned to suffer the grievous torment and crucifixion which is God's pleasure. When distractions, dryness, temptations and aversions assail you, you must say: Divine crosses, I am glad of you! I await you with a submissive heart; cause me such suffering that my self-love may be thereby crucified and obliterated. Thereupon you are to stand before God like a beast of burden weighed down by its load almost to the point of collapse, yet hoping for the help and assist-

ance of the Master. Cast yourself in spirit before the cross of Jesus Christ, kissing his sacred wounds respectfully and lying humbly at his divine feet. Be content steadily and resolutely to remain there, your passive expectancy and peaceful silence resembling those of a poor wretch who for hours at a time waits for alms upon the threshold of a great king or a generous rich man. Yet, in prayer or whatever else it be, see to it that you do not force yourself to be more recollected than God wills.

2. Avoid violence, then, in your efforts to extend recollection throughout the day and to shun the distractions which beset you. Be content to know that this state of distraction displeases you and that your longing is for greater recollection, when, and to the extent that—and only to the extent that—it shall be God's pleasure.

3. Do not be disheartened even though such distractions are sometimes so many, and though such aridity, troubles, fears and other like grievous states become so overwhelming that you cannot perform a single interior act nor conceive so much as one good thought. If, thus beset, you can hold fast to that simple interior silence of respect, submission and adoration already mentioned, and can plunge into the abyss of your nothingness, then you have nothing to fear, or rather you have much to gain. This nothingness, accepted gladly out of love of God, will be your sure refuge from these tempests. In that refuge you must remain and be content to see all God's wishes performed in you. Let it be your delight to imagine him as raining distractions, dryness, fears, agonies and every kind of wretchedness and humiliation from heaven into your soul, so that you become the sport, so to say, of his will and divine love in the way that one sometimes sees great princes amusing themselves by spattering their favourites with mud in fun.

4. Take care that you never omit any of the sacraments. Yet, you ask me, how are you to prepare for confession or for communion when fears and troubles of every kind beset you—you must ignore and disdain them, and, without discussion or argument either for or against, go always to God. When sweetly and effortlessly you have done the little you are able to do, be at peace in the great interior silence of faith and respect, of sub-

mission and trust, of love and adoration. Using no words, repeat often: May my sovereign Lord and Master do with me as he will. Amen. Amen!

5. Remain tranquil and in peace, since in all you tell me there is no voluntary sin as you seem to imagine. I am not referring to the lower part of your soul, troubled as it is, but to the higher which can, with God's help, keep peacefully still in the midst of these storms and tempests. Your agitation, it may be said, is not in the soul but in the senses, that they may be crucified and destroyed, as they need to be before you can attain to pure love and union with God. Your one task is to prevent such agitation from touching your interiorly. It is in this that up till now you have shown lack of both perception and faithfulness.

6. Indeed, while I find no trace of deliberate sin in your behaviour, I do find a multitude of faults and imperfections which will do you much harm unless you attempt a drastic cure. These include anxieties, vain fears, dejection, weariness and discouragement that are half deliberate, or at least not sufficiently resisted, and that constantly disturb in you that interior peace upon the need for which I have just been insisting. What are you to do to prevent them? First, never cling to them voluntarily; secondly, neither endure nor resist them with violent effort, since that merely strengthens them. Allow them to drop as a stone drops into water; think of other things; as St Francis de Sales says, talk to God of other things; take shelter in your refuge—the interior silence of respect and submission, of trust and complete self-abandonment.

How am I to behave, you may ask, if, whether in this connection or in others, I commit faults—even voluntary faults? On such occasions you must recollect the counsel of St Francis de Sales: neither be troubled that you are troubled, nor be anxious that you are anxious, nor be disturbed that you are disturbed, but turn naturally to God in sweet and peaceful humility, going so far as to thank him that he has not allowed you to commit still greater faults. Such sweet and peaceful humility, joined to trust in divine goodness, will calm and pacify you interiorly, and this is your greatest spiritual need at present.

I forgot to say that your intense longings for divine love,

whatever your subsequent feelings, are not at all mere imagination and fantasy; they are on the contrary very real, solid and excellent. You must cherish them, yet do so with sweet tranquillity, at no time yielding to those fervours, those imaginative raptures and that human activity which spoil everything.

You should not be surprised if at one moment you feel kindled with those fervent desires and at the next long to return to self. Let me explain by an illustration what then happens in you: When you throw on the fire a dry piece of wood for kindling, the flames catch it first of all and then burn it gently and quietly; but if the wood is still green, the flames envelop it for a moment merely, then the heat of the fire coming into contact with the moist green inner wood makes it sweat and hiss, moves and twists it noisily this way and that, until as a result the wood is dry and in a fit state to kindle. Then the flames again envelop it, set it alight and silently and effortlessly consume it. There you have a parable of the action and operation of the divine love upon souls which are yet full of imperfections and self-love's evil inclinations. These must be purged, purified and refined— which cannot be done without causing them vexation and suffering.

Liken yourself, then, to that green wood upon which the divine love acts before it is able to kindle and consume it. Or again to a statue in the hands of a sculptor who shapes and fashions it with hammer and chisel to make it fit to be set in a noble building. Had that stone feeling, and in the course of its suffering cried out to you: Sister, what shall I do? I am in such pain! your answer doubtless would be: Nothing, except rest and be still beneath the workman's hand, leaving the work to him. Without him you will remain for ever a senseless and unshaped block of stone.

Let your own motto be: Have patience, and let God do the work. For, when all is said, you can do no other. Yours is merely to say: I adore and resign myself; *fiat!*

LETTER 2: TO SISTER MARIE-THÉRÈSE DE VIOMÉNIL

Interior vicissitudes

NANCY, 1734

MY DEAR SISTER,—The various states which you have described to me in your letter are merely the interior vicissitudes to which we are all liable. The alternation of light and darkness, of consolations and desolations, are as useful—are as indispensable, I would say—in the growing and the ripening of virtues in our souls as changes in the weather if crops are to grow and ripen in our fields. Learn, then, to resign yourself to them, and to accept ordeals no less lovingly than consolations. For even the most sorrowful of these ordeals, whether they come from God's justice or his mercy, are equally just, blessed, adorable, lovable and beneficial. Often his justice and mercy join in sending them; but on this earth the operation of his justice is never wholly divided from his mercy. I am delighted that a perception of your wretchedness and your weaknesses and a consciousness of your nothingness are your normal preoccupation during prayer. It is thus that you gradually acquire complete distrust of self and utter trust in God. Thus, too, you are firmly established in that interior humility which is the enduring foundation of the spiritual edifice and the chief source of God's graces to the soul.

You must be neither surprised nor grieved at the destruction your self-love fears: if it were free of this fear it would not be self-love. Only souls already greatly detached from self long for this utter death and, far from fearing it, desire and demand it unceasingly of God. In your case you will have done enough if you endure patiently and peacefully the various stages which bring it about.

It often happens that during the day one is aware of inclinations towards God or divine things, and yet this inclination is lacking at prayers. God ordains this to teach us that he is the absolute master of his gifts and his graces, and that he awards them to whom he pleases and when he pleases. Receiving these when we expect them least, and later finding ourselves disappointed in our expectancy, we can no longer argue that they are the reward of our spiritual state, or of the work we do. This is as God designs. For though he be lavish of his gifts, he claims to reserve all their glory to himself; while he would be obliged to take them back from us, did he see us appropriate any of that glory by being vainly self-complacent.

LETTER 3: TO MADEMOISELLE DE SERRE, LATER SŒUR CATHERINE-ANGÉLIQUE

The same subject—Self-abandonment

BE steadfast, my dear daughter, in the midst of your interior upheaval, never letting go of your utter self-abandonment to God or of your trust in his goodness. Let these two obvious and unalterable principles be your strength: first, God can never forsake those who abandon themselves altogether to him and who trust themselves utterly to his infinite mercy; secondly, nothing happens in this world that is not dictated by a Providence that turns all things to the advantage and exceeding profit of resigned and submissive souls. Provided you are faithful, contrary thoughts and interior conflicts serve only to strengthen consoling truths in your mind and to plant more deeply in your heart feelings that tend to your sanctification. It is undoubtedly beyond your power to reach perfection in the state to which God calls you: to attain it, therefore, you must not merely rely little upon the self but you must distrust that self utterly. You must put your hope in none but God, depending solely upon the help and strength of his interior grace that both now and in the past has enabled so many others weaker than yourself to do what seems so difficult to you. You must, then, say to yourself repeatedly: I can no more do these things, my wretchedness and my weakness being what they are, than I can fly like a bird. Yet, with the all-powerful grace of Jesus Christ, man's impossibility becomes possible and easy of achievement: I hope for that grace from his goodness and infinite merits. In this spirit numerous young, weak and timid people, in imitation and for love of their crucified Lord, have triumphed over the cruelty of tyrants, have suffered and defied the worst outrages and the most savage of tortures.

The weariness, aversion and aridity frequently experienced by you are the usual vicissitudes through which souls seeking God are wont to pass. We should have small merit and little ability to show God our fidelity, if interior grace took charge of us and gave us throughout consolations that we could feel. The one thing needed is to be faithful in every duty and every interior and exterior experience known to our spiritual state, in dryness and aversions no less than in delights and sensible consolations. The merit is only the greater if at such times everything has to be done with effort and extreme repugnance. Only thus can our love of God be wholly rid of that miserable self-love which, to quote St Francis de Sales, by its intrusive meddling, spoils everything.

In prayer there can be a gentle and pleasurable peace. But that peace can be also bitter and barren and even sorrowful. God can effect more in our soul by the latter than by the former, liable as it is to the activities of self-love. Thus, self-abandonment is necessary in this matter as in all others. Leave him to act; he knows our need better than we. We have but one thing to fear: lest we voluntarily allow ourselves to go astray. To avoid the risk of this we have only to wish exactly what God wills at every hour, at every moment, and in every happening of the day. The surest, swiftest, and, I venture to say, the sole way of perfection lies in that. Everything else is liable to illusion, pride and self-love.

To conclude: gently and without too much effort learn to refrain from those lengthy reasonings with which your mind is busied during prayer, and incline rather to loving aspirations, to simple rest and delight in God. This, however, need not prevent you from dwelling for a little time on good thoughts when their nature is sweet, simple and peaceful, and when they seem to be spontaneous.

LETTER 4: TO A POSTULANT[1]

Darkness—Helplessness

MY DEAR SISTER,—Everything you have written in your letter seems to me so easy to deal with that God must be keeping you in very great darkness if you have not been able to grapple with it for yourself with the help of his grace. You yourself say that from time to time God gives you rays of light that dispel both your interior darkness and your doubts. Your heart responds to this light which brings it peace and the will to serve God courageously. As such light can come only from heaven you may follow it without fear; while the recollection you keep of it must suffice to guide and strengthen you in times of obscurity. Yet, as God has prompted you to apply to me, it is no difficult task to answer you, point by point.

1. You say that the snares and subtleties of self-love put true discernment out of your reach. But why seek it? Holy obedience surely provides you with an oracle that never fails; while humility and docility offer firm guarantees that you will not go astray in acting on that oracle's decisions.

2. When, in childlike simplicity, you have just consulted your superior or your mistress, live assured and in peace. Failing to live so, you will be much to be pitied, though only you are to blame.

3. To be keenly aware of your weakness yet to have no perceptible support and to see yourself for ever on the brink of a precipice is a truly humiliating ordeal, and yet a salutary one since it leads you inevitably to complete self-distrust and perfect trust in God. By no other road can you leave the kingdom of the senses and enter upon the wholly spiritual life of pure faith and pure love.

4. The dark dungeon in which you find yourself confined is the prison into which from time to time you are thrown by

---

[1] This postulant was Mme de Lesen, with reference to whom Mother Marie-Anne-Thérèse de Rosen had consulted Fr de Caussade and whom she had promised to put into direct touch with him. She entered the convent of the Annonciades at Saint-Mihiel.

God's mercy—I will not say his justice—that there you may be purified like gold in a crucible. Your one need is to remain in as quiet a tranquillity as possible. How, you ask, are you to practise virtue? The one virtue at such times is to endure, suffering in silence and self-abandonment and making humble and loving submission.

You have long since encountered that noble saying: Not to do but to endure serves a soul's advancement best. But, you argue, I sin in such a state. No, the governor of that prison will keep you from all sin.—But then I seem to view hell itself without concern!—That is a strong expression, but thanks be to God I understand its significance better than you do. It merely expresses the result of the interior operation by which God is subduing your sensibility. Be of good courage! A day will come, and that may be soon, when you will see the good work achieved in this gloomy prison; just now you must live in the hope of it, with no other light than that of faith.

5. In your state of interior fever there are doubtless paroxysms that seem to destroy you. Actually only the impure and earthly elements in the soul are so destroyed, much as the various poisons in the body are destroyed during the crisis of certain fevers. This is a sign of recovery and not of sickness. Then it will not be in my power, you ask, either to pray or to turn to God? It is true enough that you cannot do so outwardly; yet in its secret desires seen only by God the heart is constantly at prayer.

The end of your letter almost made me laugh. You said that I could guess from what you had written how poorly you had carried out your obligations—saying your Office, going to Mass and so forth. I will very willingly be responsible, my dear Sister, for all the wrong you do in such circumstances if you will concede me all the good God will work in you in the meantime. Even so your remark has given me the clue to a particular temptation which the evil spirit in his subtlety is seeking to slip into your soul.

We will, however, get back to your letter and continue my answers in sequence. It occurs to you, you say, that you have been foolhardy in taking a vow to become a nun, and that the practices of religion are too much for your strength. Had I not a long experience of the rapid progress made by the most obvious temptations when a pretence of investigating them gives them the smallest opening, I would never have believed you capable of so crude a lapse. To be brief, I have to tell you:

(1) From start to finish of your letter I have felt that the devil has rung all his changes on your soul in order to make this temptation succeed. All hell will triumph in his victory if he can bring about your fall.

(2) In God's name, and with all the authority he gives me over you, I forbid you either to listen to or to ponder upon anything further in this matter. With regard to it you are to do what you would if suddenly the devil prompted you to throw yourself into a well or to poison all your nuns.

(3) God wants you in the religious life: your entrance must and shall take place though all hell be unchained to obstruct it—what, you ask, of physical weakness and mental difficulties? —As for those, God will work miracles if it be necessary; and you must wait for them to happen if the need arise. Humiliate yourself, my dear Sister; make yourself naught in God's sight; confess to him that you are frailty and inconstancy itself. May this experience serve in the end to make you aware how, if God does not lend us his persistent support, we must distrust ourselves, our pretended courage and the seeming steadfastness of our resolutions. How inexpressibly poor, weak and miserable we are! How liable to fall into every imaginable hole and undreamed of error!

6. The sensitiveness of your heart and your mind to correction given you when your troubles are greatest, though it humiliate, must not discourage you. For it is true that on these occasions such sensitiveness can sometimes be so extreme that St Teresa herself was forced to guard against allowing a sulky peevishness towards her Sisters to appear in her. It would take too long to tell you of the great benefit God confers upon our souls by this sensitiveness and rebelliousness when they are disciplined by patience.

7. God makes you see clearly that you are beset by the snares of Satan, while at the same time his invisible hand upholds and saves you: surely you should find encouragement in this. Be

steadfast: all this will bring you great good in the end. In particular it will help to impress you vividly with your weakness, which you have never really seen in its true light. Everyone of these temptations and ordeals will be needed to convince you of it, and to uproot once and for all your vain trust in yourself. This is an evil not fully understood until its cure is begun.

I will end this letter by telling you that your state is truly crucifying, and for that very reason sound, desirable, purifying and sanctifying. You need fear no danger as long as you act on that fine saying of Fénelon's: Despond so utterly of yourself that not one whit of hope or reliance remains to you apart from that which you have in God—in God who, when it pleases him, can raise up sons to Abraham from the very stones.

LETTER 5: TO SISTER MARIE-HENRIETTE DE BOUSMARD
(1734)

Helplessness—Distractions

1. Be not wistful, my dear Sister, for the inclinations and the conscious delights God has given you and has now withdrawn from you. Many imperfections were present in the consolations you experienced in that spiritual state.

It is true that while these consolations were perceptible, they greatly gratified your nature whose desire is to see, recognize and experience them without intermission. Yet the nearer this state is to the human, the farther it is from satisfying the needs of divine love. Accordingly God is the quicker to withdraw them from a soul whom he sees to be faithful to grace. Were he not, in this respect, to practise a father's sternness towards us, we should always remain weak, liable to every kind of fault, and unable to protect ourselves against self-love's seductions and illusions.

The soul that ordeals have not enlightened and made free allows itself to drift, almost unaware, into new recourse to self. It builds its contentment and peace upon that least dependable of all things—its feelings. If it clings to God, it does so not for himself solely but much more for the consolations it expects of him. It cherishes a futile self-esteem based upon the spiritual riches it believes itself to possess, while only God can save it from falling into something like an idolatry of its imagined excellence. Even though it stop short of this last sinful extreme, it is to be only too greatly feared that, full of itself, it will remain empty of God.

God sends souls whom he loves with a love of predilection every kind of ordeal rather than expose them to so grave a disaster; he smites, humiliates and obliterates them in their own eyes. Yet how abundantly he compensates those who remain faithful to him in their ordeal for the hardships it brings them. When as a result of a complete change in your spiritual fortunes you see yourself reduced to nothingness, you find yourself suddenly stripped of vanity, presumption and every scrap of self-esteem, and possessed of humility, trust in God and love for him. Moreover, your love is now altogether pure, since self-love's last perceptible prop has been taken from it with the result that it has nothing to cling to or corrupt. Thus I find your present state of poverty of more worth than your former fine experiences which, while they seemed so wholly pure to you, provided only so much secret and delightful food for your self-love.

2. At times it seems as if faith, hope, charity, religion, every virtue and all knowledge of God had departed from us. This happens when it pleases him to rob these virtues of their perceptible savour and delight that their essence may remain and the soul go forward in pure faith. Only then do we serve God in spirit and in truth, to quote Jesus Christ's words to the Samaritan woman. This state, which has little reference to the senses, is more precious, more exalted, more refined and more lasting than any deriving from them. In it the pure delights of the spirit can be appreciated. But it is reached only by a renunciation of sensual and earthly pleasures. Various stages must gradually be passed before the region of pure light is gained at last. Nevertheless, peace is always to be found in this state, since the soul is now established in God. It begets the feelings that are now your own; I mean a consciousness of hidden and secret strength that comes of the near presence of God. This strength, invisible as it is, leaves a soul more resolute than it was when it believed itself

equal to martyrdom. Hold fast, therefore, to your peace and bless God.

3. As for the various acts of offering and resignation, most certainly beginners must by their repetition make a habit of them. Yet in your present state it is your heart that does—and must do—not merely these but more than these, however little you may be aware of it. For God most surely sees all the most secret of your intentions without need on your part to reveal them in express and formal acts. When, in the midst of your good works, there slips into your heart some secret intention of self-love, pride or human respect, you would never think of making formal acts of such desires; on the contrary we like to hide these perverse intentions even from ourselves, knowing that God sees them and will punish them. We can surely not imagine, then, that he fails to see our secret good intentions, or believe that his rewards are less liberal than his punishments are severe.

4. The fact that your thoughts wander is in your case only one more of God's ordeals, providing an opportunity for suffering and humiliation, an exercise in patience and an evidence of merit; while the grief that it occasions you is proof of the desire you have to be for ever concerned with God. Now, God sees this desire and in his sight desires whether good or bad are the equivalent of acts. Suffer, then, humbly and patiently, all these mental distractions, and take good care not to be worried about them or to investigate anxiously the source from which they come. Such investigation, arising merely from the curiosity of self-love, God would punish by sending you even greater spiritual darkness. Remember what St Teresa said on this subject: "Let the mill-clapper make what noise it will, so only the mill grinds the corn." She compares the mind's wandering attention to the mill-clapper and the inclination towards God to the mill that grinds the corn. It is for this fixing of the will on God that we must always long. What do you imagine takes place in a thoroughly worldly woman's mind while she is listening to a fine sermon? Numerous uplifting reflections pass through her mind and her imagination while her will and her heart are concerned only with the object of her passion. She is surely not the holier for this? With you the exact opposite happens. Why then be

grieved? Again: what is the meaning of this peace and tranquillity of the soul amid these assaults, these troubles and these torments, and of the little need it feels to consult others concerning them? Plainly the one explanation is that they are a notable gift of God—a clear evidence that it is he who thus subtly afflicts the heart. Be at peace, then, in your tranquil self-abandonment to God, nor bother to learn how to translate it into acts. These will be done by the secret and invisible stirrings of your heart that God touches interiorly and moves according to his pleasure.

5. The exhaustion and sense of emptiness you feel in longing to increase and in attempting to repeat your interior acts do not surprise me. These come of withstanding God's work and acting alone as if you wished to forestall grace and perform more than God wishes. This is merely human activity. Be content to withdraw peacefully into your soul, staying there as if in a prison in which it pleases God to keep you captive, and making no further attempts to escape. That holy and profitable idleness spoken of by the saints is thus acquired, and those vast tasks accomplished which need no work for their accomplishment. It is only self-love that grows weary and despondent in doing nothing, seeing nothing and understanding nothing. Yet let self-love grumble to its heart's content. Its very weariness and despondency will rid us of it in the end. By cutting it short of food, we shall make it die of hunger—a death to be desired indeed! With all my heart I long for it in your case as I long for it in mine.

6. Your method of drawing near to God by dwelling on faith alone without recourse to pictures, statues and other symbols of whatever kind, and by setting aside all to do with the self is the purest and most perfect method of approaching God. For this is the true and wholly interior prayer of the heart; the communion of spirit with spirit. Moreover, to quote the Blessed Mother de Chantal, the more simple and unforced, the more imperceptible and unfelt such prayers are, the more sublime and lasting and the more intense and efficacious they become.

The Practice of Self-abandonment

LETTER 6: TO SISTER MARIE-ANTOINETTE DE MAHUET

The same subject—Interior rebelliousness—Spiritual poverty

ALBI, 1732

MY DEAR SISTER,—1. One of the commonest experiences known to souls who have not yet had much experience in the interior ways is the fear you have told me of: I refer to the fear of wasting time in the prayer that is a simple dwelling in the presence of God. Such souls can easily be reassured, and so can you. All you need do is to remember the divine Master's precept: The tree is known by its fruits. What produces only good effects, can be nothing else but good. Now, your own experience tells you that since you have adopted this manner of prayer, you have greatly benefited interiorly. You have, then, but to thank God for the favour he has done you in substituting, as he has, the peaceful action of his grace for the feverishness of your human activity.

I wish that you were in the habit of estimating your spiritual progress and interior state generally by the one infallible standard of faith and Gospel teaching. When you perceive that your ways, your thought and your behaviour are in harmony with the teachings of faith and the practices of the saints, you can consider them good and perfectly sound. It is then impossible to fall into the illusion accompanying judgement based on the self and on impressions received through the senses, questionable as these always are. To regulate your conduct by such impressions is to make a compass of a weathercock that veers with every wind.

You can only steer through life in safety as long as you are guided by the sure and infallible rule of faith which leads to the discomfiture of sin, to love of self-forgetfulness, to entire submission to the will of God, to self-abnegation and to mortification—to interior mortification more particularly. The prayer which most effectually results in these is obviously the best.

2. As spiritual books dealing with prayer can fall into the hands of all sorts of men, and so run the risk of being misunderstood, the authors, like preachers, do wisely to make a general

appeal and to lay down rules universal enough to minimize the scope of illusion. Directors, on the other hand, who have to do with people they know, make a very different use of such books, and by their direction reassure those who have been unreasonably frightened by either reading or preaching. Because of my knowledge of your spiritual state and of God's purposes in regard to you I am unhesitatingly able to reassure you. Go on without a shadow of fear. Only if you have followed God's inclinations can you know the fruits of his blessing. The deceits and the illusions of the spirit of darkness are known by fruits the reverse of those of grace. Whenever I see that you are subject to these illusions I shall not fail to let you know. Should I not be available, others will do you a like service, always provided that you persist in showing candour and sincerity.

3. You must likewise apply the rule of faith in estimating that stupidity of which you have been conscious for some time past. If it is merely a question of being dull and stupid and even insensible to all worldly matters, faith teaches us that this stupidity is true wisdom. Yet though this same stupidity should sometimes extend to things involving salvation, this is not proof that it arises from your estrangement from God. Provided that it does not prevent you from carrying out your duties, keeping your rules and performing your pious exercises, you ought to look upon it as one of God's ordeals that you must undergo in common with all the saints. Be faithful; for in the acceptance of this seeming stupidity you will find a praiseworthy opportunity for patience, submission and interior humility. The only harm it can do is to self-love, which this stupidity slowly undermines and obliterates far more effectually than any exterior mortification.

4. When we have some great sacrifice to make, self-love and the natural man are revolted by it, exciting the heart to a rebelliousness that threatens to overwhelm us interiorly. Was not Jesus Christ himself willing to experience this on the Mount of Olives? At such times, it is enough if the interior soul be steadfast, saying like Jesus Christ: *Fiat voluntas tua.* Hence come those interior conflicts spoken of by St Paul and all the masters of the spiritual life after him; hence the truly upright man's ability to

live the life of faith and to escape the dominion of the senses; and hence those great victories that in this world are rewarded with peace and the conquest of the lower part of the soul; in the next, by the possession of God.

5. The last and most efficacious of all the remedies I have to offer you is complete surrender of the self into the hands of that God of goodness who for so long past has consistently forestalled you with the blessing of his great mercy. You must plunge into that self-surrender with the courage with which you would plunge into the sea did you know that God demanded that sacrifice of you: just as that holy martyr did of old who, through interior inclination and particular inspiration, was led to throw herself into the midst of the flames without waiting for the executioners to do their work. Such courage and holy self-abandonment, based on faith and love, charm the heart of God, and establish the soul in a peace that nothing can shake.

6. Your behaviour in avoiding unnecessary visits, distractions and waste of time generally, seems to be excellent. Be sure that exterior solitude buttresses interior solitude which, without it, is attained only with difficulty. I advise you to supplement it, so far as the household is concerned, with the greatest degree of silence possible: never speak without cause or from other than holy motives: as, for example, for the sake of reasonable recreation, when you need to relax, or for the sake of charity and religious kindliness, and of overcoming any antipathy you may feel for this person or that. In conclusion, let me remind you of a maxim I would like to imprint on the heart of every living man, and more especially on the hearts of the devout and the religious minded who are grievously concerned to see themselves poor and wretched and stripped of everything (as they say with sighs and groans). This single maxim could make them peacefully content and truly rich in their spiritual poverty. You have already guessed that it is this: True perfection, and therefore true riches of the soul, lies in making our will conform to God's. Consequently, whenever weighed down by any consciousness of my weaknesses and interior wretchedness, I feel that though by God's grace I have avoided giving him deliberate offence, I am poor in the gifts and graces in which the saints were rich, I can

and I ought to say: My desires, O God, are your desires both in the present and for as long as it pleases you.—You may ask what remedy you have if God takes you at your word and keeps you always in such spiritual poverty. You will have, my dear Sister, no other than the will of God, and that shall stand you in the place of all else. That divine and adorable will shall recompense you for the gifts you lack; it shall become your treasure; for you it shall be a spiritual fortune in the midst even of your poverty. For can we be richer in God's sight than we are in complying with his holy will in the worst afflictions? Or can we be surer of possessing pure love than when we are willingly resigned to what serves most to mortify spiritual self-love—that subtlest self-love of them all? Be very sure, my dear Sister, that the soul which can thus rejoice in its poverty, has nothing to envy even in those souls richest in God's gifts.

LETTER 7: TO SISTER MARIE-THÉRÈSE DE VIOMÉNIL
Darkness—Insensibility

MY DEAR SISTER and dear daughter in our Lord,—God's peace be with you now and always!

I realize from what you have told me that you are walking in spiritual darkness. Yet I by no means share the anxiety this state causes you. This way is usual enough in persons of your sex; while there is no doubt that it is the safer in being the less exposed to the vain complacency of self-love or the deception of vanity. This very darkness, therefore, is one of God's graces; for in this life the best means of going to God is to walk by naked faith which is always obscure. Despite this obscurity, you can understand enough about it and can give details enough of it to make it sufficiently plain to any moderately experienced director. So much for what I think of your state in general. Now to deal with difficulties in detail.

1. You say that you cannot pray. Experience has taught me that every person of goodwill who talks in this fashion can pray better than most, since their prayer is simple and humble and in its simplicity escapes being mere formal thought. This kind of

prayer involves dwelling in God's presence in faith with a secret and persistent desire to receive his grace according to our needs. Since God sees all our desires, this is the supreme prayer. For, to quote St Augustine, perpetual desire is perpetual prayer. In prayer let your guide be simplicity. Of this you cannot have too much, for God loves to see us like little children before him.

2. As for holy communion, your growing hunger for the divine fare and the strength it imparts to you are strong reasons for going to it frequently. Give up your fears, then, taking comfort from the assurance I give you.

3. Indifference to all earthly matters and detachment from relatives even are greater graces than you realize. Detachment from self by ceasing all interior self-examination is your one remaining need. Prayer and frequent union with Jesus Christ will complete the work by slow degrees, provided your work is done in forgetfulness of self and remembrance only of God to whom you must abandon all your interests, spiritual no less than temporal.

4. Whoever said that God asks of you only submission and resignation was right indeed. In these, my dear daughter, utter perfection is to be found—search for it elsewhere is so much error and illusion. A spiritual person having some inclination to the interior life has, properly speaking, but one thing to do: to be submissive and steadfast of heart in every conceivable situation, exterior or interior, in which God chooses to set her. For example: should you be ill: since God wishes it, wish it also as he wishes it and for as long as he wishes it.—But that may possibly leave me incapable of doing any work or service for the community, you may object.—Very well! once more let your attitude be: I accept in advance not only the pain I suffer but the holy abjection and humiliation that go with it. Or—another objection—in that state I may possibly tend to pamper myself somewhat, not making all the effort I could and should. Is this too God's will, assuming I have consulted my superior and my confessor and have followed their instructions blindly? Yes; again say simply: I wish it.

Let us, then, live in peace by complying with every divine desire—in that interior peace in which God himself lives and works. This, my Sister, is a sure and exalted way. Follow it faithfully, rejecting every antagonistic thought and idea as a suggestion of the devil, the least of whose aims is to spoil that interior peace in which is the soul's chief good and the firm foundation of the spiritual life.

5. You have been guilty of grave imprudence and definite disobedience in risking a three months' bout of fever. You can be quite sure that a refusal to eat meat on such occasions is stubbornness and not virtue—a mere obstinate clinging to your own will and judgement under a pretext of piety. Most devout and spiritually minded women are to be pitied in such circumstances, though to put up with them requires much patience. At times their illusion is so blind and so fantastic that an angel from heaven could scarcely rid them of it. Be submissively attentive in all things, and in all things show an endurance that is at once sweet, peaceful and patient. Let this be your spirit in performing God's will and so serve your own greatest good.

6. They have been well advised to forbid you to give way to your wish to change your work and to petition for this. I too most emphatically forbid it. So take good care not to oppose God's decree.—But your health is not good enough, you may say.—God can easily give you health.—You have not the necessary talent.—It is always within God's power to provide you with sufficient. Already he has supplied your main need—distrust of yourself in this matter. The one essential is to recognize and be conscious of your own incapacity; for then you will rely only on God; you will appeal to him in all circumstances, you will attribute nothing to yourself and everything to God; while his blessings alone will turn all things to your increasing advantage. In a word, live in peace and trust in the all-good God, placing as little reliance on yourself as you wish. Be always humbly aware of your own weakness, incapacity and stupidity: these are precisely the tools of which it pleases God to make use that his glory may be made the more strikingly evident.

7. A lack of perception in regard to the truths of religion is in some souls no bad sign. Often it is merely evidence that God means to lead them by the surest way of all—that of simple unadorned faith unaccompanied by the knowledge and delights

he gives when it pleases him. In the ways of God effort and strife are required only in regard to sin; in all things else peace and tranquillity are the essentials. When acts have been beyond your power, say to yourself: In God's sight all has been accomplished, since God, who is master, has seen my desire, and will give me the ability to act when it is his pleasure. His blessed will shall always be my law. I am in this world only to do this; in this I possess a rich treasure. Let God give others as much as he wishes of wisdom, talents, graces, gifts and conscious spiritual delights . . . my one desire is to be rich only in obedience to his will.

There, my dear daughter, you have your way. Follow it unfalteringly in peace, trust and complete self-surrender. So shall all be well with you and your safety assured.

8. The greatest need you have to further your spiritual advancement is peacefully to endure all God wishes or allows to happen to you, neither complaining nor seeking comfort from your fellow human creatures, nor wasting your energies in futile conversation nor encouraging yourself in frivolous thoughts and vain plans for the future. All these leave you empty of God, and prevent grace from working in you. So be careful.

9. This is what you must do to help yourself concentrate upon God more easily and uninterruptedly in accordance with your desires and needs: (1) find your delight in silence and solitude since these do much for recollection and the interior spirit; (2) read only enduringly worth-while and thoroughly pious books, and by pausing frequently endeavour to savour rather than to understand or retain what you have read; (3) during the day direct frequent and fervent aspirations to God in regard to whatever may befall—difficulties, temptations, aversions, weariness, contradictions, bitterness of heart and the rest.

10. The prayers you offer God for detachment from all things are inspired by grace. Persist in them, sure that sooner or later they will be granted. It is fitting that we should wait for God who for so long has waited for us; while the great graces we ask of him deserve to be desired and waited for with patience and perseverance.

LETTER 8: TO SISTER JEANNE-ELIZABETH GŒURY
(1735)
Dryness—Distractions during prayer

MY DEAR SISTER,— Your soul's inclination is very simple, and what is simple is best. It turns straight to God, and so you must follow it unfailingly yet gently, without effort or eagerness either to keep it or to recapture it when your perception of it is gone, otherwise you would be claiming God's gift as your own. Distractions and dryness are fairly frequent in this kind of prayer. Yet these endured with patience and self-abandonment are themselves excellent prayers. Moreover, though these distractions and aridity be painful, they do not hinder that sustained desire to pray that is found in the depths of the heart. Heartfelt prayer is no other than this.

1. If you have been using this excellent form of prayer for a whole year, or possibly two, a book will not help you. If, however, these periods of helplessness and aridity last for (say) seven or eight consecutive days, by all means take a book, but read it with frequent pauses. Again, if you find that such reading still further distracts or troubles you interiorly, break it off and seek to remain in God's presence in silent peace, as far as you are able.

You must not be surprised—still less must you be perturbed—if what has moved you in the past moves you no longer: such vicissitudes must be endured interiorly as changes of weather and season are endured exteriorly. Not to expect them is to show a singular lack of experience.

2. Resolutions are rarely made in this kind of prayer. Yet much more good comes of it than of resolutions made during meditation, since from time to time the heart finds itself prepared by the previous operations of the Holy Ghost. People in this state must let this express their attitude interiorly, for it is worth more than all the resolutions put together: Lord, enable me to do good and avoid evil on this occasion or at that juncture—otherwise I shall do the reverse of what I must. For I am so pitifully weak, as personal experience has taught me in the past only too well.

The sweetness and efficacy of holy recollection are often a reward and recompense for preceding sacrifices. In the beginning such interior inclination does not abolish either repugnance or involuntary rebelliousness. But it does, however, slowly weaken them, till in time there is sensible joy in the bitterest of sacrifices.

3. God permits your small infidelities that you may be the more thoroughly convinced of your weakness and that your wretched self-esteem may slowly be destroyed within you and with it that presumption and that secret trust in the self which prevent you from acquiring true humility of heart. You do not need to be told that nothing is more agreeable to God than such self-scorn when there goes with it an utter trust in God. He in his goodness, then, confers a great grace upon you when he compels you to drink, often against your will, of the chalice dreaded by your self-love and corrupt nature. Again, if you can feel and appreciate the value of this grace and your own good fortune, you are to attribute such supernatural feelings solely to the workings of the Holy Ghost.

To know happiness in finding some small resemblance in yourself to Jesus Christ is another of the works of grace. Yet be chary of such a feeling. Distrust your own weakness and in every case be afraid of some delusive coincidence.

4. You have certainly no need to fear illusion in repugnances and involuntary rebelliousness; such illusions are irreconcilable with this holiest of prayers that conquers and subdues them. Your error lies in the conviction that you will never attain either true humility or complete mortification because of the strong resistance you feel against these. If you could rely only upon your own strength nothing indeed would be more impossible. Yet, as you truly add, with the grace of God gained for you by Jesus Christ all becomes easy. It is possible for this truth itself to make no impression upon you. I am not surprised, yet the remark you make in this connection convinces me that, like all beginners, you attach far too much importance to impressions made upon the senses. It cannot be denied, however, that in the order of the supernatural operations of grace, the more perceptible things are to the senses the less stable and perfect they are, while the

more secret and spiritual are the nearer to perfection. When God withdraws from you the perception of his presence— that is, conscious recollection—strive to keep the holy desire of it in your heart: this is all that is necessary; while it is all the more pleasing to God and the more meritorious.

5. All anxiety is a sickness of the soul. Let the energy you show in resisting your anxiety about Holy Office be as great as that anxiety itself is unjustified. The desire and the will to say your office properly are always there despite involuntary distractions—as all yours are. This is obvious, since every time you perceive your attention to be straying, you feel real grief in the depths of your heart. That, surely, is the truest and best form your disavowal can take. These distractions are not voluntary in their essence when you fear the waste of time they cause, and when you recollect your thoughts during the day. Dwell in peace, therefore, and accept these involuntary miseries submissively.

6. You have told me of another source of anxiety that profits you nothing and that is based on several illusions of which you need to rid your mind. The first of these is an over-great desire for conscious delight in communion—this comes of spiritual self-love. The second is a belief that this delight is necessary if you are to make a good communion. Alas, my dear daughter, in that case where would those many holy souls be who ordinarily experience only dryness, insensibility and even aversion? In all our pious exercises we need to go to God in pure faith, itself an almost unfelt thing. Communions and prayers are normally the purer and more pleasing to God the less they are made with feelings of sweetness. For such is the way of pure spirit and of pure love that asks nothing for itself. A favourite and notable saying of St Francis de Sales used to be: Our little gratifications are not God's gratifications. Pure love lies in being content with all that contents God. Even in the holiest of our desires and actions, that pure love allows us only to wish what God wishes, and consequently what he permits, even in cases where there has been some initial fault of our own. This fine precept has been too often forgotten, or at least too often overlaid by the precious pretexts of a self-love only too ready to believe that what it en-

joys and finds satisfying is in every instance good and holy. As to this, a saintly nun used to say that God deprived her one by one of her delights, inclinations and spiritual sensibilities in all that she did, that her love, which earlier spiritual delights had left imperfect and impure, might be purified.

Be guided by your soul's simple inclination, alike in communion and your morning and evening exercises. A single one of your short acts avails you more than anything else.

Your indifference to all that can be thought or said of you comes of the work performed in you by the Holy Ghost. Persist in neither excusing nor justifying yourself unless, indeed, you are ordered to do so. That way perfection lies. May God be blessed for all things and in all things. Amen.

LETTER 9: TO MOTHER LOUISE-FRANÇOISE DE ROSEN

Distractions—Weariness—Outbursts of feeling

MY DEAR SISTER,—I have but one answer to make to all the anxieties your letter deals with and to the doubts you reveal to me. I would say with the Master: My peace be with you; be not afraid. That which troubles you should be occasion for joy. Where you see signs of backsliding, I see merely sure indications of lasting progress.

1. The almost continuous distractions, spiritual weariness and aversion experienced by you at prayer, Office, communion and confession are no more than the result of the apparent absence of God. In order to test and purge your soul, your divine Spouse deprives it of any conscious perception of his presence. This causes the soul sorrow so poignant that at times it leaves its mark even upon the body. This is the martyrdom of grace and the Holy Ghost. For, now that there are no longer tyrants to make martyrs for the faith by the shedding of blood, the Holy Ghost has adopted the device of making martyrs for the divine love by these painful and apparent absences as by many similar methods involving anguish. Those subjected to these divine torments have only to practise resignation, blind self-abandonment and unwearied patience, just as in the midst of their tor-

tures did the martyrs of old. That same Holy Ghost, who maintained the latter in peace and divine joy even upon red-hot gridirons and under the most hideous of tortures, will maintain peace in your heart, however disturbed you be in senses and in mind. Your own need is to help him conscientiously in his work by refusing any voluntary consent to the anxieties which beset you.

Make no violent effort to recover recollection when you imagine it has begun to escape you. Go so far as to resign yourself with a good grace to being deprived of sensible and active recollection. Be content with that passive recollection which persists in the depths of the heart even when the mind wanders and which is the inalienable attribute of souls free from all undisciplined attachment to this world's goods. In this state it is true that God is not always definitely the centre of our thoughts, yet he is the ruling principle of our affairs. For this state is a state of abstraction—abstraction during which we imagine ourselves to be thinking of nothing, partly because visible things do not occupy us and partly because we have so general an idea—so vague and simple a conception—of God that it loses itself in the mind; or rather the mind loses itself in the idea and seems to fade away and break free from itself. In this state we perform all that we have to do, showing neither anxiety nor overeagerness, since it is the Holy Ghost who gently prompts us. But the Holy Spirit, jealously seeking to be the one guide possessed by the soul whom it has exalted to this state, arrests and suspends our action as soon as the activities of self-love interfere with it, whereupon the soul has only to relinquish this activity in order to recover and resume its passive recollection. This recollection you see is merely a result and an extension of the prayer of quiet and silence. This prayer consists in keeping quiet interiorly and in relinquishing every thought rather than fighting against those which come to you or striving after thoughts that fail to come.

2. The outbursts of feeling, which are sometimes aroused in you and which last for some considerable period, are another and equally profitable ordeal. By causing you anguish interiorly, they confer infinite benefits on you. They purify and humiliate and belittle you to such an extent that gradually they cause you

to become as those little children whom Jesus Christ would have us resemble if we wish to enter into his kingdom. You are right in saying that on such occasions our great need is for patience, sweetness, help for oneself rather than for our neighbour—to echo the thought of St Francis de Sales.

3. Continuous vicissitudes, interiorly, are a good sign. By means of them the Holy Ghost makes us amenable to all his influences; for by dint of altering the interior form and shape, nothing remains of your own, and thus you are able to take any shape willed by the Spirit that blows when and where it listeth. In Fénelon's phrase, it is a continual moulding and remoulding of the soul. As a result it becomes as fluid as water which, having of itself neither shape nor form, takes indifferently the shape and form of every vessel into which it is poured.

4. It is anything but difficult for you to know how to act in these varying situations. You have but one simple and easy thing to do, namely, to discover—without reference to your intellect (for that would spoil everything) whither the deep-seated inclination of your heart is leading you. Let all your acts be marked by this holy simplicity, by good faith and uprightness of heart, looking neither sideways nor backwards, but always in front, living only in the present hour and the present moment of that hour. Then I will answer for all you do. It will be plain to you that this manner of acting is a perpetual dying to the self, an utter abnegation of the ego, a true sacrifice of self-abandonment to God in the night of faith.

5. You say that you feel no interior reproaches and have no consciousness either of evil or of good, and that this silence seems terrible to you. It is part of your state. All sensibility must be taken from you, for it is a state of pure faith. Once again, have no fear; go your way in peace, in simplicity and in complete self-abandonment, indulging in neither introspection nor set reflection: when such reflection is to be made, God will give it to you, or will supply it through an interior sense or secret inclination that in all things will be a surer guide for you than all your wretched reflections. Are they then so much a treasure that you must so keenly regret their loss or spoliation? Blessed are the poor in spirit, for theirs is the kingdom of heaven. Cherish that

interior poverty which despoils our inner self as exterior poverty despoils our outward. Thus is the kingdom of God set up within us.

Aversion—Idleness

MY DEAR SISTER,—I see nothing in your present state which need justifiably alarm you. The aversion, idleness and indolence which, despite ourselves, we sometimes experience, have no guilt in them provided that we endure them with resignation and that, despite such aversion, we curtail none of our pious exercises. If, insensible to all things else, we then experience an eager desire for the sacraments and a lively contrition for our faults, this is a notable sign of God's mercy that makes use of our very faults to increase our fervour and humility.

There are two kinds of interior peace: the one is sensible, sweet and delightful; while, as it does not depend upon ourselves, it is by no means indispensable. The other is almost unperceived and is to be found in the depths of the heart and the most secret recesses of the soul. Usually it is dry and savourless and it can be possessed during the greatest of tribulations. Intense recollection is necessary before it can be recognized; you might imagine that it was buried at the bottom of an abyss. It is the peace in which God dwells and which he himself calls into being that he may dwell in it as in his own element. There in the depths of our hearts he performs his unperceived and marvellous works. These are recognized only in their effects: thus it is through God's beneficent influence that we find ourselves in a state of steadfastness amid grief, violent upheavals, great difficulties and unforeseen afflictions. If you discover this bare peace and tranquil sadness in yourself, it remains but to thank God for it: no more is necessary for your spiritual advancement. Cherish it as the most precious of gifts. Slowly increasing, it will one day be your greatest delight. Conflict and victory must precede that day.

I congratulate you on having adopted my own favourite saying: God wills it! May God be blessed for all things! What comfort there is in that saying! St Francis de Sales used to say that it is a stimulant for the heart which, by virtue of it, never fails; a cordial draught which dissolves iron, steel and all the hardest and all the most disagreeable things we can be made to swallow; a balm which relieves and cures the most poisonous wounds. Let us, my dear daughter, make use of it whenever our delicate spiritual stomachs reveal their weakness and their difficulty in dealing with food not to their liking. By this simple recipe bitterness is changed into sweetness and we find everything good and palatable. Nothing is more calculated to uplift our hearts.

LETTER 11: TO SISTER MARIE-HENRIETTE DE BOUSMARD

Powerlessness—Remembrance of former faults—Weariness—Fears

NANCY, 1734

MY DEAR SISTER,—1. True recollection lies in the calm which you enjoy in solitude, and in the tranquillity of a mind and heart that are emptied of all created things and are less and less preoccupied. God deprives you of it at prayer time, because then you are too full of desires and eagerness. Stay then during prayers just as you are in solitude; I require no more concentration and eagerness from you. Keep perfectly quiet and meditative, relinquishing all ideas of created things. Then will you dwell with God, though you neither know, feel nor understand how this can be. It is a mystery you perceive only in its blessed results—dying to self and insensibility to all temporal things.

2. It is pure truth to believe that you do nothing for God, and that the little you in fact do is spoilt because your self-love mingles with it. In one way this truth is so obvious that it is astonishing all men do not recognize it and stand trembling and reduced to nothingness before God; in another way this truth is for us so wrapped round with obscurity while our minds are so closely shrouded in the trappings of self-love that we cannot thank God enough when it pleases him to make us grasp it thoroughly.

From the time when it is God's pleasure to impart this clear knowledge of himself in combination with the humility which his blessed grace inspires, we expect nothing further from self but everything from him. We rely no more upon our good works but upon God's mercy and upon the infinite merits of Jesus Christ. There you have the true Christian hope which saves our souls. Every other spiritual state, every other spiritual inclination, involves much grave risk to salvation; whereas to hope only in God, to rely only upon God, in and through Jesus Christ, is the hard rock, the firm and lasting foundation that no illusion, self-love or temptation can threaten.

How glad I am that you have reached this state! Be steadfast in it; it is the anchor of your ship and the port of your salvation.

3. I am delighted to see by your letter how God in his mercy has made you blind. You ascribe to your evil disposition those sudden recollections of the past—which fill you with horror of yourself. Yet is it not abundantly clear that this is one of the most wholesome impressions that grace could produce in you? Truly, there is nothing more calculated to sanctify you than a holy hatred of yourself which for you began with those recollections and the deep humiliations into which they plunge you when in the presence of God.

These thoughts come to you suddenly, when your mind is far removed from them, to teach you that this is a pure grace.— Why, you ask, did you formerly have such exactly opposite feelings when remembering the past?—The reason is that formerly you would not have endured this spectacle of your imperfections without complete despondency. Your need then was a surpassing hope; your need now is that blessed horror of self in which lies the heart's true penitence. When God gives you such thoughts, accept them peacefully, gratefully and with thanksgiving; and when they pass away, let them go, abandoning yourself entirely to all that God pleases to do in you, and for as long as he pleases; but do not cling on to any of the interior dispositions he may will to give you, and do not regret those he takes from you.

4. I know the difficulties of the work to which you refer and the weariness which your duty of leading the chanting can cause you on account of your weak chest, especially on feast

days. This is painful enough it is true, but it is yet more comfortingly true that God wishes and permits it obviously in order to subdue your will. Four short words can sum up what you must do in this and in all similar cases: prayer, open-heartedness, sacrifice, abandonment. Let me elaborate: first, you must ask God for guidance; then explain in simple words to your superior the state in which you are, waiting to hear from her what orders it pleases God to give you: you must be fully resolved to sacrifice to him, in complete self-abandonment, your repugnances, your health, even your life itself. You must not harbour the slightest doubt that God, who never abandons those who abandon themselves to him, will fail to inspire her whose duty it is to reveal God's will to you as to what is most needful for yourself. One of three things will inevitably happen: either you will be given relief; or God will preserve and strengthen you; or he will allow you to die, taking you to himself from out this miserable life. Now, my dear Sister, I ask you whether you could make a better end to your life than by so generous a sacrifice or so perfect an act of self-abandonment. After you have expressed your mind, be steadfast whatever happens. For it is not your concern but God's. He knows how to make all things serve your welfare and his own greater glory. What more blessed, happy and generous behaviour than that, my dear Sister? How good it is once and for all to resign yourself to obedience and self-abandonment in all things! Oh, the peace that lies in it, the sacrifice, the grace, the certainty of salvation, and above all the merit in God's eyes! What consolation for me when, if such be the case, I learn that you have died a martyr to holy self-abandonment, and that God has permitted you to make a holocaust of yourself upon the altar of his blessed, lovable and adorable will.

5. Be content interiorly with God's contentment. Rejoice in the assurance that God's good pleasure is fulfilled in you. In this way, even when you feel discontent with yourself, on reflection you will be content in God's unique contentment. For he, as St Augustine says, is never more content with us than when we are discontented with ourselves. So do we constantly, and with no need to take thought, practise pure love which consists in liking, loving and desiring nothing but God's good pleasure, preferring

his will to anything that we would or could long for, however holy it may appear to be. Two principal methods of practising this meritorious self-abandonment are open to you. Either you can say to God: Lord, I hate and detest my imperfections and my sins; with the help of your blessed grace I wish to make every effort to cure myself of them; while for love of you I accept with all my heart the grief and abjection they bring with them. Or you can say to him: I desire, O God, to please you; I desire my salvation and my sanctification, the gift of prayer, of mortification and of every virtue. I beseech you for these: I long to work heart and soul to acquire them when you grant me the opportunity. Nevertheless, in all these things, I so greatly prefer all your wishes to my own, that I want those graces and virtues only in such measure as it pleases you, and at such time as your wise Providence ordains, though this prove to be my life's last moment. For your blessed and adorable will forever shall be the rule and measure of all my desires, even the holiest and most legitimate among them. Such acts, performed in the depths of the heart, are the fruits of that pure love which, according to the doctors of the Church, are as efficacious as baptism and martyrdom in wiping away all sins, and which find illustration in the words spoken by Jesus Christ of Magdalen: "Many sins are forgiven her because she has loved much." Can we perceive anything more likely to comfort, strengthen and encourage us?

6. You love, you say, meanly and poorly—blessed be the poor in spirit. This is but an evidence of your interior humility and holy self-hatred.—Your life, you say too, has no props; that is to say it is lived in pure spirit and pure faith.—What happier state than that, though its happiness be hidden from the soul?— You walk blindly and at hazard, you remark.—In this lies pure self-abandonment: you do not feel it; you are not even aware of it, since if you felt and were aware of it, it would be not self-abandonment but the firmest guarantee of your salvation that you could desire. For what greater assurance could you have than the knowledge that throughout time and eternity you are surrendered to God? Self-abandonment is a virtue whose full merit can be acquired only in so far as you are ignorant of the existence of the merit. Live then at peace in the midst of your

fears, your difficulties and your obscurities. Let your trust, which must ask neither to see nor to feel, be altogether in God, in and through Jesus Christ. I pray that he may be always with you.

LETTER 12: TO SISTER MARIE-ANNE-THÉRÈSE DE ROSEN
(1734)
The uses of ordeals—Behaviour to be followed

BEFORE anything else, my dear Sister, I must first express a thought which your anxious doubts and your eagerness for interior guidance have suggested to me. I am forced to believe that, if we were more attentive to the wisdom of the Holy Spirit, better prepared to receive his sacred inspirations, and more faithful in following the direction of his grace, we should need scarcely anything more to reach the perfection to which we are called. For I notice that in the midst of even the most obscure interior darkness there is always in the depths of the soul a certain light of pure faith which is an unerring guide. Apart from that, there are moments when in quick bright flashes of light the Holy Ghost lets us know that he keeps us in the right way. You need to supplement these with some reserve of peace even in the midst of interior storms, and with regularity in conduct that, despite the defects of human frailty, does not deliberately stray from the infallible rules of the Gospel and the rules of perfection. A docile and faithful soul should find sufficient guarantees in this to justify its surrender in complete self-abandonment to that interior spirit which guides it so well. Usually, then, it is a sign of weakness and the result of self-love's promptings, when we have need of anything beside. This does not apply to the beginnings of the spiritual life when the Holy Ghost has not yet firmly established his kingdom within us, or to a few extraordinary occasions when violent spiritual storms prevent us from hearing his voice.

I might have left my answer in these general terms. But I much prefer to reply to you in detail.

1. This new state of darkness, dryness and aversion to which God has brought you does not astonish me. The Master always

begins by making himself known, loved and appreciated in a sensible manner. Later he deprives the soul of these consolations in order to withdraw it from the grossness of the senses and to bring it into more excellent, more intimate and more enduring union with himself in pure faith and pure spirit. To complete this purification, these deprivations must be followed by sufferings (interior if no other), interior rebelliousness, diabolical temptation, distress, helplessness and distaste for all good, which themselves can sometimes amount to a kind of agony. All these serve admirably to rid the soul of its self-love and to give it certain features of resemblance to its crucified Spouse. All these agonies are so many blows which God levels at us to make us die to ourselves. The more self-love resists this spiritual death, the more savage these blows appear and the more cruel the agonies. The divine love is a double-edged sword that smites self-love until it is completely destroyed. Our pain has its source in that stout resistance offered by this accursed love of ourselves which hates to relinquish the control it has acquired over our heart and to allow the love of God to reign there in peace. If that love of God finds no obstacle to its divine ardours and no foe to resist it, it will make none but sweet and delightful impressions upon the heart.

No longer regret, I beg you then, those days you regard as happy because on them you had delight in prayer and communion while your union with the Beloved was altogether attractive and delicious. These present days of agony and martyrdom are in their different way as estimable and as precious. They are days of pure love, since on them you love God for himself and at cost to yourself. You are no longer afraid lest self-love mingle in your relations with him, since there is nothing in these relations but what is torturing to self-love. In this state it is the pure will of God that we desire and love, and this with a love so pure that the senses have no share in it. How difficult it is to love God purely during delightful days, and yet feel no self-satisfaction or vain complacency! But in times of tribulation and interior deprivation, to be assured of the purity of your love you have only to offer no resistance and to abandon yourself sincerely. How comforting and encouraging this assurance is for whosoever has some small understanding of the value and advantage of pure love. When God has made you understand these, you will understand also why so many of the saints preferred privations and sufferings to delights and consolations, and why they so passionately loved the former that they found it hard to endure the latter. God, it may be, gives you the idea that this painful state will last throughout your life in order that you may make him a fuller sacrifice. Do not consider or hesitate for a single moment; sacrifice everything; abandon yourself limitlessly and unreservedly to him whom you believe to have abandoned you. Maintain this interior attitude unfailingly; at the moment it is most essential for you. I will go as far as to say that it is the one thing you have to do during prayer, holy communion and Mass, during your Office as during the day. Yet do it gently and effortlessly; do not strive even to make your formal acts numerous. To maintain your soul in the habitual condition of utter and unreserved self-abandonment is enough.

I forbid you then to desire voluntarily anything other than the blessed will of God. Ask him neither to increase nor diminish your afflictions. God knows better than we do the exact measure of all we need. It is often merely presumption and illusion to want to follow the example of certain saints who, having been granted a particular inspiration during their sufferings, cried out: Still more, Lord! We are too little and too weak to venture so far unless we are morally certain that God wills it so.

I forbid you also any scruple, difficulty or voluntary doubt on the subject of either Office, Mass or so forth. In this matter your right intention made in pure faith is enough. God does not ask more than that; and I venture to say that you are unable to do more at present.

2. I am indeed glad to hear you say that you find yourself so intolerable to yourself that you are for ever on the brink of trouble and anxiety and yet never, by the grace of God, fall completely into it. In other words God, in making you feel your weakness to the full, upholds you invisibly and by keeping you in humility makes victory yours. You would perhaps love that humility either wholly or in part, if you discovered a certain courage in yourself or if you felt a certain interior strength. Ac-

cording to Fénelon, one of the most important maxims is to be learned from this: it is a pure grace of God, and one of his greatest, to suffer and to conquer in a minor way, that is to say with a degree of interior weakness, with self-scorn and humility and in the belief that we have accomplished nothing, so far are we from being self-contented. This discontent with ourselves makes God's true contentment, and God's contentment must lead to our own. Nothing will be able to trouble us any more as soon as we seek that interior satisfaction—our ability to hope that God is satisfied and content with us.

3. The faithfulness to all your duties and all your rules which God gives you in your present state is again one of his great graces. I warmly approve of you for not seeking consolation among creatures even by way of talking of your difficulties to a trustworthy person. Your silence will sanctify you more efficaciously than any conversation or advice.

4. A further great grace is to feel neither trouble, nor fear, nor anxiety, whether about your present state or about the future, as though you had become insensible to all things. For that is the fruit and the happy effect of your complete self-abandonment. As you have abandoned all to God, he takes all in his care, driving from your soul all trouble, fear and anxiety. He deprives it of all sensibility to its own interests, leaving it sensible only to himself. This condition is the firm foundation of the completest security a soul can enjoy: this life has no greater happiness nor any surer sign of God's goodwill.

5. Those interior words which you have so distinctly heard most certainly come from God: the good and swift effect they have had upon you make me sure of this. Only God can in this thorough fashion impress souls with what pleases him. This makes it plain to you that divine goodness does not refuse to grant you from time to time a few crumbs of consolation and of strength to help your weakness in those deserts which that goodness forces you to pass through.

6. You must not be surprised that your interior troubles have no effect upon your behaviour towards your neighbour and that they do not diminish your patient equanimity or your kindheartedness during spiritual ordeals. Moreover, it is during

spiritual ordeals that we are possibly more fit to help, console, relieve and serve others.

LETTER 13: TO SISTER ANNE-MARGUERITE BOUDET
DE LA BELLIÈRE (1734)

The same subject

MY DEAR SISTER,—1. Your present darkness is a true grace of God that seeks to accustom you to walk in the night of pure faith. It is the surest and most meritorious way to attain holiness.

2. Aridity and helplessness are another and equally precious grace, another meritorious participation in the cross of Jesus Christ. But, as you will say, such powerlessness prevents me from asking God for the necessary help. At least it does not rob you of the desire to be able to ask for it. For you must know that in God's sight our desires are, in the words of St Augustine, true prayer. This leads Bossuet to say that a cry confined in the depths of the heart has as much worth as a cry raised to heaven, since God perceives our most secret desires and the very inclinations of our hearts. Let it be your habit to act on this principle whether in your prayers or before or after holy communion. Nothing more is needed to render our intercourse with God sound, easy and efficacious, despite all our dryness, our involuntary distractions and our helplessness.

For none of these hinder our willingness to pray, groan and sigh before God. His all-seeing eye beholds in the intentions and inclinations of our hearts every deed that we wish to do, as he beholds the ripe fruit on the trees in the mere buds of spring—to use the fine simile of the Bishop of Meaux. In God's name, my dear daughter, make every endeavour to assimilate and appreciate that maxim; it will comfort and uphold you in those many junctures when it seems that we neither do nor are able to do anything. Our willingness is always there, performing all things in God's sight even when it appears most idle.

3. The acquiescence, submission and union of our will with that of God effect our perfection to such a degree that nothing remains for us to do except to hold steadfastly to these in all

things, through all things and for all things. This accomplished, all is accomplished. Without this, prayers, austerities, works (even heroic works) and sufferings are nothing in God's sight, since the one way of pleasing him is in all things to wish only for what he wills. The more involuntary opposition this complete resignation encounters in us, the more merit it has, because of the greater effort and more thorough sacrifice required.

4. The knowledge and fear of the perpetual snares that everywhere lie in wait for us, both without and within the soul, are in themselves the grace which enables us to avoid those snares. When we combine this humble fear with great trust in God, we are always victorious, except maybe on a few unimportant occasions when God permits trivial lapses for the sake of our greater good. These lapses are beneficial to us in that they serve to keep us always insignificant and humiliated before God, always distrustful of ourselves and always in our own eyes self-obliterated.

5. As for peace of heart, you must make a habit of seeking, finding and enjoying it in the upper part of the soul, *in the apex of the spirit*, in spite of the perturbation, rebelliousness and restlessness of the lower and less spiritual part. The latter must be held of no account, since God ignores what happens in it. In St Teresa's words it may be called the courtyard of the soul's inner castle. Profit from this precept which all the saints have adopted. Act like a man who, finding himself among the unclean animals and vermin of his castle yard, ascends hastily to the upper rooms with their beautiful decorations and cultured people. You also must ascend into the sanctuary of the soul, and endeavour never to leave it, since it is there God has made his permanent dwelling-place.

6. You have been wise indeed both to abandon yourself in all things to God and to avoid any voluntary anxiety over the frequent experience you have of your wretchedness and weakness. In this way the foundation of true humility and of utter distrust of self is slowly strengthened. Both these are precious states of soul that confer every one of God's graces upon us, and induce God himself to endow us with his strength in proportion as he discovers us to be increasingly perceptive of our powerlessness

for good. It was this which made St Paul say that the weaker he felt himself, the stronger he found himself.

7. Speaking in God's name I tell you that usually—in fact, almost always—when you imagine that you are praying worst, you are praying best. Why? Because on the one hand the will and the persistent desire to pray—and to pray well—is the heart's true prayer; and, on the other, such prayers have no complacency in them, and have nothing of that futile preoccupation with self which spoils everything. They take the form of patience, silence, self-obliteration, submission and abandonment to God. You emerge from such prayer thoroughly abased and humiliated, free from any of that conscious contentment of self-love which led St Francis de Sales to declare that our pitiful satisfactions in no way make for God's contentment. You can gather from this with what scorn you should repel the fears by which the devil seeks to discourage, weary and—at the least—disquiet you.

8. A great and sincere desire to belong wholly and unreservedly to God, together with the possible price to be paid for it, is called by St Francis de Sales the strong pillar of the spiritual edifice. This pillar upholds the whole building. While by God's grace it stands erect in the apex of the soul, you need fear nothing. As for the senses, no spiritual state can be based upon them.

9. True as it is that self-love cannot be conquered without difficulty, you must reckon that conquest to be far more God's work than your own. Take advantage of trivial opportunities of spiritual strife and victory, and be quite sure that, when God sees you in good faith perform the little that you can with his ordinary graces, he will finally set his own hand to do what is beyond your power in finishing and perfecting the work. For this reason I advise you ever more strongly to beseech God unceasingly for his divine Spirit and his blessed workings. Without them your whole life will be characterized by great faults and marked imperfections and the risk of never emerging from them, of sinking ever lower and even of falling into complete perdition.

10. Holy communion is our souls' true daily bread. In it and it alone we find our maintenance, our strength, our cure and

our preservation. What a difference between those who make frequent communions and those who make few! Ah, how little the latter realize of what treasure and grace they are robbing themselves!

LETTER 14: TO SISTER MARIE-THÉRÈSE DE VIOMÉNIL (1734)

The same subject

DEAR SISTER,—To cure you of the trouble which makes you miserable, it will be enough if I show you the principles involved in it and set their opposites beside them.

The origins, then, of your trouble are: (1) Ignorance of your spiritual path. You have, I think, forgotten that divine grace arranges that souls shall have different paths. Some are delightful, others painful. In the secular world God guides some along prosperous paths, while others—and they are the great majority—he makes follow the thorny way of trouble, affliction and adversity. Similarly, in his wisdom he allots to spiritually-minded souls spiritual joys and tribulations. The work of salvation and perfection needs that each should walk faithfully, following God's call to him, whatever it be. (2) You seem to be equally ignorant of the great truth that, generally speaking, not doing but suffering furthers our spiritual advancement, and that to learn how to be patient, especially with oneself, is to do much. (3) You forget, at least in practice, the other unchallengeable truth that perfection does not lie in receiving God's great gifts—like those of recollection, prayer and spiritual relish for all divine things—but in adhering to every wish of God in every conceivable situation, whether interior or exterior, in which God may place us. (4) From this spring those troubles, anxieties and interior despondency which have embittered and increased all your difficulties; which have robbed you of that strong foundation of the interior life, your soul's peace, and which too often have led you to seek consolation among creatures, at least in unbosoming your spiritual ills to them, whereas God wished you to seek only those consolations which it pleases him to give you.

275

The remedy for all this is in other principles and in very different behaviour.

First principle. Say to yourself often: My way is painful, it is true; it is hard and bitter. Even so it is the will of God and I must submit to it, whatever it costs: (1) because God is the sovereign Master whose absolute right it is to dispose of us as it pleases him; (2) because he is our Father, a Father so good, tender and merciful that he can wish only good for his dear children, and inevitably he turns everything to the advantage of those who are subject to him; (3) because I have never found either peace, calm, tranquillity of heart, or any lasting consolation except in a humble and patient resignation in all that he ordains for me; (4) because I can take even the shortest step forward in the interior life only by following the way marked and ordained in the eternal decrees of my predestination. Can I make a way for myself? And, if I did, would it not be the way of a blind man leading to perdition?

Second principle. I must desire my advancement and my perfection only so far as God wishes it and by the means that he wishes. Such a desire can only be calm and peaceful, even when it is full of vehemence and fervour. But there is another desire for our perfection that springs from pride and an immoderate love of our own excellence. This does not depend upon God; consequently it is restless and for ever agitated. Our need to surrender our soul to the first of these and our need to put all our energy into defeating the second are equally great. All desire for our advancement, therefore, however holy it appears, must be curbed the moment eagerness, restlessness or perturbation enters into it. Such results can only come from the devil, since all that comes of God leaves us tranquil interiorly. Why, then, my dear Sister, desire with so anxious a fervour spiritual wisdom, interior awareness and appreciation, facility in recollection and in prayer, and every other gift of God, when it is not his will to give these to you yet? Is this not to wish to perfect yourself to your own liking and not to his, to follow your own will and not the divine will; to have more regard for your taste than for God's; in a word to wish to serve him at your caprice and not in accordance with his good pleasure?

Ought I then, you may ask, to resign myself to being all my life a victim of my poverty, my weakness and my wretchedness? —Yes, indeed, if this be pleasing to God. My poverty, my wretchedness and my weakness ought henceforward to be preferable and delightful above all things else, since the blessed will of God is to be found in them. Henceforward that poverty is changed into riches; for it is to be rich indeed to be precisely what God wishes, since that way lies sovereign perfection. Again, can you be ignorant that there is heroic virtue in being able to endure with constancy and patience the soul's wretchedness, weakness, interior poverty, darkness, insensibility, vagaries, follies and extravagances of mind and imagination? This led St Francis de Sales to say that when we aspire to perfection we have as much need for patience, mildness and forbearance in regard to ourselves as in regard to others. Let us help ourselves therefore in our own wretchedness, imperfections and faults, as God wishes us to help our neighbour in similar circumstances.

Yet too often in the midst of interior upheaval the will suffers from strange emotions and is on the brink of yielding to impatience. At such times be steadfast, and in this new opportunity for strife, sacrifice and patience you will find a new opportunity for victory and commendation. Even if at the outset the poor will has wavered, it has only to try at once to regain its composure by humiliating itself gently and peacefully before the Lord's infinite mercy.—Yet, you object, this interior hurlyburly takes up all my attention during my prayers, at Mass, Office and holy communion. Are then all my endeavours lost? No; nothing is lost, since the one resolve of acquitting myself well, with which I began, holds good until I retract it by a long and essentially voluntary distraction, in a word, by some recognized and deliberate venial sin. Far from having lost anything, I have gained twice over, since to the merit of my spiritual exercises I add that of having performed them in a painful, torturing and, above all, a humiliating fashion; and in this way, far from spoiling these holy exercises by a useless return to the complacency of self-love—to which I was exposed in the past when those exercises had brought me satisfaction—I perform them with that holy humility which is the foundation and the guardian of all the virtues.—Yet, you urge, this prevents me from feeling contrition.—What does that matter? The efficacy of contrition is not felt; it is in the soul and to be found in the peak of the will. A sensible contrition often serves only as food for self-love, and can never bring reassurance, since it is not what God requires. What, you ask, if I have not contrition of the will?—You must firmly hope and believe that God has given it you; yet even if, after having previously confessed your sins, you have had contrition once only, that is enough to remit all sins, both present and past, so great is the goodness of God.

Let me finish, my dear Sister, with this comforting assurance: if it pleased God to allow you to know your state as I know it, you would thank him for it rather than be grieved about it. Dwell in peace, then, in every situation in which you are likely to find yourself. That being done, all is done. Never fail to say: God be blessed for and in all things! I wish what he wishes and for nothing beside. May all his blessed desires be accomplished in me and through me! May none of my own desires be fulfilled; they are, every one of them, blind and perverted. I should be lost if they were accomplished.

LETTER 15: TO THE SAME

The same subject

DEAR SISTER,—1. We are in perfect agreement, dear Sister, since you think with me that your activity and over-eagerness are a fault. Fight against it with all your strength; I ask no more than that. You say that I would wish to see you altogether perfect and without a fault. That is so, and has always been the object of my zeal for you. Yet I do not count it a crime that you have not reached that perfection. I know that this can only come by slow degrees, through great trust in God and great fidelity to his grace. He alone can finish the work in you that he has begun; your own duty is to abandon yourself wholly to him and leave him to do his work. But do not become one of those of whom Jesus Christ said, in speaking to St Catherine of Siena, that they make little progress in perfection because they wish to say and do everything without listening to him or giving him the opportunity to act within them.

2. I am delighted that you feel God upholds you visibly in your difficulties. Live so, in as much peace as is possible and in a great interior silence.

This one practice will advance you greatly by tranquillizing your heart in God. He has given you courage and energy: these are precious talents which you must put to use. At present the divine Master asks that you should make your courage consist of patience, gentleness and resignation. But he wishes you to find this utter self-abandonment in the depths of your soul, at the apex of your spirit and not in your sensibility. Of his infinite goodness he gives it to you at the same time as he asks it of you. Join me in giving him thanks for this; for he could not make you a more precious gift. A day will come, it may be, when this resignation will become sensible. Then it will be as sweet as it is bitter today; and in your heart's joy you will taste the heavenly unction which Jesus Christ has attached to participation in his Cross. This is the reason for the unalterable peace and happiness felt by the saints and by those who in sacrificing all to God generously hold fast to the interior life and to perfection. You tell me that it seems to you impossible to acquire this interior life with your character and temperament. That is so, but what is impossible to man is easy to God. It is upon him alone and upon his grace that you must rely, through Jesus Christ. To put a kind of compulsion on you to make humility your foundation stone, the God of goodness begins by making you more keenly aware of your weakness. Yet when this feeling casts you down, at once let hope pick you up; for, as you know, it pleases God to turn our greatest weaknesses into triumphs for his grace.

3. The words that you say interiorly time after time—Lord, who art able to do all things, have compassion upon me—make the best and simplest prayer that you can offer. No more is needed to secure his powerful help. Make this your steadfast practice. Maintain your attitude of expecting nothing of yourself and of putting all your hope in God. He will do the rest without your being aware of it, while I am sure that eventually I shall notice perceptible signs of it. I am interiorly convinced

that, short of some great infidelity on your part, God will by his blessed work accomplish many things in you. Rely implicitly upon that, trying merely to put no voluntary impediment in God's path. When, unfortunately, you know that you have impeded him, humiliate yourself immediately, and return to God and your true self with a complete trust in the divine goodness.

4. We have only to cleave to God and his holy will by acquiescing in all his plans: they will unfailingly prove blessed and profitable for us. When there can be on our part only this mere blind submission to his good pleasure, we should be content with his, since in it lies all perfection and true love of God.

5. To feel, as you do, the folly and extravagance of pleasures which worldlings pursue with such eagerness is a great grace. Hence, great good is born in the soul which in this disdain of the world finds a powerful motive for giving itself to the interior life. You, it may be, will say that you are still a tyro in that life. I agree; yet you cherish and desire, strive and ask for it: all these reveal differing degrees of grace. The rest will come in its own time. Nevertheless, restrain your spiritual fervour and your holy ambition.

6. You are beginning, you say, to become a little less conscious of the favourable or unfavourable attitude people adopt towards you. This is a greater grace than you imagine. Yet there are times, you say, when melancholy and discouragement seem stronger than we are. You must then endure these as best you can, and be resigned to the grief of seeing and feeling yourself weak; for there is nothing more galling to our spiritual self-love. This particular means of destroying the latter is the most meritorious of all our sacrifices made to that end, because it is the most humiliating.

7. This desire for some prop or perceptible support in the way of God is quite legitimate; but such a desire must be pursued with moderation, sought without eagerness, made use of without obsession, and surrendered when God wills it, I will not say without difficulty, but without perturbation or voluntary despondency. The essential is that we place our reliance upon God,

depending upon him for all our wants, putting all our hope in him, running to him in all things and for all things, just as affectionate children do in regard to their beloved mother. Such blessed simplicity, such humble and child-like behaviour towards God, moves and delights his fatherly heart. Sooner or later we obtain all we ask of him, or something better than what we ask, which is often given to us without our realizing it.

8. The complaints made by our Lord to St Catherine of Siena against the exaggerated activity of souls who are eager to say and do so much that they leave him no opportunity of working in them, must be understood in the following sense: in our acts and the performance of our duties we must behave without too much eagerness or natural impetuosity, while during the day we must be, as it were, eavesdroppers of the divine wisdom. This, that we may hear him who speaks in our secret heart, using no set words, since his works in us are his speech. Further, we must go about all our prayers, reading, self-examination and aspirations towards God gently and pleasantly, effortlessly and unconfusedly, seeking peace of heart only in God. To this end we must make frequent pauses in our activities to give the Spirit of God opportunity to effect in our souls freely and at leisure what he pleases and as he pleases.

9. All that you tell me of your fear that our faults may be made the graver because of God's presence is so much illusion sent by the devil, who in this way tries to distract our attention from that divine presence and from diligence at communion. Persist in this twofold practice and have no fear. I see the results of it, and they will become so apparent that you yourself will perceive them in time.

10. I rejoice with you that God has deprived you of some of your natural vivacity. In so far as this is lightheartedness, this will be so only temporarily: it will return to you, but altogether changed—transformed into spiritual joy that is gentle and tranquil and peaceful since, like that of the saints, it will be based on God and will come only from God.

11. I greatly approve of your manner of prayer. Go on with it, performing acts when you feel drawn to do so. If good thoughts or noble sentiments come to you in the intervals and during in-

terior silence, give them gentle welcome. Do likewise with that interior peace which varies from more to less as it pleases God. In brief, strive always towards your sovereign Lord, rather with the heart's yearning than with the mind's intelligence. Moreover, be content with whatever is given you. God knows our needs better than we do. Leave the work to him, fully convinced that peace of heart, in his holy presence, however little time it lasts, is of far more worth than all we can think and say. Let that conviction induce your heart to cleave even more closely to that blessed peace, and do not break it when he gives it you; for those are the precious moments when the King of kings admits souls whom he honours with his love of predilection to his most intimate audience.

LETTER 16: TO SISTER CHARLOTTE-ELIZABETH BOURCIER DE MONTHUREUX

The same subject

ALBI, 1730

DEAR SISTER,—1. Thank you for your good wishes and even more for your prayers. I will repay you as best I can every day in the holy sacrifice of Mass. I thank the Lord for the good results he has produced in your soul by the reading of my letters. Yet you will allow me to tell you that I find you still very conscious of the state of wretchedness, poverty and spiritual impotency to which you find yourself reduced. This comes only of excessive self-love that finds such nothingness unendurable and this state of prostration abhorrent. It is inevitable, however, that we should pass through this ordeal. For we must empty ourselves interiorly before God can fill us with himself. We must die to the old life before we can live the new. Our desire to acquire the one before we lose the other is impossible. Have patience; in the depths of your soul maintain a measure of peace in the midst of these interior storms. This state of darkness and insensibility must in no way frighten you, however intense it may become: when you are in it, your one need is submission and utter self-abandonment to God. Do not trouble to feel this submission.

Feeling has nothing to do with it; it is enough if it exists in the apex of the soul.

2. You are wrong to see in your weakness a cause for anxiety. Provided that you know you trust in God he will uphold you, as he has already done, on the brink of the precipice. It may perhaps be by an imperceptible thread, yet in the hands of God that thread is as strong as a thick cable.

3. There is but one of two things to be done in the painful situations of which you tell me: either throw yourself in spirit at the feet of Jesus Christ and kiss those sacred feet; or if that be impossible, remain in interior silence of submission and adoration and be content to take up the external postures that go with them. Thus: lift up your eyes, then lower them, bowing the head slightly, and stay like that for a little time, like Jesus Christ making his prayer in the Garden of Olives. If it be possible, go in spirit to that Garden and to the side of Jesus Christ, humiliated, abased and reduced to nothingness before his God. I like to see you adopting in prayer the attitude of a poor man or a beast of burden; but I like still better the indescribable something which drives you inward, leaving you with no distinct perception except that of an arid and bare peace. When you reach this, be steadfast in it. Failing this, be content to remain in that unique and tranquillizing expectancy of which I have so often spoken to you. On yet other occasions, try to perform this act or that, or do a little reading, in every case calmly and with frequent pauses to give the interior inspiration its opportunity. Yet never forget that you must obey the slightest summons that directs you inward, and be then at peace, neither fearing activity nor seeking distinct thoughts. Such mere dwelling in the presence of God, such mere recollection, brief though it be, is of more worth in your advancement than the sublimest thoughts.

4. I congratulate you upon the grace which God has given you to overcome the rebelliousness and the repugnance you experienced in regard to continuing your work. By such difficult victories we acquire steadfastness in virtue. Every particular you give me of your painful feelings and aversions makes me aware of the goodness of God, who seeks to destroy in the depths of your heart that presumption of which you can be cured only

by this bitter medicine. These truly diabolical feelings which God permits the devil to excite in your soul are an antidote to the still more diabolical sentiment of pride. Be taught by them to leave the work to God and to surrender yourself, if he wishes it, to still greater wretchedness and interior humiliations. If he decrees these for you, he can easily rescue you from them with a great deal gained, assuming that you are for ever faithful in calling upon him in trust from the depths of your abysmal nothingness.

5. I believe that what you say is true: God wishes humiliation for you. Delight, then, to see yourself in this state, because of the likeness it gives you to your divine Spouse. The mere relish you have in the desire for humiliation will advance you further in God's ways than all other practices put together. Endeavour, then, to turn every small opportunity to account, feeding your mind with thoughts of, and relish for, humiliation, as worldlings feed theirs with thoughts of, and relish for, vanity. That profound peace which you begin to feel in the midst of humiliations and scornful rebuffs is one of the greatest graces of which you have ever spoken to me. If you but persist in it, you will soon see effected by its sole means a great change in the whole of your interior life.

6. In the matter of exterior mortification, be guided in every instance by moderation, discretion and, above all, obedience. Make up to yourself what is denied to you in this direction, by interior self-abnegation in refusing to entertain the least desire, the smallest joy, or the slightest thought which is not both of and for God, and in constantly rejecting all useless things in order that he may be your one concern. I rejoice indescribably when I see my dear daughters in that abjection which leaves them like Jesus Christ, abject, humiliated, and self-obliterated. In your case be guided by the grace of this attraction: of itself it will lead you far. As I cannot too often tell you, I shall not cease from praying that God may strengthen you in this blessed love of abjection.

I have neither the inclination nor the time to think of an evening exercise for you. Believe me you have already exercises enough; your need is to simplify yourself interiorly. The mere presence of God, the mere self-abandonment to God, the mere desire to love God and to live in union with him, are themselves exercises and attitudes which, for souls who have made some small advance in the interior ways, are more preferable than all exterior practices.

LETTER 17: TO SISTER MARIE-THÉRÈSE DE VIOMÉNIL

The same subject

DEAR SISTER,—When you have neither the leisure nor the inclination to read, try to live in simple-hearted peace before God, and be at no pains to perform other supererogatory works, except when he gives you the knowledge, impulse and ability with which to do them. Should it seem to you that you lack courage in many things, try at least to preserve in your heart a general determination to belong to God. Humiliate yourself in perceiving that this determination is far from efficacious and at all times consider that you have done nothing. The less trust you put in yourself, the more easy it will seem to put utter trust in the unique mercy of God and the merits of Jesus Christ. For that is the enduring and perfect hope which tortures and obliterates self-love completely, by taking away from it every resource upon which it has been able to rely. There is no more salutary thing than this, especially in the case of certain souls.

There are, you say, sacrifices that lead to God and others which lead away from him. This thought is an error that arises because normally in questions of piety we judge of good and evil only by our feelings. In certain sacrifices which touch the heart in no sensible fashion, we find an indescribable comfort that leads us consciously to God. But in those which greatly grieve our hearts, because we feel only the grief, we grow troubled and inclined to despond. To know the fear of enduring evil, with no gain to compensate us for it, brings us suffering in addition to the sorrow such sacrifices cause us. The false idea that these sacrifices lead us away from God springs from this. Nevertheless, it is a safe and certain principle that, the more keenly such sacrifices affect us and the more thoroughly they cause us to die to self as the result of detachment from consolation and all perceptible aids, the more near to God and to union with God they draw us. This union is the more meritorious the more secret it is and the farther removed from the senses. Self-love has, then, no part in it, seeing that it can draw no nourishment from what it neither knows nor feels. God grant that you may be convinced of a comforting truth taught by all the Fathers, and confirmed by all experience of life.

The better to understand it, you must remember that in nearly all men there is such a mass of self-love, weakness and wretchedness, that they are unable to perceive a gift of God in themselves without running the risk of debasing and corrupting it by falling back, however imperceptibly, into self-complacency; they thus appropriate to themselves the grace of God. They are thankful to be in this or the other state, and they attribute the merit of it to themselves, not doubtless after considered thought or because of lack of trust, but because of the heart's secret inclinations. Now, as God sees into every corner of our hearts and as he is and must be infinitely jealous of his glory in order to keep it for himself and to save us from our heart's secret pilfering, he must convince us of our infinite weakness by our own experiences. This leads him to hide almost all his gifts and graces from us. There are roughly two exceptions to this rule: on the one hand beginners with their need to be attracted and won by the perception and experience of such gifts; on the other, great saints, who, as a result of having been purged of self-love in innumerable ordeals, can recognize God's graces in themselves without the least complacency or the smallest return to self.

For my part I can bear witness to this consistent plan of Providence. God has so hidden from the majority of the souls whom he has put into my care the gifts and the graces which he heaps upon them, that they can perceive neither their advancement, nor their patience, nor their humility, nor their self-abandonment, nor their love for God. Consequently they have often been unable to avoid weeping at the imagined absence of those virtues and at their lack of generosity in suffering. Yet the more such souls fear and are grieved, the less their directors have to fear and be grieved for them. This should be enough to cure you of the many griefs you have made for yourself. You will understand still better, perhaps, if you ponder what Fénelon has said on this subject. "No gift is so exalted that, after having been a means of advancement, it cannot prove a snare and a stumbling-block by reason of that habit of attributing it to ourselves, which sullies the soul." Hence it is that God takes away what he has given; yet he does not take it away to deprive us of it for ever; he takes it away in order to restore it in a better form, after he has purged it of that evil appropriation of which we have been guilty though unawares. The loss of the gift serves to take away its ownership. Ownership taken away, the gift is restored a hundredfold.

The whole of this seems to me to be of such great consequence to you that it is, I believe, important for you to read this long argument again and again. By dint of assimilating it, you will emerge, I hope, from your false conception and from many errors that often perturb you, threatening the interior peace of your soul. Without that peace, as you know, little progress is made in the ways of God.

I know a woman, greatly gifted interiorly, who has absorbed this truth to such a degree that several times I have heard her say that after having beseeched God for a very long period and having made many prayers and novenas to secure certain purely spiritual graces, she cries again and again to God: "I agree, Lord, to be for ever denied knowing whether it has pleased you to grant me these graces, since I am so contemptible that for me all known good is converted into poisonous evil. I do not wish it, Lord, but such is the corruption of my heart that these accursed complacencies of self-love soil the purity of my works almost without my knowledge and against my will. Thus it is I, O God—and I know it—who bind your hands and force you, out of your goodness, to hide from me the graces which your mercy urges you to give me."

You, my dear daughter, have greater need than any to make these sentiments your own; for I have known no one who lays more stress than you upon what is called the sensible support of direction, under the specious pretext of spiritual needs. I have always thought, though I have not told you, that at last the time would come when God, jealous to be your heart's sole support, would deprive you of this tangible help, without so much as allowing you to know in what fashion he intends to make up for all he has taken away from you. Such a state is, I admit, terrifying to our human nature; yet in this terrifying state a simple *fiat* energetically pronounced, in spite of the heart's repugnance, assures the true and enduring advancement of the soul. Then God alone remains to it in its state of naked faith—a faith, that is, which is obscure and stripped of all conscious devotion, and yet which dwells, to quote St Francis de Sales, in the apex of the soul. Then also those two sayings of St Paul are fulfilled, namely, "we go to God in faith", and "the just man lives by faith".

All this will convince you that it is not out of vengeance, but out of mercy—out of very great mercy—that God deprives you of more than he deprives others: it is merely that he is more jealous of possessing all your heart and all your trust. For this reason he needed to deprive you of everything without perceptible compensation, whether exterior or interior.

So, dear Sister, no more reflections upon present or future evils. Let self-abandonment, submission, love and trust be your motto.

LETTER 18: TO MADAME DE LESEN, AFTERWARDS AN ANNONCIADE NUN

The same subject

DEAR SISTER,—You ask me several questions, but what answers can I make that pious reading, meditation, preachers, directors and more than all these, the interior spirit, have not supplied to you time after time?

1. Do you not know that utter dying to self, to live only in God and for God, can only take place by degrees, through a persistent fidelity in making the sacrifice of the intelligence, of the will, of all our passions and caprices, of our feelings and affections; finally and above all, the sacrifice that comes of a complete submission in all trials, in unceasing interior vicissitudes, and in states, sometimes painful indeed, through which

God makes us pass in order to change us completely into him?

2. Do you not know that the state of pure faith excludes all things that can be perceived by the senses? In that state we go forward stripped of everything, and find no support from any created thing; but the pure light of faith remains for ever in the highest point of the soul; and by this simple light we see not only what we must do and what we must avoid, but we learn further that, by God's grace, we live in a horror of, and flight from, evil, in love and performance of good. At such times, then, we must say to ourselves: I am in safety and run no risk to my salvation.—But perhaps I am deluded or I delude others without knowing it?—If you do not know it, you are in good faith; now, good faith pardons everything in the eyes of a God who is equally just and merciful.—Yet, despite that, many fears afflict me.—No doubt of it; for it is our lot in this life to live always in fear; perfect assurance is possible to no one. God wishes us to glorify him by a self-abandonment full of faith and love: it is the tribute of which he is most jealous. Why, then, should we alarm ourselves when he puts us into the position of offering it to him with the more merit? It is when we give up fearing that we have occasion to fear. Every state is to be suspected when it is exempt from all fear, including fear called chaste and loving—that is to say, gentle, peaceful, quiet and untroubled, on account of the love and trust that always go with it. When on the other hand we are obsessed with the fear of displeasing God, we must be reassured by the considerations just detailed: these hold good permanently, since they are based upon the unchallengeable principles of faith. In default of feelings, we must cling to that naked faith which God for ever preserves in the depths of the soul or in the upper part of the spirit.

3. Do you not know that too often the sensible presence of God tends, because of its sweetness, to satisfy self-love, and that to prevent it becoming harmful to us God deprives us of it, leaving us only the presence of pure faith which has neither sweetness, nor form, nor shape, nor any manifestation whatsoever?—But, you object, I do not know if I possess it.—At least you know that you are for ever yearning to possess it. Such yearning, it may well be, is only too fervent in you, since you are

so liable to vexation and grief when you find that yearning thwarted. Nevertheless, you do at least possess that perpetual longing for the divine presence. This longing is known to God who understands even the mere inclination of our hearts. That must suffice you. Live in peace, in trust, in submission, in self-abandonment and in grateful love.

4. Do you not know that the best state of soul for holy communion is that in which God himself works in the soul? Go to communion, then, with complete self-abandonment and in that spiritual poverty and destitution in which it pleases him to put you. Behave throughout as if you were sacrificed, obliterated and altogether lost in your own sight, precisely like Jesus Christ himself in his Sacrament, which is a kind of obliteration. Let your own be united with his. In that state in which nothing created or human survives, God is to be found. The more stripped you are of all things and the more separated from self, the more possessed you will be of God. By steadfast compliance with God's will, make yourself spiritual riches out of your very poverty. Henceforward you will be richer than those who possess the greatest gifts of sweetness and consolation. You will be rich in the blessed will of God, having no fear of self-complacency, since that will is a hardship to human nature and a humiliation to pride. Yet that hardship is sweet and salutary since it serves you as an antidote against the poison of self-love and the venomous stings of the serpent of pride.

LETTER 19: TO MOTHER LOUISE-FRANÇOISE DE ROSEN

Usefulness of ordeals, even when they are punishments

DEAR REVEREND MOTHER,—I do not intend to excuse the imperfections of the dear Sister[1] about whom you are asking my advice, but since God has himself undertaken to punish her by

[1] The nun to whom allusion is made here seems to have been Sister Anne-Marguerite de la Bellière, to whom Fr de Caussade addressed several of his letters. For giving too much time and attention to beautifying the little oratory where she was accustomed to retire she had seen herself deprived of all the lights and consolations which God had showered upon her in prayer.

stern ordeals of his own, her lot seems to me more to be envied than her faults are deserving of blame. How many such faults there are of which it can be said as the Church says of Adam's sin: O blessed fault, that has earned so glorious an atonement! This Sister, you tell me, has perceived her errors, and now, bowed down beneath the burden of spiritual ordeals, is driven to despondency far more than to obstinacy. There is nothing, then, for you to do except to revive her courage and to comfort her gently. Tell her that nothing is lost, and that, far from being abandoned by God, she is much nearer to him than in happier times when all seemed to go well with her. I authorize you to tell her from me that I consider her more fortunate than ever as a result of the spiritual crucifixion by which God has increasingly purified her, as gold in a crucible, in order that he may then unite her to himself more closely.

Both of you should take good note of this great principle: the extent of the soul's purification in its most secret recesses is also the extent of its more or less intimate union with the God of all purity. You may judge from this as to whether the poor Sister should not be the happiest of them all, provided that she can look at her sorrowful state from this point of view. Should the very sternness of the ordeal prevent her from perceiving its value and usefulness, may she rely upon faith, and glorify God by patience and unbounded submission, abandoning herself utterly to her enviable privileges. At the same time may she never slacken in her spiritual exercises and more especially in her observance of prayer and holy communion, or yield herself to a secret longing, suggested by self-love, of shaking off the yoke of God's cross.

But, she will say, such consolations would be legitimate if my state were a spiritual ordeal; as it is, I have too much reason to believe that it is sent from God only as a punishment.—I agree. Yet in this life divine justice inflicts no punishment that is not ordered by the loving design of God's mercy. This is particularly true of souls notably loved by God. Often God permits their faults, that he may draw his glory from them and turn them to the profit of those souls. The chastisements he inflicts upon them sanctify by humiliating them and making them the readier to unite themselves more closely to God in detaching themselves more completely from self. These are then, at one and the same time, chastisements and ordeals: chastisements in so far as they atone for past evils and satisfy divine justice; ordeals in so far as they are useful to the divine mercy as safeguards against the dangers of the future, and as exercises for various meritorious virtues. We cannot too often impress stricken and tortured souls with these truths, whatever be the source of their anguish.

Let us, then, remember that nothing happens which is not a decree of divine Providence or a result of God's adorable will. Supply this dear and affectionate Sister with reading of the most spiritual and interior variety: for this is her one means of diminishing and enduring her persistent tortures, of profiting by her difficulties, and emerging from them to advantage at the time ordained by divine Providence. God inspires me with a spiritual father's true tenderness for her, and I cannot rid myself of the thought that one day she will be my joy and crown in God's sight and even outwardly in the sight of men, because of her supremely edifying life. My hope is that by her ever-present remembrance of the past she will humiliate herself before God, and so lay an enduring foundation for the interior life in which her very faults will be able, after their fashion, to guarantee her perseverance and her progress.

LETTER 20: TO THE SAME

Deep peace as the result of these ordeals

1. This profound calm which you experience, this sweet and intimate peace in which you find yourself wrapped, is by no means an illusion but a true work of the Holy Ghost who speaks in the depths of your heart. Peace and love, as St John of the Cross says, come together in union; peace in a perceptible fashion and love in an imperceptible but very real manner. I am not surprised that when God deigns to accord you these precious gifts, you are not then aware of your ordinary infirmities. Your soul's interior unction is reflected in the body and expels its

woes. I know people who have never found a more certain cure for their ills than this delightful recollection in God when he is pleased to grant us it; for, as you truly say, it is not from us that it comes.

2. To be simply steadfast in the presence of God, abandoning yourself wholly to his love and to the mercy of divine Providence, is yet another inclination which the Holy Ghost puts into the soul. You have nothing to do except to remain simply and humbly in the hands of God, clinging to him and surrendering yourself to his love, that of you, in you, and with you, he may do all he deems good. Yet never stop short at this blessed peace as though it were your objective; go still farther on, for ever inclining your heart to him who gave you that peace, and emphasizing it only so far as it makes still closer your union with God who is your centre, your life and your all. Never forget that you must see yourself swiftly stripped of everything, in supreme poverty of spirit and complete starkness of faith, that you may die utterly to self. For this utter dying can come about only through a complete deprivation whose mere threat makes our human nature shudder. For it seems as if we are about to be lost irretrievably with no perceptible support to strengthen us in the cruellest abandonment.

3. I am glad indeed that God has lessened the grief of reprobation which tortured you. You can now abandon yourself with very little difficulty by this one spiritual act: "May God do with me all that he pleases; I desire by loving and serving him the best I may, to be unreservedly his. He is the God of my heart and the God of my salvation, nor can my salvation be in safer hands. I relinquish it to him in utter trust." Such perfect abandonment alone can enable us to find the assurance which self-love seeks vainly by a recourse to creatures or to ourselves. Our weakness and our blindness should rather make us tremble. Moreover, when we consider ourselves, there would be grounds for our despondency, were we without trust in the infinite goodness of God. It is, then, in him alone, through Jesus Christ, that we find reassurance, and only in proportion as we abandon ourselves unreservedly to him.

4. Your simple *fiat* embraces everything; and the conscious-

ness of your continual dependence is one of God's greatest graces. A realization of his paternal love and of his all-powerful help is the reward that goes with it. When the heart is animated by this filial trust, it is easy indeed to receive all things at the hand of this merciful Father.

5. Pure love, unmixed with selfishness or self-love, can only come from God; but the soul must pass through many privations and ordeals if it is to acquire this infinitely precious gift. There are so many operations necessary for its purification; for we tend always to cling to the delights which God gives us, unless we have learnt through sorrowful experience to love him in the most terrible privations.

I am delighted to hear that the interior spirit is dominant in your community. If blessed recollection be not everything, at least it does everything.

You have done well to omit, so far as I am concerned, all the compliments and good wishes usual at the beginning of the year. God beholds them in your heart where they act as a perpetual prayer for me, even as my desires on your behalf are a prayer in God's eyes. Our desires, St Augustine says, are to God what our words and our speech are to man. He hears them, and we can hope that he will grant them.

LETTER 21 : TO SISTER MARIE-THÉRÈSE DE VIOMÉNIL (1731)

The same subject

It is unnecessary to remind me to pray to God for you; for I take care never to fail in that, especially since I know you to be in a state so afflicting to human nature and yet still more salutary in itself. I confess to you, however, that it has never entered my head to ask God on your behalf for anything other than patience, submission, resignation to his holy will, and utter self-abandonment to his lovable Providence. This, because I am keenly aware of the great grace God gives you and the need you have of it—a need so much the greater in that you are yourself ignorant of it. When this storm is past, you will understand these things in so lively and distinct a manner that you will not know how to show God adequate gratitude in that he has himself put his hand to the work, and in a few months has effected in you what with his ordinary graces you would not have been able to accomplish in twenty years: namely, by these bitter draughts purging you of a certain depth of secret self-love and of a pride the more dangerous in being so subtle and so imperceptible. An infinite number of imperfections, many of which escape our knowledge, spring from this poisonous root—vain reflections on self, still vainer complacencies, vain fears and vain desires, little paltry hopes, suspicions reflecting on our neighbour, little slights and behaviour that is full of self-love. You ran, then, a risk of remaining long a prey to every fault, filled, though you scarcely suspected it, with vanity and trust in yourself and with never the ability or the desire to plumb the profound interior abyss of perversity and natural corruption that you bear within you. Today, God makes you feel this accumulation of miseries, not specifically—since that would move you little—but generally and vaguely in their bulk and sum total. This mass of imperfections is like a crushing weight. Do not, then, search in your conscience for that great sin which seems to you to be hidden in it. The truth is in a sense even more terrifying: it lies in the chaos of interior wretchedness; of weakness, of imperfections, of minor faults, imperceptible but continuous, caused by the self-love of which we have been speaking. God grants you a grace in making you aware of this by his enlightening wisdom: for without the latter you would never perceive it, not even in its consequences, since in this respect you would be in something like the state of blindness and insensibility shown by vicious men with regard to certain gross sins whose gravity long use conceals from them. You were equally unconscious of the leaven of corruption which you bore within you and which spoilt and poisoned all your works, even those in which grace played the main part.

The heavenly physician, then, has shown great goodness to you in applying a vigorous treatment to your sickness. He does this by opening your eyes to the interior abscesses that are eating you away, so that at the sight of the putrefaction there revealed, you should conceive a salutary horror of it. Indeed, neither self-love nor pride can bear so grievous and humiliating a sight. I conclude from this merciful plan that you ought neither to hope nor to expect to see the treatment under which you have been placed ended before your cure is complete. Until then you must make up your mind to receive many incisions from the lancet and to swallow many bitter pills. Yet continue to be of good courage and to rouse your heart to a fresh trust in the loving and fatherly hand which examines you. Humiliate yourself beneath that all-powerful hand; prostrate yourself unceasingly; allow that hand to do its work, never emerging from your scorn and horror of self, and concentrating all your thoughts on your infidelities and ingratitude. Look at yourself constantly, not in the deluding mirror of self-love but in the faithful mirror which God in his mercy holds before your eyes to depict you as you are. Forgetfulness of self, humility and esteem for your neighbour will come of this spectacle often repeated. *Come and see*, the Holy Ghost says to you. That is to say, draw near the Lord, and by the grace of the new enlightenment which he gives you, behold what you have been, and what you are, and what you would have infallibly become.

Take great care never to abstain from prayer or communion, for these must be your buckler and strength. As for sins, you will commit none of any seriousness while you fear, as you do fear, to displease God. That fear alone must reassure you: it is a gift made by the same hand that sustains you invisibly in ordeals.

Have patience: consolation will come in its own time and it will be lasting, while ordeals will quickly be over. But our poor human nature, which dislikes suffering, is impatient to see the end of it. The important thing is that we should turn our tribulations to account. Let us pray, then, and sigh for the strength which we lack and which we can never find in our own resources. You must become fully convinced of this fundamental truth as the result of your own experiences. It is for this reason that God protracts these experiences until you have thoroughly assimilated them and until your interior consciousness can never succeed in wiping them from your soul. You speak of pure love: you must know that a soul has never lived that has attained it without undergoing ordeals and undertaking arduous work interiorly. The longing to reach this blessed goal must make you delight in those works that alone can lead you to it. The more generous you are, the sooner you will see the end of the ordeal and the more profit you will draw from it.

Go forward, then, courageously on your way. Rejoice each time that you discover a new imperfection. Yearn for that blessed moment in which full knowledge of your abysmal wretchedness will finally destroy in you all trust and all vain complacency in yourself. It is then that in horror-stricken flight from the corruption of that grave you will be borne, rapturously joyous, to the bosom of God. After we have been thus completely stripped of self we arrive at the state of thinking only of God, of delighting only in God, of depending only upon and rejoicing only in God. This is the new life in Jesus Christ, and the life of the new Adam after the destruction of the old. Hasten, then, to die as the silkworm dies, to become a beautiful butterfly winging through the air instead of crawling on the earth, as you have so far done.

BOOK V

NEW ORDEALS—SUFFERINGS, AFFLICTIONS, PRIVATIONS

LETTER I : TO SISTER MARIE-THÉRÈSE DE VIOMÉNIL

Sickness and its usefulness—Rules to be followed

DEAR SISTER and dear daughter in God,—The peace of Jesus Christ be always with you!

Do not be afraid lest your sickness prove hurtful to your soul. Be sure on the contrary that you will profit greatly from it, for:

1. To suffer in sweetness and in peace and without offering any resistance is to suffer in the right way, even though you do not then make any very vigorous acts of acceptance. The submissive heart offers these, without taking thought, in the humility and simplicity of its passive acquiescence.

2. Know further, dear Sister, that you are to thank God, as though for a grace, for what you suffer meanly and weakly, that is to say, without much courage. At such times you feel overcome by your ills, upon the verge of giving way to them, inclined to grumble about them and to yield to the rebelliousness of your human nature. Indeed, this is a true grace and a great grace at that, since to suffer this is to suffer with humility and with no great spirit. If, instead, you feel a measure of courage, a measure of strength and conscious resignation, your heart is puffed up by these, and you become, yourself unaware, full of trust in yourself, interiorly proud and presumptuous. In such a state as yours, however, we draw near to God, altogether weak, humiliated and disconcerted at having suffered so feebly. This truth is sure and comforting, essentially interior, and little known. Remember it on all those occasions upon which, feeling more keenly the weight of your tribulations and sufferings, you feel your weakness also, looking always inward in peace and simplicity to all that God wills; for this is the most satisfying way of suffering. It is what Fénelon describes as becoming little in our own eyes and

298

allowing ourselves to be humbled by a perception of our weakness in suffering. Were this truth well known to all people of goodwill, with what peace and tranquillity they would suffer, knowing neither restlessness nor any reflection of self-love on their own weakness and the lack of conscious courage with which they suffer! You must apply this rule in every painful ordeal, and recall it particularly in the midst of those daily difficulties that come your way through the person you find trying, and at all times when you feel antagonistic towards others.

3. Then there is the question of the alleviations which may be useful to you. Certainly you must not believe those many officious people who imagine they can in no way better evince their charity towards the sick than in filling them with every kind of longing—as you say, their flattering remarks are only so many snares. Just as certainly you must not scruple to take humbly and in holy simplicity all that the doctors, nurses and your superiors order. The obedience and renunciation of our own will that we practise in acting in this way are much more agreeable to God than physical mortifications: a truth, ignorance of which brings it about that many devout people are very little mortified in their mortifications. Do not yourself forget the truth; for our self-love and our own will spoil and corrupt everything in practices essentially holy in themselves. How happy would he be who for love of God once and for all gave up all his own desires, ideas and opinions!

LETTER 2

Sufferings of various kinds

DEAR SISTER,—The sufferings concerning which you ask for guidance are of various kinds. Thus, there are great spiritual ordeals and trivial everyday trials. The latter, numerous as they are, make up a larger part of our spiritual riches, provided we know how to turn them to our account. Be guided by me: so far as it depends upon yourself, let not one of these little trials, which present themselves daily, escape you. For by their means God wills that we shall reach the state in which self-love is gradually destroyed. How happy should we be if, in this way, we could at last rid ourselves of that wretched vanity which everything exasperates and irritates, which is the cause of numerous faults in us, and which rend us with its interior perturbation and rebelliousness! If there be an opportunity of enduring greater sufferings, we should reflect that these, too, will pass, and, once passed, we shall get no comfort from them if we have turned them to no profit. On the other hand, what satisfaction there is in, as the saying goes, having made a virtue of necessity and a necessity of virtue! To do this, we must speak of these sufferings only when it is necessary and then as briefly as possible; we must never voluntarily be obsessed by them or the course they take; we must leave everything to divine Providence that turns all things to the greatest advantage of those who are guided by faith and surrender themselves unreservedly to it. I pray God that he will make you realize thoroughly the valuable temporal and spiritual benefits resulting from this blessed practice of complete resignation to all the holy desires of God, and of utter self-abandonment to the adorable decrees of his lovable and incomprehensible Providence, without whose orders, our faith tells us, not one hair of our head falls to the ground nor a single leaf in autumn of all the forests in all the world. Jesus Christ could surely have used no better words than these to convince us that there is no event, big or little, in the world, which this sovereign Providence does not bring about.

How comforting that is, O God, and of how much anxiety we should be relieved if for ever we would look upon you as (to use your own words) a tender Father, and regard ourselves as your dear children, remembering that you never show us greater love than when you compel us to take bitter and salutary remedies! Have pity, O Father of infinite goodness, upon the sick who, in their delirium, rebel against their loving physician and against the purges that are to ensure them life and health!

How many men there are, O God, either blind or mad, who do not wish even to hear these truths spoken of, although you have revealed them in your sacred Scriptures for our present comfort and our eternal salvation!

LETTER 3: TO SISTER MARIE-THÉRÈSE DE VIOMÉNIL

Public calamities and disasters

DEAR SISTER,—The disaster of which you wrote is, as you say, one of the most obvious of God's scourges: happy is he who can draw profit from it for the next life! These God-wrought calamities, if rightly viewed, are worth more than all worldly prosperity. For they are over in a moment, while their fruits are eternal. For some these disasters are but stages in their predestined lot. Yet it must be admitted that for others they can be at the same time acts of reprobation. This, only when they are to blame; for what can be more reasonable, or, in one sense, more easy than to make, as the saying is, virtue of necessity! Why uselessly and criminally resist the paternal hand of God, our Father, that smites us only to detach us from our pitiful worldly goods? Can he grant us a greater grace than to free us from a bond that would cause us to lose the eternal happiness promised us by faith, and leave us in perdition for evermore? On these occasions let us often and attentively ponder the passage from one of the Fathers: "Such is the goodness of the sovereign Father of men that even his wrath springs from his mercy, since he afflicts us only to rescue us from sin and to save our souls." Like a wise surgeon, he cuts putrefying flesh to the quick, to save life and to preserve the rest of the body.

Let it be our custom to see everything from the great standpoint of faith. Then all that happens in this world, whether it inspires fear or desire, will scarcely affect us. Even those eager hopes that so often trouble the peace of the soul and the tranquillity of life will make very little impression on us.

What blindness is to be found among men and what attachment to their own judgement! How rarely we are willing either to confess that we have failed, or to listen carefully, or to take good advice! St Francis de Sales was indeed justified in saying that we are full of unreasonableness; let us humiliate ourselves unceasingly before God; let us learn from this always to distrust ourselves and to be on guard against our own opinions and perverse sentiments. St Catherine of Genoa was so imbued with this that she yearned to be able to cry repeatedly in a voice so loud that all the world should hear: "Lord, help me; succour me; have pity upon me!"

In future, then, do not forget this: a simple *fiat* said of your present troubles and of those which you fear, whether for yourself or for others, will be enough to secure you a rich treasure of peace, calm and tranquillity upon this earth. Though this practice does not give you perfect peace at once, at least it will fill you with joy, and will bring you lasting comfort in all your troubles and in all your fears.

LETTER 4

Antagonistic dispositions and characters

DEAR SISTER,—Far from chiding you, I can but congratulate you on having at last had an opportunity of practising true charity. The antipathy you feel for the person with whom you are in continuous contact, the antagonism of your ideas and dispositions, the vexation she causes you by her manners and her talk, are so many sure guarantees that the charity you show in respect to her is essentially supernatural, without any admixture of merely human feeling. It is pure gold you are amassing, and the size of your hoard will depend only on you. Thank God, therefore, and in order to lose none of the incalculable advantage of your present position be strict in following the rules I am going to give you.

1. Patiently endure the involuntary antagonism which the behaviour of this Sister arouses in you, in precisely the same way as you would endure a bout of fever or a headache. Your antipathy is indeed no more than an interior fever with its shivering and its paroxysms. How humiliating, painful and torturing this fever is, and how meritorious and sanctifying in consequence!

2. Never talk about this Sister in the way, it may be, others do; but always speak well of her; for there is good in her. And who in this world has no evil in him?—Who is perfect? It is possible that, without imagining or wishing it, you try her more

than God tries you through her! "God often polishes one diamond by means of another," Fénelon says.

3. When you have committed this fault or that, straightway make a new start by humiliating yourself sweetly without voluntary vexation either against her or against yourself, evincing neither perturbation, anger nor frustration. Our faults, when we atone for them thus, become profitable and beneficial to us. By such wretchedness and daily faults God constantly makes us small in our own eyes and keeps us in true humility of heart.

4. For the rest, whatever is said or done, do not interfere unless it be your duty. Do not talk about it nor think about it. Leave everything to divine Providence. Though everything perish and come to nothing, it matters little, so only we are God's and gain our salvation.

But I foresee your question: If this or the other thing happen, what will become of me?—Let this be your attitude: I know nothing I can do, and I wish to know nothing; for I should be sorry indeed to come out of this blessed state of self-abandonment that allows me to live in absolute dependence upon God, to live from day to day, from hour to hour, from moment to moment without concerning myself with either tomorrow or the future generally. Tomorrow will take care of itself: he who upholds us today, will uphold us tomorrow with his invisible hand. The manna of the desert was given for only a day's supply at a time. Whoever, either distrustfully or out of false forethought, gathered enough for the morrow, found it went bad. Let us not set up, by our own industry and blind and restless foresight, a providence as full of faults as God's is of enlightenment and certainty. Let us rely solely upon his fatherly care; let us surrender ourselves to it utterly for all our temporal and spiritual and even our eternal welfare.

For such is true and complete self-abandonment, that binds God to take charge of everything in regard to those who abandon everything to him, thus paying homage to his sovereign dominion, his power, his wisdom, his goodness, his mercy and all his infinite perfections. *Amen, Amen.*

LETTER 5

The same subject

You are right to thank God, dear Sister, that he prompts your heart to peace, sweetness and charity towards the person who has been deputed to wait upon you. In this he grants you a great grace. It may be that he will allow her still, either through ignorance or inadvertence, or even, if you like, through caprice and bad temper, to give you an opportunity of proving your patience. Seek then, Sister, to profit by these precious opportunities that so serve to win God's heart.

Alas, every day we offend this God of goodness in many ways. Not only through ignorance and inadvertence, but with malice and deliberation. We want him to forgive us, and indeed he does so most mercifully, and yet we are unwilling to forgive our fellows! Nevertheless, every day we repeat the prayer taught us by Jesus Christ our Master: "Forgive us, O Lord, as we forgive others." Let us never forget God's great promise that he will deal with us as we deal with our neighbour: let us then show our neighbour forbearance and helpfulness, charity, sweetness and condescension; and then God, faithful to his word, will deal with us likewise. I am elaborating this point somewhat, because it will furnish you daily with opportunities for practising the rarest and most enduring virtues—charity, patience, sweetness and humility of heart; benevolence, the surrender of your own inclinations and so forth. These little daily virtues, faithfully practised, will reap you a rich harvest of grace and reward through all eternity. Thus, more successfully than by any other of your methods or practices, you can obtain the great gifts of interior prayer, peace of heart, recollection, the continual presence of God and his pure and perfect love. This one cross, borne patiently, will secure you numerous graces, while ordeals, seemingly more painful, will avail you less in detaching you perfectly from self and attaching you completely to God.

LETTER 6: TO SISTER MARIE-THÉRÈSE DE VIOMÉNIL

Vexations of various kinds

DEAR SISTER,—How can you continue to be astonished at what your experience should have long since convinced you of? As long as we are upon this earth, even were we to live only with saints, we shall need patience in order to be tolerant of one another. It is good that this is so, in order that we may have more opportunities of practising those most meritorious of virtues—charity, humility and self-renunciation. Let us, then, with a good grace, resign ourselves to this necessity; let us try to turn to advantage our neighbour's faults as well as our own by being indulgent towards the former and ridding ourselves quickly of the latter. This is the one means of preserving our peace of soul.

I agree that your situation is no easy one. Yet what rich rewards it will bring you in heaven! And what a magnificent opportunity for penance and the performance of heroic acts! You cannot fail very soon to acquire the grace of the interior life, if only you continue to practise self-abnegation and persistent renunciation—this out of charity, humility, resignation and self-abandonment to God. Such virtuous acts will speedily prepare your heart for the sweet inpouring of divine love. Consequently, I should be very sorry on your behalf if you were more easily and agreeably situated. You complain of trials which the saints, on the other hand, esteemed and eagerly sought out, because they knew the value and advantages of them in remoulding us interiorly and bringing us into true union with God.

You have been assailed for a very long time past by a temptation, which is the more dangerous in that you little suspect its danger. It is due to the fact that you have never understood nor assimilated the truth, itself an article of faith, that all that happens in the world, with sin the one exception, comes straight from God and the decrees of his will. Again, although it is certain that God never desires sin or, therefore, the slanders, persecutions and injustices of every kind of which the elect are victims, he does, however, desire its consequences. In other words

he desires that his elect shall be slandered, persecuted, humiliated and in many cases tortured in a score of different ways. I
say that this is true, too, of the consequences of our own faults: a
man, through his imprudence or even through definitely blameable acts, falls into poverty, into sickness, into grievous afflictions
of every kind. God, though he abominates the sins, does indeed
desire their consequences—namely, this poverty, this sickness
and change of fortune. That man can and must then say: "Lord,
I have thoroughly deserved it; you have permitted it; you wish
it so. May your blessed will be done: I acquiesce in all things; I
adore and I submit!"

It was his comprehension of this great truth that made that
holy man Job say: "The Lord hath given; the Lord hath taken
away; blessed be the name of the Lord!" He did not say: The
Lord hath given and the devil hath taken away—for the devil
can only do what God allows him to do. It was from this principle that Job drew his perfect submission, his courage and constancy, and his peace of soul.

Because you have never assimilated this great truth, you have
never been able to resign yourself to certain states and happenings, or, it follows, to remain steadfast and tranquil in the will of
God. Always the devil has tempted, perturbed and circum-
vented you in this matter by numerous illusions and false reasonings. Seek, then, I adjure you for the sake of your salvation and
your peace of soul, to emerge from this error: so will you have
done with all your vexations and all your heart's rebelliousness.

To that end, make it your habit to perform acts of faith and
submission in relation to all events due either to men, or the
devil's malice, or to your own misdoing, or even to your own
sins. God has permitted it so. He is the Master. May he be
blessed for it, and his holy will be accomplished in all things:
Fiat, fiat!

Your position is very painful, it is true: for that reason it is very
sanctifying. No better penance is open to you, assured as you are
that it is imposed by God himself. Everything antagonistic to it
which the devil implants in your mind is an obvious illusion intended to rob you of God's peace and to make you sad, restless
and perturbed, always discontented with your present state,

always longing for another. For this same reason the majority of those in the world are as wretched as they are blameable, since they are reluctant to appreciate thoroughly this important and comforting truth of which I have just reminded you. What torments they would spare themselves and what rewards they would reap from the worst of their tribulations, if they would convince themselves that God makes all things serve his glory and his creatures' greatest good; and that it remains for them merely to turn everything to their advantage by a blind and utter submission that knows no exception and brooks no antagonistic reasoning, at least of a deliberate kind. Ah, why cannot I engrave this truth upon your heart and mind, writing it there with my own blood? But God, I am sure, will little by little do this himself, if only you are really willing to co-operate with his grace by promptly rejecting all contrary thoughts. Once more I entreat you, submit yourself, in spite of all your repugnance and aversions, to the secret orders of that adorable Providence and you will sanctify yourself as God desires.

LETTER 7: TO THE SAME

The same subject—Rules to be followed

I ADMIT, dear Sister, that there is nothing more difficult than to maintain perfect equanimity and unswerving patience in the midst of domestic vexations and in our contact with people of a different disposition living with us. The continuity of those annoyances makes us, in a measure, powerless at times to preserve our self-control. Yet if at one moment we fall, we rise the next. The fall is a weakness; the rising again a virtue. If we avoid a fall, we resume our serenity, knowing no vexation. Slowly God gives all things to those who can wait for them patiently.

But your own desires are impetuous and you seek to be perfect all at once. We must try by degrees to moderate the turbulence and agitation of those desires which battle in our heart and threaten to break it. Now, if we are unable wholly to prevent them clashing, let us at least try to endure this affliction gently and humbly, and not set out to aggravate it by tormenting ourselves for being tormented.

The difficulties created for you and the injustices done to you by people are, I admit, thoroughly disagreeable. I felt indignant at their mere recital. Yet what remedy is there for this except that of which we have already made use to cure our other ills—we must lift up our eyes to heaven saying: "Lord, you ordain it, you have permitted it to be so; I adore and submit myself. Your blessed will be done! Your divine decree enables me to bear your cross to expiate my sins and earn me heaven. *Fiat, fiat!*"

Did I know a better remedy, I would tell you of it. Yet as I am convinced that this is the most efficacious of all, you will not expect me to look for others. I admit that on such occasions it is almost impossible not to let a few small signs of impatience, rebelliousness and vexation escape you, at least interiorly; yet you must always come back to God and your better self as soon as may be, in order to humiliate yourself sweetly and equably, beseeching God urgently for the necessary patience.

LETTER 8: TO THE SAME

Vexations caused by good people

1. The antagonism shown you has been so much the more painful in that it has come from those of whom you least expect it. Yet be sure that it has only earned you more merit for heaven. Men's ideas are different, varying according to their attitudes and disposition. Each is wedded to his own opinion and believes right to be on his side. O men! O men! to what are we reduced! What abysmal humiliation for all mankind! It is good to have touched the bottom of that abyss, for we then find it easier to put all our trust in none but God.

A mind enlightened by faith inclines the heart to submit to the plans of divine Providence who allows good men to cause each other suffering that they may be detached from one another. On such occasions we have only resignation and self-abandonment to God in which to find our strength. For both of these leave us unaffected by the apparent reasons we have for being perturbed. Whether by considering ourselves, or whether by observing the behaviour of those who try us, we shall never lack plausible motives for growing indignant or agitated. Such intemperate moods are as opposed to reason as they are to religion; while the peace of which they deprive us is a boon incomparably superior to all those for which we sacrifice it.

2. For the rest, it is legitimate to speak in confidence to a director for the sake of gaining comfort, strength and advice. Even so, discretion and charity must always be shown. The best and most perfect thing of all is silence: it is to God alone that we ought to confide these vexations, telling him everything as if we spoke to a friend and director worthy of our complete trust. This is a prayer as excellent as it is easy—a prayer that is known as the prayer of trust and the outpouring of the heart to God. By it we are strengthened interiorly; from it we draw comfort, peace and courage.

So long as you live more or less as you are doing—very imperfectly doubtless, yet with a sincere desire to do better and to make what effort your weakness permits—your soul's safety is assured. Even the fear you feel in this connection is a gift of God, providing it does not go to the length of vexing you and making you give up your observance of the sacraments, the practice of virtue, and your spiritual exercises. As for the hardness and insensibility of heart of which you complain, have patience and make offering of this difficulty to God in a spirit of penitence, just as you would offer him your sicknesses and physical infirmities. Those of the soul are still harder to endure, and, therefore, more meritorious.

LETTER 9: TO THE SAME
The same subject

I FEEL keenly, dear Sister, the painfulness of the ordeal to which God submits you, and the anguish your heart must feel at the wounds you receive daily. It is true, I agree, that you would need to be a saint to let such things pass and feel no kind of resentment. But if you cannot yet reach such perfection in such pin-pricking vexations, endeavour at least first, to banish as far as may be every thought, reflection and remark that may embitter your heart: secondly, when you cannot rid yourself of them, repeat interiorly in your most intimate soul: "O God, you have allowed this to be; may your adorable desires and decrees be accomplished in all things: I make you a sacrifice of this difficulty and all its consequences; it shall take whatever form it pleases you: you are the Master; may you be blessed for all things and in all things. *Fiat!*" Then add further: "For love of you, with all my heart I pardon the person who is the cause of my suffering; and, to show the sincerity of my feelings towards her, I beseech you to grant her every kind of grace, blessing and happiness." When your heart cries out against this, say: "O God, you see my wretchedness; at least I long to have all these feelings, and I implore you for your grace." Once you have done this, think no more of it; if unworthy sentiments continue to torment you, resign yourself to endure that torment and so comply with the divine will that allows it, contenting yourself with renewing your offering in the depths of your soul. This is a noble means of sharing in the chalice of our good Master, Jesus Christ.

LETTER 10: TO THE SAME

Seeing God in our trials

I AM surprised, dear Sister, that with the help of the maxims I have so often impressed upon you, you are not yet in a state to recognize the hand of Providence in the misunderstandings that can arise between even the best intentioned people.

God, you assert, does not initiate things that lead to trouble.— In one sense that is true, but is it not true also that God has permitted, and often permits, his servants to give way to errors and illusions that serve to test and prove them and, as a result, to sanctify them, by means of one another? Examples of this are numerous in the lives of the saints, and, in recent times, in the lives of St Francis Regis and St Margaret Mary Alacoque. Seek to be guided not by human judgement which is weak, narrow and blind, but by the divine wisdom which is sure, righteous and infallible. So shall we make all things serve our edification, yet leave untroubled the peace of our heart and mind.

LETTER II : TO THE SAME

Loss of human support

You consider yourself much to be pitied, dear Sister, because God has deprived you of the help which he has afforded you until now. You are indeed to be pitied, but solely because of your failure to resign yourself to the plans of Providence. Is it not deplorable that a soul whom God has chosen, whom he has admitted to his service and heaped with his graces, cannot content itself with him, but yearns earnestly for small exterior aids? Such aids are good when God gives them; but, when he withdraws them, how much better is it to rely upon him alone! What joy that soul, who loves him truly, experiences in saying to him over and over again: "O God, you are my all. I have only you, O Lord, but you suffice me, nor do I ask anything more except from you." The all-powerful hand of God then comes to take the place of the poor weak reed upon which it leaned. Assured of this, how can it consider itself forsaken and unfortunate? You are frightened because from now on you will receive guidance only after the event. Yet I say that after receiving so much advice and so many letters from the most enlightened directors, you ought to be in such a state spiritually that you could direct others. Again, even if in certain circumstances you are in considerable doubt, ought that to make you despond? You must lift your heart to God who cannot refuse to give you guidance now that he has taken all other guides from you. Without hesitation you must make up your mind as to what in good faith you believe most expedient and most useful for souls, and most in accordance with God's will. Whatever may happen afterwards, you will know that you have acted wisely, since you could not do better in the circumstances. You surely do not imagine that God asks the impossible? Our infinitely good God loves uprightness and simplicity; he is content when we do what we can, having previously and trustfully implored his divine guidance.

You tell me that in your lonely state you can conceive of nothing that will not involve you in difficulty and affliction. How great is that grace of God which must have developed, or which of necessity will develop, in you complete detachment from all created things! Surely it is to his most cherished souls that God gives such a grace? O daughter of little faith, yet a daughter well-beloved of God, complain in future if you dare!—God alone, you go on, can know what I suffer.—If only you do not talk so much about it, I shall congratulate you with all my heart: so used the blessed Mother St Teresa to say during her great interior trials.

It is a good sign when we find life hard and sad. Death inspires fear because of God's judgement. Yet, provided this fear has no agitation in it, it comes from the Holy Ghost: I should be fearful indeed for anyone who was without this salutary fear.

LETTER 12: TO THE SAME

A director's departure

DEAR SISTER,—I am neither angry nor astonished at your intense feeling upon the subject of your director's departure. If, far from allowing yourself to be cast down by this feeling, you can conquer it, it will provide you with opportunities for the most meritorious acts of self-abandonment to God. In this way you will slowly become detached from creatures, and unite yourself to him who alone is your sovereign good. What happiness, what assurance in the next life, what unbroken peace in this, to exist only in God and to have no riches, no support, no help, no hope other than in God alone! Would I could send you the delightful letter one of your Sisters has just written to me. She says that for a whole month the one thought—None but God: I have none but God—brought her such strength and comfort that instead of regret she has felt deep peace and inexplicable joy. To her it seemed that God took the director's place, and that he alone would henceforth instruct and correct her. It is to him alone that I commended you on leaving and to whom I always commend you. This is the farewell made to me by the

Mother Superior of . . .[1] upon the eve of my departure: "I say good-bye to you, Father, in the will of God." That evening she comforted the other Sisters and next morning she gave the conference precisely as usual. Since then she has had much to suffer, but throughout she has shown a self-abandonment worth more than any contentment—even than any spiritual contentment.

LETTER 13: TO THE SAME

The same subject

I ADMIT that a visible guide, endowed with all the qualities requisite for such difficult work, is a grace of God and a powerful support for the soul. Yet, when divine Providence refuses us this help or takes it from us, if only we can say then with all our heart: "O God, I have no longer anyone but you, and I no longer want anyone but you", this will avail us more than all else we can have through the medium of directors. It cannot be denied that God often takes away from us all exterior aid only that he may possess all our trust. Oh, if we could but give him it to the uttermost nor share one whit of it with whomsoever it be, how thoroughly compensated we should be for the absence of all help deriving from creatures! And what interior freedom we should know! If, instead, you have far different feelings, this is because you are still far removed from that purity of love which ensures our attachment to God for himself alone. Indeed there is nothing plainer: the grief and excessive anxiety to which your soul is exposed at perceiving itself deprived of exterior help can come only from an intemperate attachment to those human aids.

Such attachment arouses God's jealousy, above all when favoured souls are concerned, whose utter trust and utter affection he desires to possess. Yet be of good cheer! Since God wills that you should endure the grievous pain of such an attachment, he seeks by this very pain to decrease the attachment little by little and at last free you from it once and for all. Allow

[1] The nun here mentioned by Fr de Caussade seems to have been the Mother Superior of the Refuge at Nancy, founded by Mme Ranfanig.

313

him to effect this purification within you that is so much to be desired, and endeavour to co-operate faithfully in his plans. For this is a work of grace as salutary as it is painful; we must endure it patiently as we endure the hardship of those painful remedies used to cure certain grave sicknesses. Now, if you cannot attain this perfect attachment thus quickly, at least aspire to it with all your strength, and restrain as much as may be the sorrow that you cannot altogether obliterate; God will do the rest when he deems it expedient.

Make frequent offerings to him of all that pleases him, humbly and simply setting your wretchedness and weakness before him. This is sufficient. Your good Master asks no more of you now that this is all you are able to do. Pick yourself up again after your falls which in this matter are not sins but mere imperfections. For the rest, be content with a confessor who gives you absolution. Go to communion as usual. In all things else God shall be your support. The instructions which have been given you in the past will be sufficient guidance for you, provided you allow God to quicken them in your heart with his interior unction. As long as you wish for more than this, you will only torment yourself vainly and lay yourself open to many imperfections that will hamper you in the interior life, as other people are set back in the way of perfection by real sins.

The fear of not recognizing or of overlooking interior sins is another temptation the devil sends to perturb and rob you of your peace. I order you in God's name to calm yourself in respect to this, and to be content with including in your confessions those things for which your conscience most reproaches you. Leave everything else to God's great mercy, without in any way making a burden of it. Then your confessions will no longer be distressing but tranquillizing and, therefore, profitable. If we give way to perturbation, we get little profit from it, and so the devil gains his end. When you find it difficult to discover definite and recognized sins in yourself, mention a few specific sins of your past life, and thereafter remain in peace. This is the normal practice of wisely instructed people, and you will run no risk in following it.

LETTER 14: TO THE SAME

Self-abandonment in ordeals of this kind

DEAR SISTER,—1. I exhort you now and always to patience and self-abandonment to God, because these are your need. God alone is all and all the rest is nothing; let us cling to him then as closely, as fully and as firmly as we can. He has his ideas and his plans that he does not allow us to plumb: the one cure for all our ills, the one comfort in all our troubles, is submission and utter self-abandonment. There is no surer means of amassing a fortune in eternity, and of winning that true life which shall never end.

2. Regard your ills and infirmities as an excellent substitute for purgatory, which you would have to endure still more rigorously in the next life had you not suffered it in the present. A simple *fiat* in all your interior and exterior difficulties will be enough to gain you great sanctification. Remember the fine saying of St Francis de Sales to one of his penitents: "My daughter, repeat constantly throughout the day: 'Yes, heavenly Father, yes; now and for ever, yes.' " This is a very short and simple practice; we need no other to acquire that perfection which often we go so far to seek, when we can find it with such ease without emerging from our interior soul.

3. I am most edified by your holy reflections upon the subject of the little consolation you get from creatures. I warmly approve that you should see in this a merciful chastisement of your exceeding tenderness and excessive affection for your friends and relatives. Such an ordeal, thus endured, can only tend greatly to bring back your heart to him for whom we are made and apart from whom we can never find true peace.

4. Yet I see today, as previously, that the most painful of your ordeals is the deprivation of all visible aids for your soul. I have told you often, and I tell you again, that while such aids are truly a grace of God, yet with respect to certain people and certain temperaments I hold that the deprivation of these aids is, essentially, a still greater grace and a more effectual means of sanctification. Listen to me without bias: when God does a soul

315

the honour of being jealous of its love, the greatest grace he can give it is slowly to take from it all that can divert that love from him; for the soul would never have the strength or the courage to reach such detachment itself. Now God long since saw that, once you had been detached from every creature, your one remaining attachment would be to your spiritual guide. This attachment most certainly was not blameable; but it was of the senses, as was the attachment of the Apostles to their divine Master before his resurrection. God, who is jealous and requires to be loved purely and uniquely for himself, could not tolerate this kind of sharing; and he has taken away the object which occupied your heart's affections in equal shares with himself. It thus becomes your greatest cross, since your heart has been assailed in its most susceptible part, and since it can also find the most plausible pretexts for making its grief seem legitimate. I imagine you telling yourself that you do not regret this deprivation on account of the consolations it has taken away from you but because of the help in your spiritual advancement of which it robs you.—Error and illusion of self-love! A mere *fiat* in this kind of deprivation has more merit in God's eyes than we can acquire as the result of the noblest, most meritorious and most comforting direction in the world.—Yet, you will say, if you enjoyed consistent direction, you would not commit so many faults.—My answer is that these faults are less displeasing to God than even the slightest attachment of the heart, however pure and innocent it may seem, or essentially is. Accordingly I cannot too greatly admire God's kindness towards you, disciplining you as he does for years at a stretch by this kind of deprivation, designed to break even the least of your attachments. He assails your body with physical ills, in order to detach you from yourself; he assails the soul with weariness, aversions, spiritual insensibility and other disabilities in order to detach you, interiorly, from all sensible aids and consolations. If you allow him to work freely in you, you will come at last to cling only to him in pure faith, in pure spirit, and, to quote St Francis de Sales, in the highest part of the soul. Allow, then, the God of goodness to do his work. For it is indeed his due that you should put your trust in him.

I cannot resist saying that the longer I live the more clearly I both perceive and understand that all depends upon God, and that we have but to make surrender of everything to him to be successful in everything. I have no sooner made the sacrifice to him than I find everything fall out as I would wish.

5. You do well to reflect that there are many others who bear a heavier cross than yourself. But remember that consciousness of its heaviness does not hinder us from being submissive to God. We can easily be deprived of a submission that is at once sensible and comforting, but we shall never be without that of pure faith and pure spirit. The latter is the more meritorious in that no vain complacency can spoil it. This is why to many, who allow their souls to cry out in humiliation beneath the weight of their afflictions, God grants only the second kind of submission.

God tempers the wind to the shorn lamb; we are always given special graces with which to endure extraordinary misfortunes. Patience makes the unpreventable tolerable, to quote a pagan philosopher who had only human reason to enlighten him. Faith and religion, the sight of the cross and the prospect of eternal happiness, should surely make us think and say as much.

LETTER 15

Usefulness of these afflictions

DEAR SISTER,—When I think of the infinite value of your present tribulations I dare not wish for them to end; what I do wish is that you shall be kept in a continual state of sacrifice and self-abandonment, or, at least, that you shall strive after this, yearn for it and unceasingly beseech God for it. When our hearts are thus inclined, our wise employment of tribulations and afflictions advances our eternal welfare more than do success and consolations. In a short while our difficulties will be over, while we shall have the full stretch of eternity to rejoice and give thanks for them. This must comfort us in all our difficulties, both interior and exterior. This, too, will be our joy in paradise. Let us reflect that we have but little time left to us before we enter it, and let us seek at whatever cost to ourselves to make ourselves worthy of the infinite happiness that awaits us.

*[1] Further, dear Sister, I already see plainly the rich harvest reaped in your soul by the ordeal through which God has made you pass. Although it has brought down violent storms upon you interiorly I cannot doubt but that it has helped your spiritual progress very greatly. Through it you have learned to be crucified interiorly, to find all things repugnant, to make God constant and painful sacrifices, to discipline yourself in many things, to acquire patience, to become submissive, and to abandon yourself to God.—Yet how, you ask, can all this have come about?—It has been accomplished in the highest part of your soul and often without your knowledge, by your endurance of innumerable troubles, setbacks and dislikes, even though you have been unaware of your submission, which you often practise without realizing it. There have been times when you have been convinced that you lacked it, and that you scarcely so much as desired it. Yet then—even then—it was there in the depth of your soul. Oh, how marvellous God is in his works! Had you known, as I, the secrets of your soul you would, it may be, have spoilt everything by hidden reversions to self and vain complacency in yourself. Let us allow God to do the work; for it is only in our ignorance, our darkness and our blindness that he can work, as he wishes, without our spoiling his work. Even our humiliation when we believe that all goes badly and all is lost makes this manifest. For you the fact that I perceive your progress clearly must be enough to make you sure of it, responsive to it, and encouraged by it.

Oh, how I would that in all things you had more trust in God, more self-abandonment to his wise and divine Providence that controls even the slightest happenings in this life! In every case he turns them to the advantage of those who put their full trust in his Providence, and who unreservedly abandon themselves to his paternal care. O God, how such trust and such utter self-surrender bring interior peace, and bring release from an infinite multiplicity of cares that are so disturbing and vexatious! Yet as we cannot reach this state all at once, but only by slow

[1] The passage marked off by the two asterisks is taken from a letter addressed to Sister Marie-Thérèse de Vioménil in 1738.

degrees and by almost imperceptible advances, we must yearn for it ceaselessly, beseech God for it, and perform spiritual acts to secure it. We shall not lack opportunities: let us grasp them, and make it our endeavour at all times to say: "Yes, O God, you order it, you permit it thus; therefore, I too desire it out of love of you; aid and strengthen my weakness." All this must be said and done gently, effortlessly, in the higher part of the soul, and despite interior rebelliousness and repugnance, which we must ignore, apart from enduring them patiently and making offerings of them to God. Let us even seek to perform such acts with these repugnances and this rebelliousness, since God wishes or allows it to be so; and when we fail, let us act as it is our duty to act after every one of our faults, attempting by interior humility to regain what we have lost. Yet let this humility be gentle and tranquil without vexation or anger against ourselves any more than we feel them towards our neighbour. I mean without voluntary anger or vexation; for the initial and unintentional impulses do not depend upon ourselves; while, providing that we give no consent to them, they will enable us the more meritoriously to exercise patience, gentleness and humility.

Dangers are ceaseless and unavoidable in this wretched state of spiritual exile. The one means of safeguarding ourselves from them is to take, neither eagerly nor anxiously, the precautions prudence suggests, and then to rely upon Providence for everything. We cast ourselves into God's arms and dwell there in peace and tranquil carefreeness, like a little child in the arms of its kind and tender mother or of its nurse. O God, he who can be faithful in this practice shall surely be rich indeed in peace and spiritual merit. Seek to follow it at all times and in all places, and thus have some small share in this interior state. Nothing is more calculated to calm and curb the impetuosities and vagaries of human nature and nothing more meet to prevent or diminish its many bitter griefs and restless forebodings.*

P. F.'s state is worthy of compassion. God shows his eagerness to sanctify him, since he has brought such affliction upon him at the end of his days. It is hard, indeed, humanly speaking, to be neglected at such a time of life; yet what comfort to suffer

greatly for God, before going to him and standing before him!
To be comfortably off and well cared for is, in truth, one of
God's boons, but one very different from the former. God preserve me from such graces, for I would grow too fond of them, it
may be, and find my consolation in them. Indifferent virtue can
make good use of the one; but heroic virtue is necessary to make
good use, in God's sight, of the other. I remain, yours in our
Lord, till death and even after it, if God is merciful to me, as
I greatly hope.

LETTER 16: TO SISTER MARIE-THÉRÈSE DE VIOMÉNIL

The same subject

1. I am not astonished, dear Sister, at the grief caused you by
the painful ordeal to which our Lord has just subjected you.
This kind of happening affects us the more keenly in that it
wounds us in our deepest affections. Yet if I am not astonished
at this involuntary grief, I adjure you to make every effort to
replace it by complete resignation to all God's wishes. Oh, how
great are the treasures of grace, of merit and of peace which this
attitude brings us! For this reason I have exhorted you for so
long and exhort you yet again to perfect self-abandonment,
wishing you to be as tranquil and as happy as you are blessed.
You have not yet reached that state; but by degrees it will come,
God helping you.

2. God allows my sick relative to remain still in the same
state, that this may test and convert the whole family. If they
profit by it, as I have every reason to hope they will, from the
bottom of my heart I shall bless God for this happy mischance as
of more worth than all the wealth in the world.

3. I have just lost the best and closest of my surviving friends—
the man I most esteemed, and upon whom I could most rely.
God wished it so, his blessed will be done. *Fiat!* I commend him
to your prayers.

4. God be blessed for all things and in all things! and particularly in those things of which he can make such use to sanctify
his elect, each helping each! On this subject the holy Arch-

bishop of Cambrai has remarked notably: "God often makes use of one diamond to polish another." How greatly this thought serves to comfort us and to prevent us from being shocked by the petty persecutions in which honest men reciprocally indulge.

5. In many districts, as in your own, hail and rain have done much damage. May God give us grace to profit by each of heaven's scourges for the expiation of our sins! A mere *fiat*, sincerely said, is of more worth than all the prosperity of our dreams, since it lays up treasure in eternity. When once we are filled with these high hopes, we find ourselves far less sensitive to the mischances of this short and wretched life.

6. By dint of pondering upon death, by degrees we are able to look upon it tranquilly. The incomparable Father Bourdaloue has said finely: "The thought of death is, in truth, sad; but as the result of looking upon it as salutary, in the end it becomes agreeable"; while it is related of a great Jesuit theologian, Father Francis Suarez, that he said at his dying hour: "I should never have thought it was so sweet to die."

7. We sometimes hear it said: But I have no aid to give me strength and no instruction to give me courage.—What better opportunity for sacrifice: *Fiat, fiat!* The most strengthening instructions are of less worth than what we gain by a mere *fiat* said when exterior aids are withdrawn. The great way of final perfection is summarized in those few words of the Lord's Prayer: *Fiat voluntas tua!* You have only to frame them with your lips, or better still in your heart, as best you may; then you can be wholly sure that, given this interior inclination, nothing either will or can be lacking to you. Learn from this how to find peace in the midst of griefs and difficulties, since all things God wishes or permits are therefore good. Troubles and afflictions are such great graces that ordinarily it is only these which convert the wicked; while honest men reach perfection only by their means.

8. God can easily compensate us for everything, and he does thus compensate us, when we desire nothing but him and when in him we put all our expectations. To lead us slowly and by a blessed compulsion to that good and desirable state of soul, he often takes from us all human aids and all human comfort, even as he gives a bitter taste to worldly pleasures to disgust and

detach from those pleasures the worldly souls he seeks to save. Blessed bitterness! blessed deprivations! So should we regard them when we appreciate that they come from God's goodness rather than from his justice.

Behaviour to be shown in these ordeals

DEAR SISTER,—Could you not check both your fears and your tears, since you have so often discovered that in all which keenly affects your heart, you have been liable to indulge in delusions and to imagine non-existent terrors? If you find it impossible to prevent these deplorable vagaries of your imagination, seek at least to profit by them in making them a subject for interior sacrifices and an opportunity for manifesting complete self-abandonment to every decree of divine Providence, whatever it be.

I agree with you: I, too, have never desired—still less have I implored—either difficulties or consolations. Those sent by Providence suffice and we have no need to desire or secure them ourselves. Our need is to expect and to prepare for them. In this way we shall have more strength and courage with which to encounter and endure them, as we must when God sends them.

This is one of my most cherished practices that avails me both for this life and the next. I make offering to God in advance of every sacrifice, the idea of which has entered my mind without my seeking it. To enable us to acquire the merit of such an offering God troubles us with these ideas and fears of future misfortunes that he has no intention of sending us. When, on the other hand, he sends us consolations, whether spiritual or temporal, we must accept them with simplicity, gratitude and thanksgiving, but without overeagerness or excessive delight; for all joy that is not joy in God can only tend to inflame self-love.

Your loneliness during the absence of her upon whom you have had occasion to depend most, grievous though it has seemed, can only have been beneficial to you. How many acts of resignation in your weakness and helplessness, how many upliftings of your heart towards God, how many acts of love and blessed resolutions it must have made possible for you! Righteous intentions will save you. God beholds them in your heart. Each of us has his way that he must follow according to his lights. Seek by degrees to make use of your present situation and of your heart's bitterness and to place all your trust in God alone for all your concerns, whether temporal or eternal.

The present calamities of which you give me so moving a picture, put you under the compulsion, for your very peace of soul's sake, to make constant and meritorious sacrifices to God. These public calamities are great, and great too is your own share in them. Yet the life of sinful men, as we all are, must from first to last be spent in crosses and penitence. God shows his mercy by holding out to us the remedy we must take. His chalice is bitter, it is true, but infinitely less bitter than the flames of hell and purgatory; and since, grudgingly or ungrudgingly, we must drink this salutary chalice, let us, as the proverb has it, make a virtue of necessity and a necessity of virtue. So shall we find adversity sweet.

Interior tribulations are, as you say, the most torturing. Equally they are the most meritorious and the most purifying; while, once these purifications and interior detachments are effected, life is all the sweeter because of them. It is then the easier to achieve full self-abandonment, and filial trust in God alone through Jesus Christ.

The reflections made by you upon this subject are in truth just and reasonable, although all too humanly inspired. Our need is in every case to get back from them to self-abandonment and to hope placed solely in divine Providence; for what can men accomplish, and to what vicissitudes are they not exposed? Depend then solely upon God who is for ever unchanging, who knows our needs better than we do and who supplies them unfailingly like the good Father he is. Yet he has often to do with children so blind that they know not what they ask. In the very prayers that seem to them most righteous and most reasonable they find delusion in that they seek to foresee a future that belongs to God alone. When he has deprived us of what appears to us to be needful, he has the knowledge and the ability to make up for it imperceptibly by numerous secret means unknown to ourselves. So true is this that these mere shrinkings and afflictions of our hearts, when endured in patience and interior silence, advance a soul more than contact with, and blessed instruction from, the most skilful director alive. I have had innumerable experiences of this. This then at present is your way and the one thing God asks of you: submission, self-abandonment, trust, sacrifice and silence, all to the best of your ability, but without too much violence in your efforts.

LETTER 18: TO THE SAME

The same subject

BE guided by me, dear Sister, and let us lull all our fears and entrust ourselves in all things to divine Providence with its secret and infallible means of compelling everything to serve its ends. Whatever men can say or do, they do nothing apart from what God wishes or permits, and apart from what serves to fulfil his merciful plans. He is as mighty in achieving his ends by the most seemingly paradoxical means as he is in sustaining his servants in the midst of fiery furnaces or enabling them to walk upon the sea. We are the more conscious of Providence's paternal protection, the more filial the self-abandonment with which we put our trust in God.

I have had an experience of this very recently. Therefore with more fervour than ever I have prayed God that he shall never grant my always blind and often pernicious desires, but shall fulfil his own—just, holy, adorable and infinitely blessed as they are. Would that you knew what joy it is to find all your peace and contentment in the mere fulfilment of the wishes of a God as good as he is mighty! Then you would long for nothing beside. At no time consider a difficulty, whatever it be, as a sign of God's estrangement; for difficulties and tribulations, whether exterior or interior, are on the contrary the results of his goodness and of the visitations of his love.

Yet, you may say, what will become of me in that case?— Such a question is one more temptation from the devil. Why are we so skilful in tormenting ourselves beforehand with what will possibly never happen? Sufficient for the day be the evil thereof! Anxious forethought does us much harm; why then do we indulge in it so readily? We are the enemies of our own peace of soul. For what have we to gain by such forethought? What on the contrary do we not lose by it both in time and eternity? When, despite ourselves, we are obsessed by these insistent conjectures, let us show our fidelity by making a continual sacrifice of them to the sovereign Master. I adjure you to make such an offering: so shall you constrain God to befriend you and aid you in all things; so shall you acquire a treasure of virtues and of rewards in heaven, and with them a submission and self-abandonment which will advance you in the ways of God more than any other pious practice. It is evidently to this end that God permits all these grievous and torturing fancies in yourself.

Profit by them and God will bless you. Your mere submission to his good pleasure in deprivations will avail you more than the noblest exhortations and the most holy reading. Did you but thoroughly appreciate this great truth, what interior peace and what progress in the ways of God would be yours! Without this submission to his good pleasure, every spiritual aid avails you little. As long as we limit ourselves to exterior practices we possess nothing but the husk of that true and lasting piety which is surely and essentially contained in desiring in all circumstances and in all places what God wishes and when he wishes it. Once we have reached this state, the spirit of God has undisputed rule over our hearts, itself compensating for all things else, and never failing us in our need, provided we call on him in humble trust.

This is one of faith's truths, only too little known, alas, to all too many otherwise pious souls. Consequently we see them, owing to this deficiency, hindered or halted in the ways of God. What pitiable blindness! The turmoil and confusion in which by the decrees of God and the plans of divinely wise Providence we exist, are of as much avail as the sweetest recollection, when we can repeat constantly in our most secret heart: "Since you desire it, O God, I too desire it. *Fiat!*" Although this be uttered only in the highest part of the soul, to quote St Francis de Sales, and although the will seems to have no part or lot in it, the sacrifice is then only the more acceptable to God and the more meritorious for us.

Let this practice become a confirmed habit with you, and you will quickly perceive its excellent results. Do but combine it with a measure of peace and tranquillity of spirit, a certain gentleness of heart towards both others and yourself, avoiding any sign of vexation, disappointment or ill-humour, and then how great and meritorious the sacrifices you will make! At least humiliate yourself gently after all your faults, and return to God in trust as if nothing had happened, thus complying with the teaching to be found in the *Spiritual Combat*. As we can enjoy either happiness or peace in this miserable life only in proportion to our blind submission to the decrees of divine Providence, I therefore never tire of giving a little space to this in writing to you. Be guided by me, and depend only upon this adorable Providence, utterly and unreservedly surrendering to it your every care. In simplicity do only what you believe you ought in the circumstances to do if you are not to vex God. Yet do these things gently, tranquilly, effortlessly and without agitation, showing neither overeagerness nor anxiety, to quote St Francis de Sales. The number of anxieties, disappointments and forebodings we could in time come to save ourselves, did we but adopt so reasonable and so Christian a practice!

LETTER 19

Happiness of souls abandoning themselves to God in their afflictions

I AM not astonished, dear Sister, that you find it hard to understand the ways of divine Providence. I understand them no better than yourself. But what I do know—and what you know equally well—is that God plans and disposes of all things as it pleases him; and makes use of what he wishes to further the success of his plans at the hour and the moment of that hour which he has ordained. Let us learn with submission and trust to abandon ourselves in all things and for all things to him who can do everything, and dispose of everything, according to his plan and conception.

Can we but put ourselves in this blessed frame of mind, we shall wait patiently for all things to happen in divine Providence's own time rather than our time, or to express it more accurately, as the result of our own activities and eagerness. Self-abandonment to his blessed Providence constrains God to remedy everything, provide for everything, and comfort us in everything. Never forget that great saying: All things pass, only God stands fast. Make surrender of yourself, then—of yourself and all those dear to you—to the care of his adorable Providence. In public calamities, as in all else, we are by our trust to glorify this infinite goodness and enable ourselves one day to say with David: "We have rejoiced for the years in which thou hast afflicted us, Lord, and for the short and light tribulations by which thou hast saved our souls." Suffering, patiently endured, is the lot and the scourge of the elect. Once more let us cry with the same prophet: "Lord, I am dumb and humbled . . . because thou hast done it."

In the greatest evils there is no cause for consolation apart from the lively faith in the goodness of him who sends them, the expectancy of eternal happiness which our spiritual ordeals will reap for us, the remembrance of the sins which they help us to expiate, and the contemplation of the sufferings Jesus Christ endured for us. Impatience will serve only to aggravate these evils, while patience has the great virtue of diminishing them. In every country in the world God permits particular calamities which are so many and various rods with which he threatens and chastises our irregularities. Yet in every case these chastisements are wholly fatherly, since he threatens or smites us in this world only the better to save us in the next. May he be blessed forever!

BOOK VI

CONSEQUENCES OF ORDEALS—
FEAR OF GOD'S DISFAVOUR

LETTER I

Temptations, fears of yielding to them

I AGREE, dear Sister, that the ordeal to which our Lord is subjecting you just now is far sterner than those through which you have passed hitherto. There is nothing more sorrowful to a soul who loves God than the fear of offending him; nor anything more terrible than to have the mind filled with reprehensible thoughts, and to feel the heart, in a measure, carried away despite itself by violent temptations. Yet this which causes you such cruel anguish is for your directors a sign of your soul's safety. The more lively your fears are, and the more horror such temptations cause you, the plainer it is that you will yield no consent to them, and that, far from doing you harm, they serve only to increase your merits. In this, even more than in all other matters, you must blindly follow the advice of those who direct you. Now—and I say it without the least hesitation—all these terrifying temptations, this interior rebelliousness which perturbs you, this discouragement that besets you, this kind of hopelessness that seems to estrange you irretrievably from God—all these come from the lower part of your soul, and have no express and formal consent from the upper part. The latter, it is true, becomes then so perturbed and so blind that it cannot discern whether or not it consents. This makes the ordeal the more painful. Yet be of good courage! You must then cast yourself, in so far as you can, at the feet of Jesus Christ crucified; you must humiliate yourself, and, in a gentle and unvexed spirit, be lost in your own weakness; you must beseech the help of God through his divine Son, our Saviour and our Advocate, and through the intercession of Mary, our sweet Mother. Lastly, you must believe that he who pursues us when we flee him cannot permit us to be separated from him against our will.

LETTER 2: TO SISTER DE LESEN, ANNOCIADE NUNN
(1734)
Fear of temptations themselves

IT is illusion, dear Sister, to have too great a fear of spiritual conflict. Never shun the opportunities which God contrives that you may acquire merit and practise virtue, under the pitiable pretext that by avoiding a struggle with them you will avoid the danger of committing faults. Do the soldiers of the princes of this world act so? And are we not aware that we are the soldiers of Jesus Christ, that our whole life is but one long struggle and that the crown will go only to him who has fought valiantly?

Blush for your cowardice. When you find yourself face to face with contradiction or humiliation, tell yourself that the moment has come to prove to your God the sincerity of your love. Trust yourself to his goodness and to the power of his grace: such trust will assure you victory. Even when you chance to fall into this fault or that, the harm done is negligible compared with the gains you will make, whether by your efforts in the fight, or by the merit secured in the victory, or even by the humiliation caused you by minor reverses.

Now if your temptations are purely interior, and if it is through your thoughts and your feelings that you fear to be led astray, rid yourself likewise of this fear. Do not so much as directly struggle with these interior impulses; let them die down; struggle against them indirectly by means of recollection and the thought of God. If you cannot be rid of them by this means, endure them patiently. This distrust which leads you to flee temptations ordained by God calls down upon you others, still more dangerous, of which you are unaware; for what plainer or graver temptation is there than to think and to say that you will never succeed in your interior life? Come, come! Are not all religious people called to succeed in it, and you in particular? This very powerlessness (which your ordeal has revealed to you) to make any substantial progress in perfection or to enjoy any peace outside this one spiritual way is surely a manifest sign that God's summons to you is unusually peremptory. Let your eyes, then, be opened; recognize that all these thoughts that discourage, trouble and weaken you can come only from the devil. He wishes to rob you of all that interior strength which you need to overcome your human repugnance. I adjure you not to allow yourself to be caught in this snare and on no other occasion to let yourself look upon this rebellion of your human passions as a sign of God's estrangement. No, dear daughter; it is, on the other hand, a greater grace than you imagine: by making you perceive your weakness and your perversity, it leads you to expect nothing save from God, and to rely upon no one save him. God alone must suffice the soul who knows him.

LETTER 3

Description of the state of a tempted soul, and of God's plans for it

IT could almost be said, dear Sister, that you have never pondered the numerous texts in the sacred Scriptures by which the Holy Ghost gives us to understand the necessity of temptations and the valuable results they produce in souls who never allow themselves to despond. Do you not know that they have been compared with the furnace in which clay receives its hardness and gold its gleam; or that they are represented as a cause for rejoicing, a sign of God's regard, a lesson indispensable if knowledge of God is to be acquired? Did you remember these comforting truths, how could you allow yourself to be overcome by melancholy? I declare to you, in our Lord's name, that you have no cause for fear. Do you but wish it, you can unite yourself as much as, and more than, you did in your moments of greatest fervour. To this end you have one thing to do: endure your soul's painful state in peace and silence, with unswerving patience and utter resignation, even as you would endure a fever or other physical sickness. From time to time you need to tell yourself what you would tell someone sick when you exhort her to bear with her sickness in patience. You would put it to her that in giving way to impatience or complaining she would merely succeed in aggravating and protracting her illness. So must you put it to yourself.

I emphatically approve the order which has been given you

to approach the holy Table without a thought of your own temptations. Your confessor is right; he would have been wrong indeed had he consented to heed your own view of this matter. Yet, you will say, if I consent to the temptation and consequently find myself in mortal sin, what a misfortune for me! That is not for you to judge: yours is but to obey blindly, basing your obedience on the great principle that even should your confessor chance to be mistaken, in God's sight you, as penitent, cannot be mistaken in giving obedience in good faith to those he has given you as guides. But, you may again object, I should very much like to know how he can have more knowledge than I as to what happens in my soul during temptation? Futile curiosity! It is not a question of knowing how. It is so. Yours is to obey, not to reason or make answer.

Yet, as I am kind and helpful to souls who are ill versed in these interior subjects, I will condescend to your curiosity. For my answer will teach you important lessons. First, you must know that we possess, as it were, two souls and two personalities: an animal soul earthly and sensitive in nature, that is called the lower part, and a spiritual soul, known as the upper part, in which dwells man's free will. Secondly, that all which takes place in the lower and animal part—fancies, feelings, undisciplined impulses—all this is in us, but not of us, and is by its nature involuntary and undeliberate. All this can certainly urge, though it cannot compel, the will to that free and unforced consent which alone constitutes sin. When temptation is weak, we ourselves feel and recognize it, and far from consenting to it, reject it. But when God permits temptation to become strong and violent, then, because of the great torment in the soul's lower part, the upper has much difficulty in discerning its own impulses, and remains in great fear and perplexity lest it should have consented to the temptation. No more is needed to cast good men into that terrifying grief and remorse which God permits, once more that their fidelity may be proved. A confessor who coolly and unagitatedly forms his judgement, more clearly discerns the truth; while the great grief known to the poor soul and its excessive fear lest it has consented are for the confessor a plain proof that there has been no such consent, at least of a full and deliberate nature. Indeed, we know by experience that those who consent and succumb to evil know neither these griefs nor these fears. The greater both of these are, the more surely the verdict will favour the tempted person.

I am, then, on your confessor's side. These are my orders:

1. In the ordinary way, neither examine nor accuse yourself on this subject.

2. Endure your humiliation and your interior martyrdom in peace. For these, I assure you, are a great grace of God—a grace you will not perceive until your ordeal is over.

3. The following is the interior prayer you must offer God constantly: "Deign to preserve me from all sin, O Lord, above all in this respect. For as long as it please you I accept the grief which mortifies and is to cure my self-love, and the humiliation and holy abjection which wound and are to subdue my pride; and I thank you for these as for a grace. Permit, O Lord, that these bitter potions shall have their effect, that they shall cure my self-love and my vanity, and that they shall help me to acquire blessed humility and a low self-esteem, since these are the enduring basis of the interior life and of all perfection."

I see that you are ignorant indeed on this subject of temptations. It is true that they never come from God, who, as St James says, tempts no one; and that they always come either from the devil, the imagination or the individual temperament. Yet it is as consistently true that God permits them for our good. And must we not adore his blessed sanction of all things, with the exception only of sin which he abominates, and which we ought to abominate no less than he? Take good care, therefore, not to allow yourself to be perturbed and disquieted by these temptations; for such perturbation is much more to be feared than the temptations themselves.

You are following, you say, a very dark road. This is no other than the always obscure way of pure faith which demands of you a greater self-abandonment to God. Yet what more easy or more natural than to abandon yourself to so good and so merciful a Father who longs for our welfare more intensely than we do ourselves? Yet, you will maintain, I am always in anxiety and excessive fear of having sinned: this makes my life hard indeed and prevents me from enjoying the peace known to God's children.—I realize that this is so for the time being, but I am also aware that it is by these persistent apprehensions that the noble fear of God is enshrined in our souls, and that love of him is straightway introduced into them. It is in this way that God works so as to disgust us with this life and its false good, and to attach us only to himself. Know that we enjoy the consolations of God's children only after we have come through their stern ordeals. We purchase peace only by war; and enjoy it only after victory. If, like myself, you perceived all the advantages and all the benefits of the state in which God permits you to be, you would give thanks continually instead of grieving about it as you do.

You are, you will say, as much entangled as the worst of sinners. My dear daughter, that is merely an outcry of your pride; for are we not all of us great sinners at heart? Do we not carry within us an abyss of wretchedness and corruption which, without the grace of God, would lead us into great irregularities? This is what God would have us know and feel through personal experience, without which we should live and die and yet never have had that profound knowledge of our nothingness upon which our humility is based. Let us thank God that he establishes firmly within us that essential basis of our soul's salvation, and still more of its state of ultimate perfection.

Our perception and our fear of the strict truth of God's judgement is a great grace; but do not spoil it by allowing this fear to become anxiety and perturbation; for the good and true fear of God is for ever sweet, peaceful and tranquil, and mingled with trust. When the reverse effects result from it, reject it as coming from the devil, who is the father of anxiety and despair.

If I had followed my own inclination, you remark, I should have acted in such a manner that . . . Oh, what are you saying, my dear daughter! You must never wish to be other than God wishes. Do you not know that only by the exercise of heroic virtue can you learn to endure your wretchedness and weakness, your ill-temper and vagaries, the follies and extravagances of your imagination—since it is mainly for the sake of this that God permits these tribulations? What great riches such tribulations

333

have heaped up for saints, both men and women, by providing scope and material for their interior conflicts, for their victories, and the triumph of grace!

You say further: Of what use is it for my heart to be freed of one thing, if another, and not God, takes its place? Learn, my daughter, that our hearts are so full, they cannot be emptied all at once. This happens gradually, and as their emptiness grows greater so God's plenitude increases; but we shall know what St Paul calls *the full plenitude of God* only after that emptiness is complete; while much more time and many ordeals will be required before this work is accomplished. Be faithful and patient; have trust, and you will behold the gift of God, and experience his mercy.

LETTER 4: TO SISTER MARIE-THÉRÈSE DE VIOMÉNIL

Sundry temptations

I CAN see quite clearly from your letter, dear Sister, that despite the distress of your interior griefs and of your spiritual ordeals, you have made, all unawares, steady progress.

1. You have already achieved much in appreciating the value of interior life and of tranquillity of heart, and in yearning for these in the midst of vexations and every kind of setback. The rest will come to you in time and will result from your gentleness both towards yourself and others. Let us make it a habit to accept everything God's hand offers us, and to bless him unfailingly in all things and for all things. If in this way we welcome his designs, our greatest difficulties will profit us most. Let us trust in God, and at no time be guilty of the slightest distrust. If need be, let us make him new sacrifices hourly. In that way we shall constantly obtain new graces, and heap up treasure for ourselves in heaven.

2. Thoughts and feelings antagonistic to our neighbour, when they are neither consented to interiorly nor expressed outwardly, are a source of merit and not of sin. Be steadfast in charity, and gradually all these things will diminish and pass. If this or that exterior or interior fault escape you, be satisfied

with humiliating yourself straightway before God, doing this peacefully and unvexedly. Forthwith atone generously for the grief you may have caused, or the unedifying example you may have given. You will gain more by this atonement than you will have lost through the fault.

3. Your insensibility and hardness of heart in receiving the sacraments is certainly a great grief. Bear it with patience and humility. Do what you can, gently and in pure faith. This is the sternest penance God can impose upon a soul to purify it of self-love and self-love's satisfaction.

4. During the day seek to make everything a reason for raising your heart to God, doing so effortlessly and unhurriedly. In all things show the most childlike submission to the various plans of divine Providence; you will gain more by this one spiritual means than by all others suggested to you by your inclination and choice. Above all, let your perfection consist in wishing only and exactly what is pleasing to God, and at the time it pleases him. His good pleasure, indeed, is the gauge of all good-will and the mainspring of all perfection, whether on this earth or in heaven.

LETTER 5: TO SISTER CHARLOTTE-ELIZABETH
BOURCIER DE MONTHUREUX (1734)

Fear of lacking submission to God

WOULD that God gave me as much grace, I will not say to cure, but to make your spiritual sickness salutary, as he gives me ability to perceive it! This sickness is no new thing, and I see no change in the state of your soul. I have, therefore, no new remedy to offer you. All that I can do is to repeat in different words what I have been allowed to tell you previously. This is it, set down in precepts and practices to be followed. I beseech you, in the name of Jesus Christ, from time to time to read this letter in God's presence and in a spirit of recollection. The most fitting occasions for this reading are those upon which you are assailed by interior darkness and upheaval; for during times of spiritual tempest all reading is almost useless. Not even an angel from heaven could then enlighten or comfort you. In all the world there is no mind or might capable of wresting from the hands of God a soul he has seized in his merciful sternness to torture and to purify.

First precept: Be sure that all the stripes with which God afflicts us in this life are less the chastisements of his justice than the results of his mercy. For this reason the prophet said: "O Lord, even when your wrath is provoked against us, you still remember your mercy."

Second precept: As God, for the conversion and sanctification of people in the world, often sends them purely temporal afflictions—sickness, loss of wealth, reversals of fortune, and the rest; so for the purification and sanctification of souls more closely belonging to him—and especially those in the religious life—he sends spiritual and interior afflictions. It is thus that he deals with you; for although you are sick of body, your greatest trouble comes from a tortured spirit whose discomfort increases twofold your bodily ills, and makes them the more painful.

Third precept: As, in order to help people in the world to sanctify themselves in temporal adversities, we exhort them only to patience, submission and constant resignation, even so we preach no other thing to souls troubled and interiorly crucified save childlike self-abandonment to the hands of God.

Fourth precept: It is a certain and admitted truth that, when we reach the stage of being no longer guilty of any mortal sin or deliberate venial fault, we make far greater progress in the ways of God by suffering than we do by action. My conclusion from this is, that to make your salvation sure and your attainment of perfection certain, you have, in the strict sense of the words, but one thing to do: to endure in patience, peace and interior resignation, as best you can, the painful state in which you are. For this you must invoke the help of grace, and show a steadfast trust in the unique merits of Christ. That is the crux of my difficulty, you may object. I agree, but I have no doubt but that this practice will slowly become easier to you, provided you are willing to adopt it, following these rules.

First rule: Make, as you have done already, the word *fiat* your favourite spiritual act and your customary spiritual exercise.

Second rule: Despise and treat as of no account the constant revulsion of your heart caused by your griefs, not so much by seeking to resist them directly, as by being content to utter this word *fiat*, or better still to make an interior act of it merely. Yet, you will ask me, how may I despise and treat as of no account this revulsion that proves my submission to God's will to be neither interior nor genuine? Hear me to the end, I beg you. I am convinced that God inspires me for your good, and it may be, in a measure, for your consolation. You are mistaken, Sister—and in the mistake is the most poignant part of your grief—when you think that, because of the violent revulsion of heart, your submission is not genuine. By divine permission you somewhat resemble in this matter those people in the world who have constant and violent temptations to impurity, hatred, aversion, revenge and similar impulses whose onslaught is violent but neither voluntary nor deliberate. Temptation in such unfortunate souls is sometimes so strong; the accursed pleasure, which is called precedent and involuntary, grips them so violently; the tempter makes such a turmoil and causes such perturbation in the sensitive and lower part of their soul, that they find it impossible to perceive whether or not they have given consent in their soul's upper part. Only their confessor can know—he discerns it by various signs—that they at no time consented. In the same way and for your greater testing, God does not allow you to recognize that true submission which is made in the highest part of your soul, stealthily, and with yourself unaware. But, thanks be to God, I know and see and feel that true submission of yours, which is purely intellectual, spiritual and almost imperceptible. Yet, you will contend, how can you know, see and feel the secret recesses of my soul, when I can do nothing of the kind? I am about to tell you, though, it may be, God will not allow you to understand, or rather will permit you one mere flash of understanding, to the end that such knowledge shall in no way lessen the grief by which he wishes to purify, in crucifying, you.

Let us return to the illustration of other temptations: a woman will tell me of the great interior grief caused to her by the temptations of hatred, impurity and so forth; she will go on to

337

say that the fear of having yielded to them perturbs, afflicts and dejects her. In this, I reflect, is a plain sign of a great fear of God, of a great horror of sin, and of a great willingness to resist. Now, theology, as well as knowledge of the human heart, teaches me that a soul in such a state, interiorly, cannot yield that full, free and complete consent known as deliberate assent; that if it were so to yield, it would at once forsake the interior, and customary, state and dispositions in which it lives, and in which I myself see it living. At worst, it may happen that, given constant and violent temptation, there may have been some negligence or a few unguarded moments. For example, some small desire for revenge may have arisen, and, as they say in the schools, there may have been a half-voluntary impulse to yield to it. Yet in such a state of soul, free, full and deliberate consent cannot take place. Consequently, we see from experience that all those who actually do consent to evil know little indeed of such griefs and anxieties, such despondency and fear. Why, they are not even disquieted by it.

You have but to make application of this to your own state, and, when your soul is serene, you will see, as I do, that the more you fear and grieve over your lack of interior submission, the more of that submission you have in your soul's depths. But God does not allow you to perceive this, as I do, since the certainty of your submission would, by comforting you and ridding you of your greatest griefs, draw you out of that state of spiritual ordeal in which God wishes you to dwell for a time, the better to purify your soul in the crucible of affliction. From this I arrive at a third rule: you are to pronounce that same *fiat* in regard to the seeming absence of this submission for which you so intensely yearn, as you do in connection with other ordeals; for of all these it is perhaps the most useful.

You have, nevertheless, every reason to fear lest this keen desire be an urge of self-love, which looks for recompense for all its deprivations in the assurance that it endures them as it should. Be not astonished, then, if God, who seeks to purify your soul completely of all such promptings of self-love, refuses it that consolation; nor doubt that in this way he gives you a great grace. When, therefore, you feel yourself most afflicted on account of this seeming lack of submission, or most terrified at the idea of God's judgement, do nothing but say: "O Lord, you do not desire that I shall so much as know my state, or perceive whether I possess the submission I ought to possess, or whether I have been deprived of it. *Fiat!* I, too, wish this; I submit myself once again to your adorable Providence."

With the object of recapturing your interior peace and your courage, you can tell yourself something of this kind: "At least by God's grace, I feel that I have a longing for this submission, a longing that perhaps is only too strong and violent, since the fear of not possessing it leaves me in grief and despondency and perturbs me more than all things else. Now it follows that because I have this desire, I reap the full benefit and reward of it; for a sincere desire avails as greatly as the thing desired, and constitutes the merit, or lack of merit, of our good works."

It is when human nature and the soul's lower part are in distress, and despair of seeing either cure or comfort for these interior tortures, that self-love is reduced to extremity and is on the point of death. Ah! then may this wretched love of ourselves die! May this intimate enemy of our poor souls, the enemy of God and of all good, be crucified.

I add a recommendation that shall be the fourth rule: namely blind submission to those who direct us. And in future you must take great care not to omit a single communion which you have been ordered to make. But, you will object, what of my terrifying indifference to God? This is, Sister, merely apparent and in the soul's lower part. The upper part desires God, and God is satisfied with it, though it is not his pleasure that you should know of his satisfaction. A plain indication of the truth of what I tell you is that you admit yourself to be vexed and grieved, in all your spiritual exercises, to feel that you do not love God, and that you can only pity yourself and tell him: "O God, I do not love you." How violent must be your deep and interior yearning to love him since the mere fear of having failed to love him grieves you so greatly, leaving you incapable of anything! Be guided by me: be at peace, knowing that you can do no better thing nor bring a better state of soul to the sacraments, t han to find yourself grieved, afflicted and interiorly perturbed at the mere fear of your failure to love God. This is a sure sign that, in the place of your coldness, insensibility and seeming indifference, God has lit in you the fire of a great love which will grow and interiorly become ever hotter and more intense, by virtue of those very fears you have lest you do not love him.

Yet, you will say, why does this love remain so hidden that I can neither feel nor recognize it? This, my Sister, is the result purely of God's goodness, designed to purify you and to make you deserving of a still more perfect love. Were you now aware of it, you would be so satisfied with your love for God that you would think more of the love than of God himself, who must be its sole and sovereign object. There would come to you, to the detriment of this love, what Fénelon has observed on the subject of the sensible presence of God—a disregard of God himself due to that love's sweetness. In other words, we are so captivated by the sweetness of our appreciation of God rather than by God himself that we forget the purpose of this appreciation: the knowledge of God through faith. You will protest, saying: "What, must I then refrain even from asking for this love?" Your heart beseeches it for you though you give no thought to it. In this connection your fear, anxiety and alarm are both pleas and urgent prayers in the sight of God, who beholds the mere tendencies of your fears, of your most secret desires and even of your heart's hidden inclinations.

Be then at peace and fear nothing. If you are without a director, God himself will act in that capacity, or he will raise up the man you need. In all things aim at sacrifice, self-abandonment, peace and trust. Live by faith and wait. Meanwhile, leave all to God: he will make all things his care, and will provide for everything. *Amen, amen.*

LETTER 6: TO SISTER MARIE-ANTOINETTE DE MAHUET (13 AUG. 1731)

Fear of displeasing God can sometimes be the result of self-love

DEAR SISTER,—I have not been able to answer your letter before. In reading it for a second time, I have noticed two things: plain evidence of God's grace and marked signs of self-love. Your distress and grief, you see, grow with your anxiety. Such distress and grief are graces of God that serve to purge and exalt the soul; such anxiety is the result of self-love that grows vexed and complaining beneath this interior cross upon which God would have it die, that you may live a new life in him. You are aware of a painful incapacity to use your mind, with the result that any reasoning and reflection leave you tired. This is one more indication by which God would have you realize that he seeks to strip you of your paltry and miserable works and to substitute for them his divine operations, without which we make only slow and difficult progress. Likewise you have a great fear of wasting time. This is one more result of self-love that for ever longs for interior certainty upon which to depend, whereas God wishes that we depend only upon him.

Books and directors will tell you enough to reassure you, so far as it is desirable, concerning that futile fear of wasting time with which self-love or the devil alone can inspire you in the circumstances in which you now are.

You feel yourself in a constant state of bewilderment and in a state of abstraction that tends to amount to stupidity. Consequently you believe yourself to be in illusion. May God grant that it be no illusion on your part as to the belief you have of being in abstraction! For that state is one of the greatest graces which God can give a soul! If you are truly in it, I congratulate you. Far from being an illusion, that which you call abstraction can but be a deep recollection that is conducive altogether of good, both by reason of an abiding consciousness of God's presence and an intimate union with God, either already formed or ready to be formed within you.

You are aware of a great peace: one more grace, though you dare not believe in it. This lack of belief is one more result of self-love. You complain that you do not enjoy the sweetness of that peace: yet another and still more manifest result of self-love. Do you not know that the lasting peace which God maintains in the depths of the soul during spiritual ordeals is always without perceptible sweetness; and further, does it not follow that God must take from the soul all its consciousness of such sweetness which serves only to give sustenance to self-love? Can he give us a greater grace than to destroy this intimate enemy of ours, by denying it its favourite nourishment, namely, sensible spiritual delights? You are indeed and in truth unjust to complain of that infinitely merciful God who can purify you interiorly as you yourself could never succeed in doing. Your very complainings are only too great a proof that you have never had the courage yourself to destroy that self-love which alone hinders the establishment in your soul of divine love. Bless, then, the Lord who saves you the trouble, and who, to perform this work in you, asks only that you shall leave it to him.

You fear, you say, lest your past infidelities should prevent God's operations in your soul. No, dear Sister, it is not your past infidelities, any more than your present wretchedness, helplessness and darkness, that should excite your fears. It is your lack of submission, your voluntary vexation in times of spiritual poverty, darkness and helplessness, that alone can obstruct the divine operations. Poverty, darkness and helplessness, provided they are unaccompanied by such fears, can, on the contrary, only facilitate the divine action. You have, then, nothing to fear save your fears themselves.

Now, if you wish to know what you are to do during these interior upheavals, I am going to tell you: you must remain in peaceful expectancy, silent submission and complete self-abandonment to the divine will, just as you take shelter and wait for a storm to pass, leaving God to calm the raging elements. The difference is that patience does not prevent natural storms that raise winds and cause great disasters, but interior storms, tranquilly endured, effect the greatest good in the soul.

Your excessive fears upon the subject of past confessions are one more result of self-love, which wishes to be reassured in everything.

God, on the other hand, wishes us to be deprived of that complete certainty which would be so delightful to self-love. You are, then, generously to make sacrifice of this certainty to the sovereign Master, who has ordained it, in order to keep man in a state of humiliation and perfect dependence.

When you violently reproach yourself, you do so in the belief that you are in no way pleasing to God, because of the deficiencies of your state, interiorly.

This is another and thoroughly dangerous illusion of the devil. By means of it he seeks either to prevent you from doing good, or to throw you into grief and anxiety after you have done it. In either case he takes the greater part of your merit from you. Do not, I beg you, be caught in so plain a snare.

Despite these mistakes due to your inexperience, by God's grace I find in your soul—and I rejoice at it—the two conditions essential to the divine operation: a steadfast resolution to belong unreservedly to God, whatever it cost you; secondly, a firm and constant determination to avoid the slightest deliberate faults. Persevere in that frame of mind, taking more precautions than you have done hitherto against the promptings of self-love. So shall you see the kingdom of God established within you.

LETTER 7 : TO SISTER MARIE-THÉRÈSE DE VIOMÉNIL (1738)

Fear of lacking goodwill

YES, dear Sister, in spite of the fears that beset and vex you unceasingly, or rather because of these fears, you must apply yourself, with all the energy of which you are capable, to the practice of an utter and filial self-abandonment into God's hands.

1. It is your conviction that you are lacking in that goodwill which is the essential condition for securing God's favour; this is at one and the same time your error and your great grief. Yes, undoubtedly you are lacking in conscious and recognized goodwill; yet there is a certain goodness of will, which God preserves in the secret depths of your soul, and which I clearly perceive in you, despite all your feeling to the contrary. Let my judgement, then, serve to keep you in peace. Thank God that in depriving you of perceptible gifts that might serve as nourishment for your self-love, as a notable result of his grace he safeguards in you the far more precious gifts of the spirit.

Have no doubt at all that your self-abandonment, coming at

the time of this apparent absence of goodwill, will tend more forcibly to purify and increase that imperceptible goodwill to be found in you. This is a certainty; hold fast to this belief; ultimately your own experience will convince you of its truth.

2. What I have just said upon the subject of the absence of goodwill I assert equally of the helplessness that gives rise to another of your fears. To what does such helplessness tend? It prevents you from turning towards God by means of recognized acts. Such acts would accord with your inclination, yet when God does not desire them you are wrong indeed to put strain upon yourself. This is an infidelity, for which you pay dearly in tiredness and an increasing sense of desolation. What are you to do then? What you are able; this because you are never without that strength which lies in the simple desire for good, and that attitude of sincerity, in the light of which God beholds all the acts you would like to perform.

So give up lamenting and grieving over your helplessness. Say rather: *Fiat; fiat.* This is infinitely better than all you could do or say following your own thought or inclination. I allow you, however, because of your weakness, to say from time to time: I know that, generally speaking, I am more than willing to turn to God. Yet I cannot. But God sees my desire and this itself tells him everything, though its manifestation is hindered or prevented. I must then dwell in peace and rely upon his love.

Yet I hear you saying to me: It sometimes seems to me that I am without this desire. My answer to this is: Why do you feel such grief upon the subject of this seeming lack? Loss of an object causes grief only in proportion to the affection you have for it: if we had no regard for it, we should feel no grief at being deprived of it. Do you know great grief at being without wealth, honours, beauty, and so forth? These things do not afflict you, and you never give a thought to them. The same would apply to your desire for God, were that desire truly absent from your heart. If, then, this seeming absence afflicts you, evidently the absence is not a real one.

3. You are experiencing a dearth of grace and strength, only because at the moment God wishes nothing more of you. But at no time do you have a dearth of blessed desires, since you feel so

much grief at your inability to give effect to them. Remain, then, in peace in your great spiritual poverty, for it is a true treasure when we know how to accept it out of love for God. I perceive clearly that you have never understood the true poverty and nakedness of spirit by which God succeeds in detaching us from ourselves and from our own works, the more thoroughly to purify and simplify us. This complete despoliation, which leaves us only acts of pure faith and pure love, is the last stage to perfect union. It is a true death to self, a most secret, torturing and hardly endurable death; yet a death soon rewarded with a resurrection, after which we iive only for God and in God, through Jesus Christ and with Jesus Christ. Judge your blindness from this: you are grieved by what is the surest guarantee of your spiritual advancement. After a soul has climbed the first rungs of the ladder of perfection it can make little progress except by the way of despoliation and spiritual darkness, and the way of self-obliteration and of death to all created things, including the spiritual. It is only in such a state that it is able to unite itself perfectly with God, in whom is nothing we can either feel, know or experience. O woman of little faith, of little understanding and of little courage, who grieve and grow despondent over what should comfort and gladden you! Jeer, then, at your self-love; declare that it can despond as much as it wishes in feeling that it is sick unto death, yet your soul will rejoice in God for self-love's despondency, even though self-love may rage.

4. You have certainly no right to imagine yourself rebuffed because you sometimes experience an intense desire to belong wholly to God and yet immediately afterwards feel yourself repulsed as if by an invisible hand. Such interior vicissitudes should give you a wholly opposite conviction, since this twofold sensation is an infallible sign of the action of the Holy Ghost, who by this secret torture effects in you the complete destruction of self. Yet, let me pause. If God allowed you to understand it as I do, that ordeal would be over—would be changed into an ineffable joy. O daughter, blessed, yet ignorant of your blessedness, continue no longer to increase your griefs by reflections wholly antagonistic to God's truth.

5. Yet, you will say, what are you to do when you cannot even

make an act of self-abandonment? Abandon that self-abandonment even, by means of a simple *fiat*, so that this becomes the
most perfect self-abandonment. You object that forgetfulness of
God seems to you a very hell. That noble thought delights God's
heart, and constitutes a most perfect act of love. Profane lovers
at times attain to it in the excesses of their frenzied love: and it
is your state of deprivation and sacrifice that by degrees has led
you to this blessed excess of hopeless love: God has planned
these interior deprivations, agonies and helplessness for no
other purpose.

6. Nearly always God ordains that this kind of grief shall seem
to the soul to have no possible end. Why is this? To give the soul
an opportunity of abandoning itself endlessly and limitlessly, im-
measurably and utterly. For this way lies pure and perfect love.

7. Yet, again, you are helpless only so far as it involves doing
what God does not wish you to do and what it would not be expedient for you to have your way in doing. Yet at this juncture,
with you and through you, God effects in you something so sur-
passingly good that, did you but understand it, you would prostrate yourself in gratitude. O blessed helplessness that prevents
you from hindering, by your miserable and paltry intervention,
the work the Holy Ghost does in you almost by stealth, though
I see plain signs of it and thank God on your behalf, poor blind
creature that you are!

8. There is no need for you to be able to explain your griefs
and your doubts. These are in no way sins, but mere interior
crosses that need only to be borne with utter submission. For
this reason, too, God has left you unable to speak of them or
even to reflect upon them clearly, since nothing so greatly
sanctifies griefs as silence, interior as well as exterior. How great
a sacrifice is, then, a mere *fiat*, particularly when it is embraced
in a simple yearning from which it can scarcely be isolated! Yet
God beholds the scope and the greatness of such a sacrifice. That
yearning tells him all that we ourselves would be able to tell
him, yet leaves us unable to feel the smallest consolation or to
know the least reassurance. Hence originates a sorrowful anguish that leaves self-love in despair, and so ensures the triumph
of divine love within us.

Fear of loving creatures more than God

I AM delighted, dear Sister, that God has made use of my letter to reassure you and make you understand the reasons for that difference, which so frightens you, between the love which we have for God and that we have for his creatures. It is true that, if we were holier, probably our love for God would be more fervent and tender. The absence of such conscious tenderness can then justifiably humiliate us, yet it ought not to grieve us. It is a wretchedness that must be added to a multitude of others, and which, can we but look upon it tranquilly and unvexed by either pride or self-love, will become for us a source of graces and spiritual riches. For, to look upon such wretchedness with peace and humility and a constant effort to decrease it by God's grace, by calm watchfulness and prayer, is, it might almost be said, to lose it in God's sight. Be at pains to appreciate thoroughly a truth which is as sure as it is little recognized. Yet I have said already that this coldness of the senses towards God should not grieve us; for it is in no way a proof that we are without true love. Remember the words spoken by our Lord to St Catherine of Siena: "My daughter, I leave to you creatures the love that is of the affections and senses, but I reserve to myself that finer love which is purely spiritual." Such love dwells in the peak of the soul, in that inviolable citadel of which your free will alone has the key, and from which it rules the whole interior soul. As long as love has not been driven from that refuge, nothing is lost, even though the sentient self may have been overcome by the greatest indifference; while, if such conscious coldness, by no means a result of your negligence, is merely a sorrowful ordeal, it will but add to the merit of your soul's true love.

Take the case of a Christian mother weeping and lonely because of the death of her beloved children. However poignant her sorrow, she would not restore them to life by the slightest venial sin. Do you not recognize that for such a mother, horror of sin is merely the more heroic in that she struggles against an affection that is so much more consciously felt? The same applies to contrition and every act of our love for God. Such acts are performed spiritually, and, as it were, unknown to ourselves in the soul's upper part. It greatly profits us that we are thus unaware: during this life we are so wretched that every known gift is quickly converted by our self-love into poison. Because of this, God is in a measure forced to hide from us the graces he grants us. Did we but understand our own best interests we should look upon this salutary blindness as the most precious grace of them all; while, like the holy man Job, we should never kiss God's hand with greater love than when he seems to lay it most heavily upon us.

LETTER 9: TO SISTER MARIE-ANTOINETTE DE
MAHUET

Fear of displeasing God and misleading his creatures

DEAR LADY and beloved Sister,—I can only bless God for the prolongation of your ordeal and the increase of your interior difficulties at prayers, since I see how greatly you profit by these, and how faithfully you practise the virtues I have commended to you as a means of making complete sacrifice of all things and reaching utter self-abandonment to God's good pleasure.

Far from wishing to see you lose such opportunities for acquiring inestimable merit, I can only congratulate you and exhort you to persevere. Prayers, made thus, are indeed very painful, but they are also the most meritorious and the most fruitful. Were your great fear of displeasing God other than a pure spiritual ordeal, I should find it easy to extirpate it. It would be enough for me to ask from where it comes. Certainly you need have nothing serious on your conscience, while you feel and even know that, normally, you do not hesitate, in order to please God, to undertake the things least palatable to human nature. You are well aware that in themselves your fears are but futile fancies. Now, if it pleases God that you shall be unable to rid yourself of them completely, you have nothing to do but to drop them from you as a stone drops into water. Take no further

348

notice of flies that come and go, buzzing in your ear. Ignore them and cultivate patience.

It is indeed surprising, after all you have said and read, that you should revert once again to the interior changes and vicissitudes which you experience. This is rather as if you believed yourself obliged to note every atmospheric variation, and had to let me know that a rainy period had followed a few fine days, or that a wild winter had succeeded a beautiful autumn. Such is God's established order; such are the vicissitudes of a life in which all things change. There is not one of the saints but has experienced this. In good weather we must prepare for bad. When bad weather comes, there is no cure for it. We must endure it tranquilly, and allow the storms to blow over, waiting for the return of more clement weather.

Instead of all these violent and strenuous acts which you believe yourself obliged to make, it would be far better at such times to dwell, as I have said, in the presence of God, in an interior silence of respect and humility, of submission and self-abandonment. Self-love, however, yearns always for conscious delight. That, nevertheless, cannot be, and God does not wish it. Let us then renounce it with a good grace.

It crosses your mind, I know, that you are deceiving everybody. It must be enough for you that you know that you do not wish to mislead them. If it crossed your mind to kill yourself or to hurl yourself to the ground from a great height you would at once exclaim: I am perfectly aware that I do not want to do this—away with such follies! How can we contrive to check the follies and ineptitudes of the human mind and more particularly of the imagination! They are but so many more buzzing flies; let us put up with them patiently. When they have flown away, others will come, and these, too, we must suffer likewise in patience and resignation.

I give thanks to God for inspiring you with such blessed interior readiness for sacrifice, self-abandonment, the death of self and perfect self-annihilation. How can you ever imagine that so good a God forsakes you, when, by a notable change, he effects in you such precious works, favouring you as he has favoured the saints? For what can he give you more in accordance with Scripture, or what better and more sanctifying thing? Neither ecstasies nor revelations are worth as much as such abjection of attitude, interiorly. For it is precisely in this that holiness and perfection lie. It remains for me then only to exhort you to lose nothing of these precious gifts as the result of contrary acts. When it is God's pleasure apparently to deprive you of these gifts by taking from you all conscious knowledge of them, accept the fact. Is not he who gives, who takes away, who gives again, the master of his gifts? His holy name be always equally blessed, now and for ever!

LETTER 10: TO SISTER MARIE-THÉRÈSE DE VIOMÉNIL

Fear of not making progress and of not doing enough penance

Do not, dear Sister, be in any way surprised that you seem to make so little progress. We never progress interiorly in the same way as we do in external works. The work of our perfection and sanctification must be the work of a lifetime. I notice that your natural ardour and over-eagerness are for ever interfering: hence the restlessness, discouragement and grief which, by afflicting your heart, turn you from your purpose. Here is the cure for these; as long as you feel a sincere willingness to belong to God, a genuine appreciation of what leads you to God, and some little courage in picking yourself up again after your small lapses, you are in a good state spiritually in God's eyes. Be, then, patient with yourself; learn to suffer your wretchedness and your weakness with gentleness, as it is your duty to suffer those of your neighbour. Be satisfied to humiliate yourself for them before God, and set your hope of advancement upon him alone. This hope will not be falsified; though God will probably realize it by means of a secret operation performed in your secret soul, and will ensure that your soul shall make considerable progress although you know nothing about it.

You are disturbed on the subject of your penitential acts. Surely, dear daughter, we cannot perform a more salutary act, or one into which our own will enters less, than by suffering patiently all those crosses which come from God? Now, all our crosses most certainly come from him when they are the necessary, natural and inevitable consequences of the state in which divine Providence has ordained that we should find ourselves. Such crosses are the most grievous, as they are the most sanctifying, because they come from God. O cross of our heavenly Father, O cross of divine Providence—how much more desirable are these than any we take up voluntarily and fashion for ourselves of our own free will.

Do you, then, love your own, dear Sister, since God alone has fashioned them, and every day fashions them afresh. Allow him to do his work; he alone knows the needs of each of us. If we but remain steadfast, submissive and humiliated beneath every cross of God, we shall discover at last our soul's peace. We enjoy a peace that nothing can shatter when, by our submission, we have deserved that God should permit us to know the divine unction always associated with, and enclosed in, the cross, since upon a cross Jesus Christ died for us. Yet, you object, how is the interior life compatible with this state of trouble and darkness? —Ah, my dear daughter, how many are misled upon this point! Do not share their error. That gentle and tranquil interior life, which, in order to give you a relish for it, I have sometimes described to you, is to be found only in two kinds of men: (1) those who are removed wholly from the world and free from all its turmoil; (2) sometimes, though most rarely, those in the world who, having conquered self and become detached from all things, live in the midst of the world as though they were not of it—in a word, as if they belonged to it only in body, but neither in heart nor in spirit. Yet such absence of turmoil and of cares is far from constituting the essence of the interior life or from measuring its worth. Another interior life exists which, though it lacks delight, is only the more meritorious. It is to this that you must direct yourself; the other will follow in its due time. Now, this interior life has two requirements: (1) we must generously perform every divine wish made manifest to us, whether these be precepts God himself has given us, or our rules, or lastly, the orders and desires of our superiors; (2) we must accept everything as coming from the hand of God, duties, adversities, sicknesses, vexations and importunities. Yet at times we shall forget—we must be ready for that. What are we to do then? You already know: we are to recollect ourselves gently, resume our tranquillity with submission, humble ourselves before God, at all times avoiding discouragement and disheartenment. Above all, we are to take great care, following the teaching of St Francis de Sales, never to afflict ourselves because we are afflicted, or to provoke ourselves because we are provoked, or to perturb ourselves because we are perturbed; for all that would be to go from bad to worse, and to cause our interior tribulations to increase. In this is a great stumbling-block for people of lively temperament.

LETTER II

Fears concerning confessions

I can only repeat to you today, dear Sister, what I have so often told you: God wishes to make you do penance and sanctify yourself, using particularly to this end vexations of heart and interior crosses, and still more particularly pangs of conscience.

In all such ordeals I ask of you only a little submission and self-abandonment, rather like those you practise in life's various mischances, bereavements, sickness, disability and the rest.

I forbid you to indulge voluntarily in those anxieties which torment you in the matter of your confessions. Be at peace; blind obedience can never lead you astray. As for contrition, it alone can inspire you with a not wholly baseless fear. You have nothing at all to fear if you include in each one of your confessions a sin of your past life, confessed without details. The clearest indication of true contrition is to refrain in future from falling into grave sins, and actively to seek at all times to correct and decrease your lightest faults. Be tranquil, therefore, upon this point, enduring the successive returns of these griefs in patience. In your present weak state such troubles will take the place of fasts and chastisements, of the hair shirt and the hair cloth; but with the difference that in such penances as these your own will can enter and find satisfaction, while in the others there is only the pure will of God. Such are the penances which our heavenly Father allots to those men and women whose salvation he particularly desires.

LETTER 12

The same subject

Do you but wish it, dear Sister, a mere jot of faith and docility will be enough to rid you, once and for all, of the fears which torment you on the subject of your confessions. To this end you have only to follow faithfully the rules I am now going to outline.

1. Never beseech deliverance from this grief, for it has seemed good to God to let you know why he allows it. The reason is that he wishes to be your sole support, your sole consolation, your sole trust, with no sensible motive to taint the purity of your love. Unable to discover in you the courage which led the saints through heroic sacrifices to that perfect purity, he has guided you step by step through less painful ordeals. Thank him for his condescension, and seek to respond to his merciful plans.

2. Henceforth you must prepare for your confessions in this manner: after a quarter of an hour at most of self-examination, performed as thoroughly as you are able, you will say to yourself: "By God's mercy I live in habitual contrition, since not for anything in the world would I commit a mortal sin; I am horrified at even venial sin, although I still have the misfortune to commit it; I have then only to perform to the best of my ability an act expressive of the inclination God has, of his grace, given to my heart." For this you will need very little time—a few minutes will suffice—while the best method of performing acts of contrition is to pray God to perform them in you.

3. Yet if it be impossible, you will say, for me to recall any distinct fault, how shall I confess?—This is what you are to say: "Father, my lack of enlightenment prevents me from recognizing my ordinary faults; but I come to you to avow generally the sins of my past life, and in particular this or the other sin, for which I ask God's pardon with all my heart." This done, you must tranquilly accept the penance your confessor may impose

353

on you; and you must not doubt in any manner whatsoever that the absolution he pronounces over you will confer all the graces attendant upon this sacrament.

4. Is there, I ask you, anything easier or more comforting in the world? Moreover, if you were to adopt this method, would you not automatically be rid of all the pains that have torment-ed you to this day? I wish that this little practice was known and performed by many members of your community, who experience the same difficulty as yourself, and who, like yourself, could easily be rid of them.

LETTER 13: TO SISTER MARIE-THÉRÈSE DE VIOMÉNIL

Fear about contrition

You ask the impossible, dear Sister; you seek to perceive what is imperceptible, and to give yourself assurances that we can never be given in this life. True contrition that remits sins is, by its very nature, wholly spiritual, and, it follows, independent of the senses. It is true that, with some people on some occasions, it becomes sensible indeed. At such times it is truly comfort-ing to self-love, but it is not for this reason either more effica-cious or more meritorious. Such sensibility in no way depends upon ourselves: therefore it is certainly not essential for secur-ing the remission of our sins. A great number of souls most devoted to God scarcely ever experience this feeling, and the fears arising in these people from this deprivation are the best proof that they are not themselves responsible for it. Such conscious coldness, far from taking away from repentance, is on the contrary one of the best penances we can offer God.

What I have just said on the subject of contrition in general I now say in particular of the divine origin of this sorrow, which is normally least realized. You must beseech God for it, and wait for him by his grace to fill your heart with it. After doing this, to persist in being perturbed would be to fall into one of the devil's snares.

Nothing must so little astonish us as to find ourselves some-times hard of heart and insensible of everything after having been stirred and deeply moved. These are inevitable vicissitudes, interiorly. *Fiat; fiat!* the full remedy lies in this one word. It is certain that God at all times gives to the souls who fear him the support they need. That support is not always the most obvious or the most agreeable, or the most desired, but it is the most necessary and the most enduring. Ordinarily this is the more true the less obvious that support is, and the more mortifying to self-love; for what aids us most potently to live in God is what best enables us to die to self.

LETTER 14: TO SISTER MARIE-ANTOINETTE DE MAHUET

General confession

YOUR fears, dear Sister, have no reasonable foundation, and you must cast them from you as dangerous temptations. When in this life we make a general confession in good faith, every reflection and anxiety which come immediately after it are so many futile scruples of which the devil makes use to trouble the peace of our soul, that he may waste our time and weaken and diminish our trust in God. Let us not stupidly deliver ourselves into this snare; let us leave all the past to God's infinite mercy, all the future to his paternal Providence, and think only of profiting by the present. A mere *fiat* at all times, and in and for all things, expressed first in repeated acts of faith and developed gradually into a set attitude of mind, constitutes in full that perfection which either through ignorance or illusion we go so far to seek outside our own spiritual state.

In conclusion, do you imagine that you shock me by speaking of your wretchedness? As the result of seeing in ourselves only poverty and misery, we learn not to be astonished at these in others. To regard them in peace and humility, making ourselves little in God's sight by demanding his grace of him, and strong with his help to decrease our faults and to subdue self out of love for him, is in a measure no longer to possess those faults. This thought comes from Fénelon. May your mind assimilate it thoroughly, and with it this further observation which I find in the same author, and which I write out for you, because it seems calculated to comfort and encourage you. "Our need is to live and to die in an inscrutable uncertainty, not only of God's judgement in respect to us, but even of our spiritual dispositions. As St Augustine says, we have to be reduced to the state in which we can present to God only our wretchedness and his great mercy as our one claim through the merits of Jesus Christ." Ponder these noble words at length; in them you find peace of soul, self-abandonment, trust and the greatest assurance in uncertainty itself.

LETTER 15: TO SISTER MARIE-THÉRÈSE DE VIOMÉNIL
The same subject—Various fears

DEAR SISTER,—Since neither my advice nor my efforts can rid you of your fears on the subject of your confessions, I can see nothing better for you than to resign yourself to them. Look upon these griefs as a penance sent by our heavenly Father, yet do not voluntarily entertain them. For I am confident that, in your general confession, you reveal everything; at least, you sincerely wish to reveal everything. No more is necessary. I have no hesitation in giving you, in God's name, the assurance that no serious omission can have crept into your confession. Remain, therefore, in peace, upon this subject.

Again, you are perturbed by a certain nobility of attitude which you admire in others, yet dare not, nor are able to desire; the two following remedies will rid you of your perplexities and cause you to profit by your wretchedness: (1) Humiliate yourself and interiorly lament—this without vexation of spirit—to see yourself so far removed from this blessed attitude. (2) Yearn interiorly to have the desire for it. Such desire of desire is a first step by which we proceed slowly to true desire; while the latter, by dint of repetition and the heart's fostering of it, grows stronger and at last takes root.

Try often to remember this great precept: God has—and can—put me in the world only to know, love and serve himself. I wish to fall as little short of this goal as may be possible for me.

For the rest, he will make of me what pleases him. I abandon myself wholly to his blessed will, that yearns only for my salvation and my eternal happiness in the life to come. It is to this end that out of his goodness he makes me pass through various interior and exterior troubles. May he be blessed for it, now and for ever!

LETTER 16: TO THE SAME

The same subject—Various fears

IN nothing, dear Sister, of all you have said, do I see any reason for alarm on your part.

You are, you say, discontented with your lack of patience and submission in respect to your troubles.—Provided that at no time does discontent reach the point of either vexation of spirit, perturbation or discouragement, it will inspire you to a sincere and interior humility and a deep contempt of yourself, which will be more pleasing to God and will advance you further than patience and submission more consciously felt. For the latter would possibly serve merely to feed your self-love upon a scarcely perceptible complacency.

You cannot, you say, report anything to me, other than your wretchedness.—I can well believe you, since, as long as we are in this life, we can but find ourselves for ever most wretched and imperfect. Do you desire a remedy that will effectively cure all this wretchedness? Here you have it: while abominating the sins which are the cause of them, cherish, or at least accept, their consequences, namely, the self-abjection and self-scorn which follow them. Yet in every case do so without vexation or grief, anxiety or discouragement. Do not forget that God, though he does not desire sin, makes a very useful instrument of it to keep us at all times in abjection and self-scorn. But for this bitter remedy we should soon give way to the intoxication of self-love. Be guided by me: remain steadfast in contentment, firm and tranquil in the midst of your wretchedness, while striving to decrease it. The greater progress you make spiritually, the more such wretchedness you will encounter. It is their ever more clearly recognized perception of their insignificance which

357

strengthens the humility of the saints. Yet this humility, in God's sight, is for ever joyous and peaceful. It reaches the stage of cherishing spiritual poverty, and so automatically converts that poverty into riches. Recollect that it is beneath the dung-hill of our wretchedness that God conceals the gifts he makes us. This to protect them from self-love's complacency and our futile self-esteem.

I do not blame your tears; yet I wish that when the poignancy of your grief finds expression in them, you would take care to shed them both for, and before, God. By this means you will feel, not bitterness, but a secret spiritual sweetness that will develop interior peace within you by instilling in you complete submission to every desire of God.

As for the seeming lack of contrition which afflicts you, you must perceive in it only a snare which the devil lays for you that he may rob you of your peace. Surely you know that the apparently deepest contrition, marked by streaming tears, is far from being the best, and that—still more important—God in no way requires this of you? Even with all these external signs of sorrow, we can yet be lacking in true contrition; while, on the other hand, without any such feelings, we can still possess that contrition which serves as our justification. The latter consists in our will to hate and shun sin. It is to be found in the peak and upper part of the soul. It follows, therefore, that it is purely spiritual and above the senses. Be, then, at peace, nor take heed of self-love that wishes to know and feel this contrition and so be assured of its existence. For various reasons God does not desire this. Chief of them all is that he wishes to keep us in holy humility and in that measure of fear which must conduce to our salvation. Let his attitude be yours, and when you do not feel regret for your faults, humble yourself profoundly. In a spirit of penitence offer to God that lively apprehension you feel of lacking the sorrow you should experience. Make sacrifice to God of that heart-pang by abandoning yourself utterly to his mercy. For by the way of obscurities and fears he has resolved to lead us, just as we are, to heaven. The greatest of saints have themselves not been exempt from this law; more faithful than we, they abandoned themselves utterly to God, and at all times preserved their peace of soul by their full trust in him.

As for those reviews of conscience which souls most solicitous interiorly are in the habit of making at least once each year, it must be remembered that this is done not of necessity, but out of humility and devotion. Each, acting on his confessor's advice, makes such reviews as comprehensive as he thinks fit; and can always take it for granted that he need do and say no more in this way than he is obliged. When our dying hour arrives, a general confession is no longer incumbent upon us. At that hour, in a spirit of penitence and compunction, yet with no excessive introspection, we confess generally our most serious sins. It is far more worth our while to spend our time in making the more meritorious acts of religion, faith, hope, contrition, love for God, resignation, trust and union with the merits of Jesus Christ. Further, the most lasting preparation we can make for death is the one we make daily by a regular life and the spirit of recollection, self-obliteration, self-abnegation, patience, charity, and union with our Lord.

I do not like to see you attach so much importance to those minor reliefs which have been given you in your disability, such as rising a little later, having your bed warmed, and eating a little more at mealtimes. In all this follow obedience with the greatest simplicity; while, without paying too much attention to your own inclinations, take what in your opinion and judgement seems to be necessary to you. The essential thing is that interiorly your passions shall be subdued and that you shall be lacking in neither patience, submission and utter self-abandonment to God, nor in gentleness and humble helpfulness to your neighbour. Such virtues sanctify us more than exterior mortifications. Pious people rarely lack exterior practices; more often their great error is to make these the basis of all their holiness, and so leave their enemies, self-love and the heart's passions, entrenched. These they are unwilling to disturb, but they would have great scruples about having eaten a few extra mouthfuls on a fasting day. Such piety is like that of the Jews who had scruples about coming before Pilate, pagan as he was, while they found it consistent with their consciences to demand the death of the Just. God grant that such lamentable illusions shall never be found among those in religious life! Do you, at least, dear Sister, avoid them, and while in no way neglecting exterior practices, let your greatest solicitude be interior.

LETTER 17: TO SISTER MARIE-ANNE-THÉRÈSE DE ROSEN

Pangs of conscience—Rebelliousness of the passions

MAKE it your endeavour to reassure the soul[1] about whom you wrote to me; for there is no substance in the cause of her present imagined anxiety. The one danger is in that very anxiety.

1. When pangs of conscience, justified though they may be, cause vexation and despondency, when they discourage and disconcert, they must surely come from the devil, who fishes only in troubled waters, to quote St Francis de Sales. The first care of a soul experiencing these pangs must be to prevent and stifle them, or better still, to ignore them. With St Teresa let us cry: "What my weakness finds impossible will become easy with the help of the grace which God will give me in his own good time. Further, I ask only so much perfection and interior life as it shall please God to give me, and that only at the time he has ordained." You must try to make these two spiritual acts a habit with you, by saying them over and over in your heart.

The second of these will be of very great service in bringing about that complete self-abandonment which is the characteristic of souls yearning to belong wholly to God.

2. That rebelliousness of the passions and excess of sensibility which finds unmeasured expression at the least opportunity, must neither perturb nor discourage the person suffering from them, nor persuade her that her longing for sanctification is insincere. Such a mistake and its attendant discouragement would be much more harmful than every other temptation. To rid ourselves of these, or to struggle against them, we must be convinced that this rebelliousness and great sensibility are sent us by God to become our victorious battlegrounds, and that our trivial defeats are permitted in order to aid us in practising

[1] The reference is to Madame de Lesen.

humility and patience. Looked at from this angle, such defeats are immensely more useful to us than victories spoilt by vain complacency. There are few more certain and encouraging truths. We must be convinced—thoroughly convinced—that our wretchedness is the cause of all the weakness which we know and which God of his mercy permits. Without it we should never be cured of that secret presumption and arrogant trust in ourselves. And we should never understand, as we must, that all evil originates in ourselves, and all good in God alone. Repeated personal experiences are necessary before this twofold thought can become habitual with us—a necessity that is greater in proportion as these vices, concealed within our souls, are strong and deep-seated.

3. You must never be astonished to find that a day of great recollection is followed by another of marked spiritual dissipation; for such is the way of things in this present life. This alternation is necessary even in spiritual matters, in order that we may be kept in humiliation and dependence upon God. The saints themselves have known these alternations, and still more grievous ones at that. You must seek merely not to be the occasion of them; when unhappily this has been the case, you must humiliate yourself peacefully and without anxiety—for that would be worse than the evil itself—and seek to return both to God and yourself. All this with gentleness and restrained eagerness, as a means of blessed and utter self-abandonment to the guidance of God.

4. Your present position in regard to prayer is good. Be, therefore, steadfast in it. The heart's humble inclinations, the submissive attitude of the soul before God, are of more avail than a multitude of reiterated formal acts. For they are direct acts of the heart which are more potent and efficacious in God's sight, although often they may be less sensibly felt, less perceived, and less consoling than others. God deprives us of such reiterated acts, compensating us with something better, simpler and meeter to unite us with him.

5. The necessary love of God is not lacking in the woman about whom you write to me; but God takes away her knowledge of it, for fear lest she shall grow complacent in regard to it,

and become more attached to his love than to him who must be its sole object. As to this, let her, then, be at peace, desiring, nevertheless, to love him increasingly, without wishing to be aware of this love or to be assured of it.

6. The antagonism and the continual disagreement between thought and feeling are simply that civil war of which the Apostle speaks when he says that "the flesh lusteth against the spirit: and the spirit against the flesh." No saint has been free from this. It is true that this civil war is more violent in some people than in others, and in some directions more than in others, and even at certain ages, at certain times, and on certain occasions: yet whether this violence be little or great, it does no harm to the soul which fights with the resolution never to brook despondency and discouragement. On the contrary, the more violent the attacks, the greater use the struggles which ensue, and, consequently, the greater the triumphs, the merit, the holiness and the rewards. These happy results are the more assured the less they are felt and especially if instead of them we feel a deeper humiliation.

Ah, if we were sufficiently appreciative to accept, value, love and cherish this blessed interior abjection, we should always wish to feel it and to live in it, because we should thereby find ourselves nearer to God! Indeed our great God has himself declared to us that he draws the nearer to us the more we abase ourselves and delight to see ourselves abased. If it be useful to us to be humiliated in the eyes of others, it is not less useful for us to be annihilated in our own eyes, in the eyes of our pride and of our self-love, which bursts with spite. It is this indeed which makes self-love die gradually within us. It is for this reason that God permits interior humiliation to be brought about in so many ways. We have only to know how to profit by it—acting on the advice of St Francis de Sales—by means of acts of true humility that, sweet and peaceful as it is, expels false humility with its griefs and vexations. Grief and vexation in humiliation are as truly acts of pride as grief and vexation in suffering are acts of impatience. Let us not forget this, but take great care not to mistake lack of feeling in regard to divine things as hardness of heart. For it is mere spiritual aridity, an ordeal as inevitable and as common as that of spiritual distractions. It is a still better sign, if it be continuous, since by this means God prepares the soul to consent to being led by pure faith, which is the surest, as it is the most meritorious, of the spiritual ways.

7. To a soul in this state we ought to cry repeatedly: "Peace, peace, be at peace; stay always enclosed in your inner soul." Hold fast to this perpetual desire for the interior life as a precious thing. This inclination alone must suffice to make you live uninterruptedly with God and your interior soul. Results will show themselves in due time; be particularly on your guard against anything that withdraws you from this blessed frame of mind; avoid any threat of its loss; humiliate yourself when you have failed to maintain it. Yet never be perturbed and never be disquieted over anything at all; for nothing could do you more harm.

LETTER 18: TO SISTER MARIE-THÉRÈSE DE VIOMÉNIL

The same subject

1. In a very few words, dear Sister, I can tell you what will serve to lighten your grief and regret: all things come from God, while, on our side, everything consists in acquiescing in God's will. Whether we wish or no, it is always fulfilled; let us with all the energy of our will make ourselves at one with it, and thus have henceforth nothing to fear. Our heart-shrinkings and involuntary rebelliousness merely make the merit of our submission the greater. When we fear lest we lack this submission, we beseech God for it, saying to him interiorly: O Lord, I wish and desire this utter submission, and I make offering to you of the anguish of heart which tortures me, that it may be joined with that agony of blood and sweat of your dear Son, Jesus Christ.

2. We must seek gently to put from us every futile reflection that serves only to embitter the heart. When we are embittered, despite ourselves, we must endure the grief of it with patience; when we fail in patience it is then that we must make the greater effort to be patient even in our impatience, and to be resigned in our lack of resignation.

3. Read those chapters in the book entitled *Saintes Voies de la Croix* that bear upon your present state. In them you will find all the instruction, help and consolation it is possible for you to receive. Yet do not expect to find there what no living man can give you. God alone can withdraw you from your ordeal; wait patiently for his hour to strike. At all times you have relied too greatly upon human help. God has deprived you of this, that you may be compelled to rely upon him alone, and may abandon yourself solely to his paternal care. The more sorrowful and violent your ordeal becomes the better augury it is for salvation and perfection. This you will soon understand no less than I.

4. As Jesus Christ crucified is our sole model, and as he desires to save us because of the likeness we bear to him, he strews crosses in the path of each one of us that we may be kept in the way of salvation. If only we are faithful, these stumbling-blocks that stud our life will become our spiritual treasure. Note, too, how great indeed is our loving Saviour's mercy: once we have undergone these sternest of ordeals and undertaken these most sorrowful of sacrifices, those that follow will cost us little, while the heaviest of crosses will begin to seem light indeed. O blessed experience, as sweet in its sequel as in its beginning it seemed painful to our humanity!

LETTER 19: TO THE SAME

The same subject—Relapses

DEAR SISTER,—The account you have given me of your misfortune and, in particular, of your faults and interior rebelliousness, has left me most sympathetic. Yet when it comes to a cure, I know no other than that which I have often pointed out to you: each time you have new evidence of your wretchedness, humiliate yourself, make offering of it all to God, and cultivate patience. If you once more relapse, do not be vexed and perturbed the second time as you were the first, but still more deeply humiliate yourself and, above all, do not fail to make offering to God of the interior grief and confusion caused by this rebelliousness and those faults arising from your weakness. If you be guilty of fresh faults, with the same trust come again to God and endure as patiently as possible the further remorse of conscience and rebellious interior grief. And let this be your invariable practice. Be sure that as long as you do this, and as long as you struggle with yourself in this way, scarcely anything will be lost; in fact, much will be gained as the result of the involuntary interior rebelliousness which you suffer. Whatever the fault that escapes you, provided that you consistently seek to recollect yourself and to come back to God, in the way that has just been explained to you, it is impossible for you to fail to make good progress. Oh, how little known are enduring virtue and true interior self-abnegation! If once and for all you learn to humiliate yourself sincerely for your slightest faults by sweetly and peacefully allowing your trust in God to pick you up again straightway, you will provide yourself with a good and assured remedy for the past, and a potent and efficacious safeguard for the future.

I greatly approve of the aversion you tell me that you have for disputes. Most certainly there normally enters into these many little illusions of self-love; for this wretched self-love, as St Francis de Sales says, mixes in, interferes with, and spoils, everything. It results from that human wretchedness to which we are, all of us, at all times liable, and more or less exposed. When we perceive it in others, we have two things to do: first we must, in the light of this, find excuses for those who allow themselves to sink into it; secondly, we must fear for ourselves and watch over our actions lest in our turn we become for our neighbour an unedifying example.

LETTER 20: TO THE SAME (1738)

Despondency in ordeals—Distractions—Resentment

1. You are wrong, dear Sister, to reproach yourself overmuch for your lack of resignation; for I believe that it is in no way voluntary. Great griefs inevitably cause a certain despondency; yet souls faithful to God effortlessly recover from it by means of trust and childlike self-abandonment to divine Providence.

There are times when we seem unable to do this, or at least to do it satisfactorily. We must not be discouraged because of this, but, on the contrary, make this very helplessness the occasion of a new act of resignation to divine goodness, content with sweet and patient humility to live in our insignificance. In this way we fulfil the plans of God who allows us to fall into such helplessness and dejection that we may more clearly perceive and feel our wretchedness. It is his desire that no tittle of trust in ourselves shall be left to us, but that we shall rely solely upon his all-powerful grace.

2. I must let you know that for long past I have noticed in you a great grace of which you have had no idea: you seem to me to be more appreciative of your wretchedness and failings. Now, this comes about only in so far as God draws near to us and as we live more in spiritual enlightenment, ourselves taking no conscious thought to this end. Such divine enlightenment, as it grows more pronounced, enables us to see and inwardly feel the abyss of wretchedness and corruption within us ever more clearly; while such knowledge is one of the surest signs of progress in the ways of God and the interior life. You should keep this a little more in mind, not to grow puffed up about it, but to give thanks for it.

Your one further need at the moment is to constrain yourself to cherish blessed self-abjection, and the scorn and horror of self which follow upon this knowledge that is gained by practical experience. When you have reached it, you will have taken a still more decisive step in your spiritual advancement. Observe, then, the goodness of God! In order to enrich you he makes use of your perception of your poverty. That poverty becomes riches as soon as it is fully recognized, accepted and cherished, because God wishes it to be thus. Such joyous acquiescence in our wretchedness does not, however, exclude the desire to remedy it; for though we are to love the self-abjection which springs from our faults, we must detest those faults themselves and show great and watchful energy to correct them in ourselves.

3. The pressure of duties and the importunity and hurly-burly of this world are worth as much in the sight of God, who

ordains and permits them, as silence and sweet recollection. We must, then, substitute for the prayer of quiet that other prayer—the prayer of patience, long-suffering and resignation. Yet do we not sometimes lose patience?—Agreed: there you have that prayer's distractions; we must seek to recover from these without delay and to grow tranquil in the thought that God wishes or permits these things which vex and cause us grief. Chief of all we must take great precautions against growing impatient because we are impatient, and growing anxious because we are anxious. Accordingly we must humiliate ourselves gently, and, merely by so doing, we gain more than we have lost.

4. There is no need for me to go into much detail upon the subject of that lively and keenly felt grief of which you tell me. I understand all the varied and afflicting reflections which make a treadmill of your head, and all the anguish of your heart. Yet in these, dear daughter, you have an excellent prayer that will sanctify you far more than spiritual ecstasies, if you but know how to profit by them. How can you do so? In this way: (1) Pray constantly for the person who has caused you this vexation. (2) Keep completely silent, speaking of it to no one in order to lighten your grief. (3) Do not voluntarily think of it, but direct your mind to blessed and useful thoughts. (4) Keep watch over your heart, lest it surrender itself even in the slightest to bitterness, vexation, murmuring and voluntary rebelliousness. (5) Cost what it may, seek to speak well of this person, to be favourably disposed towards her, and to behave towards her as though nothing had happened. I realize, however, that it would be difficult for you to have the trust in her that you once had—at least, unless you were the saint you have not yet become. (6) But, at least, never fail to help her at every opportunity, and to wish her every possible good.

LETTER 21

The same subject

BE of good courage, dear Sister, and do not imagine yourself to be estranged from God. On the contrary, you have never been nearer to him. Remember our Lord's agony in the Garden of Olives, and you will realize that bitterness of heart and anguish of spirit are not incompatible with perfect submission. These are the outcries of suffering nature, and signs of the difficulty of the sacrifice. Do nothing, then, against God's decree, nor utter one word of complaint or lamentation. In this lies that perfect submission which is born of love, and of the purest love at that. At such junctures would that you could do nothing and say nothing, but dwell in a humble silence of respect, faith, adoration, submission, self-abandonment and sacrifice: then you would have discovered the great secret of sanctifying all your sufferings, and even of turning them into great sweetness. You must strive for this state and seek to make it habitual, but when you have failed in it, you must be careful not to fall into grief or discouragement, returning rather to that great silence in peaceful and tranquil humility.

For the rest, rely with an unswerving trust upon the help of grace which can never be denied you. When God sends us this or the other heavy cross which he sees us sincerely desirous of bearing bravely out of love for him, he never fails to uphold us invisibly, in such a way that the extent of our resignation and interior peace is commensurate with the heaviness of our cross, and at times surpasses it even, so great is the goodness of Jesus Christ, our Master, and the interior grace which his merits secure for us. Let us infer from this that, to assure our spiritual advancement, on our side our goodwill avails us everything, or almost everything; God, in his mercy, does the rest. Knowing the full measure of our weakness, our wretchedness and our powerlessness in every kind of good, he upholds and strengthens us, and, through his holy Spirit, himself effects the good in us.

The practice of at all times accepting the existing state in which God sets us, alone can keep our peace of heart unbroken, and enable us to make great advances, spiritually, without anxious overeagerness. Further, this practice is very simple; we must be steadfast in it, but nevertheless with complete resignation to all that God may wish in this respect.

The outstanding sign that we are not deceived in the matter

of our love for God is this: (1) Our desire for all that pleases him. (2) Our ability to suffer and forbear for his good pleasure's sake. (3) Our possession of a great horror of sin even in its most trivial form, and our endeavour to commit no sin deliberately.

As God gives you the grace of appreciating so greatly my favourite maxims of submission, self-abandonment and sacrifice, you can be sure that you practise them, if only imperfectly. But you are too impulsive in everything; at one stroke you wish to attain to the highest perfection of this state. That is impossible: we must approach it a step at a time, resigned to committing many little faults which will serve to humiliate us and enable us to recognize our great weakness in God's sight. In such circumstances, interior rebelliousness is no stumbling-block to submission by the soul's upper part. On this subject read and re-read Letter 57 in the third book of St Francis de Sales. That particular letter has always been my delight; it will give you a clear understanding of the distinctions between the soul's two wills, the exact knowledge of which is an essential for the interior life.

LETTER 22: TO SISTER MARIE-THÉRÈSE DE VIOMÉNIL

Realization of our wretchedness—Exterior vexations

I COULD, dear Sister, echo for your benefit our Lord's words to Martha: Why so solicitous and so troubled? How can you still confuse, as you do, the care of your salvation which God requires of you with that anxiety which he rebukes?

As you seek to abandon your temporal concerns to divine Providence, yet are careful not to tempt that Providence, do likewise with your spiritual advancement. Without neglecting your own care for it, leave success in it wholly to God, putting all your hope in him. Yet at no time take heed of those diabolical thoughts that would lead you to say: I am for ever the same, for ever as lacking in recollection, as prone to distractions, as impatient and imperfect. All this vexes you interiorly, burdens your heart, and leads you to a melancholy distrust and discouragement, and so plays the devil's game. By this feigned humility and this regret for your faults he rejoices to deprive us of the strength we need to shun, and atone for, those faults in the future.

Bitterness spoils everything; sweetness, on the other hand, can cure everything. Be, then, greatly tolerant of yourself; gently return to God; gently repent, showing neither exterior nor interior anxiety, but cultivating peacefulness of spirit.

This one practice, carried out with thoroughness, will, as time goes on, secure you interior calm, and will enable you to advance farther in God's way than all your agitation can ever do. When we feel a measure of gentleness and of peace in our hearts, we take pleasure in returning to that way, and willingly carry out that practice, doing so consistently, easily and almost without taking thought. Be guided by me, dear Sister; put all your trust in none but God, through Jesus Christ; in all things and for all things, abandon yourself more and more utterly to him; and you shall know by experience that he will always come to your help in time of need. He will constitute himself your Master, your guide, your support, your protector, your invincible strength. Then you no longer lack anything; for who has God has all; while to have him, you need only approach him in complete trust; need only have recourse to him for all things, great and small, without exception; need only with great simpleheartedness cry to him: O Lord, what shall I do on such and such an occasion; what shall I say? Speak, Lord; for I listen; I abandon myself entirely to you; enlighten me, lead me, support me, make me your own.

I sympathize with you in the turmoil and vexation of which you tell me. Yet do not forget that patience and submission to God, when beset by these vexations permitted by his Providence, will advance you more than the sweetest and most recollected of lives. For the latter tends always to gratify self-love; the former, on the other hand, afflicts and tortures self-love, and thereby enables us to attain to true peace of heart through union with God. When you find yourself in such distress of heart that you are unable to perform a single act, in whatever direction it may be, be careful at such times not to torment yourself or make over-violent efforts. Remain single-heartedly in God's presence, in that great silence of heart's distress. Yet do this with respect, humility and submission, much as a criminal behaves before the judge who inflicts upon him a well-earned punishment. Be sure that the interior silence of respect, self-obliteration and submission is of greater worth and avails more to purify the heart than any act you can at such a time endeavour (uselessly) to perform. For such an act will serve only to vex the soul still further.

The character of the person you sketch for me is, I admit, very good; yet while you praise God for the gifts which he has granted her, you must not despise the lot he has accorded yourself. Your need, in fact, is that you should never know bitterness of heart in any connection whatever, but should always be gentle with yourself. For is it not true that this is how you behave towards your neighbour? You would not for ever be making bitter attacks upon his character, but would try gently to induce him to reform it. Behave in this way in regard to yourself; then, should this spirit of gentleness, by slow degrees, be instilled into your heart, you will speedily and without so much difficulty make progress in the interior life. Yet if the heart be constantly filled with vexation and bitterness, we achieve little and that at an infinite cost. I emphasize the point strongly because it is one of your essential needs; while, were I in your place, I should in all things study to acquire a great interior and exterior gentleness, as if there were no other virtue open to me to practise; for in your case gentleness must needs bring you to all the rest. I appeal to your own experience; when for some time you have worked placidly, not indulging in that impetuousness and overeagerness which banishes gentleness instead of ensuring its acquirement, you yourself will recognize that by this means our gains are greater, in that we tire ourselves less.

LETTER 23: TO THE SAME

Past faults

ALBI, 23 *July* 1733

DEAR SISTER and dear daughter in our Lord,—The peace of Jesus Christ be always with you!

371

The Practice of Self-abandonment

1. I have never spoken to you in the sense in which you write, but merely as to a poor beginner, whom God in his mercy tests that she may be purified and prepared for union with him. At present these frightening reflections upon your past delinquencies are of divine inspiration; you must dwell on them tranquilly as long as it shall please God, as you dwell on others which have only sweetness in them. This keen consciousness of your poverty and darkness gives me much pleasure; since in my eyes it is a sure sign that the divine light is growing within you, unknown to yourself, to establish within you a great reserve of interior humility. May the time come when the realization of this wretchedness, which today inspires you with horror, will overwhelm you with joy and maintain you in delightful peace. It is only when we have reached the bottom of the abyss of our nothingness, and when we are firmly fixed there, that we are able, to use the words of the Holy Scriptures, to walk in God's sight in justice and in truth. Even as pride, which is an illusion, keeps God's favours from the soul otherwise most rich in merit, so does this blessed state of willed humiliation and cherished self-obliteration bestow the divine graces upon the most miserable of souls. Seek, then, no other source of help, either in your lifetime or at the hour of your death.

You should have taken refuge in this same self-obliteration and so have escaped the fears which beset you during your last sickness. Do not fail to do so if Satan at any other time attempt to catch you in the same snare. When our last hour draws near, self-love would have some conscious reassurance arising out of past good works; but let us desire only that assurance which comes of pure faith in God's mercy and the merits of Jesus Christ. From the moment when we long to be wholly God's, this assurance is all that is required. All the rest is vanity.

2. I do, however, approve of your behaviour, interior and exterior, during your sickness. I perceive that God in his wisdom has concealed from you the increase of good that it has brought you, since without this concealment much futile complacency would have spoilt everything. I have better knowledge than you as to what has happened[1] and I bless God for it. He has upheld

[1] Fr de Caussade had been given edifying particulars of the sick woman by

you in face of your weakness; you have only to give him thanks for it, paying no great heed to speculations as to whether the supernatural element has entered into all this. Leave that to God, seeking merely to forget yourself and to think only of him.

3. What are you about in making so many excuses for your melancholy frame of mind? Let others think what they like on that subject, you have only to please God. Although he allows others to think or to say of you what they wish, you yourself must not give a single moment's voluntary thought to what they think or say. For anything in that way merely serves to bolster self-love and vanity.

4. I am delighted that you found peace in the situation in which you would have least expected it. This is a sign that God wishes you to be so situated, and that he wishes you to know peace only in the fulfilment of his blessed will—in itself a very great grace. If I have been unable to show you much pity in your sickness, this is merely that I do not look upon physical sufferings as definite evils when they confer great benefits upon the soul.

5. You are convinced that you have achieved nothing, and that you are undeserving. As a result, you find yourself plunged into nothingness. Oh, how good this is, since it is certain that from the moment we are in this state we are in God who is all. How precious is this state of nothingness! We have of necessity to reach it before God can fill us; for our soul needs to be interiorly empty, before God can fill it with his own unique Spirit. Accordingly the things which grieve and vex you are the

---

another Sister who had written to him commending her to his prayers. He made the following answer to her letter: "I attach too much importance to Sister M.-T. de Vioménil's spiritual welfare and advancement to pity her greatly in her illness. This is a new grace of God designed to mould and fashion her interiorly. Everything in her had to be crucified, the body no less than the soul. Patience, submission and self-abandonment. And if she had had to die in the state in which I know her to be, I should deem her still more blessed; but seemingly she is meant to know many other crosses, and I hope to see her renewed and remoulded as an old pewter or silver flagon which has been recast to be made altogether new, brilliant and beautiful. There was no need to commend her to my prayers; by reason of what she is, she is and always will be sufficiently commended."

very things which should tranquillize and fill you with a blessed joy in God.

6. The unreserved acceptance of all things, both for the present and the future, is one of the most delightful sacrifices we can make to God. This mere act, constantly practised, is worth all that we can do. Thus your main practice should be to concur at all times in every design of Providence, whether it be exterior or interior. Be exact in performing this, and God will slowly effect all the rest in your soul. Such a practice is simple indeed and in accordance with your bent.

7. I do not greatly regret your companion's reserved manner. You must make this another offering to God. For she was less in the wrong than you were in showing such spleen. But God has allowed her to humiliate you by letting you feel what you are when he leaves you to yourself for a short while. Humiliate yourself without vexation or grief—you are aware of what St Francis de Sales says upon the point.

8. God requires us to perform our duties, but he does not require us to be curious as to whether we are deserving or not. You give too much thought to yourself; you are too greatly concerned with yourself under the pious pretext of seeking advancement in the way of God. Forget yourself, to think only of him, and abandon yourself to the decrees of his divine Providence. For then he will himself make you progress, will purify and exalt you without a doubt, exactly as, when and in the degree, it shall please him. For what have we to do but to give him pleasure, and in all things and in all places to desire what he desires? We range far and wide in pursuit of perfection, while we have it almost at our door: namely, in our longing to do God's will in everything and never our own. Yet to reach this state of affairs we must renounce and sacrifice what, in one sense, are our dearest interests, and it is this that we are unwilling to do; for we would have God sanctify and perfect us in accordance with our own ideas and inclinations. What wretched, what pitiful blindness!

LETTER 24: TO THE SAME
Lamentable results of our imprudence

I HAVE told you, dear Sister, many times already, that nothing should grieve us, not even our faults. For all the more reason, then, we ought not to allow ourselves to be despondent over the lamentable results of certain actions which are not sins, however much they may indicate imprudence on our part. Few ordeals are more mortifying to self-love; and, it follows, few are more sanctifying. It does not cost us nearly as much to accept humiliations which come from without and which we have in no way drawn upon ourselves. We are much more readily resigned to the shame caused by faults far graver in themselves, provided that there is no outward evidence of them. But a mere imprudence which has lamentable consequences that are plain for all to see is obviously the most humiliating of all humiliations, and provides, therefore, an excellent opportunity for destroying self-love. Never fail to take advantage of it. For then we have our hearts entirely in our power; we can compel them, despite their resistance, to make an act of complete resignation. It is at such times that we must repeat not once, but many times, the *fiat* of a perfect resignation; you must endeavour even to render thanks, adding a *Gloria Patri* to the *fiat*.

A single trial, thus accepted, can enable a soul to make more progress than numerous virtuous acts. I trust that you have understood me and that you no longer perturb yourself over the consequences that can be precipitated by irregularities of which you have been the fairly innocent cause. Be at peace in an intention to take, when the time is suitable, the steps necessary for peace and the union of heart with heart. Then you must leave the outcome to God, whatever it may be. Let us make it a habit to adopt the same attitude in all the painful incidents of this miserable life; for in this way we dwell in peace and merit upon the breast of divine Providence. Lacking this submission and utter self-abandonment, there is no peace for which we can hope during our life's sad pilgrimage.

Let our one thought be to please God, to content God, and to sacrifice all things to God. Let everything else pass and be lost to us; if only God remains we shall never be the losers. Be of good courage and all will be well; be neither disturbed nor astonished at this rebelliousness of the heart: I assure you that this in no way hinders submission in the higher part of the soul, and that in our own interest God hides such submission from us. When you are most violently beset, seek only to say the following few words: It is indeed right that the creature should submit to his Creator; I therefore desire and beseech that this may be so. Read the section on spiritual progress in Father Guilloré's *Vie Intérieure*; that particular chapter is supremely good. I hope that you will carry away some of its sweet fragrance with you.

In God's name do not be troubled, but try to dwell in peace, though terrible storms rage round you. Do but this and all will be well. Indeed, I see nothing but good in all that you have revealed to me. Yet that good would be good no longer were it perceived as clearly by you as by me.

When I am worried by numerous and varied thoughts which make mountains out of mole-hills, I remember what I say to others in similar circumstances, and abandon myself in all things and for all things to divine Providence; I look the worst in the face and, like St Paul, defy it to separate me from the love of Jesus Christ. I know that without my divine Saviour's grace I can do nothing. In such temptations I pray him, then, to preserve me from all sin and from all that could displease him. But when it is a question of bitterness of heart, interior crucifixion, holy abjection, or even shame in men's sight, I accept all these and all their consequences for as long as it shall please God's sovereign Majesty. In everything I yearn for his blessed will to be fulfilled, to the detriment of mine own; while I beseech him to forbid me to say or do anything that may serve to evade even the slightest of his desires. Further, if out of weakness or error or malice I set out upon such an evasion, I implore him to prevent my success in it.

In brief, I recognize that all his desires are not only blessed and adorable, but infinitely lovable, salutary and beneficial to his creatures who are humbly submissive to him; and that my own desires, on the other hand, are at all times blind or un-disciplined. Accordingly, I underline hereby my consent to all that which is ordained and written in the decrees of our heavenly Father. It is enough that this good and beloved Father has ordered it. What need have I to be afraid? Two things result from this: (1) During these storms, which are often of the tea-cup kind, I preserve so profound a peace that I myself am sur-prised at it. (2) I deem myself blessed indeed to be set interiorly in these torturing temptations and ordeals. . . . Then I say to myself: These are worth more to me than all my own paltry interests. I feel that my soul grows strong in its self-abandon-ment to divine Providence, with the result that every desire for, and attachment to, my own will is obliterated and destroyed.

LETTER 25: TO SISTER MARIE-ANNE-THÉRÈSE DE ROSEN

Rules to be followed in spiritual ordeals

You know as well as I, dear Sister, that it is God's practice to make all souls, whom he wishes to raise to perfection, pass through every kind of interior tribulation and grief, that they may be tested, purified and detached from all things. The most painful of such tribulations are those which may be due to our own fault, and in which the poor soul, censured severely by it-self, and still more severely by others, hears, either from within or without, only an answer that makes the heart sick unto death. The person of whom you have written to me is in this state.[1] There is nothing to fear on her behalf; all the details you give me prove, on the contrary, that God has particular plans for her. When you write to her, speak only of patience, submission to God and utter self-abandonment to divine Providence, as you would to people in the world suffering from affliction and temporal adversity. Above all, let her try, by means of the most filial trust in God, to shun energetically avoidable anxieties. I use the word avoidable because the poor souls whom God sub-jects to this ordeal have no mastery of the griefs and anxieties which obsess them. These are the cause of their greatest sorrow,

[1] The reference is to Madame de Lesen, later an Annonciade nun.

and the most grievous aspect of the state of humiliation in which God wills that for a certain time they shall remain. Then the one thing for them to do is to make submission to God in the matter of these paroxysms of interior grief as in all things else.

Tell this poor soul that her chief and almost continual prayer should be the silence she keeps at the foot of the cross of Jesus Christ, the while she murmurs, as once did he: "*Fiat*, not my will, O heavenly Father, but yours be done in all things! It is you who shape all our afflictions for the good of our souls; all that you wish is for my greatest good and my external salvation; do with me, then, as it shall please you; I adore and I submit."

I consider that your friend does well not to examine her thoughts; such an examination would merely trouble her mind the more. Let her leave everything to God; let her despise those thoughts and those feigned outcries of conscience, and let her go forward without heeding them, at all times when there is nothing definitely wrong in the act she meditates performing. Such vain scruples are a temptation of the devil by which he robs her of peace and so hinders her from making progress in virtue, as a sick body, because of its weakness and languor, is incapable of manual labour.

When she succeeds in maintaining herself in this peace of the will, she will slowly recover, as a weak and languishing body recovers with rest and good food. I shall set down three methods of hastening her recovery: (1) She must put out of her mind everything that grieves and disquiets it, regarding this kind of thought as coming from the devil; for all that is of God is peaceful and gentle and agreeable, and serves only to strengthen trust in him. It shares the peace in which he dwells, and in which he breeds those varied feelings of piety which lead souls to perfection. (2) She must constantly raise her mind and heart towards God, directing both mind and heart towards submission, self-abandonment and trust in that paternal goodness which at present afflicts, only to sanctify, her. (3) She must choose for her reading those books which can most powerfully contribute to bring her interior peace and to inspire her with trust in God. These include Mgr Languet's treatise, the book entitled *Espérance chrétienne*, and St Francis de Sales's Letters. For the rest, let her go her own road, altering her conduct in no way, going to confession and holy communion as usual; for the devil, in order to deceive and still further weaken her, is quite capable of using all his cunning to inspire her with dislike and untoward fear of confession, communion and other spiritual exercises. She must lend no ear to such wicked inspirations, but as a good and true daughter of the Church at all times be guided by the light of faith and the blessed practices of the Christian religion. *Amen.*

LETTER 26: TO SISTER MARIE-THÉRÈSE DE VIOMÉNIL

The same subject

ALBI, 1733

DEAR SISTER,—1. I can only congratulate you on the efforts you are making to keep yourself constantly in a state of perfect resignation and utter self-abandonment to God's will. For that way lies all perfection. Yet in this matter, as in every other, we must know how to distinguish the substance from the shadow, the feeling of consent from consent itself, the feelings from the will. There are two kinds of resignation: the one sensible and attended by pleasant appreciation and gentle peace; the other, insensible, barren and savourless, and attended even by repugnance and great interior rebelliousness. It is the latter I notice most certainly in yourself. The first is good, but gratifying to our human nature, and therefore somewhat dangerous; for it is indeed natural that we become strongly attached to what we like. The second, very painful and disagreeable as it seems to self-love, is nearer to perfection, more meritorious and less dangerous, since we can take pleasure in it only by pure faith and pure love. Strive that your actions shall be based on these enduring motives. When you have succeeded, your attachment to God will be proof against these vicissitudes. If, on the other hand, we are in the habit only of acting upon sensible attractions we do nothing when these attractions are absent. Now we cannot prevent them being often absent, whereas faith as a motive is always present.

When God deprives us, as he frequently does, of conscious

delights, it is only to induce us by degrees to act from these spiritual motives. Were he not to do this we should always remain in spiritual infancy. You must not then be surprised at the vexations and the rebelliousness of which you speak; God permits these for your advancement's sake. Now, if you are afraid that human motives may have their part in the violent efforts which you make, repeat these two things to yourself: (1) I am at present in no state to judge; we will leave reflection about this to a time when I am calm and peaceful. (2) If, later, human considerations still weigh with me, God allows this to help my weakness; when he is pleased to make me less imperfect, my actions will reveal more perfection. Then straightway be calm, and do not tolerate the slightest voluntary grief.

2. I can easily realize that the dislike of the work you do makes your ordeal the heavier; yet recollect the rewards of the martyrs, who have undergone ordeals far more sorrowful.

3. In such a state it is natural to feel an increased zest for the solitary life. Yet the life of obedience is of greater worth: it is one long sacrifice, and if there be more causes for vexation in it, there are also many opportunities of acquiring merit. Persist in being altogether steadfast in it, until you reach the state when you hesitate to say one word that may detach you from the cross of Jesus Christ.

4. The great secret of enduring wretchedness with patience is to look upon it as God's cross, to be ranked with sickness and other afflictions of this life. Were God to send you these exterior and perceptible maladies you would endure them patiently. Do you then endure your interior ordeals with the same patience.

5. Look upon all this wretchedness of our earthly life as so much treasure for the spiritual life, since it offers you an effective means of acquiring humility and self-scorn. In the light of this, love such humiliation and such abjection, as St Francis de Sales so strongly counsels you to do.

You ask me whether, in order to avoid setting an unedifying example, you ought not to hide your wretchedness. All in good time; let your one unforced endeavour be to act in such a way that your feelings have no exterior manifestation. When they do, nevertheless, appear, though you yourself are little to blame,

seek to bear with equanimity this unimportant exterior humiliation. Even when you are to blame, find delight in the abjection
which the fact brings you. In this way you will very meritoriously mortify self-love, which would have us avoid exterior
faults, not because of the offence they are to God, but because of
the humiliation they cause ourselves.

No longer give way to the grief that arises from the difficulty
you experience in concentrating your attention. Remember
that the mere desire, if habitual, of recollection can serve in
recollection's stead, and that we have only to be unfailing in our
desire to think of God, please God, and obey God, in order to
think of, please, and obey him indeed.

6. The greater your wish to learn to pray, you say, the less is
your ability for prayer.—That might well be because your wish
is not accompanied by a sufficiently complete submission and
purity of intention. Always go to prayer with the one desire to
please God, and not to draw conscious delight from it. Go to it in
a spirit of sacrifice and to get out of it all that should be pleasing
to God. Realize, moreover, that recollection is like those things
that escape our minds when we are over-anxious to remember
them, but that return to us when we treat them with a certain
passive indifference: this is the teaching of St Francis de Sales.

7. Never lose sight of that great precept which asserts that
great spiritual poverty, known, felt and loved out of love of the
abjection it brings, is one of the greatest treasures that a soul can
possess in this world, since knowledge of it keeps the soul in deep
humility. To believe, on the other hand, that you are lost because you make no discovery in yourself of clearly perceived
faith and charity, and to be thereupon vexed, disquieted or discouraged, is a dangerous illusion of self-love, that for ever longs
to see all things clearly, and in all things to have reason for self-
complacency. When we experience this temptation we must say
to ourselves: I have been, I am and I shall be all that shall please
God; yet, intellectually and in the apex of my soul, I want to belong to him and serve him, whatever may befall me in this world
or the next.

8. You are not able to describe to me what your feelings are
but I will tell you: On the one hand—in the soul's lower part—

there is every kind of rebelliousness, grief and temptation, and a constant medley of feelings excited by self-love and the devil; on the other hand—in the upper part, or apex, of the soul—there is a faint and almost imperceptible ray of light and faith to counter-balance the turbulence of the lower part. With this insignificant aid you become invincible; for in God's hands the thinnest thread is as strong as a cable, while a single hair is stronger than an iron chain.

9. Your occasional absence from the sacraments is a tempta-tion, and comes of ill-advised humility. What others do must never be a guide for yourself, for you are ignorant of their feel-ings, their motives and their reasons for their absence.

10. You say that God often withholds from you perception of his grace.—Has he given this appreciable aid unbrokenly to even the dearest of his friends? You surely would not claim to be more favoured than the many saints from whom he has withheld it more frequently and for longer periods than he has from you? At such times what was left to them save the one light of faith—of a faith that, like our own, seems no more than a dark night? Yet during this dark night of their temptation and the assaults of their passions, no more than you did they know whether God was satisfied with them. Faith teaches us that, in default of a special revelation, the saints themselves have not been certain of possessing the full certainty of grace; and yet you complain that you are uncertain of it! Such are the lengths to which this wretched self-love leads us. If it is to be satisfied, God must per-form miracles! Of all the wretchedness which brings you so much humiliation, this is certainly the greatest and the meetest to humiliate you.

11. To wish to give up your concern in yourself in order to be concerned only with God, and yet to come back continually to self is, I admit, a temptation as persistent as gnats in autumn; we must, therefore, drive this temptation away as persistently as we drive the gnats away, never becoming wearied in our efforts yet making them gently and without grief or vexation, by humiliating ourselves before God, as we do in similar troubles. We ourselves constrain God to afflict us with this wretchedness that we may be reduced to humility and a greater measure of

self-scorn. If, despite this, we reveal so little humility and so much esteem of ourselves, how would it be if we were exempt from such wretchedness?

Be guided by me, since for some time past you have seemed to me to be so aware of your wretchedness that I look upon this awareness as one of the greatest graces God could give you. Cherish, then, all that can preserve it. I remain altogether yours in our Lord. I must confess that writing so much has left me feeling tired. When I had got to the end of your own letter, I thought, like you, that I would give you my answer in more letters than one. Yet I do not now regret that I have enabled you to perceive at a glance the full direction which you are to follow faithfully in order to get all the profit possible from the ordeal to which God submits you.

BOOK VII

ULTIMATE ORDEALS—
AGONY AND MYSTICAL DEATH—
THEIR FRUITS

LETTER I: TO SISTER CHARLOTTE-ELIZABETH
BOURCIER DE MONTHUREUX

Spiritual nakedness—Self-obliteration. The temptation to despair

ALBI, 1732

DEAR DAUGHTER in our Lord,—The peace of Jesus Christ be with you now and always! Your last letter has comforted me more than any other you have written. You have no understanding of your position, but I, by God's grace, see it with daylight clearness.

1. This state of stupidity and foolishness which you describe to me with its chaotic wretchedness and helplessness is no less than God's gift, and it is this that the various interior operations of grace have slowly produced in you. It is useless for me to try to explain these to you, since in the state in which God has put you, he gives you little understanding, while that little you would have in reading my explanation would at once vanish. But at least I can give you an assurance that ought to be enough for you.

I admit that to begin with I was a little surprised that God deals with you as he does with those who are spiritually advanced; for, in the usual way, this state is the fruit of several years of struggle and effort. A soul is aware of it when God, satisfied with the zeal it has shown in seeking to die to all things, puts his own hand to the work to enable that soul to know utter death spiritually as the result of its complete deprivation of created things. He then robs such a soul of all pleasure—even of all spiritual pleasure—of all conscious joy and of all light, that in this way the soul may become insensible and stupid and as though reduced to nothingness. When God grants this grace to a soul, there is very little for it to do but tranquilly to endure this operation, carrying, as the saying is, the gift of God in a deep interior silence of respect, adoration and submission. That is your own task. In one sense it is very easy, since it is merely a question of doing as a sick woman does when, lying in bed, she is in the hands of doctors and surgeons. She suffers patiently in the expectation of a complete and perfect cure. You are in the same situation, except that your expectation has a far better foundation, in that you are in the hands of the great and loving Physician of our souls.

2. The turbulent and almost continual upheaval of your passions is a sequel to the same death-producing, yet life-producing, operation. On the one hand, it gives rise to this upheaval of the passions that you may have an opportunity of struggling and acquiring contrary virtues; while, on the other, it lays within you, by means of this very agitation, the enduring foundation of perfection, namely, the deepest humility, self-scorn and self-hatred.

3. The temptations to discouragement and despondency are another sequel to the same state, while these are still more effective in purifying us. I realize that at no time do you consent to these, because I notice that all your voluntary inclination is precisely the reverse of that found in a soul whose desires offend God. No, dear Sister, you do not offend him in these sorrowful moments. Your soul, on the contrary, is then like the gold which bubbles in a crucible; it is purified, and acquires a new brilliance. At no time are you more paternally upheld by God's arm. Could you but see your state as it is in reality, far from grieving over it you would give thanks to the God of mercies for his ineffable gift.

4. Your prayer is—and always will be—good as long as you know how to remain in peace, utter self-abandonment and, as St Francis de Sales expresses it, in a simple expectancy as peaceful as it is altogether resigned.

5. As each one of us must follow his own spiritual inclination at prayer-time, as at all other times, do not be afraid to live constantly in this great emptiness which you discover within yourself. Remain in it, without any thoughts, unperceiving, and

insensible to all things. Delight in this state since, in your case, it is God's gift and the source of all good. I have never met with a favoured soul whom God has not forced to pass through these barren wastes before it reaches that promised land which is perfection's earthly paradise.

6. Interior reproaches on the subject of the slightest faults are a plain sign of the particular attention the Holy Ghost pays to your advancement. Out of a vigilant jealousy he tolerates nothing from certain souls. It is not a temptation, therefore, but an ascertained truth that souls which are the object of this divine jealousy cannot, unless unfaithful, permit themselves what others can do without imperfection. The delicacy and jealousy of divine love are more or less great according to the measure of God's predilection. Reflect, then, as to whether you have cause to complain of the merciful sternness which he shows in regard to you.

7. You are well advised not to have any special desire for the retreat. For with you it is not the time for desires but the season of unreserved self-abandonment to all that the Holy Ghost would effect in you. It is for him to determine the time, the duration, the manner, and the results of his operations; it is for you to undergo them with submission, love and gratitude. Many of them are austere indeed; yet those which cause you the greatest and most smarting humiliation are in every case the most sanctifying. Remain, then, in a great silence, allowing the loving Physician in charge of your case to act as he thinks fit.

8. You can apply to your own case all that I wrote, last year, to Sister Marie-Antoinette de Mahuet, and draw profit from it. Yet you must not be surprised if, during this kind of interior upheaval, neither books nor my letters are of use to you. For God does not desire these to be of use; at such times he causes all feeling and all enlightenment to vanish that he alone may effect what he pleases in the depths of the soul. Yet I put it to you: Is not what God then does of infinitely more worth to you than all you could do by your own efforts? Beseech him to make you like a beast of burden that unresistingly allows itself to be led, or like a stone that beneath the blows of a hammer takes the shape the architect intended.

9. The absence of hope grieves you more than all the rest. I can believe it; for, as in your life you find nothing to give you the smallest help, so it appears to you that you face death in a frightful void. Ah! that is wretchedness indeed. I feel for you far more in this than in your other sufferings. Let me, with God's grace, try to cure you of this ill. You want, dear Sister, to find a little help in yourself and your good works? That is precisely what God does not wish; that is what he cannot tolerate in souls that aspire to perfection. What! rely upon self, count upon your good works—what a wretched survival of self-love, pride and perversity! It is to rid chosen souls of these that God makes them pass through a desolating state of poverty, wretchedness and spiritual nakedness. He wishes slowly to destroy all the trust and reliance they have in themselves; to deprive them of all their resources, so that he may be their sole support, their sole trust, their one hope, their one resource! How accursed is that hope which unreflectingly you thus seek in yourself! How glad I am that God destroys, confounds and obliterates that cursed hope by means of this state of poverty and wretchedness! O blessed poverty, O blessed despoliation that was the saints' delight and the especial delight of St Francis de Sales! Love it as they loved it! When, by virtue of it, all trust, all hope, all earthly and created aids have been taken from us, we shall have no more aid, we shall have no more trust, we shall have no more hope save in God alone. This is the right hope, the right trust known to the saints, a hope and a trust based solely upon the mercy of God and the merits of Jesus Christ. But you will have this hope only after God has destroyed in you the last clinging roots of your trust in self. This may come to pass only if God keeps you for a while yet in entire spiritual poverty.

10. Yet, you will say, of what use to us are good works if they are not to inspire us with trust? Their use is to secure us the grace of a still more complete distrust in ourselves and a still greater trust in none but God. This is the sole use the saints made of them. To what, indeed, do our works amount? They are so spoilt and so corrupted by our self-love that if God judged us rigorously, we should deserve more punishment than reward. Give no further thought, then, to your good works as a means of

enjoying tranquillity at death: merely fix your eyes upon the mercy of God, the merits of Jesus Christ, the intercession of the saints and the prayers of righteous souls. Turn them away from everything—everything—that might give you occasion to rely upon yourself, or even in the smallest measure to place your trust in your own good works.

11. The remarks you make to others—or rather the remarks God gives you to make—in this time of your greatest spiritual aridity do not surprise me at all. It is God's usual attitude, determined by the fact that his wish is to console others, the while he keeps you in desolation and self-abandonment. At such times you speak what God gives you to speak, leaving you dead to all feeling in yourself but alive in the feeling you have for others: I see no manner of hypocrisy in this.

12. To avoid dissipation in the tasks which your obedience sets you to do, you need but to go about them placidly, showing neither anxiety nor overeagerness; while to perform them in this way you have, says St Francis de Sales, but to do them wholly out of love for God and obedience to God. For, the same saint adds, since this love is gentle and persuasive, all that it inspires us to do has the same nature. But when self-love intervenes with its desire for success and self-satisfaction—that desire is its constant companion—first it imports an element of human activity and eagerness, and then anxiety and grief.

Be that as it may, you will tell me, I am quite convinced, that these tasks hinder advancement.—When, dear Sister, we love only the love of God, we wish to advance only as much as God wishes; we abandon ourselves to his divine Providence for our spiritual progress, even as good men in the world abandon themselves to that Providence for the success of their temporal concerns. Yet the great evil is that our self-love intrudes everywhere, interfering and spoiling everything—once more to quote St Francis de Sales. It is self-love which converts even the desire to advance spiritually into a subject of self-satisfaction and a cause of grief, and, consequently, into a stumbling-block to our advancement.

13. Yet another futile fear: you are afraid, you say, lest your insensibility be the secret of your peace.—Yes, indeed, it is your

insensibility which results in this, and that is why I look upon that insensibility as a gift of God. My wish is that the Holy Ghost's operations will induce in you a still greater insensibility, until you come to resemble, as far as all created things be concerned, a block of wood or a tree trunk. In the past I used to speak to you of this and you laughed at me. We come to it at last by slow degrees. Blessed be God! But for this kind of insensibility, we should have neither the strength nor the courage necessary, in many circumstances, to preserve our peace. We should need to possess the virtue of St Margaret Mary Alacoque, of whom men admiringly reported that whatever her feelings, she was at all times mistress of herself. As for the yearning for solitude known to you during your work, I shall tell you what St Ignatius told Father Laynez in a similar situation: While, Father, you retain at court, where obedience has set you, that great longing for solitude, your soul's safety is assured. Were that longing to leave you and were you to come to love your distracting duties, this would be an unfavourable sign. Hold fast, then, to this love of the call to solitude; yet as long as God shall require you to stay amid the cares and distractions of your daily tasks, make it your part to love them with a love of obedience.

LETTER 2: TO THE SAME

The same subject

ALBI, 1732

DEAR SISTER and dear daughter in our Saviour,—The peace of Jesus Christ be with you now and for ever.

Your letter has reminded me of that saying of Fénelon's: "We begin thoroughly to know and feel spiritual wretchedness only when we start to leave it behind." Accordingly, it is a very good sign if we feel ourselves wretched through and through, provided that the feeling is free from voluntary disquietude and accompanied by complete interior resignation.

1. In these states of dryness, darkness, insensibility and interior forlornness, all that we can do is to preserve in the highest part of the soul a sincere and steadfast determination to belong

389

wholly to God. Be comforted, therefore, and at peace upon this point.

2. It is true that this state, of which I spoke to you in my last letter, is God's great gift, and that in most cases it is reserved to chosen souls who have had long testing in the lower stages of the spiritual life; but at times too it is granted, out of pure goodness, to imperfect souls. For God knows nothing of set rules; he grants such grace as pleases him, and to whom he deems fit to accord it. This is your own case, you have my word for that. On your side, you have only to be at all times steadfast in a simple submission to the interior inclinations which are known to you from moment to moment, content to wish only what God wishes and for as long as he shall wish it. If you endure the ordeal faithfully to the end, you will see, when the time comes, what will result from it. I rejoice beforehand at its noble fruit, which before God I guarantee you.

3. You are suffering—and without merit—without true fidelity.—You imagine this to be so, and it is good that you do imagine it, since God permits this. Continue in that belief as long as you like, but be steadfast in submission to every wish of God. Then will I answer to you for everything.

4. You see nothing in your present state, and since you had my last letter, less than you did before.—So much the better. My wish is that this darkness will increase with each new day, for, by God's grace, I see clearly in this darkness, and that must be enough for you. In the midst of this obscure night go forward, then, by the light of blind obedience. It is a safe guide that has never yet led anyone astray, and whose guidance is more sure and more speedy than that of even the most perfect acts of self-abandonment.

5. Such acts are indeed excellent, though it is possible that you may sometimes find yourself unable to perform them. On such occasions you will be able to put yourself in a still more perfect state which consists of dwelling in the interior silence of respect, adoration and submission, of which I have written so much. Such silence tells God more than all your formal acts. Moreover, it knows no return to self-complacency and is without consolations perceptible to the senses. Here you have the true

mystical death which must necessarily precede the supernatural life of grace. Unless God perceives in you this second
death—death to spiritual consolation—you will not attain to
this wholly spiritual and interior life for which you long so fervently. Spiritual consolations are, in fact, so sweet that, were
God not to detach us from them by the violence of spiritual
ordeals, we should become even more attached to them than to
any worldly pleasure, and this would be a supreme stumbling-
block to perfect union.

6. Let it be enough for you that God knows what is occupying
you in this state, and that I know it too. It is well for you to
believe that you are reduced to complete spiritual nakedness.
Seemingly you are never to reach the blessed state known to that
servant of God who, having forgotten the meaning of human
words, can no longer talk with his fellow men. Take courage in
realizing that those things which today constitute your sorrow
and your martyrdom will in a day to come be your greatest delight. When will that blessed time be? God alone knows; it will
be when it pleases him.

7. The fact that the peace you experience tends slightly to dis-
perse and diminish immediately you begin to emerge from this
state of spiritual stupidity should enable you to guess—although
you will have no clear idea of it—what occupies you during your
seeming idleness and fills that terrifying void.

8. Give up wishing to explain yourself more clearly upon this
point. By God's grace it is daylight clear to me. You yourself
appreciate, from time to time, the blessed results of this kind
of stupidity. Emphatically, it is neither melancholy nor extravagance: it is the unique work of the Holy Ghost.

9. There are times when everything leaves you impatient and
weary. That is inevitable. St Teresa went so far as to say that in
such moments she had not the strength to crush an ant out of
love of God. We at no time attain to that utter distrust of self
and that perfect trust in God, unless we have first passed through
these various states of complete insensibility and absolute helplessness. Blessed states whose results are so marvellous.

10. Your experience in the retreat was a slight intensification
of your ordinary state, rather like a heightening of a fever. Im-

mediately you accepted this, as you tell me you did, it can only have been very salutary for you. Remain in peace; God is your guide; his grace is working, though its operation is hard and painful to bear, as are all drastic remedies. Your interior ills have need of such remedies; allow your loving Physician to do the work as he knows how; he will vary the strength of the remedy in accordance with the extent of the evil. How sick you once were, and yet knew it not! It was then that you had cause for alarm—not now when your convalescence is assured.

11. Your experience in prayer, bitter though it be, is again excellent. At such times merely keep yourself steadfast in complete resignation in the apex of the soul, to use St Francis de Sales's phrase.

12. There was infinitely more sensibility and, therefore, more satisfaction for self-love in the way in which formerly you made your retreat. Yet your present insensibility is of incomparably more value to you. Already you must feel the effects of it; for you are changed indeed from the woman you once were after those most agreeable retreats. Though you yourself do not recognize this, I recognize it for you. If you had the least capability of reflection, you would yourself see what little foundation there was for your fears. Apart from a definite operation of grace, how can you explain the fact that you have known such sadness throughout the period of your retreat, and yet that the time has passed so quickly and with so little weariness? Should you not see in this a clear proof that you have been busy indeed, though you have not known it?

13. The terrors caused by your old faults are the most hurtful and dangerous of your temptations. Hence I order you to reject all such advances of the devil, as we reject the temptations of blasphemy and impurity. Think only of the present and shut yourself up in the will of God, leaving all else to his Providence and mercy. Your stupidity and insensibility are emphatically not punishments for some hidden sin, as the devil would have you think, so that your interior peace may be troubled. They are pure graces, that have indeed a bitter taste, and yet have had good effects already, and in the future will have still more. Who says so? I—on God's behalf I assure you that it is so.

14. I should have been sorry indeed to have had the foolish satisfaction of hearing your general confession. For that would have delivered you into the devil's snare. What are you, then, to do to be rid of these fears? You are to obey simply and blindly him who speaks to you on behalf of the Master who has deputed him for the part, and, voluntarily, give no further thought to it.

15. Your insensibility and indifference to all which formerly delighted you most is, indeed, one of the greatest graces which God could give you. How has that grace operated within you? With the help of that terrifying void—of that painful state of stupidity and insensibility which seems so bitter to you. Admittedly, this cure is violent; yet what blessed results it produces, when we lovingly accept it at the hands of our soul's loving Physician.

There you have, in brief, a summary of the whole of this letter. Your sole interior practice must be to continue to dwell, as you now do, in the hands of God, much as a rough stone that is shaped, fashioned and polished by sharp blows from hammer and chisel. In patience wait for the sovereign architect to indicate that niche in his edifice in which he shall choose to set you, once he has shaped and fashioned you with his hand.

I am altogether yours in our Lord.

P.S.—I appreciate very much, though I am in no way surprised by, the account you give me of the Duke of Hamilton: we are used to seeing such manifestations of God's power and mercy. That short conversation has been a grace for you; never forget it.

LETTER 3: TO SISTER MARIE-THÉRÈSE DE VIOMÉNIL

Interior prostration

DEAR SISTER,—I have no remedy to offer you that might lighten the painful and prostrating burden which constantly weighs down your heart. A simple acquiescence, a humble *fiat*, that you can utter—possibly without knowing it—though God will hear it distinctly—will be enough to sanctify you and make you a martyr of Providence.

393

The Practice of Self-abandonment

Again, you cannot imagine how many excellent acts are contained in that feeling of prostration which results from the great burden known to your heart. It is a greater grace for you than you think: in it you will discover a most efficient means of acquiring true penitence of heart and that compunction which all the saints have so greatly valued, and the need of which God has, not once only, so keenly made you feel. Welcome your ordeal, then, with submission and gratitude. Often declare to God that even in your holiest and most salutary desires you would make his adorable will your rule and standard, longing only for that measure of virtue and eternal happiness which he has decided to give you.

Go to communion as often as they are willing to allow you, enduring in peace and submissiveness all the grief which receiving the Sacrament will cause you. Your humility and self-obliteration will take the place of the preparation which you lack; while your loss of all perceptible benefits will be amply compensated by the courage and self-abandonment that you will show in the ways by which God guides you.

Your disability and the regimen which it has forced upon you is the best penance you could do. So you are still afraid of pandering to yourself if you give up fasting while your sickness lasts?—A vain fear! Rather be afraid of lacking in interior self-abnegation because of a desire to act on your own judgement. Obey your doctor blindly; God requires this of you, while he certainly does not require you to fast. As often as you can, make your sickness an offering to him, and with it its consequences and your own fears. Yet let this offering be made by your heart only, reminding yourself to wish only what he wishes. A simple thought, a mere glance in our Lord's direction, will suffice for that.

LETTER 4

The same subject

I can only bless God from the bottom of my heart, dear Sister, in observing that he pursues his work within you. This prostrating weight which you feel deep in your heart is one of the most

394

salutary operations of that crucifying love which acts on your heart as fire acts upon wood; before flame breaks out on it, the wood crackles and smokes, and the sap with which it was filled is driven violently from it. As soon as it is thoroughly dried, it burns softly, shedding bright light about it. So will it be with your heart, once it has been purified by various griefs, and in particular by painful interior operations. You must, then, endure these operations sweetly and courageously, seeking as far as you can neither to vex nor trouble yourself interiorly. This is the great and noble penance which God requires of you. It shall avail you more than all physical austerities, although each of us must practise the latter also, as strength and health permit.

I see a most manifest sign of the good effects resulting from your present ordeal in the remark which you go on to make. It seems to you, you say, that you are for ever expecting something now lacking to you. I will give you an explanation of that expectancy; it is accounted for by the fact that your heart, estranged from all creatures and yet unable to live without delight or love, feels more keenly than ever the need of that supreme good which alone can replenish it. The greater the void already known to your heart, by reason of its estrangement from all earthly affections, the livelier is the ardour with which it yearns for knowledge of God and his blessed love. It is this for which you are waiting; while it is precisely by means of this expectancy and these secret yearnings that we at last secure that divine love. The water of life is given to those who thirst for it. Ardent desires are the money tokens with which we buy this sublime and exquisite relish for God, this heavenly nourishment which alone appeases the hunger and thirst of our hearts, whereas the love and even the possession of any created good would merely serve to inflame and irritate the heart, and never succeed in satisfying it.

LETTER 5

Emptiness of heart

I THOROUGHLY approve, dear Sister, of the patience with which you endure the great emptiness in your heart. As the result of it, you make greater progress in a single month than you would have done in several years of delight and consolation. In this matter I have only to exhort you to persist; for it is our essential need to cross this desert if during this life we are to reach the promised land.

I am not surprised that this great emptiness brings you strength. It does indeed, since God is present in it, although in a scarcely perceptible manner, no less than he is during spiritual ordeals. At all times look upon this general aversion, and apparent insensibility to all that is not of God, as a great grace. Carefully maintain yourself in this state of soul. At the moment indicated by his grace, God will come to fill that emptiness he now makes in your heart; while the ineffable sweetness with which his presence will be accompanied will arouse a new aversion in you for all this world's paltry satisfactions.

Today, then, take a general and final farewell of all creatures, and rejoice when of their own accord they turn their backs upon you; for God permits this to help your weakness. For my part, I am delighted at what has happened, and at the little regard that has been shown to you. This manifestation has undoubtedly been as salutary for you as it has been humiliating. Oh, were you able slowly to grow to love this abjection, what progress would you not make!

LETTER 6: TO SISTER MARIE-THÉRÈSE DE VIOMÉNIL

The same subject—Grief redoubled

DEAR SISTER,—Since my letters are of such use and comfort to you, wherever I happen to be during my lifetime, I promise always to answer your letters promptly.

1. Imperfections and even faults that we may commit contrary to complete submission to God's will do not hinder us from maintaining this submission in the depths of our hearts. Nor do they rob us of merit. If we are to repair the hurt these faults render us, it is enough that we humiliate ourselves for them, and return, as soon as may be, to a filial self-abandonment to the hands of God.

2. I realize better than you imagine your heart's shrinking and the weight which seems to prostrate it. I was myself for several years in that same state, and this for a reason wholly insignificant in itself, and because of its insignificance galling to my pride. I was guilty of many faults, but I sought to recover from them speedily. It was only long after the ordeal was over that I recognized its benefits: they have seemed to me since so many and so great that even yet I thank God daily that, in his mercy, he afflicted me by causing me to pass through this interior purgatory. I am thoroughly certain that in his own time God will by degrees give you the same realization. Then you will never grow tired of giving him thanks for the affliction he sends you today.

3. I, too, have known on more occasions than I can remember the paroxysms of grief of which you tell me, and which resemble those of a fever. At such times, as in serious sickness, we have but to endeavour to remain in interior silence and peace, so far as we are able; for we are then scarcely in a state to perform express acts, particularly conscious and comforting acts. Yet God perceives the submission which never fails in our hearts. And this is merit enough. In this state there is so much the more spiritual profit as there is less consolation.

4. We are not forbidden to implore God that these griefs may cease, especially when they strongly beset the heart. For Jesus Christ so implored God in the Garden of Olives. Yet with him we must add, as he added: "Yet not my will, but thine be done." Though we add these words with great repugnance and much interior rebelliousness, what matters that? It is the soul's lower part which resists and is grieved. Yet such resistance cannot destroy the upper part's resignation. On the contrary, it can only increase the soul's merit, and hasten its progress in the way of enduring virtue.

5. They do well to make you frequent the sacraments; you would be guilty of a great fault if you kept away from them. Nothing could do you more harm. Neither despondency, nor discouragement, nor grief, nor shame, nor interior trouble should ever keep you from holy communion. Such painful preparations, suffered and accepted for God's sake, are of more

worth to you than fervour and sensible consolations. The latter serve often only to nourish and sustain spiritual self-love, itself the subtlest and most delicate of all self-loves, whereas those other preparations tend slowly to cause its death. In that death, true piety and all spiritual progress are embraced, while, lacking this true self-abnegation, the majority of devout persons are devout merely upon the surface.

You must see in the poorness of your health merely the opportunity of making each day another and meritorious sacrifice. You must submissively accept all remedies prescribed for you, and even, if it be deemed necessary, resign yourself to have not even one day's abstention from meat. Your repugnance and your scruples upon this point are entirely without foundation. You must sacrifice to obedience both these griefs, and even the most seemingly spiritual of your repugnances. Anything else would be a sheer illusion which good sense should be enough to dispel, and in which, nevertheless, I have seen various deluded people, including nuns, indulge.

LETTER 7: TO SISTER DE LESEN, ANNONCIADE NUN
(1736)
The same subject

DESPITE the tenderness of my human compassion and the great affection in our Saviour which I have for the afflicted woman about whom you write to me, I can in no way be alarmed at her state, or even greatly pity it. I have told her often that after the signal favour she has received from God I am astonished at only one thing: that she, having received in so notable degree the gift of simple recollection, was not subjected sooner to the ordeals ordinarily attendant upon that state.

Enough if I tell you that when I saw the ordeal begin, I found myself unable either to be astonished or sorry. Now that I see her in spiritual paroxysm, I can only tell her again what she knows already, and what you yourself have told her, namely, that God grants her the grace of putting that recollection into practice. You and I know equally well that as long as God wishes her to remain in this ordeal an angel come down from heaven could not withdraw her from it, nor could afford her the least consolation. I am, however, quite willing to go into a few details, if that will satisfy you.

1. These are the reasons why I consider that this dear friend's state is at one and the same time an ordeal and a result of her progress in the supernatural life: (1) her sorrowful state of soul comes from a sense of faith, and her lively fear of God's judgements, of death, eternity and the rest; (2) for long past she has had great comfort in her simple self-abandonment to the hands of God and in her union with Jesus Christ in agony; (3) the painful suffering has seized her now without any apparent conscious cause and without any forethought on her part; (4) and while her disposition, character, temperament and other factors will, as always happens, have their part in it, at bottom her grief is none the less supernatural because of these, since, without apparent or conscious cause, she has travelled far beyond mere nature.

Do not, therefore, be afraid for her; for she is undoubtedly in that state which writers on mysticism call *the state of suffering the crucifying gift of God*. She is by no means the only person who has been tormented by those fears of losing her reason which leave her in dread. I have known not a few who have been driven to make that last great sacrifice with complete trust and utter self-abandonment. She will have all its merit without, I hope, God requiring this sacrifice to be fulfilled. Such are God's ways with souls: in scores of similar circumstances, as he did of old with Abraham, he requires only the sacrifice of the heart and not the sacrifice of actual deed. Accordingly, let her constantly hope against hope. All ordeals, patiently undergone, will turn to her great advantage. Do you, then, be tranquil and at peace in regard to her. As for the retreat, I am inclined to think that it would be well to abandon it. Yet, if, nevertheless, she wishes to continue it, she has but to do what you have counselled her: to meditate solely upon trust in God; to read only what may fortify her soul with the essence of simple recollection, and this with as little thought and reasoning as may be possible, and certainly without undue effort.

399

2. Let her ponder as little as possible her grief and interior distress. Such broodings, while they rob her of merit, serve only to increase and embitter her soul's sickness. Let her, with sweetness and simplicity, and certainly without effort or violence, forget self to remember only God. Let her no longer refer to her griefs, even in her prayers to God; but let her converse with him on any other matter to the best of her ability.

3. When solitude has tended to engross her, despite herself, overmuch in her anguish, I advise her then to engage in holy talk with yourself or another of her Sisters. Reverend Mother is right in cutting out her annual confession: on God's behalf I forbid it her, and command her not even to think of it.

4. It is certain, as you have wisely remarked, that this state of grief has already had blessed consequences for this soul. Nothing has ever brought her, or will bring her, such benefit. Even when the climax of her grief is entirely over, I warn her that for a considerable time she will retain a remembrance of interior humiliation which will bear marvellous results. Her fear of experiencing a return of this sorrowful state will maintain her in a profound and almost unbroken dependence upon God that will avail her greatly.

5. To conclude: though man can provide no remedy for her supernatural griefs, nothing is easier than to point out the means by which she can draw great profit from them and alleviate them greatly. These are they: submission, self-abandonment, peace, patience and trust; with these she must allow God to do his work, and not interrupt that work by too many interior acts on her part. In short, she must cultivate merely that humble and simple interior state which the grace of Jesus Christ produces in the soul, and in which she must, in a measure, co-operate, passively rather than actively; or, to express it more accurately, she must turn her activity into submission to God's action. So be it.

LETTER 8: TO SISTER DE LESEN (1736)
Violent temptations

DEAR SISTER,—1. Each must perform her spiritual exercises, including prayer, and, therefore, her retreat in accordance with her call and her needs. Take, then, some religious book which is in tune with the call that grace enables you to hear at the moment, and in all your interior preoccupations let your heart seek, before anything else, complete self-abandonment to God. Dwell in limitless trust upon the breast of divine mercy, fortifying yourself in this feeling with as great an energy as you believe yourself to have cause for fear.

What most delights God's heart, and what most he requires from you in your present state, is hope against all hope; in other words, hope against the seeming impossibility of seeing your hope realized.

2. As for the terrifying temptation of which your letter gives me an account, I confess that it would be difficult to imagine one more dreadful, either in itself or in the particular circumstances. Take good care, nevertheless, not to allow yourself to despond. Realize in the first place that these, the most sorrowful of all ordeals, are those which God usually constrains those he most loves to undergo. At this present moment I have under my direction those who are, in this connection, in spiritual states which I cannot describe, and the description of which would leave you horrified. The whole lower part of the soul is beset by darkness and plunged in the mire. God upholds and preserves its upper part—its free will—without permitting the soul any knowledge of his support. He illumines it with a light of pure faith, so wholly spiritual that the senses can perceive nothing, and the poor soul, seemingly forsaken in its wretchedness and left the prey of demons, is reduced to a state of hideous desolation and undergoes a true martyrdom. On this subject read that chapter in Guilloré in which he writes of excessive temptation.

Your need, in truth, is to be for ever afraid, yet showing neither grief nor dejection, and leaning far more towards trust. Never forget that the Almighty, who furthers his plans in his hidden ways, at such times possesses himself of the soul's recesses and divinely upholds it, unperceived by ourselves. God grants you a grace that he often withholds from others in this state: the grace of feeling—or, at least, of knowing and perceiving —that you would rather be cut into pieces than yield your consent.

3. Be in no way perplexed as to the way in which you should confess the thoughts and suggestions inspired by the adversary; there is no need to speak of them at all. While, as for the way in which you should disown them, the best, easiest and most effective for people in your state is that which you have already adopted. I mean by that a simple glance on the soul's part towards its God; an interior impulse that knows neither vexation nor agitation and that turns from both creatures and itself and towards its Creator. That is the heart's *conversion*—in the pure sense of the word—to God. In all things and for all things, so far as of his goodness he grants you this grace, turn this to your own use. From time to time you may—though you must not believe yourself obliged to this or make violent efforts to that end—perform a few acts of set disavowal. Thus, you may repeat: "O God, keep me from all voluntary consent; let me die rather than freely consent to offend you in anything at all. Yes, O God, let death rather than sin be mine! On the other hand, for as long as it pleases you I accept what may come to me of grief, heartbrokenness, interior desolation, humiliation and abjection."

4. Plainly your terror-inspiring conception of God's justice and the anguish and interior bitterness that comes of it are another of God's ordeals. It is as plain that the peace and tranquillity which go with these sorrowful feelings of yours spring from the submission which God maintains in your soul's depths. Such peace and the interior conviction that all you do in no way serves to bring you nearer heaven are less difficult to understand than you imagine, at least for directors of some experience. That peace is of God; it dwells in the depths of the soul, or, as St Francis de Sales says, in the apex of the spirit. That terrifying conviction is no more than the spirited assault the demon is allowed to make upon the soul's lower part, or, to express it differently, upon its exterior and sense-conscious part. It is the

diabolical assault that constitutes the soul's martyrdom; while it is the submission God grants it that ensures a peace that owes nothing to the senses. Were you to perceive this as clearly as I do, you would no longer be in a state of ordeal. Be glad, then, that God leaves you some small perception and some vague trace of feeling, that you are preserved in peace. Further, should even this feeling fail you, obedience must suffice you—obedience and self-abandonment. Say unceasingly with a firm will: "God will make of me all that it pleases him, yet in the meantime my constant wish is to love and serve him as best I may, and to put my hope in him; I would keep that hope even though I saw myself at the very gates of hell." It is a matter of faith that God never forsakes those who surrender themselves to him and who put their full trust in him. Repeat, therefore: "He is the God of my salvation, and never shall my salvation be more assured than when I entrust it to his hands by placing my full trust in his infinite goodness, since of myself I am capable only of coming to perdition and spoiling everything."

5. The difficulties in your soul's lower part when your griefs are most poignant can never destroy your peace of spirit, as long as your submission to God is complete. This is known as possessing the solid and undoubted peace of God. As for painful thoughts, extravagances of the imagination and other temptations, you must: (1) allow them to drop from you so far as you are able, as a stone sinks into water; (2) when you cannot succeed in this as often happens in time of ordeal, you must allow yourself to be crucified as it shall please God, and to endure your sickness of soul as you would that of the body, in patience, peace, submission, trust and utter self-abandonment, and desiring only the will of God, in union with Jesus Christ.

6. Your *fiat*, pronounced in regard to things which arouse your disapproval, provided that out of charity you conceal the outward manifestation of that disapproval, is all that God requires of you. How many souls I have known, dear Sister, who would believe themselves blessed indeed did God leave them all the comforting aids he leaves you.

7. The deep-seated desire for recollection is in itself true recollection, though no delight accompany it. If it is less con-

soling than sensible recollection, it is only the more unselfish for that, and, it follows, the more meritorious. In such a state we call nothing ours, since it seems to us that we possess nothing.

8. The impatience which is caused by the realization of your insignificance is merely a slight vexation of haughty self-love. Were it deliberate it would constitute grave imperfection; for our need is to deplore our wretchedness with humble tranquillity. "Learn," says St Francis de Sales, "to put up with your wretchedness as you must put up with your neighbour's."

9. I am not surprised that since your retreat your griefs and temptations have doubled. Did you understand, as I, the good effects they must produce in purifying even the most secret recesses of your heart, you would not tire of blessing God for them; for this is a great grace reserved to those souls whom God wishes to lead to pure love, by detaching them from everything and from self in particular.

10. It is good to do, though discreetly, some exterior penances; yet you must not indulge in too many. As long as your present ordeal lasts, you must make your renunciation consist chiefly in accepting this ordeal with complete submission. Much still remains for you to do if you are to attain to this perfect self-abandonment; and I should be unwilling for you to lose sight of this kind of mortification for the sake of practising others that are far less necessary. Realize that your interior upheaval will cease only when you have surrendered yourself unreservedly, endlessly and limitlessly to God's every wish. May God be blessed for all things and in all things! *Amen.*

LETTER 9: TO SISTER MARIE-ANNE-THÉRÈSE DE ROSEN (1734)

Annihilation and spiritual agony

DEAR SISTER,—1. The vivid awareness which you feel of your nothingness in God's sight is one of the most salutary operations of the grace of the Holy Ghost. I know how thoroughly painful this operation can be; the poor soul appears to be on the brink of utter obliteration, whereas it is only the nearer to true life. Indeed, the deeper we are plunged into our nothingness the nearer we are to truth, since our very essence is of that nothingness from which we have been drawn out by the Lord's pure goodness. We ought, then, to dwell in it unbrokenly, and thus, by our voluntary self-obliteration, render continual homage to the grandeur and infinite nature of our Creator. Nothing is more pleasing to God than this homage; nothing assures us more certainly of his favour; and, in consequence, nothing so greatly perturbs our self-love. Such sacrifice is a holocaust in which self-love is utterly consumed in the fire of divine love. We must, then, not be astonished that self-love offers so violent a resistance or that it causes—particularly when it is at its last gasp—mortal agony in the soul. The grief that we then experience is like that of a person in his death agony, while it is only through such sorrowful agony, and through the spiritual death which follows it, that we can reach the plenitude of divine life and an intimate union with God. When this sorrowful, yet blessed, hour has come, we have nothing to do but imitate Jesus Christ on the cross: we must commend our soul to God, surrender ourselves still more completely to all that it pleases the sovereign Master to do with this poor creature, and to remain in that agony as long as his good pleasure ordains.

2. As long as these crucifying operations last, everything—spirit, memory and will—exists in a terrifying void, in sheer nothingness. Let us cherish this mighty void, since God deigns to fill it; let us cherish this nothingness, since God's infinity is to be discovered in it. Let us be of good courage, dear daughter: let us assent to everything with the blessed abasement of spirit of Jesus Christ crucified. From all this our strength must come. Let us make a habit of saying, when such anguish besets us: "Indeed, Lord, I desire all that you desire, in Jesus Christ and through Jesus Christ!" In such company as his, how could we be afraid? In the most violent of temptations a simple abasement at the feet of the Saviour-God will make all things calm: he will render you victorious; while, with his strength, he will enable your weakness to triumph over all the tempter's cunning.

3. The rebelliousness of your passions, uninstigated in any way by yourself; interior excitement; anxieties and involun-

tary griefs—these and much other wretchedness are permitted within you for two reasons: (1) To humiliate you to an extra-ordinary degree by making you realize what heights of wretched-ness and what depths of corruption you carry about with you; and by showing you what you would become but for God's great mercy; (2) To that end, new interior operations having supervened, all these seeds of death, hidden in your soul, can be uprooted like so many weeds whose appearance above soil leaves them the more easily available to the gardener's skilled hand. It is only after he has completely cleaned the soil that he can promote the growth of wholesome plants, fragrant flowers and choice fruits. Allow him to do his work: leave entirely to him the cultivation of this sorry soil that, of itself, can bear only thistles and thorns; be not anxious, but be satisfied with the feeling that you are indeed humiliated and confounded; remain in deep abasement in this mire, as Job upon his dung-heap. For this is your place. Wait until God takes you out of it, and, in the meantime, let yourself be purified by him. What matters it to you, so only you are to his liking? At times princes take delight in bespattering their favourites with mud, making them fall into the water and even into the mire. At such times the favour-ite is pleased to see the prince draw his pleasure from the sight of this bespatterment.

4. When you feel impulses of cowardice or fear, humiliate yourself by repeating: "All this, and even less than this is impos-sible to me in my weakness; but all this and infinitely more than this becomes possible and easy with the grace of Jesus Christ, from whom alone I hope and expect good to come to me."

5. Yet this ordeal has in it something yet harder and sterner and more plainly in accordance with the ways in which chosen souls are led: the poignant thought that God rejects you, that he forsakes you forever as unworthy of his favours. Did you under-stand this, dear Sister, as I do—how even in this there is revealed God's loving dealings with yourself—you would know far too great a satisfaction. All I can say to you upon this subject—and I say it to you without knowing whether, in your present state of trial, it will please God to allow you to understand—is that never before have you loved God so purely as now, and never

before have you been so beloved of him. Yet this love is so hidden beneath your torments and your seeming wretchedness that a director has need of considerable experience before he can recognize it. Yet have patience: brilliant light and splendour that will delight you will succeed this terrifying darkness.

Indeed, dear Sister, you can believe in me, even though just now you cannot understand me, for I tell you only of what God has given me definite assurance. This bitterest aspect of your ordeal, this feeling of your separation from God, which leaves you in a kind of hell—this is the divinest of all the operations of divine love within you; while at the same time this operation is wholly hidden beneath the most deceptive of outward appearances. It is the fire that seems to destroy the soul in order to purify it of all self-love, as gold is refined in a crucible. Oh! how blessed you are without knowing it! How beloved without understanding it! What great changes God effects in you, in a way that is the more assured the more secret and unknown to you it is! Our weakness it is, O God, our wretched self-love, our pride, that bring it about that you are able to grant us graces only if you hide them from us, so that, in effect, we are unaware that they exist—this, lest we corrupt your gifts by appropriating them to ourselves by reason of our hidden, futile and imperceptible complacency. Here, dear Sister, you have the whole secret of this mysterious conduct of God.

In a word, dear Sister, fear nothing; be steadfast and be of good courage. God is with you and in you; you have nothing to fear, though you should be in hell itself with unchained demons ringing you round. Nothing can befall you without God's sanction, and he can sanction nothing unless it be for your benefit. So long as you trust yourself to the goodness of so faithful a Friend, so tender a Father, so powerful a Protector, so passionate a Spouse and Lover, your safety is assured. These tender and lovable titles are those which he deigns to give himself in the Scriptures, and whose meaning he makes so significant in your case.

LETTER 10: TO SISTER CHARLOTTE-ELIZABETH
BOURCIER DE MONTHUREUX

Mystical death; its usefulness

LUNÉVILLE, 1733

DEAREST DAUGHTER,—I fully realize that the state in which it pleases God to set you is indeed painful to human nature, but I am a little surprised that you have not yet understood that in this way God desires to bring about an utter death within you, in order that you may straightway live a life that is wholly supernatural and divine. You have repeatedly besought him for this mystical death. Now he grants you it. The greater your seeming wretchedness grows, the more assured you are that God is effecting that despoliation and poverty of spirit of which the mystics tell. I refer you once again to Guilloré's works, in which you will find a good explanation of your present state.

Yet what must I do, you say? Nothing, my daughter, other than allow God to do his work, and to take precautions against thwarting God's operation by uncalled-for activity. You must abstain even from acts of conscious resignation, save at those times when you feel God has given you the impulse to perform them. Live, then, like a block of wood, and later you shall see the wonders God has worked during this silent night. Yet self-love cannot bear to see itself thus stripped and reduced to nothingness. Read, not once, but many times, what Guilloré says of this nothingness, and you will bless God that he has allowed you to possess this treasure. As for me, I can but bless him for it and deem your lot worthy of envy; for you must realize that it is to few that God grants the grace of undergoing so great a despoliation.

The terrifying aridities of which you tell me are the normal sequel to this great spiritual nakedness. God upholds you imperceptibly, as you yourself feel; and so true it is that this state comes from God that above and beyond the senses you are possessed of a sense of peace, and that, before God, you would be sorry not to be in this state. Your sole needs are patience, self-abandonment and resignation: once again these attitudes of ours must be beyond the senses. Remember that God beholds in the depths of your heart all your secret desires. This assurance must suffice you: a cry withheld is worth as much as a cry uttered, says the Bishop of Meaux.

Give up those thoughts and continual introspection as to what you do and fail to do: you are wholly surrendered to God and altogether bound to him. There is no need to undertake your own correction; leave God to do everything. Your simile is most exact: God has bound you hand and foot that he alone may perform the work in you, while all you do is to writhe restlessly in the vain efforts you make that serve only to break your sacred bonds and, following the bent of your human nature, strive to do things yourself. What unfaithfulness! God requires you to do nothing except to lie still and peacefully in your bonds and helplessness. There are, of course, your duties: perform those which are exterior to the best of your ability, and I will answer for you interiorly; for on that side God has intervened in an imperceptible manner that he may withdraw you from the things of the senses. Your mere consciousness of your wretchedness and corruption reveals the presence of God—of God who is the nearer for being hidden, and the more intimately possessed in that he has seemingly fled away. Once more, read Guilloré on this subject.

God has allowed that first imprudence of yours that you, without giving thought to it, may obtain the measure of relief you need, and that at the same time your self-love may be mortified and hindered. Blessed imprudence! God, it may be, permitted your second imprudence in order to take you from your task. Since you have in neither word nor deed striven for this end, you must have no scruples on the subject. Think no more of it, but allow divine Providence to do the work. Is it not God's fatherly solicitude that has allowed you in innocence to make a false step, as a consequence of which you have at one and the same time been relieved and humiliated, while you yourself have the satisfaction of knowing that you have in no way contributed to that relief?

Allow your terrors of death and judgement to increase as much as it shall please God; do nothing actively either to seek these fervours or to be rid of them. In short, let God handle you as though you were a dead body that can be manipulated, turned this way and that at will.

In conclusion, in one sense I can conceive nothing simpler or easier than your present behaviour generally, since it amounts merely to letting God do the work and to remaining passively peaceful yourself. Yet it must be admitted that this peace is the cruellest of torture to our accursed human nature whose being is bound up in its own activity, so that the loss of that activity is as terrible to it as death and self-annihilation.

LETTER 11 : TO THE SAME

The same subject—Before retreat

NANCY, 1734

THE theme which must be yours during retreat is simple indeed, though it cannot fail to be painful on account of the interior situation in which it pleases God to place your soul at this time.

1. Do not forget, dear Sister, that after we have left behind the first stages of the spiritual life, all our advancement comes by the way of loss, destruction and self-obliteration. Our inevitable need is to die to all that is created, sensible and human, if we are to know possession in all its fullness of the life of the spirit and of God's grace. Consequently you must expect during this retreat neither perceptible light of wisdom nor delightful spiritual appreciation of God and divine things, but, on the contrary, a lapse into still greater spiritual darkness, still greater aversion and a still more complete insensibility. Make it your one duty, therefore, to accept all it pleases the sovereign Master and Lord to give you; for, after your self-abandonment to him, you must look upon your interior self as a seed-ground belonging not to you but only to God, who will sow in it all that he wills, light or darkness, liking or aversion—in a word, all that it is his pleasure to sow, even nothing at all, if that be his pleasure. Oh, how terrible is that "nothing" to self-love! Yet how good and profitable it is to the spirit of grace and the light of faith! God effects his work in us to perfection only in the measure that we

410

are firmly of our own will established in that nothingness, since it is proportionate to our will's acquiescence in that nothingness that he discovers in us a greater or a less degree of resistance and impediment to his divine operations.

2. In such a state of spiritual spoliation, you must on no account make your preparations for retreat by artificial constraint or the consideration of subjects perplexing to you. In simplicity ponder upon the life and the mysteries of Jesus Christ, as you are well able to do. Read St Francis de Sales and a few of Mother de Chantal's letters that deal with the state of grief and despoliation; and—though this be an exception—read a little of the more moving lives of saints, both men and women, or accounts of the virtues of the blessed Mothers and Sisters of your order. Such reading will serve to instruct and comfort you.

3. During the day, shut yourself up interiorly with God that you may accept and welcome all the varying arrangements of his paternal Providence with an utter self-abandonment and a thorough self-abnegation. In this way you engage in true recollection in which you need fear no sense of idleness.

When you begin to feel more inclination to, or facility in making acts or familiar colloquies with God or our Lord, you must be gently obedient to these promptings of grace, though without effort or anxiety. You will follow the counsel of St Francis de Sales, who advises that such acts should, as it were, trickle, and be distilled, through the apex of the soul. Immediately you need to make a definite effort to persist in these, straightway give them up, and withdraw humbly into yourself.

Maintain your heart's essential restfulness, detached—as Fénelon advocates—from thoughts of exterior things. By this I mean voluntary thoughts; for in the case of those which stray into your mind you can merely take no notice. Yet if you find they engage your attention despite yourself, you can then fall back upon peace, patience and self-abandonment.

I need scarcely say that you must be wholly faithful and meticulously exact in your performance of the exercises prescribed for this time of retreat.

Observe these rules and you have no need to fear any waste of time on your part; let your one fear be lest that same miserable fear, which springs wholly from self-love, shall perturb you and divert you from simple recollection. This last you must guard as you would a rich treasure, however shallow, barren and arid this recollection may prove to be. For in your own case, there is nothing more important than such recollection in God, since, in default of it, he could not effect his divine operations within you. If you but cleave fast to your union with him, you can be sure that he will perform his work within you, though his way of doing this may be imperceptible, while the result of his work, for the time being, must be to impoverish you and more and more to despoil you spiritually, rather than to enrich you and to make you spiritually full. When, with the help of grace, we have reached the stage of finding self intolerable and of knowing not the smallest satisfaction in our good works, our one remaining need is to endure that self with sweetness and to show it the same charity that it is our duty to show our neighbour. This is one of the counsels given to us by St Francis de Sales. Blessed is he who, as the result of destroying self-love, comes to esteem that self-love no more in anything, and to love it only out of pure charity as he loves his neighbour and his enemies, and this notwithstanding the kind of horror and scorn he feels towards that self. Ah! through how many further stages and ordeals must we pass before we reach the point of loving self only out of that true love which comes of pure charity! With all my heart I implore God to grant you that grace.

LETTER 12: TO THE SAME

The same subject—After retreat

4 NOVEMBER 1734

1. Let me start by confessing frankly that, much as the man in me feels compassion for you, I cannot pity you—in fact when I read your letter I gave thanks to God. It has fallen out as I ventured to predict to you, when you began your retreat.

2. You know my opinions in the matter of keen perception of our weakness and helplessness: these are, Fénelon says, so many

graces which bring us to despond of self and place our hope only in God. It is at such times, he goes on, that God begins to perform marvels in the soul. Normally, however, he effects these by stealth, keeping the soul in ignorance in order to save it from self-love's snares.

3. The way in which God compelled you to spend the feast of All Saints is hard indeed upon your humanity, but very salutary from the aspect of grace. Blind creatures that we are! Let us leave all the work to God. Far from progressing we should retrogress badly if we acted on our own ideas and desires—even the seeming saintliest of them.

4. You feel yourself to be without faith, hope or charity: this is because God deprives you of all perception of these virtues by making them abide in the higher part of the soul. In this way he puts you in a position of making a complete sacrifice of all your satisfaction, and there is surely nothing better than that. What, then, is your complaint? It comes of the fact that disconsolate humanity cries out against experiencing nothing but griefs, aridities and interior anguish. To the human element in you these are death-dealing, yet that human element has to die before you may receive the life of grace—that life which is altogether blessed and wholly divine. I am acquainted with souls who endure such frequent and terrible anguish that it seems to them, as it has seemed to you, that at any moment they might die. They can be compared to the criminal on the wheel of torture who waits only the stroke which will finish all and which, by hastening his wretched end, will end his torments. Courage, then—courage, patience, self-abandonment and trust in God! He grants you yet one more great grace and notable favour in thus allowing you to be aware at intervals of an imperceptible support.

The various shocks which your good Master has made you experience—that acute remembrance of your sins and your wretchedness—are divine operations, torturing indeed, yet designed to purify you as gold is purified in the crucible. How can I then pity you? I am called upon to congratulate you, as of old those holy martyrs were congratulated, who deemed themselves blessed in the midst of their torments and savage tortures.

5. The regret you have been tempted to feel at the thought of consolations known to you during previous retreats is merely an illusion from which you must safeguard yourself carefully. Thanks to God's grace, you have never made a more useful retreat. He even allowed you some small perception of this when he inspired you with so great a strength with which to make him a sacrifice of your spiritual delights and sensible consolations. Yet, you go on to say, God rejected that sacrifice. Here you have more temptation and illusion. God allows it to assail you once more in order to crucify you spiritually, again and again. *Fiat! fiat!* If God at times takes tranquillity away, let it go with all the rest. For ever God remains, and it is enough to love him with the greater purity in that he alone remains. At such times, therefore, it is he alone who works divinely for our perfection, effecting it by those interior deprivations which nature so abominates as its final death, its ultimate annihilation and its final loss. Let us be patient. *Fiat! fiat!* Only by the ways of loss, self-abnegation, despoliation, death to all things, complete annihilation and unreserved self-abandonment, do we make steady progress towards perfection. Let us not be astonished at the suffering to our feelings and our reason itself—that wretched reason which is so blind in the ways of faith. For it is indeed a strange blindness on its part to confine its aspirations for perfection to the ways of divine lights and of interior joys and consolations, the inevitable results of which would be to revive self-love within us and to leave it in a position to spoil everything.

6. It is precisely the lively consciousness you have of your extreme frailty which must have been one of the things which helped you most, since, in making you realize that you are liable to fall at any moment, it instils in you a thorough distrust of yourself, and enables you to put into practice a blind trust in God. It is in this sense that the Apostle said: "For when I feel most weak, then am I more powerful, because the acute sense of my weakness clothes me, through a more complete trust, with all the strength of Jesus Christ."

7. Nothing can be simpler than the attitude you must adopt in order to profit greatly from your painful and torturing state: the heart's perpetual "yes", its humble *fiat*, utter self-abandon-

ment and perfect trust—that is all. Morning, noon and night, this is all you have to do. It will appear to you that nothing is being done. Yet you will discover that all will be found to be done and done so thoroughly well that you will forever remain in deep humility, receiving no help from that miserable satisfaction which, while it leaves God dissatisfied, serves to content our self-love, to quote yet again our beloved Father, St Francis de Sales.

LETTER 13: TO MOTHER LOUISE-FRANÇOISE DE
ROSEN (1736)

The soul's purgation

DEAR SISTER,—In reading your letter I had no sooner got to the part in which you describe to me your painful state than, quite spontaneously, I threw myself interiorly at the feet of Jesus Christ to thank him for it. Innumerable experiences give me daily an increasing conviction that interior griefs purify a soul to its depths and in its most secret recesses, and sanctify it far more effectively than mortifications, penances and exterior tribulations. I can then only bless God for the goodness which he shows you, and encourage you to make faithful response to it. To this end you have merely to observe the following points:

1. Neither in the present circumstances, nor all the time your ordeal lasts, must you expect to receive consolation other than it pleases God to give you; for not even an angel from heaven could withdraw a soul from the crucible in which God has placed it, that it may obtain increasing purification.

2. Further, it is beyond doubt that interior crucifixion is the greater in the proportion that God intends to exalt the soul to a higher degree of love and union with him.

3. Fear of reprobation seems to be in no way an unusual thing; on the contrary, it is fairly common in righteous souls whom God wishes to lead to perfection.

4. In this trouble of yours God seems to be most indulgent towards your weakness, since, by reason of it, he gives you a self-abandonment and a trust in him that he desires shall on many

occasions be sensible, or at least apparent. How many souls are, in this state, deprived of this consolation!

5. In this connection, as in all others, God directs you so skilfully by the promptings of his grace that he leads you to perform exactly and persistently what he desires of you. Accordingly I will be content to make these two brief remarks. (1) Your present state seems to me the best of any you have known throughout your life, and the greatest grace that you have received; (2) God teaches you all you need to know about it; go your way, then, and be at peace.

I have read your letter for a second time, that I may discover whether God would put me in a position to make still plainer by a few explanations the already perfectly adequate direction I have given you in his name. Let me try!

(1) Every thought which depicts God for you as having ceased, in regard to you, to be swayed by that loving mercy which is his essence is merely a part of your ordeal. Such, too, are the various aspects of the deep-seated grief of reprobation which it is God's will that you shall endure. This grief is your martyrdom; while these various promptings of the adversary are so many shafts which he discharges with God's sanction. Instead of wounding your body they pierce your heart and your soul, and assuredly they are not the less meritorious by reason of that. (2) The idea and conviction that your sins are heaped full measure is certainly inspired in you by the prince of lies and not by the Holy Ghost; yet if God be not the author of it, he allows it to torment you, and he allows this in your own interest. In addition to the fact that this ordeal is indeed humiliating, the sorrow it brings with it is a fire that cannot fail to purify you the more intense its heat becomes, and the more often your soul is set in the crucible. (3) Your seeming lukewarmness, barrenness and insensibility are the sequel and result of that sorrowful conviction which is printed upon your soul. These are flames that of necessity purify, and do not consume, their victim, the better to fit her for being consumed in the fire of God's pure love. (4) I say as much of the attempts your heart makes to leap upward to God. These attempts, to which God's sole answer appears to be a rebuff, become, in the case of certain people, so violent and so

sorrowful that they give birth to what Bossuet calls despairing love or love's despair. This impulse, in which despair has only seemingly a part, is in reality the most vehement love of all. In this, as the great bishop says, grace takes as its pattern what the profane love of creatures sometimes drives love-frenzied men and women to achieve. (5) Only excessive grace enables us to perform that heroic act of St Francis de Sales, and to say: "If I am to be estranged from God through all eternity, during my life at least I must love and serve him." This desperate love is an aid of which many souls are deprived; make use of it, but do not become attached to it; for God may well take it away from you, or at least your perception of it. (6) You have acted very wisely in increasing the number of your communions in this state, in which support is so necessary to you. You must count yourself fortunate indeed in your ability to secure new strength by their help. (7) Faith, self-abandonment, trust, hope against hope— these are your most potent aids. Yet, did God deprive you of the consolation of perceiving these virtues in yourself, the one thing left for you to do would be to abandon yourself endlessly, limit-lessly, and even without conscious and perceptible support. God would then uphold you in the depths of your soul in an incom-prehensible manner; though the poor soul which in no shape or form is aware of this support, and which, on the contrary, imagines itself completely forsaken, knows a grief which turns this state into a kind of hell. In your case you are only yet in purgatory; and this purgatory is so purifying and so full of the riches of grace, that I implore God to withdraw you from it only after you have been enriched by it for all eternity, and after you yourself have been made as shiningly pure in his sight as many other virtuous souls have become through the agency of these same ordeals. (8) In the peace which is experienced by you in suffering you have the true peace of God, without fear of illusion entering into it. You find in yourself, instead of faithfulness, courage, strength and fervour in prayer, only unfaithfulness, weakness, lukewarmness and lack of devotion: it is these that must effect your annihilation before God. O blessed state of annihilation! A righteous soul said to me, a few days ago, that she dreaded to emerge from a certain terrifying spiritual state.

447

Why so? I said to her. Father, she answered, the reason is that I fear to lose my state of annihilation before God, which gives me greater delight than any conscious, sweet and comforting grace.

Here is a word or two for your dear Sister; for I notice that in regard to both of you, God leaves little for directors to do. The conclusion I draw from this, incidentally, is that both of you should consult them but rarely. Anything else would be a kind of infidelity to the great Master of spiritual things, whose wish is himself to direct both you and her.

Let me begin then:

1. So far, God appears to me to have dealt even more kindly with this dear Sister's weakness. Spiritual darkness and barrenness are in one sense the least painful of ordeals; while, nevertheless, they are profitable indeed in that the soul, seeing nothing, can spoil nothing. Further, this lack of perception leads it to the most perfect self-abandonment. Her own, she says, increases amazingly. That is the grace of graces; for all perfection is to be found in self-abandonment at its most perfect, in which our will is wholly lost in that of God. Love, thus practised, is love at its purest—is love secure from all illusion and from all vain intervention by self-love.

2. The ineffable consolations which this dear Sister experienced before she lapsed into this state of darkness and aridity, were no more than a merciful kindness of grace, designed to win completely the depths and the heart of the soul, in which God wished to take up his dwelling and to work in his imperceptible manner. These consolations were a great grace, but her present insensibility is a still greater grace.

3. Let, then, the good Sister remain as far as she is able in this state of simple self-surrender or of simple expectancy, emerging from it only upon the impulse imparted to her by interior grace and to the extent dictated by that impulse; for it is our duty neither to be deaf to our calls nor to exceed them.

Explanation of these ordeals—Spiritual direction

NANCY, 1734

DEAR SISTER,—As long as you remain in this utter self-abandon-ment in regard to God, in which I see you at the present mo-ment, I assure you on his behalf that he will never abandon you. In respect to this, the past and the present are your guarantees for the future. I realize that the way by which the Lord leads you is difficult for the senses; yet, beside the fact that he is the Master, you must reflect from time to time—he permits you to do so—upon the great advantages and the safety of this way. Reflect, too, upon its necessity: it is the ordinary way by which God leads his chosen spouses to the perfection which he plans for them, while I have known few indeed for whom he has not deemed it necessary to enter into this way, once they have given themselves entirely to him.

Yet what, then, is the reason for these painful states? Why these shrinkings of the heart that make all things seem flat, or this despondency which leaves us unable to endure ourselves any longer? Why? To destroy in souls, whose destiny is perfect union with God, a certain reserve of secret presumption; to attack pride in its last stronghold; to glut with bitterness that accursed self-love which clings only to what is pleasant, and, in the end, no longer knowing what to cling to, dies for lack of food and drink, as fire dies down for lack of wood to feed it. Yet this death does not come about in a twinkling; for much water is needed to extinguish a conflagration.

Self-love is like a hydra whose many heads must be cut off one by one; it must be successively deprived of several lives, if we desire to be wholly rid of it. There is no doubt that you won a notable victory when you succeeded in making it die in its human phase and the phase of the senses. Yet do not imagine that you are wholly rid of its obsessions. It recovers from this first defeat, and assails you from a fresh vantage ground. More subtle from that time forth, it clings to conscious piety; and it is to be

419

feared that its second hold, much less blatant and seemingly far more legitimate, will be stronger than the first.

Pure love of God, however, can no more tolerate the one than the other; it cannot endure that such sensible consolations shall share the heart with God. What, then, takes place? In the case of less privileged souls for whom his love is less jealous, God allows them peaceful enjoyment of these blessed delights, contenting himself with the sacrifice they have made to him of the pleasures of the senses. There, in fact, you have what is the ordinary course of events with devout people whose piety is mingled with a kind of self-seeking. Assuredly God does not approve their faults; yet, as he gives them fewer graces, so he makes fewer demands upon them in the matter of perfection. Such are God's ordinary spouses belonging to a lower rank, whose spiritual beauty may be less flawless and yet his heart be not too keenly wounded by the fact. But upon his chosen spouses he has many other demands to make, even as he has many other plans in regard to them.

His love's jealousy is in proportion to its tenderness. Desirous of giving himself utterly to them, he desires also to possess their hearts utterly with none to share them with him. He cannot then be satisfied with the exterior crosses and griefs that detach them from creatures. He desires to detach them from self and to destroy within them the uttermost roots of that self-love which clings to sensible devotions, finding support, nourishment and complacency in them. To effect this second death, he takes away all consolation, all delight and all interior support, with the result that the poor soul then finds itself, as it were, suspended between heaven and earth, having consciousness of delight in neither the one nor the other. Man's heart cannot live devoid of both delight and love, and to man therefore this state is a kind of annihilation. What remains to him then but to cling, not with his heart, since that is dead to all things, but with the higher part of the soul to the one God known and beheld through dark and naked faith! Ah, it is then that such a soul, its purification perfected by this double death, enters into spiritual communion with God, and possesses him in pure delight and pure love, as it could never have been able either to possess or delight in him had not its spiritual palate been thus doubly refined. Yet I have overleapt myself; let us get back to your letter.

How many false steps have you not made, you ask? But do you not yourself know the remedy for these? It is to humiliate yourself gently, to pick yourself up afresh and to take courage anew. Yet, you go on, I do so with such aversion, grief, vexation and sadness! It is precisely this which makes your merit the greater and enables you to acquire enduring virtue, since virtue is enduring only when we acquire it valiantly and at the point of the sword, to quote St Francis de Sales.

There is such sadness in everything around us. I realize that very clearly, and it is exactly in this that God attacks your heart at its most assailable point.

"Granted, daughter," St Francis de Sales would say, "this is that God may possess your poor heart utterly." Ah well! let us give it to him, though at first this may need a little effort; later, on the return of that sweet and persuasive grace which he has withdrawn from us, taking away our feeling of it, we shall give it to him more lovingly.—But I doubt my love: all I know is that I try to love.—Equally this is all that God requires of you. One of theology's axioms is: God never refuses his grace to him who does what it is in his power to do. Endeavour, then, to love, and, though such endeavours are not the results of love, they will secure you the grace of loving. Already God shows you a great favour in inspiring you with the desire to love him. I hope that one day he will take you a stage farther, and gratify the desire. Repeat to yourself: "I should be consoled—and too greatly consoled—if at present I felt for God what I endeavour to feel, but at present God desires to rob me of all exterior consolation that I may be made to die that second death which must precede the altogether supernatural and divine life of his spirit, of his grace, and of his pure love."

Now we come to a most gratifying part of your letter that has made my heart go out to God. I shall be contented, you say, to make the humblest of remonstrances and then cling to my cross, though obedience be my death. That is true courage, which God gives and inspires in you. He holds you, then, for ever in his hand; so what need to fear? No, you will not die of that, dear

The Practice of Self-abandonment

daughter, unless it be that spiritual death which is more precious than all earthly lives. But, you go on, I should nevertheless be glad indeed if God would take me from the situation and circumstances in which I find myself. The saints could have said as much upon numerous similar occasions; but the more glad we would be to be removed from either a place or a task, the more merit there is in wishing to remain in it, if that be God's wish. Be comforted, therefore; be comforted and reassured. Live in peace; God is with you, and he is a God of goodness, who suffers the weakness, the wretchedness and the frailty of his good friends with so compassionate a pity that he forbids them to be troubled by these. And his reason? Why, because he wishes an unchanging peace to be the permanent lot of those he loves.

Frequent acts of love for God, or even the mere desire of that blessed love, are a good cure for fears of divine judgement and terrors relating to predestination: I am in no way surprised at the happy results this cure has effected.

I greatly approve, too, of your answer to the person who revealed to you her fear of failing to love God with sufficient disinterestedness. It is a manifest illusion of the devil, who, taking cover behind this or that aspect of self-love, would hold back this soul and hinder it upon its way. Tell her that self-love (I refer to that self-love which, though it is not sin, affects the perfect purity of divine love) is found only in souls who make God's gifts or his rewards a motive for loving him for themselves. Yet pure love, the love practised by the saints, is love of God for his own sake because he is God, and for the reason that he is our God, our great recompense, our infinitely good and infinitely adorable Sovereign. For to love his supreme happiness—which is God himself—is to love only God. These are two terms that mean the same thing; while we can love God only for what in himself he is. Now, in himself he is essentially our sovereign good, our latter end and our eternal happiness.

Yet, someone may object, were God not our happiness, ought we not still to love him for himself? How strange and pitiable is that hypothesis! It amounts to saying—if God were not God. Let us have done with such subtleties, going our way instead uprightly and simply, *grosso modo*, as St Francis de Sales has it. Let us love God with simplicity to the extent of our power; then he will increasingly exalt and purify that love according to his pleasure. On your part maintain that interior attitude which it pleases God to give you. St Jerome knew far longer and far more violently than you fears of death and dread of God's judgement and of eternity and all the ensuing weight of these. Cherish them as long as it is God's pleasure. Our whole will must come to die—must sink out of existence—and blessedly lose itself in God's will that is always equally lovable and worthy of respect and adoration.

LETTER 15: TO SISTER MARIE-ANTOINETTE DE
MAHUET

The same subject

NANCY, 1735

DEAR SISTER,—In sending you what you need in order to perform that work of charity which I commended to you, it has occurred to me to set out for you a few of those unchallengeable truths that most comfort souls who surrender themselves to the interior life.

First truth: We can know union with God, the source of all purity, only in proportion as we detach self from all created things; for they are the source of continual corruption and impurity.

Second truth: This detachment which, carried to perfection, is known as mystical death is concerned with two things: the exterior, in other words, creatures apart from ourselves; and the interior, in other words, our own ideas, satisfactions and interests—to be brief, the *ego*.

The proof and indication of death to all exterior things is a kind of indifference, or rather of insensibility, to all exterior goods, pleasures, reputation, relatives, friends and so forth. With the help of grace such insensibility becomes so complete and so profound that we are tempted to believe it purely natural, and this God permits to safeguard us from any return of complacency, and to enable us to go forward in all things in the obscurity of faith and a great self-abandonment.

Third truth: Interior despoliation, or death to self, is the hardest of all renunciations. It is rather as if the self were torn violently from us—as if we were flayed alive. The anguish self-love feels and the cries it utters are an indication of the strength of the bonds which attach us to created life, and of the necessity of this despoliation. For the deeper the surgeon's knife cuts, the more keenly we feel it. Our resistance to death is the greater, the fuller our measure of life. The soul, then, can only attain to this blessed death and this perfect detachment by the way of deprivation and interior anguish. It would require a tried and heroic virtue to undertake this spoliation of heart in the midst of plenty, and renunciation in the midst of pleasures. On God's part, therefore, it is his grace and mercy that strip us of every sense-perceived gift and favour, even as it is a mark of his mercy to strip worldlings of their temporal wealth in order to detach their affections from it. What, then, are we to do at the time when God effects this spoliation? We must permit ourselves to be despoiled, offering no resistance, as though we were figures in stone. What of our interior rebelliousness? We must endure this without countenancing it. But if we feel that we endure it badly? We must add this further grief to that of our despoliation, and accept all peacefully and without voluntary vexation.

But we are not sure that this despoliation comes as the result of God's work within us? As in this we come to self-love's stronghold—of self-love which for its own comfort seeks impossible assurances in all things—I must answer as follows:

Fourth truth: The one thing certain is that, apart from a special revelation, God has not desired to leave us any certainty in respect to the question of eternal salvation. And the reason why? (1) To make us go forward always in darkness, and to make our faith more meritorious on account of the obscurity in which it leaves our mind. (2) To keep us always thoroughly strong in humility against the natural and violent inclination of pride. (3) To exercise his sovereign dominion over us, and to keep us in the most absolute dependence and the most perfect self-abandonment towards himself, not only with respect to our temporal existence, but also in respect to our eternal destiny. This, seemingly, is the most terrifying truth religion teaches; yet with it goes this sweet and comforting fact: I have no sooner submitted tremblingly to the sovereign dominion of God and to his incomprehensible judgements than I experience sweet consolation. For his mercy leaves me, instead of assurance, a steadfast hope that is of far more worth than assurance, and yet detracts from none of the merit of my self-abandonment, itself so glorious in God's sight and so meritorious in itself.

Upon what is this steadfast hope based? On the spiritual treasure of the infinite mercy and infinite merits of Jesus Christ; upon the many graces which have already been heaped upon me—in the opinion of directors whose part it has been to judge of my spiritual state and inclinations—upon the pure light of faith that is never deceived, and upon what my behaviour has been when it comes to the essentials, namely, avoidance of sin and practice of virtue. I perceive, indeed, that by God's grace I habitually practise virtue, and though I do so very imperfectly, alas, I desire to practise it more faithfully. Yet, despite all this, I still feel some small fear. If this be the fear that is described as chaste, peaceful and untroubled, it is the true fear of God that must at all times be cherished; for where there is no fear there would most surely be an illusion of the devil. Yet were that fear anxious and turbulent, it would be self-love's fear—a fear always to be bewailed and made a subject of humiliation.

Yet, when we have at last reached this state of despoliation, what are we to say then? Live in peace and simplicity, as did Job upon his dung-heap, and frequently repeat: Blessed are the poor in spirit who, possessing nothing, possess all things, since they possess God. Forsake everything, strip yourself of everything, the famous Gerson said, and in God you will have everything. God known, God relished and God the giver of boons, Fénelon says, is truly God: but he is the God of gifts and these leave the soul puffed up; God in darkness, deprivation, forsakenness and insensibility is God of very God—solely and starkly God—as it might be said. But that is a little hard upon self-love, that enemy of God, of ourselves and of all good; and it is by these hard blows that self-love must die within us. Shall we,

then, fear the death that brings us the wholly divine life of grace?
—Yet it is hard to spend life in this way.—What matters that?
A little more or a little less of delight during a few minutes of this
life is surely a trivial thing to him who has an eternal kingdom
before his eyes.—But I endure all this despoliation so imperfectly and so weakly!—One more unrecognized grace: God
keep you from enduring it with great courage and conscious
strength! For how much secret complacency and self-admira-
tion would then slip in and spoil God's work! An invisible hand
upholds you long enough to leave the victory yours; while the
lively perception of your weakness leaves you humble in that
victory itself. Oh, how profitable it is to suffer weakly and
patiently, rather than in a grand manner, valiantly and courageously! We are humiliated and feel ourselves weak and small
in this kind of victory, whereas in the other we should find ourselves great, strong and courageous; we should be puffed up
with ourselves, vain, confident and presumptuous, without so
much as perceiving it. Let us wonder at the wisdom and the
goodness of God who has such skill in mingling and proportion-
ing all things for our profit and advantage; whereas, left to our
own inclinations, we should spoil and corrupt and perhaps lose
everything.

LETTER 16: TO MOTHER LOUISE-FRANÇOISE DE
ROSEN (1735)

The explanation of apparent despair

DEAR SISTER,—We must never interpret in their strict sense the
more extreme expressions used by orthodox writers, but capture
the sense and thought of the authors. Righteous souls should
doubtless be forbidden to use, of deliberate premeditation,
phraseology that suggests despair; yet it would be unjust to condemn those who, transported out of themselves by the violence
of ordeals, talk and behave as if they had renounced their
eternal happiness. We must not be shocked by their language,
nor imagine that it is inspired in them by genuine despair.
Rather it is a feeling of trust hidden in the depths of their hearts

which makes them speak in this manner; much as we have occasionally seen criminals come into their sovereign's presence, ropes round their necks, declaring that they yielded themselves up to the full severity of his justice. Do you imagine that it was despair that made them speak thus, and not rather an excess of trust in the prince's goodness?

As a result, usually, we see them obtain pardon through the overwhelming nature of their sorrow, repentance and trust. Will God be less good to those souls who abandon themselves to him for time and for eternity? Will he interpret expressions literally that, in their essence, imply only raptures of self-abandonment and of trust? It is on account of your failure to share these feelings that you imagine it necessary to delete such expressions in the book *Chrétien intérieur*. On my part, when I find these in good authors, far from being shocked by them, I am greatly edified. I marvel at the strength of the self-abandonment, and I recognize an exceeding trust, the more meritorious in that it is so little perceived during these moments of rapture in which a soul speaks after this fashion. Such extraordinary states are, in the order of grace, what prodigies are in the natural order: although they do not abrogate ordinary laws, they are above them. Far from seeming to me contrary to God's wisdom, they make me admire his power.

LETTER 17: TO SISTER CHARLOTTE-ELIZABETH BOURCIER DE MONTHUREUX

The practice of self-abandonment in the midst of these ordeals

NANCY, 1734

DEAR SISTER,—Thank you for the delightful letter of which you have been so happily inspired to send me a copy. I have re-read and I shall re-read it frequently with great edification. In your case I am having an experience that I have rarely had before: after having read and re-read your letter, beseeching God's help the while, I was unable to recall either what you had said to me or my answer to you. Three thoughts relating to this have occurred to me.

427

The Practice of Self-abandonment

1. When God desires to withdraw all perceptible help from a soul, he does not allow that soul to discover any, even in its director, except in a most fleeting manner. He then constrains the soul to sustain itself by this simple thought: My state is good, since it has been deemed so by the guide it has pleased God to give me.

2. That it is scarcely necessary for God to give me a message for you, after the letter which I have deemed before God wholly to meet your need and fully to support you.

3. For all your darkness, insensibility and stupidity, your faith does not lack an unshakable though imperceptible support, since, on the pattern of Jesus Christ, your strong desire is to abandon yourself to him by whom you imagine yourself abandoned and left forlorn. It is a plain indication that in the midst of your apparent forlornness and your conscious self-abandonment, pure faith enables you to know and be interiorly convinced that in truth you are anything but abandoned, anything but forlorn. The interior grief caused by fear of your inability at such times to abandon yourself in all things, or after the fashion which you desire, surely shows the profound and hidden desire which you bear in the depths of your heart for that utter self-abandonment and that meritorious self-effacement. Does God not see such desires? and do not all desires, deeply hidden though they be, speak more eloquently to God than all your words? Most certainly, such desires are acts—the best of all acts. For if you were allowed to practise self-abandonment consciously you would find consolation once more. Yet you would lose, at least in part, the salutary perception of your wretchedness, while you would be exposed anew to the unremarked return of self-love and its disastrous complacency. You are in far greater safety at the bottom of the abyss of pure faith. Live there in peace, and await the Lord. Such peaceable and humble expectancy must keep you in a state of recollection, be counted to you for prayer, and provide you with gentle occupation during your pious exercises.

Fruit of utter death to self

MAY God be blessed, Reverend Mother, for the notable graces which it has pleased him to accord you! Your chief care henceforth must be to guard these precious gifts with watchful humility.

1. Your experience of the peace of God during prayer comes, without a doubt, from the Holy Ghost. Take care lest, by a most ill-advised multiplication of your religious acts, you emerge from that simplicity which is the more fruitful the nearer it approaches the infinite simplicity of God. This way of knowing union with him through a complete effacement of the self is based upon the great principle that our almighty and all-good God gives his children, in all things and for all things, what he knows will be most fitting for them, and that the whole of perfection lies in the heart's steadfast clinging to his adorable will. By this simple and humble behaviour, slowly our whole will is lost in that of God, into which it is utterly transformed. When we have reached that state we shall have attained perfection.

2. Though God should have enabled you to get from your sickness no other benefit than knowledge of the constant loss suffered by a soul that is little attentive to the interior movements of grace, I would still exclaim: O blessed, O most blessed sickness!

3. Talk, then, constantly, to your dear daughters of the exalted duties which divine love imposes upon them, and the precious benefits of the interior life. Oh, how few in number there are who know it, and how fewer still who practise it! Today we know and in a measure esteem only exterior exercises. God, however, is pure spirit, who must be worshipped, as Jesus Christ said, in spirit and in truth. Where then, O God, are the true worshippers, whose worship is in spirit and in truth?

4. To be in no way astonished at our wretchedness is a good foundation for humility based upon self-knowledge: while to feel that wretchedness keenly and constantly, and yet to be

429

untroubled by it, is a very great grace from which spring distrust of self and true and perfect trust in God.

5. Your devotion to the Sacred Heart of Jesus Christ and the practices you have adopted in regard to it are true spiritual treasure which suffices to enrich both you and your dear daughters. The more you draw upon this treasure, the more there remains for you to draw, inexhaustible as it is.

6. What you have learned from the Venerable Father de Condren as to the spirit of sacrifice is indeed a most excellent practice. Yet it can be constant and continuous only in the interior life which, alone, puts us in a position to take care of all things, and to be faithful in all things.

7. Humiliation of spirit and heart over every fault, whether known or unknown, placates God and confers new wisdom and new strength, with the result that almost everything is embraced in an ability to practise thorough humiliation: I mean in an ability to bear interiorly before God a spirit for ever humiliated, and a heart for ever contrite and for ever lamenting, since God then beholds us walking in justice and in truth—to use a scriptural phrase. Remote from these, we are in error and illusion, and, consequently, remote from God, who is the supreme truth.

8. A spirit of gentleness and moderation in government is a noble gift from heaven; government is the more effectual and salutary for this spirit, whether in the case of others, or in our own case, in that it causes us to avoid those faults into which indiscreet, too active, or too bitter zeal would make us lapse. Your bearing towards the older Sisters must be full of wisdom and humble charity; while you must still further increase your gentleness, condescension, moderation and prudence towards those young Sisters who are full of goodwill, though they remain somewhat weak and lacking in courage.

9. I end where I began, by blessing God for the graces which he grants you, and exhorting you to preserve them. Let nothing in the world, Reverend Mother, induce you to emerge again from this utter forgetfulness of self, which I have so often urged upon you and which the divine goodness has at last effected within you.

In fact, why be so concerned with self? The true self is God, since he is far more the life of my soul than my soul is the life of my body. God has created me only for himself: let our thought then be of him, and his thought shall be of us, while he will provide for everything far better than ourselves. When we fall, let us humiliate ourselves, pick ourselves up, and continue our way in peace. That way is at all times to ponder upon the true self which is God—God in whom we must plunge and lose ourselves, rather as we shall find ourselves plunged and lost in heaven, in the everlasting duration of eternity's great day.—*Amen! Amen!*

BOOK VIII

SPIRITUAL COUNSELS

I : FOR THE ATTAINMENT OF PERFECT CONFORMITY TO THE WILL OF GOD[1]

1. At the beginning of each day and at prayer, Mass and Holy Communion declare earnestly to God that you wish to belong to him without reserve, and that for this purpose you wish to strive to devote yourself entirely to the spirit of prayer and the interior life.

2. Make it your chief concern to acquire conformity to the will of God in even the smallest things, saying to God in the midst of the most distressing troubles and frightening prospects: "My God, I want with all my heart what you want; I submit in all things to your good pleasure for both time and eternity. And I do this, O my God, for two reasons: firstly because you are the sovereign Master and it is right that all your wishes should be fulfilled; and secondly because I am convinced by faith and repeated experiences that all your holy desires are as lovable and as good for us as they are just and adorable, whilst my own desires are always blind and corrupt. They are blind because I do not know what I ought to want or reject; and they are corrupt because I tend almost always towards things which would be harmful to me. So I give up for ever my own desires and submit to yours. Do what you wish with me, O my God, according to your good pleasure."

3. The practice of this continual submission will keep you in that interior peace which is the foundation of the spiritual life, and will prevent you from becoming anxious and troubled after yielding to faults and failings. On the contrary you will put up with them with a humble and tranquil submission which will

---

[1] These counsels were given by Father de Caussade in 1731 to Sister Marie-Thérèse de Vioménil who was twenty-eight years of age and had been professed for nine years.

do more to correct you than would an anxious sadness which would only weaken and discourage you.

4. Do not think any more about the past, but only about the present and the future. Do not worry about your confessions; you have to accuse yourself only of those faults which you can recall to mind after examining your conscience for five or six minutes. It is a good thing to add to your confession one of the graver sins of your past life. This will intensify the sorrow in your heart and dispose you to receive the graces of the sacrament in greater abundance. You cannot make too many efforts to remove the obstacles which make the practice of frequent confession disagreeable to you.

5. To avoid the anxieties which may be caused by either regret for the past or fear of the future, here in a few words is the rule to follow: the past must be left to God's measureless mercy, the future to his loving providence; and the present must be given wholly to his love through our fidelity to his grace. *Amen*.

6. When God in his goodness sends you any difficulty, such as those troubles which used to cause you so much pain, you must first of all thank God for them as for a great grace that is all the more useful for the great work of your perfection, the more it upsets the work of the present moment.

7. Strive, in spite of your interior repugnance, to be pleasant to importunate people or to those who come to inform you of these troublesome visitors; you must at once leave your prayer, reading, choir, Office and everything in order to go where Providence calls you; and you must do what is asked of you tranquilly, peacefully, without hastiness or vexation.

8. When you fail in one of these matters, you must immediately make an interior act of humility, but not of that irritated, resentful humility against which St Francis has so much to say; it must be a gentle, peaceful and unruffled humility. This point is essential for you in order to break down your self-will and to prevent you from ever becoming a slave to your exterior or interior practices of devotion.

9. Let us understand clearly that we shall not acquire true conformity to the will of God until we are perfectly resolved to serve him according to his will and pleasure, and not according

to our own. In all things seek God alone and you will find him everywhere, but more so in those things in which you most of all renounce your own will. When you have firmly convinced yourself that you are incapable of doing any good whatsoever, you will give up making resolutions and you will say humbly to God: "My God, I see from so many proofs that all my resolutions are useless. I have undoubtedly been counting too much on myself, but you have truly confounded me. I admit that you alone can do everything. Make me then do such and such a thing; and when necessary give me the thought, the impulse and the will without which I shall never do anything. I have had so many sad experiences of this in the past!..."

10. Add to this humble prayer the practice of apologizing straightway or shortly afterwards to all the people who have witnessed your little outbursts of hastiness or bad temper.

The practice of these counsels is of great importance to you for two reasons: first, because God himself wishes to do everything in you; second, because on account of your secret presumptuousness you would never be able, even in the midst of your helplessness, to ascribe everything to God as you ought, without a thousand experiences of your utter inability to do anything good. But when you become thoroughly convinced of this truth, you will say almost unthinkingly whenever you do something good: "O my God, it is you who are doing this in me by your grace." And when you do wrong you will say: "Oh, this is me indeed! I recognize myself in this for what I truly am!" Then God will receive his glory in its full purity from all the good that you do, because it will be clear that he is the sole author of it.

This is your way: all misery and humiliation for you, all blessing and thanksgiving for God. His is all the glory, yours is all the profit. Would you not be very ungrateful if you did not accept with gratitude such an equitable and advantageous division?

2: ADVICE ON THE EXTERIOR
CONDUCT OF A SOUL CALLED TO THE LIFE OF
SELF-ABANDONMENT[1]

ON awaking, raise your whole soul to God, and filling yourself with his divine presence, do homage to the Blessed Trinity in imitation of the great St Francis Xavier: "I adore you, God the Father, who created me; I adore you, God the Son, who redeemed me; I adore you, O Holy Spirit, who have so often sanctified me and are still sanctifying me. I consecrate to you my whole day for the pure love of you and for your greater glory. I do not know what is to happen to me today, whether troublesome things or pleasant ones, or whether I shall be happy or sad, in consolation or in grief. It will all be as you please. I abandon myself to your providence, and I submit to all your wishes."

We should pay great attention to what strikes us most forcibly at the beginning of the day, and to what God's grace inclines our hearts, pondering over it quietly. We should begin our prayer with this, and then abandon ourselves with simplicity to the Spirit of God and stay like this for as long as it pleases him. Imitate the good woman who used to say: "My God, since you will not give us bread, at least give us patience."

Those who are still in the ordinary ways of prayer in which the intellect is chiefly employed, must recall the subject of meditation which was prepared the night before, because if they let themselves be distracted by all sorts of thoughts at the beginning of the day, the whole day will be upset. It is like a clock which, having been wrongly set at the beginning, remains wrong the whole day.

As for dressing in the morning, do all that is necessary and appropriate, then forget yourself.

For Holy Mass, here in a few words is a way of hearing it worthily, perfectly and indeed magnificently. Set before your mind the mystery of the Cross. Climb up in spirit to Calvary and contemplate what is going on there, just as if you were seeing it with your very eyes, and admire: (1) God's justice which is

---

[1] These counsels were addressed by Father de Caussade to Sister Charlotte-Elizabeth Bourcier de Monthureux.

exacting atonement from his only-begotten Son for the sins of men of which he himself had merely the shadow, but which he had undertaken to expiate. What a victim, and what an atonement! (2) The greatness of God to whom such reparation was due. (3) The great value of our souls which are bought at so great a price. (4) The eternal happiness which Jesus Christ has won for us, and the eternal hell from which he has delivered us. What a depth of faith, trust, humiliation, contrition, gratitude and love must such divine subjects inspire in us! Those who are unable to keep up such a lofty and powerful meditation should address themselves to the Blessed Virgin present at this scene, to St John, St Mary Magdalen, the Good Thief, and finally to Jesus Christ himself so as to give him proof of their piety and to pay him their just and affectionate respects in this prodigious and incomprehensible excess of his charity and mercy.

On the subject of prayer I have only two things to say. Begin it with an entire acquiescence in God's good pleasure, whether this be for your success or to try you with the cross of dryness, distractions and helplessness. But if you find it easy and full of consolation, then give thanks to God for this without attributing it to your own efforts or dwelling on the pleasure you gain from it for yourself. If your prayer does not go well, submit yourself to God, humble yourself and go away contented and in peace even when there may have been some fault on your part, redoubling your trust and self-abandonment to his most holy will. With these two points in mind, persevere, and sooner or later God will give you the grace to pray as you ought. But never, never be discouraged, however helpless and unhappy you may feel.

As for divine Office, here are three easy and very sound methods. The first is to keep yourself in the presence of God, reciting the office in a spirit of great recollection and union with God and raising your heart to him from time to time. Those who are able to recite it in this way must not trouble themselves about any other method. The second method is to concentrate on the words, keeping yourself united with the spirit of the Church, praying when it prays, sorrowing where it sorrows, and gathering instruction from what is instructive for us; praising, adoring, thanking, in accordance with the different meanings of the verses which you are saying. The third method is to reflect with humility: I am at this moment united with saintly souls in praising God, but how I lack their holy dispositions! You must prostrate yourself in spirit at their feet saying to yourself that they are so very much more intent on God, more full of piety and fervour than ourselves. These sentiments are very pleasing to his divine Majesty and we cannot impress them on our minds and hearts too deeply.

As for confession, I want you to be firmly convinced that you must never become anxious or uneasy about your unworthiness or your sins. As St Francis de Sales says, after sorrow for our sins we must have peace. Here then is what you must do. Before all things you must fill yourself with a great trust in the infinite goodness of God, reminding yourself that his mercy is greater than all his works, that he takes glory in forgiving us, and that he is unable to show his generosity when we lack confidence in him. He loves simplicity, candour and straightforwardness; let us always go to him with complete confidence in spite of all our weaknesses, infidelities and worthlessness. This wins his heart, and he forgives everything to those who throw themselves on his goodness and his love.

Do not spend more than half an hour in preparation; more than this would be a waste of time and an opportunity for the devil to make trouble in your soul. This is what you must avoid above all things, because this profound peace of heart is a tree of life, the real foundation of the interior life, and the most essential disposition for the prayer of recollection and interior silence. The first quarter of an hour at the most should be employed in recalling your faults; after this examination of conscience, all that you may have forgotten will be as though it had never existed, and it will be forgiven you. The last quarter of an hour should be employed in exciting contrition for your sins, asking God for this grace, and stirring it up in yourself, quite gently and without any mental strain, through the remembrance of God's bounties and his very great mercy towards you in making you leave the world where you might have lost your soul, and calling

437

you to religious life in which you can so easily save yourself; or by preventing you from dying in a state of mortal sin, or in withdrawing you from a life of tepidity and imperfection, of feebleness and slackness, in which you ran the risk of losing your soul even in religion.

After dwelling for a few moments on these thoughts you must reflect that contrition is by its nature insensible because it is purely spiritual, and that feelings of sorrow are so unreliable that in spite of all the signs of sorrow which some sinners give, they are refused absolution because these feelings can be present side by side with a wilful habit of sin and even of mortal sin. The most sure sign of true sorrow, on the strength of which we absolve the greatest sinners, is that they do not fall again into the mortal sins of which they accuse themselves.

Then say to God from the bottom of your heart: "Lord, I hope that you have given me the grace to make the necessary act of contrition; I ask very humbly for your forgiveness for all the sins I have committed; I detest them as much as I can, on account of the horror which you have of them. You see, O my God, that I am very grieved not only for having committed them, but also for not feeling all the sorrow for them that I should like to feel. I submit myself to your dispositions in this. You hide this sorrow from us even while you are giving it to us, in order that we may never be absolutely certain of forgiveness or sure of being in a state of grace. It pleases you to keep us in this humble dependence so as to leave room for the faith and holy hope which are the ways by which you wish to lead us. Thus we are obliged to be content with your great mercy, to plunge ourselves in it, to abandon ourselves to it blindly, completely and without reserve. This I do, my God, with all my heart. Yes, Lord, I rely wholeheartedly on you alone, accepting this state of terrible uncertainty in which you wish to keep all men, even the greatest saints and your dearest favourites."

As regards the telling of your sins in confession, tell simply and in a few words the faults which God recalls to your mind, leaving all the rest to his great mercy, without the least uneasiness regarding all that you do not know or that you may have forgotten. You can end by accusing yourself of one of the more considerable sins of your past life. With this you can be morally certain of receiving the graces of the sacrament. There you have a means of making the practice of frequent confession easy for yourself and for so many others. To avoid still more effectively all anxiety about the past and the future, here is a most useful maxim in a few words:

Leave the past to God's great mercy, the future to his loving providence, and give the present wholly to God's love through your faithfulness and with the help of grace which will never fail you except through your own fault.

On receiving absolution, here is a thought which should fill your mind: throwing yourself in spirit at the foot of the Cross, and kissing in spirit the sacred wounds of the Saviour's feet, say: "O my God, I beg of you one drop of this precious and adorable blood which you have shed to the very last for my salvation. Of your goodness pour this precious drop into my sinful soul so as to wash it more and more clean of all its sins and especially of the greatest sins of my past life for which I very humbly beg your forgiveness again a thousand times with a firm hope of obtaining it from that exceedingly great mercy which you have so often bestowed on this vile and miserable creature."

When you have done this, I forbid you in God's name to give any further thought voluntarily to the confession which you have just made, or to your sins or your contrition, in an endeavour to know if you are forgiven and restored to grace. This is a mystery of which God has reserved the answer to himself alone, and which the devil continually makes use of in order to disturb and trouble souls so as to make them waste time and to rob them of that sweet interior peace which is the best disposition for Holy Communion, and without which one can gain almost no fruit from this heavenly banquet; for in this state one goes to receive Jesus Christ with an unquiet and troubled heart, and in consequence we have almost no taste for this divine food. Sometimes we feel even a great distaste which we must blame on ourselves for having allowed ourselves to be troubled by a thousand vain anxieties which the devil has put into our head; whereas we should have rejected them with contempt, dropping them just as we drop a stone into the sea.

With regard to Holy Communion these two points will be enough: before Holy Communion we must be Martha, and after it we must be Mary; that is to say, we must prepare ourselves by the fervent practice of the virtues and good works proper to our state without anxiety or strain; and after Holy Communion we must repose in Jesus Christ, in his infinite merits and love, and remain united with him in that ineffable peace which surpasses all mere feeling.

Nature seeks self in everything, even in virtues and the holiest practices of piety, as likewise in the actions dictated by the necessities of life. This is what used to make the saints grieve unceasingly and keep themselves on their guard, looking on themselves as their most mortal enemy. We must keep a careful watch especially on things for which we feel an attachment, in order that we may be ready to sacrifice what pleases us, to comply with the legitimate desires of our neighbour, and above all to practise obedience. God's will must always take precedence of our own desires, however holy these may appear to us.

3: A METHOD FOR INTERIOR DIRECTION[1]

1. We attain to God through the annihilation of self. Let us keep ourselves down so low that we disappear from our own sight.

2. The more we banish from ourselves all that is not God, the more we shall be filled with God. The greatest good that we can do to our souls in this life is to fill them with God.

3. The practice of perfect self-annihilation consists in having no other care but to die wholly to self in order to make room for God to live and work in us.

4. To surrender ourselves to God by a total abandonment of self, and to lose ourselves in the abyss of our nothingness so as to find ourselves again only in God, is to perform the most excellent act of which we are capable, and which contains in itself the substance of all the other virtues. This is the one thing necessary which our Lord recommends in his Gospel. O the richness of

[1] This method, like the preceding one, was given to Sister Charlotte-Elizabeth Bourcier de Monthureux.

nothingness! Why do men not know you? The more a soul reduces itself to nothingness, the more precious it becomes in God's sight.

5. To lose oneself in one's nothingness is the surest means of finding oneself again in God. Let us practise then a simple remembrance of God, a profound forgetfulness of ourselves, and a humble and loving acquiescence in God's will. By this single practice we shall avoid all evil, and we shall make all things useful for us and salutary and meritorious to an infinite degree, and pleasing to God.

6. We must not distinguish between rest and work, either interior or exterior: it is all one when we keep ourselves in complete acquiescence and interior repose. It is good to note this.

7. In our dealings with creatures we must maintain an attitude of detachment indicating an infinite aloofness from all excessive affection and sentimentality. It is inconceivable how little suffices to hold back the soul even for a long time, and often even for the whole of life. A mere nothing is capable of stopping the wonderful progress which we would make in grace. Oh, how God wants, in order to give himself to souls, a great void, empty of all the seekings of nature, even the smallest!

8. It is in the most distressing and adverse circumstances that we practise the most perfect impoverishment and establish ourselves in a firmer confidence in the first cause through the loss of secondary causes. Let us then acquiesce in all losses except the loss of God.

9. In all our affairs and in events of every kind, everything that is apart from God must be as nothing to us, and God alone must be our all.

10. Never be over-eager for anything, nor let your heart ever be crushed by anything whatsoever. Where there is only nothingness, there is neither over-eagerness nor heart-break, but an untroubled and unchanging emptiness. In this we must entrench ourselves firmly with no attachments to created things, and, in no longer seeking ourselves, we shall happily find ourselves again. Let us lose all to find all.

11. Let us reduce ourselves to the Unity which God is. Whatever is not this, is not what we want. If we can be content with

this eminent Unity, we shall no longer trouble ourselves about anything else. Oh, how this truth, when it is well understood and well practised, relieves us of so many things, even of those which appear to us good, holy and necessary, but which in reality do us harm instead of helping us to achieve our ambition, namely to become one thing with the supreme Unity.

12. Let our motto be that of the blessed Brother Giles of Assisi: "One to one", one soul alone to one God alone. Let us plunge deeper and lose ourselves entirely in this Unity. Let us forget everything, and remember nothing but the Unity, divine and infinite, God alone! This word "Unity" is most illuminating: it will make us curtail all multiplicity and superfluity, and it is very efficacious in making us devote our whole life perfectly to God and to everything that he wants of us. In it we shall find treasures of graces, of light, innocence, holiness and happiness.

4: WHAT WE SHOULD DO AFTER COMMITTING FAULTS

1. We must bear with humility before God the shame of our faults. After committing acts of unfaithfulness to grace or falling by surprise into some fault, we must retire into our nothingness, in a holy contempt of ourselves. This is the great benefit which God makes us draw even from our faults.

2. When fears for any fault that we have committed become excessive, they obviously come from the devil. Instead of giving way to this dangerous illusion, we must repel it with the utmost steadfastness, letting these anxieties drop away from us, like a stone falling to the bottom of the sea, and never entertaining them voluntarily. If however by God's permission these feelings are stronger than our will, we must have recourse to the second remedy, which consists in letting ourselves be crucified un-resistingly, since God permits it, just as the martyrs used to do, yielding themselves up to their executioners.

3. What we have just said about fears which accompany more definite faults applies equally to the feeling of disquiet and dis-tress which arises from the frequency of small infidelities. This heaviness of heart comes likewise from the devil. We must therefore spurn and fight it like a real temptation. Yet some-

times with certain souls God makes use of this anguish and excessive dread to try them, to purify them and to make them die to themselves. When we cannot succeed in driving them from the mind, no other remedy remains but to bear this crucifixion peacefully in a spirit of total self-abandonment to the will of God. This is the way to restore peace and calm in a soul that is truly resigned to God's will.

4. Fears concerning the recitation of the divine Office are again nothing but a pure temptation since actual attention is not necessary. For prayer to acquire its full merit, it is sufficient for it to be made with virtual attention, which is nothing but the sincere intention of praying well which you have at the beginning and which you do not retract by any voluntary distraction. Thus you can say your Office very well while at the same time patiently suffering continual and involuntary distractions. The distress caused by these distractions arises evidently from nothing but the desire to pray well, and so it is the best proof that this desire is still present at the bottom of your heart. Now this desire is a good and true prayer; though hidden from the soul by the disturbance which the distractions cause, it is there none the less, and it is none the less perceived by God who gives us a double grace: firstly, in hearing our prayer as he hears every prayer that is made well, and secondly by concealing this from us so as to mortify us everywhere and in everything.

5: TEMPTATIONS AND INTERIOR SUFFERINGS[1]

Principle 1. Violent temptations are in God's view great graces for a soul. They are an interior martyrdom. They are those great struggles and great victories which have made the great saints.

Principle 2. The acute distress and cruel torment suffered by a soul when attacked by temptations are the sure sign that it never consents, at least with that full, entire, known and deliberate consent which makes a mortal sin.

[1] There are good grounds for thinking that this document was addressed to Sister Anne-Marie-Thérèse de Rosen who was the confidante of the inmost thoughts of Madame de Lesen, for whom she acted as intermediary with Father de Caussade.

The Practice of Self-abandonment

Principle 3. During the violence and darkness of frequent temptations, it is very possible for a tired and troubled soul to commit small faults through frailty, negligence, surprise or weakness; but I maintain that in spite of these little faults it merits more, and it is more pleasing to God and fundamentally better disposed for the reception of the sacraments than the common run of people who being favoured with feelings of sensible devotion have almost no struggle to endure, and have to do almost no violence to themselves. The virtue of the first is much more solid for having endured and for still enduring severer trials.

Principle 4. Whatever sin may have been committed in the past by people in temptation, if nevertheless they have since stood firm for some years without yielding voluntary consent, they make all the greater progress in the ways of God because their temptations render them more humble: for humility is the foundation of all goodness.

Principle 5. The majority of people who are not very far advanced in the ways of God and the interior life esteem only the operations of sweet and sensible grace. But it is certain that the most humiliating, distressing and crucifying workings of grace are the most effective in purifying the soul and in uniting it intimately with God. And so the masters of the spiritual life agree in saying that we make greater progress by suffering than by action.

Principle 6. Just as God converts, tests and sanctifies people living in the world by temporal afflictions and adversities, so also he ordinarily converts, tries, purifies and sanctifies persons in religion by spiritual adversities and interior crosses a thousand times more painful: these are dryness, weariness, disgust, dejection of heart, spiritual listlessness, humiliating, persistent and violent temptations, excessive fears of being in mortal sin, terror of God's judgements and dread of reprobation. Now since spiritual books, preachers, directors and good Catholics are incessant in praising up the benefits of afflictions to people of the world, without which large numbers of them would lose their souls, then why not say the same of interior crosses without which an infinite number of persons in religion would never

444

attain the perfection of their state? Experience shows us daily that the most usual way by which God leads religious persons whom he loves most is that of great trials, just as for those people living in the world who are dear to God it is the way of temporal adversities. Consequently, we who preach to people in the world patience, submission and a loving resignation in their misfortunes, must say the same thing in our own trials and apply to ourselves the moral rule which we preach so well to others. Do not interior crosses also come from God? Are they less crucifying, and consequently less salutary? Does God ask less submission from us, and can our patience be less pleasing to him?

Principle 7. Through his merciful wisdom, and in order to keep his elect always in greater dependence on his grace and in a more perfect self-abandonment to his mercy and in greater humiliation, God conceals from them almost all the interior workings of his divine Spirit together with the holy dispositions he gives them, the good sentiments he inspires in them, and the infused virtues with which he enriches them.

But what means does he employ for this purpose?

Here we must admire his wisdom and goodness. He makes use of the continuity and violence of temptations, of the disturbance they cause in the soul, and of the fear which it feels of having succumbed to them. He hides from these souls the great victories they gain, by means of the small defeats they suffer; the ardent desire of making a good Holy Communion by the fear of unworthy Communions; their ardent love of God by the fear of failing in love. As long as they feel the greatest horror of small faults, he allows them to be downcast by the continual imperfections which they think they commit. He lets them believe that all their good works are badly done, and he allows them to feel shocked by the first slight movements of their passions, while all the time they are achieving victories. But while keeping them constantly in humility and self-abandonment, he does not wish them to be without a little consolation and assurance in their trials, and so he makes known their state to some enlightened director; and so long as these souls will obey with simplicity, they can be sure of never being deceived.

From these principles we can easily see how to settle doubts

445

which sometimes assail us concerning Holy Communion and the performance of our other duties.

Rule 1. The fear which comes over us before Holy Communion must never keep us away from it, especially if the confessor commands us to receive it. God does not ordinarily allow him to be misled, but when this happens, the penitent cannot go wrong in obeying him, nor can she commit a sacrilege, for blind obedience given in good faith to a director for God's sake can never lead us astray.

The redoubling of difficulties and temptations after Holy Communion, far from robbing us of its fruit, increases it when we suffer in peace with humble resignation joined to a horror of vice. This horror makes itself sufficiently evident by the suffering and martyrdom which the temptations cause, for such suffering is never experienced by people who really give way to temptations.

Books which treat of the effects of Holy Communion and which are meant for the ordinary faithful, mention only the ordinary effects, but there are many special cases in which quite contrary effects and feelings are experienced. In such cases Holy Communion produces a much more precious fruit, for in increasing the violence of temptation and the keen realization of our weakness, it increases our merits, and fosters in the heart sentiments of the most profound humility.

Rule 2. Violent efforts to prepare oneself for Holy Communion are good and pleasing to God only in the motive which prompts them; their result however can be very harmful for they upset and agitate the soul. Therefore the intensity of these desires must be restrained, because when dealing with God and the things of God, everything must be done gently, tranquilly and without strain. The best preparation for Holy Communion in this painful state is patience and resignation in this interior martyrdom. We must then at all costs preserve this peace in which God dwells and in which he delights to work.

It is not grace but self-love which tends to keep us from Holy Communion in order to avoid the torments and agonies which God causes the soul to feel so as to kill its miserable self-love. We must therefore go to Holy Communion without fear and indeed with a kind of pleasure, so as to endure the interior operations which are so purifying and sanctifying. We shall feel the very great benefits of them afterwards, but at the moment God hides them for the soul's good. The soul must then stand before him in the humble posture of a criminal and a victim of merciful justice. This indeed is the true preparation for such a soul; it will never find peace in any other.

This apparent dereliction and abandonment have no other purpose than to foster in the soul a distrust of itself, and to make it throw itself with greater abandonment into the arms of God. It sees no other support; and it does not see even this one. Faith alone has to suffice it without any support. The sensitive part of the soul is of no avail against the will, and God at this moment expects nothing from the soul but the free choice of the will which is always master of its acts.

The profound horror which the soul feels at the approach of temptation is the best of all disclaimers. A multitude of acts would serve only to upset and weary the soul; it will do better to confine itself to this one act which includes all: "Lord, you are almighty and goodness itself. It is for you to defend me and keep me from all evil, for this is beyond my strength. I accept all the pain of it for love of you; only keep me from all sin." After this the soul should maintain itself in peace in the midst of the storm; it will find itself fortified, without knowing how, by the hidden gift of God.

Rule 3. Inability to think or make acts during prayer must not sadden this soul. The best part of prayer, and indeed its essence, is the wish to do it. Before God, desire counts for everything, in both good and evil. Now this desire amounts to anxiety in a soul like this; it is merely too intense, and it needs only to be restrained. Let the soul maintain itself in peace at prayer, and come away from prayer likewise in peace. Instead of making so many resolutions, it must be content with saying to God: "My God, make me do such and such a good act, and flee from such and such an evil one; for of myself I shall do none of these things. I am only too aware of my feebleness, and my past experience guarantees that nothing will be done if you yourself do not act in me by the power of your grace."

447

As for direction of intention, the soul abandoned to God should not make too many acts, nor consider itself obliged to express them in words. The best thing for it would be to rest content with feeling and knowing that it is acting for God's sake in simplicity of heart. Good interior acts are those which the heart makes of itself, as by its own momentum, almost without thinking about them, just as worldly people, without acknowledging it to themselves expressly, have only one objective in everything, namely, the gratification of their sensuality, their cupidity and their pride. God sees this intention which their heart conceals from itself, and they will be punished for it.

The great principle of the spiritual life is to do everything, both interiorly and exteriorly, in peace, gently and smoothly, as St Francis de Sales recommends so often. From the first moment of wishing to make an act, it is already made and counted as made, because God sees all our desires, even to the preparation of our hearts. As Bossuet says, "Our desires are in God's sight what the voice is for men; and a cry that is held back in the depths of the soul is worth a cry uttered to heaven." Moreover, all acts made in great aridity are very good, and are ordinarily better and more meritorious than acts which are accompanied by feelings of devotion.

Examination of conscience regarding the future must turn only on submission to God and self-abandonment to his holy wishes; and the aim of this practice must not be to make definite acts but to keep our heart in a certain habitual attitude of watchfulness in which it seems to say to God at every instant and in every situation: "*Fiat, fiat!* Thy will be done. Yes, I want it; I accept everything; only preserve me from all sin. Yes, heavenly Father, and always yes." This yes, said with the whole heart, contains in its brevity the greatest things, and expresses the greatest sacrifices.

FATHER DE CAUSSADE'S PRAYER FOR OBTAINING
HOLY SELF-ABANDONMENT

O MY GOD, when will it please you to give me the grace of remaining habitually in that union of my will with your adorable will, in which, without our saying anything, all is said, and in which we do everything by letting you act. In this perfect union of wills we perform immense tasks because we work more in conformity with your good pleasure; and yet we are dispensed from all toil because we place the care of everything in your hands, and think of nothing but of reposing completely in you—a delightful state which even in the absence of all feelings of faith gives the soul an interior and altogether spiritual relish. Let me say then unceasingly through the habitual disposition of my heart. "*Fiat!* Yes, my God, yes, everything that you please. May your holy desires be fulfilled in everything. I give up my own which are blind, perverse and corrupted by that miserable self-love which is the mortal enemy of your grace and pure love, of your glory and my own sanctification."

A PRAYER IN TIME OF TEMPTATION

O GOD, keep me by your grace from all sin; but as for the pain which makes my self-love suffer, and for the holy humiliations which crucify my pride, I accept them with all my heart not so much as the effects of your justice but rather as the blessings of your great mercy. Have pity on me then, dear Lord, and help me.

449

If you have enjoyed this book, consider making your next selection from among the following . . .

P9-CZV-733

WHEN CORRUPTION WAS KING

How I Helped the Mob Rule Chicago, Then Brought the Outfit Down

ROBERT COOLEY
WITH HILLEL LEVIN

CARROLL & GRAF PUBLISHERS
NEW YORK

To my father and all that he stood for.
–RC
My gang: MJ, A, A & G. Done. Finally.
–HL

WHEN CORRUPTION WAS KING
How I Helped the Mob Rule Chicago, Then Brought the Outfit Down

Carroll & Graf Publishers
An Imprint of Avalon Publishing Group Inc.
245 West 17th Street
11th Floor
New York, NY 10011

AVALON
publishing group incorporated

First Carroll & Graf edition 2004
First Carroll & Graf trade paperback edition 2006

Library of Congress Cataloging-in-Publication Data is available.

ISBN-10: 0-7867-1583-9
ISBN-13: 978-0-78671-583-1

10 9 8 7 6 5 4 3 2 1

Interior design by Paul Paddock

Printed in the United States of America
Distributed by Publishers Group West

CONTENTS

INTRODUCTION   *v*

SAINTS & SINNERS

CHAPTER 1
A DEAL WITH THE DEVIL   *3*

CHAPTER 2
COP KILLER   *23*

CHAPTER 3
MARCO & THE COUNT   *43*

CHAPTER 4
CRIME PAYS   *67*

INNER CIRCLE FIRST WARD

CHAPTER 5
HIGHLIFE WITH THE LOWLIFES   *97*

CHAPTER 6
A RUN THROUGH THE GREASE   *131*

CHAPTER 7
CHICKEN WITH WING   *145*

CHAPTER 8
THE FATAL CORNED BEEF SANDWICH   *167*

ON THE WIRE

CHAPTER 9
IN THE WEEDS   *185*

CHAPTER 10
THE WORST FUCK   *207*

CHAPTER 11
CANDID CAMERA   **219**

CHAPTER 12
PARTING SHOTS FOR HARRY AND MARCO   **243**

LEGAL ASSASSIN
CHAPTER 13
WITNESS DEJECTION PROGRAM   **259**

CHAPTER 14
"SLANDER MY NAME"   **273**

CHAPTER 15
THE HARDER THEY FALL   **293**

CHAPTER 16
AFTERLIFE   **315**

NOTES   **321**

OPERATION GAMBAT RELATED CASES AND OUTCOMES   **360**

INDEX   **363**

ACKNOWLEDGMENTS   **370**

INTRODUCTION

Most cities have one overriding claim to fame. Say Los Angeles and you think about the movies; say Paris, you think art; Detroit, cars. But when people, the world over, say Chicago, they think of something less marketable: Organized Crime. It is a stain that no amount of accomplishment or image-boosting will ever wipe clean.

The city's grim reputation is rooted back in the Roaring Twenties when Al Capone emerged victorious from gang warfare and went on to become a household name. Oddly enough, far less is known about his successors and their grip on the city during the last half of the twentieth century. But that is when Chicago's Mafia became the single most powerful organized crime family in American history. While Mob bosses knocked each other off on the East Coast, in Chicago they united into a monolithic force called the Outfit. They would literally control the cops, the courts, and the politicians—a corrupt trifecta that Capone dreamed about but never came close to achieving. The Outfit demanded a cut of every criminal enterprise in the region, from a lowly car theft or private poker game to a jewelry heist. To enforce this "street tax," their hit men killed with impunity, knowing that crooked judges would throw out any case against them. Their bookies brazenly took bets in nightclubs, at racetracks, and even in government office buildings, confident that contacts in the police department (at one point as high up as the chief of detectives) would warn them before the vice squad could make a raid. Mobsters ran Chicago union locals, and even national organizations for the Laborers and the Teamsters. This unprecedented combination of brute force and political clout let the bosses feed at the public trough with no-show jobs for their goons, and with municipal contracts for themselves and their associates. Government became one of their most lucrative rackets.

In his 1969 book *Captive City*, investigative journalist Ovid Demaris called the Outfit "the most politically insulated and police-pampered 'family' this side of Sicily" and estimated, even then, that their take was in the billions. With such total domination of their home turf, they could wander far and wide. By the seventies, the FBI reported that Chicago's Mob controlled all organized criminal activity west of the Mississippi—including and especially Las Vegas. Millions were skimmed from casinos like the Tropicana and the Stardust, and bundles of cash, stuffed in green army duffel bags, found their way back to the Outfit's bosses. Meanwhile, New York's mobsters had to content themselves with the slim pickings of Atlantic City.

Although other urban areas had their share of corruption, Chicago remained unique for its mixture of Organized Crime and political organization. The extent of Mafia influence on the city is still not fully appreciated, even by long-time residents. We think of Mobs hijacking trucks or businesses—not ballot boxes. But the ability to deliver votes and manipulate elected officials provided even more muscle to the Outfit than their army of enforcers.

In the shadows, at the controls of the Mob's political machine, was an ex-felon with a vaguely ethnic name and an obscure position in the Democratic Party. Born Pasqualino Marchone, he had been a protégé of Capone and supposedly served prison time for robbery in the thirties. Over the next three decades, he shed his thug exterior and took on a mantle of respectability, along with the new name of Pat Marcy. Most weekdays, he sat in a restaurant across the street from City Hall, ensconced at a corner table with a private phone. Dressed in three-piece suits, smoking fine cigars, he looked like his fellow diners from the local banks, government offices, and law firms.

His official title was Secretary for the Democratic Committee of Chicago's First Ward. To an outsider, his domain may have sounded like some quaint throwback. But for Chicagoans, the First Ward was a city unto itself—a political precinct carved out at the turn of the century like the richest vein in a gold mine. It extended from the slums and factories south of the city, through the central business district, up to the very wealthiest neighborhoods of the Gold Coast. And to see the company Pat Marcy kept at lunch, you'd think he was the mayor. Aldermen, state legislators, judges, congressmen, city officials, police chiefs, and union leaders—all regularly shared meals or dropped by to show the deference reserved for a man of great influence.

In that same restaurant, Marcy had other, less public, meetings away from the spotlight of the "First Ward table." Thursdays he would spend a few minutes in a booth with one or the other of the Outfit's most notorious team of hit men. Out in the adjoining lobby, as office workers rushed past and where no FBI bug could eavesdrop, he barked at lawyers and politicians, demanding that cases get fixed or kickbacks get paid. In bathrooms and unmarked offices elsewhere in the building, he conferred with the elderly bosses at the top of the Outfit. During the seventies and eighties, some of them would shuffle off to prison with the advent of new racketeering laws and federal investigations, but Marcy remained untouchable—along with his coterie of politicians, judges, and lawyers who became known as the Inner Circle of the First Ward.

Although the FBI tried to penetrate the First Ward with Mob informants and wiretaps, Marcy was too careful to be caught and too valuable for the bosses to give up. Besides, his political connections extended through both parties and ran from Chicago to Washington, DC. This clout made him radioactive to the ever-changing cast of U.S. Attorneys who rotated through the Northern Illinois office. It was one thing to target a small-time magistrate or alderman for taking a bribe. It was quite another thing to go after Marcy and charge that a Mafia figure was calling the shots at City Hall and the county courthouses. It sounded too outrageous to be true—a slap not only at the politicians and judges, but an insult to Chicago's business and media leaders, who even before Capone labored to put the best face above the city's "Big Shoulders."

To crack Marcy and Mob rule in Chicago, the Feds needed a lucky break. It arrived on a Saturday afternoon in 1986, when criminal lawyer Bob Cooley popped into the local office of the Organized Crime Strike

Force. By chance, the chief attorney happened to be in, catching up on paperwork. When he asked what Cooley wanted, he replied: "I'd like to help you destroy the First Ward. I'd like to help you destroy Pat Marcy."

Cooley was the last person that Pat Marcy or the Mob bosses would have expected to turn on them. Outside of the Mafia, few others had profited so flamboyantly from the corruption. For four years, Cooley personally handled most First Ward criminal cases involving Outfit soldiers and associates, and it helped make him rich. He took payment from his clients only in cash and at times didn't know what to do with it all. He might bet hundreds of thousands with bookmakers, buy a health club, or put up the money to start an Italian restaurant. Although he had a natural flair for the courtroom and won many cases legitimately, he let his clients know he would do whatever it took to get a favorable verdict. He solidified his reputation as the ultimate fixer when he paid off a "law and order" judge to get an acquittal on a murder charge for Harry Aleman, a hit man dubbed the Outfit's "killing machine."

Unlike the other Mob lawyers, Cooley's relationship with his clients went well beyond the courtroom. He was the life of their parties, hanging out with the young bucks at the hottest bars and nightclubs, dining at swankier spots with the older bosses. He bet with the Mob's bookies, traded girlfriends with the crew leaders, and, on some occasions, got in fistfights with them. A big part of his outlaw charm was that Cooley never appeared to take anyone or anything too seriously. He parked his luxury sedan in the bus stop outside court or, on occasion, in the mayor's spot outside City Hall. He wore a gold chain and open-neck shirt in court when everyone else wore ties. He brought his dog into fine restaurants and office buildings.

But however affable Cooley looked to the Outfit from the outside, he was boiling inside, deeply conflicted about his wealth and the scummy patrons who helped make it. For three and a half years after he walked into the Strike Force office, Cooley would wear a hidden recording device on some of the most dangerous men in America, and he helped the government develop damning cases against them. Always Cooley kept pushing his investigation higher and higher to the top Mob bosses and Chicago's most powerful politicians, even as some of his federal handlers tried to limit his targets to small-fry bookies and judges.

In 1989 the Feds finally brought a halt to his investigation, which they now called "Operation Gambat," for Gambling Attorney. When Cooley suddenly disappeared, and news about his double life leaked out, panic shot through the upper echelons of the Outfit and Chicago's Democratic Party. The FBI reported that the Mob had put a million-dollar bounty on Cooley's head. All the alarm was warranted. Before the end of 1990, the U.S. Attorney General flew to Chicago to announce the first wave of several sweeping Gambat indictments.

Over the course of the nineties, Cooley repeatedly returned to the city to testify as the central witness in Grand Jury proceedings, hearings, and eventually, eight trials. Time and again, he faced renowned criminal defense lawyers. Time and again, their clients were found guilty. When Cooley and the prosecutors were done, twenty-four individuals were convicted or had taken a guilty plea.

But the significance of Operation Gambat went far beyond the head count of all those sent to prison. What had once been a matter of speculation for a few gadfly newspaper columnists and reporters was now fact. No one could any longer deny that the Mob had influence on Chicago's leading politicians. Among those Cooley helped convict were the First Ward Alderman, a Corporation Counsel, and the Assistant Majority Leader in the Illinois Senate. Before a U.S. District Court judge imposed a sentence on one of them, he lamented that democracy in Chicago was "the same as any other banana republic or corrupt regime."

No one could deny that the Mob had influence on Chicago's judicial system, either. Among those sent to prison were the presiding judge for the prestigious Chancery Court and the only judge in America *ever* convicted of fixing murder cases. In yet another legal landmark stemming from the investigation, state prosecutors overturned the Double Jeopardy provision of the Fifth Amendment and retried the hit man who had been previously acquitted (with Cooley's help) in a rigged trial.

In the wake of Operation Gambat, the establishment was finally forced to take action. The Illinois Supreme Court's "Special Commission on the Administration of Justice" reviewed the evidence in Cooley's cases and called for wide-ranging reforms in the way judges are appointed and assigned trials in the state. The First Ward was whittled down to a fishhook fraction of its former size and, with the help of Cooley's testimony, federal trustees wrested control of some unions back from the mobsters. Significant remnants of the Outfit remain, but they have lost much of their power to influence or intimidate. Gangster hits in Chicago, which were once commonplace, are now rare.

With so much impact in so many areas—the judiciary, politics, and crime—and with so many high-profile convictions, Operation Gambat ranks as the crowning achievement of the Organized Crime Strike Force. But until now, the full story behind the investigation has remained largely untold because Bob Cooley has chosen not to tell it. This has not stopped others from speaking for him, starting with the reporters who covered the many trials and his hours of testimony. Several true-crime books have also touched on individual Gambat cases or aspects of the investigation. A character clearly based on Cooley appears in the novel *Personal Injuries* by Chicago lawyer Scott Turow, as well as a quickie TV movie called *The Fixer*, starring Jon Voight.

But none of these accounts—fiction and nonfiction—begin to explain why Cooley decided to cooperate with federal authorities. There have been plenty of theories—most of them propagated by attorneys for the Gambat defendants. Some have him drowning in gambling debts to bookmakers and in fear of their enforcers. Others claim he was on the verge of indictment himself for bribery or tax fraud. Such speculation, intended to discredit Cooley's testimony, became the centerpiece of defense efforts in almost all the Gambat trials. Obviously, it never carried much weight with a jury. In the words of Tom Durkin, the assistant U.S. Attorney who worked most closely with Cooley, "Bob is every bit the hero because he didn't have to do what he did."

As Cooley tells it, several different forces drove his decision to inform. For the most part, it was an act of conscience. This may sound laughable to anyone acquainted with the wild lifestyle Cooley once led. As he is the first to admit, morality was never his strong suit. However, the seeds for his later transformation were sown back in his childhood.

He grew up in a large, loving, and devout Catholic family. His father was a truly incorruptible cop—too honest to advance far in the Chicago Police Department—and both of his grandfathers, also policemen, died in the line of duty. From the start, Cooley was encouraged to follow the straight and narrow path laid down by his parents, although he always felt the tug to stray from it as well.

If anything, Pat Marcy became the mentor for his dark side, and Cooley's struggle with the two conflicting father figures was well under way years before Operation Gambat started. At one point, he refused to betray one of his clients as an informant, and an Outfit crew leader ordered Cooley killed. Although he managed, with his typical moxie, to lift the contract from his head, Cooley lost any sympathy he had had for his Mob benefactors. Gradually, he became filled with self-loathing about what he had done for Marcy and the Outfit. Those feelings only intensified when he learned that a crooked lawyer might have rigged the trial that acquitted his grandfather's killer. When Marcy forced him into fixing one more trial—this one involving the assault on a police-woman—Cooley could take no more. With an impulsiveness that he immediately regretted, he found himself at the Strike Force door.

It's unlikely that any other mole could have taken Operation Gambat as far as Cooley did. His zeal was nearly suicidal and partly fueled by his belief that destroying the First Ward and the Outfit had become his life's mission. But there would be few earthly rewards in the investiga-tion for this lapsed Catholic. Instead, he would star in his own version of the Passion Play. The more good he did, the more he was made to suffer—with each station of the cross that much more degrading and painful. After he "came in" to the government, he became convinced that some of the Feds—the U.S. Attorney in particular—were out to stifle and demoralize him at every pass. First he was stopped from gam-bling, which provided most of his entertainment and social life; and then from practicing criminal law, which provided much of his income. Cash that once gushed into his firm now barely trickled.

When the authorities finally unveiled the full scope of Operation Gambat, Cooley's central role should have earned him some redemption for his years of wrongdoing. Instead, like John Dean and Frank Serpico before him, Cooley discovered that the public and the media reserve a special scorn for informants—no matter how beneficial their information. During the trials, Cooley lost the gold chain and transformed himself from the cocky counselor to a humble witness. Defense attorneys he once considered pathetic pretenders to his throne heaped abuse on him in court and used their media friends to vilify him in the local papers and on TV. The Illinois Attorney Registration and Disciplinary Commission moved to disbar Cooley, based on his admissions in court, before they took similar action against any of those lawyers and judges ultimately convicted in his trials. Finally, as the last nail in the cross—for the sake of his own safety—he was exiled forever from the city he loved so much.

Outside the courtroom, Cooley also broke the mold. He refused the federal Witness Protection Program, and although the government has helped him assume another name, he has not been provided with security or further resources. He trusts his own instincts better than those of the bureaucracy. He has lived in dozens of places around the country and is always ready to move again at short notice.

Despite the extreme changes he has weathered in his life, Cooley remains much the same as he was in Chicago. Garrulous as ever, he keeps in touch with a large circle of family and friends that now includes many of the agents and prosecutors involved with Gambat. In each of his new locations, he finds new hangouts and buddies.

He remains obsessed with his investigation and the legacy it has left behind in Chicago. He wonders if the city has ever come to grips with the enormity of Operation Gambat's revelations. This obsession, as much as anything, has driven him to write this book with me and to finally get his side of the story on the record.

Cooley does not try to buff up his own image. He's open about his flaws and his own illegal activities. His brutal honesty is exactly what makes his story so credible, buttressed by testimony—over hundreds of hours—that was never significantly impeached by any of the defense counsel he faced.

Unlike other witnesses against the Mafia, he offers a perspective on Organized Crime that literally extends from the thug on the street to the equally brutal, if more sophisticated, bosses at the top. Along the way, he details the centrality of gambling to Mob culture, the mindlessly violent nightlife, and the Outfit's bizarre, longstanding relationship with elements of the Chicago Police Department.

Most important, Cooley reveals how easily the criminal world intersected with the supposedly legitimate world of law and politics. Old arrest records were dismissed as ancient history. Sweetheart contracts and rigged trials were laughed off in the press as "business as usual." Cynicism took the place of outrage, and the voting public collectively turned away.

As we complete this book, some individuals from Cooley's old Mob circles are back in the news. The *Chicago Sun-Times* exposed a municipal "Hired Truck Program" that funneled millions in public funds to "organized crime figures." Meanwhile, Richard Daley, in his fifteenth year as mayor, with no challenger in sight, now calls for Chicago to have its very own casino. He assures one and all that he needs no help keeping legalized gambling free of Mob influences. In sum, conditions are ripe for remnants of the Outfit to mount a comeback, and there's plenty at stake to attract them. It is just the time for Bob Cooley to speak up again.

SAINTS
&
SINNERS

CHAPTER 1

A DEAL WITH THE DEVIL

F irst of all, you should know that Bob Cooley is dead. Actually, I committed suicide several years ago.

It's not like I wanted to be put out of my misery. I gave up a life in Chicago that anyone else would have died for. I had a fantastic career, beautiful sweethearts, wonderful friends and family. There were nonstop parties at the finest restaurants and hottest clubs. It was not just any life. It was a fabulous life.

Now it's over.

I have a different name and will never put my roots down in another city. Like a nomad, I'm here today, gone tomorrow.

The exact date of my suicide is open to debate. Some people would say I pulled the trigger in 1986, when I walked into the Chicago offices of the Organized Crime Strike Force and agreed to wear a wire on some very dangerous people. Others would argue that I was as good as dead three years later, when a dozen FBI agents fanned out across the city with indictments based on the tapes I had made, and the Mob fully realized what I had done to them. I could have easily ended up with a .22 in the head—if I was lucky. If I wasn't lucky, I could have ended up hanging from a meat hook, getting slowly charbroiled by some animal with a blowtorch.

If you ask me, my undoing really started many years before, when I made a deal with the Devil. His name was Pat Marcy, and he wanted me to fix a murder case.

• • •

It all began innocently enough: someone asking me to help his son. The year was 1977. I was thirty-five years old and pretty hot shit—if I do say so myself. After working as a cop to put myself through law school, I built one of the best criminal defense practices in Chicago. If you got in trouble—from a traffic ticket to a gambling bust to a murder—you wanted me as your lawyer. I had my own office, in a prime location, right across the street from City Hall. Mornings, after I spent a few hours in court, I would grab a massage and a steam before I got back to the office, usually in time for lunch.

I never entered my building through the lobby. Instead, I would take a walk first through Counsellors Row, the restaurant on the ground floor. It was a big, busy place with lots of tables and leather booths. Everybody hung out there: lawyers, city workers, and all the big shot politicians. Sometimes my clients would grab a bite and wait for me at a table. It was like my second office. People would even leave messages for me there.

One day, as I was doing my walk through Counsellors, I felt a hand at my elbow. "Can I talk to you for a minute?"

I turned to see John D'Arco Senior. He looked for all the world like a kindly old Italian grandfather. Round, smiling face and thick tinted glasses. You might think he was the guy who owned the grocery down the street—but one who made out very well for himself. He wore fancy suits and silk ties, usually smoked big cigars and had a diamond pinkie ring. Once he had been a pretty tough guy—as legend had it, a stickup man for Al Capone. Somewhere along the way he got involved with the Democratic Party and cleaned up his act. For a while he had been a city council alderman, and he was still head of the Democratic Regular Committee for Chicago's First Ward. But whatever D'Arco looked like from the outside, his organization in the First Ward was still part and parcel of the Mob. That much I knew.

I used to see D'Arco in Counsellors all the time. He sat in a corner, in front of the restaurant, at what they called the First Ward table. They had bricked up the window and, on the wall, hung pictures of all their favorite politicians—in those days, Mayor Richard M. Daley and Jimmy Carter. The table even had a little pedestal with their private phone.

But when he wanted to talk to me, John D'Arco didn't take me to the First Ward table. Instead, we walked to the back of the restaurant, where it was pretty empty. We sat down, and he asked, "You know my son?"

"Yeah," I replied. "I know Johnny. I know him quite well." Seven years before, when we were both going to the same college, Johnny picked a fight with me and I beat the crap out of him.

Then Senior said, "I hear you're a fantastic lawyer, and my son's a lawyer too. He's never tried a case, and I'd like to have him learn to be a real lawyer. Would you be interested in teaching him how to defend a case?"

I was caught totally off guard. "Let me think about it," I said, "and I'll get back to you."

Then I walked up to my office in kind of a daze. Whatever I thought of Johnny really didn't matter. Thanks to his father, he had become a state senator—at the age of twenty-six—so I figured he wasn't a punk any more. Besides, I had a soft spot for fathers who looked out for their sons. My own dad was like that.

But a deal with D'Arco could mean more than taking Johnny around by the nose. This was a chance to hook up with the First Ward machine and all its connections.

It's not like I needed their help to be successful. You could have looked at me in 1977 and wondered what more I wanted as a lawyer. I didn't have some big firm, but I liked it that way. I was my own boss, and I had a hand on every dollar coming in or going out. I made all my clients pay in cash; at times I had so much, I didn't know what to do with it. I could spend hundreds of thousands each day on sports bets or blow fifty thousand on a trip to Vegas. I bought the old health club where I got my rubdowns and even owned one of the city's more popular Italian restaurants with one of my bookies.

But working with D'Arco and the First Ward wasn't about money. It was about power, and that was the one thing I couldn't buy. I knew how to *work* the system; these guys *controlled* the system. They could hire and fire cops. They could even make or break judges. When it came to the clients, they were on a higher level as well. I worked with the Mob's crew leaders; they did business with the bosses.

Before long, I was back in Counsellors Row to give Senior a response. Now it was my turn to knock him on his ass—with a much bigger proposition than he was expecting. I told him I would take Johnny around with me, but in return I wanted *all* of the First Ward's criminal business. I knew they were farming it out to ten or fifteen other lawyers. In return, I would split the fees fifty-fifty. I offered to check it out first with D'Arco's son-in-law, who ran their firm, but from the way Senior nodded, I knew it was a done deal. Like all the other Mob guys, he respected my brass balls. More than I knew.

A couple of weeks later, in the middle of the day, Senior called my office and asked that I come down to meet him at the First Ward table. When I got there, he picked up the phone, and a few minutes later, Pat Marcy was staring at us through the door to the lobby.

Pat was in his early sixties, and he dressed like some corporate executive in three-piece suits. He wore tinted dark-rimmed glasses that gave him the expression of a pissed-off owl. We got up and joined him in the lobby. Senior said, "You know Pat Marcy, don't you?"

I said, "Sure, I know Pat." In fact, I knew he was secretary for the First Ward Committee of the Democratic Party. Whatever the hell that meant. I assumed he was somebody ultra-heavy, but I thought Senior was the real powerhouse in the First Ward—even though Pat was at the First Ward table more than anyone else.

The three of us were just standing there, up against the wall in the lobby, as people rushed by to jump in the elevators. Senior looked around to check that nobody was near us. "Pat wants to talk to you about something. It's important."

Pat said, "Listen, do you know a judge at 26th who can handle a case?"

When he said that, I knew exactly what he meant. The criminal court was at 26th Street and California. He wanted a judge to help him fix a case.

Then he added, "It's a very serious case. It's a murder case."

I had fixed cases before, but never a murder case. Still, partly out of curiosity, I said, "I don't know. What case is it?"

"Harry Aleman."

In those days, the name Harry Aleman invoked the same chills as the Luca Brasi character in *The Godfather* movie. The press dubbed him the Mob's "killing machine," and the Chicago Crime Commission considered Aleman responsible for at least eighteen contract murders. I remembered reading in the papers that he had been arrested and charged with killing some union guy.

Maybe I should have backed away right then and done us all a favor. But I was flattered they had approached me. "Pat," I said, "before I say I can help, I'd like to see the police reports, so I know what kind of case they have."

Senior got a little annoyed with that. "If you have somebody, fine. If you don't have somebody, don't say that you do. Because this is a serious matter. Some very powerful people are concerned about this individual, and if you say you can do it, you can't back away."

But Pat respected my response. He saw I wasn't bullshitting, and he promised to get me the police reports.

The next day, I picked up Johnny D'Arco in my Lincoln to go on our rounds of the courthouses. Johnny had started to treat me like a big brother. Whenever we hung at a bar or club, he would order exactly what I did. After spending so much time with me, he knew I loved pranks, like parking in the mayor's spot at City Hall or dropping eggs on people from the balcony of my condo. When he found out I was involved with the Aleman case, he got worried. "This is not something you can fuck around with," he told me. "If you make a mistake on this, it could be a real problem for you. You'll probably get killed."

Later, when we got back from court, I walked by the First Ward table, and Pat Marcy handed me an envelope. Then he reminded me, "I have to know as soon as possible if you've got somebody. And if they say they are going to do it, they have to do it."

Back in my office, I pulled out the police reports. They were the originals. Obviously, Pat had some deep contacts—either inside the police department or the state attorney's office. I don't think I spent more than twenty minutes on the material before I could see that it was an absolute throw-out case—the sort of stuff that would *never* convince a judge or jury that Harry Aleman was guilty of this crime.

The victim was William P. Logan, a Teamster shop steward and part-time cab driver. He was thirty-five and living with his sister after a recent divorce. Shortly before midnight, September 27, 1972, as he was getting into his car to drive to work, another car pulled up and someone called out, "Billy." He turned to run, but got nailed with three quick blasts. His nephew, who was sleeping on the porch, woke up to see him stagger between two parked cars and crumple, face first, onto the parkway. His lunch bag was still on the hood of the car.

Besides what they pulled out of his body, the state had no physical evidence. No gun and no car. All they had was a flaky statement from a neighbor. He said he saw what happened when he let his dog out. He couldn't describe the two white males in the car, but he said one of them got out and nailed Logan with a .45-caliber pistol. In fact, though, the wounds and pellet fragments showed Logan was killed with a shotgun.

The state's first real break in the case came four years later, when some Pennsylvania state troopers arrested a speeder named Louie Almeida. He told them that he was on his way "to kill somebody." Louie was a real piece of work. He had been part of Harry Aleman's crew—the kind of knucklehead who would do whatever he was asked. But somewhere inside that thick skull, a camcorder was always running. Once the coppers got him back in Chicago, they didn't have to push too many buttons before Louie's adventures with Harry started spilling out. One of them was the Logan hit. But what Louie remembered conflicted directly with the other witness. Louie said he was driving a car completely different from the neighbor's description. Also, Louie said Harry never got out of the car, but fired a sawed-off shotgun from the back seat. Of course, Louie had some credibility issues of his own—starting with a rap sheet a mile long, and ending with a prison shrink's diagnosis that he was a Looney Tune psycho. Still, the coppers must have figured Louie was more believable than the neighbor, so they had him change his statement to match Louie's. It wasn't going to take much to tear either one of these losers into shreds once they took the stand.

As for the motive, the state had some trumped-up story about the Mob and union politics. But Logan was only a shop steward, and the Mob already controlled the Teamsters, any idiot knew that.

I went back down to get Marcy and we had another little conference against the lobby wall. "Pat," I said, "they got no case here. I could take this to a jury and walk him."

But Pat didn't want to hear that. "No. No," he said. "We want a judge to handle it." He didn't want Aleman to risk a jury trial. He wanted a bench trial, where the judge would arrive at the verdict. And he wanted to be absolutely sure that the verdict would be Not Guilty. So he asked again, "Have you got somebody?"

"Let me think about it," I said. "I've got a couple of people in mind."

Actually, I had exactly the perfect judge in mind. The last person Marcy would have expected, but I wasn't going to blurt out his name until I had checked with him first.

Frank Wilson was what we called a "state-minded" judge—a hard-nosed law-and-order guy who always leaned toward the prosecution. He could be very mean on the bench, and most lawyers were scared to death of him. But he was also considered totally legit. As far as I knew, he had never taken a dime on any case, let alone a murder rap.

That night, just as I expected, I saw the judge in Greco's, the Italian restaurant I owned. I usually headed down there in the early evening, just after I finished up with my bookies. It was about six o'clock, and Judge Wilson was at the bar, getting a head start on his Canadian Clubs before his friends arrived. The judge had what they call the Irish Disease. He drank the hard stuff every day. He was a big beefy guy with white hair, and he had that stern look of a judge. I walked up to him, shook his hand, and led him a little distance from the bar, where nobody could hear us. My plan was to pop the question and then, if he got offended, to pretend he was too drunk to understand what I was talking about.

"Judge," I said, "I was just approached on a murder case. They want me to find a judge who would handle it."

"You mean the Harry Aleman case?" he asked.

"Yeah." To my surprise he didn't show any anxiety when I brought it up. But then he explained that Aleman's lawyer had already requested that Judge Wilson *not* be given their case. Defense lawyers were allowed to name two judges that they would want substituted, and given Frank's reputation, Aleman's lawyer wanted no part of him. The judge told me, "I don't think you can get the case back to me,"

"I'll check and see," I said. "But if I can get it back, would you be interested in handling the case?"

"What kind of case do they have?" he asked.

I had tried several cases in his court, and he trusted me to know what was a good case for the defense. "I've already read the reports," I told him, "and it's a weak case. It's a throw-out case."

He shrugged his shoulders. "I doubt if you can get the case back to me."

It wasn't a yes, but it wasn't a no either. When his friends came, they had dinner as usual. I just picked up the check and went about my business. I didn't talk to him for the rest of the night.

Anybody else would have been nuts to approach Judge Wilson. But I knew him better than most other lawyers did. We hung out quite a bit, usually at a bar near the courthouse or at Greco's. As a part owner, I may have been biased, but it was probably the nicest restaurant in the area. It looked like an old-fashioned wine cellar with its trellises and vines. Our cooks were the Italian ladies in the neighborhood, so it was real home cooking. The judge lived nearby, and if I saw him there, I would pick up his check. But he was no moocher. To reciprocate, he'd invite me to his country club and take care of those tabs. When he was totally wasted, I was one of the few people he'd let drive him home. Otherwise, he got in a lot of trouble with his drunk driving. Once he drove smack into the side of a house near his country club.

What really bonded us was one experience we had in Las Vegas. Since I was considered a big spender—big loser was more like it—the casinos would fly me back and forth on junkets. They didn't care how many people I brought along, so I used to take the judge. He didn't go to gamble. He went to drink, because the booze was free. Sometimes you'd see him at the craps table with a pile of chips on the pass line. He had fallen asleep on his feet and his bet would keep riding until he lost or woke up.

Once we were at the MGM Grand at three in the morning, and I found him slumped over the bar. I was going to drag him up to his room when I saw some real cute girl giving me the eye from the other end of the bar.

I went over to her and said, "You're not a working girl, are you?"

"Oh, no," she said. "I'm just here for the weekend."

I thought, "What a gorgeous little broad." And I started rapping with her. We had a couple of drinks, but then I remembered sleeping beauty. I said, "Look. My friend here is a judge, and I got to get him upstairs. He's really wasted. Then we'll go back to my place."

We walked over to the judge and woke him up. He started drooling all over her, "Oh, hi, honey." He was fumbling with her dress and everything. I thought he was going to blow this date for me.

But she wasn't fazed at all. She pulled him to his feet and said, "I'll help you put him to bed. My father was like this all the time."

The judge had always had a horrible limp, from some childhood injury, so it took forever to reach his room. When we finally got there, I opened the door and she pushed right past me. "I'll take it from here," she said and shut the door behind her. I must have been waiting twenty minutes in the hall. I figured maybe he's attacking her or something. But finally she appeared, and we went to my room. She had this whole story about just getting divorced, and what she used to do with her ex-husband. They would each take a shower, and then they'd have sex. So I figured, "What the hell." She got the shower running and I climbed inside. But the water hardly hit my face before I started thinking, "Wait! I have a good fifteen thousand in my pants pocket, a big ring and a fancy watch on the nightstand, and I don't even know this fucking broad."

I jumped out of the shower and she was already gone. I tore open the door and ran into the hall buck naked, and there she was, just getting on the elevator. I grabbed the next elevator going down. Inside, wouldn't you know, some nice older couple was headed for an early breakfast, and there was yours truly trying to cover his nuts with his hands. I went straight to the pool, so I could grab a towel and the phone, and I called for security. As it turned out, this broad was a hustler. She flew in from LA and did this all the time. They had her picture and everything. Of course, I was one pissed-off individual. I filled out all the paperwork to file a complaint in case they caught her, and then I practically crawled back to my room. I wasn't asleep for more than a few minutes before the phone rang. It was the judge. "What the fuck?" he yelled. "That girl you fixed me up with stole all my money." He probably had four hundred dollars that she took, but it was a lot for him. You could say we had both been caught with our pants down.

When I told Pat Marcy the judge I had in mind for the fix, he couldn't believe it. Frank Wilson was exactly the kind of judge he was looking for. "But we have to get the case back to his court," I said. Like Judge Wilson, I didn't think that would be an easy matter. First, the current judge had to withdraw from the Aleman case, and then there would be a computer lottery to select his replacement.

But Pat just waved his hand and said that wouldn't be a problem. He could assign that case any which way he wanted. All this bullshit about procedures and lotteries was just a game for the rest of us. Pat told me to offer him $10,000. It sounded like a lot to me, but what did I know? Up to that time, the most I had paid on any case was a thousand bucks, but I never had paid on a murder case before. I took all of those to trial, and I always got an acquittal. And in most of those cases, the state had a lot more evidence against my client than they had against Harry Aleman.

I waited a day before I called the judge at the courthouse and suggested he invite the wife for dinner at Greco's. We had been out together before. She was a real nice Irish lady and would help break the tension.

I brought along Cathy Fleming, a very attractive young woman who was working for me at the time. She was also about to become one of my girlfriends. I thought she could mix with an older couple and make the evening look like a social occasion. At the restaurant, just as we were about to get seated, I said, "Judge, can I talk to you for a minute?"

I took him into the men's room. It was a big place, with plenty of marble for an echo, so I first checked under all the stalls to make sure no one else was using a toilet. Then I said, "Judge, are you still interested in taking the case?"

"If you tell me it's a real weak case," he said, "then yes, I'd be interested."

I said, "Judge, I think we can get the case back to you if you want to handle it."

I told him he would get $10,000 in return, but then I added, "I don't want you to say yes or no now. I want you to think about it first. If you say, 'Yes' and then back away, I will have a serious problem."

He just nodded. Then we sat down and had our dinner.

A couple of days later, we met again at Greco's. We went into the bathroom, and he said, "Okay. Okay. I'll handle it." As a down payment, I pulled $2,500 out of my jacket pocket. Pat Marcy hadn't even paid *me* yet, but I wanted to lock the judge in, right then and there. Maybe, before I gave him the money, I should have thought a little more about the consequences—for our careers and our lives. But I really thought I was doing him a favor. His annual salary was $50,000 at most. He had his membership at the country club. His daughter was ready for college. Things were probably a little tight. He took the cash and almost didn't know where to put it. I'm sure it was the first time he ever took a bribe.

A few days after my first payoff to the judge, I got a call from Marco D'Amico. He was one of the Mob's Young Turks and ran a crew on the city's West Side. We had been hanging out and gambling with each other since I had been a cop. He wanted to meet me at a motel near the airport called The King's Inn. Marco owned it behind the scenes, and we had been there before, so nothing seemed suspicious.

For a motel, The King's Inn was a pretty swanky place. On the lower level, it had a bar and a nightclub. You drove down from the street into the parking area. People couldn't see you coming or going. I brought along one of my girlfriends, and Marco was waiting for us at the bar. Disco was big in those days. There were a lot of flashing lights all around, and pounding music. Marco motioned for the girl to have a seat and told me that someone wanted to meet me. We went upstairs into an empty motel room—just a bed and a little round table in the corner. I could still hear the thump-thump of the disco music coming up through the floor. Obviously, Marco had not called me to The King's Inn just to hang out and get drunk. When Mob guys pulled this cloak and dagger stuff, it was always pretty funny, but you had to play along and act surprised or they'd get mad at you. We were just about to sit down when there was a knock at the door. I had already figured out who I was about to meet before he walked in the room: the killing machine himself, Harry Aleman.

At first sight, Harry did not look all that threatening. At thirty-eight, he had a build, from working out, but he was fairly short and a very fancy dresser. Silk shirts. Leather jackets. He had brown, blow-dried hair with prematurely gray sideburns and a hawk-like nose. You wouldn't know that Harry was a killer until you looked into his eyes and saw his stone-cold evil stare. Once I watched him in my restaurant when he stared daggers at Tony Reitinger, a young Jewish bookmaker, who wasn't paying the Mob's "street tax." Two weeks later, Tony was dead—from a shotgun blast while he sat waiting for someone in a pizza parlor. And wouldn't you know, they had to kill Tony right *after* I had paid him $5,000 on a bet I lost. Poor guy, he probably thought the street tax was a game. But Harry Aleman never played games.

"Hey, how ya doing? How ya doing?" Harry pumped my hand in the motel room like we were long-lost pals. We had met before, but we'd never had much to say to each other.

He asked, "You gonna handle my case?"

"Yeah."

"Are you sure you can handle it? Are you sure this judge is going to throw the case out?"

"Sure. He's going to throw it out."

Then he took a long look at me and gave me his Evil Eye routine. "You realize," he said, "if there's a problem, you're gonna have a problem."

"I understand what's going on," I said. "I wouldn't say it unless it was so."

Harry nodded, like everything was okay, and we sat around the table. As it turns out, he had another mission for this meeting, and it related to his asshole lawyer. "I want to keep Tom Maloney on the case," he said, "and Tom wants to stay on the case."

As far as I was concerned, this was not a matter for discussion. I told him, "Maloney can't stay on the case."

There were several reasons to dump Maloney. First of all, I didn't like the prick—as a lawyer or a human being. He was a big overbearing blowhard who acted like he was God's gift to the legal profession. I hated the way he talked down to the clerks and the bailiffs. And I knew

Judge Wilson hated him, too. But I wasn't going to say any of that to Harry.

Instead, I said, "Maloney already asked for a substitute for Judge Wilson. How would it look if he suddenly turned around and accepted Wilson as the judge? It would look suspicious. You're much better off with another lawyer."

But Harry kept on pushing Maloney. I had already told Pat Marcy that we would have to change lawyers, and now I realized that fucking Maloney had talked Harry into letting him stay on the case. "Look," Harry said, "they're gonna name him a judge real soon. This may be the last case he does as a lawyer. He would be a real good friend to have."

Harry was right. Through Marcy's connections, Maloney was soon to be appointed as a Circuit Court judge to fill a vacancy. Still, if Maloney had been appointed king, there was no way I'd ever work with him. But I wasn't going to sit there and argue about it with Harry. When these guys got insistent, it was no use arguing with them. "Okay," I said. "Let me talk to Judge Wilson and see if I can get him to change his mind." In fact, I had no intention of talking to the judge about Maloney.

Harry was still not finished with me. He had hired a private investigator to check up on the witness who was Logan's neighbor. This guy was an absolute lowlife with three warrants out for his arrest. Obviously, the investigator didn't have to dig too deep to find some dirt on him. "Maybe," Harry said, "you want to meet this investigator."

"No," I said. "I don't want to meet the investigator. I don't want anyone else to know I'm involved in this. Just get me his reports."

This was not Harry's first trial, and we all knew it wouldn't be his last, but I could tell that there was something about this case that really bothered him, and he kept me in that little motel room for another half hour. When he finally got up to leave, he gave me a number and said I should call his wife if I needed to reach him in an emergency. "I don't go home much any more, but she still knows how to get ahold of me."

I told him he was never to call me on my regular phone, and he should use a code name if someone else picked up my private line. We had to be super-cautious to make sure no one could connect me to his case.

That next day, Pat Marcy gave me more bullshit about keeping Maloney as Harry's lawyer, but I held my ground. I told him, "If you want to keep Maloney you have to find another judge." But they didn't want another judge. My judge was perfect and they knew it. Maloney could fuck himself.

To replace Maloney, Marcy got Frank Whalen, an older lawyer who used to handle Chicago Mob cases, but then moved his practice to Florida. The choice was fine with Judge Wilson. He said, "Whalen's been before me, and he's a good lawyer." But the judge didn't want to meet with him. "If there's any problems, I will deal with you." He asked that I help Whalen prepare the case, and before the trial I flew down to see him twice—at my own expense. I still hadn't even asked Marcy about my fee for this deal, but the money really didn't matter to me. If I could get Harry off, I would be locked into the First Ward legal business for some time to come.

Everything looked fine to Whalen down in Florida, but once the trial date got close, and he met with Harry in Chicago, he wasn't so sure any more. He was staying at one of the old hotels in the business district. I'd sneak through the rear entrance and go directly to his room. Whalen remembered Judge Wilson and he knew his reputation, so he kept asking me, "Are you sure this judge will throw the case out? Are you sure you can trust him?"

"That's my responsibility," I told him. "You put the case on, and I'll take the heat if the judge doesn't do what we want."

But Harry Aleman wasn't going to leave anything to chance. Just days before the trial started, I got a call at four in the morning. It woke me up from a sound sleep with a very beautiful girl next to me. It was Harry. "It's important," he said. "I got to see you right away." He told me to meet him by the *Chicago Tribune* tower at a 24-hour diner—a big, cheap Greek place.

When I got there, I ordered some coffee and took a booth by the window. I was facing the loading docks for the newspaper building, and it wasn't long before I saw Harry and his partner, Butch, slinking out of the shadows. Butch Petrocelli had a face like a fist and a skunk's tail for a head of hair—a bizarre splotch of white in the middle of the black.

You could spot him a mile away. They walked into the diner, acting as though they didn't see me. They went to a booth in the back and, after a few minutes, I got up to join them.

Harry was all excited. His brother knew some girl who lived down the street from where Logan was shot. "We can get her to come in and say she saw the shooting and that I wasn't the guy who did the shooting."

"Good." I said. "We don't really need it, but every little bit helps."

"Let the judge know that. I'm sure it will make him happy."

I said, "Okay, Harry. Okay. Whatever you say." But I was thinking, "What the fuck, you asshole? You wake me up at four in the morning to tell me this? You could have waited until tomorrow."

Then Harry said, "We're gonna give her ten thousand."

"Be careful," I told him. "I don't want you talking to this girl. That could get you into a lot of trouble. Don't you *ever* be seen meeting with her."

It was like I popped his balloon. "Oh. Okay," he said. "I won't meet with her."

This girl wasn't such a prize after all. She got second thoughts and went to the police. She tried to lure Harry into a meeting, so the coppers could catch him bribing her, but because of what I told him, he steered clear of her.

Meanwhile, the case got underway. Unfortunately, things didn't go as we had planned. After the first day of testimony, I was sitting in my office when the phone rang. It was the judge. He was calling from a pay phone, somewhere outside the courthouse. "Hi," he said.

"Hello," I said. "See you later," and we both hung up. That was our code to meet at a restaurant near his home. He was there before I arrived, waiting for me at a table by the bar. He was so upset, he hadn't even had that much to drink.

"Is Whalen sick?" he asked. "He's not doing a good job cross-examining the witnesses."

"What do you mean?" I asked.

He said, "You told me it was a weak case, but it's a good case. The state is putting on a good case. You didn't tell me how difficult it was going to be for me." Then he asked me again, "Is this man sick?"

"I don't know," I said. I explained I had never seen him in court before.

"Well, he's not the lawyer he used to be," the judge said.

I told him I'd check up on Whalen and went right over to his hotel.

"The judge is pissed," I told Whalen. "He says you're doing a shitty job. What the fuck is going on in there? I gave you all the information you needed to tear apart these witnesses."

"I'm doing a great job," he bellowed back at me. "What's he talking about?"

Now I had Whalen mad at me, too.

The judge's concerns about Whalen were not a good sign, especially since I had pushed Maloney off the case. The next morning, I went over to see Pat Marcy at Counsellors Row, and we walked out into the lobby. "Pat," I said, "the judge wants to know if Whalen's sick. He thinks he's doing a terrible job in court."

This got Pat all upset. He started glaring at me. "You tell that judge he better throw this case out."

After I left Counsellors Row, I wanted to be close to the Criminal Courthouse, and I drove down to 26th Street. I even entered the building, so I could sneak into the gallery. I went up the courthouse stairs as far as the judges' floor, but from there I could see that they had set up metal detectors outside the courtroom. Since I knew the coppers who were manning them, there was no way for me to pass by unnoticed.

I walked back downstairs, thinking, "What the fuck am I going to do now?" I had the judge upset with me for putting Whalen on the case. I had Whalen upset at me for calling him a terrible lawyer. I had Pat Marcy upset with me for being upset. My life was literally on the line with this trial, and I couldn't do a damned thing about it.

So each night I arranged to be in my office in case the judge wanted to talk again. I could sense he was getting increasingly nervous. It didn't help that the papers were printing their version of the evidence, saying the state had Harry dead to rights. In truth, no matter how weak the evidence, Harry Aleman was their perfect villain. According to the press, in the whole crazy history of Chicago, this was the first time a Mob hit man was ever standing trial for a contract killing.

Finally, the judge called me again from the pay phone, and I raced out to the restaurant. Earlier that day, away from the jury, there was a hearing about Harry's brother trying to bribe the neighbor girl. The prosecutors tried to call her as a witness, but she had only met with the brother. Anything she knew about Harry was hearsay and not admissible. The judge had no problem ruling that the state couldn't call her to the stand. But he was bothered by something else: that they were going to pay her $10,000.

"Did you know about that?" he asked.

"I knew they were trying to get a witness," I said, "but I didn't know what amount they would pay her."

"I am a judge. I am a full judge," he told me. "I am going to lose my job on this thing and all *I'm* getting is ten thousand dollars. It's not fair."

"Let me see if I can get you some more," I said.

But that wasn't all he wanted to talk about. He was reading the newspapers. "I'm going to be in trouble if I find him not guilty."

I didn't like where this was going. "Wait, Judge," I said. "Before you got involved, I told you about this case. You knew what was going on. The state really doesn't have a case. If you find this guy guilty, I'm a dead man."

The next day I went to see Marcy at Counsellors Row. I told him that the judge was getting unbelievable heat in the press. I said he was frightened and realized he probably wouldn't get reelected. Meanwhile, he found out what Harry's brother was going to pay the witness. "The judge thinks he should get some more. Maybe we should give him some more."

Pat glared at me again. "That's all he is going to get. Not a nickel more. He agreed to do it for ten thousand, and he better do what he said or there will be consequences."

As if I wasn't worried enough, behind the scenes I picked up information that was total dynamite. The hit, I learned, had had nothing to do with unions and all the other crap in the indictment. It was strictly personal. Billy Logan, the victim, had been married to Harry's cousin. They had a bitter divorce and argued constantly over custody of their son. Logan used to beat her up big-time. The final straw came after one of their fights when she said, "You better be careful, because Harry won't be happy about it." And Logan replied, "Fuck that guinea." He probably could have beaten her up a few more times, and it wouldn't have mattered. But Harry wasn't going to let some Irish goon get away with calling him a guinea.

None of this came out in the trial, but if it did, you had an entirely different case than what I had thought it was. Or what the judge thought it was. There would have been a documented connection between Harry and Logan—along with all the motive in the world.

The last day of the trial, I woke up and packed a suitcase. I knew the judge was reading his decision later in the morning. I wasn't sticking around to hear what he said. I got in my Lincoln and started driving west. I didn't even know where I was going. I was probably twenty miles outside the city, when I clicked on the radio and heard the news: Judge Wilson had found Harry not guilty. I turned my car around and headed back to the office.

When he announced his decision, the judge did all he could to justify the verdict. He mentioned how the neighbor kept changing his testimony. He said you should consider "the first story" to be the one that's "trustworthy." He discounted the other witness, Louie Almeida, because he was an "accomplice." He explained, "According to the law, his testimony is subject to suspicion and to be considered with caution."

Clearly the judge could see the public outrage that would soon be falling on his head. He finished by saying, "My decision may not be a popular one. But for those who disagree, I wish to state that every defendant, and I mean every defendant, no matter who he might be, is entitled to a fair trial and must be proven guilty beyond a reasonable doubt, whether it is a gang-type shooting or the mere stealing of a bicycle."

When I walked into Counsellors Row, there was Pat, sitting at the First Ward table. He got up and I followed him into the lobby, past the elevators and through the door to the stairwell. They had a janitor's closet back there, where he stood a few steps above me. "Wow, great job," he said. "Terrific job."

"Pat," I said, "this judge is in trouble. This case is all over the papers and the rest of the media. Can't we give him more than ten thousand?"

He replied, "Look, he agreed to take it for ten and that's what he's going to get." Pat reached into his coat pocket and took out two envelopes. I knew what a lot of cash looked like and it didn't look like that much in those envelopes. He handed me one and said, "Here's the $7,500 balance for the judge." Then he gave me the other little skinny one. "And this is for you."

I was thinking, "If those are thousand dollar bills in there, it's not a lot." For what I did, I expected to get paid fifty or a hundred thousand. My own expenses were five or ten thousand, just in running back and forth to Florida to see Whalen.

But I didn't say boo. When I got inside my office, I pulled out my envelope and opened it up. He gave me a lousy $3,000. "The bastard," I thought. An extra $30,000 wasn't going to change my life in those days, but it would have told me my efforts were appreciated. I started to see how much money meant to the Mob, and how cheap they were—in so many ways.

However bad I felt about *my* envelope, I felt that much worse about the one I had to give the judge. To smooth the waters, I brought along Cathy Fleming. I knew the judge liked to see her. We met again at that place near his house. At one time it had been a pretty hot Italian restaurant. But it had changed hands, and you would go there now to drink instead of eat. When we walked in the door, the judge was sitting alone at this huge horseshoe bar. He was already getting a load on. I could hardly believe how bad he looked—like he had aged fifteen years in two weeks. His shoulders were stooped. His face was lined. He was a broken man.

Cathy took a seat at the bar, and the judge and I walked into the bathroom. It was a dirty, smelly place. He started talking to me. "The newspapers are going to crucify me. I'm going to lose my judgeship. I can't run for reelection." He was almost crying. Then he looked at me and said, "You did this to me."

"Judge," I said, "before you got involved in the case, I told you what it was. I'm in the same spot you are. I feel terrible, but there is nothing I can do about that."

I then handed him the envelope and said, "Judge, here's the balance." He looked inside. "That's all I'm going to get?" he asked. "I'm not going to get any more?"

He shook his head and started to limp out of the bathroom. I tried to tell him that I would have given him more, but he turned around and cut me off. "You destroyed me," he said, and he walked away.

As I stood in that bathroom, I was truly sorry about what happened to Frank. I should have felt sorry for myself, too.

Although the Harry Aleman fix brought me a lot more business and a lot more influence, it also sucked me that much deeper into the First Ward. I would soon see for myself how Pat Marcy had hijacked the Democratic Party, the city government, the court system, and even the police. Like an octopus, he reached inside each one and pulled the levers of power for the benefit of his cronies and the Mob. Those who got close to him, like I did, lived in fear of his wrath. Time and again, he pushed us into more criminal activity, like the Aleman fix, and time and again, we couldn't back away.

In his supreme arrogance, Marcy never conceived that anyone in his inner circle would ever turn on him. Certainly not me. But while I may have sold my soul to him, I still kept my conscience. It was only a matter of time before the disgust bubbling inside of me boiled over. When it did, I was ready to bring the First Ward machine down around me—even if I went down with it.

CHAPTER 2

COP KILLER

James Cooley will never forget that terrible night. He was 13 years old. There was a knock on the door and then he heard his mother scream. Jim ran out to find that his mother had fainted. A policeman was trying to revive her. Jim's dad, also a policeman, had just been killed by a holdup man.

Chicago Tribune, June 16, 1950

A nd so began a newspaper article about my father, James F. Cooley. Like a lot of stories in the press, this one didn't get all the facts straight. True, my grandfather was shot that "terrible night" in 1927, but he didn't die then. The bullet that hit him between the eyes took another twelve weeks to kill him. It was a slow, agonizing death.

As you read through the clips about my grandfather's murder, the whole story seems so strange but so Catholic, too—with all the drawn-out suffering. The night of the shooting, my grandfather was fifty-one and your typical Irish immigrant cop, walking the beat and chatting it up with the locals. He wore that high Keystone Kops hat. Maybe he was swinging his nightstick, too. Suddenly two men ran up shouting that they had been robbed as they got out of their car. Grandfather walked with them the few blocks back to the scene of the crime, and just then one of the robbers appeared on the steps of a nearby house. Grandfather drew his revolver and told him, "Throw up your hands," but the robber pulled out his own gun and shot him instead. Grandfather, staggered by the bullet, shot back and then fell to the ground. He was bundled into the car of one of the holdup victims, a dentist, so he could be rushed to the hospital. Only the dentist was stone drunk ("confused by his experience" is how one article put it), so he drove around with my grandfather for an hour before they ever saw a doctor. The dentist was later convicted of driving under the influence, but a lot of good that did for my grandfather.

You would think that my grandfather—with a bullet in his brain—never regained consciousness. But three days later, when the coppers dragged a suspect into the hospital for an ID, grandfather raised his head from the pillow and said, "That's the fellow. I'd know him in a million." What a quaint way of putting it. You can hear the Irish brogue and everything. The suspect, Thomas Pemberton, was quite a character himself. They arrested him in the company of a woman described as "colored," but he later admitted to being a card-carrying member of the Ku Klux Klan. When the police searched his home, they found what the press called "an arsenal" of twelve rifles and six pistols.

Poor Grandfather lingered through the winter and into the spring, mostly in a coma. At one point the hospital sent him home, probably so he wouldn't take up a bed for someone they could help. When he finally died in April, he was back in the hospital, surrounded by his wife and six kids. The funeral was a humble affair. A wake in the family parlor. A simple interment in the parish cemetery. A few years before, the neighborhood had sent off Al Capone's little brother in a cascade of roses. All my grandmother got was a pension of $79 a month and the uniform to bury her husband in.

Justice moved a little quicker in those days, and Pemberton was on trial for the murder by October. The state had him dead to rights, positively identified by the victim and bystanders, but when the trial ended, the headline read: "Jury Frees Pemberton in Policeman's Death." Grandmother heard the verdict and fainted away. It was, the prosecutor said, "the biggest surprise I ever had in my career."

However amazing that story sounds, the most amazing part was yet to come.

Dad grew into a tall somber young man, with sleepy eyes and red hair that got darker as it grew thinner. They still called him Big Red, but he was a gentle soul who never used his size to intimidate. He tended more toward the spiritual, much like my grandmother, who never lost her faith despite all the bad breaks that came her way. She was active in the church, and somehow got her sons through Mount Carmel, the South Side's best Catholic high school. Dad took the next step towards sanctification and entered Mount Carmel Seminary, a huge Canadian monastery overlooking Niagara Falls. But after three years, he decided the priesthood was not for him, and no wonder. Within months of leaving the seminary he met my mother and they got married. She was a very pretty brunette, with deep-set eyes. There was a lot more than physical attraction to draw them together. Both were devout Catholics. Both were the children of coppers, and, believe it or not, both of their fathers had died in the line of duty.

And yet, despite all the family history, when Dad and Mom moved back to Chicago with a set of newborn twins, my grandmother "gently urged him"—Dad would say—to join the police department. People may look back and wonder what possessed her to do such a thing. How could she lose a husband to police work and then push her son down the same path? Why would he have let himself be pushed? And why would my mother have let him go?

Obviously, times were different. To some extent their attitude was a sign of their faith with a dash of good old-fashioned Irish fatalism. When your time was up, your time was up and there was not much you could do about it—whether you worked in the police department or a grocery store. But Dad had other matters to consider as well. It was the Depression, and he had to put food on the table for a growing family. One way or another the city was going to stay in business and it would always need somebody to fight crime.

Although the police may have guaranteed a paycheck, it was not a very big one. My parents didn't help matters by being good Catholics and having nine kids—two girls and seven boys. My father always struggled to bring home enough bacon, and my mother struggled that much more to stretch it.

We lived on Chicago's South Side, a gritty area far from the city's skyscrapers. When we looked up, we saw smokestacks and church steeples. Our clouds puffed up from the steel mills like steam from a chugging locomotive. When the wind blew the wrong way, you had a taste like stale bread on the back of your throat.

Dad could only afford one-floor brick bungalows. They were always on the bleeding edge of the "color line," where whites were moving out and blacks were moving in and all hell was breaking out in between. When someone got killed within a block of our house, Dad would say it was time to move. Each of the houses had three bedrooms: one for the parents, one for the two girls, and another for the boys. When there got to be too many of us, we threw a couple of mattresses into the attic.

To make ends meet, Dad juggled a second and sometimes third job, selling mutual funds or insurance. He was almost never home. Mom had to hold down the fort on her own. I remember her working from morning to night, with bottomless piles of laundry, and constant cooking and shopping on a meager budget. She had a whole routine about getting to the butcher or produce stand late in the day, just as they were marking down the prices. The older kids ran interference, so she could get first in line. At the grocery store, she looked for the dented cans and asked for a few cents off. When it came to our clothes, she always found something used, from relatives or the church where she volunteered. All the work wore her down and made her gray before her time. You hardly ever saw her in makeup or fancy clothes.

If needed, Mom could still put on a good show, like the one Sunday in 1950 when our whole family was photographed for that article about my dad ("the sixth in a series describing the bravery and earnestness of typical Chicago policemen"). Mom may have worn a simple dress, but with a baby in her arm she looked as good as Rose Kennedy.

And right there, in the center of the picture, was yours truly, at the age of seven. I was the third oldest, born after a brother and sister who were twins. This day I was decked out in a double-breasted white suit, fresh from my first Holy Communion. Of course, none of my other brothers wore a suit, and I had my hand on my jacket like a little Napoleon—already a hot shit. It's ironic that they took the picture the one time in my childhood when I was dressed so nicely. Even then, I hated being poor and I hated the used clothes most of all. I wanted us to have nice things, and I didn't want to hear my mother keep saying we couldn't afford them. It just made me focus on money that much more—certainly more than other kids my age. I was always out hustling to make some extra change. I delivered papers. I hung outside the corner store and offered to carry people's groceries home. As I got older, I'd ride my bike a few miles to a drugstore that paid me for sweeping up and making deliveries from six to nine-thirty at night. I'd get seventy-five cents, a bottle of pop, and a candy bar. By the end of the week I made five or six dollars, which was a lot of money for a kid. I gave most of it to Mom (although I didn't know it then, she was putting it away for me), but I always kept one or two bucks in my pocket, so I'd have some money for snacks. Because I wouldn't eat my vegetables, I was always hungry. My mother and I went to war over that. She refused to give me more of anything else, and I wouldn't budge on the green stuff—even if it meant starving to death.

The picky eating was just one way I tested my parents. For most of my childhood, I clanged back and forth, between Sin and Sainthood, like the clapper in a church bell. My parents were on the saintly side. Every day they got up at six to go to Mass and then lived out their days in unending sacrifice for all of us. My big brother, the spitting image of Dad, followed in his quiet footsteps and ultimately became a priest. I told the reporter who did the article about my father that I was headed to the seminary too, but my brother and I were cut from different cloth. When kids used to make fun of him because of the holes he had in his clothes, he just turned the other cheek. If kids pushed him around, he never pushed back. It made me sick to see that, and I decided I wasn't going to put up with getting picked on. I was one of the smallest kids in my class, but from the time I was six, if anybody said something I didn't like, I found a way to get him back. I didn't care how big he was. I could always use a brick or a bottle.

Probably the meanest kid in my class was Tommy Dugan. Tall and skinny, he had a perpetual scowl, and little slits for eyes that made him look like a snake. The first time he picked a fight with me, I licked him but good. That actually started a friendship that would continue through much of our lives, with some bizarre twists and turns along the way. As kids, we were like two peas in a pod. Same enemies. Same friends. Always covering the other's back. We were both smart, too, and caught on to our lessons quicker than the guys we hung with. Of course, that was nothing to brag about in our neighborhood. When it came to math, Tommy was practically a genius, but he was so obnoxious, he never got special attention from the teachers. His good grades on tests made them even madder at him.

If my parents were my paragons of Virtue, Tommy Dugan was my mentor in Sin. His upbringing was mostly to blame. His father had a decent-paying job at the gas company, but after work he'd go straight to the bar to drink, and he was a miserable drunk. When he got home at seven or eight, he always found some excuse to start beating the wife and the kids. Tommy grew up hating the bastard and lost his moral compass in the process. He respected no authority, and there was nothing he wouldn't do. When we went into stores, he had me be a lookout and then he would shoplift. At times he picked up a few things for me, too. Tommy also broke into houses to steal. But that was a line I would never cross. I knew it would kill my father if the coppers picked me up for robbery.

I got in enough trouble as it was. Mom could only take so much before she would pull out the ironing cord and start whipping me with it. After a while, I learned how to grab the cord from her. She'd say, "Wait until your father comes home. You'll get it then." But Dad never had the heart for discipline. By the time he dragged in, after some second job, I pretended to be asleep and he was too tired to pull me out of bed. The next day he might say, "God will punish you if you keep doing that." I thought, "Okay," and would keep doing it anyway.

Once, I finally pushed Mom over the edge. I broke a window and we were going to be out some money to fix it. Mom waited for Dad to come home and then marched him over to me. "Now you're going to get it," she said. He took me into their bedroom, put me over the bed and shut the door. Then he pulled the belt out of his pants. For a minute I thought I was in real trouble. But when he started to whack, he just kept hitting the bed instead of me. If this was going to work, I figured, I better do some screaming. Only I yelled too hard, because my mother burst through the door to stop him. When she saw the whole charade, she got really mad and for the first time I could remember, she yelled at Dad. Then he whipped me for real, the kind of beating I never got before. I had to crawl under the bed to get away from him. He felt so bad about hitting me, he apologized for days. I told him to forget about it. He just didn't believe in physical discipline. Maybe I got off easy in the short run, but in the long run I loved him more for it. Later, when it came to committing real serious crimes, I would always think twice—unlike Tommy Dugan. I didn't want to do anything that would break my father's heart.

Dad thought he could stop my fighting by getting me boxing gloves so I could channel my aggression through some supervised outlet. He probably watched *The Bells of St. Mary's* a few times too many. When I started boxing with the Catholic Youth Organization and learned what I was doing, I got to be even more dangerous.

Dugan's family left the neighborhood before we did, but by the time I was in eighth grade, we had to move too, and we both ended up in the same neighborhood again. Tommy's idea of the Welcome Wagon was to arrange fights for me with the toughest kids in his school. We'd go to a vacant lot across the street from a friend's house, and everyone would stand around to see me get creamed. It was like throwing me to the lions, but the fact is, I enjoyed it. Somewhere along the line, I learned that fighting was more mental than physical. I knew that however big the guy, I could go straight up to him and knock him down. It took three fights before everyone in the new neighborhood got the message.

This was the last move of my childhood, and as far as I was concerned, it was where life finally began. When school was out, I caddied at the South Shore Country Club with Tommy and started to make real money. We had a little gang that would get together every night in Avalon Park, a few blocks from our homes. My parents thought I was going to sleep early, but I took the highest bunk in our room and would fix the pillows so it looked like I was still in bed. Then I'd climb out through the window. For a while, I had a ladder hidden behind some bushes on the ground below, so I could climb back in again. Dad saw it one morning and threw it away. He thought a burglar was about to rob us. It never occurred to him that I was the one who was sneaking into the house.

We had wild times in that park. It was near the rail yards, and once we figured out which trains carried the Budweiser shipments, we liberated a few cases of beer. Eventually the railroad police caught on and set an ambush. They pinched me just as I was climbing the fence. I told them I was taking a shortcut to the drugstore and they let me go. I probably looked like too much of a pipsqueak to be involved. Tommy got out of it, too. Some nights I stayed in the park so long, it was too late to sneak home, so I'd just go straight to the golf course the next morning.

I never wanted that summer to end, but when September came, Tommy and I were classmates again at Mount Carmel High School, about three miles north from our neighborhood. It was in a little campus with a couple of sprawling brick buildings surrounded by athletic fields. The administrators and most of the teachers were Carmelite priests and friars. They wore monk-like robes with big leather belts.

I always had to be the class clown. During the first weeks of school, I started in with all my grade-school antics. When the teacher's back was turned, I used a ruler to flick spit into kids' hair. In biology class, I put a wad of bubblegum on the seat of a black guy who sat in front of me. He went up to the board and this long string of gum trailed after him. Everybody broke up. Father Jordan immediately knew who was responsible. He was big and burly, with a reputation for being a strict disciplinarian. He marched me down to the front of the class and had me bend over and grab my ankles. Then he took off his belt and hit me five or six times. He didn't miss like my father did. I must have been in shock, because I didn't realize how hard he hit me until I went to sit back down. It stung so much, I popped up like a jack-in-the-box, which started everyone laughing again. That earned me ten more whacks. This time, I couldn't keep the tears from rolling down my face.

That experience made me behave better in class, but Tommy and I were still slacking off as much as we could. We both had the ability to crack our books the night before a test and get an "A." But then there was homework, and if you didn't do that, you got a beating too. So

Tommy and I would meet at a donut shop around seven-thirty each morning and wait for the "brains" to get off at the bus stop outside the store window. Then we'd drag one of them in and copy his homework. At some point, the Fathers realized we were a dangerous combination. They split us up, so we couldn't be in the same classes—even though it meant one of us would be in a room with the slower kids.

It didn't matter, because we never took the academics all that seriously. What mattered most to us was sports. Everybody wanted to go out for football, because Mount Carmel usually had one of the best teams in the state. I was too small for that. They tossed me around like a feather. Wrestling was different. There I could fight guys my own size, and I loved every minute of it. Some of my most challenging bouts came after school. All the white people had moved out of the Mount Carmel neighborhood and black street gangs were everywhere. During school hours the police were on the street, but after four o'clock, when we left practice, they were nowhere to be seen. We never knew what was going to hit us while we were waiting for the bus. You just had to be unbelievably tough or, if you were alone, know when to run for your life.

Of course, Tommy Dugan had his own demented way of solving our transportation problems. At the start of our senior year, he staked out a used car dealership in our neighborhood, and noticed where they kept the keys for the older cars in the back of the lot. He figured we could take a car for a week and no one would notice. Then we could exchange it for another car. It was quite a racket and not a bad way to get girls, either. We got on their good side by picking them up in the morning, and we could ask them out at night. This went on for a few weeks, until one day Tommy and I were called in to see the dean of students—the chief ass-kicker. He was waiting for us with a police detective. Somebody had ratted us out. The Father told us that even riding around in a stolen car—let alone stealing it—was grounds for expulsion. We could also get jail time if convicted of the crime. But fortunately for us, both the dean and the cop knew my father. "This would kill your dad if he found out," the cop said. As long as we returned the car, no charges would be brought. For punishment, we had to stay after school for the rest of the year. That didn't bother me because I had wrestling practice anyhow.

Despite all of our extracurricular activity, Tommy and I still graduated Mount Carmel with honors. Even though we refused to take what we called the "Genius Classes" that were used to prep the smarter kids, we did well on the college placement exams, and we both got into Marquette University in Milwaukee, two hours north of Chicago. Marquette gave me a wrestling scholarship to boot.

If you looked at the neighborhood where we grew up, and how most of our friends turned out, getting into college was quite an accomplishment. Unfortunately, it also made us a little too cocky. We figured that if we could beat the system at Mount Carmel, we'd have no trouble beating the system in college.

As far as my parents were concerned, with all the trouble I had caused, getting accepted at Marquette was nothing short of a miracle. My older sister had also been accepted there, but she had been a model student. I had gone from juvenile delinquency to the verge of great accomplishment, and they couldn't have been prouder. Even though money was still tight for them, they bought me the first suit I had since my communion.

The story of what happened to that suit pretty much sums up my experience at Marquette. I first wore it in August 1960, the day I showed up for college orientation. They had assigned me to the nicest new dormitory, on the floor with all the jocks. Before long I recognized a tall rangy guy with close-cropped hair like a Marine. His name was Bill Murphy. He played halfback the year his high school beat Mount Carmel and went on to win the Chicago Prep championship. He didn't know me from Adam, but I gave him a nudge and told him to follow me if he wanted a good time.

I had heard there was a brewery only a mile away from the campus. They took you on a stupid little tour, but then they brought you into a room where you got a free sample of the wares. In those days, eighteen-year-olds could drink beer, but weren't allowed in bars. Bill and I went on the tour and had our free beer. We then figured out a way to sneak into rooms where they were serving other tour groups. We did that a few times before the security guy came over and tried to throw us out. I got into a fight with him and they called the police. Bill and I had to run out the back and climb a cyclone fence to get away. As I was going over the top, I caught my leg and tore the pants from the cuff to my knee. Walking back, we passed a bunch of guys on motorcycles. One of them made a crack about my pants, and I picked a fight with him, so there was a little more pulling and tearing on my suit. But I wasn't through yet. We stopped for a hamburger at a joint across the street from the dormitory. Somebody looked at me the wrong way, and we had another fight. I was a little midget compared to Bill, but I was going to prove to him that I was the toughest guy in the world. By the time I got back to my room, the suit was already ruined. I could have rolled it up and flushed it down the toilet.

I had plenty of other escapades in store. Tommy Dugan was no different. Suddenly there were no Carmelite Fathers breathing down our necks to make sure we did our homework. All around us there were constant parties and lots of rich kids who didn't know what to do with their money. It was too much for Tommy and me to handle.

My scholarship didn't cover pocket money or books. I was supposed to get a job for that. I lasted two days at the Elks Club restaurant before I got in an argument with some old fogey customer, but I didn't have to find another job. There was a much better way to make money. I had started poker games in the meeting room on our dorm floor. We bet only a few bucks each hand but those bucks added up. I had been playing poker since I was a little kid, and I quickly realized that the college boys didn't know what they were doing, especially with a few beers under their belts. Besides my winnings, I collected a piece of each kitty for putting together the games and buying "refreshments," although I never drank myself when I was playing. Word got around, and the games went on almost nonstop. There were days I played twenty-four hours straight.

As far as I was concerned, the legit social life on campus was a joke— especially the fraternities. All anyone cared about was their parties. My friends and I decided to put on our own mixers, with everyone invited. The coeds had to pay just fifty cents, but the men paid a dollar fifty. We rented out an apartment near the campus and our only other investment was a keg of beer we'd put in the bathtub. It usually ran out in a couple of hours, but by then we had run out, too. Nobody ever made much of a stink about it, because all the cutest girls would show up. Some guys used to go out and bring back beer on their own nickel.

Of course, Dugan had his own ideas about creative finance. He got guys who worked in the student union gift store to lose a few items on the way from the box to the shelf, like sweatshirts and hats. Nobody seemed to notice that anything was missing. We then set up our own corner to sell some of that merchandise at better prices than the store. It wasn't long before Tommy and I had a reputation—the Irish gangsters from the South Side of Chicago.

Tommy didn't need that kind of encouragement to be bad. After they put him in a different dorm from me, he teamed up with a football player named Gary. He was a muscular Italian kid who hung around the strip clubs and could introduce you to the girls there. He also carried a gun in his belt—the first time I ever saw that. Tommy now had a partner to take him to new heights in crime. They started committing all kinds of burglaries and robberies, mostly inside the dormitories.

As a result, Tommy and I started going our separate ways. The jocks I hung out with didn't want him around, and I couldn't stand Gary. But one day Dugan pulled me aside and promised to cut me in on a great scheme. "If I tell you what it is," he said, "then you're in and you can't back out." I would encounter this trap a few more times in my life, and usually avoided it, but I was dying to know Tommy's brilliant plan. "Gary and I," he said, "are going to rob the drycleaners."

It was a fucking insane idea. I wanted to shoot myself for making the promise. The drycleaner was across the street from Marquette. Tommy had a friend who worked there, so he knew what evening they had the most cash. After the robbery, they would go back to Gary's dorm room and leave the money in his drawer. Then they would sneak into a party and act like they had been there for the whole night. All Tommy wanted me to do was drive the getaway car, and he'd cut me in for an equal share. He set a time to meet me at the dormitory, but I never showed up. I went with some other wrestlers to the Eagles Club, far from campus. They held big dances and had plenty of witnesses to say where I had been. Late that night, as we drove back to the dormitory, we turned on the car radio and found out there was a robbery at the drycleaner. I couldn't believe Tommy had gone through with it, especially without me. But I had to find out for sure. I went to Gary's dorm and climbed through the back window into his room. When I opened his drawer, cash flew out in every direction. I figured they hadn't even counted it. What would it matter if I grabbed a few dollars for myself? It was an incredibly weasel-like thing to do, but I was just robbing a couple of robbers. I shoved a wad into my pocket and headed over to another party.

At four o'clock that morning, there was a banging on my door. It was Tommy and Gary, and I wasn't going to open up. Finally they kicked the door in, but by that time, everybody on the floor had woken up, too, including the resident counselor. They all stuck their heads out into the hall. Tommy and Gary were insane with rage, practically foaming at the mouth. "We know you took the fucking money," they screamed. I acted like I was so drunk I couldn't understand them. They slammed the door shut and tore into my closet, going through all my clothes and pockets. They quickly found the money—three hundred bucks. If the resident counselor hadn't been waiting outside, they would have let me have it then and there, but Gary promised they would get me later.

I couldn't have threats hanging over my head. The next morning I confronted them by myself. "What I did, I did," I said. "But I'm not telling anyone about what you guys did. I'm keeping my mouth shut. If anything happens to me, somebody at school has a sealed letter he's supposed to open. Then the whole story will get out."

Tommy said he didn't want to see me again. I replied, "Good-bye and good riddance."

For the next year or so, I had nothing to do with Tommy, but my life at Marquette had already spun out of control. I was always tired, because I was up all night playing cards. Unlike high school, I couldn't just crack a book before a test and get an "A." My grades were horrible and I was put on academic probation after the second semester. During the summer, I assured my parents I'd get my grades up in my sophomore year. But when school started, I was back to my carousing. One weekend, three of us decided to drive down to Chicago to watch our old high schools play against each other in football. We rented a car and turned back the odometer to hide our mileage. After the game, we got into our car and went to a nearby park to drink a six-pack. A cop snuck up and arrested us.

The patrolman handed us over to some piece-of-shit officer who was working Vice, and he called our parents. Just earlier that week, I sent my parents a letter, telling them I had turned over a new leaf and would be studying through the whole weekend for my first exams. Imagine how they felt when they got a call that I was back in Chicago at a police station. My father came to get me with the two other fathers. "They'll let you go," Dad told us, "but they want us to pay a bribe. That's wrong and I just can't do it."

I had put my father in a lot of nasty situations in my life, but none was worse than this. As I later learned, he had paid a heavy price in the police department for taking the moral high ground. The vice cop was asking the three parents to come up with $500—which was a lot of cash in those days—but the amount wasn't the issue for Dad. Paying off a cop was illegal, and he did not believe in breaking the law. For him, it was as simple as that. The other two fathers didn't know what he was talking about. They were more than happy to buy our way out. Otherwise, an arrest could get us all expelled from Marquette. How could my father let three kids' lives get ruined by a few cans of beer? If everyone didn't go along with the bribe, it wasn't going to happen, so Dad gave in. I knew it wasn't easy for him.

We finally got out of jail late that night, but I didn't go home with Dad. I sensed the turmoil I had put him through, and I couldn't bear to be alone with him. Instead, I talked the guys into driving straight back to Marquette. I didn't call home to talk to him for two or three weeks. By then he had forgiven me.

Even that close shave was not enough to straighten me out. I was tempting fate. I *always* tempted fate. When I got back to school, I still hung out at the bars, even though I wasn't twenty-one. One night while I was in The Stratford, a place right across the street from school, the police raided it for underaged drinkers. We had some phony Wisconsin IDs, but they didn't fool the coppers any. They arrested a whole bunch of us for disorderly conduct and took us to jail in a paddy wagon. We were booked and given a trial date. The coppers let us out on our own recognizance, because we were Marquette students, and told us to stay away from that bar.

But The Stratford was *the* place to go every Wednesday and Friday. I didn't want the people there to think I was under age. As soon as I returned to campus, I went back to the bar and told them that the police checked out my ID and found everything was okay. I figured there was no way they would raid the same place again that night. But two and a half hours later, the police were back. This time it was a different vice squad. I was the only underaged person in the whole joint. They put me in the back of a squad car with a cop named Callahan. As he drove me to jail, we passed an accident scene. When he pulled over to check it out, I bolted through the back door and took off. Good Irish cop that he was, Callahan remembered the name on my fake ID, and now he came looking for me at the dormitory. For three days straight I would get called to come downstairs, but when I saw Callahan's squad car parked in the street below, I would go and hide. A week later, I was called to the resident counselor's office again. This time I didn't see the squad car. I figured that Callahan had finally forgotten about me. I went down to see what was up. There inside the counselor's office was Callahan.

"That's the one," he said, pointing at me like I was in some lineup.

I acted shocked. "What are you talking about?"

"You're the one that took off out of the squad."

"No," I said. "Wasn't me."

Callahan couldn't prove it, because he didn't book me. But the resident counselor knew whom to believe. It was one of the counts they used to throw me out of Marquette. Of course, they had plenty of other ammunition—what with the gambling and the fighting. Then there was the party room we had in the apartment off-campus. For that alone, I could have gotten canned. I wasn't the only member of the class to earn an early exit from the school. They got rid of another forty students, Tommy Dugan included.

I didn't call my parents. I was too ashamed to go home with my tail between my legs. Instead, I moved into our apartment and hatched a crazy plan to go to California. I didn't know anyone there, or what I would do, but I wanted to get as far away as possible.

A few days later I heard a knock on the door. I opened it up and there was Dad. I played dumb. "Dad," I said, "what are you doing here?"

"I know you were kicked out," he said. My older sister was still at Marquette and she told my parents what happened. "You've got to come back home with me."

I didn't fight very hard to stay. I was still a homebody, and once again my father found a way to forgive me. Only this time, I thought, I had learned my lesson. All my little gangster ways—the stealing, the card playing—had been my undoing at Marquette. I was finally ready to straighten out and go absolutely legit.

As far as my father was concerned, there was no question about continuing my education. Dad never forgave himself for not finishing college and he wasn't going to let me make the same mistake. But now I'd have to take a rougher route to that degree: night school, and day jobs to pay tuition.

I applied to Loyola in downtown Chicago. Like Marquette, the college was run by Jesuits. My grades were good enough to get in, but I was rejected when I told them I had been kicked out of Marquette. I needed Dad again. He went to the priest in admissions, and was given an impossible Catch-22. They would accept me only if Marquette would take me back. Dad took me to Marquette and we sat down with the Father who was dean of students. Dad did all the pleading. He said I had learned the error of my ways. I was ready to return home and do penance working my way through Loyola. All I needed was this one letter from Marquette before I could embark on the path to my redemption. The Father agreed to send a letter to Loyola indicating that they would "consider" my re-admission to Marquette. But he made it perfectly clear, consideration was one thing, acceptance was another. Marquette wanted nothing more to do with me. As far as I was concerned, the feeling was mutual.

Once I had gotten into Loyola, I had to figure a way to pay for it, and that was no picnic either. I was a nineteen-year-old with a high school degree. The best-paying job I could find was at the Ford Stamping Plant, where they made parts like car doors. Now I would truly understand the value of a college education. Every morning, my father woke me up at the crack of dawn and dropped me off at the plant on his way to work. For the next eight hours I went through backbreaking hell: pushing around slabs of steel, lifting whole doors on the conveyor belt, welding with sparks flying all over my face and hair. I would just get used to one job before they shifted me to another. I went through each day like a dishrag through a wringer. And after I hitchhiked home, I couldn't collapse into bed. I had to change clothes, grab my books, and then take a bus and an El train to Loyola for night school. I didn't get home until after ten. It was, to put it bluntly, a motherfucker.

After two months of this, I was not a happy camper. I was sore. I was exhausted. I was angry as hell—at the world and at myself. One night when I got home from school, my parents were still entertaining another cop who lived a few blocks from us. His nickname was Tiny and he must have weighed 270 pounds. He was a big fat slob and no doubt crooked as hell. How else could he have lived in a halfway decent house and bought a new car every few years? He used to mock my father for having a second job.

I was in no mood to talk to Tiny. My mother put some dinner out for me, and I pulled the plates over to the other end of the table. "Look who's here," Tiny said. "The guy that flunked out of Marquette. You think you're real sharp, don't you?"

"Yeah?" I said. "You're the one who's got a fucking idiot for a kid. *He* flunked out. I didn't flunk out of anywhere."

Getting "kicked out" instead of "flunking out" may have been a fine distinction, but in any case, my dad was not going to stick up for me.

"You have no right to talk back like that to our guests," he said.

"I don't have to take his crap."

Then Dad stood up and pointed toward the door. "If you don't like the rules in my house, then you get out."

Without saying a word, I got up from the table. I packed my suitcase and walked out the door. I was fed up with my job. I was fed up with school. I was fed up with my father for being such a hard-working sucker.

I didn't tell my parents where I was going, which made my exit all the more dramatic. I had hooked up again with my old friend Tommy Dugan. After he got kicked out of Marquette, he couldn't go back home. Instead, he found a shitty little apartment near Rush Street, the city's nightclub district, and a few blocks from Loyola. But this wasn't the same old Evil John. He was going to night school at another college and, like me, working during the day at some menial job.

Dugan and I were back together, like two peas in a pod. Although we were determined to clean up our act, we were still too smart for our own good. One night we got home to find that the electric company had cut off our power. Tommy had forgotten to pay the bill. We could see a light on in the vacant apartment next door to us, so Tommy broke in and we ran extension cords through the windows. The other apartment was not such a bad place. It was still furnished, and since we had gotten inside, we figured we could use it as our study hall. This went on for a few days until one night the door suddenly opened and there was the landlord, trying to show the apartment to a prospective tenant. The guy started yelling like he had caught a couple of burglars. It's not like we had stolen anything. I told him to shut up and the next thing I knew, we were slugging it out.

So much for my attempt at independent living. The landlord ended up calling the cops, and I had to hightail it out of there. I packed the few things I had, and by three in the morning, I was back on the South Side of Chicago. I snuck into the basement of our house and slept there for a few hours, until I heard my parents in the kitchen.

I trudged upstairs with a hangdog expression on my face. The Prodigal Son had returned—after just ten days in exile. Right away my mother asked, "What happened? Did you get thrown out of the place you were in?"

"Oh, no," I said, "I just decided to come home."

My father shushed my mother. "It's great to see you," he said. "Sure you're okay?"

We sat down and had a long talk. He had never expected me to pick up and leave the house that way, but he asked that I not do things that showed disrespect. I promised it would never happen again.

The clapper had swung back toward the Saints. I was home with my parents, more determined than ever to go on the straight and narrow. I really did want to finish college. But getting a good job was the problem. No way would I go back to the factory again. Although office work was easier, it didn't pay enough to make ends meet. I even enlisted in the Marines for an ROTC-type pilot training program during the summer of 1962, but as tensions started to build with the Soviet Union, the program was canceled.

Suddenly, only one occupation made any sense. It was a job that would pay a decent salary and not take me too far from home. It was a job that would pay college tuition as long as I got good grades. It was a job that was as much a part of my family as the Catholic Church and our Irish name.

That July, at the age of twenty, I would become a cop.

CHAPTER 3

MARCO & THE COUNT

There are incidents in my life that seem so unreal, they play out in my memory like scenes in a nightmare.

One night, in the summer of 1966, I woke up, racked with pain. Through a haze, I saw someone looking at me. His face was bandaged, and the skin that showed through was discolored. He waved arms at me with only bandaged stumps where hands should be.

I was in a hospital bed, and much of my own body was wrapped up in casts and bandages. My ribs and collarbone were broken, my leg crushed. But nothing hurt me more than my left hand. It had been pierced and nearly severed—as though a stake had been driven through the palm. For a while, when I was still semi-conscious, the doctors debated amputation. The guy with the stumps had lost his hands when they melted off in the furnace of a steel mill. Every time he passed my room, he had to look in on me. I guess he figured I was about to join the club.

The doctors did not have to amputate my hand, but it took several more surgeries and months of convalescence before I could leave that hospital room. I had only vague memories of the fight that put me there. I had just arrived home from work one evening. Before I stepped into the house, I decided to go to confession in the church across the street. It was probably the first time I had gone in months. As I left church, I could see the girl who had been in the confessional ahead of me. She was with a bunch of kids from the local street gang, and they were pulling her between the houses across the street. That didn't look right. I ran over and waded into the middle of the pack. When I asked the girl if she was all right, she turned and grabbed me with a look of terror on her face. I put my arm over her shoulder to lead her away from there, and the gang started kicking and punching me. I tried to fight back, but I was getting the shit beat out of me. In the distance, I could hear sirens wailing. Hoping that someone had called the cops, I tried to hold on to one or two of the gangbangers, even as they kept punching me in the head. As I lost consciousness, they pushed me into the street—just as a squad car came to my rescue. The car ran completely over my body. The other cops pulled me out from under the back wheels.

After the doctors decided I could keep my hand, they wondered whether I would walk again without a limp. There were other questions about metal rods, pins, and scar tissue. I had just turned twenty-five, entering the prime of my life. I was not ready to confront these matters of life and limb. Until this point in time, I had felt indestructible. Suddenly my body—and life itself—seemed so fragile.

I wasn't left alone to curse my bad luck. Unlike the guy with melted hands, I had plenty of visitors: family, friends, cops, and even commanders. No one came more often than my dad. He would sit by my bed for hours and talk to me. Perhaps he thought about what happened to *his* father. Maybe he was sorry he encouraged me to join the force. I was off-duty when the fight happened, but I probably would have stayed away if I had been a civilian. Whether or not Dad felt guilty, he still had his faith to fall back on. "God must have had a reason for this," he would tell me. "God must have had some reason."

Not as far as I was concerned.

I had tried to be good. No one could have asked me to work harder as a cop, or to be more fearless. I thought this earned me some measure of redemption for my carousing days in high school and college. If there was any justice in the world, I did not deserve this suffering for trying to help that girl. I had even gone to confession, for Christ's sake.

More than that, I had been a model citizen ever since I moved back with the family and joined the police force. I stuck with night school and got my undergraduate degree from Loyola, and although I had become a cop primarily to earn my way through school, I fell in love with the job right from the start.

Back then, you got just twelve weeks in the Police Academy before they put you on the street with a badge and a gun. They called it "in-service training." In fact, during the early sixties, the crime rate was sky-rocketing and commanders had to throw the rookies into the line of fire. Because I wanted to work out of a station near our house, I first got assigned to the Third District, the roughest in the city. It was home to Chicago's most notorious gang, called the Black Stone Rangers (Black-stone was the street where I lived). With all the drug dealing and gang rivalries, there were constant shootings and stabbings.

My father then got me transferred to the Fourth, not nearly as rough, but still with enough excitement to make the job interesting. I was more suited to police work than breaking my back in a factory or sitting around in an office. Most of my young life I was getting into fights all the time to prove myself. Finally I was getting paid to do it. Better yet, I'd never had a car before. In the police department I could drive around all day.

For the first six months on the force, they wouldn't let me go out in a squad car alone, so my biggest problem was finding other coppers who wanted to ride with me. They all thought I was crazy. With every dangerous call—a shooting or a man with a gun—I raced to the scene. Even when the calls weren't ours, I picked up the mike and said, "Four-oh-two. We're clear to go." I'd crank up the siren, run red lights, anything to get there first.

This got the older cops real nervous. "Relax," they'd say, "what's your hurry?" They wanted to be the *last* to arrive. They would beg me to slow down. "Listen, I got a wife. I got kids," they'd say.

I dumped the partners as soon as I could. When I rode the squad by myself, I had a nose for trouble and made some unbelievable arrests: for robbery, auto theft, burglary, rapes; you name it. I was written up in the neighborhood paper all the time. Most of my pinches came on flukes. I'd see a car that looked out of place, and I'd follow it. If the driver suddenly took off, I'd know something was wrong. When I'd go chasing these guys, I didn't like to lose them—even if I had to run a red light. Twice I had very bad accidents where I demolished the squad I was driving, but each time I walked away without a scratch. The last time it happened was just a week before my beating.

When the district commander came to visit me in the hospital, he didn't pat me on the head like everyone else. He reminded me about the car crashes and said, "It's like you have a death wish. There's more to life than this. You have to start looking out for yourself, too."

It was one of those life-changing moments. I thought, "Yeah. He's right. Here I am, busting my ass for the force, busting my ass for school, and I have nothing to show for it." I was living at home, and I still had to take second jobs to make spending money. Where was the hard work and sacrifice taking me?

There's more to life than this. Now I heard that message loud and clear. It rang even louder with another horrible event that swirled around me in the hospital. Often, so I could sleep, I got an injection of morphine from a young Filipino student nurse. One night she mysteriously missed her shift. A few hours later, she and seven other student nurses, including a girl I had dated, were found dead in a nearby rooming house. They were all the victims of a twisted vagrant named Richard Speck. The murders horrified the nation. Fate could be so insane and so cruel. Sure, I'd had a rotten break, but I was still alive and, unlike that steel worker, I still had both my hands. Friends and family, too. When he looked in my room and saw all my visitors, he probably wished for *my* luck. I had options he could only dream about. As the weeks followed, and my pain lifted, I had no interest in rushing back to work. I needed to make another plan for my future.

For the first time, I started thinking about a real "career." Two years earlier, almost on a lark, I had begun law school at Chicago-Kent College of Law, part of the Illinois Institute of Technology. My major motivation was to get a student deferment from the draft. I never took school that seriously, and would use any excuse to skip a class or drop a course. Although my injuries now meant I wouldn't have to worry about the draft, suddenly the law career looked more promising than before. As a result of the arrests I made, I sat through a lot of trials. Like other cops, I had contempt for most of the gasbags who pranced around the courtroom. But from what I could see, criminal lawyers didn't work that much, and they were certainly making more money than cops. The actual schoolwork wasn't hard for me. I just had to buckle down and do the studying.

It took a year before I returned to police duty, and when I came back, I wasn't so eager to be the crash test dummy. As kind of a Purple Heart for my injuries, the police commanders served me a bunch of plum assignments, and I was not shy about taking them. Finally, in the fall of 1968, they put me in line for the dream job of every cop in Chicago—Rush Street District Vice Squad.

Rush Street was the most happening place in the city. More than a street, it was several blocks of bars, clubs, and restaurants. They were all wedged between the fancy Michigan Avenue shopping district and the townhouses and high-rises of the Gold Coast, the city's wealthiest neighborhood. The lakefront lay just a few hundred yards away, with all its beaches and fabulous people-watching in warm weather.

The sixties' revolutions in sex, music, and drugs all converged on Rush Street's corners. Here were the city's big singles bars, where frat boys pounded beers and tried to pick up coeds. Here were the go-go clubs, where platinum blondes bounced around on pedestals, and where guys with tans and gold chains peeked under their miniskirts. People came to get high. People came to get screwed. On weekend nights there was such a crush of pedestrians, all traffic would grind to a halt. For any red-blooded male cop, whatever your age or marital condition, this was where you wanted to work *and* hang out. After all my years on the gritty streets of the South Side, I could finally spend my days and nights in Club Land. I could even wear plain clothes when I was working. Better yet, my law school was five minutes away.

My first day in the district, they scheduled me for a night shift. I went to roll call with the rest of the guys and shook hands all around. A lieutenant, who was the Vice coordinator, came over and introduced me to another officer and said he'd be my partner. That night we were assigned to cover Old Town, a mile from Rush Street, and more of a hippie place, like San Francisco's Haight-Ashbury. The lieutenant said, "I want you to get the lay of the land, but if you see anything go down, you call me or my sergeant before you take any action. Especially if it's related to a restaurant, a club, or a bar. You don't make any arrests until you get permission."

I thought that was unusual, but Vice was not as cut and dried as robbery or traffic stops. Maybe I had to get my feet wet first.

Then he looked at me out of the corner of his eye and lowered his voice. "At the first of each month," he said, "you'll find five hundred dollars in your locker. If something else comes our way, you get a percentage of that, too."

I just nodded. It didn't take a rocket scientist to figure out where that money was coming from.

I went out with my partner and we walked around Old Town. He took me to see the managers and owners of the bars and clubs, and he introduced me like I was the new fucking beer salesman. It was clear he would never bust these guys, even if we found dope fiends shooting up in their bathrooms. I got bad vibes about the whole thing. I was no Pollyanna. There were times on the South Side when somebody left some cash on my squad seat or picked up my tab at lunch; but if I caught you committing a felony, you were under arrest, and no amount of money was going to buy you out of that.

When we returned to the station house for our break, I pulled the lieutenant to the side. "I'll go along with the program," I told him. "I just don't want any money in my locker. I'm in my last year of law school. If something like this comes back to haunt me, I could lose my license. I've worked too hard for that."

He nodded and said, "All right."

We finished our shift at four-thirty in the morning and went back to the station to check out. When I passed the desk sergeant, he looked up at me and said, "Report here the day after tomorrow at eight A.M. You're back in uniform."

I lasted just one day in Vice. That was probably the world record. But it was okay with me. If they were kissing me off, I could kiss them off, too. As I took the bus home that night, I thought, "Great. My days of police work are over. I'm just going to go through the motions until I finish law school and wave good-bye."

When I showed up at the station the next day, they didn't know what to do with me, so they assigned me to the "umbrella" car. It was shit duty. You were supposed to hang around in case they needed back-up, but nobody wanted back-up from the kind of mopes they assigned to umbrella cars. You just sat in the squad all day until your shift was over.

By the time I got to the car, another patrolman was already behind the wheel. His name was Ricky Borelli. He was a big pudgy guy with walrus jowls and black curly hair. Usually, his hat was on crooked and his tie screwed around. A collar could be pointing up or a button undone. On any other day, Ricky would have been out walking his do-nothing beat. But he had committed some minor infraction, and this was to be his punishment—shoved with me into the umbrella car like two cigarette butts in an ashtray.

After the initial introductions, we cruised around the district. I had trouble getting more than a few words out of him. When we reached the Old Town area, he pulled into a side street and parked the car. He said to me, "Do you want to play some cards?"

"Sure," I said. He pulled out a pack and we started to play gin. He was an excellent gin player (it was about all Ricky could do well), but I wasn't bad either. After a couple of games, he said, "Do you want to play for something?" We spent the next few hours playing for small change. He won some and I won some. He opened up a little more and we had a chat. I let him know I was in law school and would be leaving the force before long.

The next day they assigned me to my own car, but Ricky approached me after roll call and said, "You want to come and have breakfast across the street?" They had a big diner-type restaurant there. I figured, "What the hell?" I was always hungry.

While we were eating, Ricky asked, "Have you ever bet sports?"

"No."

"I do some betting myself," he said. "What I'm looking for is some-body to call in some bets for me."

Over the next few minutes, Ricky explained to me the basics of book-making. He called his bets in to an "office"—really no more than a phone number. Bookies might have more than one office, but they never wanted too much riding on one game. So they limited each gambler to betting $500 per game. Ricky wanted me to call in and pretend I was just another gambler. But he would tell me what to bet and give me the money if he lost. If he won, I would collect his take and turn it over. At the end of the week, I could keep a hundred dollars for my services.

I knew this was all illegal, but it was fascinating as hell. I always had a gambling streak. Even when I was a kid, I pitched pennies. I made much bigger money playing cards at Marquette. I never saw the harm in a little action. Besides, I had a good head for numbers—accounting was my minor in school.

I caught on quicker than Ricky expected. After a few days, I could see that he was an addicted gambler and a terminal loser. He lost on most of the bets he had me place. I knew I could do better. After the third week, instead of putting the entire $500 on a bet I knew he would lose, I would keep $130 for myself.

Making my own bets with Rick's money was not as ballsy as it seems. Early on, I realized that success in gambling had very little to with your knowledge about a particular sport. In fact, that knowledge could be a dangerous thing—especially for a knucklehead like Ricky. He always bet his personal favorites, like Notre Dame. Instead, good bettors played one bookie off against another. If you were smart and you weren't too greedy, you either won a little money or you won a little more money, but you seldom lost everything.

To give myself a cushion, I always gave odds to Ricky that were slightly worse than the ones I was actually getting. When Ricky lost the bet, he paid me more than I had to pay the bookie.

My chance for a big payoff came on the spread—the points separating the winning and losing teams when you bet basketball and football. I could bet on the favorite with a bookie who had them winning by *six* points against the underdog. I could also bet on the underdog with another bookie who had the favorite winning by *ten* points. If the favorites won by seven, eight or nine points, I won both of my bets—a payoff of twenty to one.

The real secret to sports betting was to know as many bookies as possible. I used all of Ricky's contacts to my advantage and started to make bets on my own. At this point, my salary as a policeman was $5,600 a year. One week after I learned to cover Ricky's bets, I won $2,000—what then seemed an unbelievable sum. And the way I was playing with Ricky, there was no way I could lose. I was only concerned that he would come up lame paying off his losing bets. But he didn't. Not for a couple of years.

On rare occasions, the police force still needed our services. The commander would put out an emergency call, and we all had to show up at the station. One time it was to put down a riot at Cabrini Green, a huge complex of dilapidated high-rise housing projects. It stretched over several blocks and had more than 20,000 residents. The squad cars that responded to the first calls were hit by sniper fire from the upper floors of one building. They didn't have SWAT teams in those days. Instead, the commander's response to any crisis was to throw more patrolmen into the fray. A bunch of us were packed into a police wagon and sent over. Before I left, I took my own weapon out of my locker—an automatic carbine rifle. I had plenty of experience with riots and snipers on the South Side, and I wasn't going to get caught in crossfire with just my service revolver. That was like standing in the open with your prick in your hands.

We pulled into one of the Cabrini Green parking lots, and somebody started shooting at us as soon as we got out of the wagon. I could see it was just one guy running along the outer balconies that encircled the building. As soon as I saw the sniper climb the stairs to a higher floor, I raced into the building. He was trying to kill me. I was going to kill him first. I got off a few shots with my carbine, but I didn't hit him. He disappeared into one of the units. When I came back downstairs, I realized I was the only cop who had gone in. All the others had stayed outside, ducking for cover, including Ricky.

It was another of my crazy stunts, but it certainly earned me stripes with Ricky. He wanted me to meet someone. One day at breakfast, he brought along his cousin, Marco D'Amico. Like Ricky, Marco appeared to be in his mid-thirties. He was of medium height and build. Nobody you'd look at twice. The strangest thing about him was his high, arching eyebrows, and his constant smirk. Both made him look almost like Jack Nicholson.

The first few times we met, in the restaurant across the street from the police station, Marco couldn't have been nicer. He was real impressed that I was in law school. Ricky kept talking up how I ran into Cabrini

Green with the carbine and all the balls I had. But mostly we talked about gambling. I figured Marco was a bookie and no more than that.

Now I had all kinds of money in my pocket—for the first time in my life. I hit Rush Street with my friends at least two or three nights a week. I had finally moved out of my parents' house, first to a little studio apartment closer to work. But after I started gambling, I could afford the step up to a one-bedroom apartment in a new glass-wall high-rise that was part of a redevelopment complex. A few of the buildings shared an outdoor pool. It was not as fancy as the Gold Coast, but it was heaven for me. Perched twenty-seven stories above the ground, I had floor-to-ceiling views of the skyline and the sunset. Below me, the western suburbs seemed to stretch out forever, flat as a pool table.

I couldn't have been prouder of my new little crib, and I had my friends over to check it out. Just like in college, I started organizing poker games, only this time the stakes were much higher. I supplied food and whatever booze they wanted. Still, I would never drink when I played cards. To me, the card games were a business that could bring in a few thousand a week, and I didn't want to affect my judgment. It was fine if everyone else got drunk as skunks, because they would just play worse and worse.

Ricky and Marco were up all the time, and they would bring a couple friends of theirs to play. Meanwhile, I started making my own network of friends from Rush Street. These were all people who had money and didn't mind blowing a few thousand. One night, when Marco and Ricky didn't come, a good friend of mine from the clubs brought along a new player named Eddie Corrado. He was kind of a greasy little guy with a big mouth, but he behaved just fine during the game.

As usual, I had a terrific night. When everyone got up to go, Eddie asked if he could stick around and play a little blackjack with me. The way my luck was running, I figured there would be no harm. But my luck quickly turned. Nothing I did was right. We switched decks back and forth. He was the dealer. I was the dealer. It didn't matter. I always lost. After playing less than an hour, I owed him $6,000. I had about $2,500 in cash and I gave him a check to cover the balance.

The whole experience shook my confidence. But something didn't seem quite right. The next day, when I saw Ricky at breakfast, I told him the story, even though it was pretty embarrassing.

"Wait a second," Ricky said. "What was that guy's name?"

When I told him who it was, Ricky said, "Stop payment on that check. He's a card cheat." Ricky called Marco, who told me to arrange for Eddie to come to my apartment when they were there. They would help me work it out.

The next night, Eddie showed up at my apartment, and he was not happy. He brought along some big goon who started giving me a squinty-eye stare from the moment I opened the door.

Eddie strutted into my foyer like a tough guy. "You motherfucker," he said. "You got a lot of balls passing a bad check to me."

I shut the door behind them, and they rounded the corner from the foyer, just as Marco came out of the bathroom. The blood completely drained from Eddie's face. The goon froze, too. In that instant, I realized that Marco was much more powerful than some bookie, and much more dangerous.

Eddie practically fell to his knees. "I didn't know he was a friend of yours," he pleaded to Marco. "Please, please. I didn't realize it."

Marco was calm and matter-of-fact. He made Eddie empty the cash out of all his pockets and hand it over to me. Ricky then walked Eddie and the collector out the door. After they left, Marco counted the cash. It added up to $4,500. He gave me my $2,500 and kept the rest for himself.

It turned out that Eddie had made the mistake of winning a lot of money from Marco a year before. Marco found out that he was a card cheat and arranged for another game at his house. When Eddie arrived, they took him into the basement and beat the living fuck out of him. Marco was still pretty impressed that Eddie cheated me. After that night in my apartment, he put Eddie in card games with wealthy guys and would take a cut of whatever Eddie won.

Eventually, Marco invited me to his "club" to play cards. It was a storefront, with boarded-up windows, on the west side of town—which I took to be Marco's territory. Inside were huge rooms with card tables.

A few booths were up front. Nothing very fancy. They had a kitchen way in the back, but they rarely served food. Still, the place was always full with two or three dozen people. Except for a break on Sunday, the club was open around the clock. Everyone seemed like a bunch of fun guys, just playing cards and hanging out. At first, I thought they were all gamblers or bookies. Only later did I find out that the club members were a who's-who of West Side bad guys—burglars, car thieves, and stick-up men. Some cops and sheriff's deputies, too. Quite a cast of characters.

Eventually I'd come to learn that gambling was literally the life's blood of the Mob. It was their work and their play—almost as much of an obsession with them as making money. Even though they knew better, almost all of them bet, and it was all they talked about. My own love for gambling—whether on cards or sports—got me instant credibility and acceptance.

With the contacts I made through Marco, my sports betting circles grew wider and I started winning all kinds of money. Often Marco knew exactly how much I won. I figured that some of these bookies really worked for him. Before long, Marco asked to be my "partner." He would stake me, so I could make more bets as long as he got a piece of what I won.

This meant I could get action with that many more bookies. I said, "Great. I'll call you each day and tell you what we have going."

"No need to," he replied. "I trust you."

After I started playing with Marco, the bets started to mushroom. On any given day, I could be playing with ten bookmakers. I would meet some down on Rush Street and they would introduce me to some others. Word got out that I was good pay and had big money. It got to the point where bookies from all over the country got in touch with me. On some Saturdays during football season, I had a million dollars in play.

The gambling did not leave much time for police work, but that didn't matter. By this time, I developed a good routine to deal with my extracurricular activity. I started each morning at seven-thirty. I would show up for roll call, pick up a portable radio phone, and off I'd go. My beat was Cabrini Green. Nobody else wanted it, and they stopped letting squad cars go over there because they became targets for the snipers. But I didn't care. I would take my own car, a GTO—I was rolling in money now—and park right against a building, so the snipers couldn't get an angle to shoot at it from their windows. Then I'd grab my radio and just stroll around. They had a school there, and I might wander in and wave at the kids. Maybe help some old lady with her groceries. At most, it would take ninety minutes to do my circuit. Then I would get in my car and drive home, which was less than a mile away. I'd park my car in the underground garage, go up to my apartment, and just keep my radio on as I went about my business. On rare occasions, a sergeant might call in to check up on me. He was supposed to meet me on the beat, but all these guys were too scared of Cabrini to sneak around there. Instead, he'd have me drive to a street corner near the station house. "Is everything okay?" he'd ask.

"Yeah," I'd say. "Everything is okay." Then I was free to go on my way.

During the summer, it was even nicer. I rented a cabana by the outdoor pool my building shared in the complex. Usually the only other residents who hung out during the daytime were stewardesses between flights. I had a little refrigerator in the cabana and an extension for my home phone. The pool area was elevated, so you couldn't see it from the street. It was like my private sanctuary. Ricky would drop by and sometimes he brought along other cops he was friendly with. Even some sergeants. We'd sit around, gab with the stews and drink some beers. In the afternoon, I called in my bets from the pool. Sergeant Bilko never had it better.

I was making plenty of money and having lots of fun, but I was more determined than ever to start my legal career. Through gambling and Marco, I met a lot of people who had trouble with the law. I figured I could build a nice criminal practice around them. In the summer of 1970, I graduated law school and took two weeks off to study for the bar. I never had problems with tests, so I was sure I'd passed, but just in case, I kept my job on the police force until it was official.

One afternoon, when I stopped back in the station to return my radio, the desk sergeant said there was someone waiting for me. At first glance, I thought this was some sort of joke. My visitor was a tall muscular guy in a yellow fishnet leotard and a purple cape. He had a helmet of tight jet-black curly hair and a meticulously trimmed Fu Manchu moustache and beard. He looked like something out of a comic book. In fact, for several years he ran an ad in the back of comic books that showed him scowling and contorting his hands. The ad touted him as the "Deadliest Man Alive," and offered "The World's Deadliest Fighting Secrets" if you joined his Black Dragon Fighting Society.

He called himself Count Juan Raphael Dante, and he claimed to be descended from Spanish nobility. He owned a couple of karate schools and said that he was the master of all the major martial arts and inventor of his own form of combat called, "The Dan-Te (Deadly Hands) System." His materials made a bunch of other wild claims: that he had served as a mercenary for Fidel Castro, that in China he had won three death matches against "the world's foremost fistic and grappling arts masters," and so on and so forth. In fact, Count Dante was another crazy Irish kid from the South Side of Chicago. His real name was John Keehan. "Dante" was the name of a street near where we grew up. From a South Side perspective, he *was* something of an aristocrat. His father was a doctor, and he lived in a wealthy neighborhood, where Tommy Dugan and I would pick fights with the rich kids. It was Tommy who sent him my way. As everyone in the station house stood there gawking at us, Count Dante grabbed my elbow and looked at me with piercing blue eyes. "I have this serious problem," he said, "and I want to know if you can help me."

I took him up to a room on the second floor where we could have some privacy. The Count's "serious problem" was a murder charge, stemming from his invasion of a competing karate studio called Black Cobra Hall. The school's owner had called him a pussy or something like that, and the Count decided he had to defend his honor. Black Cobra Hall was in a strip mall, but they had the outside done up like a castle with a huge wooden door. The Count didn't wait for anyone to answer the bell. According to the police report, he made his entrance by tearing the door off its hinges. Inside, a class was being held with two dozen students, but Count

Dante, with just three of his own students, was ready to fight everybody. One Black Cobra teacher came after the Count with a mace. The Count did that thing with his fingers and ripped the guy's eye out. Unfortunately, Jim, the Count's right-hand man, wasn't that quick and he got run through with a spear. When the Count saw that, he beat a hasty retreat. Jim got a block away before he fell over dead with the spear still inside him.

The Count was arrested and charged with aggravated battery for pulling the guy's eye out. They also charged him with murder under an arcane law known as the Accountability Statute. Since the Count had broken into Black Cobra Hall and started the fight, he was being held "accountable" for his student's death.

The Count wanted no less than a total acquittal on all the charges. "I'm claustrophobic," he said. "If I go to prison, I'll go totally crazy. I can't be confined." He had already hired a big-time South Side lawyer, but the guy would not offer any guarantees. Tommy Dugan told the Count about me: how I was a cop and hung around with mobsters like Marco D'Amico. The Count figured I could pull strings that a straight lawyer wouldn't touch.

I still didn't know if I had passed the bar—I was expecting to hear any day—but as I sat there, listening to this crazy story, I truly believed I could help the Count. "If I can't handle your case," I said, "I'll find a lawyer who can."

He pulled out a wad of bills and paid me a $5,000 retainer on the spot. "I just feel I can trust you," he said, "and that you'll get me out of this."

I have yet to meet anyone else with the Count's amazing combination of talents and flaws. Besides being an expert in the martial arts, he was also a beautician (a supermarket tabloid ran a story about him with the headline "THE WORLD'S DEADLIEST FIGHTER IS A . . . HAIRDRESSER!"). In addition to the karate studios, he owned hairdressing schools. Supposedly, he got involved with martial arts while he traveled through Asia for a wig import business. He did hairstyling for *Playboy*, and somehow that gave him an entree to the whole world of pornography and led to a financial interest in a string of adult book stores. At one moment he could be extremely sophisticated and artistic, and at the next moment crude and ridiculously macho—even more than the Mob guys.

We started to hang out together during the months leading up to the trial. He was living with two different Playboy bunnies, and one was always available for his friends to screw. At night, he took me to parties at the Playboy Mansion, which was just a few blocks from Rush Street. It was a bizarre place, always packed with people. I remember some floors that were a maze of little dark rooms. You would turn one corner and bump into a movie star. You'd turn the next corner and see a couple humping. The Count loved it all, and they loved him. He was a total sex maniac, and he was as flamboyant as anyone from Hollywood. During the day, wearing the cape and leotard, he walked his pet mountain lion along the lakefront. Did that ever attract the girls in the bikinis! He was a babe magnet in every way.

But like Jim—the guy who got the spear in his chest—I discovered that hanging with the Count wasn't always fun and games. One weekend, he invited me to come to his house for a party. Despite all of his money, he still kept a home on the South Side in a pretty rough neighborhood. While the party was going on, we went out to pick up some more beer and wine. He drove a brown Cadillac and on one of the doors, he had this phony crest for the Dante noble family with some kind of Spanish writing. We parked the car in the liquor store lot. As we got out, we saw these two Mexican guys who had apparently been drinking. They pointed at that crest and started laughing. The Count said something to them in Spanish and they said something back. I thought they were all joking around. But when I looked at the Count, I saw this terrifying anger rise up in him. His head became very still. Darkness shrouded his face, and his eyes started to bulge. Then, like a volcano, he blew, whirling first at the biggest of the two Mexicans. Using the middle three fingers of his hand, he made quick raking motions across the guy's face, and in an instant, the Mexican was writhing on the ground, bleeding from his eye and nose. Then he turned on the second guy and took him out as quickly. Behind me, I saw a car door fly open and a guy who must have been their buddy came running over. I decked him myself. Even if I broke his jaw I did him a favor. God knows what would have happened to him if he had faced the Count alone.

In a matter of three minutes, we had the three guys on the ground. I said, "Count, we better go. Remember, you're still out on bond." As we drove away, I tried to explain how delicate his legal situation was. The judge had released him on a murder charge. Virtually any other arrest would put him in jail until the trial was over. But the Count didn't want to hear my legal bullshit. Instead, he kept crowing about how I had clocked that Mexican in the parking lot. He had to tell everyone at the party what a tough guy I was. The next week, when we went out, I didn't want him going to a crowded club. I figured it would only take a few bumps to set him off again. Instead, we went to a real quiet place near his house. Most of the other customers were steelworkers who had just come off a shift. They were caked with grime and sweat. The Count, as usual, was dressed in one of his crazy cape and leotard outfits. He got up to go to the bathroom, and wouldn't you know, one of those hard-hats had to call him a fruit. I heard tables and chairs crashing. I ran back in time to see the Count with one hand on some big lug's throat and the other on his chest. He then literally lifted him off his feet and threw him through the plate glass window. Everyone else just froze in shock. I grabbed the Count and again we ran for the hills. The guy was nothing less than a walking powder keg.

A few weeks later, I learned that I had passed the bar. I had a big party in my apartment to celebrate. I bought a barrel, and inside it mixed champagne with vodka and brandy. Everybody got smashed pretty quickly with that concoction, but if I made a mistake mixing my drinks, I probably made a bigger one by mixing my guests. I invited my friends from the singles bars on Rush Street, who all made their living in perfectly legitimate ways. But I invited Marco, Ricky, and their crew, too, along with some other apes who were always good for a few laughs. One of these guys, John, was in the vending machine business. He liked to act like a big shot and throw his money around. He had his own little entourage, but he was always the biggest loser at our card games. Later that night, when we were both sloshed, John cornered me. Now that he was drunk, all his anger and petty jealousy rose to the surface. He asked what I would do if he took a glass of champagne and spilled it on me. I said, "You do that, and I'll bust your fucking head open."

John replied by tossing his champagne in my face, and I slugged him. His bodyguard pushed through the crowd and punched me, but then Marco and his guys piled on him and beat both John and his goon to a pulp. Then we literally picked them up off the floor and threw them into the hall.

When I walked back inside, I saw that all kinds of things had been smashed during the fight, but worse was the look on the faces of my legitimate friends. They were all stunned. I'm sure they had never seen that level of violence. A few minutes later, every one of them left. Of course John, who took most of the beating, sobered up and approached me at the pool a few days later to apologize for being out of line. But my legitimate friends didn't get over the fight as easily as John. They had seen a part of my life that scared the hell out of them. In the future I would be careful about who I mixed with my Mob friends and clients, and, to the best of my ability, I always tried to keep the two worlds apart.

Literally from the day I quit the police force, I had legal work—clients arrested for gambling, drunk driving, or dope busts. But I figured I needed much more high-level courtroom experience before I could tackle Count Dante's trial. As luck would have it, I got a call from Bill Murphy, my old friend from Marquette. He was now a public defender and he had come across an indigent client named Donald Kristman, who badly needed representation. He had been arrested for robbing and killing a jeweler on the north side of Chicago. Bill had seen enough of the police reports to think Kristman might be innocent, but he couldn't free up the time to take on another client. "Maybe you can get some practice on this case," he said.

I went and met with Kristman in his jail cell. He was a very big, scary-looking guy who had held down a job in the sewers for several years. He just had the bad luck of cashing a check near the murder scene. The wife of the victim picked him out of a lineup. Since he was an ex-con, they got away with pinning the rap on him. I believed his story and took his case for $500, the only fee he could afford.

Marco couldn't believe I would take peanuts on a case with so much stacked against me. In truth, I would have *paid* Kristman to be his lawyer. I wanted the challenge of a jury trial with everything on the line—at least as far as Kristman was concerned. If I had joined a big firm, they would have made me wait years for such an opportunity.

When the trial got underway and the victim's wife took the stand, I wondered what I had gotten myself into. During my cross-examination, she cried and said, "I could never forget the face of the man who killed my husband."

The next day, during the lunch break, I was at a bar near the courthouse consoling myself, when I saw a policeman who had been a good friend of mine. He came over and sat next to me. He said, "Bob, they're fucking around with you and withholding a report on this case. I can't tell you exactly what it is, but I thought you should know."

I knew this cop to be a very straight shooter and I trusted him completely. I went right from the bar to the courtroom—finally with a card up my sleeve. I didn't know if it was an ace, but it was something. This judge happened to be Jewish. The victim was Jewish too, and an important part of his community, so you know the judge was not well disposed to my client. But I approached the bench very respectfully, and I said, "Judge, I just found out about a police report regarding this case that the state is not giving me, and the state's attorneys know all about it." I had to bluff if I was going to pull this off.

We went back into chambers and the prosecutors were all upset. They wanted to know who told me about the report. I said I wasn't going to give up the policeman's name, but he was very trustworthy and he had no reason to lie. When the prosecutors kept insisting that I reveal his name, I stood up and said, "Judge, if I have to, I'll go out now and find that policeman, and let him know that they are still hiding that report. Maybe he'll be so outraged, he'll reveal his identity on his own."

This didn't make the judge very happy at all. "You walk out that door," he said, "and I'll hold you in contempt for disrupting this trial."

I kept walking. I didn't know what would happen if I tried to make good on the threat. Suddenly, one of the prosecutors jumped up and said, "Wait, Judge. I think I know what he's talking about." They then went downstairs and came back up with the report. It was the Witness Identification Report that the cops had filled out when the victim's wife fingered my client. I had already seen a *copy* of that, but then I looked at the very bottom of the original. It had a "PS"—the witness called back the detectives a few hours after the lineup to say she had second thoughts about the ID. Somehow that PS got cut off on my copy. The judge wouldn't let me put the victim's wife back on the stand, but I was allowed to call the detective who took her phone call.

This was all I needed for my closing argument. The eyewitness was the only evidence the state had, and if she couldn't be sure about the identity of the killer, how could the jury convict my client? The jury returned with a not guilty.

The Count watched that final day of the trial. I think he was there to check me out, but I kept assuring him that he had nothing to worry about. We weren't going to depend on a jury. With his case we would ask for a bench trial, where a judge would arrive at the verdict. I never said specifically that his case would be fixed, but I definitely gave him the impression that it was. In truth, I couldn't believe that any judge would find him guilty of murder. The assault charge was a different matter.

The Count's judge turned out to be an old, hard-bitten guy who didn't exactly ooze with sympathy or understanding. He spent most of the trial looking like he was having a gas attack. At least he was Irish. Since he was Irish, and I was too, as well as the Count, some luck had to break our way.

Fortunately, the so-called victims were scruffy and unkempt with long greasy hair—not your most upstanding citizens. They looked like the hopheads we picked up on drug busts when I was a cop. They had charges pending against them too, for assaulting the Count and his students with the weapons. During the trial, I kept pointing out to the judge that Black Cobra Hall was not some nursery school. All the evidence photos showed giant axes, clubs, and spears hanging on the wall. I argued, "What else would you use these weapons for, other than to terrorize people?"

In my version of events, the Count didn't invade Black Cobra Hall. Instead, he came over to work out some amicable relationship with the other teacher. Of course, if he did go there to make peace, you had to wonder why he broke the door down. But when you looked at the size of the door, it was hard to believe a human being could have ripped it from the hinges.

My goal was to convince the judge that this was a fight, pure and simple, and that the Count was acting in self-defense. But my real ace in the hole was the state's attorney, Mike. As luck would have it, he was an old drinking buddy of mine from Rush Street. He had as much disgust for the Black Cobra guys as I did, and I knew he wasn't going to hurt me with this judge.

My biggest trouble during the trial was contending with the Count. I put him on the stand to give his side of the story. Although I coached him how to act—humble and unexcitable—he couldn't help himself. Even during my direct examination, he went into all his macho bullshit about how nobody could ever get away with attacking him. The judge kept yelling at him to shut up. Once again, the victims bailed us out. They got on the stand and were as belligerent as he was.

Each day, during the breaks, the judge would go back into his chambers, muttering about the testimony. You could hear him say, "They're crazy. They're all crazy." As I hoped, when he reached a verdict, he put a plague on both their houses. First, and most important, the judge dismissed the murder charge against the Count as a matter of course. The Count, he said, could not have expected his friend to get run through by a spear. That was my argument, and Mike, the prosecutor, did not put up much of a fight on that.

When it came to the charges of aggravated battery, the judge really worked himself into a lather. He screamed, "You're each as guilty as the other. I've never seen such a pack of lunatics in my life. What were you doing with weapons like a mace? What were you doing tearing somebody's eye out? These aren't medieval times. You're both wrong, and I don't see a finding of guilty either way." He dismissed the charges against the Count, and to keep everything even, he dismissed the charges against the Black Cobra people as well.

After the verdict, the Count grabbed me in a bear hug. "You saved my life," he said. "Not even my father could have done what you did."

Meanwhile, I couldn't help thinking, "I may have saved your life this time, but what about next time?" In my bones, I just knew the Count would come to no good end.

My success with the Count's case impressed Marco as well. Throughout the course of the trial, I gave him blow-by-blow descriptions of my client's crazy antics, and I think he was surprised I got him off the hook.

Marco was now ready to throw me a bone. It was a relatively small matter, but it had proved especially difficult to fix. It involved what was then called, "Boys' Court," where they tried cases for defendants between seventeen and twenty-one.

A few months before, a bunch of punks had gotten in a fight with the bartenders and bouncers at Mother's—probably the most popular singles bar in the city. It was a huge place, in a basement. These kids had caused trouble in the past, and they were ready when the bartenders pulled out the little bats they used to break up fights. They took the bats away and started beating the staff with them. They also did tremendous damage to the bar. It turned out that most of their dads were Mob bosses or crew leaders, and they didn't want their kids to have records, since they were all in college. But despite his connections, Marco couldn't make the case go away. The bartenders and the bouncers were determined to take a stand so that something like this wouldn't happen again. Worse yet, the judge was totally straight. There was no way to buy a favorable decision from him.

It seemed like a tough situation, but I felt there was still something I could do. When I was a cop, I hung out in Mother's all the time. I got in a few fights there myself, but I also helped the bartenders put a few fights down, so I became very friendly with everyone in the place. I got in touch with the main complainant, a bartender named Ronnie. These punks had pissed him off big-time, but I explained to him, "Their parents came to me and they have no way out of this. I can be a hero if we get this dismissed, and I'll make sure the little pricks don't come back. Why can't we work something out and let the parents pay the bills for all the damages?"

As a favor to me, Ronnie said he'd try to get the other bartenders to back down. Next I went in to see the judge. He was another tough nut.

He told me he wanted the case to go to trial to teach them a lesson. "Judge," I said, "these aren't bad kids." But we both knew that was a load of crap.

Then I tried to appeal to his sympathy for me. I figured that he was once a young lawyer, trying to start a practice. "Judge," I said, "please give me a chance to work this out. There are some important people involved, and this case could be the foundation for building my business."

The judge decided to give me a shot. He said, "If you can get all the complainants from the bar to come forward and indicate that they don't wish to pursue the case, then I'll dismiss it." I'm sure he never expected it to happen, but my friend Ronnie persuaded the other bartenders to take the money and drop their charges. The case was then dismissed.

My legal career was off and running. The Count sent me great business: celebrity types who got in trouble with a gun or stash of marijuana or something like that. They all paid big fees without blinking an eye. Marco was stingier, but he more than made up for that with the volume of business he could send my way.

Those first few cases taught me the sort of lessons I never learned in law school. The only thing that saved Donald Kristman's neck was my friendship with the cop who told me about the overlooked witness report. The same went for the prosecutor in the Count's case and the bartenders from Mother's. Being a good criminal lawyer in Chicago had very little to do with the law. It was about the relationships you had with your clients and the other people in the courtroom: prosecutors, coppers, witnesses, and judges. For me, there was no line between professional relationships and social relationships. They were both part of the job. I wined and dined clients to get more clients. I wined and dined the court people, so I could do better for the clients. This type of law could be a lot of fun. It could also consume your life.

As far as some people were concerned, there was another reason for my success. "Bob Cooley is a mechanic," the Count used to say. "He can fix anything."

CHAPTER 4

CRIME PAYS

t didn't take me long to find the corruption at the heart of Chicago's justice system. In fact, the very first case I had, soon after I passed the bar, was in Traffic Court—the most corrupt court of them all. My client was up for a run-of-the-mill drunk-driving ticket. I thought the case would be easy to win. First of all, I knew the cop who made the arrest, and he knew I was an ex-cop, so he couldn't play games during his testimony. As for the prosecutor, he was another good friend of mine, and an ex-cop too. And I thought I was on good terms with the judge, Dick LeFevour, the Supervising Judge for the Traffic Court. I put my case on, and, just as I thought, the judge threw the ticket out. But when I walked out of the court, I heard, "Hey, Bob."

It was Jimmy LeFevour, Dick's cousin. Jimmy was a police officer and a notorious drunk who always had the smell of alcohol on his breath. Dick had arranged for him to be assigned to the Traffic Court building. Tall and thin, Jimmy LeFevour lurked around the halls like a ghoul. I didn't have a clue what he wanted from me. "What is it?" I asked.

"The first one is on the house," Jimmy said. "But from now on, any time you have something in here, you come and see me first."

That was Traffic Court. As a cop, I knew funny things happened there, but I had never known the extent of it. Once I became a lawyer, I found out. Either you paid or your client lost. They had a whole routine set up. First you met with the judge's bagman, like Jimmy. You would let him know what kind of case you had. In other words, how serious the charge was. He would then tell you what it would cost. Usually I paid $100 for the judge, $50 for the bagman and $50 for the policeman involved. Sometimes the bagman kept the cop's money, but if he gave it to the cop, almost all the police accepted it. (I did, when I was a cop. That was the system and you were supposed to take the money and shut up about it. As a result, I rarely wrote DUI tickets.)

Each court you went into had a different set of ropes to learn. If you were going to survive, the law you most needed to know was the law of the jungle. Narcotics Court was a perfect example. It was in one of those giant old Roman-style buildings with a huge courtroom—like a coliseum. It was always packed to the rafters with spectators and lawyers. On any given day, they could process as many as five hundred cases. Meanwhile, in the corridors outside the courtroom, you had dozens of lawyers I called Hall Rats, scuttling among the chaos for a piece of cheese. They hung out at Narcotics day after day to hustle clients, and each one had some monetary arrangements with the court sergeant, the clerk, and most of the judges. If a prisoner looked unattached from a lawyer, a presiding judge or a court sergeant might steer him toward a favorite Hall Rat.

I was practicing only a couple of months before I had my first Narcotics case. I had to be in another court first, so I got there late. Just as I entered the building, I saw my client walking out. He had been arrested in a bullshit street narcotics stop, so I was only going to charge him $500. I asked what happened and he said, "Oh, a friend of yours took care of my case." He gave me the guy's card. It turned out to be one of the chief Hall Rats, the son of a judge. The client went on to explain, "I told him I was waiting for you, but he said he was a lawyer and he could take care of it for you. And *he* only charged me $300."

What was I going to do? I wished the client good luck and went inside. Now I had never been in the court before as a lawyer, and this Hall Rat didn't know me from Adam, but I recognized him from my days as a cop. He was a skinny little guy, the sort of slick dresser who wore thousand-dollar suits and fancy little tassel loafers. He was making a fortune from that place and still poaching clients from other lawyers. I approached him and asked, "Do you have a minute?" I'm sure he thought I was a potential client, because I didn't carry a briefcase (I never did).

I walked with him from the courtroom outside into the marble hallway. It had ceilings as high as a cathedral. There were all kinds of people there: policemen standing around, lawyers chatting with clients. First, I asked the Rat if he knew who I was.

"No," he said, "I don't know who you are."

"Funny," I said. "You told my client you were a good friend of mine." Then I pulled out the card he gave my client. "Is this your card?"

When he nodded, I threw him up against the wall. Everybody around us scattered. "Listen you little piece of shit," I said. "You're going to give me five hundred fucking dollars or I'm going to split your head open against this wall."

He shook in his shoes. "But he only paid me three hundred," he whined.

"Doesn't matter," I said. "That's what I was going to charge him."

He counted out five hundred-dollar bills. I could see all the cops looking and laughing. I'm sure the Rat had paid off most of them at some point, but he wasn't so arrogant this time.

Then I put my finger in his face and said, loud enough for everyone to hear, "If you ever steal a client of mine again, there's going to be a fucking problem. And you let the rest of these people know that, too."

Given the nature of my clientele, I probably could have operated my firm out of a phone booth, but I wanted a respectable-looking office in a nice building. For help, I turned to another defense attorney, Allan Ackerman, and he offered to let me share his space and some of his secretary's time. I had approached Allan because he was one of the few lawyers I watched as a cop who impressed me. I especially appreciated his grasp of the technical side of the law—the weak chink in my armor. I practically flunked out of bibliography in Law School. Besides, I hated to be cooped up in a library. For the rest of my career, I paid Allan to do my research and help me write motions. It turned out that he was also a fun-loving guy who liked to play cards almost as much as I did.

When I moved in with Allan at 100 North LaSalle Street, I didn't know how important that office building would be—to my career and my life. As far as I could tell, it was in a great location, right across the street from City Hall, a block from one of the Circuit Courts and a short walk from Federal Court. Otherwise, there was nothing very distinguished about it. The building was a classic twenties-era high-rise with a brick and terra cotta exterior. Inside, it had dozens of small law firms, many with the same smoked-glass doors that they'd had when the place first opened. There was a marble lobby with six elevators, and a restaurant called Counsellors Row.

If not for Allan, I would have never picked out the building. But in a matter of time, 100 North LaSalle became more my home than the place where I slept. It was not just where I worked; it was my club, my hangout, and my personal gambling den—in many ways, the frat house I never experienced in college. Only a year after I started my arrangement with Allan, I was ready to move into a suite of offices with four other lawyers. Just a year and a half later, I had my own suite and two lawyers working for me.

Looking back, it's hard to believe how easily and how quickly my practice grew. The business came to me. I didn't have to go looking for it. I never advertised or promoted myself. If I bet with a bookmaker and he got pinched, I had a new client. If I chatted with a guy sitting next to me at a Rush Street bar, and he found out I was an attorney, I had a new client.

Of course, Marco was a major source of my business. Whenever any of his bookies would get arrested, he would contact Marco, and Marco would get him a lawyer, namely me. I could have six of these cases a week. I'd drop by to see Marco at the Survivor's Club and he'd pay me $1,000 for each one. Later I discovered he was charging the bookies as much as $4,000 for my services.

Even if I had known about Marco's "mark-up," I wouldn't have cared. I was more than happy with what I was making from him. Working for the Mob was like any other business. You had to be productive—churn through as many cases as possible—yet make your customers feel like they were getting better service than they could get anywhere else.

In those days, most of my cases were in Guns and Gambling, a classic "money court." You rarely had trials, just transactions. One of the senior judges in the court was Ray Sodini—a happy-go-lucky guy with a drooping bloodhound face. I didn't deal with his bagman, and we hardly ever spoke before a case. Instead, I would go back into his chambers and the little closet where he hung his suit jacket. I put a hundred in the inside pocket for every case I had in his court. If it was a tough case, and he had to go out on a limb for me, I put a couple of hundred dollars in there. Once in a while, I'd have a real difficult case—what we called an "ink case," because it got a lot of press. Only then would I have to talk to him first. I knew where he had lunch, and I could approach him there and let him decide whether he wanted to throw it out in the preliminary hearing or let it go directly to the grand jury. If he threw it out too quickly, a reporter might notice. I never wanted to put him in a position where the press could embarrass him, and he trusted my instincts. That was the key to my success in working the system. Early on, people realized I wouldn't take advantage of their trust.

For the first eleven years of my legal career, almost every day I gave out bribes—and not just to judges. The other court personnel were equally important, if not more so. On my way into the courthouse, I sometimes stopped to pick up a big bag of donuts or some fried chicken. While the other lawyers lined up to go through the metal detector, I walked past it, and made my rounds before court was in session, dropping off food in this office or that chambers. Along the way, I might shake hands with certain sheriffs or bailiffs. Inside my palm, I folded up a five or ten—sometimes a fifty. We would shake, they would come away with the money and no one else would be the wiser. It's not like I paid them for anything special. It was more like an investment— for a favor they might perform in the future.

For example, when a client was arrested and brought to the Criminal Court for arraignment, he literally entered a zoo—another giant courtroom with the judges and lawyers in the front, a big gallery for spectators, and a cage in the back, where they kept all the prisoners behind bars. A client, say, in a nice suit, would have to sit there among the drug dealers, the burglars, and the drunks still bloody from a brawl. He wouldn't see his lawyer until they were both brought before the bench.

But if I hadn't met a client yet, I wanted some face time before we saw the judge. Lawyers were not allowed in the back of the court, but I'd have a sheriff take my client out of the holding cell and bring him over to a side room, where I would be waiting with a sandwich. I figured he hadn't eaten since he'd been in custody. This had a huge impact on my clients. They realized, right from the start, that I had power in this building.

Paying off the clerks was also important. I wanted to have my cases processed like clockwork—and always before lunch. I didn't like sitting in court on a sunny afternoon when I could have been out at my pool, or at a club taking a massage. I made sure my clients were always the first ones up. If the other lawyers were paying the clerks five or ten dollars for that privilege, I paid twenty. I could walk into a court with twenty lawyers lined up, hundreds of people waiting in the gallery, and I would still be the next case called. It made everybody think I was really connected to all the higher-ups. In fact, the guy who was making me look good was the lowest man on the totem pole.

In my mind, I didn't even consider these little payments as corruption. It was my way of doing business and a leg up on my competitors— just a part of the system in Chicago. And really, what was worse: handing five dollars to a clerk, or writing a hundred-dollar check? That's what you were supposed to do when they invited you to all of those "fundraisers" for judges or prosecutors. They even had so-called benefits for the police. I attended absolutely everything. I'd just walk in and say "Hi," buy some tickets or hand over a check, and leave.

That wasn't the only way to get funny with these people. Sometimes they needed a place for their fundraisers and wanted a deal on the food and drinks. The big Greek restaurants were the popular places in those days, and a lot of the owners also happened to gamble and travel in the same bookie circles I did. I could always help a judge work out a nice deal with them.

If a judge wanted special entertainment for a "stag party," I could help there, too. Early in my career I started representing prostitutes, since I knew what a joke the Vice Squad was. If a working girl was arrested, her only crime was not having friends in the right places. I wouldn't use just any madam to book the judges' parties—only Rosie Armando, because she was a class act, and I could trust her girls not to blackmail anyone, pick their pockets, or talk out of school.

Should a judge ask me to represent a friend of his who was in trouble, I'd never charge the friend or the judge. When the guy got around to paying me, I'd say, "Don't worry about your bill. Just thank the judge. He's a good man."

You still had many legitimate judges—more than there were crooked ones—who didn't take bribes or throw too many fundraisers or ask favors. I kept an eye out for them, too, when I had lunch at a nice restaurant by the courthouse. Before these judges finished their meals, I would get to the waitress and pick up their check. On the way out, they'd say, "I wish you wouldn't do that."

I'd say, "Okay, Judge. That's the last time." Then I'd do it again the next time I saw them. I would do it even before I had cases in their courts. I knew eventually we'd meet up.

At any given time, I had good relationships with about ninety percent of the judges. There were always a few who didn't like me, and I didn't like them either. If I saw one of those guys at some function, I didn't go out of my way to kiss his ass. In Cook County, we could always petition the court for Substitution of Judge. If I had a case that ended up in front of a judge I didn't like, I walked right up to the judge and said, "I want to substitute," and off I would go. I didn't need a reason. In fact, I could also say, "I don't want this other judge either." More than likely I wound up with somebody I did like.

There was no way I could buy myself out of every case. Often, I had to go to a jury trial. Even if I had the judge and everyone else in the court on my side, I still had to win over the jurors. I've never claimed to be Perry Mason, but I would still stake my record in jury trials against any other defense attorney. In fact, my success in these cases, before legitimate judges, only made it easier to pay off the corrupt ones.

Like everything else in my practice, I had my own approach to jury trials. It grew out of my experience as a cop, when I had to spend my days in a courtroom, waiting to testify against somebody I had arrested. I didn't just watch the lawyers. I watched the jurors, learning to see a case through their eyes. Most were working-class people, the sort I grew up with on the South Side. They had no illusions about human nature. Like me, they had a friend or a relative or two who had ended up in jail.

So when I became a lawyer, I never bothered to pretend my client was an angel. Jurors had the common sense to know better.

Instead, right from the start of jury selection, I made it clear that this trial did not hinge on the goodness of my client. I asked each and every juror, "As you sit here, do you understand that my client is innocent?" Most of them would nod "yes." Then I'd ask, "If the state doesn't meet its burden, do you understand that you have an obligation to find him not guilty?"

I repeated this theme over and over in my opening statement. I would never argue that my client didn't do it. I would argue instead that the state has a burden to prove he did it—and prove it beyond a reasonable doubt. In the hands of a good defense attorney, this burden of proof can be a high bar for the state to clear. Even if the prosecutors had a mountain of evidence against my client, I could always count on the prosecution witnesses to bail me out—especially my old friends, the coppers.

I had loads of personal insight into the behavior of the police during a trial. I knew the pressure they were under—from supervisors and prosecutors—to stretch the truth. For some of these superiors, no amount of evidence was ever enough. I also had the example of my own father, who time and again hurt his own career advancement when he refused to perjure himself during big trials. In his mind, perjury was a crime and committing a crime could not be justified, even to get a conviction on a more serious crime—just like one sin couldn't justify another. When I was still a rookie cop, the prosecutors wanted me to testify to something I hadn't seen. I asked my father what to do, and he said, "Regardless of what the prosecutors say, you've got to tell the truth. If they get mad, that's too bad. Let them get mad." That was my father, as honest and straight as could be.

Fortunately for my clients, the cops I cross-examined had different standards. I could see something was fishy just by reading their reports. If the sequence of events surrounding an arrest came off too perfectly, you could smell it. But I never started to cross-examine a cop by challenging him. I took my good old time to set him up. First I played up to his ego. I let him tell the jury how many years he served on the force and what kind of special training he received.

"With all this great experience and background," I'd ask, "do you think you did a good job of filling out your reports in this case?"

He'd reply, "I did a great job. As I always do." Then I'd proceed to point out error after error in the report. For example, if the arresting officer said he chased the defendant and saw him throw his gun to the side, I knew it was bullshit. I had chased a few armed thugs in my time as a cop, and I almost never noticed one do that.

"Exactly when and where did you see him throw the gun?" I asked.

"Well," he answered, "maybe I didn't see him throw it down. Maybe it was after he turned the corner." That was it. That was all I needed. The moment someone misspoke or deviated in the slightest from his report, I had him.

I'd say, "You didn't think this was important?" He'd start to hem and haw, and bit by bit, his whole façade of infallibility would crumble right before the jurors' eyes.

"You just now indicated to the jury that it happened this way. But we see it's not in your report," I'd say, holding up some paperwork. "Either you're lying or you're incompetent." Of course, he wasn't incompetent, because only moments before, he had spent so much time telling the jury that he was so brilliant.

All I needed was that one little slip. I wouldn't let go from there. I knew that the typical juror got real angry when an authority figure was caught in a lie. I could then tell the jury, "We know that this one officer is lying, and that means the other witnesses are probably lying, too. You have an obligation. You took an oath. The state must prove these charges beyond a reasonable doubt, or the defendant is not guilty. Now you have all the reasonable doubt you need to acquit."

To me, cross-examining the state's witnesses was the crux of my entire defense. When I had cases with other lawyers, I always insisted on taking the lead with cross-examination. Even lawyers with more experience than I had let witnesses weasel out of a lie. There was no way I would ever let that happen. I was like a pit bull that locked onto another dog's leg. You'd have to shoot me before I let go.

No matter what I had done to the state's case, I still put my client on the stand. People always question me on that. They see famous trials on

TV, and the defense never puts the client on the stand. I think that lawyers who don't are idiots. If you see the proceedings through the eyes of a juror, you have no choice. The juror looks at the defendant and thinks, "How can you sit in a courtroom, day after day, and have people say all these horrible things about you and not get up to deny it?" The defendant has to get up and defend himself. If he doesn't, it comes off as an admission of guilt, no matter what a judge or anyone else says. That's how the typical juror sees it.

When I started the direct examination of my client, I never tried to gloss over his past. To the contrary, I had him discuss each and every bad thing he had ever done. I had one client get up and talk about his fifty prior arrests. He went on for more than an hour. "I was arrested for this and arrested for that. I was convicted for this and convicted for that." It was like a confessional. But it was still an inoculation against the prosecution. If he could be so forthcoming about how bad he was, then the jury might believe him when he denied the charge in the indictment.

I could also argue that having a record and a lousy reputation made you a target for the cops. I called it my "Jagoff Defense." I used it with a notorious tough guy named Joey Airdo—a pudgy character with close-set eyes, kind of like the short one in Abbott and Costello. Like a lot of mobsters, he owned an Italian beef sandwich stand, and probably ate up his profits. He was a Mob thug from Central Casting, and in this case, was charged with burning out the car and house of a landlord who had evicted him. They found a can of gasoline with his fingerprints and the girl at the store who sold it to him. It was the kind of case I called a dead-bang loser. The prosecutor would not take a plea and wanted a minimum of ten years. Meanwhile, the judge was totally legit and the sort of tough, state-minded sort who would give Joey even more time. I had no choice but to take it to trial. I needed a break from the state's witnesses, and I got it when the investigator testified that Joey's prints were the only ones on the can. The girl who sold him the can and the policeman who found her must have touched it, too. Now I had the fabrication I needed to show that this was a frame-up.

But why would the cops pin a charge on Joey? When I cross-examined the officer from the arson squad, I turned around and asked Joey to stand up. He didn't expect this, so he got up slowly, kind of confused. "Look at my client," I told the officer. "You know why he's here. I know why he's here. We all know why he's here. He's here because he's a jagoff." The whole courtroom erupted in laughter. Except for Joey, who wasn't too happy with this line of defense. I went on with the cross, but when I turned around again, there was Joey still standing. I said, "Would you sit down already?" Then I looked at the jury and said, "See what I mean?"

Now they all laughed even harder until the judge banged his gavel. Later, he threatened to report me for conduct detrimental to my client. But that became moot when we won an acquittal. I would argue that my jagoff routine played a role in the final verdict.

It was fun pitting my wits against someone else. No matter how big the case was or how difficult it seemed. All the bravado and class-clown antics that got me in trouble as a kid now worked in my favor. About the only "homework" I did was to read the police reports the night before a trial. Somehow all the details would burn their way into my memory. When policemen would get up there and testify to something different from their report, I would have my case. It was almost that easy.

After he retired, sometimes my father would come to court to watch one of my trials. He was so proud to see me there. Afterwards he'd say to me, "Son, you have a talent. You have a God-given talent." Of course, he was less than thrilled with the people I was defending with that talent.

I just loved being a lawyer. I loved being in court. I loved being the center of attention. I hated neckties, and I stopped wearing them— before anyone else could get away with it. I'd have a nice sports jacket, but I wore a turtleneck or open shirt with a gold chain. Around this time, I also had a dog I loved—a boxer named Duke. I took him every-where: bars, fancy restaurants, even my office. At one point, the land-lords at 100 North LaSalle threatened to evict me if I kept bringing Duke. I told them to fuck themselves. Duke was part of my image, too.

After a while, I got infatuated with myself and I wanted to win every case—one way or the other. In fact, I went for years without losing. If one of my clients had ever been found guilty, it would have devastated me. I probably cared more about my record than my clients did. If I knew the judge was a money guy, I'd much rather go into his court, make a payment and walk on out. If I had a case that was certain to be tossed, because the cops did something real stupid, I tried to steer it to one of my money guys, so he could get an easy payday. The next time, if I came in with something tougher, he was more likely to help me.

Even in legitimate courts, I usually found an easy way out. If I was on good terms with the state's attorney, I could get him to dismiss the case. Other times, I would offer a plea in return for a lesser charge and sentence. If my client was a burglar looking at six years, I asked for probation. When the judge didn't go for that, then I'd take it to trial, but I made sure to tie up his court for weeks. Even the legitimate judges hated long trials. Like everyone else, they wanted to clear their docket. The next time I came before that judge, he was more likely to give me what I wanted.

Bit by bit, I learned every trick to work the system. Word of mouth about my cases and my results spread. My business grew that much more. But I never treated my job like work, and I never let it affect my lifestyle. Unlike most lawyers, I didn't rush into my office first thing. I rolled out of bed around eight in the morning, took a quick shave, and then went straight to court. I parked right at the bus stop in front of the building. I knew the cops who worked the street and they never gave me a ticket. Inside, I had probably ten judges who would let me use their chambers for making calls to my office and clients. If I walked into a courtroom and saw that the judge was in session, I just gave him a nod and walked back into his chambers.

Unless I had a trial, my cases were almost always over by lunch. After I ate, I grabbed a quick steam bath and a massage. For a few years, during the summer, I'd go back to my cabana and hang out at the pool. But the rest of the year, I went into the office, usually after two. I got my messages from the secretary and might see a few clients, but I never liked too many meetings. Instead, once I had my own suite, I used the conference room for card games. This was something I started when I first shared an office with Allan, but the cards became an institution when I was on my own. Gin was the favorite game during the day. We could usually fit eight around the table. Other lawyers, state's attorneys, and building tenants would drop by, including the two Greek brothers who owned Counsellors Row. I had refreshments for everyone (I still never drank when I played), and if I had a good day, I could win a few thousand bucks. When the prices went up on the restaurant's menu, everyone would laugh and say the owners were losing too much in my gin game.

I stopped the cards around five, so I could start placing my bets for the day. Through my practice and Mob connections, I met a lot of bookies and gambling became practically a full-time job. It could take ninety minutes to call in all my plays, especially during football or basketball season.

There were nights when I stuck around the office and we had huge poker games with thousands of dollars at stake. Sometimes Rosie would send over one of her girls to hide under the table, and if one of the guys was lucky, he got something better than a good hand.

Usually after work, I would go straight to Rush Street where I hung out until the early hours of the morning. Rush Street had grown up from the days of frat-type singles bars. Now there were fancy discos like Faces, swanky spots like the Playboy Club, and huge glitzy restaurants and bars. It was the era when everyone was "swinging" and one-night-stand was no longer such a di____rd. Sort of sexual nirvana for a guy like me. I could keep two _____ friends at a time. If one wondered why I had to run, I could a____ that I needed to meet a client at Night Court.

After the clubs closed on ____, I used to bring my dates to the dice games in Chinatown. F____ reet, you had no idea what was inside. You walked to an ab____torefront and knocked on the door. You had to know some____e they let you inside. Then you walked through that abandon____ross an alley and into another building. If the police ever trie____ey would have had the wrong address on the search warrant. ____ken to a big room about fifty feet long with two craps tables a____crowded around them. There were no chairs. Just some table____ack with free cold cuts and liquor.

There's nothing like the energ____ table—people yelling and

groaning with every throw. But dice is the ultimate sucker game, and I almost never played. After Marco gave out his Christmas bonus to his crew, he used to have a dice game, just so he could win all the money back. At the game in Chinatown, Mob guys always hit me up for a loan, because they knew I carried a lot of money. If they wanted $500, I would give them $300. I never expected to get it back and didn't even bother to ask. I figured they would ask me to represent them if they ever got in trouble, and it was just a cost of doing business.

After a while, I developed a different sort of reputation among the lawyers and gamblers who hung out with the tough guys. I wasn't a mobster, but I wouldn't let mobsters push me around, either. Once I had a beef with a bookie named Moe Shapiro. He used to hang out at the Playboy Club, and I called him one Friday night to settle the bets I made earlier with him. After I got off the phone with him, I realized I had the wrong score on one of our games. Instead of losing the bet, I actually won, and now he owed me money. By the time I got back to Moe, he had already thrown out his paperwork, and forgot what I actually bet. Instead of hunting through the garbage, he demanded I pay, and I refused.

Moe was connected with the Rush Street group. We used to call them the Jewish Mafia, because so many of their bookies and gamblers were Jews. The following Monday, Moe paid me a visit at my office with his group's top enforcers, Tony Spilotro and Fat Herbie Blitzstein. Tony was a little guy, with the face of a bulldog and a well-known vicious temper. Herbie was easily 300 pounds with a Mitch Miller-type beard and a giant potbelly. He looked like one of those crazy professional wrestlers.

Tony pointed to Moe and said, "He says you lost some money and you owe him some money."

I tried to explain, but Tony cut me right off and barked, "I don't want to hear that nonsense. That's a pile of bullshit. You owe us. We want the money and I'll be back tomorrow to collect the money."

He came back the next day with Fat Herbie, but no Moe. Before Tony even opened his mouth, I said, "I didn't lose it and I ain't fucking paying. That Moe's a fucking weasel."

I then told him that I knew Marco, and Tony backed down. We all agreed to meet later with him. When we did, and I could explain what happened, we agreed to call the whole things quits. They didn't owe me and I didn't owe them.

Tony Spilotro liked the fact I stood up to him. The Chicago Mob later sent him to be their main enforcer in Las Vegas. His temper ended up getting everyone in a lot of trouble, but for a few years he practically owned Vegas. He had a jewelry store near the hotels that he called, The Gold Rush. It came out later that his crew of break-in artists, the Hole-In-The-Wall Gang, used the store to fence some of his best loot.

In Vegas, Tony, Herbie, and I would hang out at Jubilation, a disco that was like Faces, the club on Rush Street. For dinner, we would go to Villa D'Est, a fancy restaurant owned by a Joey Pignatelli, another Chicago South Side guy. I was there with Tony one night when he met up with Frank Sinatra. Tony would never pay for anything in Vegas, so I ended up with the tab—for Frank, his son, and their whole entourage. It came to something like $1,800. The next night I dropped by the restaurant with a girl. When I heard Sinatra was in the private room again, I asked Joey if I could drop by to say hello, but Frank wanted no part of me. I guess he found someone else to pay that night's bill.

By the mid-seventies, it was no exaggeration to say that the cash was coming in hand over fist—easily four to five hundred thousand a year. I had not had an easy road to my law degree. When I looked back on all those dark, cold years, working my ass off to get through college, it was like a very distant memory. Now the money came so easily, I didn't respect it, and as a result, I did silly things with it.

For instance, I bought an old-time gym called Postl's. It wasn't a place to work out, but to relax. They called it a wine and cigar gym, and it was as far from a health club as you could get. Guys went up there for a steam, a rubdown, and a drink or smoke. Charlie Postl had been a wrestling champion at the turn of the century, and when he opened the gym, he had everyone from mobsters like Capone to presidents and mayors show up. My best friend at Marquette, Bill Murphy, was his grandson, and we had stopped by a few times during a break from school. When I told Charlie I wrestled at school, he took a liking to me. He was a crusty old guy, but still a local sports celebrity and they treated him like a king at the fancy steakhouses. He'd let Bill and me eat our fill while he told us crazy stories about his wrestling exploits. After Charlie died, there wasn't much color left to his gym, and the clientele stopped coming. Bill's parents tried to run it, but when Bill told me it was on the verge of bankruptcy, I offered to buy it and bail them out. In some ways it was a toy and an ego boost—to actually own such a symbol of privilege. I also saw the club as an excuse to get my father out of the house. All he did was go to church and watch TV. I hated to see him so idle. He was always willing to help me out, so once I took possession of the club, he showed up bright and early for work. But first thing, he noticed that we were serving liquor without the proper permit. Then he saw some of the old-time mobsters come around, and he didn't like that, either. It took a week before I realized this job wasn't for him.

After two years, I sold Postl's to a couple of young guys who wanted to turn it into a modern health club. Charlie would have had a laugh. By this time, though, I already had my hands full with another crazy investment. But this one worked like a charm. One of my clients, Artie Greco, was a bookie on the South Side. Depending on your point of view, I was one of his best or worst customers. I constantly beat him, but I was also there to represent him when he got arrested. Although Artie was among the few big-time independent bookies, I could see that the Feds were starting to target him like he was a Mafia kingpin. Artie needed a career change, and in 1974 he bought an Italian restaurant in his old neighborhood. Even though he didn't have any experience in the food industry, I gave Artie the cash for the down payment. I thought he had the right bubbly personality for the business. At least, we could have a good time before we flamed out.

The place we bought was called Bruno's, named after the slob who had owned it. The dining room was in a big shed of a building with a little take-out deli in the front. Bruno wanted $50,000 down, in cash, and another $200,000 on contract. I figured he had sold the dump a few times before. The buyers probably gave it back before they could finish the payments. But we had a different plan. We completely remodeled the inside, so it looked like an old-fashioned Italian restaurant with trelliswork and vines. For the chefs, we used Artie's wife and the different Italian women from the neighborhood. They all knew how to cook authentic homemade dishes. Everything was made from scratch. Artie had all kinds of other family to help serve.

We renamed the place Greco's, and it quickly became one of the most popular Italian restaurants in the city. We started busy and only got busier. We had to rip out the deli to make a bigger dining room and a nice bar. Bruno came by during construction and practically had a heart attack. He wanted to know what we were doing "to my restaurant." We told him to get the fuck out. It wasn't his restaurant, and he sure as hell wasn't going to get it back any time soon.

Greco's was always quite a scene. Like I figured, with all the contacts from his previous occupation, Artie attracted both the bookmakers and their customers—the sort of people who are always out looking for a good time. The bookies attracted other shooters in the underground economy—the guys who owned the chop shops and the car thieves who supplied them. Added to that mix were my clients, and crew leaders like Marco and the Mob bosses above them. Then, to make things even more interesting, we started attracting the politicians. Close behind followed the defense lawyers, the prosecutors, and even the judges.

We may have billed ourselves as an Italian restaurant, but looking out on all these different types of customers, I saw a big Irish stew—potatoes, meat, carrots and onions, with nothing quite mixing together. At any moment the whole kettle could boil over and turn one against the other. People were pointing each other out, staring each other down and, in a few cases, getting ready to commit murder.

Major changes were taking place in our local crime world, and they played out right in front of my eyes at Greco's. The Outfit, as they called the Chicago Mafia, was the most powerful organized crime group in America. It didn't get the publicity of the Mafia families on the East Coast, but that was because its bosses weren't killing each other. Instead they ganged up to control everyone else in town.

All of the Outfit bosses were Italian, and they had some Mafia traditions, but their organization was strictly Chicago, and dated back to the time before Capone. They were divided up into five groups, but these were known by the area they controlled and not some family name. There was the Chinatown group, the Cicero group, the South Side group, the West Side group, where Marco was from, and the Rush Street group. If you look at a map of Chicago, you can see that four major freeways radiate out from downtown and cut the metro area into five slices of pie. Each group had control of a slice. The freeways served as their dividing lines.

The five Mafia groups got along very well—like five fingers clenched into a fist. In fact, since they did such a good job of splitting things up among themselves, they decided to organize crime for the rest of the city. If you were doing anything illegal, and lived within a few hundred miles of Chicago, they wanted a piece of it—what they called street tax.

They started with the chop shops and their auto thieves. After that, they put all the bookmakers on the arm. Then they went after the loan sharks and the counterfeiters. They expected the burglars to pay a street tax, and sell all the stolen property through Mob fences so they could get another cut. They got so greedy, they shook down legitimate businesses, too, like go-go clubs and strip joints. Even Italian restaurants. Even Greco's.

To get everyone in line, they killed a few people to make examples. You opened the paper and read that another loan shark or jewel thief had been found in the trunk of a car with his throat cut. The old bosses turned to crew leaders like Marco to organize the shakedowns and, if necessary, the consequences for those who didn't pay. The newspapers called them the Young Turks, and at first the press thought that all the dead bodies piling up were signs of a gang war. The reporters never realized it was the Outfit's war against everyone else.

But that didn't mean there weren't hitches along the way. Early on, the five groups bickered over which one had the rights to which independent criminal. Mob bosses couldn't collect street tax according to their territories. What did you do about a car thief who stole in one part of the city and lived in another? Did the group get the tax based on where the crime was committed, or the location of the criminal? What about bookies? They had clients scattered all over the region and the country. Big bookmakers also had offices in different places, too.

After a few crews got caught in the crossfire, the bosses decided to change their ways. A crew could "grab" an independent criminal, no matter where he was, and as long as they grabbed him first, they could keep him and a piece of his action. This new approach to street tax touched off a Gold Rush, with each group constantly on the lookout for independents and developing their own sources for finding them. The most obvious prospectors for the Mob were the police. Coppers who fingered an independent criminal could get a piece of his tax. Some called in their arrests to the Mafia before they talked to their desk sergeants. A bookie would get pinched, and as soon as he made bail, a goon was waiting for him outside the jail.

Gamblers like me were another way for the Mob to locate independents. The bait was too good for most bettors to pass up—especially if they were already in deep to an Outfit bookie. If you found an independent bookie for the Mob, you could start playing with him. If you won, you split the winnings with your Mob bookie. If you lost, you just let your Mob contact know when the independent bookie came to collect. That's when they "grabbed" the guy and put the muscle on him. As a reward, you got a piece of all the back-taxes they charged him.

I wanted no part of that. The truth is that I liked most of my bookies, and I wasn't about to snitch on them. But one time I did let my guard down, and I got a couple of friends in some big trouble.

They were Ed and Sid, two brothers who had a little law office at 100 North LaSalle. Their father, long gone by this time, had owned some office buildings downtown, which left his sons very wealthy. They showed up at the office each day to do family business, and not even much of that. Mostly, they just sat around. Ed played a terrible game of cards. Sid was an even worse bettor, but he liked to gamble and wanted action in the worst way, so he decided to become a bookmaker. He only booked with me and a few other guys, using betting lines right out of the newspaper. This was the sign of a rank amateur, because the newspaper's lines provide much more leeway than the odds you could get from most bookies. As a result, I loved playing with Sid. He would only let me bet $500 a game, but on a good day I could still win four thousand from him. He was like my safety net.

I never saw Sid as someone the Mob would grab, but little did I know. One night I hung out with Marco at a fancy Italian restaurant on the West Side and watched Monday Night Football. The game was unexpectedly close, and a heavy favorite won by only seven points. Most of the lines had them winning by ten. Marco lost a lot of money and was crying in his beer.

"Believe it or not," I told him, "I was able to lay six points with one book, so I'll make out pretty nicely."

Marco did not share in my happiness. "Who the hell would have a line like that?" he yelled.

I told him it wasn't any bookie he knew. "He's just a square John in my building," I said. "He takes a line out of the newspaper." But I made the mistake of mentioning Sid's name. How many Sids could there be in the directory for 100 North LaSalle?

A week or so later, Sid's brother Eddy came down to see me. He pulled me into my office and shut the door behind us. He was scared stiff. He said his brother had been visited by a couple of Mob goons. They were going to kill him for bookmaking.

"They want him to pay $25,000," he whispered.

All I could do was shake my head. I prayed to God it was a coincidence, but then Ed asked, "Have you ever heard of Marco D'Amico?"

"Yeah," I said. "I know who he is."

"Is he one of the bad guys?"

"Yeah."

Ed turned even whiter at that piece of news. But inside I was boiling—angry with myself for having such a big mouth, but angrier with Marco. How could he do this without talking to me? It was like I put red meat in front of a dog. He was going to devour it first and ask questions later.

The goons told Sid to bring his money to the very same restaurant where I watched Monday Night football with Marco. "We'll pay them what they want," Ed said. "But we want to make sure nothing happens when we give them the money."

I agreed to accompany Ed when he made the payoff. His brother was still so scared, he didn't want to be within a mile of Marco or anyone else from the Mob. They had asked him to continue booking as partner. They would split the winnings fifty-fifty, but if someone didn't pay and they sent out a goon to collect, then they'd keep everything. Poor Sid didn't want to be their partner, or anything else. He had been scared straight. Unlike the real bookies, he didn't need the gambling income. As far as I know, he never made book again.

When Ed and I showed up at the restaurant, Marco himself was there to greet us. I made it look to Ed like I was acquainted with Marco but not too friendly, and Marco played along. We sat down in a booth. Ed gave him the money and got the hell out as fast as he could. Marco counted out $1,000 and pushed the bills toward me. "Here," he said. "That's for the tip." I said, "I don't want that." I stood up and I walked away. I wanted him to know I was pissed, but I wasn't going to get in his face either. I now realized that nothing was too petty for the Outfit. They were always looking for somebody to squeeze. Even if they got nickels and dimes. Most important, I learned that there was no such thing as bullshitting with a mobster. A slip of the tongue could literally end up getting someone killed. Or myself for that matter.

I was determined to do more than ever to keep my two worlds apart. I never dropped names, and if a client wondered whether I knew this or that Mob boss, I would say, "I know him only to say hello." But some of my friends and clients were fascinated by the Outfit and tried to get me to make introductions. None was worse than Count Dante. Time and again, he asked to be introduced to big shots like Marco. He was convinced he could do all these great things with the Mafia, but I knew that even someone as dangerous as the Count couldn't mix with the Mob. They would eat him alive.

Once my law career took off, I didn't see much more of the Count. An incident one night convinced me that there was no way to control the man. We were sitting in my living room, along with our girlfriends from the time. The Count was going on about all of our exploits. He was pretty smashed, and he suddenly jumped up and started ranting to my girl, "This Bob Cooley is one tough motherfucker. I bet you didn't know that he was so tough." Then he turned to me and said, "Go ahead and tell her how tough you are."

He meant to be nice by this, but he was looking a little scary with that curly hair and beard frizzed out like a mad professor. I stood up and tried to settle him down. "John," I said, "just sit a while and relax already."

He got in my face and screamed, "I said, 'Tell her how tough you are.' "

It was stupid, but with the girls there, I wasn't going to back down. "No," I said. "I'm not going to say that."

Suddenly he swung his hand up right alongside my chin. At first it seemed like he barely touched me with his finger, but I felt a searing pain, as though my skin had been ripped off.

I grabbed my face and spun away from him. It would have been suicide to put up a fight, but the Count wasn't about to hit me again. Instead, he leaned over me and blubbered, "Oh, look what I did. You're the only friend I have in the whole world. You saved my life and look what I did to you."

I didn't have to say a word. I'm sure the look on my face said it all: "You crazy motherfucker."

The Count was ready to make amends. He was going to show us a trick. "Go get your gun," he told me. "I want you to point it at me. When I say, 'Now,' you pull the trigger. I'll catch the bullet in my hands."

I replied with the same look I had on my face before. But the Count was serious and that made it even more frightening. He talked to me like he was a magician and I was up on stage with him. "Really," he said and got in front of the floor-to-ceiling window. "Just stand over there and I'll stand here, so no one else will get hurt."

"John," I said, "how am I going to explain this to the cops when I kill you?" I had to shoo him and his girl out of the apartment. From then on, I tried to keep my distance. He would send me business, and call every once in a while, but I refused to socialize with him.

Then one day I got a call from a South Side guy who had been one of the Count's karate pupils. He had made him a partner in his car dealership. He said, "Can you come out here? The Count has got a problem." I drove out, and he told me that a couple of guys came to the lot with a shotgun and were looking to kill the Count. He said their names were Sammy Anarino and Pete Gushi.

Although I didn't know it at the time, they were with Jimmy "the Bomber" Catuara, who ran a crew for the South Side group. The Count had finally met the Mob, and from the wrong end of a shotgun. Since we parted ways, he had built a little empire of adult bookstores. The jewel in his crown was a large storefront in Old Town, still a haven for hippies and headshops. It made him a ton of money. He had intimidated the previous owner, some little Jewish guy, into selling it, but then never paid him what he promised. This Jewish guy had always made his street tax payments to the Mob, so when he complained to them, they promised to get his store back. If it had been anyone other than the Count, the Mob would have tried to threaten him. But they knew they couldn't give him a beating, so they decided to just kill him instead.

I realized I needed a higher authority to save the Count. I went to Marco. To my surprise, he knew the Count and the two guys who were sent to get him. He said, "I'll arrange a meeting and you can straighten this thing out."

A couple of days later, I took the Count to a motel by the racetrack in Cicero. Upstairs on the second floor, there was a bar. When we came in, Pete and Sammy were having a drink, dressed in pullover shirts and slacks, like they were going to the track. I had come from court, but because I wore a suit, Pete was ready to call off the meeting. He said, "What are you, a cop or something?" I had to show him my card, so he could see I was the Count's lawyer.

Pete and I went to a table in the back of the room. I left the Count at the bar with Sam. I knew he would be of no use in any negotiation. It took Pete and me just a few minutes to reach an agreement. The Count could keep the bookstore. He just had to pay the Mob $25,000 and that would be the end of it. Of course the original owner got screwed, but who cared?

When we went back to the bar, we saw Sammy and the Count sitting at a table. At least, I figured, they were calm and acting like adults, but as we got closer, I saw Sammy holding a fork like a dagger. "See this?" Sammy said. "I use this to rip eyes out."

The Count replied, "I don't need that." Then he started making with the hands. "I rip out eyes with these."

Pete and I were both pissed. What did we need this macho stuff for? He grabbed Sammy and I grabbed the Count.

Little did I know that this was exactly the introduction to the Mob that the Count wanted. He agreed to come up with the money and continued to stay in touch with them. A month later, I bumped into Pete when he came to see his lawyer, who was sharing my office. He said, "You tell that crazy Count to stop calling me at four in the morning."

"Pete," I said, "you got no business talking to the Count. You guys are like poison together."

A week later, the Count came up to my office. He wasn't dressed in crazy outfits any more, and he wasn't staying in shape either. He had puffed out, like Elvis did in his last days. But he was as manic and extravagant as always. "You're one of the best friends I have in the world," the Count told me. Then he grabbed my shoulders and whispered, "So I want to cut you in on something I have going. You could pick up a million dollars in cash for your end. But if I tell you what it is, you can't back out. This is going to be the biggest thing in history."

At times like this, when I was worried about him, I didn't call him the Count. "Listen, John," I said. "I've got a better idea. You keep the million and if I need it, I'll borrow the money from you." Whatever this "thing" was, I assumed it had to be illegal. Back in college, my friend Tommy had said something similar about my not backing out and he then tried to railroad me into committing a robbery. I wasn't falling for that one again. I said, "John, I don't want to know anything about it. I don't want to be involved. Besides, in my own experience, a million dollars shouldn't come so easy. Take my advice and forget whatever it is you've got planned."

Three weeks later, I was riding in my car when I turned on the radio and heard that a gang of masked men had broken into the Purolator armored car vault in Chicago and got away with $4.3 million. It was then the biggest cash robbery in U.S. history. Instantly, I knew this was what the Count was talking about. I just hoped to God he hadn't gone and done it with the Mob guys.

Of course, my worst fears came to pass. In a matter of weeks, Pete Gushi was back to see the lawyer sharing my office—to surrender to authorities for the Purolator robbery. To show you how smart Pete was, the FBI agents caught him trying to stash a wad of bills from the job behind a seat cushion in our office just before they hauled him away. He was indicted along with seven other guys, among them a com- modities broker from Boston who was accused of trying to launder the cash. I figured he was someone else the Count brought to the party, since the Count had business interests out in Massachusetts.

Only the broker was acquitted; the others took pleas or were con- victed. A few weeks after the trial, the Count gave me a call and asked that I drop by that night to see him. He had finally settled down with a very cute little blonde I called Christa. She managed his adult book- store in Old Town and they were living in a fancy condo on Lake Shore Drive. I brought along a girlfriend, in case I needed an excuse to duck out. We didn't get there until 9 P.M. Christa let us in. The Count ignored my girlfriend and grabbed my arm. With that crazed look in his eye, he said, "Let me show you something."

I followed him back into his bedroom. He opened the closet, and inside was a cardboard box full of money. By this time I knew big money when I saw it, and I figured he had hundreds of thousands, if not a million, in there.

Clearly he was high on something stronger than booze. Sweat was pouring off him, his eyes bugged out, and he was breathing heavily. "You always thought that I was a bust-out and a loser," he said, "but look at this. Look at this." For all of his financial success with the sleazy businesses, and for all of his fame in the martial arts world, Count Dante was still a South Side Irish kid, trying to prove how tough he was.

By now, I had no doubt where he got the money, but I didn't want to hear it from him or be implicated in any way. "Count," I said, "I'm glad for you. I hope you enjoy it. Just don't tell me how you got it." I stayed another forty-five minutes, to be polite, and then I grabbed my girl and left.

Hours later, at four in the morning, my phone rang. It was the Count. "Bob," he said, "you know all that money I showed you? That was just counterfeit. That wasn't real."

"John," I replied, "didn't you hear what I said? I could care less whether it was real or fake," and hung up.

The next evening, I got a call from his girlfriend Christa. "Hurry up," she said, "you have to come over here."

I rushed over to their condo and she let me in, sobbing hysterically. Without saying a word, she led me to the bathroom. There on the floor, slumped against the toilet, was the Count. I didn't have to get too close to see he that he was dead.

"What happened?" I asked her.

She said, "I don't know. He saw some people here earlier in the day, but I can't tell you who they were. They must have done something to him." There was blood coming from his nose, which is supposed to be a sign of poison, but Christa had no interest in finding out for sure.

Like a lot of people who see the dark side, Christa didn't want justice, revenge, or anything else. She wanted to escape with her life and, at all costs, she wanted to avoid a police investigation. I called a friend of mine who owned a funeral home on the South Side and asked him to send over a hearse. Then I called the cops. While we were waiting, I asked Christa if these guys who visited the Count had taken his money. She didn't know what I was talking about. I took her back to the bedroom closet, and when I opened it, the box with all the cash was gone.

Fortunately, I knew the cops who showed up. I said, "This is a good friend of mine. Let the funeral home take the body for now, and they'll do the transport to the morgue for an autopsy." But the Count never did leave the funeral home. Christa asked the funeral director to cremate him instead, and no one was ever the wiser about the cause of death. I never had any suspicions that Christa took the Count's money. A few years later she got married, and I knew she and her husband always struggled to make ends meet. It wasn't as if she had a bundle of cash lying around.

By disposing of the Count the way we did, we only added to his myth for all those martial arts fanatics who idolized him. I'm told that they still think he was knocked off by a rival *sensei* or some such nonsense.

Mystery, too, swirled around the Purolator job, even though Pete Gushi took a plea and agreed to testify against the other defendants. By the time the case came to trial, one of the gang was found dead, and a witness was almost killed by poison in his prison cell. For some reason, the Count's name never came up, even though, from what I could tell, he was the missing link between the Mob, the Purolator guard who let everybody in, and the Boston commodities broker. Still, the Feds never recovered $1.2 million and Pete never fingered anyone higher up in the Mob. He said he dropped a suitcase with the missing money on the lawn of his crew chief, Jimmy the Bomber. Jimmy testified that the suitcase "mysteriously" disappeared, too. It was another Chicago trial that left the press clucking their tongues. People shook their heads and wondered how the Mob could get away with it. By this time, I was not shaking my head. Maybe I didn't know exactly what had happened, but I had a pretty good idea.

INNER CIRCLE
FIRST WARD

CHAPTER 5

HIGHLIFE WITH THE LOWLIFES

F rom the moment Harry Aleman was acquitted in 1977 until 1981, I had the tiger by the tail. People who once had no time for me suddenly looked at me with respect and even fear. Although I never discussed what I had done for Harry, I knew the Mob bosses all found out, because suddenly their crew leaders were coming my way with business. Money flowed into my practice beyond my wildest dreams.

But there was a price for all that raw power and success. At any moment, the tiger could turn on me and, with one swipe of its paw, tear my head off. Very soon after I earned the overwhelming gratitude of the Mafia kingpins for fixing Harry's trial, I needed a favor of my own from them. One of their boys wanted to kill me, and it was none other than my oldest friend in the Mob, Ricky Borelli.

My troubles with Ricky gave me a whole different view of the First Ward and the relationship between John D'Arco Sr. and Pat Marcy. As far as the public was concerned, Senior was the boss in the First Ward, and he certainly looked the part of the Old World politician—always with a laugh and a slap on the back. A First Ward alderman from 1952 to 1962, he was still the Democratic Party's ward committeeman. Over the years, whispers about his connections with organized crime were minimized or ignored. When his son Johnny got elected to the State Senate, it seemed to further sanitize his past. The newspapers made him another "colorful" Chicago character, like a football coach who had been picked up a few times for drunk driving.

I was no smarter than the rest. During my seven years at 100 North

LaSalle, I figured Senior was as high as you could go in the First Ward. My arrangement with his son's firm, Kugler, D'Arco and DeLeo, turned out to be as lucrative as I expected. I got all the work they used to farm out to a dozen other lawyers. Fifty percent of the fees went to me, and the rest went to the firm. Within months of our working together, they moved the firm's office to my floor to make things more convenient for the secretaries. Still, I always insisted on keeping a separate office. Johnny D'Arco was a state senator and Pat DeLeo a Chicago corporation counsel. I thought it would be embarrassing for them to be seen with my organized crime clients.

Senior and son were more than happy with our arrangement. Johnny went to court with me, like his father wanted, but he had no interest in the law or any other line of work. After college, crazy as it sounds, Johnny wanted to be a poet. He even ran away to San Francisco for a while and lived with a bunch of hippies in Haight-Ashbury—until his father sent some goons to drag him back. Senior always wanted his son to be the political success that he couldn't be, but Johnny's heart was never in it.

Still, Johnny absolutely revered his father—to a ridiculous extent. Once we were together in a Vegas casino waiting in line to get our chips. In front of us, unshaven and very disheveled, was the famous University of Alabama football coach, Bear Bryant. When the cashier refused to cash in his chips before he paid off his markers, he got all grumpy and yelled, "Don't you know who I am?" A few minutes later, when Johnny got to the window, the cashier asked him about his own markers and he said, "Don't you know who my father is?"

That was Johnny. I just looked up at the ceiling. Why would some cashier in Vegas know about an old former alderman from Chicago? At times like this, you just wanted to give Johnny a slap and tell him to grow up already.

Usually Johnny's chief concern was getting laid. By lunchtime he was off to the gym to play racquetball or work out. Many afternoons he was holed up in an apartment, getting a blowjob from one of the girls he hired as State Senate interns. With older, more sophisticated women, he was incredibly awkward. That's where he most wanted my advice. Although he regularly skipped appointments with our clients, he was always there to grab a table at a popular outdoor café. If he saw an attractive girl, he asked me to see if she would join us. If I ordered a drink, he ordered the same drink. If I ordered a steak, he ordered that, too.

My only fly in the ointment at Kugler, D'Arco and DeLeo was Patty DeLeo, Senior's son-in-law. I knew from the start that he ran the firm, but I thought he had no reason to feel threatened by me. His bread and butter had always been civil cases, not criminal ones. Patty was corporation counsel for what was then known as the License Court. Meanwhile, a partner in the firm, Dave Kugler, represented bars that were brought before Patty's court for violations like selling alcohol to minors. Before the trial, Patty would find the cop who had filed the complaint and tell him that the accused was going to take a plea. Then, when the cop didn't show for the hearing, the judge threw the case out. It was quite a racket, so Patty should have been fine with just the civil business. Besides, as a corporation counsel, he was strictly prohibited from criminal work.

Still, Patty wanted a hand in referring criminal cases to other firms. As I got to know him better, I understood why. First of all, he was probably getting kickbacks from those criminal lawyers, which meant he could screw Johnny and Senior out of referral fees. But even more important, referring the criminal work gave him an excuse to hang out with the mobsters at the bars and clubs and smoke his fat cigar. Patty just loved to act like a tough guy. He knew that once I became involved, all the crew leaders would eventually gravitate to me.

One Saturday morning, a few months after I started working with his firm, I got a call from Patty asking if I could come to his house. He lived on the West Side of the city, just down the street from Johnny. He answered the door, and I could see he had cuts and bruises all over his face.

"Hey, Patty," I said. "What happened?"

He was still very agitated. "Last night I was at the After Hours Club in Chinatown," he said. I knew the place very well. It was run by the Chinatown group, and was a block from their Italian beef stand, The

Hungry Hound. Drunks with the munchies could chow down on some beef and then stumble over for a nightcap. From the outside, all you saw was a boarded-up storefront. Inside, there was a huge bar that stayed open from 1 A.M. to 9 A.M. After Rush Street closed for the night, all the punks ended up in the After Hours Club. A lot of them were sons of the Chinatown crew leaders, in their late teens and twenties, and they would make their bones by getting in bar fights.

"I mentioned your name to some kid," Patty said. "You know, that we now work together, and he disrespected you. We got into a fight over what he said about you, and look what happened." He motioned around the bruises on his face like Marlon Brando in *The Godfather*. "Can you go straighten him out?"

In other words, Patty wanted me to hunt down this kid and beat the shit out of him—not the typical request one makes of his legal associate. I thought, "This is like we're back in high school."

But to that point in time, Patty had been cold towards me—still unhappy about my deal with his firm. I owed it to Senior to act helpful. I said, "I'll see what I can do."

That night I went to the After Hours Club, and found the manager, Larry, who also ran The Hungry Hound. He was one of my bookies, so we were old friends. I told him Patty's story, and he replied, "That's a bunch of bullshit. I watched the whole thing. DeLeo was trying to pick up that guy's girl and he give him a slap, like he deserved. Your name never came up."

I went back to Patty's house and said, "What the fuck, Pat?"

My relationship with Patty was never real warm and friendly after that, even though I came to respect his intelligence. But it didn't matter what Patty thought of me. I couldn't have been closer with Senior or Johnny, and that's all that mattered. Funny enough, the old man also made a bizarre request around the same time. He was at his beach house in Hollywood, Florida, and he put through an urgent message for me to call him. "I have a problem," Senior said. "Can you come down here right away?"

I jumped on the next plane and didn't even change out of my heavy wool suit. Senior's house was in a beautiful secluded spot overlooking the beach. He came to the door when I rang the bell and was ashen. I asked him what was wrong, and he took me to the front of his house. The picture window had been smashed. He told me his neighbor, who lived a few doors down, threw a rock through it for no reason. Senior saw the whole thing happen, and yelled at the guy. The neighbor yelled back, "Go fuck yourself."

It was an unbelievable story. Even more unbelievable, the perp was named du Pont, John E. du Pont, and he was one of the heirs to the DuPont chemical fortune. As a result, Senior felt powerless to do anything. He wasn't going to call the police, and he certainly wasn't going to sic some Mob enforcer on a du Pont. He figured he would use my services instead. Senior walked to the foot of his driveway, pointed to du Pont's house, and said, "Now you go straighten it out."

"This is an emergency?" I thought. "I had to fly down for this?" But I could see that Senior was really upset. Away from his stomping grounds, he looked like any other helpless senior citizen.

I trudged up the street, sweating like a pig in my heavy suit, and knocked on du Pont's door. I figured there must have been a misunderstanding. How could somebody do something so strange and unprovoked? But then du Pont opened his door, and I had no doubt about what had happened. He was a half-shaven lanky guy with a crazed look in his eyes—not too different from the muttering winos I pulled out of the gutter when I was a cop. "Are you du Pont?" I asked.

He nodded.

"Mr. D'Arco just told me what you did." Then I wagged my finger in his face. "You have no fucking idea who you're messing with over there," I told him. "You better go over and apologize, and then pay for that window or there's gonna be a real serious problem." Then I turned around and walked away. I could hear the door slam behind me.

I went back and told Senior I had taken care of it. Much to my surprise, he called me the next day to say that du Pont had packed up and left town. Some twenty years later, this same nutcase was convicted for murdering a wrestling instructor who lived on his Pennsylvania estate. He shot the man for no apparent reason. Senior never asked exactly what I did to scare du Pont away, but he was very pleased with the result.

From then on, he treated me like another son, and even asked me to drive him to certain high-profile events. Senior always felt better if he had a driver with a gun. Usually it was one of the Mob-associated cops, but he knew I was always packing too, since I carried a lot of cash. When one of his old political cronies died, Senior asked me to drive him to the wake. To be seen with him, at an occasion of such importance, was like becoming a part of the family—at least in the eyes of the political bigshots at the funeral home.

One good turn deserves another, so naturally I went to Senior when I had my problem with Ricky. But Senior did not jump around and show the outrage I thought he would. Instead, he listened with a grave expression on his face, and then picked up the phone to call Pat Marcy.

As far as most people knew, Pat Marcy was no more than John D'Arco Sr.'s assistant. Pat never held elected office and his only title with the First Ward Democratic Committee was secretary. Senior had a huge office in our building. Pat's was a closet by comparison. In public, Senior was the center of attention, while Pat faded into the woodwork. Senior always had a driver. Pat drove himself.

But watching Senior on the phone with Pat that day, I could immediately see who was the boss. Marcy was at home, and he asked that I drive out immediately to see him.

He had a sprawling ranch house in the suburb of Des Plaines. Marcy took me through the house, past an indoor pool as big as any in a hotel, and out to his patio in the back yard. We sat by a grill and wraparound bar. A high brick wall enclosed the entire property, so no one could see inside.

Pat and I still didn't know each other very well, mostly to say hello at Counsellors Row. After I fixed the Aleman case for him, he referred me a few gambling cases from the Cicero group. At his house, he made no attempt to be social. He didn't even bother to get me a drink. Once we were settled, he cut right to the chase and asked me about my problem. I didn't mince any words about Ricky. "I'm sure this guy was going to fucking kill me," I said.

To anyone else, Ricky Borelli looked like the last person in the world to worry about—a big teddy bear in his rumpled cop's uniform with crumbs on his tie. But I knew there was a nasty side to Ricky, and if rubbed the wrong way, he could do nutty things. For example, he told me what he and Marco did to a guy his girlfriend accused of raping her. They beat him half to death with pool cues. When the guy passed out, they threw lighter fluid on him, let it burn until he woke up, and then beat him again. It took weeks for him to recover, and Ricky kept calling him in the hospital room to say they were waiting for him when he got out. The guy left town and was never heard from again.

I also knew that Ricky had the potential to do more than assault and battery. Because he was a cop, he was licensed to carry a gun, and therefore a very valuable asset for the Mob. There were times, he implied, when he paid off his gambling debts to Outfit bookies by doing an "extracurricular." I always took that to mean he whacked someone.

After I began my law practice, I stopped keeping my little book for him. He was always coming up short, and it wasn't worth my time to make him pay. He was like a greased walrus when he owed you money. After a few years, as a favor, I would still place some bets for him, but I tried to keep it to a minimum. We still saw each other frequently. While he was "on duty," in his patrolman's uniform, he came to the office all the time to play gin with me and the other lawyers. Also, he was often around when I hung out with Marco.

Then in 1977, during the football season, he took me aside to ask a favor. For some crazy reason, Marco had let Ricky open his own booking office. "I'm getting real big action," he told me, "and I don't want to get stuck with it if the score goes the wrong way. Can I lay some off with you?" For old time's sake I let him bet $5,000 on certain games. The first week he lost a little, then he won some—which is the worst thing that can happen to a bad bettor—and the following week he lost big, about $30,000. He was supposed to pay me by Saturday, but he was short again. Ricky never changed. He was always coming up lame. I told him I wouldn't take any action until we straightened out, but he said, "Look, somebody owes me a bunch of money. He's in Vegas right now. Just let me play one more time and we'll get straight when he gets back next week."

Like an idiot, I said, "Okay fine," and like an idiot, Ricky bet and lost again. Now he owed me $50,000. I wasn't going to press him for the money. I figured he was broke and there was nothing I could do about it. But he called me the following Saturday night to say he had rounded up $10,000. He wanted me to meet him in Austin Park, on the western border of the city, just off the freeway. I had driven by the place many times. It was rundown in every way, with all the streetlights shot out to hide the dope dealers and hopheads. He said, "I'll be waiting for you outside the clubhouse."

I said, "Sure," but after I hung up the phone I started thinking. Why, with all that cash, would he be hanging outside some boarded-up building in a city park? Why didn't he want to meet in a bar or club? I called him back ten minutes later and said I had a hot date and she wanted to go out to dinner. I told him to call me up on Sunday to set up another meeting.

Usually on Sundays Ricky called after every football game, but I didn't hear from him until after 5 P.M. He told me to meet him at Marco's club. Now I really smelled a mouse in the kitchen. Sunday evening was the only time in the whole week when the place was closed. I called Frank Renella, one of the enforcers from Marco's crew. He was a likeable guy but also very tall and threatening. Frank was not afraid of anybody—especially Ricky. They had beefs from a long way back. Frank owed me a few favors, so he gladly went ahead to the club with one of his guys to see what was what. He called me back a few hours later. "Ricky was in a back room," he said. "He didn't have any money for you, but he had some other guy with him that I never saw before. I think it was going to be a problem."

It was all so unreal. I had never threatened Ricky or even bugged him about what he owed me. But suddenly, I realized my connections with Senior and Johnny made him see me in a different light. I was more than just another guy he owed money. Now he thought I was dangerous enough to collect it. This time I couldn't risk asking Marco for help. Ricky was still his cousin, and there was no telling what he would do for family.

Pat Marcy listened to my story in silence. He knew all about Ricky and Marco. When I finished, he yelled at me, "Why the hell are you gambling like that? You should know better." Like he was my uncle or something. Then he calmed down and said, "Don't worry. I'll take care of it."

The next day at Counsellors Row, I saw Senior, and he said, "You're not going to have a problem with that guy." Ricky then disappeared.

I have no idea where he went. Maybe they just banned him from Marco's club and the places they knew I'd go. I never said one word to Marco and I have no idea whether he was involved in Ricky's vanishing act. People with the Mob often dropped out of sight for mysterious reasons. Most were never seen again, but Ricky did materialize, about a year later. We said hello, and acted as though nothing had ever happened. Of course, nobody ever repaid the $50,000 he owed me, but I didn't care by then.

This whole incident with Ricky made me realize the power of Pat Marcy. Now I paid more attention when I saw him at the First Ward table in Counsellors Row. Pat always sat in the same chair, with his back to the wall and a view of both doors to the restaurant, so he could see everything coming and going around him. The pedestal phone was at his fingertips. No one else sat in his chair when he wasn't there.

Pat liked the fact he could help me, and although he yelled at me for gambling, my little beef with Ricky gave me some street credibility. Pat knew I was not the typical lawyer or, for that matter, the typical gambler. Like Marcy, I skated between the Mob world and the legit world without getting my feet too wet. He could be seen with me in public and not damage the veneer of respectability that was so important to him. He could also hang with me in private and not worry about letting his guard down.

Bit by bit, he brought me deeper into his world. To start, he invited me to sit at the First Ward table at Counsellors Row. If you wandered into the restaurant, you might wonder why that was such a big deal. The table itself wasn't fancy, and the chairs were no different than any others. But for the lawyers, the city workers, and politicians always milling around, it was like a king's court. I started to hear people talk about "Inner Circle First Ward." If you were in it, you had powers other people didn't even know about. It meant you were untouchable. No one dared give up the name of anyone in the Inner Circle—even mobsters who flipped and became government informants.

When Counsellors Row opened for business each morning, usually the first one at the table was Fred Roti, alderman for the First Ward. Fred was not the most impressive-looking guy, very short, with the face and body of a toad. But after the death of Mayor Richard J. Daley in 1976, he was considered to have more behind-the-scenes clout than any other politician in Chicago. If you watched him at breakfast, you knew it was true. He was regularly joined by local officials, like City Clerk Stanley Kusper, other aldermen, and especially Ed Burke, head of the city council's finance committee. He also met with heavyweights from the business community, especially developers and building contractors, who were the biggest campaign contributors. Roti's father, Bruno, had been a Mob boss, so he never completely tried to hide his association with the Outfit. In fact, he made a joke of it. He used to say his election slogan was "Vote for Roti and Nobody Gets Hurt."

When Marcy arrived each day, just after 11 A.M., Roti cleared his guests away, and Pat sat in his royal chair. It was immediately apparent who was in charge and who held his coat. After lunch, Roti headed off to council chambers, and Pat had the table to himself. Then you saw a different cast of characters: not the sort of people who made headlines. Instead, they were judges, police commanders, lawyers, and especially union leaders. The unions were an endless gravy train for the Outfit—a source of do-nothing jobs for mobsters and their relatives. The unions also gave mobsters extra leverage to extort legitimate businesses. A wildcat strike could have devastating consequences to a construction schedule or a crucial service like garbage hauling.

At times, when the topic of conversation got hot, Pat motioned for the visitor to follow him out the door for a "stand-up" conference in the lobby, like he had with me when I fixed the Aleman case. Other people weren't even allowed at the First Ward table. They would walk through the restaurant, catch Pat's eye, and then sit in a booth in a distant corner of the restaurant. This was the treatment he used for lawyers defending mobsters in "ink" cases. It was also how he handled visiting hit men and crew leaders, like Harry Aleman and his partner, Butch Petrocelli, who would drop in on Thursdays. Usually he sat with Butch, while Harry cooled his heels at another table nearby. I had advised Pat never to sit with more than one person when he was talking about something illegal.

After they got to know me, Senior and Pat started coming to Greco's for dinner. One night, I had them at my table when my parents walked in. I loved having them at the restaurant, and it was a major reason I kept my piece of the business. When D'Arco and Marcy got up to leave, I went to sit with Mom and Dad. My father pulled me aside. "Son," he said, jerking his thumb at D'Arco and Marcy as they put on their coats, "I used to arrest those people."

It was hard to believe. Bits and pieces of Dad's memory had started to slip at this point. As it turned out, he was on the road to Alzheimer's disease. If what he said was true, Dad would have pinched Senior and Marcy nearly fifty years before. But in the pit of my stomach, I knew he could be right. When he was a police detective, he had an uncanny ability to match names and faces. His specialty was what they called "cartage thefts," or truck hijackings, and he made some spectacular arrests that were written up in the true crime magazines.

I later found out that Senior and Pat had been arrested for armed robbery during the thirties. Senior was part of a stick-up gang connected to Capone. Once they robbed some women of their purses, and even murdered one of them. In another case, the victim picked D'Arco out of a lineup. His partner in that particular crime was found guilty, but the jury acquitted Senior. Marcy wasn't so lucky, and even served time for his conviction. In those days, he was known as Pasqualino Marchone. As far as my father was concerned, no amount of name changing, wealth, or power could ever erase the stain of armed robbery.

Pat and Senior were not the only ones with records on the First Ward Democratic Committee. Buddy Jacobson, short and stooped and in his seventies, was a constant presence at Counsellors Row. He was a partner with Senior and Pat in the Anco Insurance Company, which had a big office on an upper floor of our building. They used property insurance as another way to shake down developers, building contractors, and anyone else doing business with the city. Pat was a majority shareholder of Anco, but Buddy had started the firm.

Buddy Jacobson may have looked like a harmless old gent, but he had once been a crooked cop and enforcer for Hymie Weiss, the bootlegger who competed with Capone during the Roaring Twenties. One day Buddy was walking with Weiss in front of the Holy Name Cathedral when Capone's men drove by and sprayed them with tommy guns. Weiss died and Buddy barely survived. But he held no grudges and quickly crossed over to Capone's side.

With the money from bootlegging, Capone realized he could put his own people in positions of power to control the cops and the courts. Republican or Democrat didn't matter. He started out by taking over the GOP and then the government in the suburb of Cicero. Crews with tommy guns literally ruled the streets on election day. Capone was convicted of tax evasion and lost his mind to syphilis before the Mob got a foothold in the Democratic Party in Chicago.

After Capone, Tony Accardo was the only real Godfather to rule the Outfit. He stayed in power for nearly fifty years, until his death in 1992 at the age of eighty-six. He was known as Joe Batters for the way he whacked guys for Capone with baseball bats, but he was a lot slicker than his nickname made him sound. He oversaw the expansion of the Outfit into other cities until the Chicago Mob reigned supreme everywhere west of the Mississippi—including Las Vegas. During a half century as the boss of bosses, he never spent a day in prison.

Like Capone, Accardo saw politics as crucial in keeping his stranglehold on criminal activities in Chicago, and the key to that power was the First Ward. The city had fifty wards, but none compared to the First. In terms of power and prestige, it contained both the city's central business district, known as the Loop, and the mansions on the Gold Coast. It had the factories and packing plants on the South Side, and equally important, the slums around them, where the Mob could run its rackets and recruit its soldiers.

Accardo groomed Buddy Jacobson and John D'Arco Sr. to be his front men in the First Ward. Buddy had started out as a Republican and even ran for alderman, but along the way he got convicted of vote fraud, so he gave up any hope of getting elected. Instead, during the forties, he worked behind the scenes of the ward's Democratic committee, and eventually became executive secretary. Because he didn't have a prison record, John D'Arco was chosen to run for office. In those days, he actually bore a resemblance to Capone, not a bad image in the eyes of your typical Italian immigrant voter. Senior was first a state representative. Then, in 1950, he suddenly backed out of his campaign for reelection when he was called before the U.S. Senate's Kefauver Committee on Organized Crime. But two years later, he had no trouble getting elected as First Ward alderman. He ran unopposed in the primary and general election. At the same time, Marcy joined their team as Buddy's assistant. Before long he emerged as the real brains behind the First Ward operation.

Early on, the Mob bosses expected John D'Arco to be mayor one day, but Senior was never the sharpest blade in the drawer and didn't command the respect of his fellow aldermen. In 1962, the FBI tapped the phone of Sam "MoMo" Giancana, then the Outfit's CEO. During one wiretap, they heard Marcy telling Giancana to "dump D'Arco." According to FBI agent and author Bill Roemer, Giancana was reluctant to make a change. But soon afterwards, Roemer barged in on Giancana and Senior while they were having lunch at a local restaurant. Roemer shouted over to them, "Ho, ho, ho, it's Mo." Senior, obviously confused, acted like a politician and shook Roemer's hand. Giancana then stormed out of the restaurant. A day later, Senior checked himself into a hospital, and announced he was too ill to run for reelection. They let him stay on as committeeman, a figurehead for the Democratic Party in the First Ward. A few other Mob lardheads were "elected" alderman until Fred Roti settled in for the long haul, but the real reins of power passed to Pat Marcy.

Pat quickly showed the Mob bosses what a sharp, shrewd guy he could be, and changes in the Outfit's leadership only made him stronger. Throughout the sixties and seventies, Tony Accardo kept trying to kick himself upstairs so he could finally retire. Like in some corporation, he would be chairman of the board and some younger Mob boss would be chief executive officer. But he never found the right man who could take control for very long. A few years after Sam Giancana booted D'Arco, Accardo booted him (and later had him killed). Other choices got arrested or died.

By the mid-seventies, the Outfit was run by committee. Depending on who was in prison, one group leader would become a little more dominant than the others, but most of the time they were in agreement. If some dispute arose, Accardo or another old-timer, Joey Aiuppa, would fly back to Chicago from their retirement homes in Palm Springs. They would hash out the differences and everything would be settled without bloodshed.

This meant that each of the group leaders was like a little king inside his territory, and he didn't have to worry about anyone stepping on his toes. A good example of this was Angelo LaPietra, the boss of the Chinatown group. They called him "the Hook," because he used to hang his enemies from meat hooks when he tortured them to death. He had a big bald head, thick glasses, and the hooded-over eyes of a cobra, but he was only five feet, five inches tall. Maybe for that reason, almost all the guys in the Chinatown crews were also short. I called them the Midgets.

The Hook would have his bodyguard drive slowly through the streets of the Italian enclave in Chinatown while he sat in the passenger seat. The people in the neighborhood looked on in awe. They would point and say, "There's Angelo. There's Angelo." They would then crane their necks to see who else was in the car.

Every summer, the Hook threw a block party right behind The Hungry Hound beef stand on 26th Street. They put up a big tent and had free food. So much smoke came up when they barbecued the ribs and sausages, it looked like the place was on fire. Mobsters and their associates from all over the city would pay something for the Hook's party, even those from the other groups. The whole party, along with the donations, were supposed to be for the poor neighborhood kids. But after you took away the relative pennies the Hook spent on food, he probably had millions left over. Everyone knew it, and they would still contribute. At one point the Hook's son-in-law told me I would have "the honor" of joining their Italian-American Club, which was like Marco's Survivor's Club. Supposedly I was the only non-Italian, but I knew my membership was just another way to hit me up for all their bogus charity tickets.

The Hook's most prized racket was Chinatown itself. The Chinese loved to gamble, and their favorite place to do it was the Chinese Palace, right on the main street in Chinatown. It was like a casino inside, with traditional Chinese games and all the stuff you'd find in Vegas. The On Leong Chinese Merchants Association ran the whole operation. They bribed Fred Roti so the police wouldn't raid it, and they paid the Hook a ton of money in street tax.

Someone as heavy as LaPietra could never be seen with Pat Marcy at Counsellors Row—or any other public place, for that matter. He would just walk through the restaurant to let Pat know he was in the building. Then he took an elevator to an upper floor and walked down the stairs to an unmarked office where they met.

The more I knew about these sorts of arrangements, the more I realized how vital Pat Marcy had become to the Outfit. He was the one link between the Mob bosses and the public officials who helped the Mafia keep a stranglehold on Chicago. Marcy's reach seemed to extend into every nook and cranny of Mob business, like that of an octopus. If he answered to anyone, it was to Accardo and Aiuppa. As far as bosses like the Hook were concerned, he was their equal if not their superior. Pat became so central and so trusted, he was the one designated to receive the army duffel bag full of cash "skimmed" from the casinos in Las Vegas. He counted it, took his cut, and then distributed a share to Accardo, Aiuppa, and each of the group leaders.

A few months after he invited me to the First Ward table in 1977, Pat asked me to join him for dinner on Thursday nights. After work, we met at Counsellors Row, and waited for a big limo to swing up to the front of our building. Inside was Ben Stein, a thin dapper guy in his sixties, with both the style and sharp edges of Sinatra. Stein was another First Ward fixture with a past—an ex-con and one-time union goon who used his connections to build United Maintenance Service, the city's biggest janitorial service. He was renowned for paying off the unions not to organize his workers. He had contracts for the McCormick Place convention center and some of the largest city and federal office buildings. The papers liked to call Ben the "Mayor of Rush Street," because of his constant presence at the nicest clubs and bars. He had the best seats at sports events, too, and was pals with local and national stars from that world. For some of our dinners he brought along Harry Caray, the longtime broadcaster for the Cubs, and Tommy Lasorda, then the manager of the Los Angeles Dodgers.

Stein was married, but he always came to dinner with his girlfriend, Karen Koppel, a petite blonde in her early thirties. She had once been a stewardess. By this time, she was Ben's full-time "kept" woman, living in his Lake Shore Drive condo. Although she was young and cute, she was no bimbo. She dressed in very stylish, refined clothes. She was also smart enough to keep the players straight during our nights out and follow the thread of our conversations. If anything, she was too smart for her own good.

Our other frequent dinner companion, Dominic Senese, could not have been more different. Over six feet tall and 220 pounds, Senese sat at the table like Jabba the Hut. He mumbled just a few words at a time, if he said anything at all. He ran the Teamsters Local that controlled the produce markets and milk trucks, so he had all those businesses by the balls if he ever called a strike. Dominic was one of the few Counsellors Row regulars that Pat invited out to dinner, so he must have had power in union circles. I thought, too, he might be an old friend of Pat's, although I learned differently years later.

I figured I was invited to the dinners for entertainment, sort of the court jester. Of all the people in Pat Marcy's circle, I was the only one who joked with him or talked back in any way. He was never one to laugh, but at least I could get him to crack a smile. I talked a little business, too. I had great contacts in the court and the police force, so I could always share a little gossip. I also gave them legal advice, such as things they should do to avoid a wire, or to minimize the damage if they were caught on tape. One of the biggest reasons Pat invited me was that I always brought a different date. I think he looked forward to checking her out, even flirting a little—especially since he and Dominic came stag. It added a little spice to their evening.

During dinner, while I chatted with my girl and Karen, I listened with half an ear as Pat and Ben talked business. They were deciding how to dole out government contracts or who would run for what office and who would get appointed to what city or county job. Some of the Mob's worst hit men and goon enforcers were on the public payroll. Usually, they didn't even show up to punch in. If there was a strike going on, Pat and Ben talked about how it should get settled and whether the workers or their employers would get screwed. You could understand why Marcy and Stein were friends—from humble beginnings, with prison time between them, they had become two of the biggest power brokers in the city. The influence of the Mob truly extended from the garbage in the street to the lights on top of the tallest skyscrapers. I started to wonder whether there was any place in Chicago where they didn't have a hand. As the meal wore on, Pat would have more drinks of Crown Royal whisky—until he smelled of it. But he never seemed drunk. He was always in command, and everyone else deferred to him.

If you ever asked Pat Marcy about the source of all his influence and power in the Mob, he would say straight away, "Politics." It seemed like a strange answer, because he was so secretive and un-political. Important topics for most politicians, like the economy, totally bored him. But whenever election day rolled around, there was no doubt that he took the vote very seriously. All you had to do was walk by the First Ward Democratic headquarters in our building. On election day it would be packed with people, standing-room only, and humming with activity. Pat set up folding tables with at least ten phones, so there was no way he would miss a call. He got the results from all the precincts in the city before anyone else did, and he demanded nothing less than an overwhelming machine landslide in every First Ward polling place. He would pick up a phone and scream, "What the hell do you mean they got fifteen percent? Wait a second." Then he would shove somebody out the door and the numbers would change by the time the papers came out the next day.

To get their landslides, the First Ward did a lot of old-fashioned organizing, but they did a lot of other things that were not so legit. For example, they used the big housing projects to literally manufacture votes when they needed them. I once went with Johnny D'Arco to Cabrini Green, the rundown complex of apartment buildings that I had patrolled as a copper. He took along bags of "street money" for the party workers. Each voter got five dollars to sign for a punch card ballot and then hand it over to the precinct captain in the polling place. The precinct captain would then punch those cards himself. At the end of the day, he went through all the other cards in the precinct by hand. If he saw holes in the "wrong" places, he punched another hole to invalidate the ballot. Of course, the Republican election judges at the polling place were supposed to keep an eye on the Democrats. But Pat picked the poll workers for both parties in the First Ward. There were absolutely no checks and balances.

At first I wondered why Pat had to win by such lopsided margins. It looked suspicious. But eventually I realized that the appearance of power was more important than the questionable math of any one election. Like a schoolyard bully, if he used the right bluster, he didn't have to back it up. This was especially true with judicial races—the elections that mattered most to the Mob. If a candidate for judge dropped by Counsellors Row to ask for Marcy's support, he always gave it to him. But then, when the opponent came in, Marcy would promise to help him too. In fact, he would do nothing for either side. Merely by promising, he made the judge feel obligated when Marcy would call after the election to ask for favors. These judges had truly sold their souls by asking for his help. This made them that much more vulnerable to intimidation. How could they ever claim that Pat was threatening them when they were the ones who first came to him?

One of my law school professors, who had been appointed an associate judge, asked if I would introduce him to John D'Arco Sr. He was facing his first election and he figured he needed the First Ward's support. He was very straight, and I knew they would chew him to pieces.

"D'Arco won't talk to a stranger," I told him, "but I'll see if I can set something up behind the scenes." I didn't say a thing about him to Senior. The professor went on to win his election, but he never forgave me for not setting up that meeting. He has no idea what a favor I did for him.

To read the newspapers of the day, you would think the late seventies was a time of tremendous upheaval for the First Ward. After the death of Mayor Richard J. Daley in 1976, the Democratic machine picked Michael Bilandic in the special election to finish the term. For the next two years he stumbled through office with the kind of scrutiny Daley never had. Bilandic was too much of a nice guy to bully the press like Daley, and it made him a bigger target for criticism. Decades of corrupt purchasing and bad hires in Streets and Sanitation finally came home to roost in the winter of 1978 when the city was buried by snowstorms. Each blizzard took forever to clean up. The voters blamed Bilandic, and a few months later, he lost the primary to a so-called "reform" candidate, Jane Byrne, the former consumer protection commissioner.

The press treated Byrne's election as some sort of revolution, but at the First Ward table it was considered a total fluke. We knew Jane was no "reformer." She had been a party hack from way back, and if she hadn't gotten into a fight with Bilandic and fired from her job, she would have still been in the fold. I always wondered whether the First Ward secretly helped her, because they thought she would be easier to manipulate than Bilandic.

Her Honor was a real screamer, and like other people who make a lot of noise, it was mostly a sign of her insecurity. I loved to tick her off by parking my car in her parking spot at City Hall. Her bodyguard was a friend of mine, and he used to call and beg me to move it. "She's screaming at me to have it towed," he'd say. He knew the traffic cops in the area were my friends, too, and that none of them would call a tow on me. It was always so obvious that she had absolutely no power.

Roti and Marcy had no trouble letting Jane ride on her little ego trip as long as she didn't screw with any part of the city government that mattered to them—especially the police department.

Besides the courts, nothing was more important to the Mob than the police. Gangs had always infiltrated the Chicago Police Department, usually in the lower ranks; but by the time Jane Byrne took office, the bad apples were in positions of command. For what seemed like a few brief moments, it looked like she would clean up the mess. When the police superintendent unexpectedly retired, Joe DiLeonardi, a truly straight and honest cop, became the "acting" chief. He immediately demoted the top brass with the worst Mob connections. "Joe Di" even let detectives raid Outfit bookies. Over a period of weeks, they made hundreds of gambling arrests.

The acting superintendent and Jane walked into her office one day when Alderman Roti happened to be waiting for her. Joe Di immediately turned on his heels to get the hell out of there. With what he knew, DiLeonardi did not want to be seen in the same room with Roti or anyone else from the First Ward. According to Roti, Jane motioned for Joe Di to come back and when he hesitated, she snapped, "You come in here when I tell you."

But neither Jane Byrne nor the First Ward would bring Joe Di to heel easily. He kept up his raids on the Outfit bookies. According to Roti, he issued an ultimatum to Her Honor: either she got rid of DiLeonardi, or the municipal unions would shut down the city during the upcoming contract negotiations. Just as the Mob thought she would, Jane Byrne buckled. In six months, the Chicago Police Department's reform era came to an end, and crusading Joe Di was sent packing to a station house on the South Side. In his place, Byrne appointed Richard Brzeczek, who had been in my class at the police academy. Dick was strictly a go-along guy.

On Roti's orders, Dick and Jane appointed Bill Hanhardt as his deputy chief of detectives. Bill was probably the most notorious officer in the entire department. He certainly looked the part of the big, bluff Irish detective and had the gift of gab. There was even talk of creating a TV show based on his career. Back in the sixties, he had built his reputation on the Criminal Investigations Unit, kind of a SWAT team, formed to bust Mob crews that specialized in hijacking trucks. Although he made some good arrests, as time went on, he got too close to the people he kept arresting. Joe Di knew that Hanhardt had gone bad and was socializing with crew leaders. To get him out of harm's way, he transferred him to the traffic division. But under the new police commissioner and Jane Byrne, Hanhardt went from the bottom of the barrel to the top of the heap. He then promoted all his cronies under him.

One of the first things Hanhardt did as deputy chief was to order the vice detectives to get their search warrants approved by their supervisors. These officers then reported to Hanhardt. This meant that Hanhardt knew the addresses of all the bookie joints they were going to raid. He then tipped off the bookies so that nothing would be in their offices when the police arrived. He also prohibited vice cops from going outside Chicago, even though he knew some of the Mob bookies were in the collar suburbs just a short distance from the city line. As a result, the only bookies the police would raid were the independents, usually on tips from the Mob.

The police department under Dick and Jane had a whole system for making payoffs. No longer did the criminal lawyers have to deal directly with the detectives involved in a case. There were other more senior detectives who would act as their bagmen. Police payoffs became as routine as payoffs in the Traffic Court.

There was never any secret about Hanhardt's connection with Roti and Marcy. After he was appointed deputy chief of detectives, he showed up at Counsellors Row all the time, and sat with Roti and Marcy at the First Ward Table. He usually came in around 1 P.M., wearing the full officer's uniform with the braided epaulets. He took the next hour for lunch. Occasionally he and Pat got up from the table and went into the building's lobby for a private conference. Marcy told me that Hanhardt was the FBI's liaison with the Chicago Police Department, so he could keep Marcy up-to-date on the Feds' organized crime investigations. Pat arranged for him to meet with the Mob bosses at Counsellors, too. A few times I saw Hook LaPietra walk into the restaurant, catch Pat's eye, and then head straight downstairs where they had a basement bathroom. A few minutes later Hanhardt would get up and follow him.

I had no idea what they talked about down there; but by this point, Hanhardt had become so corrupt, I felt he would do anything for the right price. According to Harry Aleman's partner, Butch Petrocelli, when someone like a bookie or thief was on the run from the Mob, Hanhardt would have him picked up by a squad car. The cops would then deliver him to the hit men.

Personally, I never had too many discussions with Hanhardt. Whenever I looked at him, in his clown-suit uniform, it turned my stomach. My father had given so much to the department and never had a prayer of advancement—precisely because he was so honest. Hanhardt rose to the top despite his corruption, prospered because of it, and, worse yet, actively battled the decent cops who remained. Once, when they returned to the table after a lobby conference, I heard Pat and Hanhardt mention the name of Rich, a friend of mine on the gambling squad. My blood froze. Hanhardt said he was going to take care of him. I didn't know if that meant a transfer, a beating, or death. A little later, I worked up an excuse for my own lobby conference with Pat. Before we turned to go back into the restaurant, I asked if he and Hanhardt were talking about Rich. He wanted to know why I was asking, and I told him that Rich was a good friend of mine. Pat exploded, "That cocksucker is your friend? That motherfucker?"

A few days before, Rich had raided a card game in Cicero. The son of a Mob boss ran it. As the cops pushed everyone into a corner, this kid grabbed a bunch of papers and ran into the bathroom with them. Rich yelled after him, "Don't throw that in the toilet," and when the kid did, he gave him a good crack across the head.

"There's no way," Pat said, "this guy is going to get away doing that to one of ours."

"Wait, Pat, wait," I said. I had to think fast. "You can't let anything happen to him, because he helps us on all of our gambling cases." There was no truth to that, but it was the only way I would get Marcy to show any mercy. "You want to keep him where he is. I'll talk to him, so this doesn't happen again."

Later that day I called Rich and I said, "You got a problem, and I'll take care of it, but in the future, you can't put your hands on these guys."

Even though he did the Mob's bidding, Hanhardt was an outsider. There were other cops who were actually "made" members of the Mafia. Ricky Borelli was one, but a small fry. The supreme example of the Mafiosi cop was Blackie Pesoli, a big muscular guy with the chiseled looks of Sylvester Stallone. You always saw him in a neatly pressed patrolman's uniform with spit-shined shoes. Occasionally he served as Senior's driver, but he was also a regular at Counsellors Row.

I could never figure out why this flatfoot should be so important and, for his part, he didn't pay any attention to me—until I started working on the Aleman case. Then, one day, he approached me at the restaurant. Even when he was friendly, he had an incredibly intimidating manner, like he was just about to hit you. "I hear you're handling Harry's thing," he said. I wouldn't answer him yes or no, and he was impressed that I kept my mouth shut. As it turned out he was incredibly tight with Harry and Butch. In fact, there were times when he drove them on their "errands." Then he said, "If it goes right with Harry, you'll be the biggest lawyer in town, and I can bring you a lot of business."

I just nodded and didn't expect anything more to come of it. How many referrals could I get from one copper? But after Harry was acquitted, Blackie did bring me cases from all over the city and the suburbs. He knew every judge in the metropolitan area and, if a judge was crooked, Blackie also knew how to pay him off.

When most judges started out in Cook County Court, they cut their teeth in Traffic Court, and that's where Blackie ruled the roost—even though he had no official title or function in the building. If the Mob wanted tickets cleared up or reports destroyed, Blackie took care of it. Once we were in Traffic Court together, and Blackie barged into the office of Tony Bertuca, the chief corporation counsel. Tony was having a meeting with four other lawyers. I turned to leave, but in his booming voice, Blackie said, "I need the office. Now get out of here." Without a whimper, Tony cut short the meeting and left his own office with all the lawyers trailing behind him. Blackie sat down and put his feet up on the desk like he owned the place.

Blackie never ceased to amaze me. He had his finger in more pies than a Mob boss. He owned a piece of several different prizefighters, including Jumbo Cummings, who fought heavyweight champ Joe Frazier to a draw (and is now serving a life term for murder). He made deals with the black dope gangs. He also ran the company that provided security at Chicago Stadium. In the eighties, during the height of Michael Jordan mania, if I wanted to see a Chicago Bulls game, Blackie waltzed my date and me right into the building. Sometimes he sat us down in the press box with the reporters. Sometimes we sat in the crow's nest with the cameramen.

But like everyone else in the Outfit, his primary concern was gambling.

He had several bookies working for him, and he always wanted me to bet with them. I discovered there was just one problem. Blackie refused to lose. The first time I bet with one of his guys, I beat him for $5,000. But when I called back to collect, nobody answered the phone. I tracked down Blackie and asked what happened.

"Oh," he said, "that guy got killed."

Four months later, Blackie introduced me to another one of his bookmakers. I told Blackie, "I hope he has life insurance."

I beat this guy, too, the first week we played. The next week, I was down $10,000 on Friday, but hit absolutely every bet on Saturday to go up $20,000. That evening, I called to double-check my figures, and again the line on the phone was dead.

When I saw Blackie, I asked what happened this time. "Oh," he said, "that guy got arrested." If you call in bets to a bookmaker and he gets arrested, all bets are off. I later found out from Rich, my buddy in Vice, that this bookie had *not* been pinched. Of course, Blackie still expected me to pay him the money I owed before the supposed arrest. It was the last time I ever bet with him.

At some point in his police career, the brass offered to promote Blackie to sergeant, but he didn't want any part of that. He was happy being a patrolman. That way he could report each day to his own little desk in the basement of the Greyhound Bus Station, grab his patrol radio and off he'd go. Pity the poor pimp Blackie happened to catch on his way out. This had long been a problem in the station before Blackie came. The pimps would prey on the single girls who got off the buses. But Blackie had no time for filing arrest papers or sitting in court. Instead, he cuffed the guy and dragged him down into the basement, where he strung him up over a water pipe and beat the living hell out of him with his nightstick. I saw Blackie dump one of these guys like a sack of potatoes into the alley. He put a finger in his face and said, "Never come back here. If I even see you driving around the block, I'll fucking kill you."

I always thought I was familiar with the violence that men can do, seeing it firsthand as a kid growing up on the South Side of Chicago and later as a cop. But Mob violence was different from anything I had known. It was truly a depraved indifference to human life—whether friend, foe, or just some hapless stranger.

There were certainly times when I benefited from having the Mob's muscle in my corner. But aside from my beef with Ricky Borelli, I never asked for help; I got it, whether I wanted it or not. Once, I was sitting in Counsellors Row with Marco and Butch Petrocelli when George, one of the restaurant's owners, tapped me on the shoulder. "Somebody's asking for you," he said. He pointed to a big barrel-chested character standing by the cash register. I had seen him a few times at a downtown jazz bar, but never knew what he did for a living. When I approached, he said, in a distinctive British accent, "I'm here to collect the money for Hal Smith."

Hal Smith was one of my independent bookies. The previous week, I bet one way with him and lost. But I covered those bets with another bookie and ended up winning more from him than I lost to Hal. I gave the losing bookie another week to pay me and told Hal that he could wait. When he complained, I told him to fuck himself. "Listen," I whispered to the Brit. "I told Hal that I'll pay him as soon as I get paid by this other bookie."

But the Brit started getting belligerent. He said, "I want the money right away, and I'm not taking no for an answer."

I glanced over my shoulder and could see Marco and Butch craning their necks to look at us. "Believe me," I said, "this is not the right time and place for a beef." The next day was Saturday and I usually spent a few hours in my office, playing cards. I asked for his phone number and said, "I'll call you tomorrow, when it's quiet, and we can get this settled."

I went back to the table, and Butch asked, "Who was that?"

"No one," I said. "Just some guy trying to collect for Hal Smith."

Butch said, "Hal Smith? That rat motherfucker? Are you betting with him?"

Evidently the Outfit had some longstanding beefs with Hal Smith. They believed he stole business from one of their bookies. So Butch wanted to "grab" Hal's goon. I couldn't talk him out of it.

I called the Brit the next day and arranged for him to meet me at the Walgreen's on the corner of Chicago Avenue and Michigan Avenue, in the heart of the city's shopping district. The luncheonette's booths were right next to huge windows that looked out on the busy sidewalks. It was so public, I figured nothing too bad would happen there.

At around nine-thirty that Saturday morning, I pulled into the bus stop outside the drugstore. The Brit was already in a booth and looking right at me as I got out of my car. I walked through the revolving doors and slid into the booth across from him. Casually, I scanned the restaurant, but there was no sign of Butch or his guys. Maybe he had a late night and forgot all about this meeting. "Hey, how you doing?" I said. I motioned for the waitress and ordered a cup of tea.

This guy was so big, he could barely fit into the booth. After a little chitchat, he looked at me and asked, "Have you got the money?"

There was no stalling him. I had promised to bring all the money to the restaurant. I thought, "What the fuck am I going to do now?" At this point the waitress tapped me on the shoulder and asked, "Are you Bob Cooley? Telephone call." She pointed to a phone on the lunch counter. I picked up the receiver and it was Butch, calling from a pay phone on the street. He said, "Get the fuck out of there. Go take a ride."

I hung the phone up, stared straight ahead and walked right past the booth where the Brit was sitting. Out of the corner of my eye, I saw the surprised look on his face. As I pushed through the revolving door, Butch pushed from the other side. Behind him were Bobby Salerno, Fat Mike Bryant, and another hit man. When I got into my car, I saw the four shove themselves into the booth around the Brit.

The next day, I got a call from Hal Smith. "Have you got my money already?" he asked.

"I met your guy yesterday," I said, "and I gave it to him."

"I haven't heard from him since," he replied.

I said, "That's your fucking problem."

The Brit was never seen again. I hope they didn't kill the guy. Maybe they scared him back across the Atlantic. But these people didn't fool around. Not the street guys and not the bosses. You were always playing with fire.

It was one thing for them to beat up on goons. It was another when they mauled innocent people. No one was worse than Marco, who got especially nasty when he was drunk. Once, a policeman stopped him when his car was swerving all over the road. In a rage, Marco tore out of the car and jumped on the cop while he was writing the ticket. During the fight Marco bit off part of the guy's finger. To add insult to injury, the cop got fired, too, since the Mob had influence in the little blue-collar suburb where he worked.

As my business with the Mob continued to grow, and I continued to hang out with the crews, I witnessed more acts of senseless brutality. For the crews, bar fights were just another part of nightlife, like someone else might think of playing pool or seeing a show. The mobsters weren't the only ones in a bar looking for trouble. I got in a lot of beefs myself. Maybe a guy would push me out of a chair or say something to my girl. I was always able to take care of these jokers on my own. But if I was with Marco and his crew, and I knocked someone down, they would all gather around and do a stomp job on him. That's how they operated. If you got in a fight with one of them, you got into a fight with the whole gang. I didn't want their help, but I couldn't stop them either or they would have thought I was weak, and you can never let a mobster think you're weak. For my own safety, I had to walk away, but inside I hated it. I always detested bullies, and now it was like I was one of them.

As far as Marco was concerned, I was his lawyer and social director. Wherever I went at night, he followed close behind. That's what happened when I started to go to the nightclubs in the south suburbs. If I met a nice girl at Greco's, after dinner I would take her to Condessa Del Mar. It had a restaurant in the front and a big showroom in the back for the top Vegas-style entertainment of the day, from Sinatra on down. I became a regular there, and I always got one of the best tables—even if the show was sold out.

Marco decided he had to be a big shot at this nightclub too. He took his crew with him to see a very popular act in those days, Freddy Bell and the Bellboys. While they were all waiting in the bar, Marco ordered a bunch of drinks and wanted to start a tab, but the bartender insisted on being paid first. One word led to another until Marco jumped over the counter and started pounding the bartender. The crew took this as a sign to start smashing up the rest of the place, and after it was totally destroyed, they went into the kitchen, tore the sinks from the walls and turned over the ovens.

That night I was supposed to meet Marco before the show started. When I got to the club, the whole place had been shut down. I was told that the coppers took Marco and his guys off in a paddy wagon. I went to the station, but they were long gone by the time I arrived. It was another police department in the Mob's pocket. Steve, the Greek who owned the nightclub, was stomping around the station parking lot.

"How could the cops let them all go?" he asked me.

I couldn't begin to answer. Worse yet, I realized that I was the one who had brought the Marco plague into his beautiful club. It took Steve a week to get the place back in shape, and the very night he opened for business, who showed up in the bar again? Marco. He just couldn't stay away. At least he apologized and said it wouldn't happen again, but he refused to pay the $40,000 in damages. He told Steve to let his insurance take care of that.

Shortly after this incident, I sold my interest in Greco's. Being a partner in the restaurant business was more trouble than it was worth. Besides, I had moved into one of the ritziest condos in the city, right above Morton's Steak House and just off Rush Street. Now I lived only a block from my favorite hangout, Faces disco.

It would be no exaggeration to say that Faces was the hottest nightclub Chicago ever had. Although it was modeled on Studio 54 in New York, it really did act like a "club" and have some sort of bullshit membership you could buy. I never bothered with it. From what I saw, the doormen were as rude and crude to their members as everyone else. From Thursday through the weekend, people stood behind their velvet rope in lines that wrapped around the block—even in the coldest weather. But if I walked up with the Mob guys, they let us right through.

When you entered Faces, it was like a cave, with a long, low black foyer. But then you came out into a cavernous room with bright lights and glitter balls hanging from the rafters. All around the dance floor, you had booths where people sat and watched the hordes of dancers. Way in the back, behind the dance area, there was a huge horseshoe bar. We would stake out a few booths nearby that could fit about twenty people, and we'd pull over some stools from the bar. The area was literally known as "the Mob corner."

It was only a matter of time before Faces became a hangout for Marco, too. From 1977 to 1979, we met there practically every Wednesday and Friday. The schedule became as regular as my Thursday night dinners with Pat Marcy. Marco always had some of his crew along to drive him home. By this time, he had lost his license and the bosses didn't want him driving anyway. He was always so fucking drunk he was liable to kill himself.

For us, Faces had one major attraction: It was filled with the most gorgeous women in town. We tried to lure them from the bar to our corner by passing out free drinks. Nothing worked better than fancy bottles of champagne. By the end of the night, our tab could run over a thousand dollars. At some point, Marco and I started to alternate paying the bill each week. Once, when it was my turn, I was having drinks with a developer who wanted to get closer to the First Ward crowd. At closing time, the waitress brought me the bill. The developer asked for it and paid without a whimper. None of this escaped Marco's attention—even in his drunken stupor. After the guy left, he came over and said, "This doesn't count. Next week is your turn again."

I had no illusions about Marco's generosity. Like the other Mob guys, money was his god. The major reason he paid the Faces check was to impress the cute girls in our corner. Eventually, though, I had to pop that little champagne bubble. I found out his tax returns showed a minute percentage of his total income. He claimed some Italian beef stands were his sole means of support. I was no choirboy in this regard either, but at least I reported income of a few hundred thousand. "If the government wants to build a tax case on you," I told him, "they can bring in waitresses to show how you're spending all this cash. You have to have one of your guys start picking up these tabs."

No matter when I was at Faces, I almost always saw some of the Chinatown crew. They passed out drinks too, but I never saw one of them pay a bill. I figured that they were somehow connected to the owners. They were also rumored to have a piece of the fancy restaurant next door. On occasion, some poor sap would wander over from the bar and start talking to one of the girls in our corner. Almost immediately one of the Midgets would pick a fight with him. The Midgets worked out at the gym so much that they had wide shoulders, but they were not too impressive at first glance. As soon as the sap lifted a hand, a dozen guys would surround him, like a pack of wolves, and once they pushed him to the ground, they all but stomped him to death. Then, if the people around us got upset at the blood and gore, they dragged the guy out into the street and had him arrested for good measure. One of the Rush Street cops on the take would do the honors.

It got to the point where I couldn't stand the fights any more. No matter how violent the Mob was with the rest of the world, they reserved some of their most vicious behavior for each other. Probably their most effective weapon was surprise. Four times, I shared a last meal with a gangster before he went off to his death. Each one was calm and unsuspecting.

The first was Sammy Anarino, a South Side hit man who had been sent to kill Count Dante. After I arranged the deal on the Count's adult bookstore, Sam and I hung out a few times. He needed my help after someone almost shot him to death in his car. He managed to barely escape with his life, but later, while he was in the hospital, the police found a satchel in his trunk. Inside was a bottle of chloroform, handcuffs, surgical gloves, and a gun with anti-fingerprint tape wrapped around the handle. Kind of a hit man kit. The state's attorney brought weapons charges over the bag. Sam asked me to represent him, but his crew leader wanted him to also use another lawyer, Eddy Genson, who I despised. Sam met me for lunch at Greco's and tried to change my mind, but I politely refused. I wanted nothing to do with Genson. When Sam finally got up to go, he said there were no hard feelings. He left to see "a guy" at a furniture store just a mile away. Not far from the store, someone stopped traffic so that Sam's car was stuck in the middle of the block. He saw the hit men come for him, with shotguns in their hands, and jumped out of his car, but they cornered him on the sidewalk. This time they blasted away until they were sure he was dead.

A few days after Sam died, I happened to walk past Ed Genson. He was so big and fat, he needed a cane to walk. He waddled over and got right in my face.

"You better be careful what you say about me. I heard what you said to Sam Anarino, and Jimmy was not happy to hear that, either." Jimmy "The Bomber" Catuara was Sam's crew leader and one of Genson's biggest clients. He was a dinosaur from the South Side, renowned for muscling the chop shops.

With Sam dead, I figured Ed Genson and his client were in no position to throw their weight around. "Fuck you and fuck Jimmy," I said. "My friends are killing your friends, so don't you ever threaten me again."

Lo and behold, a few days later, the police found Jimmy The Bomber in his car with a couple of .22s in the back of his head—a Mafia-style early-retirement package. The timing could not have been more coincidental.

But for Genson, it was no coincidence. The next time I saw him, outside a suburban courthouse, he ran huffing and puffing to catch up to me. "The other day, when I saw you," he said, "I didn't mean Jimmy *Catuara*. I meant Jimmy *Catrone*." This was total nonsense. Catrone was Genson's law partner—a completely harmless character. But suddenly I realized why Ed was so concerned. He thought that *I* had gotten Jimmy Catuara killed. Worse yet for Ed, with Jimmy dead, he now needed all the friends and new business he could get.

I couldn't get too cocky with the likes of Genson. I had my own clients who were getting knocked off. Little Tony Borsellino was much higher up in the Mob food chain than Sam Anarino, but that didn't make him any safer. He was pint-sized, but his hair was always slicked back, and if he didn't wear a suit, he wore a sport jacket and silk shirt. He was the muscle for all the fancy clubs and bars on Rush Street. We originally met when I defended him on an assault and battery charge for a fight at Faces. After I got him off the hook, we became friends.

He supposedly made his bones as part of an elite ring of truck hijackers and served a few years for a million-dollar silver bullion heist. He was smarter and more ambitious than most mobsters, and although he didn't gamble much himself, he ran a few bookies and card rooms. He would pick my brain about the big sports events coming up and the lines his guys should have. Tony had a large crew, and when I invited him to dinner, he would bring at least five guys with him. I used to host them all at Mama DeLuca's, a family-style restaurant in Old Town. When Butch Petrocelli joined us, it would drive him crazy if Tony had a bigger entourage than he had. It got to the point where Butch would call me first to ask, "So, how many guys is Tony bringing?" It was like the Cold War missile race. One would bring nine and the other would bring ten. All their Mojos would line up at the bar while the busboys kept pulling over more tables and the owner sent out for another leg of veal.

But Tony wasn't like the other crew leaders when we went out with our girlfriends. He was more sophisticated than the rest of them and had a taste for the finer restaurants in the city, like a French place called Le Coq Au Vin, or one of Chicago's most famous celebrity hangouts in those days, Eli's Steakhouse. We would eat dinner there, chat about news of the day, and sit by the piano bar with our girls—usually until the early hours of the morning. We were at Eli's one night in 1979 when Tony got a page. He went to make a phone call. When he came back, he pulled me aside and said, "I've got to go somewhere right away and meet some friends of ours. Can you do me a favor and take my girl home?"

The next day he was found in a field on the county line with five bullets in the back of his head. The FBI had a theory that Tony helped kill some burglars who had been stupid enough to break into Accardo's house. He was supposedly whacked to cover Accardo's tracks. Although I didn't know *why* he was killed, it was the *how* that bothered me. I thought, "I'll never let anyone sit behind me in a car." Borsellino was a very cagey guy, but he still went for a ride without looking over his shoulder first.

Although I truly liked his company, I couldn't shed too many tears for Little Tony. Like Sam Anarino, he was a well-known hit man, and I'm sure he popped a few unsuspecting souls in his time. That was the business he was in.

I felt differently about Karen Koppel, Ben Stein's stylish girlfriend. In the spring of 1980, a few months after Tony was killed, she stopped joining us for Thursday night dinners. There was a mention in the press that she had disappeared and relatives were looking for her. Ben didn't look too concerned. I learned later that she and Ben had split up. Maybe she was trying to break away. Maybe Ben had found another sweetheart. Whatever the reason, when Ben ordered her out of his condo, Karen wouldn't go. This was only a few years after actor Lee Marvin's mistress won her "palimony" suit. Karen probably knew her rights, but a lot of good that did. No trace of her has ever been found.

When I asked Pat what happened to Karen, he told me, "Rick took care of that." Rick Simon was a crooked cop who had been Ben's driver and would one day take over his business. According to Pat, Ben decided to let her stay in his condo, but that wasn't enough. "She wanted $50,000 or she was going to blow the whistle on him," he said.

This was no idle threat for Ben—or Marcy, for that matter. In the years she dated Ben, Karen watched all sorts of people get close to Pat. Just during our Thursday dinners, she heard more than enough conversation to cause serious problems if she ever started talking. The poor kid thought that knowledge put her in a position to bargain. She didn't know it put her in a position to get killed. Pat said to me, "She should have fucking known better."

He was absolutely right. In fact, you could have said the same of me. I should have fucking known better myself. I was foolish enough to think that I could stay above it all and remain protected from the death and destruction all around me. In the next few months, I would find out how expendable I was.

CHAPTER 6

A RUN THROUGH THE GREASE

A t the age of thirty-six, Nick "the Salesman" Velentzas was like other Greek immigrants on the fringes of Mob society. He was in the restaurant business—he owned a coffee shop on the northwest side of the city—and he loved gambling. Short and slight, with a pleasant disposition, he was exactly the sort of person Marco and his guys thought they could muscle.

Like the Chinese, Chicago's Greeks were very big bettors. They also ran some of the most happening restaurants in the city, and let the Mob use their back rooms for after-hours dice and cards. One place in Greek-town had a whole lamb roasting on a spit right where they played craps. Guys would eat and then roll the dice, their hands dripping with grease.

Besides slinging the hash at his diner, Valentzas ran a card game and kept a sports betting book for a bunch of other Greeks. With each of these operations, Valentzas paid the Mob a street tax. But then somebody caught Valentzas at the racetracks, where he also took bets from his friends. When Marco demanded $300 a month on this action, Valentzas finally reached his limit. He refused to pay another nickel. To show Valentzas the error of his ways, Marco sent three members of his crew: my old friend Frank Renella, Donny Scalise, a former cop and Marco's main man, and Nick Boulahanis, another Greek. They slapped Velentzas around pretty good, and he promised to have their money for them in a few days. When they came back, he paid, but he still complained about all his Outfit taxes. In a heavily accented voice, he said, "All the time I pay, pay, pay, pay, pay."

Donny Scalise didn't feel very sorry for him. He replied, "For the things you've said, and the things you've done, you fucker, you should be dead. I'm gonna tell you something. You're getting the biggest pass of your life."

Boulahanis and Donny both spoke up loud and clear—and right into a wire Velentzas was wearing under his shirt. Nick the Salesman was that rare bird who didn't just get mad at the Mob; he got even. After he was beat up, he went to the Feds and offered to become an informant. Indictments for extortion soon followed against all three slappers. Now Frank Renella, who had helped me smoke out Ricky Borelli, asked a favor in return. He was desperate for me to take the case.

But if I represented Frank, it meant my co-counsel would be Eddy Genson. Marco had already engaged him to represent Donny Scalise. This was like Sam Anarino all over again. Still, I couldn't get too angry with fat Eddy. Ever since Sam and Jimmy The Bomber had been killed, he had done his best to be cordial to me. I still couldn't stand the sight of him, but when Frank Renella kept insisting that I represent him, I said I would talk to Genson and try to work something out. Ed invited me to meet him at the fancy restaurant next to Faces. He sat there, kissing my ass. "Oh, you're a good guy," he said, "and we should let bygones be bygones. You can be lead attorney in this case. You can even use my office whenever you want. I'll have one of the girls there help you."

Through the fall of 1980, Eddy and I worked together on the motions and hearings for the Valentzas case. Then, on Thanksgiving Day, about a week before the trial was set to start, I got a call from Marco. He wanted me to meet him at the Survivor's Club. It was a holiday, but I didn't mind. I could take the opportunity to collect from Marco on my other Mob cases for that week. In those days, it would have been anywhere from $4,000 to $7,000. When I got to the club, nothing seemed out of the ordinary. Guys were at the table playing cards. Ricky Borelli was sprawled out on a couch, sleeping off his turkey. Marco and I had a friendly little chitchat. We didn't see each other as much any more. I was trying to stay away from the Rush Street nightlife with the crews. "Come on," Marco said, "let's take a walk."

We always strolled around the block when we discussed serious business—just in case the Feds had planted a wire somewhere inside his club. As we walked, he said, "Bob, you don't have to worry about the Frank Renella case no more. There's not going to be any case."

I stopped dead in my tracks. "What are you talking about?"

"We're going to whack that little Greek cocksucker," he said.

"Marc," I said, "that's not going to help the case. They already have his Grand Jury testimony. In fact, it will hurt the case. They can use that testimony and we won't be able to cross-examine him."

He said, "I don't give a fuck about the case. No one wears a wire on us and lives to talk about it. We're going to run him through the grease."

This hit me like a ton of bricks. I had already been around too many killings. No way did I want to hear about a murder *before* it happened. I said, "Marc, I don't want any part of this, and you really don't want to do this either." I reminded him about another informant who was killed in the suburb of Calumet City a few years before. The Feds responded to his murder by shutting down the Mob's entire operation in that town.

Marco suddenly got real angry and cut me off. "Listen, you're our fucking mouthpiece," he yelled. "You don't tell us how to run our business. Just do what you're told. We're going to make an example out of him."

I was furious, but there wasn't a damn thing I could do. I couldn't warn the guy that something was going to happen without getting myself killed. Instead, I hoped against hope that Marco was bullshitting. Nick was supposed to be in federal protective custody. I thought, "The bastard's just trying to show off." When we got back to the club, he paid me for my cases. I sat around there a bit longer, talking to the other guys. Then I said, "I'll see you, Marc," and left.

Friday, the next night, Johnny D'Arco and I took our dates downtown to dinner and the movies at Water Tower Place, a high-rise mall and condo which had opened a few years before. Attached to the Ritz Carlton, the complex had marble on the outside and a huge glittering atrium inside. For Chicago, it was considered the height of luxury.

Meanwhile, five miles due west of the Water Tower, in a little row house on the edge of the city, Nick Velentzas met an old girlfriend for a game of cards. Marco's club was just a few blocks away. Later, as Nick walked to his car in a parking lot behind the house, a couple of guys with nylon stockings pulled over their faces came up from behind and blasted him to pieces with shotguns.

The next morning, when I opened up the paper, there was a big story about Nick's murder. It should have come as no surprise. I had been hanging with Marco and his crews for ten years. I knew they were extorting and robbing. I knew they were killing each other too. But none of those other murders hit home like Nick's. These guys had absolutely no concern for the consequences of their actions. They thought they could get away with anything. And by telling me first, Marco had practically made me an accomplice.

Soon, I got a call from Frank Renella. The Feds wanted him in for questioning about Nick's murder. They had us go to a police station in Elmwood Park, where they had found the body. The Mob had plenty of friends in that police department—from the chief on down. We got a warmer reception from the cops than the Feds did. I went into the interrogation room with Frank and listened as the FBI agents grilled him, "So where were you at nine and where were you at ten?"

It was bizarre. I don't think Frank had any idea what had happened, but there I was, sitting around like Mickey the Mope, and I knew exactly who had ordered Nick killed, and I knew about it the night before his murder.

Suddenly it was like the earth had opened up before me. Right there, in the little police station. Somehow, I told myself, I had to back away from the Mob or I would surely get swallowed up in that bottomless pit.

As if my conscience was not bothering me enough, now my father's voice chimed in too. He was getting sicker with Alzheimer's and almost never got out of the house. I tried to drop by to see him at least once a week. More and more, he would be confused about things, but he was always crystal-clear when he first saw me. He would ask if I was still involved with D'Arco and Marcy, and then he would say, "Son, you shouldn't be wasting your God-given talents on these people."

I would nod and say I was doing my best to break away from them, but inside I knew how impossible that was. I just couldn't pick up one day and say to Marcy, "I'm through. Good-bye." I knew too much for him to ever let me go.

Just a month after Nick Velentzas's death, I shared another last meal—this time with Butch Petrocelli. We met a few days after Christmas, at about 2 P.M., in a Greek restaurant called Roditys. It was a bright place with big windows and colorful murals of Greece on the walls. The food was terrific, and it was always so loud and busy that no one else could listen in on your conversation. Butch and Harry loved the place. Butch would bring practically his whole crew there for dinner, especially if he knew I was paying. For lunch, he came alone.

He had just come from a game of handball at his gym and was in a great mood. In fact, from the looks of it, he was on top of the world. The partner in all of his rackets, Harry Aleman, would be indisposed for a while—inside a federal penitentiary. The Feds caught him running a nationwide home invasion ring. Because it was a federal case, Marcy couldn't fix it like he could in the state courts.

With Harry in stir, Butch was the one collecting on all their deals and bookmakers. The Mob even had the gall to charge bettors two percent of their winnings for the Harry Aleman Defense Fund. Imagine how this went over with the bookmakers. Here's a guy who did more than anyone to terrorize them, and now these same people had to collect extra taxes to get him out of prison.

According to rumors, Butch still had the time to do an occasional extracurricular. Supposedly, he was one of the triggermen who'd killed Nick Velentzas. I wasn't about to pop that question over a plate of braised lamb. I already knew too much about the death of the Salesman. Instead, I settled up with Butch on fees he owed me for some gambling cases. Then we sat around bullshitting about nothing in particular. At one point, he looked at his watch and said, "Oops, I gotta run. I have to go meet somebody." Off he went. As usual, he stuck me with the check.

I was the last one to see Butch—or to talk about seeing him—before he disappeared. A few days later, his live-in girlfriend reported him missing. When that happened, you knew to expect the worst.

The pre-trial hearings on the Nick Velentzas extortion case continued right through January 1981. The murder of Nick barely slowed down the Feds. Just as I predicted to Marco, it was now that much harder for us to defend our clients. Every accusation Nick made to the grand jury was sure to ring true. He claimed he was being threatened by the Mob, and look what happened: They fucking killed him.

I prepared Frank for the worst, but he was the one who should have prepared me. He had a little piece of personal history that was far more dangerous to him than a federal case. It came out as Ed Genson cross-examined a policeman during the first day of trial. The cop testified that he had met Frank on a previous occasion.

Genson wanted to know what he had talked about with Frank, and the cop was evasive. Clearly, Genson knew something. He kept pressing, and the cop kept ducking and weaving. When the FBI agent got on the stand, the whole routine started over again. He had met Frank on a previous occasion. He, too, could not recall previous conversations. Something was going on.

When court recessed for the day, I got a call from the assistant U.S. attorney on the case. It was urgent and he had to see me right away. I went to his office in the Federal Building and he shut his door behind me. He said, "It's going to come out tomorrow that Frank Renella informed on some narcotics people a few years ago and got paid for the information. The agent tried to keep from saying it, but he's under oath and he has to tell the truth."

A death sentence would have been better news. As far as the Mob was concerned, once a stoolpigeon, always a stoolpigeon. It didn't matter who Frank Renella had informed on. They didn't care about what, where, or why. They would just kill him—to show what happens to informants.

Now I understood why Frank insisted that I be his lawyer on the case. Genson had a reputation for setting up his own clients when he found out they were informants. A few got whacked while he represented them. I was sure Eddy would tell Marco about Frank as soon as the Feds made it official.

From the Federal Building, I gave Frank a call and told him I had to see him right away. He gave me directions to his house, and I drove right there. He lived in a shitty neighborhood on the second floor of a two-flat. When he answered the door, he was in his T-shirt. Frank was pushing fifty, but he was still very lean and fit, with curly hair down to his shoulders and a strange, craggy face that could be terrifying. Food was on his kitchen table, and it looked like he was getting ready to eat.

"Frank," I said, "tomorrow I think the government witnesses are going to say you were an FBI informant."

Without saying a word, he went over to the kitchen drawer and pulled out a gun. He pointed it at me and said, "If you're setting me up, you're gonna be the first to get killed. If you're not, you're gonna have a serious problem."

"Wait, Frank," I said. "What are you doing? I've come to warn you. I'm your friend."

He asked, "Are you carrying a weapon?"

I unbuttoned my jacket to show him. "No."

He walked over to his refrigerator and opened the freezer compartment on the top. "If you're telling me the truth, then you'll probably need this," he said and pulled out a baggie. Inside it was a gun. A little five-shot. He handed it to me, still wrapped in the baggie, but kept his gun trained on me. He didn't bother to close the refrigerator. He opened up another drawer to pull out some bullets and gave me those, too.

He put on a jacket and looked out the window. Both sides of the street were lined with cars. I had had to park in front of a fire hydrant. Since he couldn't see anyone double-parked, it looked like he was in the clear. He motioned me toward the door. He said, "You go out first. If they're waiting for me, you're gonna get it first."

With his gun in my back, I walked down the steps and outside the building. Nobody was there. He led me down the street to his car. He got in. "You're on your own," he said. "I wish you luck." Then he drove away.

I went back home to have a quiet dinner with a girlfriend at Arnie's restaurant in my building. I had to be in court the next morning for Frank's case, so we went to bed by midnight. I hardly shut my eyes before the phone rang. It was a hit man from Marco's crew. Like a lot of those guys, I had given him money a couple of times to help him out of a jackpot. It was probably the best investment I ever made. He said, "Bob, they're gonna kill you," and he hung up the phone.

It didn't take much time for me to connect the dots. Genson must have already told Marco what he suspected about Frank. Marco must have then sent a crew after Frank. They broke into his apartment and found he had blown town. I was the only one who could have warned him.

Now I realized how serious this was. I knew Marco would be mad. I thought he might yell at me, but killing me was something else. Just a few minutes later my phone rang again. It was another member of Marco's crew. This one owed me some money and he asked that we meet later that night, so he could pay me back. The fucking idiots. Like I was a complete moron. Like that was going to work on me. I told him I was busy and hung up.

For practically the first time in my life I had trouble sleeping. If not for the warning from the hit man, I would have been dead. I couldn't let Marco think I tipped off Frank, so I came up with a crazy idea. I handwrote a statement for Frank, explaining that "he feared for his life," and that "certain persons would make sure he did not, in fact, appear in court," and signed Frank's name.

The next morning, I went to Federal Court and sat there like Mickey the Mope, waiting with everyone else for my client to show up. Court is supposed to start at nine o'clock, but by nine-twenty there was still no sign of Frank Renella.

Out of the corner of my eye I could see Genson smirking like Jolly St. Nick, hands crossed on his big belly. He couldn't have been happier with my predicament.

Finally the judge looked down at me. His name was George Leighton. He was a real straight black guy who did not fool around with the First Ward. He said, "Mr. Cooley, do you have any idea where your client is?"

I told him that some FBI agents went to see him the night before to tell him that he would be identified as an informant. Then I handed the judge the statement. He decided to proceed with the trial anyway. For the rest of the day, I sat in court and watched the proceedings without my client—like a player in a band who forgot his instrument.

The copper and the FBI agent got back on the witness stand and their testimony could not have been worse for Frank. Or me. In addition to saying that Renella had been a prior informant, the FBI agent claimed that he had also fingered Butch as one of the guys who whacked Nick. Maybe Frank figured that Butch was dead, and this would get the Feds off his back.

I knew Genson reported all of this back to Marco. I went straight home after court and didn't even go out to eat. Again I got another call, just before midnight. It was from one of my bookie clients. "We have a guy in custody," he said, "and we need to get him out. If you can meet me, I'll give you the cash for bail." It was another trap to whack me. I said I was too busy, and they would have to find somebody else.

The night before, I had hoped that Marco was having one of his fits and just lashed out in anger. But now one thing was clear: He wasn't going to give me a pass.

The next day, I repeated my little solo act in court and again my client was a no-show. Once court was in session, we all made another show about waiting for my client. Again, after fifteen minutes, Judge Leighton said, "Apparently, he's not here, so it looks like we may have to issue a warrant for his arrest."

"Okay, Judge," I said. "What can I tell you?"

Then the judge asked, "Did you get paid your full fee on this case, counsel?" Clearly he knew what was going on. "If you want to put in a request to get paid from the court, I'll consider it."

I said, "No, that's okay, Judge."

As I left the courthouse, I thought, "Now what?" I knew that Marco's people would be out looking for me. Instead of going to my office, I went back home. I threw some clothes into a suitcase, along with a big pile of cash, and headed to the airport. From there, I caught the next plane to San Francisco.

During the flight, I felt a lot of emotions—mostly anger. Marco had no fucking reason to kill me. I had done nothing wrong to him. I just didn't want someone killed again like Nick Velentzas. I was not going to step over that line.

But I was mostly mad at Marcy and D'Arco. Marco may have been an animal, but he would have never tried to whack me without their permission. I had done so much for the First Ward—things no other lawyer could do. I never crossed them or harmed them in any way. But by this time, I knew them too well to be surprised by anything. If they disgusted me, I had to be that much more disgusted with myself.

In San Francisco, I stayed with an old friend. He had a very successful business and absolutely no connections with the law or the Mob. I explained that I had to keep low for a while. I said, "Something is going on. I can't tell you what." He knew enough about my life in Chicago not to ask any further questions.

I could have hid out with him for a long time; but, after a week, I started thinking, "What am I going to do?" It was only a matter of time before I ran out of cash. If I tried to go somewhere else to practice law, the Mob would be sure to track me down. I couldn't imagine living on the run.

I only had one option: Go back and confront Marco. I had to straighten it out with him once and for all.

I returned to Chicago, but stayed very low. I didn't want any Mob people to know I was in town. I couldn't call Marco to arrange a meeting. It would give him a chance to set up an ambush. Instead, I had to catch *him* off guard. Fortunately, he was an absolute creature of habit. I knew every place he went for lunch and the day he went there. I decided that the best place to surprise him was a small, family-style Italian restaurant. It was in a storefront with big plate-glass windows.

To help me out, I called a good friend who was an undercover cop. I picked him up in my car and parked directly in front of the restaurant. The space had a No Parking sign, but I wanted my friend to be able to look inside and see what was happening there. I didn't tell him the reason for my meeting, but I warned him, "Keep your eyes open. If something goes wrong, I may need help in a hurry." I packed some personal protection as well: a snub-nosed Smith & Wesson Airweight, which I now carried all the time, and, for heavy artillery, a .45-caliber pistol.

I saw Marco's Chrysler Fifth Avenue parked down the block, so I knew he was inside. I got out of my car and quickly walked into the restaurant. There was Marco, in the center of the dining room, sitting at a table with four of the biggest, toughest guys in his crew, including Tony Doty and Donny Scalise. When I walked over to them, they all froze and stared, as though I had come back from the dead. I said, "Marc, let me talk to you for a minute."

I walked with him into the little bathroom and locked the door behind us. I wasn't afraid of him. I knew Marco wasn't packing, because the police could arrest him for carrying a gun. Physically, he was no match for me either. He would have to hear me out. I said, "I'm telling this to your face: Frank wasn't doing anything to cause you people a problem. A few years ago, he worked with the Feds to put away some dope dealers. That was it. He was never cooperating against you. I knew you were going to kill him, but he was my client and I had to warn him. I owed him that."

Marco gave me his squint-eyed stare and said, "What the fuck is the matter with you? You should know better. You were working for us, not your fucking client."

Then, referring to Ed Genson, he said, "The Fat Man did the right thing when he told us about Frank. You report to us first. You, you ass-hole, had to stick your nose where it didn't belong. What kind of example does that set for the other lawyers? As far as I'm concerned, you'll never get business from us again."

I said, "Marc, that's fine. I don't care about the business. I know you guys are pissed about Frank, but I've done nothing wrong. I did nothing to hurt you people. If you're looking to do something to me, it ain't going to happen. I ain't taking no beating. I'm packing and I'm packing wherever I am. If anyone comes around me, I'll fucking kill him. I got somebody out in front with me right now. He knows exactly what's going on. If I think something is going to happen, I'll kill you right now as we stand here."

When I opened the bathroom door, I didn't know what to expect, but there was Marco's crew, sitting at the table exactly where we left them. Classic mobsters. You took away the boss and they didn't know what to do—like a snake with its head cut off. I walked out of the restaurant, got into my car, and drove off.

The next day I went to court and then drove to my office at 100 North LaSalle. Like the old days, I parked my car in the bus stop, right in front of Counsellors Row. When I walked through the restaurant, I saw Pat

Marcy sitting there at the First Ward table. Suddenly, he was all hale and hearty. "Hey, how you doing, Bob?" he said. "Gee, haven't seen you in a while. Where you been? Vegas?" It was one of the few times I ever saw him laugh.

I nodded and went to my office. Pat may not have known where I was, but he definitely knew why I left. He never once called my office during the entire week I was away. For years he had been calling me at least two or three times a week.

Later that day, I saw Johnny D'Arco and Patty DeLeo. It was like nothing had ever happened to me. Like I hadn't even been gone for an hour. Nobody bothered to ask, "Where were you? What were you doing? Was something wrong?" Obviously, they knew that there was a problem.

Now, more than ever, I just had to get away from these people, but I had to be careful how I did it. If they thought I was totally pissed off or afraid, they might worry about me going to the Feds. I needed some other excuse.

In fact, I still wasn't sure that my problem with Marco was completely over. I carried my guns all the time. Getting shot or even killed was not my biggest worry. My worst fear was torture. These feelings would only be reinforced with the discovery of Butch Petrocelli's body, just a few weeks after my return from California. He was found in March 1981, on the floor of a car parked in some lousy neighborhood on the South Side. The remains were partly decomposed, but they could tell that Butch's mouth had been wrapped shut with duct tape. In that same way, they had bound his hands to his chest. Worse yet, the pathologist said his eyes and nuts had been melted away with a blowtorch, but it was the suffocation that killed him. He literally screamed to death. A few open cans of gasoline were alongside him in the car near some blackened upholstery. The police figured that someone threw a match inside, but then shut the door with the windows closed. The glass got scorched, so you couldn't see inside, but no air was left to keep the fire going.

A few days after the body was found, I happened to bump into Harry Aleman's brother, Anthony, and said, "Geez, that's terrible what happened to Butch."

Anthony's face turned red, and he hissed, "That fucking dirty no-good rat. He was a stoolpigeon cocksucker." Unlike Harry, Anthony was not a real bad-guy type. I never heard him talk that way before. Still, I didn't argue with him. "Okay," I said. "That's a shock to me." But I was thinking, "Butch was no more a stoolpigeon than the man in the moon."

Besides, if Butch had been a stoolpigeon, they would have left his body out in the open somewhere—as an example. They wouldn't have tried to burn the corpse. Eventually we got another explanation for why he was killed, and this one made more sense. At some point, the bosses did the math and figured Butch had kept some of the money for the Harry Aleman Defense Fund. They probably tortured him to find out where he hid it.

I had no illusions about Butch Petrocelli. Like Tony Borsellino, he was a vicious killer. But he was always loyal to the Mob bosses. I saw with my own eyes how he would meet Marcy at Counsellors Row practically every Thursday afternoon. If they could turn on Butch and torture him so horribly for a piece of cheese, they could turn on anyone.

CHAPTER 7

CHICKEN WITH WING

For a long time after my beef with Marco, I became unbelievably cautious. I always carried at least one gun on me, even when I went to court (the guards let me walk around the metal detector). I kept another pistol in the glove compartment of my car. I became much more careful about the places I went. When I had to collect on fees or bets, I didn't go anywhere strange; when I met with people for the first time, I did so only in public. I would never get into a car with someone sitting behind me. If I was offered a lift, I'd say, "I'll drive. I have to be somewhere later." I got into the habit of getting on my hands and knees to check under my car each morning. When I drove, if I looked through my rearview mirror and thought someone was following me, I'd take a sharp turn into an alley, or, on the freeway, would suddenly slow down to see if he'd pass.

My whole lifestyle changed. There were no more Thursday night dinners with Pat Marcy. I stopped going to Faces and other clubs where I knew the crews hung out. I didn't want to be with those people at two in the morning and get caught from behind in a parking lot.

Now, in the worst way, I wanted to break up my partnership with Kugler, D'Arco and DeLeo and get my office out of 100 North LaSalle. But I needed an excuse. Otherwise, they might get suspicious. Fortunately, Patty DeLeo came to my rescue. He asked me to help out a bookmaker and told me it was a "Ward case." This meant the bookie was someone connected to the First Ward, like a precinct captain, and I should do it for nothing. I was always happy to help their workers. I took this bookie to court, and, in short order, his case was thrown out. A few weeks later, I bumped into him at a benefit for Johnny.

Just joking around, I asked, "Are you staying out of trouble?"

"I can't afford to get caught," he said. "You guys are too expensive."

I thought, "What the fuck?" but I didn't act surprised. "We didn't charge you that much, did we?"

"*I* think you did," he said. "A thousand dollars! And you were only in court for a few minutes."

I tried to commiserate and explain the cost of overhead and other such happy bullshit, but out of the corner of my eye, I saw Patty DeLeo walk into the room. I excused myself and went up to him. I pointed out the bookie. "Patty," I said, "I just saw your friend over there and he told me something interesting."

"What's that?" Patty took a quick look at him but was pretty nonchalant.

"He told me he paid you a thousand dollars on his case."

Pat's face took on a surprised look. "But I told you that, didn't I?"

I said, "No, Patty. You didn't. You told me that he was a Ward Case."

Patty pulled a billfold from his pocket and counted out $500—a total admission that he had cheated me. In any other circumstances, I would have been pissed, but now I couldn't have been happier.

The next day, I put on a gloomy face and sat down with Senior. I said, "I think I want to break away from our relationship."

His mouth dropped. "Why?" he asked.

"Patty cheated me," I said. "And I'm sure he's cheating Johnny, too. I just don't want to deal with that."

"What? Are you crazy?" Senior said. "You really want to give up the kind of money you're making with us?"

I said, "I'll work out arrangements with Johnny when he comes back from Springfield. It's time we part ways."

Senior kept shaking his head. "Give it some more thought," he said.

Of course I had to run this by Marcy, too. He suggested I have it out with DeLeo in front of Senior. I replied, "I'm not going to have Senior choose between his son-in-law and me. You guys have to have DeLeo around, but I can't trust him as a partner, so I really shouldn't be involved with the firm any more."

Marcy nodded. What could he say? We both knew that Patty DeLeo could be a snake, but he was also smart and ambitious in ways that Johnny was not. I was sure that they were grooming DeLeo to take over the First Ward after Pat Marcy died.

Fortunately, the lease on my office had just run out. With the partnership dissolved, I had a good excuse to move a block down LaSalle Street to share offices with another lawyer. I explained that I was helping him out and saving on rent in the process. That made sense to everyone and didn't ruffle any feathers. I still did a lot of gambling business, especially with independent bookmakers who were paying street tax. Besides, even after I broke off the partnership, a lot of the other First Ward people kept their cases with me. The only exception was Marco, and I wanted nothing to do with him anyway.

Although my office was not in 100 North LaSalle, I dropped by Counsellors Row for lunch almost every day. I did my best to keep away from the First Ward table when Pat Marcy or Johnny were there. I would say, "Hi," or give them a friendly nod, but would not spend much time talking to them.

My strategy was always two steps forward and one step back. Although I tried to put more distance between myself and the First Ward, I wanted to be visible, so no one would ask, "Where's Bob?" and worry about what I was doing or who I was talking to.

But after a few months of this new life, I was still looking over my shoulder all the time. I knew that people in the Mob had long memories. When they were ready to whack you, they wanted you to think everything was all right so you would drop your guard. In fact, I had seen that happen four times: with the bookmaker Anthony Reitinger, Sam Anarino, Tony Borsellino, and Butch Petrocelli. All were equally clueless when they got up from their "last meal" with me and went to their deaths. Besides, I had already watched Marco in action and how he could lash out in a rage—for no apparent reason.

To feel safe again, I had to know that I was still important to the First Ward. If I worked for them on big cases, no one would be allowed to touch me. It was the only way to find peace of mind. Wherever I moved or whatever I did, everything still circled back to Pat Marcy. Once more, I needed his approval.

It came in July 1981, when I got a call from Alderman Fred Roti. He said, "Pat Marcy wants you to represent some people on a case."

I breathed easier than I had for months. The Marco beef was finally in the past and they were ready to use me again.

The case was only weeks from trial, but it sounded pretty straightforward: something to do with a shooting between two Chinese gangs in Chicago's Chinatown. One group was known as the Ghost Shadows; behind the scenes, they had become the enforcers for the On Leong Chinese Merchants Association in Chinatowns across the country. Among the four defendants in the case was Lenny Chow, one of the Ghost Shadows' top hit men. If he was convicted and started talking to the Feds, he could cause problems for a lot of powerful people in the Chinese community.

"Go meet this guy, Wilson Moy," Fred told me. Moy was like the unofficial mayor of Chinatown, and I knew he paid Roti to keep the cops away from the Chinese gambling parlors. He didn't want to be seen with Roti or Marcy, so close to the Lenny Chow trial. Fred said, "Don't bring him around Counsellors and don't meet him in your office, and when you see him, don't indicate you have a relationship with us."

When I got back to my office, there was a message from Moy and I returned his call. For a minute, I wondered if this wasn't a ploy to set me up, so I arranged to meet Moy for lunch at Arnie's Outdoor Café, just off Rush Street and alongside my apartment building. If they were going to kill me, it would have to be in plain sight of a busy street corner.

But Moy walked in all alone. Tall and thin, in his late fifties, he was dressed in a conservative suit and had the look of a professor. As he filled me in on the case, he was extremely nervous. Up to this time, he explained, On Leong had paid for an experienced criminal defense lawyer, but Moy thought the lawyer charged too much. "If you can guarantee an acquittal," he said, "we will switch our lawyers."

I would *never* tell anyone straight out that I could fix a case, or guarantee a verdict. For all I knew, he was wearing a wire. Instead, I told him that I almost never lost a trial. The real issue was what fee I should charge. Before I could tell him that, I had to look at the police report. If the state had a good case against Lenny Chow, I would charge a high fee. If not, I would charge a lower one. I said I'd call him back after I checked into it.

The next day, I met Marcy at Counsellors Row. Moy did surprise me with one piece of information: Pat had gotten the case assigned to Judge Thomas J. Maloney. Before Pat made him a judge, Maloney had been a criminal defense lawyer, and I bounced him from the Harry Aleman trial, despite Harry's objections.

"There might be a problem with me handling the case if Tom Maloney is the judge," I told Pat. "You know Maloney and I don't get along. He hates me."

Marcy totally dismissed my concern. "That won't be a problem. I'll take care of that," he said. Pat just wanted to make sure Moy would hire me.

"I'm sure I can convince him," I said.

"Then try to get $50,000 if you can," Pat said.

Once again, Marcy used his contacts to get me the police report for the case, and I read it over before I met Moy. The state's evidence against Lenny Chow depended on the testimony of the victim's three fellow gangbangers, who were nearby when he was shot. They were all in a renegade offshoot of the Ghost Shadows, and had tried to muscle protection money from Chicago Chinatown businesses. After they beat up a restaurant owner, the On Leong called in Ghost Shadows from New York to straighten these guys out. When the bad boys pulled their car up in front of the On Leong headquarters, Lenny Chow and the other Ghost Shadows appeared on the balcony with automatics. They sprayed the car with at least twenty bullets. The victim, William Chin, couldn't get out from behind the wheel. Somehow he survived the shooting, but he was still in bad shape.

The whole case looked pretty shaky for the prosecutors. First of all, their key witnesses were admitted gang members who had done bad things. Secondly, they didn't speak English that well. Who knew what words the cops had put in their mouths during translation? This was a classic throw-out case for a bench trial.

I met with Wilson Moy again the next day. I was still careful about what I said. I didn't come straight out and say I would fix the case. Instead, I offered him something like a Chinese menu. I said, "I'll charge you $50,000 for a jury trial. But you know, you can never be certain about a jury verdict. If you go for a bench trial, with just a judge and no jury, that will cost $100,000." I told him that the verdicts were always more predictable with a bench trial.

"That's a lot of money," Moy said. "Can you do it any cheaper?"

I stuck to my guns, and Moy said he would have to check with the national leaders of On Leong in New York. The next time we met, he shook my hand and said, "We're going to hire you, but we want the $100,000 trial."

I told him to give me a check for $10,000 as a retainer. "Is it okay if I give you cash?" he asked.

"Oh, sure," I said.

After seeing Moy, I went back to Counsellors Row and told Pat I could get $100,000 from On Leong. He couldn't believe it. But when I asked for $50,000 as my cut, he said, "Oh, no, no. We can't do that. You know the judge will want a lot, too." I settled for $25,000.

I then started my work on the case. Even if it was fixed, I wanted to give the judge good solid reasons for an acquittal. Moy arranged for me to meet the witnesses. To set everything up, On Leong brought in Chan Kwok Wing, probably the biggest Chinese guy I ever saw. He had a barrel chest and legs like tree trunks. He was supposed to be very proficient in karate, and he walked around with one of those dark martial-arts stares. All the gang members knew about him, and they were scared to death of him. When he showed up, people could die.

They booked a suite for Wing at the Ambassador West, an older hotel just off Rush Street. He could stay in one room and we could meet the witnesses in the other. When I saw the three witnesses, I couldn't believe how young they looked—like three little kids.

Wing gave each one a withering stare, and he spoke to them in harsh barking tones. They were literally shaking in their shoes.

I said, "I know you guys don't speak English that well and when the police interrogated you, they might have misunderstood you."

They all nodded their heads.

"From what I'm told, you didn't recognize Lenny Chow during the lineup, but that's not what the police wrote in their reports."

They nodded again. In truth, they really didn't speak much English and were probably illegal immigrants. The gangs smuggled them in from China to do their dirty work. I told Wing to set up a meeting with a leader of the Ghost Shadows so we could get these three back in that gang and on their payroll.

During the weeks leading up to the trial, Wing and I became good pals. Now that I was working with Marcy again, I wasn't worried about going to the clubs on Rush Street, and I took Wing along. I also arranged for him to stay with Rosie the Madam. He had a thing for her blonde call girls. He ended up saving a lot of money on hotels, but I'm not sure he got much sleep.

Everything seemed to be going smoothly until the victim, William Chin, went back into the hospital and died from infections to his bullet wounds. Now, the charge of attempted murder became actual murder. Typically, a judge would put the defendant back into custody and demand a higher bail. That certainly would have made sense for my client, Lenny Chow, who didn't have ties to Chicago and had never surrendered his passport. But Maloney ruled that we could "transfer" the attempted-murder bond to a new bond for the murder charge. When the prosecutors tried to object, in his typical fashion Maloney barked, "Don't speak up in this court."

No one could believe that Maloney would do something as fishy as transferring the bond. The trial hadn't even started and it smelled like the fix was in. But nothing Maloney did surprised me. In fact, just before the bond hearing, Marcy pulled me aside at Counsellors Row and said, "You have to bring in Herb Barsy on this case."

"Who is Herb Barsy?" I asked.

"He's a lawyer and a friend of Judge Maloney, and the judge wants you to use him. In fact, the judge wants him to be the lead."

This was classic Maloney: a last-minute move to humiliate me. He knew it was too late for me to back out or put up a fuss. I said to Pat, "Okay, I'll hire him." I went to meet Barsy, and, much as I thought, he was a milquetoast guy who usually carried the bags for the more powerful lawyers in his firm. When I said I would only pay him $2,300, he quickly agreed. I had my own ideas about who would be the lead lawyer on this case, but I wasn't going to discuss them with Barsy or Marcy before the trial.

If you looked at our backgrounds, you would have thought that Tom Maloney and I might have been friends instead of such bitter enemies. Like me, he came from the South Side; went to Mount Carmel, where he did some boxing; and started out as a cop. But from there, all resemblance ended. He was a graduate of the University of Maryland and John Marshall Law School. Hulking in size, he had flowing white hair and a ruddy complexion. After he became a lawyer, he put on airs along with his fancy suits. Unless you were someone who could help his career, he talked down to you, like you were hard of hearing or mentally defective. Meanwhile, Mr. High-and-Mighty was defending some of the worst scumbag narcotics dealers in the city, fucking their girlfriends, and hanging out in the bars where they did their deals. He was under federal investigation when Marcy got the state's Supreme Court to appoint him a full Circuit Court judge immediately after the Aleman trial (just as Harry predicted).

Once he got behind the bench, Maloney grew even more pompous and overbearing. He screamed at court clerks and bailiffs like they were his servants. He had no problem with waltzing into court late and kept everyone around into the night when that suited him. If defense lawyers were not paying him off, he belittled them in court and buried their clients under ridiculously severe sentences. He put as many men on Death Row as any judge in the system, and held himself out as the ultimate protector of Law and Order. In fact, for the right price, he would let anyone off for any crime. Absolutely anyone. I couldn't stand his bullshit hypocrisy. We were bound to be on a collision course—just by being in the same courtroom.

The state's case against Lenny Chow and the three other shooters opened with the investigating detective. The coppers had someone approach me before the trial to see if I would pay them all off to alter their testimony. Because I turned him down, they decided to embellish on all the things they put in their reports. When it was time for cross-examination, I got up to tear the detective a new asshole.

Before I could speak, Barsy tapped me on the shoulder. "What are you doing?" he asked.

"The cross."

Under his breath, Barsy said, "But the judge wants me to do it."

"Come on," I told him. "I'm doing this for his own good."

By the time I finished cross-examining the cop, he looked like a total idiot. But later, when I went back to Counsellors Row, Pat Marcy glared at me and motioned toward the rear of the restaurant. "You were supposed to take a back seat in this case," he hissed. "The judge is all upset because you're trying to be a big shot again."

"Pat, I'm trying to give the judge a case," I said. "How can you expect me to sit there and watch it fall apart? If I don't cross-examine the witnesses when they get on the stand tomorrow, there's no telling what they will say."

He waved at me in disgust and walked away.

The next day, another policeman came to the stand again. He testified that in the hospital, shortly after the shooting, William Chin made a "Deathbed Statement," identifying Lenny Chow as the shooter. Usually Deathbed Statements carry a lot of weight with a jury. You tend to think a dying man will be truthful if he knows he's about to meet his Maker.

But Chin did not make the supposed statement on his deathbed. He was released from the hospital and died months later. There was plenty of time in between to take a normal statement. Secondly, there was conflicting testimony about what he actually said in the hospital—from the nurse and copper who were with him. The nurse testified that he mumbled something, but she couldn't make it out. After she left the room, the detective claimed, Chin suddenly spoke up loud and clear, and said, "Lenny shot me." This was quite a feat, since he barely spoke English.

I couldn't let the copper get away with that bullshit, so I got up to cross-examine him. Out of the corner of my eye, I could see Maloney turning different colors of red, once again in a rage that I took the lead.

This time the judge was going to show me who was boss. Against all the prior case law and common sense, Maloney admitted the Deathbed Statement into evidence. I couldn't believe it. He just made it harder on himself to throw out the case.

After he finished reading his decision, Maloney gave me a smirk. This whole trial had become a game of chicken between him and me, but I sure as hell wasn't going to blink first. The gang members were called to testify and, again, I told Barsy I would lead the cross-examination. "These kids recognize me," I said. "If they see you, they may think you're the prosecutor and who knows what they'll say."

When I got up, Maloney looked at me with daggers. He kept staring at me like that for the rest of the day. Meanwhile, Wing, from his seat in the spectator's gallery, was doing his own laser stares right through each witness. According to plan, they recanted the incriminating testimony they had given the police.

I brought Wing back to Counsellors Row to celebrate, but Marcy was in no mood for a party. I left Wing at the bar and followed Marcy as he stormed into the back of the restaurant. This time he screamed loud enough for everyone in Counsellors to hear. "I told you to keep your mouth shut and to sit there and do nothing, and you wouldn't listen."

"Pat," I said, "when I told you last night that I had to cross-examine the witnesses, you walked away. You never told me *not* to cross-examine."

He couldn't argue with that. "This fucking Maloney is nuts," I said. "There was no way any other judge would allow a Deathbed Statement into evidence. He's made a case where there wasn't one. I'm trying to give him grounds to throw it out."

"You're like two fucking kids," Pat said.

I promised him I'd keep quiet the rest of the trial.

Wing and I stayed out late that night, and the next morning we had a nice leisurely breakfast. Maloney had yet to show up for court before 11:00. I was going to be goddamned if I sat around waiting for him again. We walked into court at 10:45, and wouldn't you know, it was the one day the judge was on time. Everybody else—the prosecutors, the witnesses, Barsy—was waiting for us. As soon as he saw me, Maloney started yelling, "Counsel, do you know what time court starts?"

I said, "Judge, the last two days, you didn't come in here until after eleven, and since I had an important matter to take care of . . ."

"Just sit down," he said. As I went to my chair, I could see all the court personnel smiling big-time.

I let Barsy do the rest of the cross-examinations, and the state brought its case to a close. According to the script for your typical fixed bench trial, we then made a motion for a Directed Finding. This was the perfect opportunity for the judge to throw out the case. Maloney had every reason to do so, because the main witnesses to the shooting had recanted their testimony.

But instead, to ram it up my ass one more time, Maloney overruled the motion and told us to put on our case. "Go ahead," he said, "and call your first witness."

Herb looked at me and said, "What are we going to do?"

I said, "Herb, we're not putting anybody on the stand. We rest."

Herb almost died. "What are you talking about?"

"Herb," I whispered, "I'm not calling a witness to let this jagoff judge make a case where there is none." I then stood up and announced to the court, "We rest."

I sat back down and kept my eyes on Maloney, thinking, "Okay, you idiot. What are you going to do now?"

Maloney didn't know what to do. He sputtered and hemmed and hawed.

I truly didn't give a fuck if he found Lenny Chow guilty. We had received only $10,000 up front from Moy. I thought, "Let him face the wrath of Pat Marcy, if he blows this case and $90,000 for us."

Finally, Maloney said, "Well, I'll make my decision tomorrow."

Later, when I saw Marcy at Counsellors Row, I said, "I did what I could to protect the judge. He's a total jagoff. You better straighten him out or he's going to fuck us."

"I've already talked to him," Pat said.

Walking into court the next day, I had no idea what Maloney would do—whether his ego and hatred of me would overcome his fear of

Marcy. Wing let me know we had something else to worry about. He said, "I should tell you. The family of William Chin is going to have all of us killed if the judge finds Lenny not guilty."

We then sat back and watched as Maloney read out his decision. It was almost worth the aggravation of the trial. In essence, he said, yes, he did admit the Deathbed Statement, but no, that didn't mean the dying man knew what he was talking about. How could he have seen Lenny Chow shoot from the balcony if he was behind the wheel of the car? It was the most convoluted piece of bullshit I ever heard.

I had Wing hustle the three witnesses out of the courthouse and into my car. When we drove them back to their hotel, I called some detective friends on the police force. I asked them to take the kids to O'Hare Airport and stay with them until they got on the plane to New York.

From the hotel, Wing and I went back to my apartment. I had a couple of guns on me, but I got another for Wing. I said, "We're going to go to Chinatown and collect that $90,000."

Wilson Moy waited for us in front of his gift shop surrounded by a delegation of other Chinese merchants. It was like a meeting of the Rotary Club. Once we were in his store, he handed me $40,000 in cash in something that looked like a fat FedEx envelope. When I asked for the rest, he said I would have to go to New York and see the On Leong national president, Eddie Chan. "He wants to meet you in person," Moy said.

I took the money back to Counsellors Row. Alderman Roti led me to his City Hall office across the street, where he took out the bundles of cash and counted them. He gave me my $5,000, and stuffed the rest in his jacket and pants pockets. I grabbed copy paper from his desk and put that in the FedEx envelope, so when I took it out of his office, it looked as full as when I brought it in.

Later, when I told Pat about going to New York for the remaining $50,000, he wasn't too happy, but what could he do? Grudgingly he agreed, and he added, "Don't make any stops in Atlantic City on the way back."

I flew to New York with Wing. Ghost Shadow gang kids waited for us at the gate to carry our luggage. Outside the airport, they put us into one Mercedes and a group followed us in another. We drove right to a funeral home on Mott Street in New York City's Chinatown. This was the headquarters of Eddie Chan, national president of the On Leong Merchants Association. We walked upstairs to a reception area where the walls and doors were made of mahogany. Wing went into the office and came out with Eddie's two bodyguards. One was a huge black guy who looked like some kind of weightlifter. The other was a short, dumpy white guy. As I found out later, he was a U.S. Marshal, which meant he was licensed to carry a gun on a commercial airline. Eddie never went anywhere without a U.S. Marshal.

They led me into a huge office, and Eddie rose from behind his desk to give me a greeting. He was a man in his fifties, round-faced and over-weight, with a military bearing—like those Chinese generals you saw in the newsreels. All over the walls, there were pictures of Eddie shaking hands with mayors, presidents, and governors. He had been a staff ser-geant for the Hong Kong police force and, in 1975, when the government there investigated police corruption, he moved to New York and brought forty crooked cops with him. Besides investing in souvenir shops, restaurants, and funeral homes, he tried to control the gangs like the Ghost Shadows so he could get a piece of their narcotics and gam-bling business. A novel and movie called *Year of the Dragon* was based on a character with a similar background. When I sat down by Eddie's desk, he leaned close to me and said, in somewhat broken English, "Give all your money to Wing."

I looked at Wing and thought, "What's this about?"

Wing said, "He doesn't want you to spend any money while you're our guest. I told him how you took care of me in Chicago and picked up all the bills. Now we can do the same for you."

This was a shocker. The Mob bosses in Chicago were so tight, they squeaked. "Can't I have a little money for tips?" I asked.

"No, no," Eddie said. "You don't spend any money here." I emptied my wallet and Eddie put the money in one of his drawers.

We then headed over to a street in Chinatown that was lined with restaurants. We went into one and climbed the stairs to a private ban-quet room on the second floor. It was filled with On Leong people from all over the country. Like Eddie and Moy, they were prosperous-looking guys in suits. Eddie took me around the room, and I had to shake hands and say hello to each one. We then sat down at a huge round table. Eddie was on one side of me, and Wing on the other. They had a banquet spread out on beautiful china serving dishes, and the whole table spun like a lazy susan. I was probably looking at the finest Chinese delicacies, but there was not a single thing I wanted to taste. I was still the picky eater who drove my mother crazy. Anything with vegetables or funny sauces just turned my stomach. Everyone in the hall sat watching, waiting for me to eat. Finally, I turned to Wing and said, "Explain to Eddie that I'm allergic to vegetables."

This created a whole commotion, and the next thing I knew, they were making a special banquet for me with just steak and seafood. As we ate, and I listened to Eddie, I realized that Wing had laid it on thick about how well I did during the trial and all the connections I had in Chicago—with the cops and the Mob. Later on, Eddie said, "We want you to be our lawyer and travel all over the country for us."

"Sure," I replied. Now this whole event made sense. Eddie wanted to pave the way for me with the other On Leong leaders.

"I would like to come to Chicago some day," Eddie said, "but I can't."

"Why not?" I asked.

"Because some people there want to kill me. If I come, can you make sure I'm safe?" he asked.

"I can arrange that," I said. "I'll have someone pick you up and stay with you the whole time you're in the city."

In fact, I would have never introduced Eddie to any Mob guy for his protection. Instead, I worked out a deal with Gerard, a maitre d' at Arnie's, one of my favorite restaurants. He always carried a little gun in his pocket, and he put on a good show. He was a big, tough-looking Italian with a handlebar moustache. I told Eddie that he was a vicious hit man. Eddie paid him $500 a day whenever he came to town. Eddie usually had a U.S. Marshal with him, and all Gerard really had to do was drive them around.

For the next three years, I represented the On Leong Merchants Association in cities around the country: Boston, New Orleans, San Francisco, and Houston. Usually, one of their kids had killed a kid from another gang. Over that period, I became very tight with Eddie. If something came up during a case, I would fly to New York to see him on it. Every time we met, he had $5,000 in cash waiting, even if all we did was chat.

On Leong gave me the perfect excuse to move farther away from the Chicago Mob. They knew I was out of town a lot, so it was no big deal if I didn't show up in Counsellors Row every day or the clubs at night. Practically no one noticed when I moved to an apartment in the sleepy southwest suburb of Countryside. Just as quietly, I later moved my office to a place near Midway Airport, closer to where I lived. Once, an affluent, flashy image had been so important to me. Now, only my security really mattered.

On Leong also gave me an excuse to be much more picky about the cases I took. Although I still handled gambling arrests, I turned away the other garbage the Mob wanted me to fix, like narcotics cases. I had always refused to work on anything involving rapists or child molesters.

Sometimes, when I turned down a case, and the crime or the criminal disgusted me, I went behind the scenes to make sure it wasn't fixed. Once a drug dealer approached me because he knew the judge was a friend of mine. This judge would have probably given me every break in the world, but only because he was a real good guy. He would never have taken money for it. After I turned down the case, the dealer told me he had found someone else who could get to the judge. I knew that was bullshit, but I didn't want my friend to get a reputation. Before the trial, I called him and said, "I just turned this case down. You should know that the new lawyer says he's a good friend of yours, too. That's why he got the case." Enough said. The dealer got his bench trial, and the judge found him fucking guilty.

In December 1981, I helped stop the fix on another case that really bothered me. The defendants were two cops who beat a vagrant to death at a South Side El stop. They asked him to stop smoking, and when he didn't, they handcuffed him and pounded the living shit out of him. After they dumped him into a squad car, another cop piled on, but the guy was as good as dead by then, and charges against that cop were eventually dropped. Besides being a former mental patient, the victim was also black, so his death got the attention of the Reverend Jesse Jackson, and a bunch of protest rallies followed.

This was a classic "ink" case, but an important part of the story never made it into the press. One of the cops was related to Angelo LaPietra, the little king of the Chinatown group, and Hook wanted to make sure the case was fixed. Blackie Pesoli first approached me at Counsellors Row to handle it. I begged off, explaining I had trouble with cop cases and just didn't take them.

Instead, the First Ward turned to Samuel V. P. Banks, who was, in my humble opinion, the biggest buffoon practicing criminal law in Chicago. He even dressed the part of your Mob lawyer, with crazy shark-skin suits and loud ties. There was only one way to defend this case: Have one cop point the finger at the other for delivering the fatal blow. Each would need his own lawyer for that strategy; but despite this client conflict, Banks represented both cops. Hook's relative was probably the more culpable of the two, so the other cop really got the short end of the stick. Obviously, Banks expected a little help from the judge. That was his one and only ace in the hole.

If there had not been so much publicity, Marcy would have assigned the case to a judge like Maloney. But he would not have wasted Maloney's reputation on these small potatoes. The Mob reserved him for its own murderers or big payoffs. Instead, the case was assigned according to normal procedures and ended up with Circuit Court Judge Arthur Cieslik. Alderman Ed Burke was the political connection who had "made" Cieslik—in other words, he pulled the strings to get him appointed to the court. Burke assured everyone in the First Ward that he could get this judge to do what he wanted.

It so happened that I knew Cieslik pretty well and dropped by his chambers all the time to chat with him. Meanwhile, I also knew Burke, who was a lesser light at the First Ward table in Counsellors Row. Even though I didn't take the case, during the ten days of the cops' trial, I was pretty actively involved.

Once I had been friendly with Ed Burke and his wife, Anne. Along with Patty DeLeo and his wife, the Burkes had had dinner with me at Greco's several times. Ed and I were about the same age, and, like me, he had been a cop for a few years before he passed the bar. But Ed's father had been an alderman, and he had always been groomed for a political career. The second youngest alderman ever elected to Chicago's City Council, Ed was smart and handsome, and had a full head of silvery hair. If it hadn't been for the Daley dynasty, I think he would have seen himself as mayor some day. But Ed was always a little too slick for his own good. On the one hand, he wanted to project a squeaky-clean public image as a churchgoing, devout Irish Catholic, but on the other, he hung out with Marcy, Alderman Roti, and the rest of the First Ward crowd. Behind the scenes, he worked quite a few lowlife deals for the Mob. At least Fred Roti had the decency to stay out of the limelight. Ed Burke always wanted it both ways.

With the cops' trial, Ed tried to pull a typical Pat Marcy. He gave Judge Cieslik a full-court press to acquit the cops. Only Ed didn't know the judge like I did. This guy was no pushover. Short and ornery, with a dark, craggy face and a beetle brow, Cieslik had a knack for rubbing everyone the wrong way. Even though he was a state-minded judge, the prosecutors hated him as much as the defense lawyers. The first time we met, I tried to get a good plea out of him for my client, and when he wouldn't give it to me, I took the case to a jury trial. I got an acquittal. In the bargain, I won his respect too. From then on, he would call me into his chambers and sometimes talk out of school about an ongoing trial or decision he was about to make. I think he appreciated my understanding of juries or how the public might see things. But nothing I could say would ever make him do something wrong. He was as honest and incorruptible as a judge could be.

During an early part of the cops' case, I stopped by Cieslik's chambers to chat. He was amazed that both cops were using Sam Banks as their lawyer. He asked me, "Why didn't they get someone to represent the other one?"

I just shrugged my shoulders.

He then said, "The state has a case. It has a good case."

I said, "Then do what you think is right."

He kept mumbling, "Why didn't he get someone to represent the other one?"

In Counsellors Row, after the first day of trial, I saw Patty DeLeo and Sam Banks at the First Ward table. I went to sit down with them. At that moment, Ed Burke entered the restaurant through the lobby door and joined us. They all started talking about the trial, and Sam whined to Patty DeLeo, "This judge is giving me a hard time."

Burke snapped at him, "Don't worry about it."

But Patty was worried—probably about pissing off LaPietra if his relative got convicted. Patty said to Burke, "Are you sure? There better not be a problem."

"It's only a fucking nigger," Burke said. "I can't see what's the big deal."

By this point, Burke's Fourteenth Ward, on the Southwest Side, probably had more blacks than whites. I thought, "Boy, if some of his voters could hear him now."

The more Banks moaned about the judge, the more my respect grew for Cieslik. The next day, I again popped into his chambers to help keep him strong.

He said, "Ed Burke keeps telling me that this is a First Ward case. That the First Ward will be very upset if I find the cops guilty." He knew about the First Ward's connections with the Mob and was worried they would physically harm him or his family. But I knew the First Ward would never touch a judge, so I lied a little to calm him down.

I said, "I saw Eddie Burke last night at Counsellors Row. He's the *Fourteenth* Ward. He's the only one pushing you on this case. The First Ward is not involved. They have nothing to do with this."

Now I had to see this trial for myself. The next day I watched a few hours of testimony. Witness after witness got up to describe the way the two cops mercilessly beat the victim while he was in handcuffs. Banks tried to claim he was resisting arrest and threw himself to the ground headfirst.

When I went in to see Cieslik later that afternoon, he was pacing around his chambers, his eyebrows practically touching his nose. "The state has got a good case," he said. "And the cops' lawyer can't properly defend, because they can't blame each other."

"Judge," I said, "you just got to do what you think is right."

Cieslik found them guilty of involuntary manslaughter and official misconduct. That night Burke, DeLeo, and Banks were in an uproar at Counsellors Row. I shook my head and clucked my tongue to commiserate, but I thought, "Would they go nuts if they knew what I was telling that judge." Now they started plotting ways to make the judge give the cops probation.

During the sentencing hearing, I continued to see the judge each day after court. He would say, "I just can't give them probation for this type of crime."

I would simply say, "Just do what you think is right." He wound up sentencing the cops to time.

I got more satisfaction from seeing those cops sentenced than from winning my own cases. Cieslik really did do the right thing, and, by providing him some moral support, I may have helped. I liked the way that felt. Now, more than ever, I questioned the life I had made for myself as a lawyer. These feelings grew stronger as my father got sicker.

While I was representing the On Leong, I was out of town a lot and I didn't see him much. I would call and he'd only say a few words before he passed the phone to my mother. He suddenly stopped going to Mass and Communion every day. Sometimes he wandered out of the house half-dressed, even in the middle of winter. Worse yet, his personality changed, and he became mean and violent with my mother. When she told me this, I could hardly believe my ears. His whole life, he had been so gentle. We now know that these are all telltale signs of Alzheimer's disease. But back in the early eighties, it was not as well understood.

When people came to visit my father, he forgot their names, but he always seemed to recognize me. After my mother left the room, he would pull me to the side and whisper, "Son, don't let them put me in a nursing home. I know you won't let them."

But eventually there was no choice. It was too hard on my mother. We put him in a place in the south suburbs. The first time I went to visit, he was strapped to his bed and had crapped all over himself. I went screaming for the nurses. When one arrived, I demanded to know why she had tied him up, and she told me he had been violent. He seemed like a puppy with me. He motioned to the straps and the tubes they put on him and said, "Son, look what they're doing to me."

I sat and tried to chat. He said, "I want to go downstairs and commit suicide." He spoke so clearly and there was no mistaking what he said. For a devout Catholic, taking your own life is a mortal sin. I tried to console him and tell him things would get better, but who was I fooling?

I saw him as much as I could when I was in town. The nurses would put him in a wheelchair, and I would push him around to some corner where we could be alone. I never knew what would come out of his mouth. One moment he made sense, and the next he spoke total gibberish. But one day he looked at me and said, "Son, remember, you have to get away from those people."

"Sure, Dad," I said. "Sure." I told him I had broken away, but the truth was that I had not totally broken away.

Then, out of nowhere, he said, "One of those people. One of Capone's people killed your grandfather."

I had never heard him say that before.

Then he said, "And a crooked lawyer got the killer off. A crooked lawyer."

I knew a jury had acquitted my grandfather's killer, and I knew my grandmother fainted when they announced the verdict. I never figured a crooked lawyer was involved, but it seemed so obvious as soon as the words left my father's mouth. It was why it hurt him to see me associated with Marcy and D'Arco. He was just too nice a guy to come out and say that to me—until his illness took the gloves off.

Dad died in February 1983. It was a blessing when he passed. He had been such a good and caring person, he did not deserve what Alzheimer's did to him at the end. My mother did not deserve to watch him go through that either.

Like other people do after a parent dies, I looked back on my own life and what I had made of myself. I remembered lying in the hospital bed after I was run over by the car, and wondering why I had survived. If God had given me a second chance, I did do something with it. I enjoyed success beyond my wildest dreams. I was generous with the money I made. I used my influence to help friends and family, who were good and decent people.

But as my father feared, I had also become a crooked lawyer. Like the lawyer for my grandfather's killer, I helped murderers get off the hook. And not just any murderers, but professional murderers like Harry Aleman. Could this really be the mission that God or anyone else intended for me?

CHAPTER 8

THE FATAL CORNED BEEF SANDWICH

My work with On Leong soon came crashing to a halt. During one visit to New York, Wing picked me up at the airport. Instead of driving to the funeral home in Chinatown, he took me to the parking lot of a high-rise on the east side of Manhattan. Wing went into the lobby and called up. A few minutes later, Eddie came down to our Mercedes. He handed me an envelope. Inside was a picture of a Chinese guy from Houston standing next to a car.

Wing pointed at his picture and told me, "We want to get this guy killed, because he killed some of our people. We got his partner, but we can't kill him." Evidently their target was always on the lookout for a Chinese hit man, so they couldn't get their people close enough to do the job. They wanted me to find them a white hit man from Chicago.

I just stared at the picture, caught totally off guard. After all these years of working with me, they still thought I was totally Chicago Mob. I realized then that I wanted nothing more to do with On Leong.

Wing asked if he could start meeting with my people to set up the hit.

"That's not how they work," I said. I had to figure a way to get out of this situation without causing them to lose face or get suspicious. "My people have problems doing things like this with strangers," I said. "But I'll see what they say." Of course I didn't contact anyone in the Mob when I got back. I waited a day, and called Wing to say that my contacts wouldn't do it. Wing was pissed. He could probably hear in my voice that I wanted no part of this. Although I continued to call Gerard when Eddie Chan came to town, I did no more legal work for him.

Once more, my law practice was rooted in Chicago, and I tried to expand my base of clients on the southwest side of town where I had my office. My partner, State Senator LeRoy Lemke, was your typical small-time political operator. I had met him when he hired me to get his son out of a jam. Our offices were in a house we shared with a U.S. congressman. With my background in criminal work and his local connections, he thought we could drum up a lot of business together, and he was right. I made a point of showing my face at Counsellors Row, but I didn't need the First Ward. After On Leong, I never went back to them for anything else and, for a while, I got no more calls from Marcy.

If you read the newspapers, you would have thought that 1983 was the beginning of the end for the First Ward. In the spring, the city elected its first black mayor, after Harold Washington beat both Jane Byrne and Richie Daley in a bitter primary. That summer, rumors started to fly about Operation Greylord. For three years, an undercover attorney and judge wore wires to catch fixed narcotics and traffic cases. It looked like the Feds were finally going to clean up the courts. Then, before the year was over, indictments for skimming cash from Las Vegas casinos were announced against fifteen Mob leaders in five cities, including Joey Aiuppa; Tony Accardo's right-hand man, Angelo "the Hook" LaPietra, the little king of the Chinatown group; Jackie Cerone, the boss of the West Side group (Marco reported to him); and Tony Spilotro, the Outfit's enforcer in Las Vegas. The Feds called this investigation "Strawman II." They had already used "Strawman I" to take out Joey Lombardo, the boss of the South Side group.

But despite all these major federal investigations, when I walked by the First Ward table at Counsellors Row, nothing seemed different. There were Roti, Marcy, Patty DeLeo, and Johnny D'Arco, wheeling and dealing as always. Like Byrne before him, Mayor Washington let the same bad guys run the police department. White Democratic machine aldermen, led by Fred Roti, Ed Burke, and Ed Vrdolyak, pretty much controlled city council and the rest of Chicago's government. Johnny D'Arco was more powerful than ever in the State Senate.

As for Marcy, Operation Greylord did not scare him a bit. Even after they were convicted, none of the lawyers or judges nailed by the Feds dared to name anyone who was Inner Circle First Ward. The judges still on the bench may have been more careful, but Marcy went about his business as though nothing had ever happened. In fact, in October, the same month that the Strawman II indictments came down, he fixed a murder case involving Tony Spilotro. His trial featured the usual suspects: Thomas J. Maloney was judge, Herb Barsy the associate defense lawyer. Making a guest appearance as the out-of-town lead attorney was Oscar Goodman. (A flamboyant Mob lawyer from Las Vegas, Goodman was elected mayor of that city in 1999.)

Each day after court, I would watch the same little routine unfold in Counsellors Row. Oscar strolled into the restaurant first, soon followed by Spilotro and his sidekick, Fat Herbie Blitzstein. They would take a booth along the wall and order a couple of drinks and something to nibble. Marcy would walk by and, a few minutes later, Tony Spilotro would get up to follow him.

One night, while I was standing at the pay phone, they passed by me. I don't know what had happened in court that day, but Tony had a pained expression on his face. I heard him say, "Are you sure everything is going to be okay? Are you sure?"

Marcy said, "Don't worry about it." He used the same dismissive tone with him that he had often used with me.

When I saw Pat later and asked him why Tony looked so upset, he said, "He's got nothing to worry about. I've taken care of everything."

It was all so brazen—there for the world to see. If you bothered to look. This was not just any trial. It was probably one of the most notorious cases in Organized Crime history. Although the press called it the M&M Murders, it had nothing to do with candy. Billy McCarthy and Jimmy Miraglia were low-level Mob thugs who got into a bar fight with two brothers. Without first getting permission, they killed the brothers and, worse yet, they did it in Elmwood Park, the western suburb where the Mob controlled the police department. No whacking was allowed there.

To make an example of M&M, the Mob commissioned Chuckie Nicoletti and Milwaukee Phil Alderisio, two longtime brutal hit men.

Tony Spilotro, only twenty-four at the time, tagged along like an apprentice, because he had been friendly with Billy McCarthy. To make McCarthy give up Miraglia's name, Tony tortured him for hours. At one point he put McCarthy's head in a vise and turned it until one of his eyes popped out.

The M&M Murders had happened in 1962. The only reason the state could dredge the charges up twenty-one years later was that they now had a key witness: a man who had made the call that helped Tony trap McCarthy and later heard the details about the killings from Spilotro. This witness, Frank Cullotta, was one of Tony Spilotro's crew, and also a lifelong friend—until Tony tried to whack him. In federal cases to come, Cullotta's testimony would win many convictions. But in the state's M&M case, Maloney did not find Cullotta credible. Surprise, surprise. He acquitted Tony Spilotro of all charges.

The M&M fix was all the proof I needed that the Feds had not come close to Marcy. Even as all the corruption and Mob cases came to trial in federal courts over the next few years, Pat only seemed to get stronger.

At first, I was unbelievably happy about Greylord. All the judges and their bagmen had gotten too greedy. If the whole system changed, I would never have to make another payoff. A state's attorney named Terry Hake set the whole investigation in motion. He got fed up with the corruption he saw on a daily basis. Somebody heard him complain, and the FBI asked if he would wear a wire. Over three years, Hake recorded more than thirteen hundred hours of conversations, first pretending to be a corrupt narcotics prosecutor and, later, a defense attorney who could get cases fixed. In the end, he helped convict forty lawyers and a few dozen cops, deputy sheriffs, and other assorted court personnel. But the investigation team's real targets were the judges (the name Greylord came from the gray wigs the judges wore in England), and they convicted fifteen of them, including Dick LeFevour, who had his cousin Jimmy shake me down in Traffic Court just after I got out of law school.

But for me, Operation Greylord was a disappointment. Despite the body count, it never reached as high as the prosecutors promised. The investigation primarily cleaned up the small-time graft in the narcotics and traffic courts: lawyers and judges at the bottom of the food chain—not the ones working with major felonies or murder cases. It did nothing to change the way judges were appointed or assigned. That entire corrupt system remained absolutely intact. If anything, Greylord helped Marcy. With the conviction of each judge, he had another opening to fill, and if you wanted to be named an associate judge, his charge rose to $25,000.

Operation Strawman was definitely more painful for the Mob. A lot of old bosses went off to prison to die, and important crew leaders joined them. But there were literally dozens to take their place. Territories remained the same. Any differences between the bosses were hashed out. Meanwhile, murder cases were still fixed for the hit men, and the hit men were still killing people left and right.

The Outfit was like an octopus. If you cut off an arm, another grew back. To kill it, you had to go for the head—and that was Pat Marcy. He was the one person the Mob protected at all costs. Like Accardo, he was immovable; but unlike Accardo, he could not be replaced. In the whole organization, he was the only one who held all the strings—to the politicians, to the courts, to the unions, and to the cops.

When all the indictments blew by Pat Marcy without so much as messing a hair on his head, he got even more arrogant than before. It was then, in the last few months of 1985, that he called me again.

Oddly enough, he wanted to meet about a client I already had—a 28-year-old baker from Elmwood Park named Mike Colella, who had been charged with nearly beating a policewoman to death. Although the papers made him out to be a monster weightlifter, he wasn't as big or muscle-bound as all that. Instead, he was maybe five feet, eight inches tall and solid, but did not look so terrifying. However, he was obsessed with weightlifting and that's what got him into so much trouble. He had been referred to me through another kid I represented who was breaking into drugstores. I think he was stealing steroids. Whatever he and Mike were taking, it made them both nuts. At the drop of a hat, they would flip out and fight people. Before the incident with the policewoman, Mike had not been pinched in his life, but suddenly he became notorious. He got into a typical barroom brawl and was arrested for that. Then he got in a shouting match with a couple of suburban cops in an all-night diner, and he was charged with assault and resisting arrest.

Mike came into my office with his father. He seemed high to me and started giving me some lip. I would have thrown them both out, but the father was such a nice guy, I felt bad for him. He reminded me of my dad and the way he saw my good side when everyone else saw the bad. I said to Mike, "I won't even represent you until you're straight." Then I told the father to put him into a thirty-day rehab program.

They returned a month later, and I couldn't get over the difference the rehab had made. When he was sober, Mike was actually a decent kid. He seemed genuine about wanting to straighten out his life. I thought the dad didn't have much money, so I told him I wanted only a $500 retainer and would charge an additional $2,000 for the trial.

According to the press, the police had an open-and-shut case. The policewoman stopped Colella on New Year's Eve for driving the wrong way down a one-way street. When she had him get out of the car, he supposedly jumped her, broke her jaw, and would have killed her if other cops hadn't arrived to pull him off. But according to Mike, the story was more complicated than that. He had been out drinking all night in an Old Town bar, and he was cruising down that street looking for prostitutes. When the policewoman stopped him, he gave her an attitude and said, "I wasn't doing anything wrong."

She had him get out of the car. Then she told him he was drunk, and she was going to arrest him. When she ordered him to turn around, so she could put the cuffs on him, he refused. According to Mike, he was struggling with her when the backup cops arrived and they piled on, swinging away with their nightsticks. I had been in melees like that when I was a cop. You start clubbing with those long sticks and you're as likely to hit another cop as the perp. It was totally possible that's how the policewoman's jaw was broken. There was no doubt that they beat the living shit out of Mike. When they dragged him into the police station, the booking officer sent him to the hospital. They never mentioned his injuries in the police reports. I had medical records as proof, and I could use them to show that the cops were lying. Despite all the bad ink, I thought I had a good chance with a jury.

I had been on the Colella case for just a few months when I got a call from Marcy—the first I'd heard from him since I moved my office to the Southwest Side. He said, "I want to talk to you about something. Can you come down to Counsellors?"

It took me about twenty minutes to drive over. Pat Marcy was at the First Ward table with a guy I had seen around but only knew as Nunzio. Pat motioned for me to follow him out the door.

When we were standing in the lobby at 100 North LaSalle, he said, "Look, you're representing this kid Mike Colella."

"Yeah," I said. "As a matter of fact, I am."

"We'll let you keep him," he said, "but I'm going to make sure the case is thrown out."

Even though I thought the kid had gotten a bum rap, I still wanted no part of fixing a case that involved the police—especially if a cop was supposedly the victim. I said, "Pat, I want to take it to a jury. I can win this case."

He said, "You're not taking it to no fucking jury. We'll handle it."

I said, "It's not a big deal. I've read the police reports. The police are all lying, and I can tear them apart in court. I can win this case."

Now he got pissed off. "Just do what you're told," he said. "You'll take a bench and you'll do what you're told. Can you get ahold of the coppers on this case?"

Actually, I did talk to some cops who knew the policewoman. I told them we could help bring a dram shop lawsuit against the bar where Mike was drinking and make everyone rich in the process, but they did not want the kid to get off the hook. "I tried," I told Pat, "but the coppers are still beefing."

"Then fuck them," he said.

Pat then had Nunzio join us in the lobby. It turned out that he was Mike's uncle, and the one who had told Pat about the case. His full name was Nunzio Tischi, and he was a supervising attorney for the public defender's office. Pat said, "If you need a file or he can help in any way, you let him know."

I drove back to my office pounding my steering wheel all the way. No fucking way would I fix a case with cops. I had to show Marcy that there was another way on this case—that I could take Mike before a jury and win.

I asked Nunzio to get me files on the more recent case against Mike, where the suburban cops charged him with resisting arrest and assault. From what Mike had told me, the police at the diner recognized him from articles about the policewoman. Although they egged him on, he never swung. Instead, he told one cop, "If you ever came to my neighborhood without your uniform, I'd kick your ass." It was not a smart thing to say, but it didn't meet the legal definition of assault either. He did not do or say anything that represented an *immediate* threat.

It so happened that this case was before Judge Adam Stillo, who would have fixed it for me. But I told the judge, "I'll take it to a jury and I'll win." That's exactly what happened.

I went back to see Pat Marcy at Counsellors Row. When we were out in the lobby, I told Pat how I had just won my first jury trial for Mike in the suburbs. I had less to work with than on the policewoman case. I said, "Let me take her case to a jury too. If it's just a bench trial and a judge throws it out, the sky will fall. Believe me."

"No," he said. "You just go before the judge, put the case on, and get rid of it already."

I had asked for a Substitution of Judge, and Pat had the case assigned to Lawrence Passarella, a liberal judge. He must have been as soft as a grapefruit to take on a case like this, but maybe Marcy gave him no choice. Although Passarella did lean toward the defense, no judge could go easy on crimes against cops. In truth, I never liked Passarella all that much. He was one of your classic high-and-mighty judges. When I used to see him at Counsellors Row, he wouldn't even bother to make small talk. Once, he was alone at the First Ward table when I sat down.

"Waiting for Pat?" I asked.

"Pat who?" he said.

Still, even if Passarella was a pompous ass, I figured he couldn't be completely stupid. He might welcome a plea to get out from under this heater case. The minimum sentence for attempted murder was six years in prison. I didn't want Mike to do any jail time. From what I could see, the kid was like a whole new person and finally straightening up his life. If the judge reduced the charge to just aggravated battery, he could get away with giving Mike probation.

I called Mike and his father back to my office. I never said a word about what was going on behind the scenes with Marcy and Nunzio. I told them, "What I can maybe do is work out a plea with this judge and get you probation."

The father said, "Whatever you think is right, I will go along with it."

Once again, I went back to Pat Marcy. I said, "I talked to the kid and his dad and they're willing to take probation. Let me work out a plea on this."

Marcy did not want to hear about a plea. "Just go and do what I told you to do." Obviously, through Nunzio, someone had offered a lot of money to the judge for a not guilty.

But whatever Marcy said, I was still determined to work out a plea. Since Pat wouldn't let me talk to the judge, I tried to go first to the assistant state's attorney. They had a special prosecutor on this case because of all the publicity. I said to him, "I'd like to work out a plea if you can reduce the charge from attempted murder to just the battery."

He said he needed to check with his superiors. He came back the next day and said, "No. We're not going to reduce it. Either you plead guilty to attempted murder, or we go to trial."

I wanted to say, "Listen, you fucking asshole, you're not going to win this case, and you don't even know it." But I bit my tongue and said, "Okay. We'll go to trial."

I approached Pat one last time about working out a plea, but Marcy refused to listen. "Just go in there," he said, "and stop with this."

But I didn't go to trial. Three times before our date came up, I went into court and asked for a continuance. I avoided Pat, so he wouldn't ask me about the delay. I hoped against hope that something would develop to get me out of this.

By February 1986, I realized I couldn't stall the Colella case much longer, and I did everything I could to distract myself. I stayed up late, I drank more than usual, and I gambled like a demon. Because I wasn't thinking clearly, I made silly bets—violating all of my own rules about covering both sides of a line. When the year started, I was on a winning streak, but now it was like I had been cursed. All my numbers went the wrong way. In the first few weeks of February, I went in the hole for $350,000. On just one day, I lost eighteen out of twenty college basketball games, where I bet from $5,000 to $10,000 a game. Never in my life did I have a day like that. Maybe it was the Catholic in me, or just plain superstition, but I started to think I was being punished.

My biggest mistake was playing with Bob Johnson, an independent bookie from the south suburbs. He was big and burly, more than six feet tall, and had been a boxer, so he thought he could throw his weight around. I had nearly had a fight with him once before. Worse yet, he was a cokehead, and had his own debts piled high. At times it made him desperate. I owed him $55,000, and he started calling me several times a day to collect. He'd tell my secretary, "Your boss is a bust-out fuck. Tell him I want my money, or I'm coming there to get it." At one point he called me at home and, to get him off my back, I told him, "I can't talk now. I'm being raided by the IRS." That kept him quiet for a few days, but then he started calling again.

I had been in the hole to bookies before and, with enough time, I played my way out of it. But Johnson and the approaching fix started throbbing away like a cavity. I had no desire to save the tooth. I just wanted it out and done with.

Finally, I had to let the Colella case come to trial—on the last Wednesday of the month. The case was heard in the criminal courthouse on 26th and California Street. Spectators were kept behind bulletproof glass, so they heard the testimony through speakers. As I expected, the gallery was filled with reporters, cops, and officials from the Fraternal Order of Police. This was the sort of trial my father would have attended when he was a union officer.

The whole proceeding lasted no more than three hours; but, for me, it seemed to go on and on like a slow-motion nightmare. It started with the testimony from the policewoman. She described how Colella reached into his car before he turned on her. She said, "He came up with this bar of cold, rolled steel. He said, 'That's it. I'm going to kill you.' "

This quote appeared in the newspapers the next morning. They did not bother to report on my cross-examination of the policewoman or the other cops. As for the steel bar, the cops said they found it behind the car. How did it end up there, if Colella was under a pile of cops? Also, they never bothered to dust it for fingerprints. Clearly this so-called weapon and her claim about his threat to kill her were ways to trump up the charges to attempted murder. When I asked the cops about beating Mike, they wouldn't even admit he bled, let alone that he needed all the stitches and had all the contusions listed in his medical report.

Unfortunately, the evidence—or lack of it—would have mattered only if I had had a jury focused on a verdict, but this entire proceeding had nothing to do with the law. Instead, I was stuck in a crazy charade. On the inside, I had a judge who knew his ruling before he ever took the bench. Meanwhile, on the outside, reporters and the rest of the public had their minds made up too, before they had heard one word of testimony.

But the worst part of the trial did not come until the very end—when Passarella announced his ruling. He switched off his microphone and whispered to the court, "Not guilty," and then all but ran out of the courtroom. He never gave any further explanation for his verdict.

At first, the spectators thought he was going to lunch, or needed a bathroom break; but when they saw the prosecutors jump to their feet and get all pissed off, there was pandemonium.

As I walked out, the policemen started yelling at me: "You should be ashamed of yourself. You should be ashamed of yourself."

I just ignored them and pushed my way through the crowd, but inside I was seething. Every day of my life, I looked at the hole in my hand from the beating I got as a cop. How could anyone give *me* crap about a police beating? But then again, I had allowed myself to be associated with a total travesty of justice. All of my feelings were twisted inside-out like a pretzel.

As I drove to Counsellors Row, I thought about Passarella. No matter how much I disliked the man, I felt sorry for him. I thought, "This is an exact replay of what happened to Frank Wilson in the Harry Aleman trial. This fix will be his ruin."

When Marcy saw me enter the restaurant, he got up from the First Ward table and walked into the lobby. Once again, he led me past the elevators and through the door to the staircase. He stood above me on the steps leading to the janitor's closet. Again, he reached into his pocket and took out an envelope.

He said, "Here's the other $2,000 you have coming." I had never told him about my fee arrangement with Colella's father. Obviously he had been talking to them, or someone close to them.

As I took the envelope, I said, "This judge is going to have a serious problem. The media is all over this. This guy will probably lose his job."

He said, "That's none of your business. It's not your concern what happens to him."

"But what if he beefs on us?" I asked.

"Nobody would dare fuck with us," he said.

I thought, "Maybe you're looking at someone who will."

The moment I had the thought, I looked away. As crazy as it sounds, I wondered whether he could read my mind or see something in my eyes. That was the kind of power he had over me.

After I left Counsellors Row, I tried to get the trial off my mind and go about my business, but I didn't sleep well. I had bad dreams. I saw dead people out of my past. The innocent ones, like the bookie Anthony Reitinger, and the not-so-innocent, like Butch Petrocelli, who were killers themselves. I kept hearing my father say, "I used to arrest these people." Or "You shouldn't be wasting your God-given talents on these people." These people.

I also heard Marcy's voice. Over and over again, I heard him say, "Nobody would dare fuck with us." Then I started thinking: "Maybe, after I was almost killed so many times, this is the reason I was left alive—to fuck with Marcy and the First Ward."

My father used to say, "The Lord has a plan for all of us, and there's a reason why things happen." Now at night, I started thinking: "This is my destiny: to take down this horrible organization."

But then the next morning, with the light of day, I said to myself, "Why would I pick a fight with Marcy? It would be like committing suicide, and I have a fantastic life. I worked my ass off to get a law license.

TOP: My family in 1951. In the center of the picture stands yours truly at the age of seven, fresh from my first Holy Communion—already a hot shit. (*Chicago Tribune* photo by the *Chicago Tribune.*) **ABOVE (LEFT):** Count Dante in his famous comic book ad. I have yet to meet anyone with his amazing combination of talents and flaws. **ABOVE (RIGHT):** Marco D'Amico, 1994. He once said to me, "Nobody wears a wire on us and lives to talk about it."

LEFT: The four major freeways sliced the Chicago metro area into pieces of pie—one for each of the Outfit's main groups. **BELOW RIGHT:** Tony Spilotro in 1974, then the Mob's main enforcer in Vegas. He liked the fact that I stood up to him. Later, we had one of my "last meals" together.

BELOW: Tony Accardo (center of photo, wearing glasses) and Joey Aiuppa (far left), have a sit-down with some of their bosses in 1978. The five Mafia groups got along very well—like five fingers clenched into a fist.

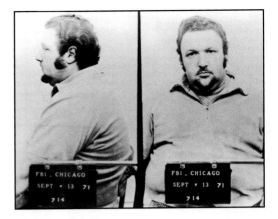

ABOVE (LEFT): Angelo LaPietra, the little king of the Chinatown Group. They called him "Hook," because he used to hang his enemies from meat hooks when he tortured them to death. **ABOVE (RIGHT):** Herb Blitzstein, Tony Spilotro's sidekick. He looked like a combination between Mitch Miller and a weird professional wrestler. **RIGHT:** The First Ward table itself wasn't fancy, but for the lawyers, city workers, and politicians always milling around, it was like a King's Court. (*Chicago Tribune* photo by the *Chicago Tribune*.)

ABOVE (LEFT): John D'Arco, Sr., 1952, in Council Chambers. The resemblance to Capone actually helped his career. The Mob bosses expected him to be mayor one day, but Senior was never the sharpest blade in the drawer. (As published in the *Chicago Sun-Times*, Inc. Copyright 2004 by *Chicago Sun-Times*, Inc. Reprinted with permission.) **ABOVE (RIGHT):**

Johnny D'Arco in 1990. He yelled at the prosecutors, "Slander my name all over the world—you!" Then he marched out of the courtroom, leaving his wife behind to bawl her head off. (As published in the *Chicago Sun-Times*, Inc. Copyright 2004 by *Chicago Sun-Times*, Inc. Reprinted with permission.) **LEFT:** From left to right: Yours truly, wearing a hat and sunglasses, with Alderman Fred Roti, John D'Arco Sr., and Sam Banks on our way to criminal court in 1978 during my heyday. I loved being a lawyer. I loved being the center of attention. (As published in the *Chicago Sun-Times*, Inc. Copyright 2004 by *Chicago Sun-Times*, Inc. Reprinted with permission.)

TOP (LEFT): Pat Marcy (right), 1990, with lawyer Terence P. Gillespie. "Nobody would dare fuck with us," Marcy once told me. I thought, "Maybe you're looking at someone who will." (Photograph by Brian Jackson. As published in the *Chicago Sun-Times,* Inc. Copyright 2004 by *Chicago Sun-Times,* Inc. Reprinted with permission.) **TOP (RIGHT):** Harry Aleman in 1977. He bore in on me with that Evil Eye and asked, "Are you sure you can handle it? Are you sure this judge is going to throw the case out?" **ABOVE:** Judge Frank J. Wilson, running from reporters after he acquitted Harry Aleman. When I paid him off, he said, "You destroyed me." (Photograph by Larry Graff. As published in the *Chicago Sun-Times,* Inc. Copyright 2004 by *Chicago Sun-Times,* Inc. Reprinted with permission.)

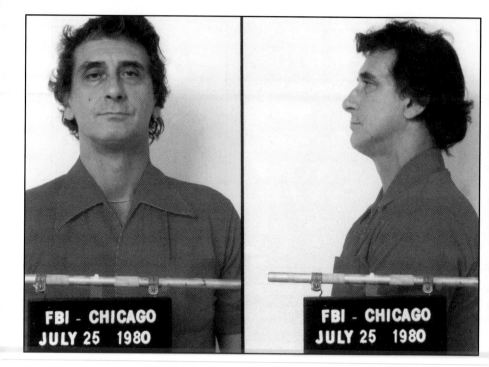

ABOVE: Frank Renella in 1980. He went over to the kitchen drawer and pulled out a gun. He pointed it at me and said, "If you're setting me up, you're gonna be the first to get killed." **RIGHT:** Judge Thomas J. Maloney in 1977. The arrogance of the man knew no bounds. For the right price, he would let anyone off for any crime. Absolutely anyone. (Photograph by Jim Frost. As published in the *Chicago Sun-Times*, Inc. Copyright 2004 by *Chicago Sun-Times*, Inc. Reprinted with permission.)

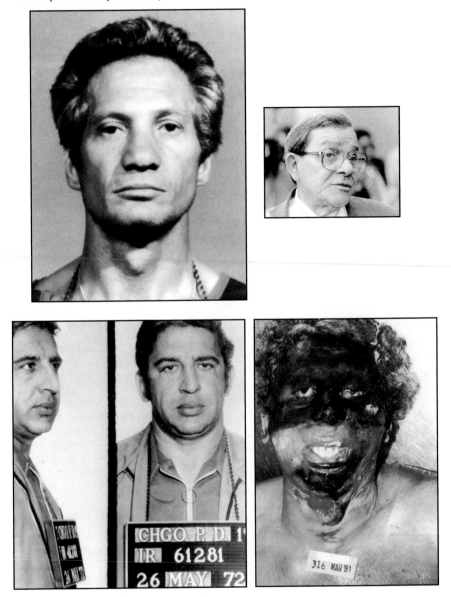

ABOVE: Butch Petrocelli, living in 1972, and dead in 1981. If they could turn on Butch and torture and burn him so horribly for a piece of cheese, they could turn on anyone.

ABOVE (LEFT): Alderman Ed Burke and his wife Appellate Judge Anne Burke (2000). I wanted the Feds to look at two cases they were involved with: a wife stabber out for insurance money and a high school principal who abused his students. (Photograph by Brian Jackson. As published in the *Chicago Sun-Times*, Inc. Copyright 2004 by *Chicago Sun-Times*, Inc. Reprinted with permission.) **ABOVE (RIGHT):** John DiFronzo in 1992, when he was CEO of the entire Outfit. As I walked through his showroom, I wondered if he had installed a sophisticated device to detect wires. **LEFT:** Attorney Ed Genson in 1998. He staggered to the judge, pointed at me, and said, "This man is a legal assassin. Every time he opens his mouth he plunges a dagger into my client." (Photograph by Bob Black. As published in the *Chicago Sun-Times*, Inc. Copyright 2004 by *Chicago Sun-Times*, Inc. Reprinted with permission.)

Why would I want to give everything up for nothing? I don't want to give it up."

The day after the Colella trial, when I got back to my office, I got another crazy call from Bob Johnson. He was screaming, "I want my money! I want my fucking money!"

I slammed down the phone and got in my car. I had a lunch meeting scheduled at Counsellors Row, and got angrier as I drove. If I was going to stomach a fix like Colella, the least the Mob could do was get these fucking bookies off my back. When I walked into the restaurant, I passed Marcy, going in the opposite direction.

"Pat," I said, "can I talk to you a minute?"

"I'm busy," he said. It was an absolute brush-off—maybe his way of getting back at me for beefing about the Colella fix.

As I sat through my meeting, I couldn't get my mind off Marcy and the "injustice" of it all. One way or another these people were going to help me with *my* problem.

I had another idea. With all the bosses in prison, the Mob had given Marco control over most of their gambling operations in the Chicago area. I figured he should have clout with any bookie—even the independent ones. After I left Counsellors Row, I drove to his Survivor's Club—for the first time in years. Marco was there playing cards. I asked to talk a few minutes, and when he got up from the table, I told him about my problem. He couldn't be bothered, either. He said, "Put the names down and come back and see me in a day or two."

Now I was really pissed. I figured: "Fuck it. If Marco won't help me, I'll just go over his head to Johnny DiFronzo." After Jackie Cerone was convicted in Operation Strawman, DiFronzo had become the head of Marco's West Side group. Accardo also anointed him the boss of the other bosses—the latest in the Outfit's long line of acting CEOs. John was a different breed from the other Mob bosses. He may have done some dirty work to make his bones, but over the years he had polished up his act considerably. Fit and trim at fifty-eight, he always wore a suit. He had razor-cut hair with a distinguished patch of gray at the temples. He spent most of his time at his Chrysler dealership on the West Side, and he definitely looked the part of a wealthy car dealer. When I walked into his office in the back of the Chrysler showroom, he gave me a warm greeting and asked, "What can I do for you?"

I said, "I'm sorry to bother you with this, John, but I have a problem. I owe a few people some money on bets I made. If I can get a little more time, I can straighten out with them. I just need a little more time."

Like I thought he would, John took a real interest in my problem. I had recently represented his kid on a case, got the charges dropped, and never even sent him a bill. He said, "Give me a list of the people who are bothering you, and I'll have someone look into it. Then get back to me tomorrow."

When I went back to the dealership on Friday, DiFronzo told me his people had contacted all the bookies on my list, except one. He asked, "Who is this Bob Johnson?"

I said, "He's a guy on the South Side."

"Who's he with? Nobody knows who he's with."

I said, "I don't know." I realized Bob Johnson was not paying the Mob his street tax. I had just gotten him into a lot of trouble.

John then sat me down, and he said, "Bob, I don't want you paying Bob Johnson—or anybody else, for that matter. You don't pay anybody anything. As far as I'm concerned, you are now clear." Then, just like Marcy did years before, he scolded me. "And I don't want you gambling any more, either. You get yourself in trouble. You've always been a big gambler and you should know better already."

I nodded my head, but some day I fully intended to pay my debts so I could start gambling again. All I needed was enough time to win back everything I had lost. I thanked John for his help and promised to mend my ways. By the end of the day, two of the bookies called to assure me that they would not collect. One of them, Dominic Barbaro, said, "I never threatened you. You make sure you tell your friends I never threatened you." For the first time in a long time, I didn't hear anything from Bob Johnson.

But the bookies were not my problem. I still didn't sleep well. I still couldn't get the Colella case off my mind. Just as I expected, the papers crucified Judge Passarella. Only a week after the trial, Passarella met with the chief judge of the Circuit Court and asked to be transferred out of the criminal division. Richie Daley, then the Cook County state's attorney, charged that the verdict showed "total disregard of the facts of the case." But Daley put all the blame on Passarella's judgment and said he had come up with similar bad decisions in the past.

The press figured something else was going on. I got a call from John Drummond, then Chicago TV's premier crime reporter. He brought a crew to my office to tape an interview. Right in front of the camera, he asked me if the Colella case was fixed. I replied that the state had no case, and I truly believed that. "The police got up on the stand and they all lied," I said. "The judge did the right thing." Of course, he did the right thing for the wrong reason, but I didn't say that.

When Saturday rolled around, ten days after the Colella trial, I was still in turmoil, just boiling inside. That morning, for a little fun, I went downtown to play gin with my old lawyer pals at 100 North LaSalle. The group included Allan Ackerman, the first attorney I had shared an office with. We had our laughs, and it was like the good old days again. I totally forgot my troubles. We finished up early in the afternoon, and I wanted to grab some lunch before I went home. My favorite deli, the Dill Pickle, was only a few blocks away, so I decided to take a stroll. Getting a corned beef sandwich was my only purpose in life. When I turned the corner onto Dearborn Avenue, I happened to pass the Federal Building. It seemed to draw me like a magnet. Suddenly I thought, "Maybe I should see who's up in the Strike Force office."

The Organized Crime Strike Force was a federal agency set up specifically to go after the Mafia. I figured that the attorneys and FBI agents reported directly to the U.S. Attorney General in Washington, D.C., with no local stops in between. That's all I knew. I didn't even know anyone who worked there.

I walked into the lobby, and there was a security guard behind a little desk. When I asked if anyone was in the Strike Force office, he called and got an answer. I told the guard my name and that I was an attorney, and he was told to send me up.

Only one person was in that day—Gary Shapiro, chief attorney for their entire Chicago operation. He was in his shirtsleeves, probably catching up on paperwork.

"I'm Bob Cooley," I said.

"What can I do for you?" he asked.

"I'd like to help you destroy the First Ward," I said. "I'd like to help you destroy Pat Marcy."

ON
THE
WIRE

CHAPTER 9

IN THE WEEDS

O nce I walked into the Strike Force office and opened my mouth, it was like I had stepped off the ledge of a sky-scraper. There was nothing I could do to save myself. Even-tually I would hit the ground. I just didn't know how long it would take.

What do you want?

That was the question Gary Shapiro kept asking. It was the question all the Feds would ask. He said, "If you're coming here to help us, what do *you* want in return?"

Immediately I had second thoughts about the whole thing. I was talking to a federal agent—a stranger—about illegal things I had done or known about. "What *am* I doing here?" I thought. "Have I gone crazy?"

"Do you need money?" Gary asked. "Do you need protection? Do you need anything?"

I said, "I don't want anything. I don't need anything. But I think I can help you people. I think I can help you people take down the First Ward. That's the cancer behind the courts and everything else in this city."

In my own mind, I didn't have a clear picture of what I could do. I imagined they would want me to wear a wire, like Terry Hake, who developed all the Greylord cases. But that meant I would be a witness, too, and I knew the defense would attack my testimony by claiming that I had come to the authorities for personal reasons—to get myself out of a jackpot. That's how *I* would destroy a government informant:

first get him to discuss his motives for cooperating—such as a lighter sentence or money—and then destroy his credibility in the eyes of the jury. How did I know that the Feds or the state didn't already have me on tape or have me as a target in one of their investigations? If I was coming in to save my own neck, I'd be a stoolpigeon and my testimony would be worthless.

I said to Gary, "What I want you to do is check that I don't have any problems of my own. If I'm under investigation already, then I can't help you."

"But what do you know about the First Ward?" he asked. "What can you tell me? I'm sure we don't have any investigations against you."

I wouldn't take his word for it. I said, "I want you to check with all the federal agencies and really make sure there's nothing out there." I gave him my card. "If I have no problems, then get ahold of me and we'll sit down. Maybe we can do something."

Only a few minutes passed while I was in Gary's office, but after I walked out of the Federal Building, I was in a different world. Once again, I looked over both shoulders when I walked, nervous as a cat. I realized what a stupid thing I had just done. What if Gary was connected to the First Ward? He'd be calling Marcy or Roti at that very moment, and I would have just signed my own death warrant. Meanwhile, I had given him a reason to make *me* the target of an investigation. There were plenty of reasons why the Feds never went after the First Ward, but there was nothing stopping them from coming after me. My case could be bundled up with all the attorneys they indicted in Greylord.

A week went by, and I was relieved that Gary Shapiro didn't call. I figured he had forgotten the whole thing. That was fine with me. I now had no interest in helping him.

On Tuesday, March 18, I spent the morning in court and drove back to my office after lunch. When I walked into the reception area, I could see by the look on my secretary's face that something was wrong. "Bob," she whispered, "are you in some kind of trouble?"

"Why?" I asked. "What's wrong?" For all I knew, Bob Johnson had paid a call.

She said, "I think there are some FBI agents in your office."

My heart sank. I walked back and saw them sitting there: a man and a woman; very square types with neat hairstyles and conservative suits. In other words, they looked exactly like FBI agents.

They got up to greet me, and we shook hands all around. When we sat down I could see them giving my office the once over.

The man, Steve Bowen, did most of the talking. He wanted to know why I looked so surprised. "You told Gary we should check if you had any problems and then come see you."

"I'm surprised," I said, "because I thought I would get a call from Gary first."

"Well, we did all the checking and you don't have any problems," Steve said. "So what can you tell us? How can you help us?"

"I thought I could do something," I said, "but now I'm not really sure."

But with the two of them sitting in my office, I couldn't tell them to get lost. They already checked into my background and knew about all my notorious cases. I had opened a Pandora's box. If I kept my mouth closed, they had reason to stay focused on me until they found something to make me talk. There was no stopping now.

Then Steve said, "Are you sick? Do you have some kind of terminal illness?"

"No," I said. "I'm feeling fine." At first it seemed like an odd question, but I realized that he was totally mystified by my motivations.

He asked, "So why do you want to talk to us?"

"Because it's something I feel I have to do," I said. I was too embarrassed to mention my father. Besides, how could I talk about something so personal when I had just met them? I said, "The average citizen in this town doesn't have a prayer when he goes into court. You had this Operation Greylord and it just made the First Ward more powerful. It's business as usual for the court system. Somebody has to stop it. Nobody else has the balls and nobody else will."

Then again, Steve asked the question: "But what do *you* want for this? We don't have cases on you anywhere."

I said, "Fine, then all I want is 'use' immunity." This meant they could not use anything I told them to bring charges against me. "If you can build cases some other way, so be it." As a next step, I asked that they arrange another meeting with the U.S. Attorney to make sure I had the protection I was looking for. I said, "Just tell Gary to get ahold of me."

Gary called back and set up a meeting with me two days later at the Holiday Inn in the western suburb of Oak Brook. I had no idea why they picked that location. With its fancy golf courses and big new sub-divisions, Oak Brook was the new "residence of choice" for the Mob bosses. Marcy himself had just bought a home there.

When I walked into the lobby, I saw Steve Bowen, one of the FBI agents who had come to my office. I was supposed to pretend I didn't know him and go upstairs. He followed, and then led me to one of the rooms on the second floor. Inside was the other agent who came to my office, Marie Dyson, with Gary Shapiro. They brought along another agent, Jack McCoy, a bull-necked drill sergeant type. We had to pull the chairs near the bed so everyone could have a seat.

Gary then said, "I had a conversation about you with Anton Valukas." He was the U.S. Attorney for the Northern District of Illinois. "We decided that 'use' immunity for you would not be a problem."

Although I was glad to hear about the immunity, I was not happy he had talked to Valukas. Evidently the Strike Force had to work with the local U.S. Attorney. Although I didn't know anything about Valukas— he had just been appointed a few months before—I did know some-thing about his predecessors. After they left office, almost all of them ended up working for one of the two big Chicago firms that the Mob bosses and politicians used when they got into trouble. It was a revolving door. One month they supposedly investigated the bad guys, and the next month they defended them. If Valukas saw that same career path for himself, would he want me to take down his future clients?

But Gary wasn't finished with the bad news. He went on to say, "We want you to understand that if you work with us, you can no longer do anything illegal. You can no longer fix cases, and you can no longer gamble. . . ."

Crazy as this sounds, I never thought my gambling would be an issue for them—maybe because I didn't consider gambling to be *that* illegal.

I held up my hands and said, "Whoa. Wait. My problem is that I owe some money to some bookies. I had a few real bad weeks. If I can just keep playing a little longer, I'll win back enough to straighten out."

But Gary wouldn't hear of that. He said, "You can't gamble any more. Period. If you are going to be a Cooperating Witness, there are certain rules you have to abide by." Then, he went on to give me *more* rules. I could no longer do any work in Federal Court whatsoever. Also, I couldn't handle any serious case where a client might get a lot of time, because later he might complain that my government work interfered with his defense.

I let them know they were cutting out a big chunk of my income. Gary said, "If you need money, we'll give it to you in return for the business you're turning down."

"I don't want your money," I said. "If I take money from you, then it looks like I'm a stoolpigeon, just doing something to help myself. Juries will never believe me."

When they asked how I would get along without their money, I said, "I'll handle it myself. I can build my civil practice."

As far as the gambling debts were concerned, Gary wanted to give me the money to pay those off. I told him about Dominic Barbaro, Bob Johnson, and a few others. "We want to build cases against some of these bookies," he said. "Will you make payments to them?"

"I saw John DiFronzo about Bob Johnson," I said. "He specifically told me not to pay Johnson back."

Jack McCoy jumped up from the bed. "You saw *who*?" he asked.

When I explained what had happened at DiFronzo's dealership, McCoy laughed. "You've got to be kidding."

McCoy had been a hard-ass from the moment I met him, and now he all but called me a liar. I said, "If you don't believe me, let me put on a wire and I'll confirm what I'm telling you."

I did not expect to start this relationship by wearing a wire on *the* top boss in the Mafia (Accardo was mostly retired by this time). But now my honesty was at stake. I had to prove myself, or I'd never get off on the right foot with the Feds.

Then, for the next few hours, I told them the story of my life: my youth on the South Side, my years as a cop, how Jimmy LeFevour tried to shake me down in Traffic Court my first few days out of law school—even about Count Dante. At first, I thought they only wanted to hear about the courts, but when I told them how Marcy fixed the cases for Colella and Lenny Chow, McCoy acted skeptical again. "You really think you can take down Marcy?" he asked. Evidently he specialized in organized crime for the FBI, and he knew how hard the First Ward was to crack. He asked me what I could tell them about Fred Roti, John and Johnny D'Arco, Patty DeLeo, and Marco D'Amico. I still wasn't ready to talk about the Harry Aleman case, but I told them how I fixed a case for Harry's brother-in-law, Richie Kimball, when he kicked an FBI agent in the head during a bar fight. I thought they'd enjoy that story.

But there was one name McCoy did *not* want to hear. At one point I said, "Next to Marcy, no one is more dangerous than the police department's chief of detectives, Bill Hanhardt."

I started to explain what he was doing to protect the Mob bookies, when McCoy interrupted me and said, "You don't like him, do you?"

"Sure I don't like him," I said, "but what does that have to do with anything?"

Then he asked: "Is that why you're making these things up about him?"

I said, "I'm not making anything up. I'm here to help. You asked me what I knew and I'm telling you." Hanhardt had been the Chicago Police Department liaison with the FBI. In the process, he might have become McCoy's friend, too. (Hanhardt retired from the police force a few months after this meeting.)

If McCoy was against me, he was the only one in that hotel room. Gary Shapiro and the other two agents looked pretty excited. After that meeting, McCoy faded out of the picture. The next morning, when it came time to get ready for my meeting with DiFronzo, just Steve Bowen and Marie Dyson showed up at my apartment.

In time, I got to know Steve and Marie pretty well. They were two of the straightest arrows you could ever find. Steve was slim and bald, and he carried himself like a Marine. Marie had dark short hair. She was very proper and reminded me of a no-nonsense teacher you'd have in grade school. They always did everything strictly by the book. Each and every time before I put on a wire, I had to sign my own consent form saying that I put on the body recorder "voluntarily" and without receiving threats or promises. Only after we completed the paperwork did Steve take me into the bedroom so I could "attach" the wire.

The FBI used a body recorder made by a Swiss company called Nagra Audio. It came in a silver metal case the size of an old-fashioned whiskey flask. Inside was a mechanism as precise as a Swiss watch: two tiny reels with thin tape that threaded through a series of gears and posts.

Steve wrapped an Ace bandage around my thigh with a pocket for the case. From there, he ran two wires under my shirt. They had microphones at the tip, and he taped each one under my collarbone. Everything still seemed so unreal; it was like I was watching him do this to someone else. Once Steve left the room to let me finish getting dressed, I grabbed my Smith & Wesson Airweight and attached it to a holster on my belt. I would need more protection than an Ace bandage if DiFronzo caught me with that fucking Nagra.

Steve and Marie wanted to follow me in their car and then wait near the dealership in case I had a problem, but that was too risky. I didn't want anyone strange to be seen around me in that West Side neighborhood, since it was crawling with Marco's crew. Instead, we agreed to meet in a nearby park after I saw John.

If I had been in a daze up to this time, once I got in my car and drove to DiFronzo's dealership, the full impact of what I was doing hit home. My entire body broke out into a sweat. Marco's words rang in my ears: "Nobody wears a wire on us and lives to tell about it." After I wore a wire on DiFronzo, there would be no turning back. I was a registered informant, and the Mob would kill me if they ever found out.

As I walked through DiFronzo's showroom, I started to wonder if he had installed a sophisticated device to detect bugs or wires in the building. John was sharp enough to do something like that. The Ace bandage on my thigh felt like a cast. I kept glancing down to make sure there was nothing funny about the way my pants hung.

A guy in a suit sat at a desk outside John's office door. He was supposed to look like a salesman, but he was really one of DiFronzo's bodyguards from a West Side crew. I'm sure he was packing, too. He recognized me and let John know I was there. DiFronzo chased some people out of his office and had me come in.

I half-expected a bell to go off when I walked through the door, but nothing happened. Instead, once again, John gave me a warm hello, and that put me at ease. All I had to do was thank him, I thought. There was nothing suspicious about that.

I told John how quickly some of those bookies got back to me and how scared they sounded. He got a kick out of that. But then I said, "I appreciate what you did, but I'm going to make a couple of payments to these guys."

That got John upset. He yelled, "What the fuck are you making payments for? I told you not to. You're not afraid of them, are you?"

I said, "Bob Johnson has been calling and harassing me."

He said, "You're not afraid of him, are you?"

I said, "No."

He said, "Then I don't want you paying him. You're not supposed to. He's not with anybody."

I didn't really say I would *not* pay the bookies. I just told John not to worry, shook his hand to thank him again, and got the hell out of there.

Later, I met Steve and Marie in the park. I delivered the Nagra, and my little tape sure delivered the goods. Once the Feds listened to it, they couldn't believe their ears. For the first time, they had ample evidence that John saw himself as the top Mob boss. Meanwhile, the tape gave me a future "inoculation" in case a Mob lawyer ever questioned my motives for coming in. DiFronzo made it clear that I didn't have to pay the bookies back, so no one could say I helped the Feds because I owed money on my gambling debts. Most important, the tape proved to Gary and the agents that I wasn't some idle bullshitter—like McCoy made me out to be.

But still, the Feds were in no rush to put a wire on anyone in the First Ward. Instead, they kept my sights lowered—as far as they could go—and had me focus on the bookies. The first one I called was Dominic Barbaro. He was still scared by the warning he got from DiFronzo's people to stay away from me. I told him I would pay him back, so we could start playing again. Poor Dominic couldn't help himself. He was scared of DiFronzo, but he really wanted that money. We arranged to meet at an Italian beef joint a few blocks from my apartment in Countryside.

Steve Bowen and Marie Dyson showed up again at my place to get me ready. First they counted out fifteen hundred-dollar bills and noted the serial numbers of each one. Although I owed Barbaro $24,000, we were going to pay him a little at a time. The Feds used each payment as a separate count in the indictment. This time, they brought a special Nagra recorder for me. Compared to the first model I wore, it held more tape—enough for three hours—and included an on/off switch that came up through a hole in my pants pocket. Although Barbaro had not been my client, I had represented a bookie who worked for him. On the chance I might bump into him or any of my other clients, I could reach into my pocket and shut off the recorder, so I wouldn't violate attorney–client privilege. But this new, bigger recorder didn't fit in the special pocket of the Ace bandage. Instead, Steve used the bandage to wrap the Nagra to my leg.

I drove the few blocks to the beef stand. Inside this joint, you ate at a counter that ran along a plate glass window. I pulled into a parking spot right in front of the place where Barbaro sat and stuffed his mouth with a sandwich. He was a little, skinny guy with a ferret face. He could see me through the window and gave me a nod. I opened my car door, but when I put my leg out, I felt the bandage give way. The Nagra fell through my pants and clattered to the ground. I was still behind the wheel, but when I looked up, there was Barbaro staring at me. I had no idea how much he saw. Immediately, I pointed to my right. When he turned his head, I pulled my leg back into the car and the Nagra came up with it. I slammed the door shut and backed out of my parking spot. Barbaro watched me pull away, frozen like a statue—with his mouth open and the beef sandwich in his hand.

Steve and Marie had parked up the road, and they were equally shocked to see me drive off. I'm sure they wondered where I was going with their $1,500. I drove straight back to my house. Soon after I walked inside, they rang my doorbell. I told them what had happened and for a few minutes, we were all in a state of panic.

"I don't know if he saw it," I said.

"If he did," Steve said, "you have a serious problem."

Then my phone rang. It was Barbaro, calling from the beef stand. "What happened?" he asked.

I said, "Didn't you see those coppers sitting in the gas station parking lot? I pointed to them. It was like they were staking you out."

"Oh," he said. Dominic had just gotten pinched a few weeks before. In fact, he wanted me to represent him in that case. Then he said, "Do you have my money?"

I told him I'd meet him behind a restaurant down the street.

After I got off the phone, Steve said, "Are you sure you want to go through with this?"

I said, "I'm not worried about him." Barbaro talked like a tough guy, but I could break him like a twig. Still, before I left, I pulled the Nagra and the Ace bandage off. When I saw Barbaro, he didn't have a clue that anything was wrong, and I handed him the money. Although I couldn't record the transaction, we had him set up to receive future payments. For the next meeting, I had him come to my office. Besides my wire, we also had a hidden video camera filming him through a hole in an attaché case. But during this visit, he said he didn't want my money. He wanted me to pay him back by handling his case. There was no way I could do that, but I told him, "I'll think about it."

He said, "Remember, you tell your friends I never threatened you, and I never will threaten you. You're a nice guy."

Then he asked me if I had heard from Bob Johnson. "I was told they're going to kill Bob Johnson," he said. "They're going to kill him because he threatened you. And he ain't paying street tax, either."

This was more information than we wanted to hear. Now the Feds had to pay a visit to Johnson and warn him that someone from the Mob might be looking to kill him. The next night, Bob Johnson called me at home. The FBI had attached a recorder to my phone, and I turned it on as soon as I heard his voice on my answering machine. I picked up the receiver and he was practically crying. "Your friends are going to kill me," he whined. "You got to help me. You got to put a stop to it."

I said, "Bob, I don't know what you're talking about. Why don't you meet me in my office and we can talk about it?"

He said, "I'm not coming anywhere near you," and hung up.

Then he called a day or two later. This time he was loud and belligerent, slurring his words together like he was high on something. "Where's my fucking money?" he screamed. "I want my money. Where's my fucking money?"

"Bobby," I said, "if you come on down to my office, I'll give you some money."

There was no way he'd come to my office. Instead, he sent someone else to collect for him, an ex-con who was involved with the South Side group. Like I did with Barbaro, I only gave him $1,500 each time he showed up. A few days later, Johnson would get high, and then call again to threaten me. This helped build a case for extortion in addition to bookmaking.

Bit by bit, as I dug myself deeper into this double life, my habits and my surroundings had to change. I became sensitive to the fact that my apartment was on the ground floor with big windows, so I moved to a place on an upper floor without a view. My longtime secretary was a sharp young woman, who would eventually figure out what was going on, so I had to let her go. State Senator LeRoy Lemke was not so sharp, but I didn't want him to suffer collateral damage, either, so I forced him out of our partnership.

The hardest change was to stop gambling. It was such a huge part of my social life, my relaxation and my recreation. Just a week after I got my instructions from Gary, one of my best buddies, a crazy dentist, asked me to put some money on a big game for him. When I called in the bet, I couldn't help but place one for myself. As soon as I did, I realized what a mistake I made. One stupid bet could destroy the entire investigation. I said to myself, "If I'm going to do this, I can't lie to the Feds." The next time I saw Steve Bowen, I told him I had something to say. It was as bad as going to confession when I was a kid. "Steve," I said, "I gambled." I gave him the name of the bookie and the amount I gambled, and I never did it again.

But I didn't go through all these changes just to nail a bunch of bookies. I wanted to go after big game already. During the spring of 1986, I continued to brief the FBI agents about all my activity with the First Ward, so I could start wearing a wire on Roti and Marcy. One story always led to another. I would start talking about the Lenny Chow fix with Judge Maloney, and the next thing I knew, they were picking my brain about the On Leong Chinese Merchants Association.

We now met at a more convenient place for me, a Countryside motel near my apartment. In May, Gary Shapiro and another assistant U.S. attorney attended the session, and I expected they would finally have the written agreement for my "use" immunity. But once again, Gary started our meeting by saying he had had a discussion about me with the U.S. Attorney, Anton Valukas. "When we told him about all these different things you were involved in and that some of them were illegal acts on your part, he said it might be a good idea if you pled guilty to a misde-meanor." Gary then stopped and asked, "What do you think of that?"

I was so angry, the blood was pounding in my ears. I said, "What the fuck are you talking about?"

Gary said, "He just thinks that because you've admitted to all these things, it might be a good idea if you plead guilty to some misdemeanor."

I said, "You fucking people have got to be kidding. I came in to help you. I'm giving up my life. All I asked for was 'use' immunity. Now you're telling me to take a plea and maybe go to jail. If I go to jail, I'm a dead man. Besides, I can't plead guilty and be of any help to you. It will negate all I'm trying to do. It will totally destroy my credibility. It will look like I was in trouble and that's why I came in to you." I got up from the chair and said, "I made the mistake of my life." Then I stormed out of the room.

I walked the few blocks back to my apartment, kicking myself all the way. I had been too trusting. I ate all their bullshit about not gambling or practicing criminal law. I wore a wire on the most powerful mobster in Chicago. And what did I get in return? The jackpot.

When I got home, I was still so hot that I decided to go cool off by the pool. I grabbed my portable phone, stomped downstairs, and had just settled into a lounge chair, when I got a call. It was Gary. "Why did you leave?" he asked. "What's the matter?"

I said, "Fuck you. I don't need this bullshit. I better get myself a lawyer. I'm going to need one." Then I hung up and called my old friend from Marquette, Bill Murphy. He had become a very successful defense attorney. I said, "Bill, I met with the Feds and I was going to cooperate with them."

He couldn't believe it. Bill was always warning people to stay away from the Feds. He said, "Bob, are you crazy? You know you can't trust them."

"You're probably right," I said. "I think now I'm going to need some representation. I thought I had a deal with them, and now they're backing out."

"But what did you do?" Bill asked.

"I can't even tell you," I said, "but now I don't know what I can do."

Bill and I arranged to meet the next day, but before I even left my apartment that morning, Gary called me again. I told him, "You people have really wronged me. I got myself a lawyer and now you have to talk to him before I say another thing."

Gary said, "But we changed our mind."

"What?"

He said, "I told you '*Valukas* thought it was a good idea to take a plea.' But if you don't think it's a good idea, we'll just forget about it. If you have a lawyer, that's fine, but be careful. It's dangerous for you to talk to anyone else."

"Okay," I said, "I still want something in writing." In fact, I didn't get my "use" immunity in writing for another year and a half. But what was I going to do? I had already crossed the line, and like I told myself in the parking lot of DiFronzo's dealership, there was no going back.

A few hours later, I got together with Gary and the rest of the team at the Countryside motel. It was probably the most productive session I had with them. I put together a list of all the judges I had paid off—either "hand to hand" or through a conduit, like Pat Marcy or a clerk. Also, for the first time, I gave them the details behind the Aleman fix.

But even after all I told them, the Feds would still not let me go after the First Ward. Instead, they pointed me toward another distraction. This one involved a defense attorney named Joe Ettinger, one of my professors in law school and one of the city's leading experts on ethics. He was representing Big Bill Hill, probably the city's biggest dope dealer at that time. Evidently, he had gotten Hill to come up with $25,000 to pay off the judge. One of Ettinger's cop friends was going to be the conduit, but the bagman suddenly died of a heart attack and the judge never got the money. Ettinger was now in a fix himself. He couldn't ask the client for another payoff, and if he didn't deliver the expected results during the trial, Big Bill could get very mad at him. Mr. Ethics went to Blackie Pesoli for help, and since Blackie knew I was a friend of the judge, he sent Ettinger my way. I notified the Feds. Although they authorized me to wear the wire on Ettinger, they didn't want me to do anything to help fix the case. I had Ettinger meet me in my office, so we had him on tape and on the hidden video camera. I couldn't help but find the whole scene amusing. Here was a lawyer everyone thought was legit, trying to buy the sort of fix he condemned from his media soapbox. I got him to tell me the whole story all over again. Ettinger was clearly terrified of Big Bill. He said, "It's very important. Whatever you want, I'll pay you. I have to get a not guilty."

By the time Ettinger left my office, I thought the Feds had a rock-solid case against him. But they asked that I meet him again and get him to tell me what he would pay for a fix. We met at one of my favorite Greek restaurants. I pretended that I had already talked to the judge, and that he was afraid the Feds were watching this trial. I told Ettinger what strategy he could use if he took the case to a jury, but he cut me off and said, "I don't want to take it to a jury."

I had a lot of trouble getting him on tape that day in the restaurant. Maybe he suspected something or thought we would be overheard. He talked in whispers, so even I barely understood him. When I asked what he would pay, he decided to be cute, and wrote the figure on the back of a napkin. I kept my eye on the napkin, and when he wasn't looking, I put it into my pocket. It was an airtight bribery case. When FBI agents later questioned him, he out-and-out lied to them, which was another felony. But like so many of my other investigations, for some mysterious reason this one never resulted in charges.

By June, it looked like the Feds wouldn't let me do anything but chase these small fry. I decided to take the bull by the horns. I went through the old files in my office, looking for something that might get Marcy to talk to me about one of the cases I had fixed. I found a grand jury transcript from New York. It had been sent to me by another lawyer who worked on On Leong cases. One of the witnesses repeated a story he had heard about how we fixed the case for Lenny Chow.

This time, I wasn't going to ask the Feds for their permission *before* I talked to Marcy, so they could tell me, "No." Instead, I first went down to Counsellors Row without a wire and had Marcy come out in the lobby with me. I said, "Pat, somebody's going to send me a copy of a grand jury transcript. It's supposed to say something about On Leong and that the case was fixed with Tom Maloney."

He said, "You're kidding."

I said, "Yeah. When I get it, I'll show you."

"Oh, yeah, do that," Pat said. "Most certainly."

Now that the door was open, the Feds had to let me walk through. I called Dave Grossman, one of the FBI agents assigned to me. He then had me meet with Tom Durkin, an assistant U.S. attorney. Tom was a big hefty guy with glasses. He had been an accountant before he went to law school, and from the outside he looked like a fairly mild-mannered CPA, but he was an absolutely ferocious trial lawyer and an expert on racketeering. He quickly became my strongest ally among the federal prosecutors. I told Tom, "If you can just let me wear the wire when I show Marcy this transcript, I can get him to implicate himself in the On Leong case."

Somehow Tom and Gary Shapiro got the permission for me to wear the wire on Marcy. I waited a few days and on Thursday, June 5, went back to Counsellors Row with my Nagra. I took Marcy into the lobby to look at the transcript. Not until I pulled it out did I notice—for the first time—that there was a date on the upper corner of each page, and it was from years before. I pulled it back from him and held my thumb over the corner of the transcript, and acted like I was helping him flip to the important pages. "Look here," I said to Pat. "I got a copy of the whole transcript this time."

Then I showed him some of the testimony and said, "This little fucking punk is saying I told him the case was fixed. I never told anybody that we fixed the case. In fact, everybody thinks I'm enemies with Tom Maloney. Nobody knows that he or you were involved and nobody is going to know you were involved."

I was laying it on thick. Too thick. But so much was at stake; I couldn't help but overdo it. Pat looked at me and he looked at the page for a minute. Then he said, "Bob, didn't you go down there? You went to New York, didn't you?"

"Uh-huh," I said. Marcy had told me exactly what I wanted to hear. He confirmed he knew all about the On Leong fix down to my trip for the final payment.

"Who was the judge?" he asked.

"Maloney," I said. "Maloney was the judge." Later I asked, "Don't you think you should warn him?"

Pat shook his head no. He said, "If there's a problem, he'll get ahold of me. He knows how to handle himself. I ain't going to shake him up."

I walked out of Counsellors on a cloud. The statute of limitations had long since passed on the On Leong fix, but if we made a new case, we could link it with On Leong and show a pattern of racketeering. Now, I thought, we were ready to rock and roll. I could stop spinning my wheels on bookies and build a case against the First Ward.

After they heard the Marcy tape, all the prosecutors and the FBI agents on the Strike Force were finally convinced I was telling them the truth, and they could see the potential of my investigation. There were no objections when I asked to put a wire on Alderman Roti to show that he was also involved with the On Leong. The next week, unannounced, I dropped into his office at City Hall. The secretary told me he was in the city council chambers. She called him there, and he told her to have me come over.

I went back down to the second floor of City Hall, and as I turned the corner, I saw that they had installed a metal detector right in front of the council chambers. There had been some raucous protest the day before and the police didn't want to take any chances during the city council meeting. I would have turned around, but Roti was on the other side of the metal detector, talking with a couple of people, and he spotted me. He waved for me to come on in. I walked towards him down the long hall with its cathedral ceiling. As I got closer, I looked to see if I knew one of the coppers by the metal detector, so he would let me walk around it, but I didn't know any of them. I got a few feet away when I just stopped in my tracks, turned on my heels, and walked back down that long, long corridor. I could feel Roti's eyes on me each step of the way.

I went right from City Hall to my car and pulled the wire off. Then I went across the street to Counsellors Row and left a message at Roti's office that I would be waiting for him to call me at the restaurant.

After an hour or so, when I didn't hear from him, I left Counsellors Row. I met the agent and handed my Nagra back to him, and then went to my office. I still didn't get a call from Roti. I couldn't stand waiting to hear from him or wondering what he was thinking. The next day, without the wire, I went to Counsellors Row when I knew he'd be eating lunch. He was sitting at the First Ward table with Marcy and a few other people. When he saw me, he said, "Why wouldn't you come through that metal detector yesterday?"

I tried to laugh, and then bent over to whisper, "What do you think? Because I was wearing a piece. I can't walk through those things and have them find that."

"Oh," he said. "So what did you want anyway?"

I came up with some excuse to ask for a bullshit favor. He acted like he'd be happy to help. I waved good-bye and left.

Now even I was spooked. I wondered if he really bought my expla-nation. Out of the corner of my eye, I saw Marcy give me a funny look—or what seemed like one. The Feds didn't have to keep me away from Counsellors Row any more. Until I was sure where I stood with the First Ward, I wouldn't go back to the restaurant—with or without a wire.

If I was edgy that summer, I had a good excuse. One week after the incident in City Hall, I had another of my last meals—this time, dinner with Tony Spilotro and his younger brother Mike. Earlier in the year,

Tony had survived another prosecution when he was acquitted for the burglaries committed by his Hole-in-the-Wall Gang. Oscar Goodman represented him again, and a "surprise" witness for the defense was the recently retired chief of detectives for the Chicago Police Department, Bill Hanhardt. He discredited the Feds' chief witness, Frank Cullotta, who had been Tony's old pal. Spilotro got another break—or so it seemed—at the start of the Strawman trial for casino skimming. He developed a legitimate heart condition. His case was then severed from that trial. His co-defendants, including some very top Outfit bosses, were found guilty. As I looked at Tony across the table, he looked much older than his forty-eight years. His hair was now gray and his bulldog face had gone puffy. I thought, "No fun being a tough guy. Not any more."

Little did I know. Tony thought he was in town for a sit-down the next day with his new crew leader. Instead, he and his brother were beaten to death with baseball bats and buried in an Indiana cornfield. A farmer found the bodies a few weeks later. Evidently, the bosses were not happy about the trouble hotheaded Tony had caused in Vegas. Worse yet, his behavior may have touched off the Strawman cases, but then he got off the hook when so many of his elders went away. The use of the bats said it all. The Outfit did not play games. They played for keeps.

I climbed down from the mountaintop, and was back in the weeds with the Feds as they tried to build more bullshit cases. In the middle of the summer, they asked me if I would fix a "contrived case" before Judge Adam Stillo in the Maywood branch of the Cook County Circuit Court. I said, "Sure."

The Feds used to call Maywood the Mafiosi court. A lot of the Mob's cases ended up there, because it was smack in the middle of the Italian suburbs. There were as many Italians inside the courthouse as outside—judges, lawyers, and court personnel. Terry Hake, the mole in Operation Greylord, broke his pick trying to crack it. The place was too damn insular. Johnny D'Arco had introduced me to Judge Stillo at a fundraiser and, as I told the FBI agents, I had paid him off dozens of times. He was a jolly old guy, always pleasant, but no dummy either. He was very careful about how we exchanged money, and I was sure he'd be extra-careful after Greylord.

In August, wearing my wire, I approached Judge Stillo in his chambers to see if he would still work with me. He said he might—as long as it wasn't a gambling case. I told him I wouldn't bother him with bullshit. "Unless it's real important, I won't even talk to you," I said.

So what did I get as my "real important" case? The Feds concocted the most bullshit traffic stop I could imagine. Supposedly an *off-duty* state policeman pulls a guy over after he sees him drive erratically. (He had to be off duty, so the Feds would not have to wrongly account for a state police car.) When he looks in the car, he sees an open can of beer. Then he finds a few grams of marijuana in the glove compartment. Worse yet, to play the part of the driver, the Feds used some corn-fed blond FBI agent from Oklahoma and gave him the name James David Hess. When I met the guy, I said, "You look just like an FBI agent."

Later I told Tom Durkin, "This isn't going to work. It just doesn't ring true. Why would a guy who looks like this have the open beer *and* the dope?"

I suggested they put a gun in the glove compartment instead. But for some reason the Feds weren't allowed to fake a gun charge—even if it had a broken firing pin. Against my better judgment, I decided I should be a team player. At least they were trying to make a case. "Okay," I said, "we'll try it."

Two months later I put on my wire and went back to Stillo's chambers. He wanted to gossip a bit about the D'Arcos and some of the Mob figures I used to see in Senior's Florida beach houses. I told him that I had no idea why Senior would sell those beautiful homes. The judge joked, "Bugs in them."

At some point, I slipped in the news that my "important" case had been scheduled. "I got something coming up in about two weeks," I told him. "It's some guy with some 'grass' in the glove compartment of his car." I explained that he'd have no trouble throwing it out, because the arresting officer made an illegal search. But then he said, "You know my nephew Joey? Talk to him."

That was bizarre. Judge Stillo never had a bagman before. I always paid him off directly, but it was another sign he was trying to be careful. His nephew, Joey Stillo, was a tall thin snake of a guy—almost the polar opposite of his uncle. They both lived in the suburb of River Forest, but Joey was a criminal defense lawyer, and he loved hanging out with the bad guys in the Italian restaurants and bars on the West Side. After I broke up with Johnny D'Arco's firm, the First Ward started steering Mob cases toward Joey.

I took Joey to lunch, and he, too, wanted to chitchat about Johnny D'Arco. We finally got around to the "Hess" case, and I explained why it would be so easy for his uncle to throw out. I didn't ask outright for a fix. I would never have done that in the old days, and I wasn't about to change my habits while I was wearing a wire. Instead, I said, "You tell me what's fair and we'll take care of it then."

Joey said, "All right."

"As I say," I said, "I never complain about the numbers."

Before I left, Joey assured me that he'd work things out with his uncle. "Don't worry," he said. "I'll make the call."

The Hess case went to trial November 5, 1986. Just the day before, we had elections in Cook County, and three judges were thrown off the bench—including Lawrence Passarella. The press and everyone else blamed his downfall on the Mike Colella case. Judge Stillo must have seen that in the morning papers. Not the best timing for a fix—especially with me.

The trooper who was supposed to have arrested Hess was the state's most important "witness." I tried to coach the guy beforehand. In our twisted world of make-believe, I wanted him to say things that would make it *easier* for Judge Stillo to throw the case out. "Testify that you used your flashlight," I told him. "Then we would have an illegal search."

This trooper got pissed off with that suggestion, because he knew the law. "I *never* use a flashlight," he said. "I'm not going to lie."

"But you didn't really arrest him, either," I said. "This whole case is a lie."

When he got up on the stand, the trooper ignored my coaching and said exactly what I told him *not* to. It was like he was going in for the kill on a real case. I didn't think it mattered much. But Judge Stillo ruled that the search was legal, and he found my client guilty. He gave him a $50 fine and a year of supervision. Maybe he thought he was doing me a favor, because the sentence could have been as much as $1,000 and a year in prison.

But I was stunned. I had never lost a case before this judge. After I left the courthouse, I regrouped with the FBI agents and the prosecutors. We were all in shock. I wondered whether now, after Judge Passarella's defeat, I was too hot for another fix. One of the prosecutors suggested I should still pay off Joey in return for the light sentence. I rejected that idea. Then the Stillos would know for sure I was trying to set them up. "Let me go see Joey anyway," I said, "and see if I can turn this around."

I put on the wire and went downtown to Joey's law firm. When we were alone in his office, I started to beef about the state trooper's testimony. I told him I could understand why the judge found Hess guilty, but then Joey cut me off. "That's not why he did it."

"Then why?" I asked.

"Something about this guy coming from Oklahoma," Joey said. "He looks like an FBI agent."

I tried to laugh it off as Greylord paranoia. "This judge is seeing FBI agents in his soup."

But when I turned over the tape, the Feds didn't see the joke. They thought I had to leave town. If Stillo had figured out I was working with the FBI, they said, my cover was blown. It was a matter of time before everyone knew.

I wasn't leaving town—not over this stupid case. I said, "Let me see the judge and see what I can do with him." That very afternoon, I put on the wire and went back into Judge Stillo's chambers and caught him right after lunch. When I asked what happened with my "client," he said, "He didn't sound right. He sounded like a plant. I just started having bad vibes out there." When the judge ran a check on Hess's license plate, no name or address came back, which is usually what happens with a law enforcement vehicle.

Inside, I was seething. How could the Feds be so careless? But on the outside I kept acting like this was one big joke. "Judge, you have to be kidding," I laughed. "This guy's a bookmaker. I've known him for years." Thinking fast, I said he was with the Rush Street group. I figured

Stillo wouldn't know any mobsters from that part of town. I explained that Hess wanted to be a commodities broker, but now that he was on supervision for this offense, he couldn't get his license.

The judge bought my explanation and offered to make it up to me. I went back to him a few months later to get the supervision terminated, just to keep my story straight, but at this point he didn't ask for money, and I didn't give him any.

Even though no money changed hands with the Stillos, their intentions were clear on the tape. The Feds had been too quick to give up on the case and me, I thought, when all it took to seal the deal was one more wire on the judge. His comments alone about "the plant" gave the Feds enough ammunition to bring charges against him and the nephew. But I didn't care much either way. The Stillos were strictly penny-ante, like something out of Operation Greylord. But while we were playing around with this bullshit case, we did get our first big break—totally out of the blue—and it would lead to none other than Judge Thomas J. Maloney.

CHAPTER 10

THE WORST FUCK

Everything in the Maloney case started with an "innocent" phone call from Billy Swano, a criminal defense attorney. When I had first met him years before, Billy was a public defender and a real sharp lawyer. We started going to the same places at night, and sometimes we would hang together. He had dark good looks and a frat-boy mentality about partying, but then he started to dip too much into the cocaine and would do crazy things when he got high. Once, his girlfriend called me to say he was beating her up and stalking her. I straightened him out, and Billy left her alone. Not a totally bad thing, since she became my girlfriend for a while. Another time, a client asked me if he could trust Billy to buy some dope for him. Again, I had to confront Billy and get angry with him. I said, "Are you fucking nuts?" But he would listen to me like I was a big brother.

After he left the public defender's office, Billy became a private criminal attorney. When he put his mind to it, he could be an effective lawyer. He won some high-profile cases and I sent a few lowlife clients his way. But when he called me in September of 1986, I hadn't seen him for a year. He said, "Can I meet with you?" Coincidentally, he lived in an apartment complex close to my own in Countryside.

In my bones, I felt this could be important. I called Steve Bowen, and when I mentioned Billy Swano's name, he said, "Are you kidding? Will you wear a wire on him?" Evidently something was up with Swano, but Steve couldn't tell me.

By the time Billy appeared on my doorstep, Steve had dropped off the Nagra. This time I tried to put it inside one of my cowboy boots, but that turned out to be another fuck-up. Every time I moved, my boot squeezed the metal case and shut down the recorder. It didn't matter, since Billy didn't say anything too earthshaking. He mostly wanted to talk about Paul Baker, a client I had pawned off on him. Baker was a weird violent guy who ran with a bunch of hick thieves and drug dealers called the Hillbilly Mafia. The last time I saw him, he was lying on his couch with a needle sticking in his arm. I never wanted anything to do with him after that. Whenever you turned around, Paul Baker had another murder or attempted murder charge against him. To escape the latest rap, he started talking to the Feds. An assistant U.S. Attorney showed Swano what Paul said about him and me—about how he wanted to gamble with me, how he paid Swano in cocaine and so on. Most of it was a bunch of bullshit, but some of it was true. Billy started talking like a tough guy. He wanted me to find someone who could "whack" Baker.

"Whoa, Billy," I said. "You don't even want to think like that or you're just gonna make more problems for yourself."

He decided to withdraw from Baker's case the next day. First he would see the judge and then he'd break the news to Paul, who was in Cook County Jail. He asked me to go with him when he saw Paul. I couldn't believe Swano was so scared of him. But Baker did have a cross-eyed psycho look. I had made him wear thick glasses when I defended him before a jury in a murder case. He smashed the glasses on the table as soon as he heard, "not guilty." But Billy didn't need me to protect him from Paul. Baker was already in jail. What could he do to Billy there?

I got the wire and met Billy the next day at the Criminal Courthouse. They were holding Baker in a cell behind one of the courtrooms. We went in together to see him. I told Paul, "I found out you gave the Feds some information about me. Why would you do that, after all I did for you?" Of course, Baker denied it. I said, "Swano indicates you have a beef with him. You better work it out in a nice way." Then I left the two of them alone.

When Billy came out, he said, "I have to go upstairs to see Judge Maloney. You want to walk with me?"

I figured, what the hell. I didn't have anything better to do. Besides, I could see Billy was stewing over something. We got in the elevator, and he said, "He fucked me."

"What?" I replied. Was Maloney the one who fucked him?

Then Swano asked me, "What's the worst fuck that somebody can do to you?"

To bust his balls, I said, "Steal your girl?"

He said, "No. Worse than that." Then out of the corner of his mouth, he added, "He takes the money and still finds them guilty."

"On a case?" I asked.

"A murder case," he said.

"You're kidding."

"But I got the money back," he said.

I thought to myself, "Is he really talking about Maloney?" Just to make sure I got this on tape, I repeated back what I heard him say: "He takes the money, finds them guilty, and then gives the money back?" I asked. "What good does that do you?"

Now I remembered. He had just worked a big case in front of Maloney that was in all the papers. It involved a contract killing for the city's most notorious street gang, the El Rukns.

We got out of the elevator, and Swano left me for a minute. He poked his head into Maloney's chambers, but then came back when he saw the judge was out. I asked Billy if he was talking about the El Rukns trial.

He nodded and said, "Listen, I mean Maloney and I have been like this for years." He held his two fingers together. "He always thought I was a great lawyer. I've always won up there." Then rubbing his thumb over his index finger, he added, "His track record has always been excellent. But now he's nuts. He's not to be trusted."

When I kept telling him I couldn't believe it, he shot back, "Just trust me. It just happened."

At that very moment, the elevator doors opened, and who got out but Judge Thomas J. Maloney himself. At first he looked shocked to see me standing there with Billy boy, but then he gave me his usual scowl and went huffing off down the hall. Billy chased after him.

Now I understood why the Feds were so interested in my meeting with Swano. Later, they went nuts when they heard the tapes with him. Evidently they had a few high-placed snitches in the El Rukns, along with some wiretaps on their phones, and knew a fix was coming down. During the entire trial, they had watched behind the scenes, hoping to catch Swano and Maloney in the act. At the last minute, with all the press that the trial was getting, Maloney must have gotten cold feet. He found Swano's two clients guilty. Then, to add insult to injury, he held their sentencing hearing before a jury, and they both got the electric chair.

It didn't matter that Maloney gave back the El Rukns' money. He had still originally intended to fix the case. Swano knew more than enough to implicate him. Meanwhile, my tape with Marcy about the On Leong fix could help build a racketeering charge against Maloney, too.

Suddenly, the misery I had gone through to wear the wire seemed worth it. Next to Marcy and Roti, Maloney was the symbol of all that was wrong with Chicago's criminal justice system. He wasn't fixing traffic cases and misdemeanors like Stillo. He was fixing *murder* cases, and no judge in America had ever been caught doing that.

Still, to get anywhere on Maloney we needed Billy Swano, and just hours after I left him outside the judge's chambers, he called to say he wanted to meet again that day. I told him to come to my office.

I put on the wire, and we set up the hidden video. Once he sat down in my office, I told Swano I had heard things about the El Rukns trial. He knew I had sources in the police department and the FBI—he used to see me hanging out with agents in the bars on Rush Street. "Billy," I said, "they're investigating this case. They know about the El Rukns and the money being transferred. You may find yourself with a problem. You should try to get yourself immunity and work something out."

He said, "I never said anything about fixing the case or passing money."

Now I knew why he had come to my office. He was trying to "clean up" and throw cold water on everything he told me in the courthouse. Maybe after I left him, Maloney had mentioned to Billy how much we hated each other. Maybe Billy had seen a lawyer. Before he said another word, I cut him off. "You're talking in a strange way for some reason," I said. "I think we better end the conversation right here, because you're talking into a microphone or something now if you're talking like that."

Here I was, accusing *him* of wearing a wire, but it calmed Billy right down. He almost apologized. "I'm not talking into a microphone," he said. "I appreciate your help." We shook hands and I showed him out of my office.

Nothing was going to come easy for us. I would need a lot of time before I could turn Billy around. The most important thing was not to bug him about it, or he would get suspicious. I had to wait for him to call me again to check out my "sources."

When I first started working with the Feds, I had fantasies about making cases for them one after another, and being done with the whole investigation in a year. But now, winter was rolling around again, and I hadn't done shit.

Then, I got a call from one of the FBI agents on my case. Anton Valukas, the U.S. Attorney for Chicago, was finally ready for a meeting. He asked that I go to the Palmer House, an old hotel in the center of the city's business district. When I got there, I went through the usual routine: I saw Steve Bowen in the lobby, and he followed me into an elevator. We went to a room on an upper floor.

Valukas was waiting for us there, wearing his suit and tie like he was ready for court. He had reddish hair and a pinched, pale face with a stern expression. He never extended his hand. He only said, "I'm Anton Valukas."

I said, "I'm Bob Cooley."

So much for pleasantries. He then said, "You paid off Judge Sodini, didn't you?"

"That's right," I said. I had given the FBI agents Ray Sodini's name along with a list of other judges I had bribed. I used to pay Ray for guns and gambling cases by going to his chambers closet and leaving money in his jacket pocket. He had been indicted the year before as part of Greylord, and his case was coming to trial. Valukas made himself the prosecutor—probably because the case would be a slam-dunk conviction.

"I want to know what you can tell me," Valukas said. "I want to use you as a witness."

"What?" I couldn't believe my ears.

He repeated, "I want to use you as a witness."

If he used me as a witness, my cover would be blown and the whole investigation would be over. I said, "I haven't done anything yet."

"I need you on this case," he said.

"But please don't call me as a witness on this case," I said. I was practically begging him. "If you give me a chance, I can do so much more than Sodini. I can destroy the whole First Ward. I can take down all the Mob people."

But nothing I said seemed to matter to him. "To assure a conviction on this case, I need you as a witness," he said.

He needed me like he needed a third eye. So many lawyers had paid off Ray Sodini, Valukas could have lined them up around the block. He kept me in the room for another half-hour, asking when I had paid Sodini and how much each time. I could feel the steam coming off the top of my head.

As soon as he let me go, I found a phone in the hotel and called Gary Shapiro. "This is bullshit," I told him. "I've given up my law license. Once I'm exposed, I'll have given up my life. All this, to be one more witness against Ray Sodini?"

I was told that Gary had to go to Washington to keep Valukas from putting me on the Sodini witness list. They could still have called me to testify during the trial; but then, in January 1987, Sodini pled guilty. Who knows? If poor old Ray hadn't thrown in the towel, my whole investigation could have come crashing down around him.

Still, over the course of 1987, I wondered what I could ever accomplish with the Feds. They just kept me busy on bullshit assignments that never went anywhere.

At the beginning of the year, it looked like they wanted me to make a gambling case against DiFronzo and some of the crews. I went to a couple of Super Bowl parties with a very cute young woman, who was an FBI agent from the East Coast. We were both wearing wires. Marco and his crew hosted one of the parties at a West Side Italian restaurant.

John DiFronzo was there at one of the tables with the chief of the Elmwood Park Police Department. At one point, they sold "squares" for point combinations in the upcoming game. You paid $1,000 and picked a square. If your square contained the last number of the winning team's score, you could make a lot of money. To determine the numbers that went with each square, they picked cards from a deck. Marco's right-hand man, Donny Scalise, pulled my "girlfriend" over and said, "To make this honest, we'll have her shuffle the cards and cut the deck."

I thought, "Donny, you have no idea how honest she can be."

Later, the agent and I attended a similar party at Faces, run by the Chinatown group. There, too, I bought a square.

We had enough to shut down both places, but the Feds didn't make a case against anyone for the Super Bowl parties. They also refused to let me put a wire again on any of the First Ward heavyweights. Meanwhile, the ropes they wrapped around my practice were starting to rub me raw. I was now careful to report my income to the IRS, but I had to pay my back taxes, too. I was getting chopped down to size an inch at a time.

Even more frustrating, when I knew a case was about to be fixed, the Feds wouldn't let me do anything about it. The first time was a child abuse trial that started just after I came in. The molester was a wealthy car dealer from the South Side who had abused a grandchild. I used to see him eat at Greco's all the time. I notified the Feds, but they told me, "You can't interfere with a live case." Just as I predicted, it went to a bench trial before a bad judge. He threw out the confession and acquitted the bastard.

Late in 1986, Blackie Pesoli approached me to see if I would "handle" another, more notorious child abuse case. This one involved a Chicago high school principal named James Moffat. He was accused of molesting five students (four boys and a girl) at least eight times. I told Blackie this sort of case turned my stomach, and he didn't bug me any more about it. But then I saw that the case ended up with Alderman Ed Burke's wife, Anne, and a high-priced lawyer named Lawrence O'Gara. It was to be decided in a bench trial by Francis Mahon, one of the Circuit Court judges Ed Burke had made. Everyone thought Mahon was straight, and maybe he was, but this time I didn't ask the Feds for permission to intervene. Instead, I called the judge's personal bailiff and disguised my voice. I said, "The Feds know that Eddy Burke is behind fixing this case, so they're paying real close attention." The judge found Moffat guilty and called the evidence "shocking and ugly."

Of course, Anne Burke screamed to high heaven about the verdict, but this was no flimsy case. The state had the school's staff testify about how Moffat kept taking the kids into his private office and then went to their teachers to change their grades. I got some small measure of satisfaction from that outcome, even though there was nothing else I could do with it.

But meanwhile, Mr. and Mrs. Burke were working on another disgusting case—this time with Pat Tuite, another of the First Ward's high-profile criminal defense lawyers, and also their good friend. The Feds would let me use my wire on this one, but once again there was nothing I could to do affect the eventual verdict. The defendant, Herbert Cammon, was a social worker accused of stabbing his wife to death to collect on her life insurance policy. There was all kinds of circumstantial evidence against him: He married the woman after a "whirlwind romance" and she would be killed just a few months later; despite the marriage, he kept his gay lover; he insisted on a $250,000 policy for the wife when the insurance agent advised him that $50,000 was enough; a janitor saw him in their apartment building just before the killing, but he later told police he had been nowhere near; there was even evidence that Cammon called the insurance company to see if the policy was in effect shortly before the wife's murder. When the case went to trial in 1984, the jury deadlocked, voting ten to two for conviction. After that close call, Cammon was evidently willing to pay *anything* to make sure he wasn't convicted in the retrial.

Pompous Pat Tuite liked to think of himself as a great lawyer, but nobody—not even Clarence Darrow—could have saved Cammon in a legitimate retrial. To acquit this character, Tuite needed a bench trial and plenty of help from the judge. He had just one problem— the judge on the case was ornery little Arthur Cieslik. After his experience with the killer cops case, Burke knew he couldn't trust Cieslik to give him the verdict he wanted. Instead, he pushed Cieslik to recuse himself.

But Cieslik dug in his heels. He didn't know why the case should go to another judge. Then, Tuite brought in Anne Burke as his co-counsel. She told a reporter that working with Tuite on this case was her law school "graduation gift." Since Cieslik had "political ties" to Burke's husband, Tuite and Anne Burke filed a motion asking the judge to withdraw.

Still, Cieslik wouldn't let go of the case, and the appeals courts agreed with him. He could sniff out what the defense intended to do, and for the next three years he fought their motions. At one point, he got an angry visit from Alderman Burke. Cieslik told him that there was a lot of evidence that Cammon had killed his wife. According to the judge, Burke then said, "It's only a fucking nigger." (Both Cammon and the wife were black.) I heard Burke use that same line when he talked about the vagrant the cops had killed.

Cieslik said he replied, "She was a human being, Ed. She was a human being."

A few times during 1987, I went to visit Cieslik in his chambers while I was wearing a wire. Although he didn't know it, I got his version on tape and hoped Cammon would be the basis for a case on Burke. I tried to keep the judge strong, but I could see they were wearing him down. He was convinced that Burke and Tuite were orchestrating a campaign against him in the press. An article appeared about him in the *Chicago Tribune*, charging that he used harsh sentences to punish defendants who chose jury trials. Later, he was reprimanded for "disparaging" comments he made to female attorneys. Finally Cieslik had had enough and he let the Cammon case go. If there really was a campaign against Cieslik, it succeeded. During the next election, he was thrown off the bench—with the help of the *Tribune* editorial page. No one could ever call the judge "politically correct," but as I knew too well, he had far more honesty and integrity than most of the judges the paper endorsed.

Once Cieslik let go of the Cammon case, it was assigned to none other than Thomas J. Maloney. Now, I thought, the Feds had all the necessary pieces to follow a classic fix as it developed: first, how Burke maneuvered behind the scenes to get an honest judge off the case, and then how the First Ward machine could rig the so-called random assignment to Maloney. The final piece would come with Maloney's ruling, which was sure to be a not guilty. To pull Burke, Marcy, and Maloney into one indictment would have been a Strike Force trifecta.

In my mind, we already had a good case against Maloney with the El Rukn trial. As I hoped, Billy Swano finally did give me another call, in March 1987 (six months after I threw him out of my office). We met in a diner parking lot near where we lived in Countryside. Billy got into the passenger seat of my car. Since I had seen him last, the El Rukn prosecutors had put on more pressure. For legal help, Swano turned to Ed Genson and his partner, Jeff Steinback. As he sat in my car, Swano told me that Steinback had approached the prosecutor directly and asked if the Feds had Swano on tape. The prosecutor said, "No."

I had to bite my tongue. Obviously, the prosecutor didn't know about *my* tape with Billy. But how could he have answered that question at all? He pissed away all of his leverage. "Billy," I said, "the prosecutor is lying."

They were building a case on him, I said, whether or not they went after Maloney. Again, I told him, he had to make a deal. Billy wasn't ready to go there yet. "I would never roll over," he said. Clearly, he was scared to death of Maloney and the First Ward. Also, if he did prison time, he could meet up with some El Rukn inmates, and that wouldn't be fun either. As far as he was concerned, his only option was flight. "If they give me a lifetime in jail," he said, "I'm gone."

I shrugged my shoulders and wished him luck, but I did everything I could to seem disinterested. It's not like we were close friends, and I didn't want him to think I was pumping for information. He would have to get in touch with me again.

Almost three months went by before he called. He asked if I was going to be in my office for the next few hours. As soon as I got off the phone with him, I called Steve Bowen. He rushed over to bring me the Nagra. By this time, I knew myself how to set up the hidden video camera inside the attaché case. I liked to have both the video and the wire running in case one or the other broke down. I had a feeling that the third time with Swano would be the charm.

He arrived only a few minutes after we had everything set up. I could tell he was under enormous pressure and maybe a little high. The whole time we talked, he kept sitting down and standing up, rubbing his face or twirling his sunglasses. I got the impression he had just come from his lawyers and that they had gotten more calls from the U.S. Attorney.

One more time, Swano wanted to know how my sources got their information. I told him, "Somebody was telling them what was going on, step by step: what happened, how it happened, when it happened, where it happened."

"I wonder who that is," Swano said. "Are they saying that they have somebody tight with Maloney that was talking to me? If I fixed the case, who did I bribe?" Realizing what he said, he backtracked a bit and added, "Just, you know, hypothetically?"

"They have information that you bribed Maloney," I said.

"That's wrong, that's ridiculous," Swano said. "Maloney would have to say, 'Swano gave me money.' Right? Maloney ain't gonna do that. They'd have to have proof that I gave Maloney money."

For some reason, this didn't make sense to him. He said, "I wonder if they had Maloney wired. His phone might have been wired."

Clearly there was something else missing in what I told him—and it gave him hope that my "source" didn't know shit. Then he said, "They'd have to have somebody between Maloney and me."

Suddenly I realized what he was talking about—a bagman. Maloney would have never taken a payoff directly from Swano. There must have been someone else who took the money from Swano and gave it to the judge.

Now Swano got even more specific. He asked, "There was no mention of another lawyer involved?"

I answered, "There is somebody else."

Swano got up from his chair and, without knowing it, stared directly into the attaché case camera. "Well, that would be a liability," he said. "That'd be a real liability right there." He then let loose with a sigh—a sigh like all the air had been let out of his lungs. Billy could see his future, and it wasn't looking too good. You had to feel sorry for the guy.

As far as I was concerned, right there we had all we needed to make a case on Maloney. Once Swano knew I had him on tape, he would have no choice but to cooperate with the Feds and testify about the cases he had fixed with the judge.

After his close call with the El Rukns, you would think that Maloney would have sworn off fixes for a while, but the arrogance of the man knew no bounds. In January 1988, the Cammon murder case came before him in a bench trial. In another of his infamous convoluted rulings, Maloney called Cammon "a schemer, crooked, ignorant and callous," and then acquitted him for murdering his wife. Cammon died soon after, from AIDS. The only justice in this case was to come from the insurance company. After reviewing the evidence in the trials, the examiners refused to pay on the policy. If nothing else, I hoped that Tuite, Maloney, and the Burkes never saw an extra nickel for their fees.

I didn't know if I had enough evidence for the Feds to go after Ed Burke on this case, but Maloney was a different story. One way or the other, I thought, his day would come.

y the start of 1988, I still had not managed to do anything of substance against the First Ward. I kicked myself for putting the wire on Marcy so early without having much of a case. Now I needed to have Pat, Roti, or Johnny D'Arco approach me on something current. Otherwise, I would never get permission to tape them.

For the first few months of the year, I tried to make something happen just by showing up in the right places. It was like trolling. In January I went to Florida and called Johnny D'Arco to let him know I was in town. We had lunch with Larry Oberman, the developer who picked up my bills at Faces to get closer to the First Ward. A few years before, in a truly bizarre incident, he was arrested for a plot to assassinate Mayor Harold Washington (who died from a heart attack in 1987). Although Larry first asked me to represent him on the case, Oberman was eventually steered to another First Ward lawyer. Maloney acquitted him in a bench trial.

After lunch with Oberman, Johnny asked that we get together again when we were both back in Chicago. I made a point to look for him the next time we were both in Counsellors Row, and he told me he did have a case for me to "handle." A chiropractor friend of his had been caught in a billing fraud. But Valukas wouldn't let me follow up with a wire. He told the assistant U.S. attorneys it was too "dangerous." That was such bullshit. I had already worn a wire on John DiFronzo. Was a state senator more dangerous than a Mob boss?

At one point, while I was in Counsellors Row with Johnny, Pat Marcy walked by. He acted a little more friendly than he had been in the past. Still, nothing developed from these chance meetings. I was trying to make a fire by piling up twigs and waiting for lightning to strike.

Meanwhile, Valukas decided to make my personal life that much more miserable. He said I had to stop doing criminal work of any kind. He had cut off my arms when he stopped me from taking on big cases or federal cases, and now he cut off my legs too. This all came about because of a case totally unrelated to me. A witness to a murder had approached me and offered to change his testimony for $200,000. I wasn't the lawyer, but I knew the defendant's father, a state senator. I could have kept the whole thing to myself and no one would have been the wiser. But I did the right thing and informed the Feds. Valukas saw the incident as a reason to go to Richie Daley, then the Cook County State's Attorney, and let him know I was working with the government. Just talking to Daley could have put me at risk, since Marcy had friends and relatives working assistant as state's attorneys (I reported one of them to the FBI). After Daley and Valukas spoke about me, they decided that *any* criminal work was now a "conflict" for me.

I had been making a decent living with the nickel-and-dime misdemeanor work. Once they took that away from me, I needed extra income. Although I built a civil law practice, I brought in another attorney full-time to help. I couldn't pull more money from him. Now when the Feds offered to make up for my lost business, I had to say yes. I took just $1,800 a month—enough to cover basic expenses—but I hated to take *any* government money. Down the road, when we finally got to trial, I could see it coming back to haunt us.

One day, while all of this was going on, Dave Grossman, one of the FBI agents, appeared at my door. He said, "You have to leave town. We have to get you into Witness Protection."

I said, "What are you talking about?"

"We just got information that your life might be in danger," he said. "You've got to go right away. I have some people coming by in a short while to help."

He was trying to save my life, and at the same time he was giving me a death sentence. That's what leaving Chicago meant to me. "I can't leave," I told him. "I haven't done anything. I haven't done what I set out to do. The least you can do is tell me why you think I have a problem."

"Someone came to a grand jury and testified that he did something illegal with you," he said. "The only other person he mentioned was just killed. We think he's giving you up because he knows you're next on the list."

"Let *me* worry about that," I told him. "I'm not going anywhere on that basis. End of conversation."

Whenever threats like this popped up with the Feds, I always laughed them off; but inside, I did know the risk I was taking. Now, I carried two guns with me at all times—the five-shot Airweight and a .45 with nine rounds. If Marcy had even a suspicion I was working with the Feds, he'd have me killed. I had no doubt about that. If I needed an example to keep me on my toes, I could look at our old Thursday night dinner companion, Dominic Senese. In January 1988, he got out of his Lincoln to open the security gate to his Oak Brook subdivision. Two guys walked up to him and one emptied a shotgun into Dom's face. He was 71, but still as big as a horse. After they ran off, he somehow crawled back in his car and managed to drive home. Over the next few days, the papers were full of stories about the failed whack job in Oak Brook. Supposedly Dom had fallen out with the Mob over control of his Teamsters local. Whatever the reason, Dom didn't talk—in fact, his jaws were wired shut—and he never cooperated with the Feds. Instead, he quietly stepped down from office. Of course, none of the reporters mentioned Marcy in their stories, but I knew who was responsible for the hit. Just a few months later, Johnny D'Arco had a fundraiser in the ballroom of a Gold Coast hotel. I saw Dom come in, his face covered with bandages like a mummy. He walked right over to the table where you handed in your donation. When he saw me, he stopped to say hello in a strange, strangled voice. Even through the bandages, I could see that the lower half of his face had been blown away. Then, I watched him shake hands with Johnny. Pat Marcy sat right nearby, but Dominic—who I once thought was Marcy's best friend—kept his back turned to Pat and then left the room.

By the spring of 1988, I realized that my time in Chicago had become very short. I had to make something happen soon. If some other Mojo shot his mouth off to a grand jury, Valukas would just as well be rid of me. I could no longer wait for a phone call, like the one I got from Swano, or a chance meeting at Counsellors Row. Instead, I had to brainstorm with Tom Durkin and Steve Bowen to get the investigation off the dime. If they could concoct some stupid traffic stop for Judge Stillo, why couldn't they come up with something a little more elaborate to catch Marcy and Roti in a sting? If they had restrictions with criminal cases, why couldn't they try civil ones? I suggested they fabricate a lawsuit for the Chancery Division of Cook County Court. That's where disputes were settled over huge amounts of money—even sweeter honey for a sting.

In early April, I put on a wire and met with Marcy at Counsellors Row. We went into the lobby, and I told him some bullshit story about two partners in a tax shelter racket. They now hated each other, and my client was suing to get $350,000 out of the bank account of their busted business. I wanted to make sure the case got in front of Judge Anthony Scotillo. I had bribed him in the past, and I knew Pat kept him on a short leash. When Pat heard about all the money involved, I could see his eyes light up. He told me he'd look into it and I should get back to him in a week. But when we met again, Pat wasn't his arrogant old self. He had spoken to the top judges, and they didn't want to screw with Chancery assignments. Greylord trials were still in the papers. "These guys are scared to death," Marcy said, "and I'm not gonna fuck around with them. I know they're gonna flip if they squeeze their neck a little. I don't need that shit."

Like it or not, we had to enter the lawsuit in the Chancery computer and wait for it to randomly assign the case. "There's no way to get around the machine," Marcy said. "I tried that a year ago."

We decided to take our chances with the computer. It was like throwing dice, but that was always fine with me. For the next few weeks, the Feds put flesh on the bones of our contrived case. My "client" was named Jim Nichols and they called his ex-partner Paul Wilson. In fact, everybody involved, besides me, was really an FBI agent with a pseudonym, including the lawyer for the other side. In July, I filed the complaint for Jim Nichols. The assignment came back a month later and bang, I rolled craps. Instead of a real corrupt judge, like Scotillo, we got David Shields, presiding judge for the entire Chancery Division. Every lawyer who was ever in his court held him in total esteem—including me. I had tried a dozen cases in front of him. He never found my clients guilty, but he never asked to be paid and I never thought of paying him. He was the last judge I considered to be a money guy. In fact, he was supposedly on track to be Chief Judge for the entire Circuit Court of Cook County, one of the largest unified court systems in the world.

But there was nothing I could do about the assignment. I had to tell Marcy. The subject came up while we were having lunch at the First Ward table. As long as we didn't speak about any illegal act, Marcy often brought up topics of previous conversations while we were eating. He asked who we got for my tax shelter case, and I said, "We got Shields."

"I wouldn't go near him with a ten-foot pole," Marcy said—just as I thought.

At that very moment, Patty DeLeo was sitting down for lunch. As usual, he couldn't help but overhear our conversation. A few minutes later, he pulled me aside and asked why I mentioned Shields to Marcy. I told him about my bad luck with the assignment, and that we couldn't work with Shields.

"No," Patty said, "he'll do whatever we want." He rubbed his thumb over his index finger. "All he's worried about is this."

I couldn't believe it. Of course, Patty DeLeo did his fair share of bullshitting, but he seemed totally confident. If he was right, my only regret was dragging Judge Shields into the investigation. But it was too late. Patty was on tape, and like it or not, I was committed to follow through. If he could make this happen, I told Patty, there would be $5,000 in it for him.

Three days later, on the morning of my hearing with Judge Shields, Patty and I walked into a bathroom in the Daley Center, the main office tower and courtroom complex for the Circuit Court. First I checked to make sure no one was sitting in one of the stalls. Then Patty said, "Give me the money, and I'll give it to him."

Into Patty's hands I counted out fresh, government-issued hundred-dollar bills. I said, "One, two, three. . . ." When I wore the wire, I always made a practice of counting out loud. If I got killed before we went to trial, I wanted the tapes to speak for themselves.

Patty was only too happy to play along. During one $2,500 payoff, after I counted out the hundred-dollar bills, he asked, "Was that twenty-five?"

From the bathroom, we went up to the 24th floor, where Patty ducked into Judge Shields's chambers for a moment, and then came out. Judge Shields told Patty he couldn't take the money until he granted the temporary restraining order (TRO) during our hearing. Shields would take a bribe, but he was being honorable about it.

When the Feds got my tapes back, they were ecstatic. The fact that Shields was a presiding judge made this a very big catch for them. I felt horrible that he was involved. He had always been such a fine and decent person. But if he had to suffer, at least it was for a good cause. With a case against Patty DeLeo, I was finally putting a crack into the foundation of the First Ward.

As it turned out, the first Shields payoff was not enough for the prosecutors. They always wanted one more nail in the coffin, and then another. They had tailed DeLeo after the hearing, when he went back into Judge Shields's chambers with the cash, but they were not sure he actually handed it over. To get the judge himself to confirm the payment, they asked me to wear a wire on him. I refused. I had never paid Shields in the past, I said, and for me to ask now would be suspicious. In truth, I didn't want to make things worse for him. Besides, I was hoping against hope that Patty kept all the money for himself.

But the Feds cooked up another excuse to bribe the judge. At the end of the month, at their urging, they had me ask Shields for more hearings. First, I requested to turn the TRO into a preliminary injunction. Then, when my client's ex-partner filed an emergency motion to release some funds, I asked the judge to stall the case, so we could force him to settle. After the second payoff, Patty told me the judge "was like doing somersaults."

Patty DeLeo and I never got along better. But then, during all this action, rumors about me cropped up in First Ward circles. One of my judge friends tipped me off that Pat Tuite, the criminal defense attorney, was telling people, "Cooley can't be trusted" and that they should be careful around me. Tuite had a lot of reasons to give me shit. If nothing else, he knew I had bucked up Judge Cieslik during the Cammon case. But problems for the Mob were happening wherever I went—and for good reason. I had taken undercover FBI agents to the racetracks and pointed out bookies there. That summer, the Feds raided their booking offices and held people for questioning at the tracks, including the Cicero group's top boss, Joe Ferriola. He had just had a heart transplant, and he didn't appreciate the anxiety.

I couldn't take the chance that Patty would hear stories about me from Tuite or someone else. I had to take the offensive. After one payoff to Judge Shields, while we were riding down the elevator, I mentioned what Tuite was saying about me.

Patty acted like it was funny. "Maybe you are a beefer," he said.

"Huh?" I said.

"It's possible," he said. "Better men than you have gone down that drain, haven't they?"

For a moment, I didn't know if he was being funny or calling me out. I replied that this wasn't something for Tuite to be "joking about."

Patty agreed. "You should never say anything like that. That's one of the worst things you can say about someone."

From then on, I never worried that Patty would be suspicious of me. He went along with each twist and turn on the Shields case, so he probably didn't suspect a thing. At the end of September, when we were done with all the proceedings, I gave him $6,000—$5,000 to keep and $1,000 to pass on to the judge for future services.

We never knew if Patty made the final payment to Shields, but the Feds had all they needed for an indictment. In fact, unknown to me, they had planted a bug in Shields's chambers, which helped lock it down that much more. This one case vindicated all the FBI agents and the assistant U.S. attorneys who supported me. More important, it got Valukas to back off and let my investigation run its course.

After more than two and a half years on the wire, I was finally on a roll. With the contrived cases and a little luck, I could do some real damage. In the next twelve months, I helped build four more major indictments and contribute to several others. Two of those cases were textbook examples about how closely the Mob was tied to Chicago's elected officials and court system.

Johnny D'Arco became the glue for a couple of those cases, after I finally figured out how to get a wire on him. I was in Counsellors Row with the Nagra to see Marcy. When Johnny approached me, I simply left the tape running and recorded him as he asked me to fix a case. With this totally unsolicited request, I got permission to wire Johnny directly. But I didn't want to just fix a case with him. I wanted to do something much bigger than that. I wanted Johnny to help me pass a state law.

Despite all his laziness and screwing around, Johnny had become one of the most powerful politicians in Springfield. By this time, he was assistant majority leader in the State Senate and chairman of the Insurance Committee. As far as I was concerned, his influence throughout the state capital was directly related to the First Ward back in Chicago. This meant he had the clout to push a bill through the legislature *and* get the Republican governor to sign it into law. In those days, the governor was Jim Thompson, another former U.S. attorney and a guy with a reputation for being super straight, but Johnny seemed as close to him as any Democrat. I had watched them meet on a couple of occasions at the health club and sit together in the steam room when they had to talk about something confidential.

In the fall of 1988, Johnny would have breakfast with me at a newly opened restaurant near his South Loop townhouse. Believe it or not, the place was decorated in a Capone-era gangster theme with tommy guns on the wall. Whenever we ate together, Johnny was always critical of my diet. In the morning, I liked eggs and ham, which I would wash down with a Coke. He would be picking at granola or fruit and telling me about his cholesterol count. He looked too fucking skinny, if you asked me. He had recently divorced, and when we met at this tommy gun place, he left his new girlfriend at home to watch his kids. Sometimes he would use our breakfasts as an alibi, and then cut out early to see another girlfriend. Even in his mid-forties, Johnny was up to his old tricks.

On Monday morning, October 31, I wore my wire to breakfast with Johnny. After a little chitchat, I told him I had a big client from the East Coast looking to pass some insurance law. About ten years before, when we were in Vegas with another state senator, Johnny said he would pass legislation in return for a fifty-fifty split of lobbying fees. When I asked if I could take him up on that offer, he said he would be my "co-counsel." He told me that insurance companies paid lobbyists $50,000 to get bills passed. I said I could probably get that and promised him $5,000 up front. Johnny suggested a "tax dodge" he had used in the past. We would sign up a licensed lobbyist as our front man, and pay him a nominal fee. In return, he would report to the IRS that we paid him the entire $50,000. That way we wouldn't have to pay taxes on our cut. He gave me the names of lobbyists who could "keep their mouths shut," including Arthur "Ron" Swanson. (In 2003, the Feds indicted Swanson for various kickback schemes involving the administration and friends of Governor George Ryan, who was later indicted as well.)

Just a few weeks after our breakfast, on December 23, I was counting out fifty hundred-dollar bills to Johnny as he sat in the passenger seat of my car outside Counsellors Row. I didn't even know what law I was bribing him to pass. The Feds were debating that question. They didn't want him to ram through legislation that could actually affect the state's insurance industry. Eventually, they came up with something silly: a law to permit one specific travel agency to sell trip-related insurance. Why would anyone have paid $50,000 for that? Fortunately, Johnny was never one for details. He just complimented me on my car and shoved the money in his pocket. Before he left, he wished me Merry Christmas.

While I was building a case on Johnny, I was putting something together on Marco D'Amico, too. For obvious reasons, I did not want to leave him out of the picture, but I was forbidden from walking into his Survivor's Club with a wire. Now the Feds told me I was too valuable to take that risk—or some such bullshit like that. But I didn't give up hope. Almost every night, I went to the Maywood Park Racetrack and hoped to see Marco or his people there. One night, in March 1989, while I was watching the races, I saw Tony Doty. He had become Marco's top guy. He said, "Hey, Bobby, how you been?"

I said, "Okay."

He said, "Gee, how come you're not playing with us any more?"

Of course, the Feds didn't allow me to make sports bets any more, so I told him, "I don't have to gamble any more. I've got my own book."

He said, "You do?"

I said, "Yeah. I've got a bunch of guys from the commodities exchange and some lawyers. I'm picking up around $10,000 a week doing that."

The next day, I called Steve Bowen and told him to get the paperwork ready for a wire on Marco.

Steve got upset. He said, "We told you, you can't do anything against Marco."

I said, "But I have a feeling either he or his people are going to call me first."

That's exactly what happened. Only a few hours later, Tony Doty called and said Marco was looking for me. I put on the wire and went to see Marco in his club. He took me outside and we walked around the block. I acted like a dummy; like I didn't know I really had to pay street tax for my little book. Marco was only too happy to spell out exactly what he wanted and why. He said, "Bob, even I can't protect you. You gotta pay tax if you got a book. No matter how small it is. You know the rules. If you don't pay, something is going to happen and I can't help you."

A few days later, I returned with my first weekly payment of $2,000. Marco took me to the back of the club. While I was counting out the money, I had an idea.

I said, "Marc, I need to borrow $50,000. Can you get me some money?"

At first, he balked—like he was afraid I'd gamble it away.

Then I said, "I need it for Johnny D'Arco. He's going to pass a law for us in the State Senate, and he has to grease the palms of all those senators."

I could see the wheels turn in his head. He nodded and said he would think about it. I thought, "What could say more about Chicago politics than this? You take juice money from the Mob so you can bribe a state senator to pass a law."

But the street tax and the juice loan were just the beginning of the case I built on Marco. One day, when I was in the club counting out cash, Marco asked, "How come you're not betting with us any more?"

I said, "Remember, Marc. I have my own operation."

He said, "Why don't you move some money our way? You must be overloaded on some games."

I needed some bullshit answer to distract him. If I really did have a book, I *would* want to move money. "Maybe I could," I said. "But I'm involved in a big card game."

"Where's the game?" Marco asked.

Again, I had to say something. "It's over at the Water Tower apartments."

"How much money is in the game?"

I said, "Oh, you got to bring $10,000 to sit down. I make real good money at it."

He said, "We can hit the game and you'd get twenty-five percent."

"No, Marc," I said. "It's too dangerous."

He said, "What do you mean?"

I said, "It's at the Water Tower. That's a fancy building. They got all kinds of security."

He said, "No. We hit a game there before. My guys come in with shotguns. What are they gonna do? Nobody's gonna balk. Do any of your guys have weapons?"

I still put him off. "Let me think about it, Marc."

In fact, this idea was my dream come true: a phony card game as a sting, with FBI agents as the players, so we could catch Marco's crew in the act of armed robbery. Still, I had to be careful about entrapment. I never wanted the tapes to show that I was eager for something illegal to happen or that I was encouraging it. Instead, I wanted to show that I tried to talk him out of it first.

For the next few months, Marco and I continued to talk about the card game. In my bones I could sense that my investigation would be drawing to a close before the end of 1989. If I played my cards right, Marco's raid on the card game could be my grand finale.

While things were picking up with Marco, I got another break to get me back inside the First Ward. This one came from my younger brother—a totally straight lawyer who knew nothing about my work with the Feds. He had clients who owned property in a gentrifying First Ward neighborhood, and they wanted to change the zoning from manufacturing to commercial. Like everyone else in Chicago, my brother's firm took the request to the alderman, in this case Fred Roti. As soon as he heard the name Cooley, Freddy asked my brother's partner if the "Cooley" in the firm was related to me. He then said I should call to follow up with him on the matter.

This mystified my brother, because he knew I didn't do much real estate work. But when he asked for my help, I immediately understood where Roti was coming from. Old Freddy knew the zoning change would make the property valuable, and he wanted a bribe in return. Coincidentally, that very week, the Feds wanted me to meet some FBI agents who had investigated Roti for three years. They still hadn't gotten to first base on him. Now they wanted to buy a trucking company for $200,000 and then bribe Roti to put up No Parking signs by the entrance. I said to the agents, "I can save you guys a whole bunch of money."

I arranged with Freddy to have our zoning chat during his morning hours at Counsellors Row on June 5. By the time I got to the First Ward table, around eleven o'clock, he had already been holding court for a few hours. I sat down across from him. Like this was all new to me, I pulled out a pen and a little notebook from my pocket. I said, "Freddy, tell me what the procedure is now."

Freddy grabbed my pen and pulled my notebook over to his side of the table. He then wrote the numbers "75" on a corner of the page and underlined it. Then he slid it back at me.

"Hmmm. Okay," I said.

"You know what I'm talking about?" Freddy asked.

"Yeah," I said. "Little ones, not big ones."

Freddy got a kick out of that. "Nooooo," he laughed.

"Okay."

Then he just came out and said, "Seventy-five hundred."

"Hmm?" I said. I wanted to make sure I got that on the tape.

"Seventy-five hundred," he said, even louder.

I motioned Freddy to follow me into a quiet corner of the restaurant. We sat down at an empty table. He had his back to the door.

I pulled out some money and said, "Let me give you five hundred now so you got some lunch money in your pocket."

As I was counting out the bills, who should walk into the restaurant but Uncle Pat. He saw the two of us sitting there, away from the First Ward table, and immediately knew something was up.

He marched over and barked, "What's going on?"

Fred went bolt upright, like he had just gotten a jolt of electricity, and shoved the money into his pocket. "Oh, Pat," he said. "See, you weren't here, so I figured I'd start it."

As soon as Pat found out we were talking about zoning, he sat down and jumped right in. He said, "Tell me who the fucking owners are."

I mentioned the name, but he didn't recognize it. He wanted to know if it was a big project. I told him it wasn't, but he waved me off. He said he'd find out more about it on his own, and let Freddy know what they should pay us.

Three days later, I went back to Counsellors Row, to give them the first installment on the bribe. Marcy saw me enter the restaurant and then led me to the back. When I asked if Roti's figures were right, he said, "The figures are okay."

"Let me give you thirty-five hundred more now," I said. Again I counted the bills out, but Marcy then recounted to make sure.

A week later, I made my final payment on the zoning bribe to Freddy. Again, we went to an empty table in the back of Counsellors Row. "Let me give you the rest of this," I said. "Did you talk to Pat?"

"Yeah," Roti said.

"Okay," I said, "Because I gave Pat thirty-five. Here, check it. Those are fifties. There should be fifteen."

After I was done counting it, I said, "Here's two thousand more. That should be the whole thing then." A few months later, when my brother and I had to make a presentation to the city council, Roti didn't even bother to show up for the meeting. He had his lackey, Alderman Bernie Stone, get up and say that Freddy thought it was "a good project."

From beginning to end, the zoning bribe was the most rock-solid case I built against anyone. There was absolutely no doubt what Marcy and Roti wanted or what I paid them. The Feds were very happy. Still, for me, it was all just icing on the cake. Zoning kickbacks were a dime a dozen in Chicago. The First Ward's control of the courts was something entirely different. That's what I really wanted to expose.

Ever since we finished the Nichols case with Judge Shields, I had been after Tom Durkin and the agents to cook up another civil suit for Marcy to fix. But this time it had to be assigned to Judge Scotillo. As far as I was concerned, he was the most corrupt judge, and practically Marcy's precinct captain inside the Circuit Court. When Pat put up candidates for associate judge, Scotillo lined up the votes from the other judges.

To get the case to Scotillo, the FBI agents just kept entering it in the computer—over and over again. We called it *Eldridge v. Carr* and used another bullshit story about battling partners. This time, my "client," Alan Carr, was the defendant and quite a little weasel (played once again by an FBI agent). Eldridge (another agent) caught him stealing $210,000 from their business. If these Chancery Court judges had ever talked to each other, they would have wondered why this one stupid case was on so many dockets. It took about twenty tries, and several months, but it finally popped up for Scotillo at the end of June.

In some ways, the delay worked out for the best. Only the week before, I made my last payment on the zoning bribe and was back in the good graces of Marcy and Roti. I dropped by Counsellors Row to let Pat know about the Chancery case. We went into the building lobby to talk, but it was full of people. Pat didn't like the looks of it. Maybe he was starting to feel nervous about things. When I made my last payment to Roti, Patty DeLeo took me aside to say that the FBI had questioned Judge Shields about my previous Chancery case. This was news to me, but Patty wasn't concerned in the least. "They got nothing on him," he said.

Marcy might have thought differently. He pushed through the revolving doors and led me out to the street. We talked just a few moments. I let him know I had a new case to handle with Judge Scotillo and that something would be happening any day now. He nodded, happy to hear it, and we then walked the few steps to the front doors of the restaurant. I held my arm out for him to go first, but for some reason Pat decided to be the gentleman that day. He stepped back and pushed me ahead of him. With the warm weather, I was wearing the Nagra body recorder in a harness over the small of my back. Pat put his hand right on the unit. The moment I felt him touch me there, a complete shock went through my system. I kept walking into the restaurant. I had no idea if he felt anything or had a surprised look on his face, and I couldn't turn around to see if he did.

Normally, I would have left Pat and gone about my business, but now I couldn't walk away or show any concern about what happened. I followed Pat back to the First Ward table and watched him take his seat. All of the other chairs were taken, mostly with Mob-connected union people. I stood there for a few minutes and then arched my back. To no one in particular I announced, "Wow. I strained my back and now it's killing me." Then I said good-bye and walked away.

The next day, I made a point to go back to Counsellors Row—but without the wire. I bought a back brace and walked around stiffly, hoping someone would notice, so I could make another explanation. But no one said anything, and I just sat around bullshitting.

Once again I debated with the agents about leaving town. But after a week of hanging around at Counsellors Row, I saw no change in Marcy's attitude towards me. We agreed I should go forward with the *Eldridge v. Carr* case.

By now, the tension became second nature for me. Even if I was scared as hell, I got it out of my head by thinking, "This is something I have to do." I was mentally prepared to die. At one point, I thought about getting cyanide capsules. I did not want to be taken alive and put on a meat hook. I could deal with the idea of poison, or a sudden blast from shotgun or .22. If it was time to pay the price, so be it.

For the first time in two weeks, I put on the wire and went back to see Marcy. I told him that my Chancery case had now heated up. Eldridge had discovered the bank account where my client, Carr, had hidden $210,000. That morning, Eldridge's attorney (actually an agent) had filed an emergency motion with Judge Scotillo to stop Carr from withdrawing the money. I opened up a folder and showed Marcy the motion. If Scotillo could stall for two days, I told him, my client could get back to town and withdraw the money.

Marcy went to his phone by the First Ward table and called Roti to join us. A few minutes later, Freddy came running over. As we stood in the lobby, Marcy opened the folder and showed the papers to Roti. I tried to fill him in on the background, but Marcy cut me off. "Just tell him what you want," he barked.

They knew that Judge Scotillo's court was in session and only someone important could interrupt him while he was on the bench.

I said, "I want the judge to stall tomorrow when the other lawyer comes in."

"Hold it, hold it," Freddy piped up—like a kid raising his hand in school. "Why don't I go see. . . ."

"Call our friend Buck," Marcy said, finishing the thought for him. They meant Pasquale "Buck" Sorrentino, presiding judge of the entire Cook County Circuit Court's Law Division. "All right," Marcy told him. "Go see Buck."

Freddy grabbed the folder from me and waddled off to the Daley Center. In the span of just a few minutes, I had seen Marcy, the Octopus, in all his glory—first reaching to pluck the seniormost Alderman from City Hall, and then using the chief judge as his errand boy to fix a Chancery Court case.

I hung around Counsellors Row for a while and waited for Freddy to come back. After my scare from the previous week, I was still a little antsy. I walked over and said hello to George, one of the brothers who owned the restaurant. I chatted with some lawyers having breakfast. At one point, I glanced at the First Ward table. Pat had caught the eye of someone who had just entered the restaurant. But instead of Roti, it was Rocky Infelice, probably the most feared crew leader in the Cicero group. He was big and bear-like with a bald head and deep, close-set eyes. He went straight downstairs where they had a bathroom and a party hall that was usually closed. Marcy hurried after him.

Rocky was not a guy with a sense of humor. I never tried to pal around with him. I knew the Mob bosses reserved him for their most vicious and important hits. The Feds believed he had organized Tony Spilotro's baseball-bat execution—if he hadn't in fact done the deed himself. He was later convicted for the torture murder of the independent bookie, Hal Smith.

I went back to my schmoozing. When I looked again at the First Ward table, Marcy was standing there next to Roti. Freddy had a big grin on his face. Evidently the mission was accomplished. They motioned for me to go out in the lobby with them.

According to Freddy, he pulled the chief judge off the bench while he was working on another First Ward case (FBI agents shadowed Roti every step of the way and then followed the judge). After Buck got his instructions from Roti, he went directly to Scotillo's courtroom. Roti said, "He walked over there in person and he gave him a piece of paper."

It seemed we should all be happy. But Marcy looked pissed off. He then motioned for me to follow him outside again. I chased after him down the sidewalk toward the old city parking garage in the middle of the block. In all the years of our secret meetings and payoffs, he had never taken me there before. I suddenly realized I had not seen Rocky Infelice leave the restaurant, and I looked over my shoulder. Were they on to me?

Pat walked through the entrance of the garage and up some steps. I stayed just behind him. He pushed open a rusty metal door. There was a dark, stinky bathroom inside. In the moment before I followed him, I thought, "That bastard Rocky is waiting in there. They're going to grab me and check me for a wire." All this time, Pat had not said one word to me. I walked in after him and the door shut behind me. Pat just opened his fly, stepped over to the urinal, and took a piss. I had already reached for one of my guns. After he zipped up his fly, he turned around and said, "We're gonna have to take care of Scotillo *and* Buck now."

But we still didn't know what Scotillo would do. "Is he going to help us for sure?" I asked.

"Positively," Marcy shot back. The next day we had our emergency hearing with Scotillo. The judge played his role to the hilt, barking at me like I was the biggest idiot in the world. But he refused to grant a temporary restraining order to the plaintiff—just as Roti ordered—and continued the case.

On Thursday, I was supposed to meet Roti to discuss what to pay everyone, but this time I walked into Counsellors Row without a wire. I was still spooked by my walk to the garage with Marcy. If he had been testing me, I did not want to push my luck for a second day.

Roti led me to a table in the back of the restaurant. First he wanted to know my fee for the Chancery case. I told him it was $25,000 and asked what the judges would want. He grabbed a napkin and wrote "2500," and then circled it. When I asked what he and Marcy wanted, he put "7500" under the other number. Then, he added them up to "10,000" and underlined the total. "That's what we need," he said.

I told him I had just $2,500 on me. I counted it out and handed it to him under the table. I crumpled the napkin with his numbers like I was going to throw it out. When he turned away, I shoved it in my pocket. That would have to do for evidence on this payoff.

I made the next payment on Friday, a week later. By this time, I felt better about wearing the wire, so I caught Roti on tape asking me, "You got an envelope?"

I said, "Yeah. I'm gonna give ya thirty-five hundred more today. I don't want to take too much out of the bank at one time."

I arranged to make the final payment to him or Pat on Monday, July 10. I was hoping I'd wire Marcy for at least one payment. As usual, Steve Bowen met me at my apartment that morning to bring the Nagra and paperwork. While I was driving downtown, I called Counsellors Row from my car to see if Pat was in. George, the owner, answered. I asked for Marcy, and the next thing I knew, Roti was on the phone. I said, "I'm just checking to make sure somebody's there for me."

He said, "Pat's here, but I'll meet you outside."

As soon as he said that, I knew something was wrong. I parked my car in the alley next to the restaurant and called Steve. I said, "Steve, something is wrong."

He said, "What do you mean?"

I said, "Because Roti got on the phone and he wants to meet me outside. Something must be going on."

I hung up the phone and got out of the car, and there was Steve standing right behind me. For the first time in a long time, he had followed me into town. He said, "Are you going to make the payment?"

I said, "I guess so, but something must be wrong."

As we stood there in the alley, Mike, the beat policeman, who happened to be nearby, walked up to us. "Guess what?" he said to me. "They found a bug in the restaurant."

I couldn't believe it, but from the look on Steve's face, I saw this wasn't news to him. It was why he followed me.

At that moment, I heard someone call, "Bob."

It was Roti. He spotted me from the sidewalk and motioned for me to come right over. Fortunately, Steve was wearing a suit that day, so he looked like just another lawyer. I said to Mike and Steve, "I've gotta go."

I hustled over to Freddy, who had a frown on his face. He made a little circular motion with his hand—as if to say we couldn't talk around there. "They found something in the booth right by our table," he said. "Come on. Let's go across the street."

As I followed him, I was still trying to digest the news. Why did the Feds need a bug when I was getting all we needed with the wire? This could blow my last payoff.

Roti led me through the side door of City Hall. "I know you're careful," he said.

"You gotta be," I said.

We took the elevator to his office on the second floor. It was a set of massive rooms with pillars and high ceilings. I'm sure most mayors didn't have anything as big. Usually his secretary was in the reception area, but today she was gone. I followed him into his inner office. As soon as I went through the door, he turned around and locked it.

My first thought was, "This is a fucking setup and I got a wire on." I expected to see some muscleheads come from behind the corner. I reached for my gun, ready for a battle. But Roti walked over to each of his two windows and lowered the blinds. Then he turned and said, "What have you got? Four?"

He was talking about my last payment of $4,000. Now I was at ease. "Yeah," I said. "Four. That's the end of it."

He took the money from me and started counting it.

"Well, there are no other problems, are there?" I asked.

Fred shook his head.

Later, I heard how a busboy had found the bug the previous Friday. It was actually a tiny camera, mounted in the booth across from the First Ward table. At first, the owners didn't know what to make of it. They waited through the weekend, and finally decided to call the FBI on Monday morning.

For me, the camera was total overkill, and it certainly put my investigation—if not my life—in jeopardy. I had clearly told the Feds that Pat Marcy never talked dirty at the First Ward table. Worse yet, nobody told me about it beforehand—or even after it was found. The FBI agents knew I was walking into Counsellors Row with a wire to make my payoff exactly when everybody would be most paranoid about surveillance.

For the next few days, the papers were full of stories about "the bug in the soup" at the First Ward table. They even had a diagram in the paper that showed the view from the hidden camera and the placement of various microphones.

But after the smoke cleared, it was pretty much business as usual. Marcy found some expert to sweep the restaurant and all of his offices to make sure there were no other bugs. The next time I sat down with Roti at the restaurant, I asked if he was worried about anything that the camera picked up. He shook his head. He rubbed his thumb over his index finger to indicate cash and said, "It never changes hands here." In fact, I had paid off Fred in the restaurant several times—although not at the First Ward table. It seemed so obvious to me: At the very time I return to Counsellors Row to start fixing cases again, a bug shows up. But fortunately nobody put two and two together.

Although we had good evidence against Roti and Marcy for the Chancery fix, the Feds were still not satisfied. Once again, they were concerned about their case against the judge. They wanted me to wear a wire on him, so we could hear Scotillo confirm that he had gotten paid. But I knew this judge pretty well. He was very, very sly, which is why he survived Greylord without a nick. You couldn't meet him for lunch or give him a call and expect a straight answer from him. To try to put the judge at ease, I had another idea. I knew where he lived on the Gold Coast and how he walked to work. One August morning, I "accidentally" bumped into him on the street.

"Oh, hey, hi, Judge," I said.

He was a big distinguished-looking guy with a full head of black hair. He had gotten a little soft around the middle, but he always wore an immaculately tailored suit. "Oh, hi, Bob," he said. I asked him if he had time for coffee, but he said he was in a rush. I said good-bye, but then turned back and said, "Judge, wait a minute. Let me talk to you a second."

I told him that the *Eldridge v. Carr* case worked out great for me, and he confirmed that the chief judge "delivered a message" in time to help. But when I asked if Buck took care of him, he said, "Just between you and I, no. He just took a pass on me. He didn't do anything."

"Oh, no," I said. "That's terrible." I told him how I had given $10,000 to Roti and Marcy, and that $3,000 was meant for him and the chief judge.

"You know how they are," Scotillo said.

I thought, "You bet I do."

I could see the judge's sixth sense kick in, and he started to pull away. As we said good-bye, I laughed about him getting angry with me during the hearing.

"Oh," he said. "That was just an act."

I left there thinking we had all we needed to indict Scotillo. He clearly indicated that he knew the case was fixed and he helped it go our way. But the Feds still felt we didn't have enough evidence because the judge got no money. We had to come up with a new excuse to bribe him, which meant another episode in the story of the dueling partners, Eldridge and Carr. To add some spice to the situation, we brought in a new character, my client's girlfriend (another of those cute FBI agents). According to this twist in the plot, she still had access to the account and Eldridge was suing to block it.

This time, to play the role of bagman, I turned to our distinguished state senator, Johnny D'Arco. I knew Scotillo was tight with Johnny and would feel more comfortable taking money from him. I had been seeing Johnny throughout the summer, and despite all the uproar over the camera at Counsellors Row, he wasn't worried one bit. On one of my wires, he laughed that the only thing the bug would pick up at the First Ward table was some political gossip and "dirty jokes." In September, I gave him $2,500 more for my bogus law. He promised that when the legislature had its spring session, "I'll slip something in and nobody will know the difference." I thanked him again and mentioned how much it cost me to get the zoning change from Roti. Johnny said, "You shoulda came to me. I would have done it for ya a lot cheaper."

He was only too happy to help bribe Scotillo—for a piece of the action. Once again, I wanted the judge to stall a temporary restraining order—this time against the client's girlfriend. I told Johnny how Marcy or Roti stiffed the judge the last time I tried to pay him off.

At first he laughed, "Roti would stiff his own mother." But Johnny understood what had happened. "They feel they made him," he explained. Still, if he was going to help me make a payoff to Scotillo, he said, I shouldn't tell Roti or Marcy about it.

Johnny then had me drive him directly to the judge's apartment, so we could talk about it with him in person—which would have been a wet dream for the Feds—but the judge wasn't home. Johnny had to handle it without me. In October, I handed him $2,500 while he was eating his Cream of Wheat at a downtown hotel. I told him to give the judge $1,000 and keep the rest for himself.

To confirm that Scotillo got the money, I prepared another "accidental" meeting with the judge two weeks later. I went to the restaurant where I knew he had lunch, and I made sure to bring two very attractive young ladies with me. Scotillo walked in, along with the chief judge, Buck Sorrentino. As soon as they got a load of my guests, they came running over to say hello. In between the chitchat, I slipped in a question to the judge: "Now, Johnny took care of you this time, right?"

He replied, "Yeah. He did." With that reply, I thought, we had a solid case against Scotillo and a new case against Johnny.

My investigation had not gotten serious until the spring of 1988, but by the end of October 1989, I knew we had all the evidence we needed to bring down the Octopus, Pat Marcy, and the rest of the First Ward—Fred Roti, Patty DeLeo, and Johnny D'Arco. In the process, we also pinched the Circuit Court's most powerful judges, including David Shields, Anthony Scotillo, and, worst of all, Tom Maloney. I even thought we had enough to make a case against Chief Judge Sorrentino and possibly Ed Burke. If nothing else, I figured, Illinois' court system would have to be overhauled from top to bottom when all this came out.

For reasons that weren't made clear to me yet, the Feds let me know that there was only a few weeks left before I had to leave town. But at this stage, even if we did have the First Ward locked up, I still had some unfinished business: I wanted one more stab at making a case on Harry Aleman, and I had a few scores left to settle with Marco D'Amico.

CHAPTER 12

PARTING SHOTS FOR HARRY AND MARCO

O f all the bad things I had ever done, the one I most wanted to undo was fixing the murder case against Harry Aleman. The whole idea of putting him on trial again for the Logan murder was like an impossible dream throughout the investigation. When I first started talking about it with the agents and prosecutors, everybody laughed at me. They said, "What? Are you nuts? He was found not guilty. That's double jeopardy." The Fifth Amendment says you can't be tried twice for the same offense. On the other hand, a defendant can't tamper with the jury either, and as far as I was concerned, that's exactly what Harry did when he had Marcy get me to bribe Judge Wilson.

I said to the Feds, "We can go on the basis that there was no jeopardy because Harry knew ahead of time that the case was fixed."

But there was no way to connect me with Harry Aleman—there was no proof he even knew me—and there was no evidence to connect me with his case. My first ploy was to get help from Judge Wilson. Earlier in 1989, the Feds let me visit Frank where he retired, in Scottsdale, Arizona. They still had no hope of building a case against Aleman. At best, they told me, we could add a few counts to Marcy's federal racketeering charges for fixing another trial.

To be honest, I had one more reason to go. I wanted the Feds to give me a nice warm-weather vacation. To make the experience complete, I hooked up with Cathy Fleming, an old girlfriend, who had moved to Lake Tahoe and was working as a cocktail waitress. She had been with me when we met with the judge and his wife before the Aleman case. I remembered that the judge's wife liked her, and I thought she could help put them at ease. The FBI had no problem with my bringing Cathy along. They figured she made it look like a vacation for me. To play it up to the hilt, they put us in a luxurious resort. For a few days, it was like old times.

After we settled in to our room, the agents gave me Frank's home number. He answered the phone and I told him I was in town on vacation. I invited him to bring the wife and have dinner with us, since the hotel had such a fabulous restaurant.

When the judge met me at the bar, he looked like his gruff old self, only his limp had gotten worse. I said it must have been six years since we last met. "No," he said. "It's been nine years. I've been here dying for nine years."

Cathy didn't have the effect on him that I expected. At the sight of her, he seemed to stiffen, and then he practically clammed up for the evening. Our plan was for Cathy to go to the ladies' room during dinner, and we figured the judge's wife would follow. But Mrs. Wilson stayed rooted in her chair the whole time we were there. Meanwhile, as we ate, I could see the judge sip wine, but not the hard liquor he used to drink. He seemed on guard.

My only chance to speak one-on-one with Frank came after dinner while we were walking to his car. Cathy stayed back chatting with Mrs. Wilson, so the judge and I could put some distance between them. I told him that subpoenas were going out to people involved in the Aleman murder trial. If I was called, I said, "I'm gonna testify. I'm not gonna take the rap on this. The only way I can get in trouble is by perjuring myself." It was my way of telling him to cooperate. I truly didn't want him hurt even worse by this case. "What are you gonna do?" I asked.

"Don't worry about me," he said. Even with his horrible limp, he was walking faster and faster, trying to stay away from me. I was practically jogging to keep up with him.

"I'm sure they know the whole story," I told him, "but they can't do anything to us. See, the five years is long gone. This statute [of limitations] is long gone."

But whatever I said, he replied, "I don't know anything about anything."

Then he got in his car and, with the window down, started backing out and pulling away—even though his wife and Cathy were still far behind us.

Only later, when I was alone with Cathy, did I discover why the judge was so upset to see her. She was with me at the bar when I gave the judge the final payment for the Aleman fix. After I went to pick up the tab, he said to her, "Stay away from that Cooley. He's a bad man."

In 1989, he had to wonder why she was still with me after what he said, or why she had come with me to see him. It must have smelled like a setup. But Cathy's memory alone made the trip to Scottsdale worthwhile for the Feds. Later she could testify about my connection to the judge, and that he did something with me that Frank considered "bad."

But we still had to prove that Harry knew about the fix. When I found out that Harry was hanging around Maywood Park Racetrack during the day, I wanted to approach him there with a wire and get him to implicate himself. Some agents tried to talk me out of fooling around with Harry. This monster was certifiably dangerous. But by October, I wasn't so concerned about the risks. The whole investigation had been a death wish. How could I deny myself one more score, so close to the end?

That morning Steve met me at my apartment with the Nagra. He and Jim Wagner wanted to follow me around the racetrack, but I told them to stay away. Harry was sure to have people looking out for him. I figured he'd stay out of public areas, so I went to an upper level of the clubhouse, where they had private boxes. I walked past the party room. Most of the lights were off, but I could make out someone sitting alone in the corner. It was Harry. I wandered into the room, like I was lost and looking for the sky, and then I bumped into his table.

"Hey, Harry," I said.

He looked up and gave me his evil eye. Maybe thinking I was a cop, he said, "Who the fuck are you?"

"Harry," I said. "Don't you recognize your old pal? I'm Bob Cooley."

A light came on in his eyes. "Hey, Bob. Yeah. How ya doing?"

I took a deep breath and sat down with him. I said, "Harry, you're looking great." It was true. His hair was gray, but the weightlifting he had done in prison left him pretty fit for a guy pushing fifty. "Doing the time did you some good."

Harry didn't think that was so funny. He gave me his stare again. "I ain't never going back in," he said.

"Not if I have something to say about it," I thought.

Out of the corner of my eye, I could see Harry's brother-in-law, Richie Kimball, walk in. He was the guy I once represented for kicking an FBI agent in the face at a nightclub. I hadn't seen Richie in fifteen years. He squinted as though he didn't recognize me and left the room.

I had to be quick before someone else barged in on us. I said, "Listen, Harry, let me talk to you for a second." And I walked him back to the far end of the room, where they had a bar and some stools. I sat down at one and he sat down next to me.

He seemed to be looking at me kind of funny. Maybe he could tell I was nervous. I said, "Some lawyer said you were pissed at me about something."

He said, "What are you talking about?"

While he was in prison, Harry asked me to give a job to his kid, who was a law student. The cocky little shit used to show up drunk or high, so I had to fire him. I said, "I thought maybe because of your son."

"No, Bobby," he said. "That ain't the case. If I was mad at you. I would tell you."

I thought, "Sure, Harry. You would tell me with a .22 in the back of the head." I said, "That's good to know. I wouldn't want to be on your wrong side."

He said, "Oh, Bobby, no. You're a great guy."

Then I took a deep breath. "You know who I just bumped into?" I asked.

Harry leaned closer to me.

"The judge," I said.

Harry pulled away. "What do you mean, 'the judge'?"

"The judge on your case," I said. "Frank Wilson."

As soon as he heard the name, Harry jumped off the stool. "I don't want to talk about it," he hissed. "Don't ever mention that name again. Don't ever say nothing again."

"Motherfucker," I thought. I once instructed this guy to never discuss anything illegal from his past. What could be more illegal than fixing your own murder trial? "If someone brings it up," I used to tell him, "assume you're talking into a wire."

Richie and two buddies came back into the room. Harry sat down at a table by the wall, but he never took his eyes off me. With his arms folded, he gave me an absolutely evil stare.

I couldn't leave now and get Harry even more suspicious. Instead, I walked over to Richie and started to shoot the breeze. All the time we talked, I could feel Harry staring at me. I had my two guns, but I had the wire, too, and I felt like it was burning a hole right through my leg.

To explain why I was hanging around, I told Richie I had a horse in the next race. When I went to make the bet, I looked back and saw Richie hiding behind a pillar to watch me. Now I had to blow a few hundred bucks to show I was serious. I went out to the track to watch the race. After it was over, I wandered back into the party room with Harry one more time. I wasn't going to run and hide. I wanted to show I had no reason to be afraid. I stuck around until no one seemed to notice me, and then I left.

Even though I didn't get much out of Harry, I got enough to make the wire valuable. First of all, it showed, beyond a doubt, that he knew me. Also, the way he acted when I mentioned Judge Wilson's name showed that he was hiding something. I still had no illusions about how difficult it would be to retry him. But at least I had done all I could. To take him to trial for the murder, I would need to convince state's attorneys instead of federal prosecutors, and that couldn't happen until I left town.

As I kept building cases against Marco, I pushed my death wish up another notch. If I was going to go out with a bang, it would come with his raid on my card game. But I wanted to make sure I was there when it happened. It would have to be the very last act of my investigation, and then I could leave town.

In November, with everything else winding down, the Feds realized they should let me start betting again. I was in Marco's club each week to pay my street tax. I might as well do double duty and help them make a few last gambling cases against some bookies. The day they gave me the go-ahead, I zipped over to the club to bet. When I walked in, there was Ricky Borelli, the fat slob, lying all over the couch. Marco had let him have his own book again. I thought, "This is payback. This is double payback." Either I would beat him for serious money or, if I lost, I would never have to pay him. But when I put my mind to it, there was no way I could lose to Ricky. In a matter of two weeks, I won $40,000 and managed to collect half. I started betting with two other West Side offices: one run by Marco's right-hand man, Tony Doty, and the other by his brother-in-law Bobby Abbinante. Marco had just sold the beef stand Bobby used to run for him, and Bobby was desperate to make some extra money.

With the okay to gamble, I had another excuse to hang around Marco's club. Whenever Marco saw me, he wanted to go outside and walk around the block. He had moved his club out of the West Side storefront and into a nicer building in a residential neighborhood of Elmwood Park. We would stroll around a little park across the street or walk in the nearby schoolyard. Just like I thought, he couldn't get the robbery caper off his mind. He kept asking, "What about the game?"

When I first approached the Feds with the idea of staging a card game for the robbery, they went ballistic. They said, "It's absolutely too dangerous to have you in a room with these guys swinging shotguns." They didn't want to cause problems in a fancy place like the Water Tower or any other apartment building, for that matter, even if all the players were SWAT team FBI agents. Too much could go wrong in a confined space.

I then asked, "What if we can do it somewhere that's totally under our control?" I suggested the resort town of Lake Geneva, Wisconsin, just an hour from Chicago. Marco and some other mobsters would vacation up there and were trying to take over the dog track nearby. They knew about all the wealth in the area. We could find a house with plenty of land all around it, so no innocent bystander would be in harm's way.

To set this up for Marco, during one of our walks I said, "Lately, Marc, when we have our games, we don't just go to one place. We're going to different people's places."

"Like where?" Marco asked.

"Last week, we went to Lake Geneva. What a great place." Then I acted like an idea suddenly dawned on me. I said, "But wait. The more I think of it, the more I think something could be done there. It's right out in the open. It's pitch black, and they only got local nitwit cops running around."

Marco got all excited about this idea. Then the next time I saw him, I mentioned that sometimes we had a couple of dope dealers in the game, and how they would bring briefcases with one or two hundred thousand in cash.

It was like we were writing a movie script together, only he didn't know it. Meanwhile, I had to deal with my nervous Nellie producers back in Washington.

Marco had some concerns himself when he heard about the drug dealers, because he knew they carried guns. He wanted to make sure "there would be no heroes."

I told him, "No, as long as your guys don't get nervous."

"They don't get nervous," he said. "They're professionals." He claimed they were real experts at this sort of operation and worked all over the country. Getting these guys out of circulation would be another bonus.

A few days before Thanksgiving, the Feds told me I would have to leave town the following week. It was like they had given me my date of execution. Valukas had decided to step down as U.S. Attorney. Just as I thought, he was going back to his old firm of Jenner & Block, and would soon be representing the same scumbags we were looking to lock up. During the press conference announcing his replacement, Valukas wanted to break the news about me. The Feds even thought about having U.S. Attorney General Dick Thornburgh come in for the occasion. By this time, nothing Valukas did could surprise me, but the irony of it all was beyond belief. At every turn he tried to squash my investigation. Now he had finally succeeded in shutting it down, so he could tout it as the greatest achievement of his term.

Like it or not, my time would be up in just a matter of days. Before I left Chicago, I had to break the news to my family. At the time, my mother, four brothers, and a sister lived in town. I invited all of them and the in-laws downtown for dinner at a nice new restaurant. My mother was in her seventies, still sharp and active, and I loved seeing her have a good time with everyone. As far as they were all concerned, this was just another of my dinner parties, so no one imagined anything was up. As the evening wore on, I took each of my brothers aside. I told them, "I've been working with the government for three years. I'm going to do what I can to change things, but it means I have to leave, and I won't be able to contact you for a while." They took it really hard. I promised each one that I'd figure out a way to tell Mother before the dinner was over, but I couldn't bring myself to do it. We were all laughing and joking, and she was having so much fun. After she left, my brothers stayed behind and wanted to pound me for not breaking the news to her. I couldn't blame them.

It's hard to describe my feelings during those last days in Chicago. There was a great sadness inside of me, and a dread about my future, but also a tremendous anger. All of these emotions combined to put me into a frenzy to tie up every loose end that I could. I chased down Ricky Borelli and the other bookies to collect on my bets. I also arranged to pick up the juice loan from Marco that I was supposed to use for bribing Johnny. Marco had Tony Doty deliver the $50,000 in the parking lot of a West Side White Castle. He got into my car and handed me a paper bag stuffed with cash. I wasn't wearing a wire, but I left my car phone on. Jim Wagner listened in from his car around the corner. This whole scene smelled like too much of a setup for the FBI, and they wanted to make sure no one grabbed me.

At this stage, I truly didn't care if I got hit. I kept priming Marco for the robbery, and I set things up so the FBI couldn't leave me back in Chicago. But with all the arrangements being made in Wisconsin, and Valukas screwing around with his press conference, I still didn't have an exact day for the game. Then, on the morning of Wednesday, November 29, I was told they were ready to go—that night. Right away, I went to see Marco at his club. I pulled him outside and said, "It's going to happen tonight."

Marco was pissed. "Those guys are out of town," he said. "I can't get them back in time."

We needed a Plan B. "What about Bobby?" I asked, referring to Bobby Abbinante, Marco's brother-in-law.

Marco shrugged his shoulders and then nodded okay.

Ever since Marco told Bobby about our plan for the card game, Bobby was pitching me to rob it. He told me that he did home invasions, too, and that his crew was as fast and efficient as the one Marco wanted to use. Bobby was a weightlifter, more than six feet tall and probably the toughest guy in Marco's gang. He was ambitious, too. Besides making book, he had some kind of job as a tow truck driver with the City of Chicago.

I was expecting Bobby to meet me at the club with the money I won betting with him. He didn't show up until two o'clock in the afternoon. I told him, "Marco has decided to let you do the card game, but it's tonight."

Bobby said, "I'll get ahold of the boss." He didn't mention a name, but it was probably a guy I would have recognized.

After I left the club, I called the agents on my cell phone. I said, "You should put a tail on Bobby. He's rounding up the crew for the job." But he was off before they could follow him.

I drove from the club back home to pack. The plan was for me to leave for the airport as soon as we were done in Wisconsin. The Feds warned me not to bring any suit or clothing with a label that could identify where I was from. I could only take two suitcases. Everything else I left behind.

I drove up to Wisconsin with Jimmy Wagner, the FBI agent on my investigation who specialized in organized crime, and the one who coordinated a lot of the details for the sting. I had told Bobby I would come up with some excuse to leave the game around nine o'clock and go back to the hotel where I was staying. He could call my room and I'd give him directions to the house.

I checked into the hotel, and when I went into my room, there were five FBI agents waiting for me. They were all with the Milwaukee SWAT team. The supervisor was a hard-ass, and he didn't want a civilian like me anywhere near the action. But I hadn't come all this way to sit on my ass by the swimming pool. When the phone rang, Bobby was on the other end. He told me that they had come up in two cars. One would be the "work" car, which was probably stolen. They would drive that to the house and then ditch it after the robbery.

The agents had put a wire on my phone, and as I spoke with him, I tried to be the voice of reason. I said, "I don't want anyone to get killed."

He said, "Nobody's going to fuck with us. We've got these big shotguns and carbines. We're all set." This was really all we had to hear. Even without an actual robbery, we could build a case against him just for taking automatic weapons across state lines to commit a felony.

When I asked him where he was, he told me he was right outside the hotel in the parking lot. He wanted to follow me back to the house. He said, "We'll see you when you're coming out."

I said, "I'll be out in about twenty minutes."

After I hung up, the supervisor got angry with me. "What did you tell him that for?" he asked. "You're not going anywhere."

I said, "Sure I am."

He said, "No. We'll have somebody put your clothes on."

Bobby wouldn't fall for that. He knew what I looked like. I said, "I have to go."

Jimmy Wagner agreed with me. He said he would get in the car with me to make sure I was all right. Besides, the supervisor was not about to pull the plug on this whole operation, given all the resources they had already put into it. We let the Milwaukee agents get a head start. Then Jimmy and I left the hotel and got into my car.

Wagner had picked the perfect place for the raid. It was a big A-frame post-and-beam house on a dirt road cul-de-sac. To one side there was a trail leading into the woods. Another house was in the distance on the other side of the subdivision. A bunch of Jaguar-type luxury cars were lined up in the road as additional bait. You had to park your car in the cul-de-sac and then walk a few dozen yards across the lawn to get to the house.

It was pitch black out there, just like I told Marco, but the agents had planted flash grenades all over the grounds, and were ready to light everything up as soon as the bad guys made their move. Curtains were drawn over all the big windows in the house, but you could see lights and smoke coming from the chimney, so it looked like something was going on inside.

The front door opened for us, and we walked into a huge split-level living room crammed with agents. They were all in bulletproof vests and armed to the teeth with machine guns and rifle barrels sticking out everywhere. Clusters of agents had set up to shoot in practically every direction.

Now the supervisor barked at me to go upstairs to the master bedroom and lock myself in the bathroom. If shooting started he didn't want me to catch any stray bullets. At this point, I couldn't argue with him, but I left the door open, and I could hear the reports from all their lookout points. They must have had some agents with night vision hidden along the trail. They also had a surveillance plane making sweeps overhead.

At one point I heard, "Here comes the car. It might be them. There are four males in the car. They're slowing down. Someone got out of the car. Now, the car is speeding up and taking off again."

There was a circular drive that went all the way around the subdivision. They didn't come back for another hour. They shut off the headlights and slowed down.

I heard someone say, "They're probably ready to come in."

But then the guy they let off got back in the car and it drove away. After two more hours went by, there was still no sign of the car. We thought, "What the fuck?"

It was probably 4 A.M. Jimmy Wagner knew I had a 7:30 plane to catch. He said, "Let's get out of here."

The agents figured that the robbers had seen something suspicious and then ran off. But I could never let something go that way. I had to find out what happened and see if there was anything more to salvage from all this. At around 5:30, when we got closer to the city, we stopped at an undercover FBI office. Using a monitored phone, I called Bobby's house. I got his wife and she woke him up for me.

"What happened?" I asked.

"Oh, fuck," he said. "We were all set and ready to go. It looked perfect. We were going to come in through the sliding doors on the porch. But after we dropped a guy off, we drove around a little and we saw a fucking copper sitting there." Later, I found out that the FBI had warned the local sheriff that there might be a ruckus. His asshole deputy got curious and parked nearby to rubberneck.

Bobby and his crew parked behind him and watched for a while. "We give him a chance to leave and he's still there," Bobby said. "We figure he's sleeping or fucking something, so we decide we were going to do it anyway. We went to get the work car, but when we start it, a hose broke."

Bobby said they even tried to find a mechanic in town to fix the work car, but everything was closed at that point. Now, he wanted to use the other car, but the boss of the crew was more careful and he called it off.

Even though they didn't go ahead with the robbery, Bobby's description to me over the phone was corroborated by the surveillance. Together, along with the weapons violations, it made a good case against them all. Still, I could get Bobby and his crew to try again. I said, "Then maybe we'll do the game next week."

He said, "All right."

After I hung up, I said to Jimmy, "We can do this thing next week. We can find out who these stickup men are." I was concerned about getting that group off the street. Besides, it would give me more time to collect the $100,000 the bookies owed me.

But Jimmy told me I wasn't doing anything next week. "You have to leave town today," he said. "Valukas has everything arranged."

We went straight to Midway Airport. Jimmy handed me my ticket and watched me get on the plane.

For some reason, Valukas never got his press conference with the U.S. Attorney General. But a few hours after I left town, FBI agents fanned out across Chicago to serve subpoenas. It soon became common knowledge that the requests for information stemmed from wire recordings I had made for the last three and a half years. One of the agents went to City Hall and happened to see State Senator John D'Arco Jr. as he talked in a lobby phone booth. The agent would later tell the court that

Johnny heard something over the phone that made him drop the receiver. "He gasped like he was in pain, almost as if the wind had been knocked out of him," the agent testified. Then Johnny stumbled backward out of the booth, fell to the floor and, holding his head in his hands, cried, "Oh, my God."

LEGAL
ASSASSIN

CHAPTER 13

WITNESS DEJECTION PROGRAM

November 29, 1989. One life had ended for me, but if you asked what would come next, I couldn't have told you. When Jimmy Wagner took me to the airport, I literally had no idea where the Feds were sending me until I looked at the ticket and saw that the destination was Fort Myers, Florida. I was in a daze the whole flight. All I had to my name were those two suitcases and about $5,000 in cash.

Jimmy told me that another FBI agent would be waiting for me at the airport, but when I got off the plane, there was no one at the gate. As I went for my luggage, I saw a sign that read: "Turn left to Marco Island." This was just not some funny coincidence. Marco D'Amico and a bunch of the other Mob bosses and crew leaders had started to buy land in Marco Island, about fifty miles south of Fort Myers. That was their new hangout. What were the Feds sending me here for? Once again, I had to ask myself if they knew what they were doing.

I went to a pay phone to call Jimmy. He said, "Go to the motel by yourself. Just give me a call and let me know when you check in."

They put me in a decent place near the airport, where I could lie around by a pool. When I got to my room after I checked in, I flipped through the channels on my television and saw they carried WGN out of Chicago. The noon news was on and the next thing I knew, I saw John Drummond, the crime reporter, with a breaking story. He was talking about me, and they flashed one of the tapes with me on the screen. He announced that I had been exposed as an undercover agent, working for the federal government, but then he started in with all this bullshit about me being involved with cocaine and having gambling debts that drove me to become an informer. Immediately I could see what was happening. Once the big criminal defense attorneys like Pat Tuite and Ed Genson got a look at their clients' subpoenas, they realized they would be facing me in court, so right away they had to cut me down in the minds of potential jurors. They had to make me look like somebody who got caught by the government. Then they could argue that I would say anything to get off the hook, just like a rat.

I grabbed the phone and called John Drummond at WGN. I said, "John, what they're saying is a bunch of bullshit. That's not the way it is. These lawyers are trying to smear me and ruin my credibility before I give any testimony. I wasn't forced to come in. It was just the opposite. I'll call you back later, and tell you the true story."

I always knew the criminal lawyers would try to crucify me. I just didn't think it would happen this soon. My mother didn't even know I'd left town, and I didn't want her to find out this way. Fortunately, when I called, she still hadn't seen anything on TV. I tried to prepare her for what would come out. "Don't pay attention to the stuff about me in the media," I said. "Most of it won't be true."

But then I told her I had left town. "I'll be gone for a while, but I'll stay in touch and let you know I'm okay," I said. I promised that over the next few days, I would be calling the reporters. "I'll straighten it out with them and make sure they don't destroy the family name."

Of course, this all seemed so strange to my mother—it was almost like telling her I had a terminal illness. There were times when I heard her crying on the other end of the line. As soon as I hung up with her, the phone rang again. It was Dave Grossman, the FBI supervisor. He said, "Valukas wants to talk to you," and he transferred me to another line.

The next voice I heard was Anton Valukas. He only had a few hours left in his stint as U.S. Attorney. That was still plenty of time to make my life even more miserable. He said, "We heard that John Drummond was on television earlier today, saying you would be talking to him."

I said, "Yes. That's right."

"Please don't talk to anybody," Valukas said. "You might affect the cases."

"But wait," I said. "My family is back there, and the defense lawyers are dragging my name through the mud with all this stuff about drugs and gambling debts."

He thought that was funny. "Oh, don't worry," he laughed. "All the truth will come out when you go to court. Let them say whatever they want right now."

"Can't you have someone come forward and deny these things?" I asked.

He said, "No. We can't do that now. But if you want your investigation to be successful, you can't say anything. You'll have your day in court, believe you me."

And, like a jackass, I listened to him. I never called back John Drummond or anyone else from the press. The next morning, the *Chicago Tribune* article about my investigation had the following lead: "A Chicago lawyer who feared for his safety because of gambling debts. . . ." Nobody from the government ever came forward to defend me during this period, and the defense lawyers were left alone to dirty the jury pool.

Judge Cieslik used to tell me how easy it was for lawyers like Pat Tuite to manipulate the press. To some extent, you can understand it. When stories break, reporters are desperate for any information they can get. Prosecutors are as much to blame as defense attorneys when it comes to leaks, but prosecutors come and go. The high-paid, high-profile criminal lawyers stick around, and they're the ones with the crime reporters in their pockets. I had a few myself. But I never floated gossip in the press that I couldn't back up in court. I didn't want jurors to walk into court thinking one thing to find out another. They tend to take that out on your client.

To make matters worse, the Feds called my investigation, "Operation Gambat"—for Gambling Attorney. I certainly don't deny that I gambled, and loved doing it, but that name turned everything back onto *my* activities and *my* motives. As a result, whenever the newspapers wrote about me, my first name was always "crooked" or "corrupt." One reporter created a whole new adjective for me: "corrupt-lawyer-turned-government-informant." Meanwhile, they had different descriptions for Pat Marcy, such as "businessman" or "an influential member of the First

Ward Democratic Organization." In all the months leading up to his trial, no one ever wrote that he was an ex-convict. For that information, the reporters had to look as far as their own newspapers' clip files.

From the start, almost all the press reported that I was in the Witness Protection Program, but nothing was further from the truth. First of all, I always thought Witness Protection was something for stoolpigeons and rats—people who informed for the money and had nothing better to do with their lives. A year before I left Chicago, the FBI had someone from the program come to talk to me to change my mind. He told me how four people would pick me up and stay with me at all times; how we would keep moving from hotel to hotel; how I wouldn't be allowed to call home. That sounded like jail to me. I asked him very nicely to leave my apartment and never come back.

Those who knew the truth thought I was brave to opt out of Witness Protection, but to be honest, I had to wonder how much protection the program would give me. Most people think the FBI or the Secret Service run the program. In fact, it's the U.S. Marshals Service. My life would have depended on a bunch of guys who weren't making all that much money—under $30,000 in those days. What would they do if the Mob put a huge bounty on my head?

After I had been in Fort Myers for a few days, I got a visit from another agent. He told me that Tony Accardo, the grand old Godfather of the Outfit, had come out of retirement to fly back to Chicago and deal with the fallout from my investigation. One wire caught another old boss saying, "They ruined the First Ward." The FBI was more convinced than ever that the Mob would have me killed, and once again this agent pleaded with me to go into Witness Protection.

But I wouldn't change my mind. The FBI didn't like it much, but they decided to work out their own special program to keep me in hiding until my trials were over. When the agent asked where I wanted to live, I didn't have a clue. He told me that the Denver area was nice, and I decided to give it a try. Steve Bowen met up with us and I flew with him to Colorado. Before we looked for an apartment, he took me to a Denver courthouse. There, we legally changed my name and they gave me a new Social Security number to go along with it.

I chose to live in Littleton (now known for the student shootings at Columbine High School), a very picturesque town outside of Denver. After I signed the lease for my apartment and my car, I sat down with Steve and figured out my monthly expenses. Whenever it came to government funds, I always gagged a little. I didn't want to take too much and have the defense lawyers throw that back in my face during a trial. It was like my Vow of Abstinence. I let Steve add only $150 a week for spending money. My total income came to $3,200 a month. There were nights at Faces when I had spent more than that for the bar tab. Eventually, when I had to show up in court and needed to buy some suits, they gave me a raise to $3,400 a month. Because of some silly government regulation, it was easier to do that than write up an expense report for clothing. I never let them raise my monthly allowance beyond that amount. Before he left town, Steve introduced me to the Denver-area FBI agents. I would meet them once a month to get my pay in cash.

My apartment was in a nice new subdivision. I had no complaints about it, but obviously I felt totally isolated in a very strange place. The first night I was there, the temperature was sub-zero, weather that was much colder than anything I had experienced in Chicago. Inside, it was warm, but I still had trouble getting to sleep. Then, at three in the morning, there was a knock on my door. My first thought was: "Who could that be? I don't know anybody in this town."

But the knocking got louder, and then I thought, "Good Christ. They found me."

I tried not to panic. How stupid would a hit man be to knock? Typically they just burst in, but because of the weather, the front doors in these apartments were too big and thick for that. When I looked out through the peephole, I saw a guy standing there, and it looked like he had some kind of rifle cradled in his arm.

I no longer carried my guns, so now I had to scramble to find something I could use as a weapon. I don't even remember what I grabbed, just that it was big and solid. As the guy kept pounding, I quietly took off the chain. Then I suddenly yanked open the door to brain him.

It was the maintenance guy with a crowbar and a sledgehammer. He must have thought I was some kind of crazed paranoid psycho, but I couldn't have been happier to see him. He said, "The pipes are frozen and I may have to knock a hole in your wall. Is that okay?"

I said, "Fine. Fine. Go ahead and knock down the wall if you want."

About the second day I was there, I decided I would go out and hit the nightclubs. I wanted to make some friends and see what life was like in my new hometown. I was sitting in the bar, minding my own business, when a guy came over and sat down next to me, smoking. I quit smoking when I was a kid, and I just hate cigarette smoke. I said, "Excuse me, could you move the cigarette so the smoke doesn't keep blowing in my face."

He said, "Why don't you move?"

The next thing I know, we're exchanging words, and he's asking me outside to fight. As soon as we reached the parking lot, the guy waved me off and left. When I went back into the bar, people came up to me and said, "This guy's always causing trouble, and we were hoping to see him finally get a beating."

But then, as I sat there, I started thinking, "Am I fucking nuts?" With the mood I was in, who knows what I could have done to him? If I got arrested in this strange town, it could have caused some serious problems. I was supposed to be in hiding. I had to learn to take a little shit and keep a low profile.

The FBI wanted me to spend my days going over the hundreds of tapes I had recorded with my wire. Their secretaries tried to transcribe them, but had every other line marked "IA" for inaudible. They gave me earphones and a little steno machine. Often, I had to listen to the same thing over and over again. It was incredibly tedious and boring work— especially for a guy like me who has trouble sitting still.

When Christmas Eve rolled around, did I ever feel alone. I couldn't even call my family. The Feds were still concerned the Mob might find a way to trace calls to their numbers. When I turned on the radio or the TV, all I heard was holiday music, and it made me even more homesick. I finally decided I had to get out of the apartment.

I got in my car and drove into the mountains. When the road ended, I turned off on one of the trails. I went as high as I could go, and then backed up to turn around. I had leased a cheap car with front-wheel drive, not like the big Chryslers or Lincolns I had back in Chicago, and it got stuck in the snow. No matter what I did, I couldn't push it out. I waited to see if anyone would drive by, but no one did. I remembered passing a volunteer fire station on the way up, so I got out of the car and walked back down the mountain. The station was much farther away than I thought, maybe four miles, and when I finally reached it, it was closed for the night. I had to keep trudging through deep snow and bitter cold without boots or a heavy coat. After a few hours of walking, I wondered if I would ever get back without freezing to death. I really started to feel sorry for myself. Like everything else in my life, I had taken this stupid outing without any regard for where it would take me, and once again I was paying the price. Finally, I reached the road and flagged down a car to give me a ride.

If I needed something to make me feel even worse, it came a few weeks later when I got a call from one of the FBI agents. On the day I left town, he went to Arizona to interview Judge Frank Wilson. He told Wilson, "Bob Cooley has been working with the government and they have you on tape. You may be called as a witness."

But Frank was no more forthcoming with him than he was with me. He kept up with the same line, "I don't know what you're talking about." But then, in February, they called him again to say that he'd be granted immunity if he testified before the grand jury. After he put down the phone, the judge went into his back yard with a handgun and blew his brains out.

When I heard this, I just felt horrible. He was the most decent of all the people involved in my cases, and the bribe he took for Harry Aleman was probably the worst thing he ever did in his life. Still, he wouldn't have gone to jail if he cooperated. He was just too embarrassed and humiliated to do that. Of course the family claimed he was depressed over health issues, but the timing told me otherwise. If I hadn't gone to the Feds, he would have been left alone to live out his years.

I also felt badly for my family. They didn't deserve the infamy I brought to our name, or even my father's story. When I took on the zoning change for my brother's clients and turned it into a sting, I never thought about the impact this would have on my brother's law firm or his career. Neither he nor the clients knew about the bribe, but their names and the property were dragged into the papers with news about the Roti and Marcy subpoenas.

That whole winter was like a black hole for me. But eventually I realized I had to get over it. If my investigation hurt good people, at least it was something I had attempted for a good cause, and it was that much more important for me to make successful. As for myself, I had already jumped off the building when I became an informant. The life I had once loved so much was over, and there was nothing I could do about it. Instead, I had to find a way to enjoy what was left to me.

I decided to stay in touch with family and friends back home—even after I learned that the Mob had put a million-dollar bounty on my head. I actually let one buddy come out to visit me. His name was Bobby Whitebloom. He had been a lawyer for the secretary of state's office, and I originally met him through Johnny D'Arco. After he retired from the state job, Bobby worked for an insurance company. During my last years in Chicago, he became one of my closest friends. He was short and slight, and very quiet, but he loved to hang around me and watch the crazy crowd I attracted. Sometimes he'd join me when I'd have a group of people at a Greek restaurant. He always left early, but he usually picked up the check on the way out.

I became Bobby's entire social life, and he was devastated when I left town. After we talked on the phone a few times, I decided that Bobby could fly to Littleton and see me. I totally trusted him to keep my location a secret. But shortly after he got back to Chicago, he called me and said, "Johnny D'Arco came to see me at work. He said, 'I'm sure you know where Bob Cooley is. Tell me or you're going to have problems.'" Johnny said he would be back in a week.

I was furious. D'Arco knew that Bobby had health problems, but the kid also had brass balls, and was not going to knuckle under to anyone. I called the Feds and told them that D'Arco was intimidating Bobby. I knew that agents had already gone out to Mob leaders like M and warned them that there would be consequences if anyone harassed my friends and family. But now the Feds figured they might have another count against Johnny if they could get Bobby to wear a wire. Like an idiot, I agreed, and helped talk him into it.

Bobby did get Johnny D'Arco threatening him on tape, but we'll never know what could have been done with his evidence. Bobby already had a weak heart, and after this incident, he had more problems with it. A few months later, he wound up in the hospital and the doctors wanted to operate. The night before surgery, we talked and Bobby was nervous. I tried to assure him. I said, "Bobby, you're going to be okay. You have great doctors and you're in a great hospital." But what did I know. He died on the operating table. I felt partly responsible for dragging him into my situation, but now I lost any pity I ever had for Johnny D'Arco. He deserved everything he had coming.

Back in Littleton, I kept going out to the nightclubs to meet people. My best friends were one couple from the area. She was going to law school and, without revealing my identity, I could regale her with stories about my years as a criminal attorney. She had to go to Chicago for a conference, and her boyfriend asked me to pick her up at the airport when she returned. I met her at the gate. First thing, she said, "I thought I saw you on TV." The FBI had me wearing a toupee to change my appearance, but it didn't fool her any. Coincidentally, flying on the same plane was the Cook County State's Attorney, Cecil Partee. I had known him for years, but he walked by me at the gate like I wasn't there.

Obviously, it was a matter of time before word got back to Chicago that I was in the Denver area. The FBI yanked me out of there, and I moved next to Richmond, then Charleston, Charlotte, and Atlanta. Each time, the Feds got a tip that the Mob knew where I was and that the hit men were coming to get me. I stopped buying furniture or too many nice clothes, because the warnings would come so suddenly, I would have to leave everything behind.

Even when I was on the run, I couldn't help but build new cases for the government. I had just been in Atlanta for a few days when I heard about the Buckhead area, and I walked into one club there. It reminded me of the places back in Chicago where the mobsters used to hang. I struck up a conversation with a guy at the bar. "I'm just here from Denver," I said, and gave him my new name. "I'm an attorney." One thing led to another, and I realized that my new friend was a mobster who specialized in fixing traffic cases. The judges and lawyers would come to this club to meet him. He also did some bookmaking and gambling, so he loved my advice on betting lines.

The next morning, the Atlanta agents assigned to help me couldn't believe who I had met at the bar. He was a crime boss on the level of Marco D'Amico. They had been trying to make him for years, but the last informant who got close to him ended up dead. They asked me to build some cases on him, and I was only too happy to help. I thought this was great. Here were all the mobsters in Chicago looking for me, while I was working on these other bad guys in Atlanta. I went back to wearing a wire and hosted dinners for the crime boss and his friends. I started to meet women through the local singles ads, and I had them come along, too. A few more agents were added to the mix as my associates—two males and a female. One of those agents was a single guy who liked to show off for the woman. One night, when he was drinking with her at the bar, he started to brag to her about his exploits. Later, the bartender took me aside and asked, "You're not an FBI agent, are you?"

"What are you talking about?" I said. "Who gave you that crazy idea?"

"Your buddy over there," he said. The bartender pointed at the single-guy agent. "He's been talking all night about making raids with a SWAT team."

That was the end of my Atlanta operation, and now I had to ride out of town again. Too bad, because I had really started to love Atlanta.

But I couldn't let any of these detours distract me from the investigation in Chicago. My main purpose in life was to convict everybody I had made cases against. That's why I had to stay alive and why I had to move if there was ever a hint that the Mob knew my whereabouts. If they got me, then they won. I wasn't going to let that happen.

In September of 1990, I made a trip back to Chicago to testify before a grand jury. They took me into the Dirksen Federal Building through a basement garage and up to a room that looked like a lecture hall. Grand jurors sat where the students would be. Tom Durkin, the assistant U.S. attorney, asked me questions, and most of my answers were "yes" and "no." After this went on for a couple of days, I realized the sheer number of charges that were lining up behind my testimony—like freight cars at a rail crossing.

Finally, a few days before Christmas 1990, the Feds had the big press conference that Valukas thought he would get. Fortunately, in his place was the new U.S. Attorney for Chicago, Fred Foreman, along with U.S. Attorney General Dick Thornburgh and FBI Director William Sessions, who both flew in from Washington for the occasion. They announced three indictments. There was one against Patty DeLeo and Judge Shields, and another against Johnny D'Arco. But by far, the biggest case was against Pat Marcy and Fred Roti and their "enterprise" known as "the First Ward." The charges included fourteen counts and six acts of racketeering that touched on everything from the phony Chancery case of *Eldridge v. Carr* to the zoning bribe and the fixes for Harry Aleman, Lenny Chow, and Mike Colella. There was only one charge in the indictment that I didn't develop—a bribe Marcy took from someone who wanted his brother to be an associate judge. (The Feds found out about it when they tapped Marcy's phone at Counsellors Row.)

The next day, the *Chicago Tribune* front-page headline read: "Five Indicted in 'Corruption Feast.' " It quoted Fred Foreman when he said, "Whatever type of corruption you wanted, you could get, and this movable feast went from the First Ward to Springfield, to City Hall, to the Circuit Court of Cook County; even to the highest levels of the Chancery Court."

With just these three indictments, the paper said, "The charges in Operation Gambat surpass in both money and scope the corruption unearthed in the infamous Operation Greylord investigation into judicial corruption."

When a reporter asked whether the investigation would produce any more indictments directly tied to organized crime, Attorney General Thornburgh replied, "Stay tuned."

But I had a few questions about the indictments myself—especially about the unindicted. If they could accuse Marcy and Roti for fixing the Eldridge case, why wasn't there a charge against the judge, Anthony Scotillo? What about all the cases I had against Marco and his crew?

What bothered me most was that they didn't indict Maloney—and, according to my grapevine of FBI agents, they didn't plan on doing it in the future, either.

A few months after the press conference, the Feds brought me back to the Federal Building in Chicago to start our preparations for the first trials. As usual, the FBI agent took me in through the garage and let me off by the elevator while he parked the car. At that moment, the U.S. Attorney, Fred Foreman, walked by.

At first, he was startled to see me. He thought I was in protective custody like everyone else. I had dealt with him years before, when he was the DuPage County State's Attorney. I always thought he was a straight shooter and we got along just fine.

Fred said, "Bob, what are you doing here?"

I said, "I'm waiting to go upstairs."

He said, "Are they taking good care of you?"

"Sure," I said.

As he started to get on the elevator, he added, "If there's anything I can do, you let me know."

Then I said, "Fred, wait. There is one thing you can do."

"What's that?" he asked.

I said, "You can indict that scumbag Maloney."

"We had a meeting on that," he told me. "The assistant U.S. Attorney who had the case indicates he doesn't have enough evidence for conviction."

I said, "This man is probably the worst judge we ever had in the system. It would be good to indict him even if he gets acquitted, so people realize you can't get away with that behavior. If we indicted Shields, we can indict Maloney. The case on him is better."

He said, "I'll take another look at it."

I knew his real problem was not the case but the prosecutor who got the assignment. So far, all the Gambat indictments had come through Tom Durkin. He was bright and aggressive, but he couldn't prosecute all of my cases. We needed another sharp attorney to go against Maloney. I told Durkin and Foreman that my favorite candidate was another assistant U.S. Attorney, Scott Mendeloff. I was already working with him on one of the last Greylord cases, involving a sheriff's deputy named Lucius Robinson, who had been bailiff and bagman for some very corrupt judges. Although Robinson took a guilty plea for accepting a bribe, he lied during his grand jury testimony to protect all the judges he helped pay off. Now the Feds were coming after him for perjury. Since I had passed money through Lucius a few times, Scott asked me to be a witness.

In June 1991, I was in a hotel in Wisconsin, working with Scott on the Robinson case. I hated preparing for a trial. I had hated it when I was a lawyer, and I hated it just as much when I became a witness. When I was the attorney, I used to read the police reports just once and was ready to go. Now, I would read a transcript from my wire just once and I was ready to go. But that wasn't good enough for Scott. He's very methodical, and he wanted me to go over everything again and again. One day while we were doing this, it just started to get on my nerves, and I said, "What's happening with Maloney? The statute must be coming close." I figured it would soon be five years since his El Rukn trial with Swano.

Scott said, "That's really none of your business. Why don't you concentrate on this case?"

I said, "Why am I wasting my time here on this bailiff, this go-fer, when Maloney—the worst scumbag of all—may skate because he's politically connected with Ed Burke?"

That got Scott really mad. He said, "You can't take these cases so personally. You're not supposed to push for prosecution. You're not a prosecutor. You're only a witness."

We went back to a transcript and started to bicker again about a word on the tape. I was frustrated, but I could see I had raised an issue that got him equally frustrated. Finally Scott said, "Either you're going to work with me and do what I tell you, or I might not call you as a witness."

One of the agents was there, and I said to him, "Maybe you should change my airplane reservation to tomorrow." I got up and started to walk out the door.

Scott said, "Come on. Stop it already. Let's go back to work."

Soon afterwards, he got paged and went to another room to make a phone call. He came back a few minutes later. "Now you can be happy," he said. "We just indicted Maloney."

It turned out that the statute of limitations for the El Rukn trial was closer than I thought. The indictment against Maloney and Swano came on the very last day that the government could bring charges.

CHAPTER 14

"SLANDER MY NAME"

n the days after the first Gambat indictments were announced, the papers and TV stations went back to speculating about my motives for becoming an informant. I knew this was really audition time for all the stories that the defense attorneys would tell the jury. Once again, they trotted out the bullshit about my gambling debts and that I was afraid of Bob Johnson and Dominic Barbaro. Pat Marcy hired Genson to represent him, and fat old Eddy was quick to dismiss all my cases by saying, "They are the ravings of a sick mind, and Mr. Cooley will be shown as such in court."

But in the same article where this Genson quote appeared, *Tribune* reporter Ray Gibson added some new perspective. He found out about my beef with Marco and my disgust with the Mike Colella fix. He also mentioned that my brothers served with distinction as police officers, and my father's reputation for honesty. He wrote, "Friends say reports that [Cooley] was in fear of his life because of gambling debts are untrue. . . . He had simply become fed up with corruption."

Who was the real Bob Cooley? A lot of people were waiting to see, but my debut on the witness stand would not come with an Operation Gambat trial. Instead, I was asked to testify in a wide-ranging case the Feds had brought against the On Leong Merchants Association. Originally, they had more than thirty-three defendants from all over the country, but most of the counts involved the gambling operation that the Chicago On Leong ran out of their headquarters on Wentworth Street in Chinatown. From the balcony of that building, Lenny Chow had shot William Chin.

I had known for some time that the government was investigating the On Leong. After I came in, the Strike Force had me wear the wire on Wilson Moy to confirm that he had paid to fix Lenny Chow's murder case. We also got evidence that he was paying off Roti to keep the police from raiding his games. The Feds even paid me to go to an On Leong convention with Moy in Taiwan. While we were still in Taiwan, Moy and I met up with Wing and Eddie Chan, the former national leader of the On Leong. Eddie fled the U.S. as soon as he found out the Feds were on his trail. I tried to talk Eddie into coming back, but he knew better.

A few weeks before I was supposed to testify at the trial in Chicago, I went to an Iowa hotel to meet the assistant U.S. Attorney leading the prosecution. His name was Stephen Anderson, and he looked to be a young guy who might have bitten off more than he could chew with this case. When I first walked into his room with the FBI agent Steve Bowen, Anderson went overboard with all the compliments. "What an honor it is to meet you," he said. "I realize what you've done and all the sacrifices you've made." He laid it on so thick, it was embarrassing. Finally, I said, "Okay. Let's get started already."

I was with him in the hotel for two days, going through all the details of the Lenny Chow trial. When we were ready to leave town, Steve Bowen dropped Anderson and me at the airport. I said good-bye and we went our separate ways. I'm sure Anderson thought Witness Protection was picking me up (the FBI never wanted me to tell anyone where I was going). But while I was walking around the airport, I saw Anderson again at a phone booth. I remembered something I forgot to tell him. I walked up from behind just as I heard him say, "How would you feel if you were stuck in a room with a stoolpigeon for the weekend?"

I spun around and walked away before he could see me, thinking, "What a phony piece of shit." I was supposed to call him before I came back to town to testify, but I was still so fucking mad, I never did.

While the Lenny Chow fix was an important charge in the On Leong indictment, it was still a small part of the whole trial. There were dozens of other charges against eleven defendants, and I could only testify about two of them, Wilson Moy and Wing. But as far as the media was concerned, On Leong was all about me. Throughout their coverage of the trial, the reporters called me the star witness. It was like the sideshow had taken over the circus. When I made my first appearance, July 1, 1991, the case had already dragged on for three months, but the *Chicago Tribune* front-page headline read: "Cooley's Credibility On Trial."

The article made it clear that the defense lawyers saw much more at stake in my testimony than the verdict for the On Leong trial. The reporter, Matt O'Connor, wrote: "If defense lawyers have their way, Robert J. Cooley, the lawyer turned government informant, will be on trial as much as the defendants when he testifies Monday for the first time in federal court." Because of my "corrupt behavior," O'Connor predicted, my "character and credibility are expected to come under blistering attack" by the defense attorneys.

You didn't have to read too much between the lines to see what he was driving at. The lawyers saw this trial as a just a first skirmish. For them, the most important battles—over the First Ward—were yet to come, and anything they could do to weaken me would help.

In fact, prior to my arrival in Chicago, various court documents had already been leaked to the press to muddy me up in advance. One was the "proffer" that the government submitted in which I listed my illegal acts. An article on that leak had the headline: "U.S. Says Informant Bribed 20 Judges"—actually, it was 29. The other leak was a motion filed by Ed Genson for Johnny D'Arco. It tried to stop me from testifying in his case, because I was "simply [and] inherently unreliable." Genson filled the motion with every negative thing about me that he could find. It was clearly written more for the press than the judge. He dragged in bullshit charges made against me by my ex-client Paul Baker (who was also Swano's client) when he talked to the Feds—the sort of stuff that would never be allowed in court. He even dug up the time I was arrested in Milwaukee back when I was going to Marquette.

You couldn't look at the papers or watch TV without seeing this crap about me, and I knew it had to be getting through to the jurors. They probably expected me to show up in court covered in slime like the Creature from the Black Lagoon.

My first day of testimony, I entered the Dirksen Federal Building through the basement garage. I had no idea about the commotion this was causing on the street with the news trucks or with all the reporters in the lobby. I went up through the judges' elevators and then down the halls past their chambers. It was like entering a theater from the backstage.

The government held the case in what was called the Ceremonial Courtroom, because of all the lawyers and defendants involved. It was probably the biggest place for a trial in the city of Chicago. When they brought me through the side door and out into that huge room, it was standing room only. Besides the press and all the spectators, I saw a whole aisle full of lawyers who were waiting to pound me in the upcoming Gambat trials. Johnny D'Arco, Patty DeLeo, and Eddy Genson were crammed in among them on a gallery bench.

I could see by the looks on their faces that they weren't expecting the new Bob Cooley. In the words of the *Tribune*, I was "distinguished in a dark blue suit and striped tie." No more turtlenecks and gold chains. My demeanor changed as well. As a lawyer, I was a bantam rooster as soon as I stepped into a courtroom. But as a witness, I was a little nervous and shy. I even spoke in a softer voice, and tried to answer, "Yes, sir," and "No, sir," when a lawyer asked me a question.

To start off the direct examination, the assistant U.S. Attorneys would lead me through a confessional—just like I used to do with my clients. I went over each and every bad thing that I had done: from the little cash tips I got as a cop, to the bribes I gave out as a lawyer, the cases I fixed, and my IRS problems during the investigation. I even explained how I withheld information about certain people and activities when I started talking to the Feds and only fully disclosed later. This part of a trial is never easy—the legal version of a rectal exam. Unfortunately, I had to go through it for the first time with Steve Anderson instead of Tom Durkin, a prosecutor who knew me well. Anderson went along like he was reading a laundry list. The *Tribune* would sum up my first day's testimony with the headline "Bribes Were My Way of Life, Informer Says." Meanwhile, anything I said about the Lenny Chow fix was practically reduced to a footnote in the press coverage.

Representing Wilson Moy was pompous Pat Tuite. From the moment

I appeared in the courtroom, he made a big deal about my security and complained that it would bias the jury into thinking, "This witness has to be afraid of somebody." From then on, I always entered before the jury did and was sitting at the witness stand when they arrived.

As I went over my litany of bad acts with the prosecutor, Tuite sat ramrod-straight at the defense table, mugging and tsk-tsking for the jury. The night before he was to cross-examine me, I saw Tuite on the TV news. He used to hold his little press conference in the hall of the Federal Building. He kept telling the reporters how he couldn't wait to get me on the stand. Boy, did that charge me up. I couldn't wait to see him, either.

The next morning, when they brought me into the Federal Building, Steve Anderson asked to meet with me first. The other prosecutors told him I had developed information on the Cammon case that Tuite had fixed with Ed Burke and Judge Maloney.

Anderson said, "When you go into court, I don't want you causing a disruption during the cross-examination. This trial has been going on for a couple of months, and we can't afford a mistrial if you make any charges about Pat Tuite."

I said, "Then you better protect me and keep that piece of garbage from playing games with me."

But Tuite played every game in the book and Anderson hardly lifted a finger. He spent hours going through my proffer, while he took on all these airs and made little comments along the way, like: "I'm disgusted to be a lawyer in your presence." Or at another point, when I explained again how I detailed my illegal activity to the Feds, he said, "That took an awful lot of time, I bet."

At one point, he asked if I admitted taking tips when I was a policeman. When I told him I did, he said, "You became a five- or ten-dollar whore; isn't that right?" He continued in that vein, saying again: "As you look at it now, weren't you whoring your profession as a police officer by taking those five and ten dollars?"

Now this would have been hard enough to take from a straight lawyer, but not someone as rotten and corrupt as Tuite. Through all of this, Anderson sat with his finger up his ass, hardly ever making an objection.

Later, Tuite handed me something to read. I didn't hear his instruction to read it to myself. When I started to read out loud, he shouted, "Are you trying to pull some shots, Mr. Cooley?"

I started to apologize, but then he shouted again, "Judge, would you admonish this *snake* to listen?"

I couldn't look angry or flustered, but, by the end of the day, I decided I wasn't going to take it any more. Tuite got close to me and said, "I doubt that you ever knew an ethical lawyer if you saw one."

I replied, "That's two of us."

Tuite spun around like I had punched him, and a hush went over the courtroom. Then he pointed at me and said, to the judge, "I resent the comment. He made a comment to me, and I resent it."

But the judge hadn't heard what I said. When he asked, another defense counsel yelled out, "Judge, I heard the comment. He said, 'That makes two of us.' "

Now everyone laughed, and of course, this exchange became the lead for the TV news shows and the next day's papers. When he left the courthouse, Tuite ran the other way when he saw the cameras coming.

The other big bombshell of the day came when Tuite asked if I had gone to the Feds because I was afraid of my bookies. I told him that they had been contacted and told to do whatever I wanted them to do.

He laughed. "Who did you contact to contact them?"

"John DiFronzo," I said.

Again, everyone—even Tuite—was stunned. Then he laughed me off like I was bullshitting. "And he supposedly talked to these people, right?" he asked, his voice dripping with sarcasm.

I answered, "I know he talked to these people."

Tuite mugged some more for the jury, but he knew better than to challenge me. It would only give the prosecutors a chance to play another tape.

The On Leong trial continued long after I finished my testimony. Finally, facing open rebellion from the jury, the judge forced it to a close. The jurors returned a split decision, acquitting the defendants of all the major charges, and finding just Wilson Moy and a couple of the restaurant owners guilty of tax evasion. Of course, I mostly testified against Moy, but as far as the papers were concerned I was the reason the government lost the case. According to the *Tribune*, the jurors "divided over the credibility of Robert Cooley, the corrupt-lawyer-turned-federal-informant who is a key witness in the government's Operation Gambat probe of First Ward corruption." The article quoted one juror as saying that someone put "the Snake" next to my name on a bulletin board in the deliberations room. When asked about me, the jury foreman said, "I don't think much of him."

From what little I saw of the case, the Feds tried to pack too much against too many people into one trial. Jurors even had trouble keeping the names straight. But I learned some things from those juror comments about me. In future trials, I tried to make eye contact with each and every juror at some point in my testimony and otherwise try to build a rapport with them.

Fortunately, by the time the On Leong verdict came out, we were already deep into the first real Operation Gambat trial, against Patty DeLeo and Judge Shields. This time, I was totally confident about the prosecution. In addition to Tom Durkin, who had just been promoted to first assistant U.S. Attorney, we had Mike Shepard, another long-time federal prosecutor and a tough trial attorney.

As for the defense, you couldn't have had two more different lawyers. Representing Judge Shields was Dan Webb, the former Chicago U.S. Attorney during Operation Greylord. He was renowned for taking apart Ollie North in the Iran–Contra hearings. Like so many before him, when he left the Justice Department, Webb had pushed through the revolving door to Winston & Strawn, another Chicago-based firm that specialized in defending wealthy white-collar criminals. He was considered the finest trial lawyer money could buy.

But then, sitting at the other defense table, representing Patty DeLeo, was a lawyer as far removed from Webb as I could imagine—the clown prince of the criminal courts, Sam Banks. He was just an idiot in every way. I suspected that he charged Patty no fee for the case, because so much of Sam's business came out of the First Ward. But this was no time for DeLeo to be a cheapskate. He had a lot at stake—like years in prison. I thought, "How stupid can Patty be to use an incompetent like this?"

Despite the presence of Banks, this case was no slam-dunk for the government—even with my tapes and the recordings from the bug in Judge Shields's chambers. First of all, Patty DeLeo was the only person who saw the judge taking the bribe, so Dan Webb could argue that Patty pocketed all the money I gave him and that the judge only ruled in my favor because my "client" was in the right. In fact, the FBI agent who played my opposing lawyer in the case did not put up much of a fight during the hearings. Supporting this line of defense was the sterling reputation of Judge Shields, and I was not about to tarnish the man with my testimony.

When Webb asked if I had ever bribed Shields in the past, I told him "No." When he asked if the judge had ever indicated he wanted money, I also said, "No." Like a good trial lawyer, Webb sensed my positive feelings about Judge Shields, and he milked them for all they were worth. I ended up saying that Shields was always a gentleman to me, and very professional whenever I dealt with him.

This part of my testimony did not thrill Tom Durkin and Mike Shepard, and they ripped into me after court adjourned for the day. They didn't want me to lie, but they didn't want me to be so complimentary, either. "Don't worry," I told them. "You watch what happens when Sam Banks cross-examines me. I guarantee he'll mess it up for Judge Shields."

That's exactly what happened. Banks started off by asking some silly questions about my "sordid past." First, whether I took money as a cop. Without mentioning his name, I told him how Alderman Edward Vrdolyak left some cash on my passenger seat after I let him go in a traffic stop. Then he wanted to know how much I spent gambling. When he asked me about the bribes I paid in Traffic Court, I gave him my standard reply: "It happened every day I was in there. Anyone who worked in the courtroom on a regular basis either paid or lost."

But as I talked, I could see the wheels spinning in Sam's head. He knew that if he wasn't careful, I could testify about the murder case *he* tried to fix. I was in Counsellors Row all those nights he worked with Ed Burke on the killer cops trial. Like I thought, Sam didn't probe too much into this area.

Then, Banks committed the cardinal sin for trial attorneys: He asked me an open question and had no idea about my answer. "Now you had no problems paying judges, did you?"

I replied, "There were some judges I couldn't pay personally."

Thanks to this moron's question, the jury realized that a corrupt judge might take money from one lawyer, but not another. It followed that maybe DeLeo was the only lawyer Shields trusted to be his bagman.

Dan Webb almost had a fit. He pulled Judge Shields and their table away from Patty and Banks to literally put space between them.

For me, the best part of Banks's cross-examination came with his final questions. Previously, he had me estimate my income as a lawyer. I told him that in my good years, I could make two to three hundred thousand a year. When he asked about my current income from the government, I answered, "$3,400 a month."

With a furrowed brow, he did the math. You could see him realize that this added up to a lot less than what I used to make. Clearly I did not cooperate with the government to increase my income. Finally, Sam sputtered, "And that is by your own choice, is it not?"

"Well, yes," I said, "it is my own choice."

One episode during the trial most defined the character of Judge Shields. Webb tried to pound home that Patty was slippery enough to take my bribe and never turn it over to the judge. Of course, I had several stories to support that theory. I could start with the time I caught him red-handed, cheating me on what I thought was a Ward case. That incident gave me an excuse to break from his firm. Before I could start the story, Sam Banks jumped up and down. He demanded a separate trial.

The judge, Ilana Rovner, was a no-nonsense lady who didn't stand for this kind of commotion. First she rejected Sam's motion, and then she excused the jury. I told her the story, and she decided that the jury could hear it, too. During this time, I could see Judge Shields talking with Webb. Then, before the jury returned, Webb got up to say his client had instructed him to withdraw the question. Even though it was in his interests, Judge Shields would not trash Patty's character any further.

As the trial came to a close, Webb put Shields on the stand—a desperation move for a lawyer like that. The judge came off very well in the direct examination; but during the cross, he opened the door for Tom Durkin to ask about the time he was stopped for drunk driving. He had shown the arresting officer his judge's card. A year after this arrest, as head of the National Conference of State Trial Judges, Shields wrote that judges "cannot use their judicial office for the purpose of advancing a personal interest." This embarrassing story may not have seemed like a big deal compared to the other charges, but I believe it did plant seeds of doubt with the jury: namely, that the defendant was pretending to be something he was not.

The jury deliberations went on for four days. According to the papers, most of the time was spent listening to the tapes. First they listened to what was recorded on my wire when Patty DeLeo confirmed what I wanted from the judge. Patty had said, "We want to stall it till next week."

I replied, "Fine, that's all we need."

Then, a few minutes later, the bug in the judge's chambers picked up Patty saying, "Stall it till next week, and the case will be settled."

Since the bug was installed in an old radiator, the sound would go in and out with the steam. But after listening over and over, the jury became convinced that Patty really did say the word "stall." The judge clearly replied, "All right," and stall is exactly what he did for me when he presided over the hearing a few minutes later.

"The jury was probably sorry to hear it," Mike Shepard later told the reporters, "but it's there." Evidently they liked the man as much as I did, but they had to do their duty. They found both Shields and Patty DeLeo guilty.

When it came time to sentence them, the Shields personality did not win over Judge Rovner. She sentenced the judge to 37 months and said, "What you have done has shamed many honest judges, but more importantly impaired the public's belief in a fair, impartial judiciary." It was exactly Judge Shields's reputation, she said, that made his conduct "particularly tragic," because "all over Cook County, lawyers and litigants are saying, 'If Dave Shields could do this, then any judge is capable of doing this.' And what is being said is, 'Who is there left to rely upon, when those who are so trusted prove themselves to be so untrustworthy?' "

Shields may have hurt himself most with her by continuing to deny responsibility. I guess that was his pride talking. Judge Rovner pointed to the evidence from the wires and the bug. She told him, "As much as you wish it otherwise, those words are on that tape. You were convicted by your own words—and once again by your false denial at trial."

Surprisingly, she sentenced Patty DeLeo to a few months less than the judge, but she gave him a tongue-lashing too. She told him to listen to the tapes with Shields as they plotted to stall the case in his chambers. "Listen to them," she said, "and it is obvious to all that it is simply business as usual going on there in that locked chambers. The citizens of Cook County have unfortunately seen this scenario played and replayed. And, Mr. DeLeo, we are all tired of it."

To his credit, Patty took it like a man. Instead of denying it, he told the judge that the trial was a "very devastating experience." He said, "If there are lessons to be learned, believe me, I have learned them."

Patty may have learned lessons from the convictions, but none of those rubbed off on the political or legal establishment in Chicago. Harry Comerford, chief judge for the Cook County Circuit Court, called Shields and DeLeo an "isolated case." He claimed that the court system had already gone through enough reforms after Greylord and didn't need any more.

In October 1991, the trial began for Johnny D'Arco—only two weeks after we finished with Shields and DeLeo. As far as the press was concerned, the jury was still out on my credibility. Reporters kept pointing to the bug in the judge's chambers as the crucial piece of evidence in the first Operation Gambat conviction.

Normally when my testimony was over in a trial, I was supposed to leave town, but a couple of times I didn't. After the FBI agent dropped me off at an out-of-town airport, I would rent a car and come back to Chicago and spend time with family or with girlfriends. I felt secure, because I figured nobody would think I'd be in town.

Sometimes I did crazy things during a trial, too. I'd tell my girlfriend where I was staying, and have her wait for me in the lobby with a little champagne and other party favors. She'd pretend not to know me when I walked in with the agents after dinner. They took rooms on either side of me. Once I could hear their doors close, I'd call down to the desk and have the receptionist send my girl up to join me. I'm sure the Feds would have gone nuts if they found out about this. Still, I needed something to make me happy at night, since my days were spent hearing what a lowlife scumbag I was.

Of all the trials, none was more vicious or personal than Johnny D'Arco's. I was the source of almost all the evidence, either through the tapes from my wire or through my testimony. As a result, Ed Genson decided to turn the entire defense into an attack on me.

In his opening remarks, Genson dismissed the tapes. "There was nothing here but talk," he told the jury. "A lot of smoke, a lot of fantasy." Then, waddling around the courtroom and gesticulating with his cane, he dismissed me. "The man is a paragon of corruption," he said. "The man is walking slime. And this is the man who is going to explain the tapes?"

After the defense attorneys were done with their opening statements, court was adjourned. Usually, I came in before the jury did, so they wouldn't see me enter the courtroom through a side door or with security guards. When I first took the stand, all I could think about was Bobby Whitebloom, and how D'Arco had hounded him to death. I made sure to catch Johnny's eye. He started to glare at me, but then I gave him a wink and a smile, just to bust his balls. From that moment on, as even the *Tribune* noted, he "looked toward the gallery, and avoided glancing at Cooley."

Meanwhile, as the jury filed in, Genson walked right up to me at the witness stand, like we were the best of friends. He said, "You're looking pretty good, Bob. Are you feeling all right? Are they treating you okay?"

This was not only the guy who had just called me "walking slime." He had also nearly gotten me killed when he told Marco I warned my client Frank Renella about being named an informant. "Ed," I said softly, with a pleasant little smile on my face, "go fuck yourself. Just go and fuck yourself."

My direct examination by Mike Shepard took four days. Again, we went through my confessional. Again, I explained why I came in. I said, "I offered my services to help put a stop to some of the corruption in the court system and some of the organized crime corruption here in Chicago."

Once more I was careful about my demeanor, and tried to be polite and soft-spoken at all times; but throughout my testimony, Genson would jump up and make objections or call for sidebars—especially when I explained what some of the tapes were about. As I told the jury, I never mentioned the words "fix" or "bribe" outright. Instead, we all spoke in code.

At one point, when Mike Shepard asked me what it meant when I said, "Go shake some hands," I explained that it meant passing bribes. Suddenly, Johnny's voice piped up and, making some lame stab at sarcasm, said, "You're the best, Bob. You're the best." Genson put his arm around Johnny's shoulder and told him to shut up. Then, for the rest of day, when I said something he didn't like, Johnny would put his face in his hands and shake his head.

I thought the tapes had enough incriminating statements from Johnny to seal a conviction. But according to the media, the verdict would hinge on my cross-examination by Genson. The *Chicago Tribune* headline said it all: "Focus Still On Cooley's Motives." Like Tuite before him, Eddy had promised in his opening statement to take me apart on the stand.

I had no fear of Genson. I knew how lazy and sloppy he was. Still, in the first few minutes of his cross-examination, I came the closest to breaking down in Federal Court. He was going on about all the oaths I took and violated. He went through the ceremony I had gone through in Springfield to become a lawyer. He asked if I raised my hand to swear in, and when I told him I did, he added, "With your father standing next to you, a Chicago policeman?"

"He was there," I said.

As soon as he mentioned my father, my eyes clouded over. I got so incredibly angry, but I couldn't show Genson that he had hit a weak spot. Instead, I tried to focus on giving him the shortest answers I could. If I kept thinking about my father, I knew I would choke up.

That was the roughest patch, even though Genson had me on the stand for weeks during his cross-examination. I could have told you what questions he would ask before he asked them. At one point, he said, "You tried [jury cases] with some success. Isn't that correct?"

Immediately, I realized that this was a trap. If I bragged on myself about being a great lawyer, why would Johnny or anyone else need me to fix trials? Or so Johnny's jury might think.

I answered, "I won some. I lost some."

If Eddy had asked for specific numbers, I would have answered that I probably won forty-eight and lost two. Instead, he didn't press any further. He just turned over a bunch of pages on his legal pad and started another line of attack.

In each of my Operation Gambat cases, the defense always looked for some magic bullet to explain why I went to the Feds. For Genson, it was Operation Greylord. I had admitted bribing Judge Wayne Olson, who was convicted as part of the Operation Greylord investigation. He then became a government witness, and Eddy argued that I expected him to rat me out.

But the opposite was true. "I was told he wasn't naming any of us," I testified.

"Who were you told by?" Genson asked.

"By some friends of yours," I answered.

I could see Eddy choke on that. Of course, he had to ask a follow-up, and I got to mention Pat Marcy. Later, I explained to the jury that I was never worried about the Greylord witnesses. "I was in the inner circle of the First Ward," I testified, "and I knew they wouldn't name me." When I came in, one of the first assistant U.S. Attorneys to interview me was Charles Sklarsky. Coincidentally, he also interviewed Judge Olson. Later in the trial, Sklarsky was called to the stand and confirmed that Olson had never named me, and that I was not under any government investigation when I walked into the Strike Force.

Genson's other big argument was that I went to the Feds because I was desperate for money: a drunk, a loser, and a bust-out. But Johnny, he claimed, was my opposite number: sober, successful, and influential. This became Eddy's theme throughout the trial; that I was a photo negative of

Johnny. The reporter for the *Chicago Daily Law Bulletin* played right along. She described me as "pink, bald, overweight," with "yellow-tinted glasses." On the other hand, she wrote that D'Arco was "dark, handsome and slightly built. He likes to read and go to the gym."

Eddy made a big deal about Johnny's wife, Maggie, who sat behind him in court, and the fact that I never got married. Of course, I could only chuckle inside, knowing how Johnny used to screw around and ask my advice about women. In fact, one of the last conversations we had had was about Maggie. I asked him why he didn't marry her already. He said, "I'm not going to marry her. Why do I have to marry her?" At some point, Johnny must have realized I had this conversation on tape. Who knows if that got him to finally pop the question?

According to Genson, Johnny only humored me out of pity, because I was "shabbily dressed" and "driving an old car." I have no idea why Genson picked on my clothes or my car. But I do know one thing for sure: He never bothered to read all the transcripts from my wires. The prosecutors later reviewed tape transcripts that showed Johnny complimenting me on my sports jacket, and asking where I got it. In another tape, after he got into my car for a payoff, he asked me who made it and said it looked just like a limo.

But even without those tapes, Genson's arguments were nonsense. "*I* was passing out money to *him*," I testified. "I had my pockets full of money all the time, so I would not assume that made me out to be a bust-out."

In fact, the longer Eddy kept me on the stand, the more problems he made for his client. He kept asking open-ended questions that let me introduce other illegal things Johnny had done that were not part of the indictment. At one point, he went over a discussion we had had, during breakfast, about my bribe for passing the state law. Genson charged that I was using "double-talk" and had no reason to believe Johnny wanted a bribe for passing the law.

I replied, "I know what he's done in the past."

When he asked what that could be, it was like he loaded the gun and then handed it back so I could blow his brains out. I answered: "Sir, I was present in Vegas when he talked to Richie Guidice how he was going to work this deal." Giudice was a state senator Johnny talked into becoming a lobbyist. I went on to testify that Johnny explained how he would split our lobbying fees fifty-fifty, and then told us how to avoid paying taxes on our share.

Eddy started to sputter, realizing what he had done. He demanded to know why I didn't bring this story up during my direct examination. I answered, "I was told I couldn't, unless I was asked on cross-examination."

Before long, Eddy was whacking the defense table with his cane. "This is totally improper," he shouted, "and I move for a mistrial."

Now Johnny was on his feet and yelling, "This is ridiculous. He's absurd."

Judge George Lindberg sent the jury out of the courtroom. But Johnny still wasn't done with his tantrum. He slammed his chair against the table and yelled at the prosecutors, "Slander my name all over the world—you!" Then he marched out of the courtroom, leaving his wife behind to bawl her head off.

Eddy next staggered over to the bench, one hand clutching his chest and the other pointing at me. "This man is a legal assassin," he hissed. "Every time he opens his mouth, he plunges another dagger into my client."

I was dismissed, too; but later, when I went over the trial transcripts, I could see all the comments Eddy would make during the sidebars. As far as the judge was concerned, Genson took "risks" when he asked his open-ended questions, but Eddy blamed me for how things were unraveling. He told the judge, "I have known Robert Cooley for twenty-five years. He is as crafty a human being as there is. This is no accident. We are not dealing with some street guy that likes to talk. He's taking shots. . . . I've been doing this a long time, and I don't get these shots pulled on me."

But before the judge brought me back into the courtroom, he admonished Eddy, "Mr. Genson, I am going to ask that you restrain yourself. I realize that there is a certain amount of gesticulation associated with your presentation . . . but I don't think you are entitled to belittle the individuals who are representing the government. . . ."

Poor Judge Lindberg. This was only his second criminal trial and, as he admitted, "I am a very mild-mannered judge." But he was presiding over a madhouse. We adjourned for the weekend and when we returned, he tried to take back some control. He told me that I was "not a lawyer in these proceedings" and should keep my answers to "yes" and "no."

But then he said to Genson, "Next time I see that cane misused, it's going out the door." He warned both Johnny and Eddy that if there was another outburst, "I am not beyond arranging different housing."

Genson finished his cross-examination a few days later, but he had helped me open a Pandora's box filled with Johnny's other illegal activities. The prosecutors needed three more days of redirect to go into everything. Before I left the stand, Eddy still had to give me one more shot. "Is there any lie you won't tell to win?" he bellowed.

I calmly replied, "Do you expect me to perjure myself and put myself at risk?"

By the time I finished, I had spent fifteen days of testimony as a witness. Usually, after I was done with a trial, I would go to another floor in the building and wait for an FBI agent to take me to the airport. This time, when I walked into that room, it was full of agents with submachine guns and flak jackets. During the trial, someone had called in a tip to a reporter. He said that the Mob knew I was living in Richmond and planned to kill me before Christmas. I pulled up stakes again.

Meanwhile, back in the courtroom, Johnny and Eddy still had a few more dramatic moments for the jury. The day after I wrapped up my testimony, Genson put Steve Bowen on the stand. Eddy accused the FBI of pursuing Johnny as part of a vendetta against his father. At the mention of Senior's name, Johnny burst into sobs and "shook with emotion," according to the *Tribune*. I read that and had to think how Senior had started this all, when he pulled me aside in Counsellors Row and asked me to help his son. Johnny was never cut out to be the player his father wanted him to be. Who knows what Johnny would have become if Senior hadn't tried to live his dreams through him?

Like Judge Shields, Johnny, too, had to take the stand in his own defense, but then the defense got even more inane. First, Johnny testified that he never knew I had asked for a bribe. "Many times I didn't understand what he was talking about," Johnny said of me. "A lot of times I would not listen to what he was saying or just not pay attention."

Still, Johnny had to explain away the times I gave him money. In the beginning of the trial, Genson argued that I pocketed the money and never paid Johnny off. As proof, he played the tapes when I counted money to pay Marcy, Roti, and DeLeo. When I gave the $5,000 to Johnny in my car, I didn't count out each bill. It was crazy for Genson to bring up all these other payoffs, because it only confirmed the things I said about First Ward corruption.

But now, with Johnny on the stand, Genson totally reversed course. They would no longer deny that I paid off D'Arco. "Unfortunately," Johnny testified, "I took his money." With the Scotillo bribe, he claimed that he pocketed the $2,500 I paid him, and never intended to give the judge a $1,000 bribe.

"You lied to Cooley for a thousand bucks?" Mike Shepard asked.

"I lied to him because he kept bothering me," Johnny replied.

He told the court that he considered my $5,000 payment for the state law to be a "retainer" from my client, which Johnny described as a "national or international corporation."

Shepard then asked, "You were going to be paid by this national-international corporation in cash? In a car?"

"That's correct," Johnny answered.

In a bizarre appeal for sympathy, Johnny blurted out to the jury that he expected to be indicted for paying off Scotillo. Tom Durkin and Mike Shepard objected, but as far as I was concerned, he was just banging more nails into his own coffin.

In his closing argument, Mike Shepard told the jury: "You learned all about bills, Senator D'Arco-style. You learned how he takes in dollar bills, you learned how he puts through bills in the legislature, and you learned how he tried to sell you a bill of goods when he got caught on tape."

But in his closing statements, Genson acted like I was the one on trial. He called Johnny a sensitive poet and a "family man," who rose above his roots. But I was a "drunk," a "gambler," and a "womanizer," who was still mired in the gutter. "You can't reform a sewer rat," Genson told the jury. "The attempt to make [Robert Cooley] look like a reformed sinner was pitiful. He has been a trial lawyer for twenty years. He is as slippery as an eel."

Genson's description of me made the TV news, but it didn't have much effect on the jury. It took them seven hours to find Johnny guilty.

Again, when the newspapers discussed the case with the jury, they had to ask them about *my* credibility. But this time, the *Tribune* reported: "Because of the strength of the tapes' contents, forewoman Connie Kelly said, the jury did not even discuss the credibility of Cooley, formerly a longtime crooked lawyer.

" 'I wouldn't date him,' Kelly, a nurse from the west suburbs, said of Cooley. 'But I think he was a credible witness.' "

Judge Lindberg gave Johnny three years. Also, as part of the sentence, he ordered him to "never seek employment by any state."

Johnny didn't cry in court this time, but his response was typically wacky. "Somehow," he told the judge, "I must learn to live with myself." Evidently that meant living someplace else. He had already relocated to Florida with his wife. Just before he got out of prison, they let him take a plea on bribing Judge Scotillo. In return, he only had to serve another six months for that crime. For reasons I don't understand to this day, Scotillo was never indicted.

The day of the D'Arco verdict, the Feds finally decided they couldn't let defense attorneys like Tuite and Genson continue to smear me without some official response. Chicago U.S. Attorney Fred Foreman— in total contrast to Valukas—held a press conference to set the record straight. Tom Durkin and Mike Shepard joined in as well. Foreman praised me for having "opened a window to corruption."

Tom, for the umpteenth time, told the reporters that I had not been under investigation when I approached the Strike Force. In terms of my motives, Tom explained, "He was sick of what he was doing and sick of what he saw."

Only a few reporters attended this press conference. At least one of them was Matt O'Connor from the *Tribune*. He picked up their comments in the bottom of the story about Johnny's verdict, and the paper set the tone for future coverage with the next day's headline: "D'Arco Conviction Has Probe On A Roll."

CHAPTER 15

THE HARDER THEY FALL

could not wait for the case to begin against Pat Marcy and Fred Roti, but the trial didn't start until December 14, 1992—just about a year after Johnny's conviction. Some of the delay came from the typical back-and-forth over evidence, but most of it was related to the defendants complaining about their health, first Roti and then Marcy. By this time, Fred was seventy-two and Pat was seventy-nine, but I thought they were faking it. I knew the old Mob bosses had this deathbed stuff down to a science. There were even certain clinics they used to get phony diagnoses. Still, even the government doctors agreed that Pat had a "terminal" heart condition. To lessen the strain on him, the judge agreed to keep court in session only four hours a day and four days a week.

With all the counts in the indictment, the prosecutors needed the first day just for their opening statements. The defense took half of the next day for theirs. To my utter and total amazement, Eddy Genson represented Pat Marcy. I figured Marcy must have been getting a First Ward freebie from Genson—like Patty DeLeo got from Sam Banks. Eddy had failed so miserably in the D'Arco trial, I didn't see how anyone could use him for another Gambat case. Maybe money really did mean more to Marcy than life itself.

Once more, from his opening statement, Genson made me the focal point of the trial. "Other than Cooley, no one else will testify that Pat was any way involved in this case," Genson said. "It is only the word of Cooley regarding Aleman, regarding Chow and regarding Colella, the word of a lawyer who has prepared witnesses to lie and prepared himself to lie in this case. It's a word of a liar, a drunk, a bribe giver, a bribe taker, who took and gave money to let the drunk driver drive again, the killer kill again and the dope peddler sell dope again."

If Eddy was trying to play to the press, it wasn't working so well any more. In fact, the papers were not just referring to me any more as the "corrupt lawyer." Sometimes I was also the "government mole"—not yet your sterling citizen, but at least a few rungs up the animal kingdom ladder from snake and rat. Meanwhile, the media wasn't referring to Marcy as just a businessman. Both major papers finally reported that Bill Roemer, the former Chicago FBI agent, had identified him as a "made member" of the Mafia during a U.S. Senate hearing.

But Genson argued in his opening that if Marcy had done anything wrong, it was not criminal—it was political. "This case does not involve fixes," he told the jury. "It's about old men, brought up in a different system. It involves favors that are clearly political but not against the law. That's all politics is—favors. This, ladies and gentlemen, is old-time politics."

Engineering the acquittal of hit men was just politics? I had to hear how Eddy worked that one out with the jury.

When I entered the courtroom on my first day of testimony, I really looked forward to seeing Pat. I expected that with all the talk of illness, he might be shriveled or frail. But when I took the stand and glanced over at the defense table, there he was, sitting next to Genson, and he looked exactly as I remembered him—even with the pissed-off glare. I stared back as if he wasn't there; but when Genson looked the other way, I flashed Pat a wink and a smile. His glare got even darker, but then something caught in his throat, and he started to breathe more heavily.

Tom Durkin took me through the direct examination for the rest of the day. Once again, he was brilliant at laying out a complicated case in very simple terms for the jury, with great charts and photos. Counsellors Row had gone out of business shortly after Marcy and Roti were indicted, but there it was again, up on the easels. The prosecutors marked out the location of the table and the path Pat would take into the lobby of 100 North LaSalle and back past the elevators into the janitor's closet. Whenever I made a reference to organized crime or hit men, Genson would jump up with an objection. But what other words could I use to describe Johnny DiFronzo, Marco D'Amico, or Harry Aleman? Out of the presence of the jury, the judge instructed me to refer to anyone associated with organized crime as First Ward or First Ward associate. I thought that was a laugh. The judge didn't know how right he was.

We skipped the next day, a Wednesday, as part of the judge's shortened schedule for Marcy, and then returned after lunch on Thursday. Although I spent most of my testimony looking at Tom or the jury, I could still see Pat out of the corner of my eye. He kept bringing his hand to his mouth, like he was ready to cough. By late in the afternoon, I was up to the fixed case for Mike Colella. Suddenly, Pat started coughing again, in two long jags. At first, I tried to ignore it, thinking he was trying to distract the jurors, but after the second fit, the judge called a brief recess. When Pat came back, he was still sucking wind.

We adjourned less than an hour later. That was the last I ever saw of Pat Marcy. He went straight from the Federal Building to the intensive care unit of a suburban hospital. The doctors reported that he had suffered a heart attack at some point in the previous twenty-four hours. They predicted that he would need another half year before he could return to trial, but he didn't live that long. He died three months later. Still the guy with the upper hand—right to the very end. He was going to deny us the chance to see him humbled, even if it killed him.

The remaining trial against Fred Roti was an anti-climax—like seeing the shadow instead of the monster in a horror movie. At least I was done with Genson. Roti's lawyer, Tom Breen, was much more slick and competent, and he knew where he was going in the cross. He wasn't out to score points in some bigger battle against Gambat and me. He was trying to reduce the sentence for his client. The tapes with Freddy were too damning for a not guilty across the board.

Eventually, Breen admitted that Roti took the zoning bribe and claimed the Chancery fix was one of those "old-fashioned" political favors. But when it came to the On Leong fix, he denied everything. Of course, the Lenny Chow trial happened before I became a government informant, so I never had Fred's voice on tape from back then. I'm sure

I could have gotten him to talk about the case when I was wearing the wire, but the day that I had approached him, he was behind the metal detector in City Hall. I only mentioned Roti's name in passing to Pat Marcy when we discussed the On Leong grand jury transcript outside Counsellors Row. Our best evidence was a tape I made with Wilson Moy. He told me that he had been paying Roti off for other things as well. Moy said, "I found out, with him, money first, money first, money first." But with his accent, Moy's comments did not come across clearly on the tape—especially when he said, "Alderman Roti."

For this trial, Tom Durkin gave his most powerful closing statement. "You can get away with murder in Chicago," he told the jury, "if you have a fix in the First Ward and the money to pay for it." During the course of the trial, he assembled a chart with pictures of all the judges and politicians involved in the cases that were fixed. Pointing toward the chart, he said, "At the top of this chain of corruption, this rogue's gallery of photos, stood Pat Marcy and Fred Roti. They pulled the strings."

Breen used his closing to attack me. Because I was "sly and treacherous," he said, I could trap Roti into committing a couple of minor offenses. But with the On Leong fix, he suggested, I kept all the money I got from the Chinese. He then described me as "a dishonest, conniving manipulator, who had not done a decent thing in his life."

Mike Shepard picked up on that line in his rebuttal and said, "He caught Fred Roti. That's a pretty decent thing."

The jury deliberated two and a half days, and Breen's strategy paid off. Freddy got a pass on the On Leong charges—a potential nine-year sentence. But he was found guilty on eleven other counts for the zoning and Chancery bribes. After the trial, the jurors explained that my tapes on the murder fix were not as clear-cut as the ones for the other charges. Maybe we had just set the bar too high with all the other evidence we had.

But the judge, Marvin Aspen, had no doubts about Fred Roti's guilt, and he threw the book at him during sentencing, giving him the maximum term of four years, an additional three years of supervision, and fines over $125,000. For Judge Aspen, the case didn't have to do with the specific illegal acts, but the holes in the system that permitted them. He said, "The power of the First Ward to effectuate that kind of corruption in the judicial system . . . was not an isolated case." Commenting on Marcy's influence on the appointment of judges, he asked, "What does that judge do down the pike when that judge receives a telephone call . . . from Mr. Marcy or the First Ward? We know what that judge does, because we've seen it in this case. Whether it's Judge Wilson, Judge Maloney, or other judges who have been implicated in this case as being the order-takers from the First Ward. It is truly a chilling spectacle."

In asking the judge to go easy on Roti, Breen described him as a "role model" to other aldermen. Judge Aspen replied: "The specter, Mr. Breen, of Mr. Roti being a role model, of counseling other aldermen in the City of Chicago . . . is not a very happy one. Mr. Roti's corruption and greed spread over many years. Whether it's courts or zoning, or other types of activity, Mr. Roti has committed serious crimes. . . ."

The judge went on to explain that the crimes were not "against individuals alone," but also against the reputations of honest judges and city officials. Then he added, "But there is a bigger victim, and that's the whole democratic process. When you have courts of law that are fixed, when you have city government that is fixed, what you're doing, really, is attacking the core of democracy. You're saying that this democracy . . . is the same as any other banana republic or corrupt regime."

During the trial and the sentencing hearing, nothing was more pathetic than the slavish little lackeys who showed up as witnesses and boosters for Roti. Prime among them was Alderman Bernie Stone from the 50th Ward on the northern tip of the city. Many times he had joined me, Marcy, and Roti for breakfast at the First Ward table. I had several of those chitchats on tape. Bernie is Jewish, but Marcy and Roti hated Jews—even more than they hated blacks. It seemed like every time Bernie was at the table, they found a reason to start badmouthing different Jewish people or start telling "cheap Jew" jokes. Bernie Stone just sat there and listened. He never said a word. This wasn't accidental or just insensitive. They intentionally wanted to insult him to put him in his place. Those were the sorts of people that Roti and Marcy were. To later watch Stone jump up to vouch for their *character* turned my stomach.

I wanted to say to him, "Those people never had an ounce of respect for you." But a guy like Bernie probably had no respect for himself either.

The trial against Judge Tom Maloney started a month after the Roti conviction. The indictment had him fixing five cases—three of them for murder, including the Lenny Chow trial. As we went on from one Gambat trial to the next, there was always some new hurdle to clear. This time, we had no incriminating tapes with the judge on them. Instead, we had tapes and testimony of the people around him. After he was indicted, Swano finally decided to cop a plea and cooperate with the Feds against Maloney. After the court bailiff, Lucius Robinson, was convicted for perjury, he also agreed to testify against Maloney for a lighter sentence.

The judge's co-defendant was Robert McGee, a lawyer the government accused of being the bagman on some of the fixed cases. He was a Casper Milquetoast, like Herb Barsy, the attorney Maloney had forced down my throat as the co-counsel in the Lenny Chow case. I had to believe he was terrified of Maloney, or he would have flipped too. The government would have gladly cut him loose, like they did with Billy Swano. Instead, McGee was like a ghost in the courtroom. Nobody paid much attention to him one way or another. Whenever there was a sidebar, he'd go to the coatroom in the back of the court and pace back and forth.

At sixty-seven, Maloney was as big and beefy as ever. He sat behind the defense table like he was still on the bench, with his arms crossed over his chest. As one reporter wrote, he "scowled." He scowled at the witnesses. He scowled at the prosecutors. Even at the judge and jury— almost like he was telling them, "What right do *you* have to judge *me*?" He had retired just a few months before the Marcy and Roti indictments, so he must have known something was up, but he also believed that Swano would never flip on him. According to Billy, the last time they talked, he asked, "Are you standing tall?"

Swano replied, "I hear they are trying to put a tax case on you."

He said Maloney got "red-faced" and then replied, "Don't worry about me. You take care of yourself."

After Swano heard that I had him on tape, he did take care of himself, and agreed to cooperate with the government. I certainly wasn't the central witness in this trial, but I was the one who got Swano to flip, and without him the government had no case. When I took the stand, Maloney's eyes narrowed, his faced turned red, and he kept mouthing the words, "Motherfucking liar. Motherfucking liar." Sometimes he said it loud enough for me to hear.

His brother, a retired copper, sat behind him, and he glared at me the whole time too. It was quite a sight to see these red-faced Irish guys with white hair jawing at me—like some kind of "motherfucking" choir. When no one was looking, I'd give Tom a big wink and a smile, and watch his face get redder.

In his opening remarks, Maloney's lawyer, Terry Gillespie, called me, Swano, and Robinson "three rotten eggs." He said, "They're con men extraordinaire, three of the best in the business, and they're going to try to con you."

"Con man" was about the nicest thing any defense lawyer had called me. But Gillespie, who was a good lawyer, put his finger on the problem for the prosecution. Swano and Robinson—who were closer to Maloney's illegal activity than I was—really were stoolpigeons. They testified in this trial to reduce their own sentences. What they said about Maloney *before* they flipped had more credibility than what they said under oath, because it would help corroborate their testimony. Terry Hake, the mole in Operation Greylord, came in to confirm that Robinson had fingered Maloney as one of the judges who could be "approached" for a fix in criminal court. My job was to walk through my tapes and videos of Swano, as he told me what happened behind the scenes in the El Rukn trial.

When it came time for my cross-examination, Maloney tried to run the show with his defense team. I was told later that he wanted his lawyers to take me over the coals and smear my family. Evidently they talked him out of it. Gillespie didn't even do my cross-examination. He left that to the co-counsel, Tom Breen. He was businesslike, just as he had been in the Roti trial, and smart enough to realize that they shouldn't make me their focus. That had to be Billy Swano, and the defense couldn't have asked for a more tempting target. As Gillespie put

ROBERT COOLEY WITH HILLEL LEVIN

it, he not only represented the El Rukns, "he did dope with them." He also went back and forth a few times with the Feds before he decided to come in. I was told he seemed shifty on the stand—not able to look anyone in the eye.

Besides my tapes, the government had other evidence to corroborate Swano's testimony, but there was one missing link. At a critical point in the El Rukn trial, Swano exchanged phone calls with Robert McGee, Maloney's bagman. According to Swano, McGee called the judge in his chambers to discuss the fix and then called Swano to tell him the fix was off and that Maloney was giving "the books back." The government had records for Swano's calls to McGee, but not McGee's calls to Maloney.

The day the prosecutors were winding up their case, we learned that McGee's phone records still existed. Most big phone companies throw those out after eighteen months, but the apartment complex where McGee lived used a little local firm. When that company sent someone to testify to McGee's home number, he brought along the records for every call McGee had made. An assistant prosecutor noticed them in his briefcase and, bang, the Feds suddenly had very important new evidence.

In the words of the *Sun-Times*, the phone records fit Swano's story "like a long-lost glove." The calls from McGee went out to Maloney's chambers exactly as he had said in his testimony. With this unexpected corroboration, Billy's credibility got a huge boost with the jury.

There was also one other piece of circumstantial evidence that really clinched the case for the jurors. Over several periods of time, the Feds observed Maloney buying money orders. Later, during deliberation, the jurors asked themselves, "Why would a big-shot like Maloney stand in line for a money order?" They figured he must have had something to hide.

This is the common sense at the heart of our jury system, and it's more important than any fancy arguments or high-tech evidence. Juries are what the First Ward tried to avoid at all cost. And a jury finally took down the high and mighty Maloney. For fixing four of the five cases in the indictment—including all three murder trials—they found him guilty of racketeering, racketeering conspiracy, conspiracy to commit extortion, and obstruction of justice.

For the sentencing hearing, prosecutor Scott Mendeloff practically staged another trial to make sure the judge threw the book at Maloney. In his opening remarks, Scott said, "It is the view of the government that this is, simply, the most pernicious course of judicial corruption in the history of this state." Scott then explained that the hearing would help "complete the picture of Tom Maloney's life of corruption." In addition to testifying on cases Maloney fixed as a judge, witnesses would testify on cases he had had a hand in fixing as a defense attorney. This included what Scott called "one of the most notorious case fixes in the history of the county, *People vs. Harry Aleman*." Maloney had been Harry's attorney, until I had Marcy replace him with the out-of-town lawyer, Frank Whalen.

In many ways, this hearing was our dress rehearsal for retrying Aleman. Scott even brought in my former girlfriend, Cathy Fleming, to corroborate my relationship with Judge Wilson. Also, for the first time, I testified about the things I saw at Counsellors Row during Tony Spilotro's M&M murder trial, and how Marcy indicated the fix was in for that case.

After Cathy and I were done with our testimony at the sentencing hearing, Scott brought in a bunch of other witnesses, including a former cellmate of Harry and a former client of Maloney who was in Hook LaPietra's crew. The whole proceeding took more than two days, and, at the very end of it, Judge Leinenweber gave Maloney a chance to speak. He went on for two hours.

Remembering that the old windbag had once been a boxer in college, the *Sun-Times* wrote, "Thomas J. Maloney went down swinging." Although he hadn't testified in his own trial, Maloney went through the evidence, point by point, and denied everything. Along the way, he had some choice words for everyone involved in the case—even some reporters who followed it, like Carol Marin, the investigative reporter and anchorwoman for WMAQ-TV. Of course, the choicest words were saved for the three people who put him in this jackpot: Swano ("a conniving slime rat"), me ("a corrupt, inept slob"), and even Scott ("devious, and I don't think the truth is in him").

By the time he was done, Maloney stamped out any shred of sympathy that might have remained for him. There he was, an arrogant piece of shit in all his glory. To have him say something bad about you was like a badge of honor.

After listening to all of this Maloney baloney, Judge Leinenweber said, "What you told us here today is too little too late." He explained that they would not retry the case during the hearing, but then he added: "I personally agree one hundred percent with that jury verdict. I don't know what caused you to go wrong . . . whether it was money or whether you have ties to organized crime, I don't know. But you did agree to fix these particular cases."

Scott was hoping the judge would give Maloney twenty-five years. Leinenweber gave him fifteen instead; but, with federal guidelines, he had to serve at least thirteen—practically a death sentence for a guy pushing seventy years old. All in all, I couldn't have asked for too much more.

The Stillo trial opened in July 1993, just three months after Maloney's conviction. By this time, Gambat had such a head of steam behind it, there was no stopping us. The timing could not have been worse for Judge Stillo and his nephew, Joey. On the surface, this seemed like our weakest case. The judge did find my "client," the FBI agent, guilty, and no money ever did change hands.

Joey had attended almost all of the previous Gambat trials, and tried to stare me down each time. He probably watched me every day that I testified against Johnny D'Arco. Besides giving me dirty looks, he apparently didn't watch anything else going on in the courtroom, because he ended up choosing Ed Genson as his lawyer.

True to form, Ed went on to bungle the case for Joey and Judge Stillo, too. Once again, he tried to put me on trial, except now he called me "the most corrupt attorney in the history of Cook County." He took bits and pieces that came out in our previous cases (some involving his previous clients) and tried to tie them together like cans on a dog's tail. The On Leong fix, the Colella fix, the money I owed to the bookies, the money I owed to the IRS—for all these reasons, he charged, I went running to the Feds.

By trying to tar me, he just reminded the jury that all my cases had ended up in convictions. When he cross-examined me, this time for seven hours, he only boosted my credibility. The government had two other lawyers testify about paying off Judge Stillo, including Billy Swano, but the jury only convicted him for the charges that involved me—even for cases I fixed with the judge long before I wore the wire.

The prosecutors wanted a sentence of ten years for Judge Stillo, but Judge Leinenweber told them, "I'm dealing with a 77-year-old man," and gave him just four years. He only served a third of that before his parole. Joey got just two years, and served eight months at the federal pen in Oxford, Wisconsin, where all his Mob friends used to go. Then, after he did his time, he came home and suddenly died. Very strange, right to the end.

As we were wrapping up the Stillo trial, I was in the papers for another hearing—my own. A few years back, when I first appeared on the stand, the state's Attorney Registration and Disciplinary Commission opened an investigation into my conduct. This was usually the first step in getting you disbarred.

It was nothing less than a kick in the teeth. Even though the government had *indicted* Johnny D'Arco, Judge Shields, Patty DeLeo, and Maloney, the Disciplinary Commission had not opened an investigation into their conduct. Just mine. I had already suspended my license and I never planned to practice again, but for me, this was a matter of justice, pure and simple. I petitioned the Illinois Supreme Court to let me surrender my law license, so there would be no need for a hearing. But the court declined my request and told the Disciplinary Commission to proceed with their hearing. The Illinois legal establishment was clearly looking to slap me down. When asked about the Disciplinary Commission's actions, Barry Miller, the head of a Chicago legal reform group, put it this way: "A series of circumstances have created the appearance that the system may be 'punishing' Robert Cooley for cooperating with federal authorities in exposing judicial corruption."

To add insult to injury, the Disciplinary Commission scheduled my hearings in the middle of the Maloney trial. For evidence of misconduct, their investigators submitted the transcripts of my testimony in previous trials. The proceeding was like a kangaroo court. The board took less than an hour to recommend disbarment. I sent the commission a letter asking for another hearing. I explained that I had no desire to practice law again. Instead, "This concerns whether my legal career should be allowed to end with some salvage of dignity, or as an exceptional example of professional disgrace."

When my letter leaked to the press, the *Tribune* thought it was very funny. Their article began, "Poor, misunderstood Robert Cooley." It said that I was crying because: "The criminal-defense bar is focusing on his past career as a bribe-paying lawyer and a fixer. . . ." In my letter to the commission, the paper said, I was "peddling" a "message" that "we should be filled with admiration for his work as an undercover informant and key prosecution witness in the federal Operation Gambat investigation."

Actually, there was another message I was peddling. What about looking at *all* the lawyers and judges in the Gambat investigations who were caught doing unethical and illegal things? Like Alderman Ed Burke, Judge Anthony Scotillo, Chief Judge Buck Sorrentino, Joe "Mr. Ethics" Ettinger, and Judge Lawrence Passarella. For whatever reason, the government didn't indict them, but why didn't the Disciplinary Commission open up investigations on them? I sent a letter that offered to provide the necessary information, but never got a response. The Feds told me they would hand transcripts of my wires over to the Disciplinary Commission for further investigation, but I knew that would never happen. It would raise questions about why the government never brought charges.

Clearly some of these people were protected, either because of their personal connections or because of the lawyers they chose. A couple of years after I left Chicago, the FBI had me fly in to Milwaukee to help develop a case on Ed Burke. Cammon had just died of AIDS, but obviously Maloney was a hot topic for the Feds, and now they were willing to take a second look at all of his bench trials. They put me up in a hotel and even got a conference room for the day. The agents told me they were finally ready to investigate Burke. I just laughed at them. "Why are you wasting my time?" I asked. "Nothing is going to happen to him."

"Oh, no," one agent said. "We're here to build a case."

"Then call Judge Cieslik," I said and gave him his phone number. "You have to get to him right away. He's getting up there in years."

Two months later, I got a call from a new FBI agent on the Burke case. "Do you have that phone number for Judge Cieslik?" he asked. "We lost it."

After the Stillo case, I realized that Gambat had reached as high into the political and judicial establishment as it was going to go. I had to get resigned to that, and turn my attention back to the lower-level hoodlums—especially Harry Aleman.

In the early nineties, the Feds had done their best to make life difficult for the Outfit. They convicted Johnny DiFronzo and some other Mob bosses for trying to take over an Indian casino in California and collect on Tony Spilotro debts in Vegas. A few months after I left town, they went after Chicago-area gambling operations by arresting Rocky Infelice, Harry Aleman, and seventeen other muscle guys—mostly from the Cicero group. The charges related to the street-tax racket and how they killed off independent bookies like Hal Smith to keep the others in line. I was ready to testify about the time Harry wanted me to find independent bookies for him to grab. But Harry was not about to risk a jury trial—especially if I was going to testify against him. Despite his tough talk at the racetrack about never going back to prison, he copped a plea. It was a smart move. Rocky Infelice went to trial, got convicted, and the judge sentenced him to life. With good behavior, Harry expected to be released by 1998 or, worst case, the year 2000.

But I had other ideas. I kept after Tom Durkin and Gary Shapiro to share my testimony about the Harry Aleman trial with the Cook County State's Attorney. Finally, the Feds arranged for me to meet with Pat Quinn, an assistant state's attorney in charge of the Organized Crime Unit. We had a little rendezvous in Arizona. He was my kind of lawyer— a big, balding, round-faced Irish guy who loved a good joke. We ended up in a bar that was a hangout for some Chicago Mob people. The place had a little gimmick where you would sign a dollar bill and they would post it on the wall. Pat had me sign one "Bob Cooley," just to bust the balls of any Outfit guy who happened to pass by.

Pat told me that he had discussed retrying Aleman with the lawyers in the state's attorneys' appellate office. These were considered their best legal minds, and they told him that there was absolutely no way to beat double jeopardy. But Pat was convinced otherwise. He had the theory that Harry had never had *any* jeopardy during the first trial, because the bribe assured him of a not guilty verdict.

On December 8, 1993, the Cook County State's Attorney, Jack O'Malley, held a press conference to announce that the state had indicted Aleman again for the murder of Logan. "Justice took a hit in 1977," O'Malley said. "A murder case was fixed." O'Malley was one of those rare Republicans elected to office in Cook County, and at first I thought he was a gutsy, independent guy, but he turned out to be a politician like the rest of them. When Mike Wallace and *60 Minutes* wanted to do a story about the case, O'Malley gave the go-ahead—until he found out that Mike Wallace had no intention of interviewing him. He then prevented me from talking to Wallace, which killed their story. Funny enough, they already had the interview with Harry in the can.

Harry's lawyer was my old gin-playing pal, Allan Ackerman, and a technical battle like this was right up his alley. When the press asked him about the indictment, he quoted from the Fifth Amendment provision—"nor shall any person be subject for the same offense to be twice put in jeopardy of life or limb." Typical Allan. Then he told the reporter, "The public prosecutor cannot subordinate constitutional protections for political gain."

Putting Aleman on a pedestal of constitutional protection was like dressing up a pig in a tuxedo. But I'm sure Allan had to tell himself something to justify defending a monster like Harry.

The *Tribune* called the indictment "Mission Impossible," and quoted a "double-jeopardy authority," from the University of Chicago law school. "There might be some hope if the state could show that the defendant was really a prime mover of the bribery effort against the judge," he said. "Even then, it would be a very difficult case to win."

But we got an important break when the case was assigned to Circuit Court Judge Mike Toomin, a super-smart guy with the guts to back a tough decision. In a forty-five-page opinion, he ruled that a fix really did negate double jeopardy. If the defendant knows a judge has been bribed, he argued, then "the claim of jeopardy is more imagined than real." In reaching his decision, Toomin said he researched common law back to the Magna Carta.

But next, we had to prove to him that the Logan case really was fixed—and that Harry had a hand in it. I don't think any preliminary hearing was ever more important. You could even say it was more important than the trial.

The hearing was held in the judge's courtroom in the old Criminal Courthouse on 26th Street and California. To protect me, it was held in secrecy. Allan Ackerman and Aleman didn't know about it until the last minute. When I took the stand, I didn't bother to smile or wink at Harry. You can't play games with a stone-cold creep like that. But when I did look at him, I was surprised to see that he had gone completely gray.

The whole proceeding was very businesslike. Judge Toomin did not allow any grandstanding from the lawyers or digressing by the witnesses, and he hurried us all along. I had already told the Aleman fix story so many times, I could have done it in my sleep, but for the purposes of the hearing, I gave more details about Harry's personal involvement: my first meeting with him when Marco brought me to The King's Inn motel; how Harry gave me his wife's number to relay a message; how he and Butch met with me about bribing a witness; and how they took my business cards after his acquittal and referred me a bunch of new business. Also, I discussed how Cathy Fleming was with me when I paid off the judge. Her presence that night had become crucial in connecting me with Frank Wilson.

In his cross-examination, Allan Ackerman zeroed in on our biggest obstacle in proving the fix and getting a conviction—the passage of time. One after another, he asked about the key people in my story: John D'Arco Sr., Pat Marcy, Judge Wilson, Butch Petrocelli, and Harry's out-of-town lawyer, Frank Whalen.

"Living or dead?"

The answer—for all of them—was dead. As Allan later joked in his closing argument, the trial would be like a "séance." Which would make me the medium. I was the government witness who would do most of the talking for the deceased.

The only other government witness at the hearing was Vincent Rizza.

During the first Aleman trial, he had been a Rush Street vice cop. And also an independent bookie, a drug dealer, and a cokehead. Harry "grabbed" him and became a fifty-fifty partner in Rizza's book. He saw him practically every day to collect the street tax, and sometimes they would chat. Rizza testified that Harry had once said, "Committing murder in Chicago was okay if you killed the right people."

During the murder trial, Rizza remembered, he had seen Harry and told him that "it looked bad" and "the newspapers were crucifying him."

But Harry was unconcerned. According to Rizza, Aleman said, "It wasn't a problem. It was taken care of."

Of course Rizza was not your most upstanding witness, and Allan went to town on Rizza's rap sheet, which included perjury. But Harry could not deny that he knew Rizza or me. When he copped a plea on the Rocky Infelice street tax case, Harry admitted his association with Rizza and that he had asked me to help him find and grab independent bookies like Rizza.

The only defense witness at the hearing was the nephew of Frank Whalen. He had helped his uncle prepare Harry's case and, as expected, he testified that he never saw me. But during the cross, Pat Quinn brought out the fact that this nephew was only a few years out of law school. Why would Whalen have stayed in Florida and relied on this kid for a murder case if he didn't know the fix was in?

Assistant State's Attorney Scott Cassidy gave the closing argument. He summed up our testimony, plus all the incriminating circumstantial evidence: how Harry first asked to substitute for Judge Wilson, and then turned around and accepted him; how Whalen was incredibly lazy in preparing for the trial. Based on this record, Cassidy argued, the trial "shouts of impropriety. The stench reeks."

It smelled for Judge Toomin, too. One month later, he ruled that Harry was not protected by double jeopardy and should be retried for the murder of Billy Logan. In most other preliminary hearings, judges only need to find probable cause. But this time, Toomin had to find that a fix actually had taken place and blame Harry in the process.

In his ruling, Toomin made a judgment about me, too, because my testimony was central to the state's case. The judge wrote: "I find [Cooley] to be a credible witness. He was persuasive. He had a good memory. There was clarity to his testimony, and there was very little contradiction."

Speaking for his client, Ackerman said that Harry was "utterly amazed that any sworn judicial officer could believe an informant like Robert Cooley."

Again, the *Tribune* turned to its so-called "double jeopardy expert" for his opinion, and he predicted that the Appeals Court would overturn Toomin's ruling. "Bribing a judge is an extreme case," the so-called expert said. "But once you start creating exceptions to double jeopardy protection, you undermine a great deal of its value."

Well, this joker was wrong again. A panel of the Appellate Court unanimously affirmed Toomin's ruling, which went all the way to the U.S. Supreme Court and beat back every challenge. From the time the State's Attorney first issued the indictment, it would take more than four years to finally get Harry's trial under way.

In the meantime, we were able to clean up the leftover mobster garbage from my investigation. There were the bookie cases against the likes of Dominic Barbaro. (We never indicted Bob Johnson, because he was arrested on another charge and supposedly hanged himself in the federal lockup.) We also brought an indictment for perjury against Blackie Pesoli. While I was wearing a wire, he had asked me to help him fix a divorce case for an insurance executive. He copped a plea and got an eleven-month prison sentence.

In November 1994, just as the statute of limitations was running out, the Feds indicted Marco D'Amico and nine other members of his crew, including Bobby Abbinante, Tony Doty, his brother Carl, and my old copper pal Ricky Borelli. Besides charges for bookmaking, extortion, and racketeering, the indictment also included conspiracy to commit robbery—Marco's little plot to rob my card game in Wisconsin. According to the papers, at the time of his arrest, Marco was "second-in-command" to Johnny DiFronzo.

Marco had once said to me, "Nobody wears a wire on us and lives to talk about it." Fortunately, I lived, and I was more than happy to talk about it, but I knew that Marco wanted no part of me in that court-room. Five months after his arrest, he copped a plea. Although he admitted his guilt, his agreement with the government stipulated that he "refused to cooperate with the government." Marco knew what happened to stoolpigeons.

During the sentencing hearing, Marco's lawyer talked about his "devotion" to his family and then introduced "his wife—of 35 years—and four daughters." I guess all the mistresses couldn't show up for the occasion. According to the *Tribune*, the lawyer then told the judge that Marco "had visited Skid Row dressed up as Santa Claus, sponsored youth baseball teams, had a restaurant he operated give free food to poor children and anonymously left boxes of basketballs at play-grounds."

The judge was not impressed. She gave him twelve years and three months. Ricky got off much easier, with ten months of prison and two years of supervision.

Besides my work in the courts, during the mid-nineties, I testified at hearings about the Mob's influence in the unions. Bit by bit, the Justice Department was trying to take back the Chicago locals from the Mafia, especially for the Teamsters and the Laborers' International Union of North America. If the government's hearing officer could make a credible link between a union official and organized crime, he could throw him out of office and replace him with a trustee.

The Laborers Union represented the lowest level of unskilled workers. Most of the members were ditch diggers and street sweepers who worked for the city. For decades, their local had been the personal property of Hook LaPietra and the Chinatown group. Frank Caruso and Bruno Caruso, the brothers who ran the local, took down six-figure salaries. No-show laborer jobs and union positions were filled with Mojos, their family and friends.

I had no trouble linking the Carusos with LaPietra and the rest of the Chinatown group. They were like fixtures at all my favorite places on Rush Street and in Chinatown. The Laborers Union hearings were usually conducted in a hotel ballroom, but for me they had a special session in an FBI conference room. For hours I talked about the old days, hanging out at Faces, making bets at the social clubs and race-track, or dropping by the late-night dice games in Chinatown. It made me remember how much fun I had once had.

I'm sure my testimony did a lot of good for the unions and the city, but I was still biding my time until I was back in court with Harry. This would be the final curtain—on Operation Gambat and my life in Chicago.

Finally, on September 22, 1997, the State of Illinois took its second crack at Harry Aleman. In the words of the *Tribune*, the trial opened "a new chapter in the history of American jurisprudence." Pat Quinn, the prosecutor who had done so much to get Harry retried, had been elected to the Appellate Court, but we still had Scott Cassidy on the case, along with another veteran state's attorney, Neil Linehan. Oddly enough, for his lawyer, Harry reached out of state to a guy from Kentucky named Kevin McNally. Evidently he had just reversed a death sentence for one of the killers in Harry's old crew, and Aleman was convinced he could work a miracle for him, too.

I had never had security like I did for this case. Months before the trial, the guards at the federal prison caught Harry slipping a note to his stepson. It read: "The two will be taken care of if this goes to trial, one after the other." The Feds considered me to be one of the "two." An FBI agent on my cases, Vic Switski, spent two weeks preparing special protection for my route in and out of the courtroom. This time, when we drove to the city from my out-of-town hotel, it was in a motorcade with cars in front and in back. As we got closer to Chicago, they shut down traffic on the freeway and then the surface roads leading to the old Cook County Criminal Courthouse. Since there was no basement entrance like at the Federal Building, I was surrounded by SWAT TEAM FBI agents with flak jackets when I got out of the car. Inside the courthouse, they had another two dozen agents with machine guns, and they led me to the judges' elevators. All the courtrooms were locked down while I walked through the halls. To get into Judge Toomin's court, you were searched and then had to go through a metal detector.

Still, when I walked into the courtroom, it was standing room only. I saw FBI agents, lawyers from my other trials, and family members of the victim, Billy Logan. The first witness had been Logan's sister, and she remembered how he had died in her arms. Harry sat there at the defense table in a brown sport jacket over a polo shirt—like some guy eating lunch at a country club. He had his family there, too. Reporters wrote that he blew kisses to his wife each day. He also had some other friends as spectators. One goon kept staring daggers at me. He looked familiar, and I pointed him out to Vic. When the FBI ran a check on him, they found out he was a hit man for the Mexican Mafia. He still had an outstanding warrant, so they could lock him up.

Aleman's lawyer, McNally, referred to me in his opening statement by saying, "The only reason we are here is because of a corrupt lawyer."

Boy, was that ever true. In every way.

He went on to argue, "This is a murder case. This is not a bribery case. . . . Mr. Aleman did not bribe anyone. Mr. Aleman does not know anything about a bribe. Frank Wilson was an honest judge."

In just those few words, he had set up the challenge for my testimony. I had to convince the jury that Judge Wilson had not been honest, that he did take a bribe, and that Harry knew all about it. Unlike my other Gambat trials, this case was not built on tapes and transcripts. Absolutely everything I said—about things that had happened twenty-five years ago—would have to come from my memory with very little corroboration from other sources.

But by this time, after all the testifying I had done, remembering was not such a big deal. I had a way of putting myself back into those moments the lawyers asked about. When the assistant State's Attorney, Neil Linehan, asked me about Counsellors Row, I could see the First Ward table in the corner and then the lobby outside, where Senior introduced me to Marcy. I heard Pat tell me about an important case and ask, "Do you have somebody that can handle it?" It was like the whole scene materialized before my eyes.

It was the same when I described The King's Inn motel and my meeting with Harry. He walked into the room and pumped my hand, "Hey, how ya doing? How ya doing?" And then bore in on me with that evil eye, and asked, "Are you sure you can handle it? Are you sure this judge is going to throw the case out?"

When I got to the point in my testimony where I made the final payoff to Judge Wilson—in that stinky bathroom—I saw him, too. Right in front of me in the courtroom. Standing there, rumpled and half-drunk, a little off-balance on his gimpy leg.

"I gave him the money," I testified.

"What money?" Neil asked.

"The seventy-five hundred," I said. I started to break down.

"What was his reaction?" Neil asked.

I could see Judge Wilson looking at me and I put my hand up to my eyes. Tears were running down my face. "He was . . . He was . . ." I cleared my throat. Then I said to the court, "He was a broken man."

I looked again at my vision of the judge, and saw him standing there with the envelope. I heard him ask, "That's all I'm going to get?"

I saw him turn his back on me when I tried to explain. I saw him start to walk out of the bathroom, and then turn around to say, "You destroyed me."

He was right. I destroyed him.

And I destroyed myself, too.

AFTERLIFE

Harry's lawyer didn't put up much of a fight during my cross-examination. He kept me on the stand for a few hours, and then I was gone.

The surprise witness for the defense was Billy Logan's ex-wife, who is also Harry's second cousin. She had already said that Logan beat her, but now she had something new to add. She testified that she had dated Harry's old partner in crime, Butch Petrocelli. She told a story about a time when Logan tried to break into her house while she was with Butch. She said that the two guys went out into the alley, and she heard Butch threaten to kill Logan.

You had to laugh. Harry probably had been the one who asked Joe Ferriola to have Petrocelli tortured and killed. Now, to get himself out of this jackpot, he was ready to dig up Butch for help.

The jury didn't buy it. After four hours of deliberation, they found Harry guilty. According to the *Tribune*, Logan's brother and sister were weeping with joy. Harry blinked a couple of times.

With this case, the prosecutors did more than beat double jeopardy. It was also the first time a hit man had been convicted for murder in the history of Chicago. Some record for the town that Al Capone made famous. Scott Cassidy, the assistant state's attorney, said, "It's a great day for American justice."

When it came time for the sentence, Judge Toomin did not take any chance that Harry Aleman would ever get parole. He gave him from one hundred to three hundred years. As important as all that time is the fact that it's state time. Once Harry completed the sentence for his street tax charge, he had to leave the cushy federal pen in Oxford, Wisconsin, and go back to a nasty state prison in Dixon, Illinois, where he'll serve out the rest of his days.

The moment Harry's guilty verdict was announced, I should have been as happy as the Logans. Instead, I felt a terrible void. It was like I had nothing more to live for.

The years since then have blown by me without much purpose. I still come to Chicago every once in a while, to see family and friends, but I do it without warning, and don't stay too long. Mostly I'm a nomad. I've already roamed across the country and stayed in what seems like a million different places. When I make new friends, I have to be careful about what I say. After a few years, I feel the need to move again.

Mostly what I have left is the investigation. I know if my father is looking down, he has to laugh. Operation Gambat was really my life's work—part of the Master Plan that he would say God had mapped out for me. In a bizarre way, everything I did leading up to it prepared me to help the government get all those convictions.

So what did Operation Gambat really accomplish?

For one thing, there wasn't another Mob hit in Chicago for ten years after I left town, and it's been a rare event ever since. This is not a small thing in a city where, for most of a century, mobsters were whacking each other on a regular basis. Finally, even the Outfit's lowest-level street thug realizes that cases can't be fixed; that you can't get away with murder.

In 1993, after the first eleven convictions in Gambat, a report about my investigation was written for the Illinois Supreme Court's Special Commission on the Administration of Justice. Reforms were recommended, and eventually made, in the Cook County Circuit Court that affected the way judges are appointed and cases are assigned, so it would be impossible for another Pat Marcy to manipulate trials. In addition, the court now has an independent watchdog as a kind of check on the judges.

These days, the old Outfit is a shadow of itself. To put the big bosses away, the Feds used several successful investigations. But I believe that Operation Gambat took out the hit men and the protection of the courts, which had been the foundation for the Mob's power in Chicago. No Young Turks will ever organize street crime the way they did for Tony Accardo. I even played a part in reducing the influence of the Mob on some unions. I know a garbage strike can be a pain in the ass for most people; but for me, it's a sign that the union leaders are finally looking out for the interests of their members, and no longer taking payoffs from the companies that employ them.

Getting Maloney off the bench was another great accomplishment. There's no telling how much more damage he could have done. Of the nine men Maloney put on Death Row, six have now been granted new trials. Two were sentenced to life, but two were aquitted, and the remaining two stand a good chance of release as well. In the words of Judge Ilana Rovner, now an appellate judge: "We may no more treat Maloney as an impartial arbiter for constitutional purposes than a delusional megalomaniac who locks a judge in the closet, dons a black robe and hoodwinks everyone with a credible impersonation of Oliver Wendell Holmes." The lawyers called me to testify in one of these lawsuits, but decided they couldn't use my testimony because I was already so outspoken in my hatred for the man.

Probably the single greatest symbol of my investigation's success is what became of the First Ward itself. After I took down the political organization, Mayor Richie Daley literally took apart the aldermanic district. He split off important parts of the ward until just a little fishhook was left. City Hall claimed that reputable downtown businesses no longer wanted to be associated with the First Ward. Meanwhile, I'm sure the mayor didn't want to see all that power and influence concentrated in one ward any more. So if someone says Bob Cooley changed Chicago's political landscape, it would be true in more ways than one.

All in all, I can take satisfaction from this. A lot of good did come from the investigation, despite the trouble I made for myself, and despite the fact that some decent people were caught up in it, like Judge Shields and Judge Wilson.

But in the last few years, when I've read the newspapers from Chicago, I've seen the accomplishments of Operation Gambat slowly chipped away. One recent *Chicago Tribune* article reported that Operation Gambat ended up with *four* convictions, when the actual number is twenty-four and this doesn't count my contribution to the Rocky Infelice case that resulted in the conviction of nineteen more mobsters. Now, when I read stories about Maloney, they say he was convicted as part of Operation Greylord.

Maybe these are your typical reporter errors or oversights. But I think there's something else at work, too. There are still powerful people in Chicago and Washington who want to pretend that Operation Gambat never happened. Some are embarrassed by the real connections we showed between the courts, our government, and organized crime. Some would like us to forget about all the corruption and cover-ups that remain. Since my investigation never went as far as I wanted it to go, I still hope that there are areas where the Feds and local reporters will pick up the pieces and attend to unfinished business.

For example, in 2002, Bill Hanhardt, former chief of detectives, and once the third-most powerful man in the Chicago Police Department, was convicted of running a jewelry theft ring that stole more than $5 million. This trial came more than sixteen years after my first report to the FBI. Testimony showed that he started the jewel thefts while he was still in the department. No way was Bill Hanhardt just one bad apple. To this date, no one has ever taken a second look at all the officers he promoted and supervised in his last years as chief of detectives. Most Chicago cops are honest and hardworking, but there is also a culture of corruption in the force that makes it harder for the good policemen to do their jobs. It's no surprise to me that the mayor, Richie Daley, continues to promote commissioners from inside the department. Any qualified outsider would start lifting up some rocks, and you can bet that person would find a whole bunch of maggots underneath.

In 2003, Anne Burke, wife of Alderman Ed Burke and now an Illinois appellate judge, was appointed to head the National Review Board monitoring priest abuse for the United States Conference of Catholic Bishops. Did the bishops know that she had once represented a child molester during her years as a defense attorney? Especially a child molester as notorious as James Moffat, the high school principal who was convicted of abusing five of his students? If you knew anything about the Moffat case or the Cammon murder case, even from what you read in the newspapers, why would you ever trust Anne Burke to get to the bottom of a child abuse case? Or even serve on the Appellate Court?

In 2004, the *Chicago Sun-Times* discovered that Chicago was giving $40 million to people with trucks that could be used for city business. The reporters found that most of these trucks just sat in a driveway somewhere and that ten percent of these contractors were Mob associates. Others were politically connected with the Daley administration. Supervising this program for the city was Nick "The Stick" LoCoco. Once, I had represented Nick when he was arrested for bookmaking. I thought I was working without a fee, because he was a "Ward case." When I found out that Patty DeLeo still charged him a thousand dollars, I had an excuse to break from the firm.

You see? Even after all these years, my Mob friends keep popping up with city jobs or contracts. I can guarantee that this trucking program is just the tip of the iceberg. The First Ward spent half a century "embedding" mobsters into city and county government. It's going to take more than a few years to weed them all out—if the mayor and the public really have the stomach to do the job.

Maybe corruption in Chicago is no longer king, but it's still somewhere in the deck. If the city isn't careful, it could start rising to the top once again. When U.S. District Court Judge Marvin Aspen sentenced Alderman Fred Roti, he quoted the philosopher who said, "Those who cannot remember the past are condemned to repeat it."

NOTES

Other sources provide further verification and amplification for Cooley's story or add different perspective. I note these below with my own comments.

Hillel Levin

INTRODUCTION

v. *Chicago's Mafia became the single most powerful organzed crime family in American history.* This statement is not disputed by organized crime historians, but may come as a surprise to casual readers of Mafia books. Some of the most seminal non-fiction works have focused on New York crime families, such as *The Valachi Papers* by Peter Maas, *Honor Thy Father* by Gay Talese, and *Wiseguy* by Nicholas Pileggi. The novel, *The Godfather*, and its screen adaptations may have had the greatest impact on popular imagination, especially in regards to which Mafia families controlled illegal activities in Las Vegas. In fact, by the seventies, Chicago's Mob had chased the last remnants of the New York Mafia out of Vegas. Their victory is chronicled in *War of the Godfathers* (New York: Ballentine, 1991) by former FBI agent William F. Roemer. In his non-fiction book, *Casino* (New York: Simon & Schuster, 1995), Pileggi further details how Chicago mobsters controlled the Vegas gambling industry. In *Accardo: The Genuine Godfather* (New York: Ballentine, 1996), Roemer quotes Pileggi as telling him that during his research on Casino, he "discovered that it was Tony Accardo and the Chicago Mob who really made Las Vegas what it became." (*Accardo*, 220.)

v. *While Mob bosses knocked each other off on the East Coast . . . never came close to achieving.* See notes below for page 83, and "Highlife with the Lowlifes."

vi. *In his 1969 book,* Captive City *. . . in the billions.* (Ovid Demaris, *The Captive City* [New York: Lyle Stuart, 1969], 5.)

vi. *By the seventies, the FBI . . . the Tropicana and the Stardust.* (*War of the Godfathers*, 177; *Casino*, 179 and 267.)

vi. *Bundles of cash . . . to the Outfit's bosses.* (Michael Corbitt, Sam Giancana, *Double Deal* [New York: William Morrow, 2003], 280.)

vi. *Although other urban areas . . . political organization.* In *The Captive City*, Demaris explains how several Capone cronies transformed themselves from street thugs into influential members of Chicago's political establishment. Demaris starts his chapter, "The Clout Machine," with the following 1951 quote from Senator Estes Kefauver, who led the first congressional investigation of organized crime:

"Everywhere we went, the committee found a certain amount of political immorality, but in Chicago the rawness of this sort of thing was particularly shocking . . . There was no doubt in the minds of any of us, after the sort of testimony we heard in Chicago, that organized crime and political corruption go hand in hand, and that in fact there could be no big-time organized crime without a firm and profitable alliance between those who run the rackets and those in political control." *(Captive City,* 93-232.)

vi. *Born Pasqualino Marchone . . . robbery in the Thirties. (Captive City,* 42.)

vii. *Although the* FBI *tried to penetrate the First Ward . . . Marcy was too careful to be caught . . .* Tom Durkin, assistant U.S. Attorney for the Northern District of Illinois, 1980-1993, explains: "It was impossible to infiltrate the First Ward corruption with undercover FBI agents. Pat Marcy only worked with people he had known for years." (Thomas M. Durkin, interview by Hillel Levin, May 2004.) According to Jim Wagner, a former Supervisory Special Agent for Organized Crime Investigations in the FBI's Chicago office, "Literally generations of [FBI] agents had tried to crack the First Ward and got nowhere. We were well aware of their Organized Crime connections." (James W. Wagner, Interview by Hillel Levin, June 2004)

viii. *Harry Aleman, a hit man dubbed the Outfit's killing machine.* (Maurice Possley, "The Mob's Killing Machine," *Chicago Tribune,* May 10, 1998.)

ix. *Before the end of the 1990 . . . Gambat indictments.* (John Gorman and Ray Gibson, *Chicago Tribune,* "5 Indicted In 'Corruption Feast,'" Dec. 20, 1990.)

ix. *When Cooley and the prosecutors . . . a guilty plea.* See notes below for "The Harder They Fall" and chart, "Operation Gambat Cases and Outcomes."

ix. *In the wake of Operation Gambat . . . take action.* See notes below for "Afterlife."

x. *Operation Gambat . . . Organized Crime Strike Force.* See notes below in "Afterlife."

x. *A character clearly based Cooley . . . movie called* The Fixer, *starring Jon Voight.* Turow calls the character, Robbie Feaver, and his book's jacket copy reads: "When the flashy, womanizing, multimillion-dollar personal injury lawyer is caught offering bribes, he's forced to wear a wire." Turow never met Cooley, but had an assistant call him. Voight plays Jack Killoran, who *TV Guide* describes as "a corrupt lawyer in Chicago's political inner circle."

xiii. The Chicago Sun-Times . . . *"organized crime figures."* (Steve Warmbir and Tim Novak, "Mob ties run throughout city truck program," *Chicago Sun-Times,* Jan. 25, 2004.)

xiii. *Meanwhile, Richard Daley . . . Mob influences.* (Gary Washburn and Ray Long, "Daley places his bets on casino for Chicago," *Chicago Tribune,* May 11, 2004.)

CHAPTER 1
A DEAL WITH THE DEVIL

4. *I turned to see John D'Arco Senior . . . for Al Capone.* See notes below for "High-life with the Lowlifes," p. 107.

4. *But whatever D'Arco . . . parcel of the Mob.* In 1969 Demaris wrote, "Of the wards under the aegis of the Syndicate, the First Ward remains one of the most representative in the system." *(Captive City,* 136.) See other notes below in "Crime Pays" and "Highlife with the Lowlifes."

4. *They had bricked up . . . and Jimmy Carter.* Mayor Richard J. Daley often fended off charges of First Ward involvement with Organized Crime. In 1969, when the Crime Commission listed D'Arco's company, Anco Insurance, as "Mob-linked," Daley refused to cut off city business from the firm, explaining, "It's one thing to have facts and another to report hearsay." (John O'Brien, "Daley Questions D'Arco Gang Tie," *Chicago Tribune,* Nov. 7, 1969.)

6. *A couple of weeks later . . . the First Ward table.* In several different trials, Cooley has described his first meeting with Pat Marcy and the subsequent events involving the case he fixed for him. He provided the most detail in *State of Illinois v. Harry Aleman,* No. 93 28787 (Sep. 23, 1987) Transcript of Proceedings at 8-103.

7. *The press dubbed him . . . contract murders.* ("Mob's Killing Machine.") A Chicago Police Department rap sheet from this time shows that Harry Sam Aleman had been arrested on at least 19 occasions from Jan. 1960 (when he was 21) to April 1975, for offenses ranging from malicious mischief to aggravated battery, burglary, grand theft auto, armed robbery, false statements on a mortgage application, gambling and aggravated kidnapping. In most of the cases he was sentenced to probation or the charges were dismissed by the judge. (City of Chicago Department of Police, "Arrest Record of Harry Sam Aleman," IR 12312, Feb. 2, 1975.)

8. *The victim was William P. Logan . . . a shotgun.* (James Griffin and Robert Shanahan, "Homicide Report for William P. Logan," RD#M397025, Chicago Police Department, Sep. 28, 1972.) The initial police report, begun on the night of the murder, included statements from Bobby Lowe, the neighbor witness. These would prove inconsistent with the evidence and other witness accounts—especially his description of the car, murder weapon and number of shots fired. Although he would later depart from these initial comments, and bring his testimony in line with the other witnesses, Lowe's credibility always remained problematic for the prosecution.

8. *Once the coppers . . . spilling out.* One of the first interviews with Almeida was conducted by an FBI agent and police officer. (John J. O'Rourke, *Federal Bureau of Investigation FD-302,* Oct. 18, 1976.)

13. *[Marco D'Amico] was one of the Mob's Young Turks . . . West Side.* During this period, reporters and Mob observers used "Young Turk" to designate the Outfit's top crew leaders like D'Amico, Harry Aleman and William Joe "Butch" Petrocelli (Chicago Crime Commission, "William 'Butch' Petrocelli," Searchlight, Jan. 1979, 7). Although hits committed by Young Turks were first thought to be power grabs, they were in fact enforcement measures sanctioned by the older Outfit bosses. (See "Crime Pays," p. 84.) D'Amico would eventually become the head of all the Mob's sports gambling operations in Chicago and the suburbs. (Daniel J. Lehman, "Gambling Charges Hit 9," *Chicago Tribune,* Nov. 19, 1994.)

14. *Once, I watched him . . . in a pizza parlor.* State prosecutors later considered charging Aleman for the crime, but concentrated on the Logan murder instead. *(United States v. Thomas J. Maloney and Robert McGee,* 91 CR 477 [N.D. Ill. July 19, 1994], Tr. of Proceedings at 235.)

15. *Through Marcy's connections, Maloney was soon to be appointed as a Circuit Court judge to fill a vacancy.* (Jerold S. Solovy, The Illinois Supreme Court Special Commission on the Administration of Justice: Final Report, Dec. 1993, 19.)

19. *The hit, I learned . . . Logan replied, "Fuck that Guinea."* Cooley was given this information by Butch Petrocelli. He first reported it to the FBI (John "Steve" Bowen, FBI 302, on May 13, 1986) and then discussed it again with assistant State's Attorney Patrick J. Quinn when he considered whether to retry Aleman for the murder.

20. *When he announced . . . a bicycle."* (*Illinois v. Harry Aleman,* No. 76 C 6958 [May 24, 1977], Tr. of Proceedings at 674-679.)

CHAPTER 2

COP KILLER

23. *Jim's dad . . . a holdup man.* (Patricia Leeds, "Commandments Daily Guide of This Policeman," *Chicago Tribune,* June 16, 1950.) *The bullet that hit him between the eyes took another twelve weeks to kill him.* ("Policeman Dies From Wound In Holdup Battle," *Chicago Tribune,* April 5, 1927.)

23. *The night of the shooting . . . saw a doctor.* ("Cop Shot in Holdup, Taken on Wild Ride," *Chicago Tribune,* Jan. 24, 1927.)

24. *The dentist was later convicted of Driving Under the Influence . . .* ("Policeman Shot In Bandit Battle Is Near Death," *Chicago Tribune,* Jan. 25, 1927.)

24. *Grandfather raised his head . . . described as "colored . . ."* ("Man Identified As Robber Who Shot Policeman," *Chicago Tribune,* Jan. 27, 1927.)

24. *He later admitted . . . six pistols.* ("Accuse Man In Shooting Of Policeman," *Chicago Tribune,* Jan. 28, 1927).

24. *A few years before . . . a cascade of roses.* A sociologist from the era, John Landesco, writes, "Al's brother was given a spectacular funeral. The coffin was silver-plated and the flowers were said to have cost more than $20,000." (John Landesco, *Organized Crime in Chicago* [Chicago: The University of Chicago Press, 1929], 179-180.)

24. *Grandmother heard the verdict . . . in my career.* The prosecutor added, "I can't understand a jury returning such a verdict in the face of the evidence." When she recovered, Cooley's grandmother told the reporter: "I am astounded, dumbfounded." ("Jury Frees Pemberton In Policeman's Death," *Chicago Tribune,* Oct. 22, 1927.)

26. *If needed, Mom could . . . about my Dad.* ("Commandments Daily Guide.")

27. *Probably the meanest kid . . . along the way.* We use a fictitious name for this individual who never became a public figure. Although he would eventually make a fortune in the world of finance, he suffered reverses, partly due to alcoholism and resumed the illegal activities of his youth. When he was last in touch with Cooley, he was in a state penitentiary for home invasion.

33. *I was a little midget . . . guy in the world.* Murphy, today a Chicago attorney, remembers that first day of escapades with Cooley and says: "Bob was wild and out of control. Also, for a little guy, he could be very tough in a fight. Part of the problem was that he was away from home for the first time. He came from a deeply religious family and now he was free to sow his wild oats." (William P. Murphy, interview by Hillel Levin, June 2004.)

CHAPTER 3
MARCO & THE COUNT

46. *A few hours later . . . named Richard Speck.* The eight murders were committed during the late night hours of July 13 through the early hours of July 14, 1966. (Steve Johnson and Sharman Stein, "Speck's death fails to end the pain of victims' relatives," *Chicago Tribune,* Dec 6, 1991.)

51. *One day at breakfast . . . no more than that.* According to police records, D'Amico would have been 34. Although well-known to authorities as a rising power in the West Side crew, to this point he did not have a significant record—only one gambling arrest when he was 21. ("The D'Amico Enterprise," *Illinois Police and Sheriff's News,* www.ipsn.org, Nov. 26, 2003.) D'Amico also had several Italian beef stands, often run by members of his crew. (Peter F. Vaira, *In The Matter of Bruno Caruso,* et. al., Docket No. 99-12D, Office of the Independent Hearing Officer, Laborers' International Union of North America, Jan. 10, 2001, p. 25.)

56. *In fact, for several years . . . contorting his hands.* An example of this ad could be found in *The Stalker.* ("Issue #2," DC Comics, 1975.)

56. *He called himself Count Juan Raphael Dante . . . grappling arts masters . . ."* The legend of Count Dante can still be found on the web site, CountDante.com, which is run by his former student, William V. Aguiar.

56. *In fact, Count Dante . . . a wealthy neighborhood.* In one of his last interviews, Count Dante admitted his real name and that his father was a doctor, although he still claimed Spanish heritage. (Massad F. Ayoob, "Count Dante's Inferno: What it's really all about," *Black Belt,* Jan. 1976.)

56. *The Count's "serious problem" . . . the spear still inside him.* (Tony Sowa, "Karate School Feud Flares, 1 Killed, 1 Hurt," *Chicago Tribune,* April 24, 1970.) John Keehan, aka The Count, was no stranger to feuds with competing martial arts schools. He was caught trying to bomb one five years before. ("2 Plead Guilty, Get Probation In Bomb Plot," *Chicago Tribune,* Oct. 29, 1965.)

57. *A supermarket tabloid . . . "The World's Deadliest Fighter Is A . . . Hairdresser!* The front page headline had the subtitle, "Will Cassius Clay Accept Count Dante's Challenge?" (*National Informer,* July 21, 1968.)

58. *During the day . . . along the lakefront.* A lion owned by John Keehan and partner in a karate school was reported to have bitten the mayor of Quincy, Illinois during a photo shoot. ("Chicago Lion Sinks Teeth in Quincy Visit," *Chicago Tribune,* Oct. 8, 1964.)

63. *My biggest trouble . . . macho bullshit . . .* In a story Keehan wrote himself, he says the confrontation was provoked when one of his instructors was "threatened" and he was then challenged by the Green Dragon Society, which operated the Black Cobra Hall. (In court documents and some articles, Green Dragon and Black Cobra are used interchangeably.) He called Koncevic, who ran a nearby school, to help. Keehan writes that he, Koncevic and a student faced twelve armed men. "The police later told me I was crazy to have walked in, but to me the greater the odds the better the fight." Although he concludes, "I blame myself," for Koncevic's death, he adds, "I still look with disgust on the cowardly actions . . . of the complete Green Dragon instruction force . . ." (John Keehan, "Death in Chicago: Count Dante's Own Store of the Killing of Jim Koncevic," *Official Karate,* Oct. 1971.)

CHAPTER 4
CRIME PAYS

67. *It was Jimmy LeFevour . . . on his breath.* In a book about Operation Greylord, the investigation that eventually caught up to the LeFevours, the authors write, "In twenty-eight years as a police officer, [Jimmy LeFevour] never rose above the rank of patrolman in a career that was distinguished only for his drinking." (James Tuohy and Rob Warden, *Greylord: Justice, Chicago Style* [New York: Putnam 1989], 90.)

70. *One of the senior judges . . . his suit jacket.* "During the 1970s and into the 1980s, Sodini franchised gambling court to the highest bidders." (*Greylord*, 16.)

71. *For the first eleven years . . . just to judges.* When Cooley admitted this on the stand during later trials, a defense attorney used his words to label him "the most corrupt attorney in the history of Cook County." In fact, when Cooley started his practice, bribes had become a widespread practice in the court system. In regards to traffic court, the authors of *Greylord* write, "All new judges assigned to major courtrooms were tested immediately by [presiding] Judge LeFevour, and those who did not accept bribes were not reassigned there." (*Greylord*, 27.)

73. *I've never claimed . . . defense attorney.* Cooley's college friend, Bill Murphy, who went on to become a highly-regarded Chicago defense attorney says of Cooley, "He had good trial skills. He was competitive. He wasn't a legal scholar, but he could go to court and be effective." (Murphy, interview.) Another lawyer who watched him in action says, "He could be incredibly skilled at identifying himself with members of the jury. He prevailed in most jury cases that I know about." (Confidential Source, interview.) Ironically, Ed Genson, a renowned criminal defense attorney competing with Cooley during this period would later try to turn his success at jury trials against him when Cooley became a witness (see above, p. 286). But not all lawyers who knew Cooley are unanimous about his ability. One says, "To call him a 'great trial lawyer' is ridiculous. He never prepared for trial like great trial lawyers do. I doubt if he knew how. Instead, he walked into court like he had the verdict in his pocket, and many times, in bench trials, he did." (Confidential Source, interview.)

79. *After the clubs closed . . . in Chinatown.* Cooley testified extensively about the dice games during hearings about Mob influence on the Laborers' International Union (LIUNA). He often saw union leaders in attendance. (Office of the Independent Hearing Officer, Laborers' International Union of North America, *In Re: Trusteeship Proceedings Chicago District Council*, No. 97-30T [July 22, 1997], Tr. of Proceedings at 1058-1066.)

80. *Tony [Spilotro] was a little guy . . . vicious temper.* In *Casino*, Pileggi quotes an FBI agent who spent years listening to Spilotro wiretaps: "[Spilotro] lost his temper faster than anyone I ever knew. There was no slow burn. He went right from being nice to being a screaming, violent maniac in a second." (*Casino*, 150.)

81. *He had a jewelry store . . . his best loot.* The FBI would later charge that the store was a "veritable warehouse of stolen jewelry." (William F. Roemer, Jr., *The Enforcer. Spilotro: The Chicago Mob's Man Over Las Vegas* [New York: Ballentine, 1994], 124.)

81. *Charlie Postl . . . mayors show up.* Demaris writes that FBI agents observed John D'Arco Sr. and Pat Marcy, among other members of the First Ward having "conferences" at Postl's with Mob bosses. (*Captive City*, 152.)

83. *The Outfit, as they called . . . killing each other.* In 1981, *Tribune* crime reporters quoted federal authorities as saying, "All territory west of the Mississippi River belongs to Chicago." (Ronald Koziol and John O'Brien, "Mob's gathering in café gives insight to hierarchy," *Chicago Tribune*, Jan. 25, 1981.) But the power of Chicago's Mob was known long before that. In 1976, FBI agent Jim Wagner arrived in Chicago after six years in the New York City office. (He retired from the FBI in 2000 and spent all but the first of his 31 years at the bureau on Organized Crime.) Comparing the Mafia in the two cities he says, "Chicago was more brutal in its control of their people and interests, and more impatient with people who didn't cooperate." As far as Chicago's control of everything west of the Mississippi, he says, "That information had been received by so many different informants and sources, it became common knowledge early in the seventies." (Wagner, interview.)

83. *They were divided up . . . family name.* Wagner explains the wisdom behind the Outfit's territorial organization. "The New York Mafia's infighting was caused by the fact that it was so fractionalized: first by the family divisions and then by the boroughs they were in. In recent years, New York has moved closer to the sort of cooperative models that Chicago's Mob created." (Wagner, interview.)

Although some law enforcement authorities and mobsters have used different names for the groups listed by Cooley, there is general agreement that there were five that divided the metropolitan area along the four major freeways. In 1983, before the U.S. Senate Permanent Subcommittee on Investigations, then FBI agent Roemer presented a chart listing the prominent members for each of Chicago's five groups. He credited the Chicago Crime Commission for their assistance and used the chart in the preface of his books (e.g. *The Enforcer*, xvi-xvii). The "geographical" organization was also discussed during the LIUNA hearings. (Vaira, 24.)

84. *The five Mafia groups . . . called street tax.* With Cooley's information, the Organized Crime Strike Force would use the street tax system as the basis for a future prosecution that netted crew leader Ernest 'Rocco' Infelice and 17 others, mostly from the Cicero group. (See "The Harder They Fall," p. 305 and further notes for that chapter below.)

90. *I heard that a gang . . . in U.S. history.* A book about the robbery that mentions the missing money was co-written by *Tribune* crime reporter O'Brien: Edward Baumann and John O'Brien, *Chicago Heist*, South Bend: And Books, 1981.

91. *Only the broker . . . were convicted.* The broker, Luigi DiFonzo, was represented

by famous criminal defense lawyer Joe Oteri and gave him a Rolls-Royce as a reward. (Cris Barrish and Jerry Hager, "For the defense, Joe Oteri," *Delaware News Journal*, June 14, 1998.)

93. *For some reason, the Count's name . . . Boston commodities broker . . .* Although the potential involvement of John Keehan (the Count) with the Purolator heist was not widely reported, connections between the robbery and his death were made a few days later by longtime *Chicago Sun-Times* reporter, Art Petaque, in his crime column. Petacque interviewed Christa ("Keehan's wife"), who told him that Keehan was questioned by the police about Purolator and passed a lie detector test, but never left their condo during the three-week trial of the accused robbers. (Art Petacque, "Purolator link? Probe karate whiz's death," *Chicago Sun-Times*, June 1, 1975). Petacque describes the cause of Keehan's death as "shock and internal bleeding," but Christa also talked to the *Black Belt* writer who conducted Keehan's last interview. According to him, "His pale, delicately beautiful young wife found [Keehan] stiff in his bed one morning, his insides full of clotting blood." In this version, Christa attributes his death to an untreated ulcer and "high, hard living." ("Count Dante's Inferno.")

CHAPTER 5

HIGHLIFE WITH THE LOWLIFES

97. *As far as the public was concerned . . . or ignored.* When Cooley first met him, D'Arco had received a pass from the media and the first Daley administration ("Daley Questions D'Arco Gang Tie"), but controversy would later flare around his Mob connections in 1980 when he supposedly influenced Chicago Police appointments by Mayor Jane Byrne (see notes below for page 107).

100. *[The After Hours Club] was a block from . . . The Hungry Hound.* In his report, the LIUNA's Independent Hearing Officer called the Hungry Hound "a convenient meeting place for the main organized crime family in the area." (Vaira, 25.)

101. *Some twenty years later . . . no apparent reason.* "Multimillionaire John E. du Pont was found guilty of murder yesterday, but jurors spared him a possible life sentence, deciding that mental illness played a role in his fatal shooting of an Olympic wrestler:" Maria Panaritis, "Du Pont guilty of killing wrestler but mentally ill," *Associated Press*, Feb. 26, 1997.

102. *Pat never held . . . was secretary.* When FBI agent Roemer testified before the U.S. Senate Permanent Subcommittee, he charged that Marcy was a "made" member of the Chicago Mob and his appointment as Secretary was engineered by one-time Outfit CEO, Sam Giancana. Much of Roemer's information was

based on wiretaps. (William F. Roemer, Jr., *Roemer: Man Against the Mob* [New York: Ballentine 1989], 100.).

106. *But after the death . . . politician in Chicago.* Roti was often portrayed in the press as a puckish Damon Runyan character. "Patronage is a fine art for [Roti]," one article muses. "Nine Rotis are on the city payroll, and as many as 17 relatives have been there at one time. Nephew Fred Barbara received a $10 million hauling contract in 1988 over a minority firm that was low bidder. Another nephew and his son got city grants." (Hanke Gratteau and Ray Gibson, "5 Indicted Men Political Veterans," *Chicago Tribune*, Dec. 20, 1990.) Typically these stories did not mention that Roti's father, Bruno "the Bomber" Roti, had been a mobster or that his nephews—Bruno, Frank and Leo Caruso—were the discredited and brutal leaders of the Chicago local of LIUNA. The Independent Hearing Officer used the Carusos association with Roti as one of the grounds for revoking their membership from LIUNA and barring them from ever holding office in the union. (Vaira, 118.)

106. *He used to say his election slogan was "Vote for Roti and Nobody Gets Hurt."* ("5 Indicted Men.")

107. *Senior was part . . . jury acquitted Senior.* Although there are no records of convictions for D'Arco, his early arrests and association with Capone are documented in several newspaper clips from the time. One has him picked up in a car without a license plate after leaving the funeral for a Capone bodyguard. ("Rio, Al Capone's Guard, Buried In Gangland Style," *Chicago Tribune*, Feb. 28, 1935.) In a far more serious case, at the age of 21, he was one of four arrested in the purse-snatching murder of a 49-year-old woman and "mother of four children." ("4 Youths Held As Police Probe Woman's Murder," *Chicago Tribune*, May 24, 1930.) Although D'Arco was acquitted, one of the others was later convicted. (John W. Tuohy, "Battaglia Brothers," *AmericanMafia,com*, July 2001.) From court files, Demaris cites another instance in 1931 when D'Arco was arrested for armed robbery. Again, a friend, also charged in the crime was convicted, while D'Arco was not. (*Captive City*, 140.) Marcy wasn't so lucky, and even served time for his conviction. In those days, he was known as Pasqualino Marchone. Besides identifying Marcy as an ex-convict, Demaris says his brother, Paul, also did time for robbery, but eventually became an administrative assistant for the Cook County Board of Zoning Appeals. (*Captive City*, 142.)

107. *Pat [Marcy] was a majority . . . the firm.* Demaris shows how an interest in Anco prevented a previous First Ward committeeman from a cabinet appointment by then Governor Adlai Stevenson. (*Captive City*, 141.) Marcy's majority share of the firm was disclosed in his federal indictment. ("Second

Superseding Indictment," *United States v. Marcy & Roti,* No. 90 CR 1045 [N.D. Ill. Sep. 1990], at 3.)

108. *Buddy Jacobson may have . . . to Capone's side. (Captive City, 139-140.)*

108. *With the money from bootlegging, Capone realized he . . . Democrat didn't matter.* According to sociologist Landesco, gang leaders in Chicago had once aspired to become elected officials or party activists on their home turf. But Capone, he writes, was "totally mercenary." He did not want to be elected to office. Instead, he wanted control of the government wherever he ran his various rackets to protect "the profits of illegitimate or contraband commerce." Political ideology did not matter in the least, so Capone tended to take over the party in power. In the suburb of Cicero, which practically became his headquarters, it was the GOP. Capone's Mob took a similar tack with politics in the city, targeting whatever party was in power in each ward. (Landesco, 178.)

108. *After Capone, Tony Accardo . . . made him sound.* FBI agent Roemer writes, "Nobody in history has ever made the impact in organized crime that Accardo has . . . I feel that Accardo's ability to remain un-incarcerated while serving his organization in the very top positions for so long, with all our powers of law enforcement focused against him, is indicative of his immense performance." (*Accardo,* 384.) Roemer claims that the nickname was bestowed on Accardo by Capone himself. (*Accardo,* 41.)

108. *Like Capone, Accardo saw . . . to the First.* At the turn of the century, the First Ward was a "red-light" district. Rival gangs of politicians literally fought (and killed each other) for control. (Landesco, 36-39.) Although the ward eventually expanded to encompass the business district and wealthy neighborhoods, Mob elements retained their control in the apparatus of the Democratic machine. (*Captive City,* 136.)

108. *Buddy [Jacobson] had started . . . executive secretary.* He ran for Alderman in the 20th Ward in 1927. He lost and was convicted of vote fraud in the process (*Captive City,* 140). He lost another race in a bid to be the GOP Committeeman for that ward three years later (*Chicago Tribune,* April 16, 1930). Jacobson changed party affiliation when his 20th Ward was merged with the overwhelmingly Democratic First Ward in 1947. (*Captive City,* 130.) By 1952, he was Secretary for the First Ward Democratic Committee. ("Civic group asks Dems to purge Hoodlums," *Chicago Tribune,* March 6, 1952.)

109. *Then, in 1950 . . . general election.* (Brian J. Kelly and Pat Wingert, "The Man City Hall Whispers About," *Chicago Sun-Times,* April 20, 1980.)

109. *During one wiretap . . . for reelection. (Man Against the Mob,* 194-197.)

110. *By the mid-seventies, the Outfit . . . were in agreement.* These constant changes in Mob leadership are documented by Roemer in *Accardo,* 405-407.

110. *The Hook would have . . . passenger seat.* Cooley described these scenes for the LIUNA Hearing Officer, since the Caruso brothers were closely allied with the Chinatown group. (*In Re: Chicago District Council* at 1093.)

110. *At one point . . . Italian-American Club . . .* In fact, the LIUNA Independent Hearing Officer (IHO) found that here were non-Mafiosi members: "The Italian-American Club was open to all Italian-American persons, many of whom joined for social purposes and were not connected to organized crime. . . . The IHO notes that while some members of organized crime chose to transact organized crime business at the club, it was not the type of club to which only the [Mafia] could be admitted." (Vaira, 45.)

111. *The On Leong Chinese Merchants Association . . . in street tax.* Although the On Leong societies in Chinatowns across America looked, from the outside, like harmless civic groups, they evolved from tongs or gangs. Besides gambling, they became involved with drug smuggling. (Gwen Kinkead, *Chinatown: A Portrait of a Closed* Society [New York: Harper, 1992], 47-49.) For more on the On Leong's involvement with Roti, see "Chicken With Wing."

111. *I realized how vital Pat Marcy . . . on Chicago.* FBI agent Jim Wagner says, "When I came to Chicago, it was astounding for me to see the influence of Organized Crime in the political arena. I wasn't aware of anything at all similar in New York. I looked at Pat Marcy as the connection between politics statewide and the Outfit. As far as the general public was concerned, he was low profile. But those in the know realized that he was the powerhouse. He had the ability to make decisions or get decisions made." (Wagner, interview.)

111. *Pat became so central . . . in Las Vegas.* In his book, *Double Deal,* former suburban police officer and Outfit associate, Michael Corbitt, describes how money made its way out of Las Vegas. For a time, he provided the last leg of the courier service and made the delivery himself to Marcy and Aiuppa. (*Double Deal,* 280.)

111. *Stein was another . . . his workers.* (*Captive City,* 42-43; Also, "Ben Stein, King of the Janitors," *Illinois Police and Sheriff's News,* www.ipsn.org, June 24, 1997.)

112. *[Dominic Senese] ran the Teamsters Local . . . a strike.* Peter F. Vaira, then Attorney in Charge of the Chicago Strike Force co-wrote an internal report for the U.S. Department of Justice. He voiced alarm about the Mob's stranglehold on unions, especially in the Chicago area, and writes: "The picture that it presents is thoroughly frightening." He describes Senese and his local as follows: "[Local 703] represents the produce haulers. The Secretary Treasurer is Dominic Senese, a Chicago syndicate member and a relative by marriage of Anthony Accardo, Chicago Syndicate head. Senese is a powerful man in the Teamsters Union, and has been rumored for a job

with the international. He is currently under investigation for taking pay-offs for awarding health and welfare insurance contracts for his union to a syndicate company." (Peter F. Vaira, "Organized Crime and the Labor Unions," *Organized Crime Strike Force Internal Document*, 1978.) Senese and Ben Stein were rumored to have dipped into Local 703 pension funds to buy a dilapidated hotel. They then sold the property as the site for the James R. Thompson State of Illinois office building. ("Ben Stein.").

113. *Some of the Mob's worst hit men and good enforcers were on the public payroll.* The press reported that Tony Borsellino had a high-paying union job at the city's convention cente one year after he was paroled for hijacking trucks. ("John Anthony Borselliono Among Kingpins Working at McCormick" *Chicago Tribune*, Aug. 1, 1974.) Butch Petrocelli received a salary from the engineering division of the park district. (*Chicago Tribune*, Jan. 17, 1969.)

116. *Joe Di[Leonardi] was sent . . . a go-along guy.* DiLeonardi told one reporter that Byrne demoted him because he would not stop the vice squad com-mander from raiding Mob bookies. Brzeczeck, the new chief, responded by casting aspersions on DiLeonardi. (Bob Weidrich, "Ex-chief refused to oust Duffy," *Chicago Tribune*, April 20, 1980.) During this fray, John D'Arco Sr. became a lightning rod again. When the *Chicago Sun-Times* looked into his past, the paper said the new police chief defended him, saying, "none of the allegations against [D'Arco] had ever been proved." ("The man City Hall whispers about.")

116. *Although [Hanhardt] made some . . . crew leaders.* More than just a friend with the Mob, Hanhardt practically became family, explains FBI agent Jim Wagner. "His daughter married the son of one Mob boss." (Wagner, interview). For much of his career, Wagner tried to build a case against Hanhardt, ultimately succeeding. In 2001, Hanhardt pled guilty to operating a jewel theft ring that stole more than $5 million. (Matt O'Connor, "Hanhardt gets nearly 16 years." *Chicago Tribune*, May 3, 2002.) See further notes on Hanhardt in "In the Weeds."

119. *Blackie never ceased . . . Jumbo Cummings . . .* (O'Connor, "Ex-Cop Charged As Probe Focuses On Divorce Court," *Chicago Tribune*, May 16, 1992.)

122. *No one was worse . . . was drunk.* D'Amico's drinking and temper caused an arrest in 1978 for "street fighting" on Rush Street, and aggravated battery in 1980. In 1983, he was stopped for D.U.I. and then resisted arrest in the suburb of Palatine (and bit the arresting officer). All these charges were even-tually dropped. ("D'Amico Enterprise.")

126. *I was with my girl in the corner talking to two leaders from the Chinatown crew, Larry Pusiteri, who managed the After Hours Club, and Richie Catazone, an older bald guy.* During his LIUNSA testimony Cooley identified Pusiteri as the manager of the

Hungry Hound and, with Catazone,, a member of the Chinatown group. He also placed them both at the dice games. (Vaira, 37 and 52.)

129. *[Borsellino] supposedly made his bones as part of an elite ring of truck hijackers, and served a few years for a million dollar silver bullion heist.* ("John Anthony Borselliono Among Kingpins Working at McCormick," *Chicago Tribune,* Aug. 1, 1974.)

129. *The next day [Borsellino] was found . . . of Accardo's house.* According to Roemer, the FBI tied seven deaths to the break-in, not just the burglars, but their ex-cop fence and a friend who happened to be with him at the wrong time. Supposedly Borsellino was killed to cover Accardo's tracks. (*Accardo,* 13.) Later, when Frank Cullotta, a former member of Tony Spilotro's gang, became a cooperating witness for the government, he identified Borsellino and Butch Petrocelli among the Outfit's most prolific killers. (Ronald Koziol, "Informer ties 4 dead 'hit men' to 24 murders," *Chicago Tribune,* Sep. 20, 1982.)

130. *When I asked Pat . . . over his business.* According to the *Illinois Police and Sheriff's News,* the last time Koppel was seen, she was with Simon at Flapjaw's Saloon. ("Ben Stein.")

CHAPTER 6
A RUN THROUGH THE GREASE

131. *In a heavily accented voice . . . of your life."* (Jay Branegan, "Separate extortion trial set for missing mobster," *Chicago Tribune,* Jan. 8, 1981.)

134. *The next morning . . . Nick's murder.* (Terry Dvorak and John O'Brien, "Witness in Mob Extortion Trial Shot Dead: Scheduled to testify Dec. 8," *Chicago Tribune,* Nov. 29, 1980.)

135. *A few days later . . . expect the worst.* According to *Tribune* reporters, before Butch disappeared, "he was reportedly under investigation for charges of obstruction of justice in connection with the murder of Velentzas." (Jay Branegan and John O'Brien, "2d mobster missing in trial here," *Chicago Tribune,* Jan. 7, 1981.)

138. *The copper and the FBI agent . . . who whacked Nick.* Cooley also made public the handwritten statement he wrote for Renella to counter the agent's testimony. (Jay Branegan, "Separate extortion trial set for missing mobster," *Chicago Tribune,* Jan. 8, 1981.) Police eventually found Renella in Vancouver after tracking his various girlfriends (although he left all of his clothes back in Chicago, they noticed he took his cologne). He pled guilty and was sentenced to seven years for extorting Velentzeas. ("Hid from authorities for 7 mos.," *Chicago Tribune,* March 1, 1982.)

142. *The remains were partly . . . a blowtorch . . .* Although details about the burns and suffocation appeared in the papers ("Informer ties 4 dead"), the information about the blowtorch was provided to me by a Chicago police detective assigned to Organized Crime who helped identify the body.

143. *At some point, the bosses . . . Defense Fund.* The *Chicago Sun-Times* reported a similar theory and had Aleman himself ordering the execution and torture. ("Decomposed body of reputed top mob boss identified," *Chicago Sun-Times,* March 16, 1981.)

CHAPTER 7

CHICKEN WITH WING

148. *It came in July 1981 . . . in Chicago's Chinatown.* Cooley testified extensively about this case in *U.S. v. Maloney.* (*United States v. Maloney & McGee,* No. 90 CR 444 [N.D. Ill. March 19, 22, 1993], Tr. of Proceedings 1802-2122.)

148. *One group was known . . . across the country.* At first, the national On Leong organization was out to curb the gangs, but eventually decided to use them to control all illegal activity in their communities, much as the Outfit did in its territory. (Kinkead, 92.)

148. *"Go meet this guy . . . gambling parlors.* Growing up in the Chinatown area, and then as First Ward Alderman, Roti was well-known to the Chinese and likely to be spotted if he tried to meet with Moy. (O'Connor, "Sentencing Of 'Chinatown Mayor' Closes On Leong Case," *Chicago Tribune,* May 16, 1995.)

151. *I went to meet Barsy . . . in his firm.* Although Cooley did not hold Barsy in high regard, FBI agent Roemer identified him as a prominent defense lawyer and one of the few he "respected." (*The Enforcer,* 222.)

151. *Like me, [Maloney] came . . . John Marshall Law School.* Maloney provided information about his education as a witness. (*Roger Collins, United States v. Welborn,* No. 93 C 5282 [N.D. Ill. June 16, 1999], Tr. of Proceedings at 11). Other biographical details could be found in such articles as: O'Connor, "Ex-Judge Gets Final Fix," *Chicago Tribune,* July 22, 1994.

151. *He put as many men . . . Law and Order.* Maloney had nine cases where he sentenced the defendants to death. (Also, see p. 317 "Afterlife.")In at least one of these cases, Maloney appointed a discredited attorney to defend against the capital charges and permitted the prosecutors to pack a jury with whites when the defendant was black. This defendant has since charged that Maloney's harsh sentence helped camouflage his decision in the Chinatown case. (Ken Armstrong and Steve Mills, "Death Row Justice Derailed," *Chicago Tribune,* Nov. 14, 1999.)

157. *[Eddie Chan] had been a staff sergeant . . . and gambling business.* Chan also quickly bought favor with local authorities by contributing heavily to local politicians. (Kinkead, 92.)

160. *Ed and I were . . . Chicago's City Council.* ("Alderman Edward M. Burke," CityofChicago.org, as of June 11, 2004.)

163. *Cieslik found them . . . misconduct.* During the trial, the medical examiner testified that the victim died of "massive" injuries. Fifteen bones were broken. Meanwhile, Jesse Jackson was not happy with the judge either—for acquitting the third cop. ("Policemen Convicted of Involuntary Manslaughter in Beating Death," *Associated Press,* Dec. 23, 1981.)

164. *Dad died in February 1983.* Cooley spoke to the paper for the rest of his family. "My father was well-liked as a policeman," he was quoted. "He had been in the seminary and he was ultrahonest." ("J.F. Cooley; policeman added to family legacy," *Chicago Tribune,* February 15, 1983.)

168. *The Feds called this investigation . . . South Side group.* The operation got rolling when the FBI bugged the home of a Chicago patrolman related to a Kansas City Mob leader. They could then monitor a meeting of the Outfit's top bosses that included Aiuppa and LaPietra as they discussed selling their Las Vegas hotels to the Kansas City Mob. The feds listened in as they weighed the purchase prices against the amount they were skimming from the casinos. (*The Enforcer,* 244-247.)

168. *Like Byrne before him . . . police department.* In a series of articles, Tribune reporter David Jackson revealed links between Mob associates and Washington's police superintendent, Matt Rodriguez. The chief was reluctant to take action against a dozen cops identified by the FBI as potential mobsters. (David Jackson, "Forbidden Friendships Between Cops and Criminals," *Chicago Tribune,* Oct. 24, 2000.)

169. *Each day after court . . . to follow him.* Cooley testified on this scene extensively in *U.S. v. Maloney* at 76-102.

170. *[Frank] Cullotta's testimony would . . . of all charges.* Roemer devotes a few pages to M&M in his book on Spilotro and calls it a "weak case" (*The Enforcer,* 219-224). This assessment has pleased Maloney, who quoted from the book when lawyers questioned him about his verdict. (*Roger Collins,* 32.)

170. *In the end [Terry Hake] helped convict . . . and they convicted sixteen of them, including Dick LeFevour . . ."* (Solivey, Appendix II.)

170. *But for me Operation Greylord was a disappointment . . . or murder cases.* Although Greylord did not take down the First Ward, it was still among the most successful federal investigations, just in terms of the sheer number of corrupt officials and lawyers convicted. More important, according to FBI agent

John "Steve" Bowen, "Greylord laid the foundation for future investigations by giving us pro-active investigative techniques, like contrived cases, to go after people who were looking for bribes." (John "Steve" Bowen, interview by Hillel Levin, June 2004.) But those techniques had their limits, according to Assistant U.S. Attorney Tom Durkin, who like Bowen worked on Greylord cases. "With Greylord, we attacked fairly notorious corruption. It was so widespread, you could infiltrate it with undercover agents, who were new on the scene. But when it came to the First Ward, only a true insider could penetrate the higher levels of corruption where you had Marcy and Roti and the most powerful judges. They only trusted a limited number of people, which is why they got away with so much." (Durkin, interview.)

173. *I had been on the Colella case . . . to Counsellors?"* (*United States v. Marcy & Roti*, No. 90 CR 1045 [N.D. Ill. Dec. 14, 1992—Jan 12, 1993], Tr. of Proceedings at 421-442.)

176. *[The policewoman] said, "He came . . . kill you.* '" (Linnet Myers and Philip Wattley, "Judge In Cop Beating Case to Transfer," *Chicago Tribune*, March 6, 1986.)

180. *Just as I expected the papers crucified . . . Judge Passarella.* One headline in the *Tribune* read: "An Incomprehensible Verdict" (*Chicago Tribune*, March 9, 1986.)

180. *Passarella met with . . . of the case."* ("Judge in Cop Beating.")

CHAPTER 8

IN THE WEEDS

185. *"Do you need money?" . . . in this city."* As they talked, Shapiro remembers thinking, "Why me?" Although Cooley remembered him from a previous encounter with a client, Shapiro had no memory of Cooley, but immediately he understood his potential. At the time, he says, "Chicago's Mob was still enormously powerful. It was just smarter than the Mafia groups. It was organized smarter—by crews instead of families, and it was run smarter, with the bosses handing union jobs to mollify everyone. Accardo and Aiuppa were just another level above your typical Mob leader, but the key to their success was Pat Marcy. He was the most significant unknown powerbroker in Chicago and his influence was unbounded." (Gary Shapiro, interview with Hillel Levin, June 2004.)

187. *Then Steve said . . . terminal illness?* Bowen explains that after checking into Cooley's background, they still needed to meet him to complete their evaluation. In fact, Dyson's specialty was psychology. Bowen says, "You always want to know where someone is coming from in those first few meetings.

With Bob, we went for a long time really not knowing what his motivation was." (Bowen, interview.)

188. *I was not happy . . . U.S. Attorney.* In fact, the Chicago Strike Force office had to coordinate closely with the Chicago U.S. Attorney (and would be eventually absorbed into each local office). Although Shapiro's title was "Attorney in Charge, Chicago Strike Force," his bailiwick was really Organized Crime. He explained, "The U.S. Attorney had first dibs on Public Corruption, and that's where we determined Bob could help most. Besides, we had the best Public Corruption program in the country. Finding a corrupt official in Chicago was like shooting fish in a barrel." (Shapiro, interview.)

In fact, Bowen was one of the FBI agents assigned to corruption. For Cooley, this division made no sense—the Mob in Chicago was all about public corruption.

189. *I could no longer . . . a lot of time . . .* In fact, Shapiro says, "There was a lot of concern in Washington about Bob maintaining a law practice. It paralyzed things for a while." (Shapiro, interview.)

189. *McCoy had been . . . I'm telling you.*" Looking back, Bowen thinks McCoy's challenge was appropriate. "You always start testing the waters to see if he's serious." (Bowen, interview.)

190. *But there was one . . . do you?*" Cooley's comments about Hanhardt were in fact recorded by McCoy in a separate 302. (Jack S. McCoy, John S. Bowen, Marie L. Dyson, *FBI 302*, March 20, 1986.

Although FBI agent Jim Wagner long had suspicions about Hanhardt, these were not shared by agents who knew him best. "It seemed like [Hanhardt] was a friend of the bureau. You could say he even endeared himself to certain agents and supervisors. For example, he was very helpful working on big easy-turnover cases like cartage theft. Nobody wanted to consider the fact that the guy was dirty. As he went higher in the force, Hanhardt became a more difficult issue, because he could affect your day-to-day working relationship with the CPD." (Wagner, interview.)

191. *Steve and Marie wanted . . . I saw John.* Bowen says, "I'm sure we were watching him. Sometimes we were on him and he didn't know it." (Bowen, interview.)

192. *But still, the Feds . . . the bookies.* Bowen remembers, "All that time we were waiting for guidelines from the [Attorney General]. It was as frustrating for us as Bob. At least we could keep him busy with the bookies, and although that was Organized Crime [as opposed to Public Corruption], that side was glad to let us do it." (Bowen, interview.)

196. *"When we told him . . . think of that?"* Shapiro says, "I don't know how Bob heard that, but I was not trying to negotiate a plea or any other sort of deal with him. That was not my job. That was something he had to work out with

the U.S. Attorney [Valukas]. I really wanted to be the guy at the Justice Department he didn't have to worry about—someone he could always talk to." (Shapiro, interview.)

197. *I said, "Fuck you . . . Bill Murphy."* Shapiro says, "If I thought he was serious about talking to a lawyer, I would have stopped talking to Bob and have talked to his lawyer. No matter what. I always respect a witness's right to representation and would never discourage it." (Shapiro, interview.)

Murphy does remember receiving the call from Cooley at that time and remembers being "overwhelmed" by what he heard. He says, "To this day, I think Bob made a mistake. If you knew him, you knew he had a tendency to act impulsively, and I think the decision to cooperate was an impulsive act. He had a good career and he threw it away. Despite his sacrifice, I don't think too many people in the government care about him in the least. They just wanted to use him and say goodbye." (Murphy, interview.)

199. *Somehow Tom and Gary Shapiro . . . on Marcy.* Unlike a bug or a wiretap, prosecutors did not need consent from a judge. However, they still had a fairly complicated process to follow. David Grossman, an FBI agent who became a public corruption supervisor, explains, "We always needed 'predication.' You have to have a good reason to believe someone is involved with criminal activity. In a typical situation, Steve Bowen would draft a request, and I would review it. My boss, the Assistant Special Agent in Charge of the Chicago division, would have to approve and then it would have to get by an assistant U.S. Attorney." (David Grossman, interview by Hillel Levin, May 2004.)

200. *Then I showed him . . . the case."* Cooley discussed a transcript of this recording in *United States v. Marcy & Roti*, No. 90 CR 1045, (N.D. Ill. Dec. 28, 1992), Tr. of Proceedings at 861-862.

200. *I went back down . . . Council Chambers.* Wire procedures eventually changed for public buildings first. Federal agents would get the recording devices inside the building first and install them once the informant was inside. (Grossman, interview.)

202. *A "surprise" witness . . . Tony [Spilotro's] old pal.* Hanhardt retired shortly after Cooley fingered him in his debriefing with the Feds. Roemer bends over backwards to justify Hanhardt's testimony and seems to find nothing fishy about it. (*The Enforcer*, 259.)

202. *Little did I know . . . an Indiana cornfield.* The medical examiner determined that the brothers died from "blunt force injuries from around the neck and head." (*Casino*, 346.)

202. *In the middle of the summer . . . Cook County Circuit Court.* Bowen remembers Cooley being more resistant. "Bob kept saying these contrived cases were 'Greylord nonsense,' and he hadn't come in to just do that." (Bowen, interview.)

203. *"Unless it's real important . . . I said.* (Charles Nicodemus, "Jury Hears Tapes Of Judge Talking About 'Plant' Fears," *Chicago Sun-Times,* July 17, 1993.)

203. *I told him . . . in them."* (Robert Cooley, Adam Stillo, Sr., *Federal Bureau of Investigation Electronic Surveillance* [Raw Transcription], Oct. 6, 1986.)

203. *"You know my nephew Joey? Talk to him."* (Nicodemus, "Jury.")

204. *"As I say," . . . the call."* (O'Connor, "Stillo Found Guilty Of Corruption," *Chicago Tribune,* July 30, 1993.)

205. *"Something about this . . . FBI agent."* (O'Connor, "Judge's Sixth Sense Recounted At Bribe Trial," *Chicago Tribune,* July 9, 1993.)

CHAPTER 9

THE WORST FUCK

209. *"What's the worst . . . not to be trusted."* (O'Connor, "Returned Bribe Discussed On Tape," *Chicago Tribune,* March 20, 1993.)

211. *"You're talking in . . . like that."* (Rosalind Rossi, "Videotape Shows Lawyers Discussing Payoff To Judge," *Chicago Sun-Times,* March 23, 1993.)

212. *I was told that Gary had to go to Washington . . . crashing down around him.* Shapiro denies that he had to go to Washington to overrule Valukas. "If there was a decision to keep Bob out of the Sodini case, I'm sure it was made by Tony [Valukas]. He didn't need pressure from me or anyone in Washington." (Shapiro, interview.)

Scott Mendeloff, an assistant U.S. Attorney, also defends Valukas and says categorically, "I never saw Valukas do anything to interfere with any investigation." (Scott Mendeloff, interview by Hillel Levin, June 2004.)

Attorneys who prefer not to be identified believe that Valukas was simply focused on the Sodini trial and saw Cooley's value to other cases as still unproven. One says, "Tony is very self-centered. He was relatively new on the job, and I think he was being selfish to get as much evidence as he could to win one of the first big cases on his watch." (Confidential Source, interview.)

Another member of the team says, "A lot of us fought like cats and dogs to keep Bob out of the Sodini trial. It was not pretty. And, for a while, we really thought they would call him as a witness and blow everything." (Confidential Source, interview.)

One investigator from the time does believe that Valukas felt threatened by Cooley, and says most of the U.S. Attorneys before him would have felt the same way. He says, "You just had to look at the way we were organized. There was Organized Crime and there was Public Corruption. In most cities that works. However, in Chicago, the Mob actually used corruption to become

more powerful. Some U.S. Attorneys had a mindset that it was too embarrassing for the city to make that connection between public officials and
mobsters. Valukas started out with that mindset. He lived here and knew he
had to return to private practice here. (Confidential Source, interview.)

214. *Anne Burke screamed . . . change their grades.* Besides his position as principal,
Moffat was reported to have political clout and was, at one time, "second in
command" for the entire city school system. A teacher told reporters he was
"worried that Moffat's power would win him an acquittal." (Linnet Myers,
Casey Banas, and Terry Wilson, "Ex-Principal Convicted of Sex Abuse,"
Chicago Tribune, March 24, 1987.)

214. *The defendant, Herbert Cammon . . . the wife's murder.* (John Gorman, "Insurer
Sues to Bar Death Claim," *Chicago Tribune*, June 29, 1988.)

215. *. . . Tuite brought in Anne Burke . . . to withdraw.* (Steve Neal, "GOP Rival's
Ally Tries to Smear Anne Burke," *Chicago Sun-Times*, Aug. 30, 1993.)

215. *An article appeared . . . jury trials.* (Joseph R. Tybor and Mark Eissman,
"Judges Penalize the Guilty for Exercising Right to Jury Trial," *Chicago Tribune*,
Oct. 13, 1985.)

215. *Later, he was reprimanded . . . female attorneys.* (Charles Mount, "Judge Reprimanded for Sexist Remarks," Aug. 1, 1987.)

215. *Finally, Cieslik had . . . the help of the* Tribune *editorial page.* ("Voters: Kick Out
Three Judges," *Chicago Tribune*, Nov.7, 1988.)

216. *"I would never roll over," . . . I'm gone."* ("Maloney Trial," *Chicago Sun-Times*,
March 23, 1993.)

217. *"I wonder who . . . right there."* ("Video.")

218. *Maloney called Cammon . . . murdering his wife.* (Linnet Myers, "Man didn't
kill wife for cash, judge rules," *Chicago Tribune*, Jan. 13, 1988.)

218. *After reviewing the . . . the policy.* ("Insurer Sues.")

218. *I hoped that Tuite . . . fees.* In fact, by the time the case went to trial before
Maloney, Anne Burke had withdrawn as counsel. This is disclosed in a column
by *Sun-Times* political writer Steve Neal that tries to be supportive of the
Burkes, but probably calls too much attention to the Cammon case in the
process. ("GOP . . . Tries to Smear Anne Burke.") See more on Burke and
Neal's column in notes for p. 318 below.

CHAPTER 10

CANDID CAMERA

219. *A few years before . . . a bench trial.* (Bowen, FBI *302*, Jan. 4, 1988.) Oberman
was the developer who tried to curry favor with Cooley and the First Ward by
buying drinks at Faces. (See "Highlife with the Lowlifes," p. 125.)

219. *But Valukas wouldn't . . . a Mob boss?* Steve Bowen explains, "Someone may have told him it was a danger issue, but it was probably just an administrative issue. Because of his position as a state senator, D'Arco was at a new level and that delayed us because we had to do the predication paperwork all over again. These things are a pain, but you can understand why the government wanted to keep us focused in our investigations." (Bowen, interview.)

220. *After Daley and Valukas . . . "conflict" for me.* Gary Shapiro says, "The conflict of interest issues are not something Bob can blame on Tony [Valukas]. I don't think he ever knew about the battle that Tony fought behind-the-scenes to try to work out the problems inherent in an attorney working for the government and simultaneously representing clients being charged by the government. There were people in Washington who wanted him to shut down his practice from Day One. The kinds of conflicts of interest that an undercover attorney wearing a tape recorder all day would have with his clients made his keeping his law practice impossible." (Shapiro interview.)

221. *In January 1988, [Senese] got out . . . drive home.* (Ronald Koziol and Robert Blau, "Gangland-Style Attack Breaks the Immunity of Oak Brook," Chicago Tribune, Jan. 24, 1988.)

221. *Dom didn't talk—in fact . . . down from office.* (Ronald Koziol and James Strong, "Union Chief Reportedly Cuts Mob Deal," *Chicago Tribune,* Feb. 18, 1988.)

222. *Chancery Division of Cook County Court . . . a sting.* "Everyone tends to focus on the criminal courts," says Tom Durkin, who was an assistant U.S. Attorney. "But we were limited with contrived cases. We couldn't create a case with serious criminal charges. Meanwhile, Greylord never cracked the civil courts. Because of the sums involved, Chancery was very prestigious and all those judges seemed very insulated." (Durkin, interview.)

222. *[Marcy and I] went into the lobby . . . shelter racket.* Cooley concocted this tale from the real-life adventures of his childhood friend (whom we call Tommy Dugan). Cooley used to regale Marcy with Dugan's wild and wooly business antics. "Tom and I would have skull sessions with Bob to come up with the contrived cases," Bowen says. "We'd ask ourselves, 'Would this work or would that sound better?'" (Bowen, interview.)

222. *"These guys are scared . . . a year ago."* (*U.S. v. Marcy* at 488.)

223. *[Marcy] asked who we got . . . a ten-foot pole," Marcy said—just as I thought.* (*U.S. v. Marcy* at 491.)

223. *"No," Patty said, . . . about is this."* (*United States v. Shields & DeLeo,* No. 90 CR 1044 [N.D. Ill. Aug. 19—Sep. 24, 1991] at 363.)

224. *Into Patty's hands . . . "One, two, three . . ."* (*U.S. v. Shields* at 383.)

224. *Shields would take a bribe, . . . honorable about it.* (*U.S. v. Shields* 391.)

224. *After the second payoff . . . somersaults."* (*U.S. v. Shields* at 460.)

225. *I had taken undercover . . . bookies there.* Shapiro explains, "Bob was like our Encyclopedia Britannica of the Outfit. We may have known most of the faces, but he knew connections between groups and individuals that we hadn't dug up before." (Shapiro, interview.)

225. *"Maybe you are a beefer," . . . about someone."* (*U.S. v. Shields* Tr. of Electronic Surveillance CG 183B-2181.)

225. *I gave him $6,000—$5,000 . . . future services.* (*U.S. v. Shields,* ElSur.)

225. *In fact, unknown . . . that much more.* The bug in Shields's chambers was only the second ever authorized for a judge (the first was for Operation Greylord). Steve Bowen says it was installed only days after DeLeo "nonchalantly" claimed he could pay off Shields. Bowen brought in an affidavit for the federal judge to authorize the surveillance. "You could just see the shock on his face. Shields had so much respect in the legal community. Nobody would have expected him to be involved in this kind of fix." (Bowen, interview.)

225. *This one case vindicated . . . run its course.* Durkin says, "I remember taking Valukas the first tape with DeLeo saying he could make Shields 'do whatever we want.' He was as enthusiastic as everyone else and wanted us to take the investigation as far as it would go." (Durkin, interview.)

226. *When Johnny approached . . . fix a case.* A chiropractor friend of the state senator's had been charged with fraudulent billing. (Marie L. Dyson, FBI 302, Jan. 19, 1988.)

227. *On Monday morning, October 31 . . . insurance law.* (Bowen, FBI 302, Oct., 31, 1988.)

227. *He gave me . . . Arthur "Ron" Swanson.* (O'Connor and Ray Long, "Ryan pal lied to grand jury, U.S. alleges: Ex-senator, lobbyist Swanson indicted," *Chicago Tribune,* Aug. 28, 2003.)

227. *Fortunately, Johnny was . . . "Merry Christmas."* (O'Connor, "U.S. Says D'Arco Took $5,000 Bribe On Tape," *Chicago Tribune,* Oct. 10, 1991.)

227. *Now, the Feds told me . . . bullshit like that.* But agents remember there was a legitimate concern about Cooley's safety. Ironically, he had been so successful making cases against high-level officials, some assistant U.S. Attorneys now did not want him to take risks against low-level mobsters. FBI agent Jim Wagner, who specialized in organized crime wasn't informed about Cooley until 1989 and wanted his help with Marco D'Amico. But he remembers, "There was reluctance on the part of those in public corruption to allow him to work on organized crime. There was a concern for the danger involved and the possibility that Bob could be suddenly terminated." (Wagner, interview.)

228. *I thought, "What could say . . . pass a law."* As they did with every payoff, the FBI made note of the serial numbers for each of the bills Cooley used for each

street tax payoff. A report also notes his discussion with Marco about the juice loan for the D'Arco bribe, and mentions that Bob gave a $200 loan to a crew member in a card game, but did not believe the player "will ever pay it back." (Bowen, FBI 302, March 7, 1989.)

229. *In fact, this idea . . . armed robbery.* It was almost too good to be true for Jim Wagner, too. D'Amico had been a tough nut to crack. He explains, "Marco trusted very few, conversed with few, passed money with very few. He was long acquainted with Bob and that was the only reason Bob could get so close." (Wagner, interview.)

230. *[Roti] then wrote the numbers "75" . . . even louder.* (U.S. v. Marcy at 518.)

231. *[Marcy] marched over . . . fucking owners are."* (U.S. v. Marcy at 509.)

231. *[Marcy] said, "The figures . . . to make sure.* (U.S. v. Marcy at 527.)

231. *A week later, . . . the whole thing then."* (U.S. v. Marcy at 667-668.)

232. *As far as I was concerned . . . the Circuit Court.* (U.S. v. Marcy at 481.)

232. *This time, my "client," . . . from their business.* (U.S. v. Marcy at 19-22.)

233. *[After Marcy accidentally puts his hand on Cooley's back where the recording device is strapped.] Once again . . . town.* Steve Bowen, the FBI agent who worked most with Cooley, remembers the incident. He says, "That did scare me. I'm not doing my job if I'm not scared. At times like that we seriously considered shipping Bob out of town and putting an end to the investigation." (Bowen, interview.)

233. *[I] went back to see Marcy . . . for him.* (U.S. v. Marcy at 560-565.)

234. *They meant Pasquale "Buck" Sorrentino . . . Law Division.* Sorrentino had also once been President of the First Ward Democratic Organization and considered D'Arco Sr. his political mentor. (Solivey, 35.)

234. *Rocky Infelice, probably . . . baseball bat execution . . .* Roemer adds that Infelice was a decorated paratrooper in World War II who was dropped behind enemy lines during the Normandy invasion. (*The Enforcer*, 265.)

235. *He was later convicted . . . Hal Smith.* (John O'Brien, "Infelice latest mob boss headed for prison," *Chicago Tribune*, March 11, 1992.)

235. *[Roti] pulled the Chief Judge . . . a piece of paper."* (U.S. v. Marcy at 571.)

235. *FBI agents shadowed . . . the judge.* (Solivey, 35.)

235. *Pat walked through . . . Marcy shot back.* (U.S. v. Marcy at 575-576.)

236. *[Roti] grabbed a napkin . . . my pocket.* (U.S. v. Marcy at 580.)

236. *I made the next payment . . . at one time."* (U.S. v. Marcy at 667-668.)

237. *I couldn't believe it . . . he followed me.*
Although Steve Bowen hid his surprise, he says that this was also the first time that he learned the bug had been discovered. (Bowen, interview.)

237. *"I know you're careful," [Roti] said. "You gotta be," I said . . . Roti walked over*

to each of his two windows and lowered the blinds. Then he turned and said, "What have you got? Four . . ." "Yeah," I said. "Four. That's the end of it." (*U.S. v. Marcy* at 623-624.)

238. *Later, I heard how a busboy . . . on Monday morning.* The discovery created a splash in local and national news. A few days later, a front page story in the *Tribune* quoted an inside source as saying the camera was part of an investigation that would be "the next step of Greylord." But reflecting the divisions in the U.S. Attorney's office, another source suggested that the discovery of the bug "caught the government off guard and may call into question the ultimate success of the case." (Dean Baquet and Joel Kaplan, "Spy camera tied to Greylord Organized crime, court links sought," *Chicago Tribune*, July 16, 1989.)

238. *For me, the camera was total overkill . . . never talked dirty at the First Ward table.* To this day, it has been assumed that the Counsellors Row bug was an integral part of Operation Gambat. In fact, it was fought by prosecutors and FBI agents most closely involved with the investigation. One says, "You will find that the Counsellors Row bug is a very touchy topic for us. It was pushed through by an FBI supervisor who had not been in his position very long. He believed that we had to pick up something useful, but it was a very high-risk install and was not worth blowing the access we already had with Cooley." (Confidential Source, interview.) Although little useful evidence was gained with the camera, the tap on Marcy's phone did lead to the charge that he solicited a bribe in return for a judicial appointment to circuit court.

238. *For the next few days . . . various microphones.* Much of the coverage quickly made light of a development that would have been cause for more concern in other cities. (Wes Smith, "Jeepers Peepers: Smile, Covert Cameras May Be Catching Your Act, *Chicago Tribune*, July 17, 1989.)

238. *[Roti] shook his head . . . "It never changes hands here."* (*U.S. v. Marcy* at 624.)

239. *[Judge Scotillo] confirmed that . . . just an act."* (*U.S. v. Marcy* at 645.)

239. *We had to come up . . . to block it.* (Solivey, 37.)

240. *[D'Arco] laughed that . . . a lot cheaper."* (*United States v. D'Arco*, No. 90 CR 1043 [N.D. Ill.], Tr. of ElSur CG 194A-828 for Sep. 14, 1989.)

240. *[D'Arco] laughed, "Roti would stiff . . . the judge's apartment . . .* (*U.S. v. D'Arco* Tr. of ElSur Sep. 27, 1989.)

240. *In October, I handed him $2,500 . . . the rest for himself.* (*U.S. v. D'Arco* Tr. of ElSur, Oct. 5, 1989.)

240. *I went to the restaurant where I knew [Scotillo] had lunch . . . [I asked,] "Now Johnny took care of you this time, right?" He replied, "Yeah. He did.* FBI agents also followed Scotillo as he walked from the court to lunch. (Bowen, *FBI 302*, Oct. 19, 1982.)

CHAPTER 11

PARTING SHOTS FOR HARRY AND MARCO

244. *"No," [Judge Wilson] said . . . nine years."* (*U.S. v. Marcy,* Tr. of ElSur [CG 183B-2442] May 16, 1989.)

244. *I said, "I'm gonna . . . about anything."* (*U.S. v. Marcy,* Tr. of ElSur May 16, 1989.)

245. *[Wilson] said to her, "Stay . . . bad man."* (*Illinois v. Harry Aleman,* No.93-28286-87, Tr. of Proceedings Feb. 9, 1995 at 253.)

245. *I wanted to approach . . . certifiably dangerous.* Agent Jim Wagner says he was among those who cautioned Cooley about Aleman. "Bob took risks that I believed he should not take, but he was very convinced of his invincibility; that his wit and mouth could always get him out of a tough situation. You need a huge ego to pull that off, and Bob was that sort of unique individual." (Wagner, interview.)

245. *That morning Steve met . . . to stay away.* Wagner did try to follow Cooley at a distance and crossed paths with Aleman. Wagner remembers, "We locked eyes for a moment, and I must say he did have the killer's look." (Wagner, interview.)

248. *I zipped over to the club . . . double payback."* Later court records show Cooley bet a total of $140,000 with Borelli and $775,500 with Abbinanti between Oct. 29 and Nov. 26, 1989. (Vaira, 15-16.)

249. *[D'Amico] wanted to make sure . . . "They're professionals."* (O'Connor, "Reputed Mob Boss Enters Plea," *Chicago Tribune,* May 2, 1992.)

249. *During the press conference . . . the occasion.* In fact, others involved with the investigation question whether Valukas would or could have a press conference. See notes below for p. 254.

250. *He got into my car . . . around the corner.* Inside the bag were "rubber banded" bundles of fifty-dollar and hundred-dollar bills, all adding up to the $50,000. (Wagner, FBI 302, Nov. 21, 1989.)

251. *[Abbinanti] was ambitious, too . . . City of Chicago.* Abbinanti was on the city's payroll as a truck driver for the Department of Streets and Sanitation. (O'Connor and Ray Gibson, "Reputed Mobster Indicted As Statute Of Limitations Nears," *Chicago Tribune,* Nov. 19, 1994.) He managed some of D'Amico's beef stands and was also a precinct captain for a ward near O'Hare Airport. (IPSN, "D'Amico Enterprise.")

252. *Wagner had picked . . . the raid.* Wagner remembers, "I spent weeks looking for that house. It had to meet a lot of conditions to keep this project as safe as possible." (Wagner, interview.)

254. *But Jimmy told me . . . everything arranged."* Wagner remembers, "This was as frustrating for me as it was for Bob. I put a lot of work into it, and we knew we

could catch some bad people in the act, but there was absolutely no way we could get a second opportunity. The decision had been made by the U.S. Attorney [Anton Valukas] that Bob had to leave town." (Wagner, interview.)

254. *For some reason, Valukas . . . Attorney General.* None of the prosecutors or agents I talked to say that a Valukas press conference was in the works. Gary Shapiro told me, "Valukas would have never held one at that point. Getting the media involved could have jeopardized everything we did." (Shapiro, interview.) Dave Grossman, then the Supervising Special Agent for Public Corruption agrees. "There is no way we would have stopped an investigation for political reasons." (Grossman, interview.) Then assistant U.S. Attorney Tom Durkin adds, "It would be very unfair to say that Tony Valukas ended Gambat early for his own purposes. He was a very legitimate and determined prosecutor." (Durkin, interview.)

But others involved with the investigation say that Cooley could have been led to believe that an event was coming that would force Gambat to a conclusion. One says, "For Bob's own good we had to get him to stop. He had played out his string and was taking some pretty big risks for low-level mobsters. To be honest, we were all burned out." (Confidential Source, interview.) Another says, "It's no coincidence that Gambat stopped the same week as Valukas's term. You can't tell me he didn't want credit for the investigation. But he deserved it, too. Once things got rolling, he was very supportive of what Bob was doing—in many ways that Bob would not have known about." (Confidential Source, interview.)

254. *One of the agents . . . "Oh, my God."* (*U.S. v. D'Arco* at 4958.)

CHAPTER 12
WITNESS DEJECTION PROGRAM

261. *[Valukas] said, " . . . if you want . . . believe you me."* Tom Durkin says, "I would have told Bob the same thing. Making extraneous statements gives the defense quotes that they can later use against you. Bob was a smart guy and once we explained that, he understood why he shouldn't talk to reporters. As far as I know, he didn't." (Durkin, interview.)

261. *The next morning . . . gambling debts . . ."* (John O'Brien and Ray Gibson, "FBI Sting Targeting Corrupt Judges, Zoning," Chicago Tribune, Dec. 2, 1989.) At some later time, the *Tribune* tried to amend this account of Cooley's motivations. Today, the digital copy of this article contains the following preface: "Corrections and clarifications: Stories published in some editions of the *Chicago Tribune* on Dec. 2, Dec. 3, and Dec. 5, 1989, stated that Robert Cooley turned government informant because of gambling debts and threats against

him because of the debts. Testimony in a subsequent trial showed that this statement about his motivations was not correct."

261. *To make matters worse . . . and my motives.* In fact, FBI agent Steve Bowen came up with the name. He says, "As I got to know Bob and his motivation for helping us, I had tremendous respect for him. He truly did have a conscience and made a pretty gutsy move when he came to us. I never intended for the name 'Gambat' to reflect badly on him. But you have to come up with these names quickly and don't have time to think about it. I had always heard that 'Greylord' really came from the name of a racehorse that one of the FBI supervisors owned. I can see how that could happen." (Bowen, interview.)

261. *Meanwhile, they had different . . . newspapers' clip files.* Despite what Ovid Demaris had written about Marcy in 1969, and despite what Roemer had testified about him to the U.S. Senate in 1983, only after Marcy's indictment did reporters indicate that Marcy had past Mob associations; and even then in a most elliptical way, such as the following: "For most of his years as secretary of the 1st Ward Regular Democratic Organization, Pat Marcy Sr. was a man about whom little was known and much was rumored. Even his name was a fiction, changed after his entry into politics from Pasquale Marchone. But his indictment Wednesday sharpened the focus on one of the 1st Ward's most elusive figures. Over the years, Marcy's name has surfaced repeatedly in discussions of mob activities." (Hanke Gratteau and Ray Gibson, "5 Indicted Men Political Veterans," *Chicago Tribune*, Dec. 20, 1990.)

262. *From the start, almost . . . the truth.* Although FBI agents directly involved with Operation Gambat know that Cooley was not in the Witness Protection Program, many others did not. It's possible that some members of the prosecution team were confused as well. Steve Bowen explains, "I wouldn't even tell the prosecutors where Bob was. Many times when they met with Bob, it was in a 'neutral' location—somewhere outside of Chicago but pretty far from where Bob was actually living." (Bowen, interview.)

262. *Most people think . . . U.S. Marshals Service.* "The Marshals Service provides for the security, health and safety of government witnesses—and their immediate dependents whose lives are in danger as a result of their testimony against drug traffickers, terrorists, organized crime members and other major criminals. The Witness Security Program was authorized by the Organized Crime Control Act of 1970 and amended by the Comprehensive Crime Control Act of 1984." ("Witness Security Program.," *United States Department of Justice Web Site* [usdoj.gov], as of Jan. 25, 2004.)

262. *One wire caught . . . the First Ward."* (Wagner, interview.)

263. *My total income came to $3,200 . . . to $3,400 a month. (U.S. v. Shields* at 1016.)

264. *I knew that agents had already gone out to Mob leaders and warned them . . .* The FBI did warn Mob bosses not to harass Cooley's friends or family. Jim Wagner says, "I arranged a meeting with Marco at his attorney's office to specifically tell him that Bob was working with us. I let him know that this was official notification and I didn't want to see any repercussions for Bob, his friends or his family." (Wagner, interview.)

265. *[The FBI agent] told Wilson, "Bob Cooley . . . a witness."* (O'Connor, "US Fights Key Tapes By Cooley," *Chicago Tribune,* July 26, 1991.)

265. *But then, in February, . . . and blew his brains out.* An FBI report also indicates that "Wilson had just been served a subpoena in connection with Chicago case entitled 'United States v. Rocco Infelice; et. al.'" Harry Aleman was among the additional defendants in that case. (Peter J. Wacks, FBI *302,* April 13, 1990.)

269. *I had dealt . . . along just fine.* Some of the assistant U.S. Attorneys working on Gambat cases did not share Cooley's view that Foreman was better than his predecessor, Anton Valukas. One says, "Fred was exactly the sort of politically connected lawyer who should have never had that job. He was not nearly the U.S. Attorney that [Valukas] was." (Confidential Source, interview.)

269. *The next day, the* Chicago Tribune *. . . Attorney General Thornburgh replied, "Stay tuned."* (Gorman and Gibson, "Five Indicted in 'Corruption Feast.'")

270. *I knew [Foreman's] real problem . . . the assignment.* Then assistant U.S. Attorney Scott Mendeloff had previously prosecuted judicial corruption, and contrary to Cooley, he did feel that Maloney would be a tough case. "Maloney had a reputation for being a tough no-nonsense guy who was not supposed to be in the pocket of anyone, because he favored the state so much. He knew what trying a case meant and his decisions, even with the fixed cases, had some rationale." (Mendeloff, interview.)

272. *It turned out that . . . could bring charges.* To meet the statute of limitations and not affect another Gambat case already underway, the government kept the indictment under seal for nearly four months. (O'Connor, "Ex-Judge Maloney Charged With Taking Bribes In 3 Murder Cases," *Chicago Tribune,* Sep. 28, 1991.)

Chapter 13
"Slander My Name"

273. *[Genson] was quick to dismiss . . . with corruption."* (Ray Gibson, "Cop, Lawyer, Informant: Odyssey In 1st Ward," *Chicago Tribune,* Dec. 24, 1990.)

273. *Originally, [the case] had more than . . . in Chinatown.* (O'Connor, "On Leong Case Gets Split Verdict," *Chicago Tribune,* Aug. 28, 1991.)

274. *After I came in, the Strike Force . . . Moy in Taiwan.* Cooley also reported to the FBI that former retired Chief of Detectives Bill Hanhardt was paid off by the On Leong while he was Chief of Detectives. (Edwin C. Barnett, Thomas M. Bourgeois, *FBI 302*, May 6, 1987.)

275. *When I made my first appearance . . . by the defense attorneys.* (O'Connor, *Chicago Tribune*, July 1, 1991.)

275. *An article on that leak . . . 20 Judges . . . "* (Ray Gibson and O'Connor, *Chicago Tribune*, June 27, 1991.)

275. *The other leak was . . . to Marquette.* ("Cooley's Credibility on Trial.")

276. *In the words of the Tribune . . . "Bribes Were My Life . . . "* (O'Connor, *Chicago Tribune*, July 2, 1991.)

276. *From the moment I appeared . . . afraid of somebody."* (*United States v. National On Leong Chinese Merchants Ass'n,* No. 90 CR 760 [N.D. Ill. July 1, 1991] Tr. of Proceedings at 59.)

277. *The night before . . . Federal Building.* Patrick A. Tuite and Edward M. Genson were then two of the best-known defense counsel in Chicago. They represented nearly fifty Greylord defendants and "had reputations for taking many cases to trial" in both federal and state court. (*Greylord,* 152.) "Tuite speaks softly, politely, and if angry at a witness on cross-examination, he is more likely to use sarcasm than volume. Genson is loud, outraged, and can be grating." (*Greylord,* 155.)

277. *[Tuite said,] "I'm disgusted . . . I bet."* (*U.S. v. Ntl. On Leong* at 332.)

277. *At one point . . . and ten dollars?"* (*U.S. v. Ntl. On Leong* at 216.)

278. *[Tuite] shouted, "Are you trying . . . snake to listen."* (*U.S. v. Ntl. On Leong* at 324.)

278. *[Tuite] said, "I doubt that . . . two of us.'"* (*U.S. v. Ntl. On Leong* at 368-369.)

By sheer coincidence, one of the other defense counsel that day was Bill Murphy, Cooley's friend from Marquette. Of the exchanges between Tuite and Cooley, he says, "I've been doing this for 36 years and I've never seen anything like it. That cross-examination was incredibly personal. Even if you didn't know them, you could sense that each had an intense distaste for the other." (Murphy, interview.) See notes on page 302 for a description of Cooley's cross-examination by Genson.

278. *[Tuite] laughed, "Who did you . . . to these people."* (*U.S. v. Ntl. On Leong* at 368.)

278. *The jurors returned a split decision . . . much of him."* ("On Leong Case Gets Split Verdict.")

279. *From what little . . . into one trial.* One writer who followed the trial blamed the government's central witness, who she describes as "bizarre." She also comments, "The defense leapt on Cooley as an object beneath contempt." (Kinkead, 122.) Gary Shapiro adds, "It was a tough case, and while I thought

Bob did well, our other witnesses were awful. On top of everything else, we had to do simultaneous translation in Chinese, probably the worst language for trial testimony." (Shapiro, interview.)

FBI agent Steve Bowen remembers that On Leong was a depressing start to Cooley's career as a witness. "The day after Bob testified, the press really beat him up, and I remember he was pretty down about that."

279. *[Dan Webb] was considered . . . could buy.* The Web site for Webb's firm, Winston & Strawn, adds that he is "listed in The Best Lawyers in America for both business litigation and criminal law . . ." (Dan K. Webb, Attorney Profile, whywinston.com.)

280. *Like a good trial lawyer . . . I dealt with him.* (*U.S. v. Shields* at 574-577.)

280. *Banks started off . . . either paid or lost."* (*U.S. v. Shields* at 760-783.)

281. *"Now you had no . . . pay personally."* (*U.S. v. Shields* at 810.)

281. *When [Banks] asked about . . . my own choice.* (*U.S. v. Shields* at 1034.)

281. *Then, before the jury returned . . . any further.* (O'Connor, "Cooley calls DeLeo his cohort in bribery," *Chicago Tribune*, Aug. 23, 1991.)

282. *[Shields] showed the arresting officer . . . a personal interest."* (O'Connor, "Shields Grilled On Drunk Driving Arrest, Tape," *Chicago Tribune*, Sep. 5, 1991.) Durkin remembers, "We found that article in an old issue of *Litigation*. He is a smart, articulate guy, and he presented well on the stand, so I think it helped counter that." (Durkin, interview.)

282. *First [the jury] listened . . . "but it's there."* (O'Connor, "Jury Plays Tape Until All Agree Shields Is Guilty," *Chicago Tribune*, Sep. 25, 1991.)

282. *[Judge Rovner] sentenced the judge . . . denial at trial."* (*U.S. v. Shields*, Tr. of Proceedings, March 2, 1992 at 35-40.)

283. *Surprisingly, she sentenced Patty DeLeo . . . all tired of it."* (*U.S. v. Shields*, Tr. of Proceedings, March 2, 1992 at 29.)

283. *[DeLeo] told the judge . . . learned them."* (O'Connor, "Ex-Judge Shields Gets 3-Year Term," *Chicago Tribune*, March 3, 1992.)

283. *Harry Comerford, chief judge need any more.* ("Jury Plays Tape . . .")

283. *As far as the press . . . of evidence . . .* But inside the U.S. Attorney's office, Cooley's credibility and value to the investigation were riding high. Then assistant U.S. Attorney Scott Mendeloff remembers, "Shields looked like a very tough case for the government to win. When we did, it was a real boost to the entire office, and we really needed that after what happened with On Leong." (Mendeloff, interview.)

284. *Genson dismissed the tapes . . . explain the tapes?"* (*U.S. v. D'Arco* at 297-298.)

284. *From that moment on . . . at Cooley."* (O'Connor, "U.S. Says D'Arco Took $5,000 Bribe On Tape," *Chicago Tribune*, Oct. 10, 1991.)

285. *Again, I explained why . . . here in Chicago."* ("U.S. Says D'Arco . . .")

285. *Suddenly, Johnny's voice . . . to shut up.* (O'Connor, "D'Arco Has A Few Words For Cooley," *Chicago Tribune,* Oct. 11, 1991.)

285. *The* Chicago Tribune *headline said it all . . . on the stand.* (O'Connor, Oct. 18, 1991.)

285. *[Genson] added, "With your father . . . there," I said.* (*U.S. v. D'Arco* at 637.)

286. *[Genson] said, "You tried jury cases . . . lost some."* (*U.S. v. D'Arco* at 1534.)

286. *"I was told he wasn't . . . yours," I answered.* (*U.S. v. D'Arco* at 701.)

286. *Later, I explained to . . . wouldn't name me."* (*U.S. v. D'Arco* at 2027.)

286. *Later in the trial, [Charles] Sklarsky . . . the Strike Force.* (Mary Wisniewski, "Cooley came in on his own, ex-prosecutor says," *Chicago Daily Law Bulletin,* Nov, 5, 1991.)

287. *The reporter for the . . . to the gym."* ("Cooley came in . . .")

287. *According to Genson, Johnny only humored me out of pity, because I was "shabbily dressed" and "driving an old car."* (*U.S. v. D'Arco* at 1527.)

287. *Tape transcripts . . . my sport jacket . . .* (*U.S. v. D'Arco,* Tr. of ElSur Oct. 5, 1989.)

287. *In another . . . like a limo.* (*U.S. v. D'Arco,* Tr. of ElSur Dec. 23, 1988.)

287. *"I was passing . . . a bust-out."* (*U.S. v. D'Arco* at 1529.)

287. *I replied, "I know . . . work this deal."* (*U.S. v. D'Arco* at 1480.)

288. *He demanded to know . . . He's absurd."* (*U.S. v. D'Arco* at 1486-1487.)

288. *[D'Arco] slammed his chair . . . her head off.* (O'Connor, "D'Arco Flies Into Rage At His Trial," *Chicago Tribune,* Oct. 26, 1991.)

288. *As far as the judge . . . human being as there is . . ."* (*U.S. v. D'Arco* at 1145.)

288. *[The judge] admonished Eddy, . . . representing the government . . ."* (*U.S. v. D'Arco* at 1501.)

289. *[The judge] admitted, "I am a very . . . different housing."* (*U.S. v. D'Arco* at 1709-1711.)

289. *"Is there any lie . . . at risk?"* ("15 Days Of Testimony Ends In D'Arco Trial," *Chicago Tribune,* Nov. 6, 1991.)

289. *At the mention of Senior's name . . . to the* Tribune. (O'Connor, "D'Arco Breaks Down During His Trial," *Chicago Tribune,* Nov. 8, 1991.)

289. *"Many times I didn't . . . not pay attention."* (O'Connor, "I Didn't Understand Cooley, D'Arco Says," *Chicago Tribune,* Nov. 15, 1991.)

290. *As proof, [Genson] . . . out each bill.* ("D'Arco Jury Hears Tapes . . .")

290. *"Unfortunately," . . . money."* (O'Connor, "D'Arco Admits Cooley Paid Him," *Chicago Tribune,* Nov. 16, 1991.)

290. *"You lied to Cooley . . . Johnny answered.* (Mary Wisniewski, "D'Arco admits taking money," *Chicago Daily Law Bulletin,* Nov, 18, 1991.)

290. *In a bizarre appeal . . . paying off Scotillo.* (O'Connor, "D'Arco: I Expect 2nd Indictment," *Chicago Tribune,* Nov. 20, 1991.)

290. *Mike Shepard told the jury . . . an eel."* (O'Connor, "Jury Deliberations To Begin On D'Arco," *Chicago Tribune,* Dec. 5, 1991.)

291. *"Because of the strength . . . a credible witness.'"* (O'Connor, "D'Arco Convicted Of Bribe Taking," *Chicago Tribune,* Dec. 7, 1991.)

291. *Judge Lindberg gave Johnny . . . with his wife.* (O'Connor, "D'Arco Gets 3 Years, Is Barred From Returning To Government," *Chicago Tribune,* May 21, 1992.)

291. *Just before he got . . . for that crime.* (O'Connor, "D'Arco Doesn't Fight New Charges," *Chicago Tribune,* Oct. 20, 1994.)

291. *For reasons I don't . . . never indicted.* Prosecutors and FBI agents involved with Gambat are divided about the decision not to indict Judge Scotillo. A prosecutor says, "I've heard the two tapes with Bob [in the street and at the restaurant] and I just don't think there's enough there to indict. If Scotillo had been home the day Johnny and Bob came calling, I have no doubt he would have been indicted and convicted." But an investigator, also familiar with the recordings, argues, "We took Shields with a lot less tape than we had on Scotillo." Another prosecutor adds, "Scotillo is the one case Bob can truly chalk up to politics." (Confidential Sources, interviews.)

291. *U.S. Attorney Fred Foreman . . . "D'Arco Conviction Has Probe On A Roll."* (*Chicago Tribune,* Dec. 8, 1991.)

CHAPTER 14
THE HARDER THEY FALL

293. *Still, even the government . . . four days a week.* (O'Connor, "Marcy Sent To Intensive Care Unit," *Chicago Tribune,* Dec. 19, 1992.)

293. *"It is only the word . . . in this case . . ."* (*U.S. v. Marcy* at 94.)

294. *Both major papers . . . U.S. Senate hearing.* (Rossi, "Curtain To Rise On 1st Ward Bribery Trial," Dec. 10, 1992; O'Connor, "FBI Tapes Will Start In Roti, Marcy Trial," *Chicago Tribune,* Dec. 14, 1992.)

294. *"This case does not . . . old-time politics."* (O'Connor, "Cooley Ties Judge Bribe To Marcy," *Chicago Tribune,* Dec. 16, 1992.)

295. *He went straight . . . live that long.* (O'Connor, "Marcy's Heart Attack May Delay Trial For 6 Months, Lawyers Say," *Chicago Tribune,* Dec. 22, 1992.")

295. *[Marcy] died three months later.* Even with his death, the newspaper headlines still dealt gingerly with their characterization of Marcy. The *Chicago Sun-Times* was boldest: "Pat Marcy Dies, 1st Ward Power Linked To Mob," (Tom Seibel, March 14, 1993.) The *Chicago Tribune* was remarkably circumspect, "Power Broker Marcy, 79, Dies," (Don Babwin and Michael Lev, March 14, 1993) but it did lead with the following line: "Pasquale 'Pat' Marcy, a Chicago political power broker in the notorious 1st Ward and reputed mob link to City Hall, died early Saturday."

295. *Breen admitted that Roti . . . denied everything.* (O'Connor, "Roti Fixed Zoning, His Lawyer Concedes," *Chicago Tribune*, Jan. 13, 1993.)

296. *"You can get away . . . pretty decent thing."* ("Roti Fixed Zoning . . .")

296. *Freddy got a pass . . . the other charges.* (Rossi, "Roti Verdict Split," *Chicago Sun-Times*, Jan. 16, 1993.)

296. *But the judge, Marvin Aspen . . . over $125,000.* (Rossi, "Roti's Sentence: 4 Years, Fine, Imprisonment Costs," *Chicago Sun-Times*, May 14, 1993.)

297. *[Judge Aspen] said, "The power of . . . or corrupt regime."* (*U.S. v. Fred Roti*, No. 90 CR 1045 [N.D. Ill. May 13, 1993], Tr. of Proceedings at 3-7.)

298. *As one reporter wrote, [Maloney] "scowled."* (Rossi, "Ex-Judge Maloney Guilty Of Fixing Murder Cases," *Chicago Sun-Times*, April 17, 1993.)

298. *[Maloney] asked, "Are you . . . take care of yourself."* (*U.S v. Maloney & McGee* at 2765.)

299. *I was the one . . . had no case.* Assistant U.S. Attorney Scott Mendeloff, believes Swano may have flipped no matter what. He says, "I think that underneath it all that Swano was a decent person, and he did not want to be dragged into a trial where he would be tarred with the El Rukns. Whatever his motives, Swano's testimony had to be credible, and Bob [added to that]." (Mendeloff, interview.)

299. *Maloney's lawyer, Terry Gillespie . . . to con you."* (O'Connor, "Maloney's Court Ruled By Greed, Jury Told," *Chicago Tribune*, March 5, 1993.)

300. *[Swano] not only represented . . . with them."* (Rossi, "Trial Opens For Ex-Judge Charged With Fixing Cases," *Chicago Sun-Times*, March 5, 1993.)

300. *McGee called the judge . . . to Maloney.* (O'Connor, "Phone Records Back Testimony Of Trial Fix, Maloney Jury Told," *Chicago Tribune*, March 5, 1993.) 300. *When that company . . . McGee had made.* (Mendeloff, interview.)

300 *The phone records . . . long-lost glove."* (Rossi, "Ex-Judge Trial Winding Up," *Chicago Sun-Times*, April 12, 1993.)

300. *Later, during deliberation, . . . a money order?"* ("Ex-Judge Maloney Guilty . . .")

301. *Scott said, "It is the view . . .* People vs. Harry Aleman." (*U.S. v. Maloney*, July 19, 1994 at 13-14.)

301. *"Thomas J. Maloney went . . . truth is in him".* (Rossi, "Ex-Judge Gets 15 Years, Rips Accusers," *Chicago Sun-Times*, July 22, 1993.)

302. *Judge Leinenweber said, "What you . . . particular cases."* (O'Connor, "Ex-Judge Gets Final Fix: 15 Years," *Chicago Tribune*, July 22, 1993.)

302. *[Genson] called me, "the most . . . a dog's tail.* (Charles Nicodemus, "Mole Sticks To Story In Stillo Bribery Trial," *Chicago Sun-Times*, July 21, 1993.)

The *Sun-Times* reporter also observed, "Genson's angry description of Cooley's history, successfully objected to by assistant U.S. Attorney Scott

Mendeloff, came after two days of cross examination had left Cooley unflustered and his story of corruption unshaken." ("Mole Sticks . . .")

Mendeloff had similar feelings about Genson's performance. "Usually, Ed is most effective when he uses his humor. But with Bob there was a stridency that did not help him or his client. You could see that this had become very personal for him." (Mendeloff, interview.)

303. *Judge Leinenweber told them, "I'm dealing . . . two years . . .* (O'Connor, "Judge Stillo Gets 4 Years For Fixing String Of Cases," *Chicago Tribune,* July 12, 1994.)

303. *Then, after he did his time . . . to the end.* Mendeloff felt sorry for the younger Stillo. "I think he was very marginal to the case, but there was no way the jury could convict the uncle without convicting him. He was always very civil and decent with me. I understood he had a weak heart and that's what killed him." (Mandeloff, interview.)

303. *"A series of circumstances . . . judicial corruption."* (William Grady, "State Agency Appears To Be Punishing Cooley, Lawyer Group Says," *Chicago Tribune,* July 12, 1994.)

304. *Their article began, "Poor, . . . Operation Gambat investigation."* (William Grady, Bill Crawford, John O'Brien, "Informant Wants 'Salvage Of Dignity,'" *Chicago Tribune,* July 13, 1994.)

304. *The agents told me . . . happen to him."* When *Sun-Times* columnist Steve Neal made a tortured defense of her role in Cammon, Anne Burke indicated to him that she had been contacted by the U.S. Attorney's office: "Mrs. Burke, who wasn't the co-counsel in the second trial, said that she cooperated with federal prosecutors who had questions about the 1984 trial. Court records from the case were subpoenaed after a federal undercover witness recorded conversations with Judge Cieslik in which the Cammon case was discussed." But the prosecutors and FBI agents who worked with Cooley and listened to the Cieslik tapes do not believe they were sufficient to get an investigation off the ground. "One says, "We may have had a judge talking about Burke putting pressure on him, but we never had enough to predicate Burke as having fixed other cases." (Confidential Source, interview.)

305. *They convicted Johnny DiFronzo . . . debts in Vegas.* ("Chicago mobsters sentenced for scheme to take over casino," *Chicago Tribune,* May 27, 1993.)

305. *[The Feds] went after . . . the year 2000.* (John O'Brien, "Infelice latest mob boss headed for prison," *Chicago Tribune,* March 11, 1992.)

Strike Force prosecutor Gary Shapiro explains that Cooley was instrumental in tying Aleman to the Infelice indictment. "Until I talked to Bob I didn't know how they were connected. I met him in a neutral location and spent a day with him. That's all it took to charge Aleman and give him another 11-year sentence."

306. *On December 8, 1993 . . . murder case was fixed."* (John O'Brien, "Acquitted Mobster may Not Be Off Hook," *Chicago Tribune*, Dec. 9, 1993.)

Although then assistant State's Attorney Patrick J. Quinn, helped put the retrial in motion, he says, "Jack O'Malley is the one who pulled the trigger and he deserves a lot of credit for that. You can bet that the vast majority of state's attorneys would have let a case like that drop, especially because it was such a long shot." (Quinn, interview.) Another lawyer involved is less charitable. "O'Malley had an election coming up. What better publicity could he ask for?" (Confidential Source, interview.)

306. *[Ackerman] quoted from . . . life or limb."* (Gary Wisby, "Aleman Charged Again In Murder Despite Acquittal," *Chicago Sun-Times*, Dec. 9, 1993.)

306. *The* Tribune *called . . . case to win."* ("Acquitted Mobster.")

306. *[Judge Toomin] ruled that a fix . . . real."* (John O'Brien, "Exception To Double Jeopardy: Bribery Cited As Reason For New Aleman Trial," *Chicago Tribune*, Oct. 13, 1994.)

307. *Ackerman zeroed in . . . —was dead.* (*Illinois v. Aleman*, Feb. 9, 1995 at 211-213.)

307. *As Allan later joked . . . like a "séance."* (*Illinois v. Aleman*, Feb. 9, 1995 at 259.)

308. *Rizza testified that . . . taken care of."* (*Illinois v. Aleman*, Feb. 9, 1995 at 52-53.)

308. *When he copped a plea . . . like Rizza.* (*Illinois v. Aleman* at 255.)

308. *Pat Quinn brought out . . . fix was in?* (*Illinois v. Aleman* at 197.)

308. *Cassidy argued, the trial . . . reeks."* (*Illinois v. Aleman* at 248.)

308. *One month later, . . . Billy Logan.* (Gary Marx, "Aleman Can Be Retried: Double Jeopardy Doesn't Apply," *Chicago Tribune*, March 10, 1995.)

309. *The judge wrote, "I find . . . of its value."* ("Aleman Can Be Retried . . .")

309. *A panel of the Appellate Court . . . every challenge.* (Possley, "'Fixed' Murder Case To Resurface: Stage Set For Retrial Of Reputed Mob Hit Man," *Chicago Tribune*, Aug. 29, 1997.)

309. *There were the bookie cases . . . Dominic Barbaro.* (O'Connor, "3 More Plead Guilty In Gambling Ring," *Chicago Tribune*, Dec. 17, 1992.)

309. *[Pesoli] copped a plea . . . prison sentence.* (O'Connor and Ray Gibson, "Ex-Cop Says He's Guilty Of Perjury," *Chicago Tribune*, May 5, 1993.)

309. *In November 1994 . . . Ricky Borelli.* (O'Connor and Ray Gibson, "Reputed Mobster Indicted As Statute Of Limitations Nears," *Chicago Tribune*, Nov. 19, 1994.)

310. *Five months after his arrest . . . two years of supervision.* (O'Connor and Ray Gibson, "Mob Leader D'Amico Gets 12 Year Term," *Chicago Tribune*, Oct. 4, 1995.)

310. *I had no trouble linking . . . Chinatown Group.* The Independent Hearing Officer mostly cited Cooley's testimony for the decision to kick the Caruso brothers out of the union. (Vaira, 117-121.)

311. *In the words . . . American jurisprudence.* ("'Fixed' Murder Case . . .")

311. *I had never had . . . this case.* Assistant State's Attorney Scott Cassidy says, "I had never seen that level of security at the criminal courthouse for anyone before, and I haven't seen it since. I'm told there was something similar for the trial of Jeff Fort [El Rukn gang leader], but I think that's the only thing close." (Scott Cassidy, interview by Hillel Levin, June 2004.)

312. *Reporters wrote . . . each day.* (Lorraine Forte, "Aleman's Retrial In 1972 Murder Fills Courtroom With Drama," *Chicago Sun-Times,* Sep. 28, 1997.)

312. *Aleman's lawyer, McNally, . . . an honest judge."* (Possley, "Mob Fixer Tells How He Bought Aleman Judge," *Chicago Tribune,* Sep. 24, 1997.)

312. *Unlike my other Gambat trials, . . . from other sources.* The prosecutors who had worked with Cooley in the past believed he was up to the task. After the Maloney and Stillo convictions, assistant U.S. Attorney Scott Mendeloff went on to other high-profile trials, including the government prosecution against Timothy McVeigh for the bombing at Oklahoma City. He says, "Bob Cooley was the finest witness I ever had. Bar none. And I've had a lot of experience with witnesses in corruption cases. Everyone talks about how good a witness Terry Hake was in the Greylord cases—and I'm a big fan of Terry—but Bob was ten times the witness. You could ask him to describe an incident and then ask for the same thing five months later. The two descriptions would not vary in the least. Jurors loved him and, most important, really believed him." (Mendeloff, interview.)

313. *"I gave him the money," . . . "You destroyed me."* (*Illinois v. Aleman,* Sep. 23, 1997 at 94.)

CHAPTER 15

AFTERLIFE

315. *[Billy Logan's ex-wife] told a story . . . kill Logan.* (Possley, "Aleman Defense: 2nd hit man Did It: Teamster's Ex-Wife Describes Fistfight," *Chicago Tribune,* Sep. 30, 1997.)

315. *According to the* Tribune, *. . . American justice."* (Possley and Judy Press, "Aleman Guilty On 2nd Time Around," *Chicago Tribune,* Oct. 1, 1997.)

315. *When it came time . . . three hundred years.* (Possley, "Mob hit man Aleman Gets 100-300 Years," *Chicago Tribune,* Nov. 26, 1997.)

316. *For one thing . . . rare event ever since.* From 1991 to 1996 (until he was elected to the Appellate Court), Pat Quinn headed the Organized Crime Unit of the Cook County State's Attorney's Office. He says, "During the years I held that position, there were no murders related to organized crime. I directly attribute that to Bob Cooley and his testimony. After him, the hit men

couldn't trust anyone. Even the lowest-level street guys realize that you can't fix a murder case in Chicago. Not any more." (Quinn, interview.)

317. *Of the nine men Maloney . . . release as well . . .* (Ken Armstrong and Steve Mills, "Death Row Justice Derailed," *Chicago Tribune*, Nov. 14, 1999.)

317. *Judge Ilana Rovner [wrote]: "We may . . . Oliver Wendell Holmes."* (Lawrence C. Marshall, "Righting the Wrongs in our Criminal Justice System," *Chicago Tribune*, June 16, 1997.)

318. *After I took down . . . fishhook was left.* (John Kass, "Remap imperils City Council vets," *Chicago Tribune*, Oct. 29, 1991.)

318. *One recent* Chicago Tribune *. . . four convictions . . .* (John Chase and Gary Washburn, "Illinois' Bane: State of shame; Scandal has home in land of Lincoln," *Chicago Tribune*, Dec. 18, 2003.)

Those who were closest to Operation Gambat are the most mystified by this relative lack of recognition for Cooley and his investigation:

Scott Mendeloff is now a partner at the firm of Sidley Austin. He says, "It's hard to overstate the importance of what Bob has done for Chicago, because what he's done has been so far reaching. Getting rid of the First Ward people was essential to cleaning Organized Crime out of City Hall and our court system. This city used to suffer serious miscarriages of justice on a regular basis. Generations of prosecutors and FBI agents know this and realize what Gambat accomplished. Maybe the general public doesn't appreciate it as much because they didn't know how bad it really was here. Ironically, by cooperating the way he did, Bob took a hit to his reputation that cannot be easily removed, but in the process he delivered such a gift to this community. (Mendeloff, interview.)

Tom Durkin is now a partner at Mayer Brown. He says, "What is so unusual about Gambat is how important one man was to the investigation. If he had not walked in the door, it's likely that none of these old cases would have been solved and Bob would have still been practicing law. Without Bob, government prosecutors had no way to get at these people or their transactions. We couldn't even get close. When you look at the Gambat cases, you realize that this was not an inevitable set of prosecutions, waiting for someone else to stumble over them. They each needed someone with his access and initiative for both the indictment and the convictions. Now the city, the legislature and the judiciary are the better for it." (Durkin, interview.)

Gary Shapiro is now First Assistant U.S. Attorney in the Chicago office. He says, "If Bob had done no more than help jail Maloney and Aleman, he would have made a major contribution to the safety of Chicago, but obviously he did much more than that. Even beyond the specific cases he helped us win, he taught us things about the Mob's metabolism and their worldview that led to many more convictions and continue to pay dividends." (Shapiro, interview.)

318. *For example, in 2002, Bill Hanhardt, . . . than $5 million.* (O'Connor, "Hanhardt gets nearly 16 years," *Chicago Tribune,* May 3, 2002.)

For decades, FBI agent Jim Wagner was on Hanhardt's trail. He found success just before he retired. "I finally did it by building a 'Chinese' wall between the investigating agents and the Chicago police assigned to the bureau. Those officers still suffered retribution when we indicted Hanhardt. I think it truly damaged their careers. Their supervisors had expected a warning." (Wagner, interview.)

318. *In 2003, Anne Burke, . . . the United States Conference of Catholic Bishops.* On May 2, 2003, after two years on the board, Anne Burke announced she was stepping down. Two other high profile board members joined her—trial lawyer Robert Bennett, and former White House chief of staff in the Clinton administration, Leon Panetta. It has been assumed that the move was to protest the Bishops' slow progress with the Board's audits into Priest child abuse. (Geneive Abdo, "Anne Burke to leave priest abuse panel," *Chicago Tribune,* May 2, 2004.)

319. *In 2004, the* Chicago Sun-Times *. . . Nick "The Stick" LoCoco.* (Steve Warmbir and Tim Novak, "Mob ties run throughout city truck program," *Chicago Sun-Times,* Jan. 25, 2004.)

319. *When U.S. District Court Judge Marvin Aspen . . . repeat it."* (*U.S. v. Roti* at 2).

Operation Gambat Related Cases and Outcomes*

[1]Conviction (C) or Guilty Plea (P); [2]Supervised Release; [3]Restitution; [4]Probation

Name	Case #	Position Held	Counts/ Charges	C/ P[1]	Date Conv Or Plea	Sentence
John D'Arco, Jr.	90 CR 1043	State Senator	2-Extortion 1-False Tax Return	C	12/6/91	3yrs. prison; supv[2]; $10,000 fine; $7,500 rest[3]; 360 hrs Community service
Pat DeLeo	90 CR 1044	Chicago Corp. Counsel	4-Extortion 1-Racketeering	C	09/24/91	33 months prison; 2 yrs supv; $7,500 fine
Thomas J. Maloney	91 CR 477	Judge	2-Bribery 1-Extortion, Racketeering 1-Obstruction of Justice	C	04/16/92	15 yrs prison; supv; $200,000 fine
Pat Marcy	91 CR 1045	Secretary, First Ward Democratic Committee	1-RICO (conspiracy) 1-RICO 6-Bribery 6-Extortion			Died during trial
Robert McGee	91CR 477	Attorney	1-RICO (conspiracy) 1-RICO 1-Extortion	C	04/16/92	6yrs prison; 5yrs prob[4]
Samuel "Blackie" Pesoli	92CR 374	Chicago Police officer	2 Counts Perjury	P	05/03/93	11 mos prison; 2yrs supv; $5,000 fine.
Fred Roti	90CR 1045	Alderman First Ward	1-RICO (conspiracy) 1-RICO 5-Bribery 4 Extortion	C	1/14/92	4 yrs prison; 3 yrs supv; $75,000 fine, $17,500 restitution; $550 fine; $1,492/mo prison cost; $1,318/mo supv cost
David Shields	90CR 1044	Presiding Judge Chancery Court	4-Extortion 1-RICO 2-False Statements	C	09/24/91	37 mos prison; supv; $6,000 fine
Joseph T. Stillo	91CR 795	Attorney	1-Extortion	C	07/29/93	2 yrs prison; $10,000 fine
Adam Stillo Sr.	91CR 795	Judge	1-RICO (conspiracy) 1-Extortion	C	07/29/92	4 yrs prison; $100 fine
William A. Swano	91CR 477	Attorney	2-Bribery	P	07/15/91	4 yrs prison; $1,000 fine

Name	Case #	Position Held	Counts/ Charges	C/ P[1]	Date Conv Or Plea	Sentence
Dominic J. Swano	92CR 483		2-Gambling 12-Tax (failure to file)	P	10/8/92	20 mos prison; 1 yr prob
Mark E. Guidi	92CR 483		2-Gambling 10-Tax (failure to file)	P	12/16/92	10 mos prison; 2 yrs prob
Mark D. Hollendonner	92CR 483		2-Gambling 2-Tax (failure to file)	P	12/16/92	4 mos prison; 3 yrs supv; $2,000 fine
Anthony Nolfe	92CR 483		2-Gambling 2-Tax (failure to file)	P	12/16/92	1 month prison; 5 yrs prob
Marco D'Amico	94CR 723		2-Firearms 1-RICO (gambling) 4-RICO (extortion) 2-False Tax	P	05/01/95	12.5 yrs prison; 3 yrs supv; $6000 fine
Anthony R. Dote	94CR 723		1-RICO (gambling) 2-RICO (extortion) 2-False Tax	P	05/03/95	4.25 yrs prison; 3 yrs supv; $10,000 fine
Robert M. Abbinanti	94CR 723	Truck Driver, Chicago Street & Sanitation	1-Firearms 1-RICO (gambling) 2-RICO (extortion) 2-False Tax	P	04/28/95	6.75 yrs prison; 3 yrs supv; $3,000 fine
Roland "Ricky" Borelli	94CR 723	Chicago Police Officer	1-RICO (extortion) 2-False Tax	P	05/09/95	10 mos prison; 2 yrs supv; $100 fine
Frank Catapano	94CR 723		2-RICO (extortion) 1-Contempt	P	05/11/95	15 mos prison; 5 yrs supv; $4,500 fine
Carl R. Dote	94CR 723		1-RICO (extortion)	P	04/13/95	3 yrs prob; $2,000 yrs fine
Frank Maranto	94CR 723		1-RICO (extortion) 1-Contempt	P	05/01/95	15 mos prison; 3 yrs supv
Robert L. Scutkowski	94CR 723		1-RICO (extortion)	P	04/18/95	3 yrs prob;
William L. Tenuta	94CR 723		1-RICO (extortion)	P	05/11/95	15 mos prison; 2 yrs supv
Harry Sam Aleman	93-28786-87		1st Degree Murder	C	09/30/97	100-300 yrs prison

* Sources: U.S. District Court, Northern District of Illinois; except Aleman, Appellate Court of Illinois, First District, Fifth Division

INDEX

A

Abbinanti, Bobby, 248, 251–54, 309
Accardo, Tony ("Joe Batters"), 128, 168, 171, 179, 317
   role in The Outfit, 108–11, 189, 262
Ackerman, Allan, 69–70, 181, 306–9
After Hours Club, 99–100
Airdo, Joey, 76–77
Aiuppa, Joey, 110–11, 168
Alderisio, Phil, 169
Aleman, Anthony, 142–43
   Aleman, Harry ("killing machine"), 152, 269, viii
   Bob Cooley and, 97, 106, 118–19, 165, 197, 293, 295
   Butch Petrocelli, 107, 117, 119, 135, 142–43, 315 case reopened, 241
      Double Jeopardy, 243, 305–9, 315
      Frank Wilson, 243–47
      retrial, 301, 305–9, 311–13, 315–16
      first trial, 6–22, 149
Almeida, Louie, 8, 20
Anarino, Sammy, 88–90, 126–27, 129, 132, 147
Anderson, Stephen, 274, 276–77
Armando, Rosie, 72, 151
Aspen, Marvin, 296, 319

B

Baker, Paul, 208, 275
Banks, Samuel V. P., 160–62, 279–81, 293
Barbaro, Dominic, 180, 189, 192–94, 273, 309
Barsy, Herb, 151–55, 169, 298
bench vs. jury trials, 9, 62, 73–78, 149, 155
Bertuca, Tony, 119
Bilandic, Michael, 115
Blitzstein, Fat Herbie, 80–81, 169

Borelli, Ricky, 51–52, 118
   death threat on Bob Cooley, 97, 102–5, 121, 132
   gambling, 49–53, 55, 59, 248, 250
   indicted, 309–10
Borsellino, Tony, 127–29, 143, 147
Boulahanis, Nick, 131–32
Bowen, Steve, 187–88, 195, 211, 263–64, 274, 289
   Bob Cooley wires, 190–94, 207, 216, 228, 236–37, 245
Breen, Tom, 295–99
bribes. See fixing cases/bribes
Bruno's (restaurant), 82–83
Bryant, Bear, 98
Bryant, Fat Mike, 122
Brzeczek, Richard, 116
Burke, Anne, 160, 213–15, 218, 318–19
Burke, Ed, 106, 168, 213–16, 218, 241, 280, 304, 318
   Arthur Cieslik, 160–63, 214–15
   Cammon case, 214–16
   James Moffat case, 213–14
   Thomas J. Maloney, 215–16, 271, 277
Byrne, Jane, 115–16, 168

C

Cabrini Green, 51–55, 113–14
Callahan (Milwaukee cop), 37
Cammon, Herbert, 214–15, 218, 225, 277, 304, 319
Capone, Al, 24, 81, 164, 226, 315
   John d'Arco "Senior," 4, 107
   The Outfit and, 83–84, 108–9, v–viii
Captive City (Demaris), vi
Caray, Harry, 112
Carter, Jimmy, 4
Cassidy, Scott, 308, 311, 315
Catrone, Jimmy, 127
Catuara, Jimmy ("the Bomber"), 89, 93, 127, 132

Cerone, Jackie, 168, 179
Chan, Eddie, 156–59, 167–68, 274
Chancery Court Division, 222–23, 232–33, 236, 238, 269–70, 295, ix
Chicago's Mafia. See Outfit, The
Chin, William, 149, 151, 153, 155, 273
Chinatown, 83–84, 99–100, 110–11, 125, 148, 156–59, 168, 273, 310–11
Chow, Lenny, 148–56
  Operation Gambat cases (passing mentions), 190, 196, 199, 269, 273–74, 276, 293, 295, 298
Christa (Count Dante's girlfriend), 91–92
Cicero group, 83–84, 102, 108, 118, 225, 234, 305
Cieslik, Arthur, 160–63, 214–15, 225, 261, 305
Colella, Mike, 171–81
  Operation Gambat cases (passing mentions), 190, 204, 269, 273, 293, 295, 302
Comerford, Henry, 283
Cooley, Bob as government informant, 181–82, 185–86, 188–90, 191–92, viii-x
  Cooperating Witness rules, 188–89, 195–96, 213, 220, 228, 247–48
  credibility, 259–61, 273–80, 284–87, 290–94, 296, 302–3, 309, xi-xii
  disbarment, 303–4
  Frank Wilson meeting, 243–45
  leaving Chicago, 250–51
  at Organized Crime Strike Forcedoor, 182, 185–86, 286, 291, vii-viii, xi
  'use' immunity, 187–88, 196–97
  wired, 227–28, 241
    Adam Stillo, 202–3, 205–6
    Arthur Cieslik, 214–215
    Atlanta, Georgia, 268
    Billy Swano, 207–11, 216–18
    Bob Johnson, 194–95
    Dominic Barbaro, 193–94
    Eldridge v. Carr (contrived case), 232–33, 269
    Fred Roti, 200–201, 230–32, 234–38, 274, 290
    Harry Aleman, 245–47, 269
    Jim Nichols (contrived case), 222–23, 232
    Joe Ettinger, 198
    Joey Stillo, 205
    Johnny D'Arco, 226–27, 239–40, 250, 254–55

Johnny DiFronzo, 191–93, 197, 212–13, 219
  Marco D'Amico, 227–28, 241
  Pat DeLeo, 223–24, 232, 240, 290
  Pat Marcy, 199–200, 210, 222–23, 231–36, 238, 290
  Tony Doty, 250
  Wilson Moy, 274, 296
Witness Protection Program, 220–21, 262, xii as government witness
  DeLeo/Sheilds trial, 279–83
  Fred Roti trial, 269, 293–98
  Harry Aleman retrial, 306–9, 311–13, 315–16
  Johnny D'Arco trial, 283–91
  On Leong trial, 273–79
  Pat Marcy trial, 293–95
  Stillo trial, 269, 293–98, 302–3, 305
  Thomas J. Maloney trial, 272, 297–302
  union testimonies, 310–11
  legacy/reforms, 316–19, ix-x, xii
  lifestyle, 3, 5, 10–12, 78, viii
    after becoming informant, 254, 259–68, 283–84, 289
    gambling, 33, 35, 78–80, 188–89, 195–96, xi
    sports betting, 49–54, 85–87, 103–5, 120–22, 175–76, 179–80
  Mafia affiliation
    100 North LaSalle Street, 69–70, 77, 85–86, 97–98, 141, 145–47, 181
    fixing cases/bribes, 159–63, 213–14
    clerks, 72
    Colella, Mike, 293, 302
    Count Dante, 62–65
    Criminal Court, 71
    Guns and Gambling Court, 70–71
    Harry Aleman, 6–22, 293
    Lenny Chow, 148–49, 293, 295, 302
    Traffic Court, 67–68
  pre-Mafia affiliation
    Chicago-Kent College of Law, 46, 55
    as cop, 41, 43–51, 54–56
      Cabrini Green, 51–55
      Rush Street District Vice Squad, 47–48
    family/childhood background, 23–28, xi
    high school days, 30–32
    Loyola University, 38–39, 44

Marquette University, 32–38, 275
Saint/Sinner conflict, 22, 28, 41, xi
Cooley, James F. (father, "Big Red"), 23–26,
74, 82, 107
Alzheimer's, 107, 134, 163–65
discipline and son Bob, 28–32, 36,
38–41
God's plan for son Bob, 44, 77, 78, 316
Corrado, Eddie, 52–53
Counsellors Row, 4, 105–7, 111–12, 117,
147, 294. See also First Ward
bugged, 236–40, 269
Ed Burke, 160–63
Fred Roti, 230–31, 234–36
Harry Aleman case, 6–7, 18–20
John D'Arco "Senior," 289, 312
Johnny D'Arco, 219, 226
On Leong, 150–51, 153, 155, 201
Mike Colella, 173–74, 177–79
Operation Greylord effects, 168–69
Pat Marcy, 199–201, 222, 226,
233–36
Count Juan Raphael Dante (John Keehan)
(Count Dante), 56–60, 62–65, 87–93,
126, 190
crew leaders, 84
Cullotta, Frank, 170, 202
Cummings, Jumbo, 119

D

Daley, Richard J., 106, 114–15
Daley, Richard M. (Richie), 4, 168, 181,
220, 317–19, xiii
D'Amico, Marco, 13, 123–25, 259, 268,
273, 295
Bob Cooley relationship, 70, 83, 179
Count Dante, 57, 59–60, 64, 89
Frank Renella, 136–41, 284
gambling, 51–55, 80, 86–87, 121–22,
212–13, 229
indictment, 309–10
informing on, 190–91, 269
Lake Geneva, Wisconsin, 248–54
Logan case, 307
Mothers (bar) case, 64–65
Nick Valentzas case, 132–34
Ricky Borelli, 103–5
wired, 227–28, 241
D'Arco, John ("Senior"), 4–7, 97, 107–9,
114, 289
du Pont incident, 100–102

informing on, 190, 307, 312
Pat DeLeo, 145–47
Ricky Borelli, 104–5
D'Arco, Johnny (son of "Senior"), 5–7,
97–99, 133, 142, 145–47, 221
Adam and Joey Stillo, 202–4
elections, 113–14
indictment/trial, 269, 283–91, 293,
302–3
informing on, 190, 219, 266–67
On Leong indictment, 275–76
wired, 226–27, 239–40, 250, 254–55
D'Arco, Maggie, 287
Dean, John, xi
DeLeo, Pat (Patty), 98–100, 142, 145–47,
160–62, 168
Operation Gambat, 190, 225, 276
indictment/trial, 269, 279–83, 293,
303
wired, 223–24, 232, 240, 290
Demaris, Ovid, vi
Democratic Party, 22, 113–14, 168,
261–62
First Ward Committee, 4, 6, 97, 102,
107–9, vi
DiFronzo, Johnny
Bob Johnson, 179–80, 189
Operation Gambat, 266, 278, 295,
305, 309
Dominic Barbaro, 192–93
wired, 190–92, 197, 212–13, 219
DiLeonardi, Joe ("Joe Di"), 115–16
Doty, Carl, 309
Doty, Tony, 140, 227–28, 248, 250, 309
Double Jeopardy, 243, 305–9, 315
Drummond, John, 181, 259–61
du Pont, John E., 101
Dugan, Tommy, 27–35, 38, 40, 56–57
Durkin, Tom, 199, 268, 270, 276
contrived cases, 203, 222, 232
credibility of Bob Cooley, 291, x
DeLeo/Sheilds trial, 279–80, 282
Harry Aleman retried, 305
Pat Marcy trial, 294–96
Dyson, Marie, 188, 190–94

E

Ed and Sid (bookies), 85–87
El Rukns (street gang), 209–10, 216, 218,
271, 299–300
Eldridge v. Carr, 232–33, 239, 269

elections, 113–14
Ettinger, Joe, 198, 304

F

Faces (disco), 124–25, 128, 145, 263, 310–11
Ferriola, Joe, 225, 315
First Ward, 108, 113–14, 269, 295, 297, vi–viii. *See also* Counsellors Row
  "First Ward table," 4, 20, 105–6, 111, 117, 160, 168, 223, vii
  Inner Circle of the First Ward, 105–6, 168, 286, vii
  reforms, 316–19, ix–x, xiii
Fixer, The (Voigt), x
fixing cases/bribes, 72, 77–78, 99, 159–63. See also Maloney, Thomas J.; Passarella, Lawrence; Wilson, Frank
  Cammon, Herbert, 214–15, 218
  Colella, Mike, 171–81, 269, 302
  Count Dante, 62–65
  Criminal Court, 71
  Eldridge v. Carr, 232–33, 269
  Fred Roti, 230–32, 269, 295
  Guns and Gambling Court, 70–71
  Harry Aleman, 6–22, 306–9
  Joe Ettinger, 198
  Lenny Chow, 148–49, 269, 274, 295, 302
  Thomas Pemberton, 24
  Tony Spilotro, 169–70, 301
  Traffic Court, 67–68
Fleming, Cathy, 12, 21, 243–45, 301, 307
Foreman, Fred, 269–70, 291
Frazier, Joe, 119

G

Gambat. *See* Operation Gambat
Gambling Attorney. See Operation Gambat
Gary (football player Marquette University), 34–35
Genson, Ed (Eddy), 127–28, 132, 216, 259
  Frank Renella trial, 136, 138–39, 141
  Joey and Adam Stillo trial, 302–3
  Johnny D'Arco trial, 284–91, 293
  On Leong trial, 275–76
  Pat Marcy trial, 273, 293–95
Gerard (bodyguard), 158, 168
Ghost Shadows (Chinese gang), 148–49, 156
Giancana, Sam ("Momo"), 109

Gibson, Ray, 273
Gillespie, Terry, 298
Gold Coast, 47, 52, 108, 239, vii
Goodman, Oscar, 169, 202
Greco, Artie, 82–83
Greco's (restaurant), 10, 12–13, 82–84, 107, 123–24, 128
Grossman, Dave, 199, 220, 260
Gucci, Pete, 88–93
Guidice, Richie, 287–88
Guns and Gambling Court, 70–71

H

Hake, Terry, 170, 185, 202, 299
Hall Rats, 68–69
Hanhardt, Bill, 116–18, 190, 202, 318
Hill, Big Bill, 198
"Hired Truck Program," 319, xiii
history of organized crime, Chicago, v–vii
Holmes, Oliver Wendell, 317
Hungry Hound (Italian beef stand), 100, 110

I

indictments. See Operation Gambat; Operation Greylord
Infelice, Rocky, 234–35, 305, 308, 318
informants/moles, 185–86. *See also* Cooley, Bob; stoolpigeons
  Frank Renella, 136–37
"ink cases," 71, 106, 160
Inner Circle of the First Ward. See under First Ward

J

Jacobson, Buddy, 107–9
"Jagoff Defense," 76–77, 155
Jackson, Jesse, 160
"Joe Batters." See Accardo, Tony
Johnson, Bob, 309
  gambling with Bob Cooley, 176, 179–80, 186, 189, 192, 194–95, 273
Jordan, Michael, 119
judges. *See Individual names of judges*
judiciary vice, 9, 22, 67–68, 114, ix
jury vs. bench trials, 9, 62, 73–78, 149, 155

K

Keehan, John. See Count Juan Raphael Dante

Kimball, Richie, 190, 246–47
Koppel, Karen, 112, 129
Kristman, Donald, 60–62, 65
Kugler, D'Arco and DeLeo, 98–99, 145
Kugler, Dave, 99
Kusper, Stanley, 106

L
Laborers and Teamsters. See union politics
Lake Geneva, Wisconsin, 248–54
LaPietra, Angelo ("Hook"), 110–11, 117, 160, 162, 168, 301, 310
Las Vegas, 10–12, 81, 108, 111, 168–69, 287–88, vi
Lasorda, Tommy, 112
LeFevour, Dick, 170
LeFevour, Jimmy, 67, 170, 190
Leighton, George, 138–39
Leinenweber, (judge), 301–3
Lemke, LeRoy, 168, 195
License Court, 99
Lindberg, George, 288–89, 291
Linehan, Neil, 311–13
LoCoco, Nick ("The Stick"), 319
Logan, William P. (Billy), 8, 15, 17, 19–20, 243
   Harry Aleman retrial, 306–9, 311–13, 315–16
Lombardo, Joey, 168

M
Mahon, Francis, 213–14
Maloney, Thomas J., 160, 206, 219, 241, 270–71
   Billy Swano/El Rukn case, 207–10, 216–18
   Harry Aleman first trial, 14–16, 18
   Herbert Cammon case, 215–18, 277
   indictment/trial, 272, 297–303, 317
   Lenny Chow case, 149, 151–56, 196, 199–200
   Tony Spilotro/M&M Murders, 169–70
Marchone, Pasqualino. See Marcy, Pat
Marcy, Pat, 3, 109, 261–62, 316, vi–viii, xi
   Anthony Scotillo, 239–40
   Arthur Cieslik, 160–61
   Bob Cooley relationship, 139, 145–47, 168, 178–80
   Cooley informs on, 182, 186, 190, 197, 216
   Dominic Senese, 221

First Ward table, 106–7, 111, 141–42, 201, 312
Harry Aleman, 135
   case fixing, 6–9, 12–13, 15–16, 18–22
   retrial, 243, 307, 312
   indictment/trial, 266, 269, 273, 293–95, 298
Karen Koppel, 129
On Leong, 148–49, 151–53, 155–56
Mike Colella, 173–75, 178
Operation Gambat cases, 286, 297, 301
Operation Greylord, 168–71
Ricky Bortelli, 97, 102, 104–5
   wired, 199–200, 210, 222–23, 231–36, 238, 290
Marin, Carol, 301
McCarthy, Billy, 169–70
McCoy, Jack, 188–90, 192
McGee, Robert, 298, 300
McNally, Kevin, 311–12
Mendeloff, Scott, 270–72, 301–2
Miller, Barry, 303
Miraglia, Jimmy, 169–70
M&M Murders, 169–70, 301
Mob culture, 5, 54, 123, xiii
mob violence/torture, 129, 133–34, 221, 234–35
   against mob members, 126–29, 135–39, 142–43, 201–2, 234–35
Moffat, James, 213–14, 318–19
moles/informants. See Cooley, Bob; informants/moles; stoolpigeons
Mother's (bar), 64–65
Moy, Wilson, 148–50, 155–57, 274, 276, 278, 296
Murphy, Bill, 32–33, 60, 81–82, 197

N
Narcotics Court, 68–69, 170–71
New York, viii
Nichols, Jim, 222–23, 232
Nicoletti, Chuckie, 169

O
Oberman, Larry, 219
O'Connor, Matt, 275, 291
O'Gara, Lawrence, 213
Olson, Wayne, 286
O'Malley, Jack, 306
On Leong Chinese Merchants Association, 111, 163

Eddie Chan, 156–59, 167–68, 274
Lenny Chow case, 196, 199–200, 210,
    273–79, 295–96, 302
    trial, 148–50
Operation Gambat (Gambling Attorney),
    261, 276, 286, 304–5, 316–18, ix–xi
    Adam and Joey Stillo trial, 302–3
    Blackie Pesoli indictment, 309
    DeLeo/ Sheilds trial, 279, 293
    Dominic Barbaro indictment, 309
    Fred Roti trial, 295
    Harry Aleman retrial, 312
    indictments, comments on, 269–70,
        273, ix–xi
    On Leong trial, 279
    Ricky Borelli indictment, 309–10
Operation Greylord, 185–86, 202–3, 206,
    238, 283, 318
    indictments, 168–71, 211, 270–71,
        279, 286
    paranoia, 205, 222
    Strawman I and II, 168–69, 171, 179, 202
    Terry Hake (mole), 170, 185, 202, 299
Organized Crime Strike Force, 181–82,
    ix–x. *See also* Operation Gambat
Outfit, The, 83–85, 108–11, 305, 316,
    v–vii

P
Partee, Cecil, 267
Passarella, Lawrence, 174–77, 180–81,
    204–5, 304
Pemberton, Thomas, 24
People vs. Harry Aleman. See Aleman,
    Harry
Personal Injuries (Turow), x
Pesoli, Blackie, 118–20, 160, 198, 213, 309
Petrocelli, Butch, 121–22, 128, 139
    Harry Aleman relationship, 16–17,
        106–7, 117, 119, 315
    killed by mob, 135, 142–43, 147, 178,
        307
Pignatelli, Joey, 81
police force vice, 36, 47–48, 115–20,
    152–53, 168, 318. See also Borelli,
    Ricky
politics and criminal activity, 22, 108,
    113, 168, 226–27, 230–32, 294–95,
    vi–ix. See also Democratic Party
Postl, Charlie/Postl's Gym, 81–82
Purolator robbery, 90–93

Q
Quinn, Pat, 305–6, 308, 311

R
reforms, 316–19, ix–x, xii
Reitinger, Anthony (Tony), 14, 147, 178
Renella, Frank, 104, 131–34, 136–39,
    141, 284
Republican Party, 108, 114, 306
Rizza, Vincent, 307–8
Robinson, Lucius, 271, 298–99
Roemer, Bill, 109, 294
Roti, Bruno, 106
Roti, Fred, 106, 109, 168, 186, 190, 210,
    239–40, 266
    indictment/trial, 269, 293–99, 319
    Jane Byrne, 115–17
    On Leong, 111, 148
    Pat DeLeo, 161
    Pat Marcy, 117, 148
    wired, 200–201, 230–32, 234–38, 274,
        290
Rovner, Ilana, 281–83, 317
Rush Street group, 47–48, 52, 79–80,
    83–84, 111–12
Ryan, George, 227

S
Salerno, Bobby, 122
Scalise, Donny, 131–32, 140, 213
Scotillo, Anthony, 222–23, 232–35,
    238–41, 270, 290–91, 304
Senese, Dominic, 112, 221
"Senior." *See* D'Arco, John
Serpico, Frank, xi
Sessions, William, 269
Shapiro, Gary, 181, 185–90, 195–97,
    212
    Harry Aleman retrial, 305
    Johnny DiFronzo tape, 192
    Pat Marcy wire, 199
Shapiro, Moe, 80
Sheilds, David, 223–25, 232, 241, 317
    indictment/trial, 269, 270, 279–83, 289,
        303
Shepard, Mike, 279–80, 282, 285,
    290–91, 296
Sid and Ed (bookies), 85–87
Simon, Rick, 129
Sinatra, Frank, 81, 123
Sklarsky, Charles, 286

Smith, Hal, 121–22, 235, 305
Sodini, Ray, 70–71, 211–12
Sorrentino, Pasquale ("Buck"), 234–35, 239–41, 304
South Side group, 82–84, 88–89, 108, 127–28, 168, 180
Speck, Richard, 46
Spilotro, Mike, 201–2
Spilotro, Tony, 80–81, 168–70, 301, 305
   killed by mob, 201–2, 234–35
Stein, Ben, 111–13, 129
Steinback, Jeff, 216
Stillo, Adam, 174, 202–6, 210, 302, 305
Stillo, Joey, 204, 302
Stone, Bernie, 231, 297–98
stoolpigeons, 136, 143, 185–86, 189, 274, 310
Strawman I and II. See Operation Greylord
"street tax," 14, 84–85, 131, v
   Bob Cooley, 228, 247–48
   Bob Johnson, 180, 194
   Hal Smith, 305
   Harry Aleman, 315–16
   Vincent Rizza, 308
Survivor's Club, 70, 132, 179, 227
Swano, Billy, 222, 275, 303
   Thomas J. Maloney case, 207–11, 216–18, 271, 298–301
Swanson, Arthur ("Ron"), 227
Switski, Vic, 311–12

T
Thompson, Jim, 226
Thornburgh, Dick, 249, 269–70
Tiny (Chicago cop), 39
Tischi, Nunzio, 173–75
Toomin, Mike, 306–9, 311, 315
Traffic Court, 67–68, 119, 171
Tuite, Pat, 225, 260–61, 285, 291
   Herbert Cammon case, 214–15, 218
   On Leong trial, 276–78
Turow, Scott, x

U
union politics, 8, 106, 111–13, 116, 310–11, 317, v
'use' immunity, 187–88, 196–97

V
Valentzas, Nick ("the Salesman"), 131–36, 139
Valukas, Anton, 222, 225, 254, 291
   Johnny D'Arco, 219–20
   leaving office, 249–50, 260–61, 269
   Ray Sodini case, 211–12
   'use' immunity, 187–88, 196–97
Voight, Jon, x
Vrdolyak, Edward (Ed), 168, 280

W
Wagner, Jimmy, 251–54, 259
Wallace, Mike, 306
Ward Cases, 145–46, 319
Washington, Harold, 168, 219
Webb, Dan, 279–82
Weiss, Hymie, 108
West Side group, 13, 83–84, 168, 179, 248
Whalen, Frank, 16–18, 301, 307–8
Whitebloom, Bobby, 266–67, 284
Wilson, Frank, 265, 297, 301, 307–8, 312–13, 317
   Harry Aleman first trial, 9–22, 317
   Operation Gambat, 243–47, 265, 297
   Harry Aleman retrial, 301, 307–8, 312–13
Wilson, Paul, 222
Wing, Chan Kwok, 150–51, 153, 156–58, 167, 274
Witness Protection Program, 220–21, 262, xii

Y
Young Turks (crew leaders), 13, 84, 317

ACKNOWLEDGMENTS

We owe the biggest debt of gratitude to the mutual friend who introduced us. He is the supreme investigator and teller of hard truths. Along with many others, we also want to thank Vic Switski and Steve Simon of Acumen Probe, Steve Bowen, Dave Grossman, Jim Wagner, Frank Marrocco, Tom Durkin, Scott Mendeloff, Gary Shapiro, Pat Quinn, Scott Cassidy, Bill Murphy, Mark Coe, Jim Bernard, Marc Brown, and Marc Winkelman.

Finally, our thanks for their patience and insight to our literary agent Nat Sobel, and our editors at Carroll & Graf Publishers: Philip Turner and Keith Wallman.